Presented to the

Library, Westmar College

by Wayne R. Detloff, M.D.

Class 1942

BOLLINGEN SERIES XX

THE COLLECTED WORKS

OF

C. G. JUNG

VOLUME 2

EDITORS

†SIR HERBERT READ

MICHAEL FORDHAM, M.D., M.R.C.P.

GERHARD ADLER, PH.D.

WILLIAM MC GUIRE, *executive editor*

EXPERIMENTAL
RESEARCHES

C. G. JUNG

TRANSLATED BY LEOPOLD STEIN

IN COLLABORATION WITH DIANA RIVIERE

BOLLINGEN SERIES XX

PRINCETON UNIVERSITY PRESS

LIBRARY OF CONGRESS CATALOGUE CARD NUMBER: 75-156
ISBN 0-691-09764-X
MANUFACTURED IN THE U.S.A.

EDITORIAL NOTE

Jung's creative use of association tests was a part of the pioneering research going on at the Burghölzli in Zurich under the rigorous aegis of Eugen Bleuler at the beginning of this century. Freud's investigations, at the time known though little accepted, were clearly in Jung's mind as he observed the perplexing behaviour of associations; so instead of brushing these to one side and considering them only as aberrant features or as "failures to react" amongst classifiable groupings, he applied the interpretative method and formulated the theory of "complexes." Thus he rescued the association method from "scientific pedantry . . . and reinvested it with the vitality and interest of real life."[1] The papers in this volume marked, in their day, a revolutionary advance in the use of experimental techniques. All Jung's writings setting out his experimental point of departure and method are included in this volume. Another work of major importance in which the tests were used incidentally is placed in Volume 3 of the Collected Works: Jung's celebrated investigation of dementia praecox. In "On Simulated Insanity," in Volume 1, Jung uses the more formal surface classification of associations, and in a later paper, "A Review of the Complex Theory," in Volume 8, he gives his mature reflections on the place of association studies in his general view of psychic structures and processes.

Perhaps the most vivid account of the association theory will be found in the Tavistock Lectures (1936),[2] in Volume 18.

*

The principal contents of this volume are Jung's six contributions to the famous Studies in Word Association (*Diagnostische Assoziationsstudien*). The experiments underlying the Studies were carried out under Jung's direction at the Psychiatric Clinic of the University of Zurich, beginning about 1902. Jung at that

[1] C. A. Mace, "On the Eightieth Birthday of C. G. Jung," *Journal of Analytical Psychology*, I:2 (1956).
[2] First published 1968 as *Analytical Psychology: Its Theory and Practice*.

time was senior assistant staff physician at the Burghölzli Mental Hospital (where the Clinic was); its director was Eugen Bleuler. The Studies appeared from 1904 to 1910 in the *Journal für Psychologie und Neurologie*; they included contributions also by Bleuler, Franz Riklin, K. Wehrlin, Emma Fürst, Ludwig Binswanger, and Hermann Nunberg.[3] They were reprinted in two volumes, 1906 and 1909. The entire series was translated by a leading British psychoanalyst, M. D. Eder, in a single volume, *Studies in Word-Association*, published by William Heinemann, London, 1918, and Moffat Yard, New York, 1919 (reissued in a facsimile reprint, 1969). The Eder translation has been consulted in the preparation of the present volume.

Jung's lectures under the heading "The Association Method" at Clark University in 1909 were translated by the American psychoanalyst A. A. Brill immediately afterwards for the *American Journal of Psychology* and for a volume issued by the University (both 1910). With little or no change, they were included by Constance E. Long when she edited Jung's *Collected Papers on Analytical Psychology* (1916). The Brill translation has also been consulted for the present volume.

The three other association studies in Part I of this volume appear for the first time in English. "The Psychopathological Significance of the Association Experiment" was Jung's inaugural lecture upon his appointment to a University lectureship. The three studies in Part II originally appeared in American and British journals, two of them being collaborations with American psychiatrists who came to the Burghölzli to participate in research. Four of the brief works in the appendix are also appearing for the first time in English; the fifth was originally published in Sydney, Australia.

In one or two details, the present translation does not follow the terminology evolved in other volumes of the Collected Works; these are cited in footnotes. The translation of "The

---

[3] See the bibliography under their respective names. Jung published two abstracts of the Studies: (1) At the request of the French psychologist Alfred Binet, an "analyse bibliographique" of Vol. I of the *Studien* in Binet's journal, *L'Année psychologique* (Paris), XIV (1908), 453–55; (2) Summaries of both volumes of the *Studien*, in "Referate über psychologische Arbeiten schweizerischer Autoren (bis Ende 1909)," compiled by Jung, in the *Jahrbuch für psychoanalytische und psychopathologische Forschungen* (Leipzig and Vienna), II (1910), 366–74; see Volume 18 of the Collected Works.

Association Method" and "The Family Constellation" was completed after Dr. Stein's death (1969) by Jean Rhees and revised (as the entire volume has been) by Diana Riviere.

Acknowledgment is made to Professor C. A. Meier, of Zurich, for editorial advice and for the loan of a diagram reproduced in the first paper in Part II.

The Editors are deeply indebted to Dr. Stein and Miss Riviere for undertaking the difficult translation of these studies, with their exceptional problems of terminology and of rendering the stimulus- and reaction-words in the tests. The German originals of the lists of test words will be available in due course in the Swiss edition of Jung's collected works.

TABLE OF CONTENTS

PART II: PSYCHOPHYSICAL RESEARCHES

APPENDIX

I

STUDIES IN WORD ASSOCIATION

THE ASSOCIATIONS OF NORMAL SUBJECTS[1]

by C. G. Jung and Franz Riklin

1   For some time past, attention has been paid in this clinic to the process of association. In order to produce scientifically useful material for this, my director, Professor Bleuler, has compiled a list of 156 stimulus-words and experimented with them on all types of psychosis. In these experiments a very considerable difficulty soon presented itself. There existed no means of precisely and quantitatively separating association in abnormal subjects from that in normal ones. No work had been done giving any facts on the range of normal subjects and formulating the apparently chaotic coincidences of association into rules. In order to fill this gap to some extent and thereby to pave the way for experiments on pathological associations, I decided to collect more material on association in normal people and at the same time to study the principal conditions involved. I carried out this plan with my colleague, Dr. Riklin.

2   The main experimental methods are as follows: Initially we collected associations from a large number of normal people, with the intention, first, of examining the reactions to see whether they are at all subject to any law; and, next, of

[1] [First published as "Experimentelle Untersuchung über Assoziationen Gesunder," *Journal für Psychologie und Neurologie* (Leipzig), III (1904), 55–83, 145–64, 193–214, 238–308, and IV (1905), 24–67, 109–23. Republished in *Diagnostische Assoziationsstudien: Beiträge zur experimentellen Psychopathologie*, edited by C. G. Jung, Vol. I (Leipzig, 1906; 2nd edn., 1911; 3rd edn., 1915), pp. 7–145 (I. Beitrag). Translated by M. D. Eder in *Studies in Word-Association* (London, 1918; New York, 1919).

[Franz Riklin (1878–1938) was assistant physician on the staff of the Burghölzli at this time. From 1907 to 1913, he and Jung were active in the International Psycho-Analytical Association. For his principal publications, see the Bibliography.]

3

discovering whether individual patterns occur, i.e., whether any definite reaction-types are to be found. We combined with this a second experiment of a general psychological nature.

3   The mechanism of association is an extraordinarily fleeting and variable psychic process; it is subject to countless psychic events, which cannot be objectively established. Among the psychic factors that exert the main influence on the mechanism of association, *attention* is of cardinal importance. It is the factor that in the first place directs and modifies the process of association; it is also both the psychic factor that can most easily be subjected to experiment and the delicate affective apparatus that reacts first in abnormal physical and mental conditions and thereby modifies the associative performance.

4   Attention is that infinitely complicated mechanism which by countless threads links the associative process with all other phenomena of the psychic and physical domain in consciousness. If we know the effects of attention on the process of association, then we also know, at least in general, the corresponding effects of every psychic event that attention is capable of affecting.

5   These considerations led us to investigate the effects of attention on the process of association, hoping to clarify as precisely as possible the following questions:

1. What are the laws governing the range of association in normal subjects?

2. What are the direct effects of attention on the association process? In particular, does the valency of the association decrease with the distance from the focus of consciousness?

6   Our experiments have revealed a series of facts that not only encourage us to follow the paths on which we have set out into psychological regions but also, as we believe, fit us to do so.

C. G. JUNG

PART ONE

I. GENERAL EXPERIMENTAL PROCEDURE

7   The experiments were carried out alternately by the two authors so that each one in turn undertook a series of experiments on the subjects concerned. Altogether thirty-eight people took part: nine educated men, fourteen educated women, seven uneducated men, and eight uneducated women; the age-bracket was 20–50 years. Care was taken to use, as far as possible, normal subjects for the experiment. This, however, led to unexpected difficulties, particularly with the educated subjects, as precisely on this level the concept of normality must be very elastic. Nevertheless we hope we have not deviated too far from the norm in our selection of subjects for experiment. We give the numbers of the subjects in detail and in many cases combine with this a short description of the personality, which will facilitate the understanding of possible anomalies. Naturally the two authors have also carried out the experiment on each other.

8   In noting associations we have entirely limited ourselves to those produced by calling out stimulus-words. We used altogether four hundred different stimulus-words. These, grammatically classified, are as follows:

nouns	231
adjectives	69
verbs	82
adverbs and numerals	18

9   The number of syllables was not taken into account (the stimulus-words have one, two, or three syllables). Nor were the stimulus-words arranged in definite categories as Sommer, for instance, has arranged them. On the contrary, as much care as possible was taken to see that stimulus-words of similar

5

forms or meaning should not follow each other, so as to avoid the subject adapting to a particular topic after one or two re-actions. Through an unfortunate coincidence it happened that among the first hundred stimulus-words there were about thirty that can easily be associated according to temporal or spatial co-existence; in the second hundred there are only about twenty of these, which caused a notable difference of the co-existence association in the first and second hundred. The shortage of stimulus-words of this kind is made up by verbs. It was considered important completely to exclude difficult and rare words, in order to prevent mistakes or lengthened reac-tion-time due to lack of knowledge on the part of the subjects. The stimulus-words were therefore taken as far as possible from everyday life.

10   This consideration was all the more essential for us, as with most of our subjects we had to work under somewhat abnormal linguistic conditions. In German-speaking Switzer-land the vernacular consists, as is well known, of the Swiss-German dialect or dialects, which not only deviate considerably from standard German but also show significant phonetic dif-ferences among themselves. In the schools children learn stand-ard German as if it were a foreign language. In later life edu-cated people gain a fairly complete knowledge of and facility in the German language. The uneducated man, however, un-less he has spent a considerable time in Germany, retains at best those German phrases that he has learned at school and later learns little or no more. Nevertheless, literary German is familiar to him in printed or written form and he also under-stands it as a spoken language without being able to speak fluent, correct standard German himself. We tried therefore in many cases to call out the stimulus-words in the dialect form, but we soon noticed that the uneducated subjects did not understand dialect words as well as standard German. They reacted to the dialect words more laboriously and tried to react in standard German. This somewhat paradoxical phenomenon can be explained by the fact that Swiss-German is a purely acoustic-motor language, which is very rarely read or written.

11   Everything printed or written is in standard German. The Swiss is therefore not used to experiencing words individually but knows them only in acoustic-motor connection with others.

If he has to say a single word without an article he will usually choose the standard German form. We therefore avoided dialect words completely in our experiments. In most cases a correct standard German reaction was given, but any reactions that were in dialect were fully accepted. The reactions were, of course, written down in the form in which they were given. To subjects who had never taken part in such experiments, their significance was first explained and practical examples of how they had to react were demonstrated to them. Not a few of the uneducated subjects thought that it was a kind of question-and-answer game, the point of which was to find an appropriate word connection to stimulus-words, e.g., *house* / *house-cat, wild* / *wild cat*. The experiments were never started till it was certain that the subjects understood the experiment. We stress that a case of not understanding never occurred and that general lack of intelligence was much less disturbing than affects, particularly a fairly frequent emotional obtuseness. It is of some significance that many of the uneducated came with a certain "schoolroom" attitude and a certain correct and stiff demeanour.

12   We organized our experiments as follows: The *first two hundred reactions* were noted without further conditions. The reaction-time was measured with a 1/5-second stop-watch, which we started on the accented syllable of the stimulus-word and stopped on the uttering of the reaction.[2] We do not, of course, presume to have in any way measured complicated psychological times by this simple procedure. We were merely concerned with establishing a general idea of a roughly average reaction-time which is in many cases not without importance, being very often of value in the classification of reactions.

13   After two hundred reactions, these were as far as possible classified, with the help of the subjects. With educated subjects this was always done; with uneducated subjects, who only rarely have any capacity for introspection, it was of course impossible. We had to limit ourselves to having the connection explained in particularly striking associations. The results of the experiment were divided into a first and second hundred and

---

[2] A later paper will report on time-measurements. The times were not measured in all subjects. [See below, "The Reaction-time Ratio in the Association Experiment."]

these were written down separately. During the experiment the psychic state of the subject was as far as possible established, both objectively and subjectively. If for any reason physiological fatigue occurred, we waited till the next day before doing the second experimental series. With the educated subjects fatigue almost never occurred during the first experiment, so that we could continue at once with the second series in nearly every case.

14   The *second series of experiments* consisted of one hundred reactions which were recorded under the condition of internal distraction. The subject was asked to concentrate his attention as much as possible on the so-called "A-phenomenon" (Cordes) and at the same time to react as quickly as possible, i.e., with the same promptness as in the first experiment. By the "A-phenomenon" we understand, with Cordes,[3] the sum of those psychological phenomena that are directly stimulated by the perception of acoustic stimulus. To establish whether the subject had observed the A-phenomenon he had occasionally to describe it after the reaction, and this was noted. On completion of this experiment new classifications were again made. Of course, for this experiment only educated people could be used and of these unfortunately only a selection, because it takes a certain psychological training to be able to observe attentively one's own psychic phenomena.

15   The *third experimental series* was sometimes not carried out till the second day. It consisted of one hundred reactions and was based on the condition of external distraction. The distraction in this experiment was brought about in the following way: The subject had to make pencil marks of about one centimetre, in time with a metronome. The beat for the first fifty reactions was 60 per minute and for the second fifty reactions 100 per minute. The classification results of the first fifty reactions and the second fifty were recorded separately and for ease of calculation brought to one hundred. With a very few subjects the metronome was speeded up at every twenty-fifth reaction in order to exclude an all too quick habituation. The beat was in these cases increased from 60 to 72 and from 100 to 108 per minute.

[3] Cordes, "Experimentelle Untersuchung über Assoziationen" (1899), p. 30.

16   The factor of habituation, in any case, unfortunately plays a large part in these experiments, as one would expect. Many people very quickly get used to a purely mechanical activity in which, in the second phase of the experiment, only the beat changes. It is difficult to introduce other disturbing stimuli of equal continuity and variability without adducing word-images, particularly when one does not wish to make too great demands on the intelligence and will-power of uneducated subjects.

17   In trying to find a suitable disturbing stimulus we were above all intent on excluding that which might have had an excitatory effect on verbal imagery. We think we did exclude such effects by our experimental procedure.

18   From these experiments three hundred to four hundred associations, on an average, were obtained from every subject. We also tried to supplement our material in other directions, in order to obtain a certain connection with Aschaffenburg's results, and for this purpose we took associations from some of our subjects in a condition of obvious fatigue. We were able to obtain such reactions from six subjects. Associations were also taken from one subject in a state of morning sleepiness after a night of undisturbed sleep, in which the factor of fatigue was completely excluded. With one subject associations were taken when he was in a state of acute moodiness (irritability) without fatigue.

19   In this way we obtained about 12,400 associations.

II. CLASSIFICATION

1. GENERAL

20   Anyone with practical experience of work on association has been confronted with the difficult and unrewarding task of classifying the results of the experiments. On the whole we agree with Cordes[4] when he says that in earlier association experiments the false assumption prevailed that the fundamental psychological phenomenon corresponds to the stimulus-word and that the connection between stimulus-word and reaction is an "association." This somewhat too simple interpretation

[4] Ibid., p. 33.

9

is at the same time too pretentious, for it maintains that in the connection between the two linguistic signs there is also a psychological connection (the association). We do not, of course, share this point of view but see in the stimulus-word merely the stimulus in the strict sense of the word and in the reaction merely a symptom of psychological processes, the nature of which we cannot judge. We do not, therefore, claim that the reactions we describe are associations in the strictest sense; we even wonder if it would not be altogether better to drop the word "association" and talk instead of *linguistic reaction*, for the external connection between stimulus-word and reaction is far too crude to give an absolutely exact picture of those extraordinarily complicated processes, the associations proper. Reactions represent the psychological connection only in a remote and imperfect way. Thus, when describing and classifying linguistically expressed connections, we are not then classifying the actual associations but merely their objective symptoms, from which psychological connections can be reconstructed only with caution. Only in psychologically educated subjects is the reaction what it really should be—namely, the reproduction of the next idea; in all others a distinct tendency to construct something is mixed with the reaction so that in many cases it is the product of deliberation, a whole series of associations. In our association experiments we stimulate the language apparatus. The more one-sided this stimulus is, the greater the number of linguistic connections that will appear in the reaction. As we shall see, this is mainly the case with educated subjects, from whom a finer differentiation of psychological mechanisms, and therefore a greater ability for isolated application, can *a priori* be expected. One must therefore guard against the fallacious assumption that the educated subject has in any way more external associations of ideas than the uneducated.[5] The difference will be a psychological one, as in uneducated subjects other psychological factors insinuate themselves. In the second part of this paper we shall refer to this difference.

21   As long as we still know so little about the connection be-

[5] Ranschburg states that in uneducated subjects inner associations predominate. With Balint, "Über quantitative und qualitative Veränderungen geistiger Vorgänge im hohen Greisenalter" (1900).

tween psychic events, we must refrain from formulating the principles for a classification of external phenomena from inner psychic data. We have therefore confined ourselves to a simple logical classification, to which as a precaution it is in our view essential to limit oneself, till we are able to derive empirical laws from psychic associations.[6] The logical principles of classification must also be adapted to the special experimental conditions, that is, to the verbal reaction. We must therefore, in classifying the associations, take into account not only the logical quality but also, if possible, all those external circumstances occurring as a result of this particular experimental design. The use of the linguistic acoustic brain mechanism naturally is not without influence on the associations. The purely intrapsychic association cannot become the object of another's consciousness without being transformed into the familiar symbolism of language. Thus a completely new element is added to simple association, which exerts a great influence on the latter. In the first place, the results will be determined by the subject's verbal facility; i.e., James Mill's generally valid "law of frequency" directs the reaction even more selectively towards what one is accustomed to. Thus one of the chief principles of our classification will be that of verbal facility.[7]

22   We proceeded with the classification of associations essentially according to the Kraepelin-Aschaffenburg scheme. We preferred this system to others because in our opinion it is heuristically the most valuable. When Ziehen describes the Kraepelin-Aschaffenburg attempt at classification as a failure, this is surely a rather strong term. No one will maintain that Aschaffenburg's classification is exhaustive; Ziehen would not want to claim that even for his own.

[6] Aschaffenburg, too, is cautious about this and confines himself entirely to the relation between stimulus and reaction as it is reflected in speech. He insists on this, since the linguistic reaction does not by any means always tally with the simultaneous inner associations. ("Experimentelle Studien über Assoziation" (1896), p. 220.)

[7] Trautschold says: "First and foremost in this respect is practice or habit, which facilitates certain associations so much that in the end they occur quite mechanically, and there can be no question of other reactions" ("Experimentelle Untersuchungen über die Assoziation der Vorstellungen" (1883), p. 221).

23   Ziehen's classification has certainly opened up most valuable vistas, but it is itself not completely satisfactory. First of all, the differentiation between "jumping association" and "judgment association" is a very doubtful one, if it is completely dependent on the presence or absence of the copula, a fact which Claparède[8] also strongly criticizes. The complete failure of Aschaffenburg's schema should first be proved, but this has in fact not been done; on the contrary, the results based on this classification are very encouraging, so that at present one can still venture to use it, although bearing in mind its one-sidedness. The other schemas of classification are, however, biased in other ways. The criticism that Aschaffenburg's schema is biased on the side of logic is not valid, as it makes sufficient allowance for logical data as well as for sensual and perceptual connection, and also for the linguistic factor. Faced with reactions in the form of sentences, however, the schema is more or less powerless. On the other hand it must be stressed that with normal subjects sentences occur very rarely. One factor of great practical significance deserves to be stressed. Aschaffenburg's schema has been tested on a great deal of material, part of it pathological, and has proved itself of value. His *conditio sine qua non* is not the subsequent questioning of the subjects about the reaction phenomenon, as in the schemas of Ziehen, Mayer and Orth, and Claparède; it also allows at least an approximately correct classification without the help of the subject, which is of particular importance in psychopathological experiments.

24   As we regard this work merely as a preliminary to psychopathological experiments, we have not hesitated to give preference to Aschaffenburg's schema. Those of Münsterberg and Bourdon appear to us as too much weighted on the side of logic; Ziehen's criticism of these, that they are unpsychological because they abstract completely from the context, is valid. Claparède's extremely subtle and penetrating suggestion (p. 226) does, however, deserve serious consideration, but should perhaps first be used on a wider range of material to test its application in practice.

25   In attempting the classification of acoustic-verbal associations one must never forget that one is not examining images

---

[8] Claparède, *L'Association des idées* (1903), p. 218.

but their verbal symbols. The examination of associations is an indirect one and is susceptible to numerous sources of error caused by the great complexity of the process.

26   In our experiments we examine the resultant of an appreciable number of psychological processes of perception, apperception, intra-psychic association, verbal comprehension, and motor expression. Each of these activities leaves its traces in the reaction. In view of the great psychological significance of motility, particularly of the speech function, one must attribute above all a main role to linguistic facility. It is mainly this factor that is to be considered in classification. This principle of classification can be criticized for introducing an extremely variable and indeterminable magnitude into the calculation. We must admit that verbal facility is an extremely variable magnitude and that in an actual case it often causes difficulties, and that therefore the logical character of the classification also suffers. It introduces an arbitrary element into the classification that one would like to avoid. But, for the reasons stated above, we have nevertheless, *faute de mieux*, decided on this mode of classification, taking as a guiding line certain empirical rules that we shall discuss later.

27   By these restrictions and a thorough consideration of the subject, we hope to have avoided being arbitrary in applying this principle.

28   In the following nomenclature (flight of ideas, associations etc.,) it must be remembered, after what has just been said, that by this we mean primarily speech-phenomena from which we have allowed ourselves to make deductions about psychological events. Here we are fully aware that we are examining a relatively limited area, that is, associations that are for the most part reflected in the speech mechanism. Thus, when we speak of "flight of ideas," we mean by this the speech phenomenon that is an external manifestation of internal processes. Of course, the psychological event is not necessarily reflected *in toto* in the form of word associations, but is only expressed in linguistic signs of that type when it affects the speech mechanism. In the flight of ideas, the actual thinking would naturally present a totally different picture if it could manifest itself directly. Thus, for example, the flight of ideas resulting from predominantly visual parts of images constitutes a special aspect

that can hardly manifest itself adequately enough and is therefore hardly accessible to external examination; particularly in mania, it will as a rule not be accessible to examination, because of the linguistic agitation. We shall find an opportunity in a later publication[9] to discuss the visual form of flight of ideas.

2. SPECIAL CLASSIFICATION

A. Internal Association[10]

29   (a) GROUPING. We classify under this heading all associations connected by co-ordination, superordination, subordination, or contrast. The perusal of the cases in question leads to the following special classification of co-ordinations:

30   (α) Co-ordination. The two parts are linked by a similarity of content or nature; i.e., a general idea, in which both parts are contained, underlies them. Examples:

(accumulation of water)

lake   ocean

(fruit)

cherry   apple

(measurement)

long   narrow

(injustice or vice)

unjust   faithlessness

---

[9] [No such publication has been traced.]

[10] Ziehen (*Introduction to Physiological Psychology* (orig. 1891), p. 205), arguing against internal association, gives as examples the following: *guest/chest, pain/ rain*, and remarks that these so-called internal associations are purely external and are almost completely limited to the acoustic image of words that have similar sounds. One can readily agree with Ziehen, for surely no one will want to call these examples of inner association.

We consider, with Wundt, that associative affinity is the principle of internal association and practice the principle of external association (or similarity = internal association, contiguity = outer association).

31   Association by co-ordination must take place within the framework of a clear-cut common general concept, but may be the result of more or less vague similarity. The similarity may be very great, so that only a nuance prevents it from being identical, e.g., *to forbear / leniency*. The similarity can also be very remote, so that the common meaning of the two concepts is not an essential one but a more or less coincidental attribute of the stimulus-image. In such cases the reaction appears very loosely connected with the stimulus-word and thus is distinguished from other co-ordinations. The distance of the association is, as it were, greater. Therefore these co-ordinations can to some extent be separated from those already discussed. In the loosely connected associations two categories can be distinguished:

(1) The stimulus-image is linked to the reaction by a meaningful but otherwise coincidental attribute, e.g.:

father (worried)	worry
play (of child?)	youth
War (peace-league)	Bertha v. Suttner[11]
murderer (to hang)	gallows
sentence (contains something)	content
star (romantic, night?)	romanticism

(2) The stimulus-image is linked to the reaction by an unessential, external, mostly quasi co-existent attribute, e.g.:

pencil (long)	length
sky (blue)	colour
sea (deep)	depth
table (particular shape)	style

32   These two modes of co-ordination may be called "the connection of images according to internal or external kinship." The first category contains by far the more significant co-ordinations, and justifies to some extent the terms internal and external. The co-existence of attributes in the second category indicates that the formation of these co-ordinations is due to external association.

[11] [Baroness von Suttner (d. 1914), Austrian writer and pacifist, recipient of the first Nobel Peace Prize, 1905.]

33   As a last category of co-ordination we should like to propose "co-ordination through example." This category primarily contains reactions that are nothing but the inversions of the two previously discussed patterns:

worry	father (e.g., of the father)
content	sentence (e.g., of the sentence)
colour	sky (e.g., of the sky)
misery	old woman (e.g., an old woman is in misery)

34   Now, there is a series of reactions to adjectives and verbs which, although it is true that they are not grammatically co-ordinated to the stimulus-word, can nevertheless perhaps best be grouped with co-ordinations, particularly those of the examples:

to give in	peace-loving	foreign	emigrant
to pay attention	clever man	to pray	pious man
to despise	wickedness	to help	good man

35   These associations can, if the expression be permitted, be called analytical; they are conceptions that are given, so to speak, implicitly with the stimulus-word to which they have been subordinated or superordinated. But as it is difficult, if not impossible, to distinguish this relationship with certainty in concrete cases, and as in addition the concept of the whole and the part cannot be applied to adjectives and verbs, we count these reactions also as co-ordination through example, inasmuch as among the possible nouns certain typical ones always appear in the reactions. The reactions in these cases are always extremely general and closely dependent on the stimulus-word.

36   The special classification of the co-ordinations would then be as follows:

(1) by common general concept
(2) by similarity
(3) by internal relationship
(4) by external relationship
(5) by example

Examples

(1) father   uncle
(2) father   God
(3) father   worry

16

(4) father   our house
(5) to pay attention clever man

37 It must be added that with these examples the rich variety of co-ordinations is by no means exhausted. With individuals who associate intensively according to subjective constellations, a whole series of different co-ordinations, which cannot really be placed in any of these categories, is possible. In these cases one can safely admit one's inability and simply content oneself with the classification "co-ordination." One can console oneself with the idea that the individual possibilities are innumerable and that no schema could ever be invented that would make possible a clear-cut classification of all associations. But there is a number of co-ordinations that could without undue strain be placed under different headings, i.e., they have no clearly defined character; one can either leave it at that or perhaps group these reactions with the type they most resemble. The headings set out above are not meant to be absolute, compulsory categories, but merely a name for empirically found types which, on occasion, however, may merge into each other without sharp boundaries. More must not be expected in our present state of knowledge of association.

38 (β) *Subordination.* The reaction is considered as a part or a minor (subordinated) concept of the stimulus-word, e.g.:

   tree beech

39 Here we include all reactions that specify the stimulus-word, i.e., that represent special instances of the general stimulus-concept, e.g.:

   house   house on X street
   horse   Mr. X's horse
   railway station Baden

40 In some cases there may be doubt whether the association should be considered as subordination or as predicate, e.g.:

   food today's (viz., food)

41 (γ) *Superordination.* The reaction is considered as the whole or general concept of the stimulus-word, e.g.:

   Ofen[12] town
   cat   animal

[12] [See infra, par. 423, n. 47.]

17

Here too the separation from the predicate is difficult, e.g., *thirteen / unlucky number.* Is *unlucky number* in this case a general concept and as such includes thirteen with other unlucky numbers? In our opinion there is a predicate here; on the other hand we would include Aschaffenburg's association *baptism / ancient custom* as a superordination, as *ancient custom* is a general concept that includes many other subordinate concepts.

42 (δ) *Contrast.* The concept can be understood without difficulty. The classification and evaluation of the contrasts is much more difficult, however. Contrasts are as a rule very closely associated images, not only conceptually but also perceptually and above all linguistically. There are even languages in which only one and the same word exists to express typical contrasts. It must have been a considerable psychic achievement in the beginning of language and conscious thought to separate contrasts in speech and concept. Today, however, we have these ancient achievements in thought already formulated in the language; they are taught to us from earliest youth together with the first concepts of speech, with the first songs and reading material. We are verbally very practised in these closely connected concepts, which are very often supported by quotations and rhymes; e.g.:

sorrow	joy	sour	sweet
pain	pleasure	light	dark
good	bad		

Sauersüss and *helldunkel*[13] are even colloquial words in German. For these reasons we have grouped a large number of common contrasts with external associations. Here we only count associations that are not current, such as:

friendly	angry	sense	stupidity
good	sinful	vengeance	to forgive
animal	plant		

43 In spite of this detailed classification of the groupings there are still associations that cannot be put into any of the subgroups. For these there remains simply the general term "co-ordination," e.g., the association *high / silk.* The stimulus-word

13 [Sour-sweet and light-dark, i.e., *chiaroscuro.*]

high [German *hoch*] has been understood as a proper name; the bearer of this name [Hoch] has a silk shop; hence the reaction *silk*. This cannot be merely a case of co-existence; the reaction consists of two specific images that are spatially co-existent; it is therefore a rather complicated formation. One could perhaps place it under the heading "co-ordination through external connection," though admittedly on slight evidence. Therefore it is safest, for the moment, to admit that such co-ordination cannot be further classified.

44   Summarizing, we arrive at the following schema:

Grouping
- (α) Co-ordination:
  - (1) by a common general concept
  - (2) by similarity
  - (3) by internal relationship
  - (4) by external relationship
  - (5) by example
- (β) Subordination:
  - (1) Actual subordination
  - (2) Specification
- (γ) Superordination
- (δ) Contrast
- (ε) Groupings of doubtful quality

45   (b) PREDICATE. We include here, in agreement with Aschaffenburg, all judgments, properties, and activities that in any way refer to the stimulus concept as subject or object (summarized by Kraepelin under the name "predicative relationships").[14]

46   It is well known that Kant divides judgments into analytic and synthetic.[15] This principle of logical classification is of value to us only in so far as, in an analytic judgment, a part of the concept (i.e., a predicate) is presented that is necessarily inherent in the concept. Thus only that is given which already implicitly exists. But in the synthetic judgment something is added to the concept that is not necessarily already contained

[14] *Psychol. Arb.*, I, p. 222.

[15] "In an analytical judgment I do not go beyond the given conception, in order to arrive at some decision respecting it. If the judgment is affirmative, I predicate of the conception only that which was already cogitated in it; if negative, I merely exclude from the conception its contrary. But in synthetical judgments, I must go beyond the given conception, in order to cogitate, in relation with it, something quite different from that which was cogitated in it . . ." etc. Kant, *Critique of Pure Reason* (trans. Meiklejohn, 1934), p. 126.

in the concept. As regards associative performance the synthetic judgment is in a way superior to the analytic. If we approach this question practically, we find (in so far as this method of classification can in practice be applied at all) that in simple judgment-reactions the analytic judgment exists mainly in the naming of a co-existent perceptible attribute, while the synthetic judgment is mostly a value judgment with a more or less marked ego-reference. Thus we see here a relationship analogous to that between "co-ordination by external relationship" and "co-ordination by internal relationship." In the association *pencil / length, length* is essentially contained in the concept or is co-existent, while in *father / worry* the concept *worry* adds something new and therefore causes a shifting of concept. We should readily accept the grouping of judgment-reactions into analytic and synthetic if there were not a considerable practical difficulty: we have no way of knowing in the individual case whether the analytic predicate is an essential part of the concept or not. One can only attempt to decide this question if one can differentiate in individual cases between a concrete and an abstract concept. We know that Ziehen considers that he has done this by direct questioning, even of children. We not only consider this method most unreliable, but also find the distinction between concrete and abstract concepts particularly difficult. If I give a name to a mental picture, then the picture consists of a condensation of many memories, whose more concrete or more abstract aspect depends on minimal differences of perceptual vividness. In many cases even psychologically educated people would be at a loss if they had to decide whether, for example, in *house / roof* they had visualized a concrete or an abstract roof. Of course we are far from denying the existence of abstract concepts; but in concrete cases of acoustic-verbal experiments we cannot help suspecting that the so-called abstract concepts are merely words that lack individual content, only not so much because they are abstract concepts as that they are mostly linguistic formations of a motor kind, in which the other sense-impressions participate only very slightly.

47   For the answer to the question whether we are faced with an analytic or synthetic judgment we should have to know exactly whether the thought was concrete or abstract: e.g., *snake / green* is objectively entirely synthetic. It is not necessary

to think of *green* together with *snake*; only in the case of the image of a definite snake must green be already implicit, in which case it would be an analytic judgment. Apart from these reservations, there are other, mainly practical, difficulties which interdict this mode of classification.

48   In order to arrive at a special classification of the predicate we must consider the different possibilities:

(1) The stimulus-word is a noun, the reaction an adjective.

(2) The stimulus-word is an adjective, the reaction a noun.

49   We have no reason to separate these two cases, any more than the other forms of predicative connection:

(1) The stimulus-word is the subject, the reaction its active or passive activity.

(2) The stimulus-word is the active or passive activity of the reaction. Or:

(3) The stimulus-word is the object, the reaction is the activity referring to it.

(4) The stimulus-word is an activity, the reaction is its object.

50   Let us consider the first forms: the predicative connection of noun and adjective. Two main possibilities are to be distinguished:

51   (*a*) The adjective describes an essential and internally meaningful characteristic of the stimulus-image. One can call this type of predicate "internal." It can easily be divided into two groups:

(1) Objective judgment, e.g.:

snake	poisonous	war	bloody
glass	fragile	grandmother	old
mild	spring	winter	raw
thirst	intense		

These predicates describe an essential and meaningful addition to the stimulus. Their purely objective character distinguishes them from the second group:

(2) Value judgment, e.g.:

father	good	pupil	good
to stink	unpleasant	soldier	brave
to ride	dangerous	wood	useful
mountain	beautiful	murderer	base
book	interesting	water	refreshing

21

In these reactions the personal element is more or less prominent; but where the ego-reference is clearly expressed in the
form of wish or rejection, one can speak directly of "egocentric
predicates." We do not however want to separate such reactions
from value judgments as a distinct group, for reasons stated
below. We also count the following as value judgments:

iron	useful metal
water	one of the most interesting chemical substances
scoundrel	disgrace

52   Value judgments expressed in the form of an activity, e.g.:

smoke	stinks
apple	tastes nice

are best placed with the predicates.

53   We also count as value judgments reactions in which a value
is not stated but demanded, e.g.:

good	one should be
diligent	the pupil should be
to threaten	one must not

54   Such reactions are not frequent in normal subjects; we
merely mention them for the sake of completeness.

55   (β) The adjective refers to an external, less significant, possibly co-existent, and perceptible characteristic of the stimulus.
For this type of predicate we should like to use the term "external":

tooth	protruding	exercise-book	blue
water	wavy	salt	granular
tree	brown	etc.	

56   We assess the predicate-relation between adjective as stimulus-word and noun as reaction according to the principles
explained above. Thus, in classifying, we evaluate *green /
meadow, meadow / green*, as more or less equivalent.

57   Aschaffenburg has with some reason considered interjections as predicates, but we have interpreted them differently
(see below).

58   A further sub-group of predicates is made up of the "relationships of noun and verb."

59 (a) *The subject relation*. The noun as the stimulus-word or the reaction is the subject of a definite activity:

resin	sticks	to cook	mother
hunter	to shoot		

60 (β) *The object relation*. The noun as the stimulus-word or the reaction is the object of a definite activity:

door	to open	to clean	brass
to recruit	soldiers	throat	to strangle

61   The predicates so far discussed cannot easily be distinguished from the above-mentioned "co-ordination by example," if the attributive part is the stimulus-word. For this diagnosis we consider decisive the subject's evident effort to find a reaction-word (i.e., a noun) as appropriate as possible to the stimulus-word and with a general validity, as in:

to pray	pious person
to despise	wickedness
to give in	peace-loving

Thus we count *to clean / brass* as an object relation and *to clean / shining metal* as co-ordination by example.

62   Specifications of place, time, means, and purpose are somewhat loosely connected with the group of predicates (Ranschburg's[16] "end-defining association").

place: to go	into town
time: to eat	12 o'clock
means: to beat	with a stick
purpose: wood	for burning

63   One can sometimes, with these reactions, be in doubt about whether perhaps they are to be interpreted as specification and therefore belong to subordinations. But in most cases the decision will be easy, so that error will not be too great. Definitions or explanations of the stimulus-word, which in general occur very rarely, have a certain connection with the group discussed above, for which reason they too have been placed in the group of predicative relations. Examples:

door	noun	star	heavenly body
blue	adjective		

---

16 Ranschburg and Balint, p. 715.

23

64   The predicative relations are thus made up of the following groups:

Predicative Relations
- I. Noun and adjective
  - (a) Internal predicate
    - (1) Objective judgment
    - (2) Value judgment
  - (β) External predicate
- II. Noun and verb
  - (a) Subject relation
  - (β) Object relation
- III. Determination of place, time, means, and purpose
- IV. Definition

65   (c) CAUSAL RELATIONSHIP (Münsterberg). Stimulus-word and reaction are linked by a causal connection. Examples:

pain	tears
to cut	painful

B. External Associations

66   (a) CO-EXISTENCE. The connection of co-existence is *contiguity or simultaneity*, i.e., the link between the two concepts is not exclusively similarity or affinity but also temporal co-existence or immediate succession. Spatial co-existence is included in temporal contiguity as spatial co-existence results from succeeding sense-impressions. Examples:

ink	pen	pupil	teacher
exercise-book	knife	table	chair
table	soup	lamp	family
Christmas	Christmas tree	mother	child
Sunday	church	institution	warder

We also include here reactions like:

to ride	horse	to ride	saddle
eye	to see	ear	to hear
pencil			
paper			
exercise-book	to write		
to sing			
to calculate			
school			

The associations with *to write* are complexes of school-memories, the connection of which is conditioned by simultaneity; the other examples concern reactive images associated with the stimulus images by co-existence.

67   (b) IDENTITY. The reaction contains no shift or development of the sense, but is a more or less synonymous expression for the stimulus-word.

68   (a) The synonymous expression is taken from the same language as the stimulus-word. Examples:

grand	magnificent
to pay attention	to take notice (in Swiss-German usage, essentially synonyms)
to squabble	quarrel

69   (β) The synonymous expression is taken from a language other than the stimulus-word, i.e., it is a *translation*. Examples:

stamp	timbre
Sunday	dimanche

70   (c) LINGUISTIC-MOTOR FORMS. (Ziehen:[17] "Current word-compounds and associative word-complements." Kraepelin-Aschaffenburg:[18] "Linguistic reminiscences." Trautscholdt:[19] "Word association.") In this sub-group of external associations we collect together all connections of images, which have been canalized through verbal practice, although logically and historically they may have a different meaning and therefore could be put into one of the types mentioned above. In dealing with *contrasts* we have already mentioned a series of reactions that we interpreted as being of such common verbal practice as to be canalized. We classify them as

71   (a) *Canalized verbal associations.*

    (1) Simple contrasts. Examples:

dark	light	white	black
sweet	sour	like	unlike

[17] Ziehen, "Die Ideenassoziation des Kindes" (1898), p. 29; *Sammlung von Abhandlungen aus dem Gebiete der pädagogischen Psychologie*, I (1898), p. 6.
[18] *Psychol. Arb.*, I, p. 223.
[19] "Experimentelle Untersuchungen über die Assoziation der Vorstellungen," p. 213.

(2) Current phrases. Examples:

hunger	to suffer	something	more
house	and home[20]	force	to apply
of age	to come	bread	to earn
goods	and chattels[21]	head	to bow
thanks	to give	bird	bush
gallant	to be	water	to drink
trials	and tribulations	to swim	to be able to
world	and people	tram	to ride
old	frail	to go	for a walk
right	to do	revulsion	to arouse
to come	(and) go	cat	mouse
place	time	to break	the news

72   (β) *Proverbs and quotations.* Examples:

everywhere	and nowhere	war	and peace
liberty	equality	more	light[22]
everywhere	I am at home	meat	drink
eye	tooth		
do's	and don'ts		

73   (γ) *Compound words.*

(1) The reaction-word complements the stimulus-word and forms a compound word. Examples:

table	leg	frog	blood[24]
needle	case	book	marker
mat	hanging[23]	head	scarf
piano	player	tooth	ache
vengeance	to thirst for	institute	women's

The reaction may also be such that the stimulus-word is repeated in the reaction, e.g.:

tears	tearduct[25]	foot	football[27]
to knock	to knock at	star	starlight
to hear	to hear out[26]	sweet	sweetmeat

20 [In German, *Grund/und Boden* (bottom/and ground), an expression referring to the hospital grounds.]
21 [In German, *Kind/Kegel* (child/bastard); *Kind und Kegel* is a folk expression for "the whole family."]
22 [Goethe's dying words.]
23 [*Matte/Hänge = Hängematte*, 'hammock,' originally a hanging mat. Some of these compounds are untranslatable.]
24 [Referring to someone who is "cold-blooded."]
25 [The actual example, *Tränensack*, refers to the lacrymal sac.]

(2) The reaction is essentially only a grammatical variation of the stimulus-word (Wreschner:[28] "Association with inflexional form").

to die	dead	to find	found
kindling	to kindle	love	to love
to hammer	hammer	cab	cabby
school	scholar	murderer	to murder

74   (δ) To this should be added a small group of reactions that can be termed anticipatory. Examples:

| dark red | light | grandiose | small |
| slow | short | | |

75   (ε) Interjections, which only rarely occur, have been placed in the category of "linguistic-motor connections" although, as Aschaffenburg stresses, they represent a predicate. We justify our interpretation by pointing out the highly imperfect linguistic form of the reaction, which moreover contains a very strong motor component. Examples:

| grand | ah! | to love | oh! |
| to stink | pooh! | | |

C. Sound Reactions[29]

76   The content of this group corresponds to Aschaffenburg's group of "stimulus-words acting only by sound."

77   (a) WORD COMPLETION. We interpret these words in agreement with Aschaffenburg, only including here reactions that together with the stimulus-word, form an indivisible word. Examples:

| wonder | -ful | modest | -y |
| love | -ly | friend | -ly |

---

26 [The German, *aufhören*, means to listen attentively.]

27 [In the German language there is the generic term *Spielball*, meaning a ball used for any game.]

28 Wreschner, "Eine experimentelle Studie über die Assoziation in einem Falle von Idiotie" (1900), p. 241.

29 ["Sound" = German *Klang*, also translated in the *Coll. Works* as "clang."]

We also consider addition to the stimulus-word, to form a name, as word-completion. Example:

Canter   -bury
Winter   -bourne[30]

78   (b) Sound. The reaction is conditioned solely by the sound of the whole stimulus-word or its beginning.[31] Examples:

enchain	enchant	intention	intestine
mercenary	merciful	to roast	roast beef
		humility	humidity

79   (c) Rhyme.[32] Examples:

dream	cream	king	ring
heart	smart	crank	plank
leave	grieve		

80   To divide sounds and rhymes into "meaningful and meaningless," as Aschaffenburg does, is not worthwhile, owing to the rarity of the "meaningless" ones. We have therefore refrained from doing this.

D. Miscellaneous

81   This not very large group comprises reactions for which no place can be found in the rest of the schema, but which have only a very limited connection with each other.

82   (a) Indirect Association. Aschaffenburg, as is well-known, contrasts the indirect mode of reaction with all other reactions, which he regards as "direct" ones. We have rejected this quantitatively most disproportionate contradistinction, because with uneducated subjects one can never know how many different contents of consciousness stand between stimulus-word and reaction. We cannot even *ourselves* always state how many conscious, half-conscious, or unconscious constellations affect our reactions. We will not enter here into the academic contro-

---

[30] [The examples given by Jung are *Laufen* (to run)/*burg* and *Winter*/*thur*, both giving the name of a town.]

[31] [Jung's examples (except for *to roast*/*roast beef*), being untranslatable, have been replaced by similar pairs of English words.]

[32] [Some of the rhyming pairs have been replaced by English equivalents.]

versies about indirect association (that is, whether the intermediate link is conscious or unconscious) but confine ourselves to stating the phenomenon of the indirect mode of reaction within the framework of our cases. We call "indirect association" that mode of reaction that is intelligible only on the assumption of an intermediate link different from the stimulus-word and the reaction. We distinguish five forms:

83   (a) Connection by common intermediate concept. Examples:

white far	dozen 144
snowfield	heap
false blonde	turbid shallow
Miss X is false and blonde	water
repentance black	red scent
mourning	flower
to close round	bicycle round
to turn	wheel
to disgust odourless	to walk pear
to stink	under pear-trees
fast to whistle	to turn earth
locomotive	to rotate
hay green	rich 5-franc piece
grass	roll of money

84   It must be noted that in these associations the intermediate link is usually clearly conscious. Such reactions are very rare and occur almost entirely in individuals of markedly visual type.

85   (β) *Centrifugal sound-shift* (Aschaffenburg's "paraphasic indirect association"). There is an inner reaction that is to a greater or lesser extent clear and meaningful, which, however, in the process of articulating it, is replaced by a canalized association with a similar sound. We therefore designate this

29

group of indirect associations as "centrifugal sound-shift." Examples:[33]

decision to slide
(to decide)

stubborn foolish
(mulish)

to quarrel to shoot
(dispute)

hair blue
(blonde)

sacrifice to castrate
(casket, sacristy)

ears typhus
(tubes)

to dress excessive
(overcoat)

society unit
(union)

earth house
(heap)

medal fastness
(fastened)

love crate
(hate)

pair hoot
(boot)

86   Cordes wants to exclude these reactions from the indirect ones, admittedly, from his point of view, with some justification. The direct inner association appears to be a genuine association and not a sound reaction; so there exists an entirely appropriate and direct intention which, however, at the moment of enunciation, is shifted towards a similarity of sound to the detriment of the meaning. Such shifts can only occur when the inner image to be expressed does not command the intensity of attention necessary to set going the appropriate speech-mechanism. Deviations into by-ways only occur when what has to be enunciated is not intense enough, i.e., it does not reach a sufficient degree of consciousness. Therefore we also assume that, in spite of correct intention, the intermediate link has remained abnormally obscure, which agrees completely with the accounts of subjects who can observe themselves. Some had no more than a feeling that they had not said the right thing, without being able to point to the intermediate link. Whether in such cases the shift towards similarity of sound occurs at the sending station or the receiving station seems to us irrelevant to the evaluation of the reaction.

87   (γ) *Centripetal sound-shift.* The stimulus-word is internally replaced by a sound similarity, which in its turn determines the reaction. Usually the intermediate link is in that case half-con-

[33] [Most of the original examples are not translatable, so equivalents have been found.]

scious or unconscious. It must be noted that in all cases here classified the stimulus-word has been correctly understood, so that it is not merely a case of misunderstanding. Examples:[34]

to ride slip (slide)	lazy mist (hazy)
to wallow bird (swallow)	to rust fair (just)
strong sin (wrong)	room to caw (rook)
malt pepper (salt)	stroke cigar (smoke)
politics hefty (policeman)	to wallow throat (swallow)
stroke knot (string)	to love turtle (dove)
to hit to bite (to smite)	pleasure tape (measure)
malt vinegar (salt)	

88   In our experience by far the largest number of indirect associations are shifts through sound similarity. What we have said in the preceding paragraph about the consciousness of the intermediate links also applies here. The occurrence of a sound association points to a stimulus-word with an inadequate feeling-tone.[35] Reaction to the intermediate sound-link is likewise a result of insufficient feeling-tone of the stimulus-word. In this case the sound association is, in our experience, as indistinct as the stimulus-word, and at first the subject is even unsure of the kind of stimulus-word. The reaction is innervated before the act of apperception has taken place.[36]

[34] [Many of the original examples, being untranslatable, have been replaced by English equivalents.]

[35] Intensity of attention; see above, par. 86.

[36] Münsterberg maintains that, in order to stimulate associations, the external excitation does not first have to be converted into a conscious process, but that, between external excitation and conscious central excitation, there is a non-conscious stage in which an association-process takes place that does not reach consciousness (*Beiträge zur experimentellen Psychologie*, IV (1892), p. 7). Nevertheless, Münsterberg denies the occurrences of indirect associations through conscious intermediate links (ibid., p. 9).

89   (δ) *Centrifugal and centripetal shift through word-completion or linguistic-motor association.* Examples:

standard	filter		head	block
	(solution)			(blockhead)
false	faithfulness		angel	heart
	(faithful)			(hard)
rats	poisonous		clean	flea
	(poison)			(unclean)
to cook	coachman		painter	beautiful
	(the cook)			(painting)
avarice	patient		lockjaw	teeth
	(pathological)			(jaw)
armlet	foot		permanently	to certify
	(arm)			(deranged)
horrible	grey		to roll	round
	(gruesome)			(roller)
look-out	strike		fox	finger
	(lock-out)			(foxglove)

90   (ε) *Shift by several intermediate links.* The intermediate links may be associations that are mechanical yet of high valency. The reactions in this category are very rare and are mostly of abnormal origin. All the types described above can of course be found among these reactions. Examples:

ink	acid		revenge	rector
(red	litmus)		(right	rectify)
bird	mouse			
(flutter	bat [*Fledermaus*])			
lithe	big		tough	headache
(lice	small)		(tooth	ache)

91   We shall not at present look further into the theory of indirect association in acoustic-verbal experiments. For the moment let us simply say that these associations are closely connected with variations in concentration.

92   (b) MEANINGLESS REACTIONS. In moments of emotion or embarrassment reactions are sometimes given that are not words or are not associations.

93   We of course separate assonances as sound reactions from

32

mere sounds. Among the non-associated words there are hardly any of inexplicable origin. They are mostly names of objects in the surroundings or of coincidental concepts that are not connected with the stimulus-word. Some nonsense reactions are perseverations of type b (see below).

94   (c) FAILURES. The absence of a reaction we call a failure. The cause of the failure is usually emotional.

95   (d) REPETITION OF THE STIMULUS-WORD. A very small group that could equally well be put into the category of failures! There are, however, normal individuals who cannot help quickly repeating the stimulus-word to themselves and then giving the actual reaction, a phenomenon that can be observed outside the experiment in ordinary conversation. This reaction is not included in any of the normal categories. Repeating the stimulus-word is, in any case, also an emotional phenomenon (Wreschner[37] is of the same opinion).

96   This completes the specific classification of associations. There remain only a few general points that help to clarify the types of association.

E. The Egocentric Reaction

97   It is striking that certain individuals tend to form ideas of reference during the experiment; that is, to give highly subjective judgments that are clearly influenced by wish or fear. Such reactions have something individually characteristic and are indicative of certain personalities.

98   (a) DIRECT IDEAS OF REFERENCE. Examples:

grandmother	I
to dance	I don't like
unjust	I was not
praise	for me
to calculate	I cannot

99   (b) SUBJECTIVE VALUE JUDGMENTS. Examples:

to be lazy	pleasant	piano	horrible
to calculate	laborious	love	stupid
blood	gruesome		

[37] "Eine experimentelle Studie über die Assoziation in einem Falle von Idiotie."

33

F. Perservation[38]

100   By perseveration we understand a phenomenon[39] that consists in the fact that the preceding association conditions the next reaction. We have made it a rule to consider the effect on only the immediately following reaction. Thus we have excluded an effect that bypasses uninfluenced reactions; we prefer to consider this type of effect under the general heading of constellation. Here we do not want to be prejudiced about the nature of the phenomenon of perseveration. We must point out, however, that perseveration may be caused by psychophysical factors at present unknown as well as by specific feeling-constellations. In practice, two cases of perseveration are to be distinguished:

101   (a) The reaction is an association to a previously used stimulus-word. Examples:

winter ——	skates
lake ＼	ice
to melt ——	hot
slow ＼	fire
water ——	fall
to dance ＼	to fall

102   (b) The reaction is not an association to a previously used stimulus-word. Examples:

lid ——	box
rats ＼	basket
softly ——	she comes along
gallant ——	up the steps

103   If at the moment of the experiment consciousness is dom-

---

[38] Aschaffenburg's "association to words previously used."

[39] We use the word "perseveration," as in Müller's and Pilzecker's experiments ["Experimentelle Beiträge zur Lehre vom Gedächtnis," 1900], to denote merely the continuance of the preceding image in so far as it is manifest in the following reaction. The term is intended to be purely formal and is not intended to explain anything. We offer no opinion on whether the perseveration is a cortical or a cellular (nutritional) process (Gross) or whether the result is a particular associative constellation. In any case, we wish to stress that our concept has no connection with the "perseveration" in organic cerebral processes any more than with the hypothetical "secondary function of brain cells" which is said to explain the psychological after-effect of the vector-image.

inated by a strongly feeling-toned complex, then a longer series of heterogeneous stimulus-words will be absorbed into the complex, each reaction being influenced by stimulus-word and complex-constellation. The more powerful the complex-constellation, the more the stimulating image is liable to assimilation (Wundt), i.e., it is not comprehended in its actual and usual sense but in the special sense adapted to the complex.

G. Repetition

104   In each experiment the same reactions were counted; the first and second hundred of the associations in normal subjects were counted separately. One could perhaps differentiate between repetition of content and of particular stylistic form. Since in normal subjects particular stereotype-reactions constructed with auxiliary words are extremely rare, we have decided not to count repetitions of form.

H. Linguistic Connection

105   It is a striking fact that associations are linked to each other not only by meaning (i.e., the principles of *association, contiguity*, and *similarity*) but also by certain solely external motor-acoustic properties. To my knowledge Bourdon was the first to tackle this question experimentally. In his remarkable work "Recherches sur la succession des phénomènes psychologiques," he describes investigations into the phonetic linking of association. Bourdon noted, from the top of every page in books chosen at random, the first noun, adjective, or verb. In this way he compared five hundred pairs of words. The total of phonetically similar pairs was 312, assuming a phonetic similarity if the words have one or more phonetic element in common. It must be noted, however, that Bourdon interpreted this similarity somewhat widely, e.g., *toi* and *jouer* because of the "w" sound! Bourdon examined especially the *ressemblance phonétique, graphique* (one or more common letters), and *syllabique* (a common syllable). He found the following comparative figures:

Ressemblance phonétique:	0.629
"	graphique:	0.888
"	syllabique:	0.063

106   Bourdon finds: "Il reste néanmoins vrai, que les mots s'as-

socient entre eux plutôt par leur signification que par leur ressemblance phonétique."

107   In accordance with these investigations, we have assembled a group that contains external linguistic factors.

108   (a) THE SAME GRAMMATICAL FORM. We simply counted how often the form of the word was the same in the stimulus-word as in the reaction, that is how often noun / noun, adjective / adjective occurred together. We arrived at this question because we had observed that large individual variations exist.

109   (b) THE SAME NUMBER OF SYLLABLES. We counted how often the stimulus-word and the reaction contain the same number of syllables, with the object of finding out more about the influence of rhythm.

110   (c) PHONETIC AGREEMENT.

(1) *Consonance.* We counted how often the first syllable of the stimulus-word and of the reaction agreed at least as regards the vowel.

(2) *Alliteration.* Here we noted how often the stimulus-word and the reaction alliterated in the first vowel or consonant.

(3) *The same ending.* Here we examined the phonetic influence of the ending of the stimulus-word on the ending of the reaction, that is, the tendency to rhyme. Here we only noted whether the final syllables tallied.

SUMMARY

111   *A. Internal Associations*

(a) Grouping
    (α) Co-ordination
        (1) By common general concept
        (2) By similarity
        (3) By internal relationship
        (4) By external relationship
        (5) By example
    (β) Subordination
        (1) Actual subordination
        (2) Specification
    (γ) Superordination
    (δ) Contrast
    (ε) Groupings of doubtful quality

(b) Predicative relationship
    I. Noun and adjective
        (α) Internal predicate
            (1) Objective judgment
            (2) Value judgment
        (β) External predicate
    II. Noun and verb
        (α) Subject relationship
        (β) Object relationship
    III. Determination of place, time, means, and purpose
    IV. Definition or explanation
(c) Causal relationship

B. External Associations

(a) Coexistence
(b) Identity
(c) Linguistic-motor forms
    (α) Canalized verbal associations
        (1) Simple contrasts
        (2) Current phrases
    (β) Proverbs and quotations
    (γ) Compound words and word-changes
    (δ) Anticipatory reactions
    (ε) Interjections

C. Sound Reactions

(a) Word-completion
(b) Sound
(c) Rhyme

D. Miscellaneous

(a) Indirect associations
    (α) Connection by common intermediate concept
    (β) Centrifugal sound-shift
    (γ) Centripetal sound-shift
    (δ) Shift through word-completion or linguistic-motor form
    (ε) Shift through several intermediate links
(b) Meaningless reactions

(c) Failures
(d) Repetition of the stimulus-word

E. The Egocentric Reaction

(a) Direct ideas of reference
(b) Subjective value judgments

F. Perseveration

(a) Connection with a [previous] stimulus-word
(b) No connection with a [previous] stimulus-word

G. Repetition of the Reaction

H. Linguistic Connection

(a) The same grammatical form
(b) The same number of syllables
(c) Phonetic agreement
   (1) Consonance
   (2) Alliteration
   (3) The same ending

112   We have classified our material according to the principles laid down in the schema. In order not to complicate the presentation of the results unnecessarily by a plethora of figures, the graphs published in Part Two reproduce only the figures of the main groups, allowing the extensive material to be grouped more clearly than with a detailed report of the figures for all the sub-groups. For reasons of scientific integrity we considered ourselves obliged to give an exact account of the kind of consideration that led us to the classification of the associations in one or other main group. Also it seemed to us of general interest to state the different empirical possibilities of the associations so far as they are known to us.

113   Thus our figures concern merely the following main groups of the schema:

   I. Internal Associations
      1. Grouping
      2. Predicative relationship
      3. Causal relationship

II. *External Associations*
  1. Co-existence
  2. Identity
  3. Linguistic-motor forms

III. *Sound Reactions*
  1. Word-completion
  2. Sound
  3. Rhyme

IV. *Miscellaneous*
  1. Indirect associations
  2. Meaningless reactions
  3. Failures
  4. Repetition of the stimulus-word

A. *Perseveration*
B. *The Egocentric Reaction*
C. *Repetition of the Reaction*
D. *Linguistic Connection*

  1. The same grammatical form
  2. The same number of syllables
  3. Alliteration
  4. Consonance
  5. The same ending

PART TWO

RESULTS OF EXPERIMENTS

A. RESULTS OBTAINED FROM INDIVIDUAL SUBJECTS

114   Subjects reacted very differently to disturbing stimuli. Producing internal distraction was the most difficult, as already stated. It was not even possible to achieve with all educated subjects. External distraction by metronome-beats was somewhat easier. But here too great differences are apparent between individual subjects. It therefore seemed necessary to give the figures of each subject fully. Here a plethora of tables cannot be avoided. All figures are percentages.

I. EDUCATED WOMEN
Fourteen subjects with 4,046 reactions

115   *Subject 1.* In general the character of these associations [see table] is very objective and almost entirely uninfluenced by subjective constellations. In the normal state external associations prevail over internal ones. Between the first and second hundred of the normal reactions a clear difference is apparent, there being an increase of 9 per cent in the sound group. We attribute this change to a certain lassitude appearing in the reception of the second hundred, which psychologically has no more significance than a relaxation of attention.[1] There can

---

1 Aschaffenburg says: "Our attention is so enormously unstable, the non-controllable and unavoidable changes in our psychic life so great, that we should not use short experimental series. On the other hand one must not forget that in the course of longer experiments signs of fatigue occur, so that it is not, for example, permissible to compare the first 25 associations with the last 25 of a series of 200 reactions, without taking this fact into consideration" ("Experimentelle Studien," I, p. 217). Thus Aschaffenburg has noted the same phenomenon, but in our view has not interpreted it correctly.

Subject 1. About 22 years of age, very intelligent

SPECIAL QUALITY	NORMAL		DISTRACTION		
			Internal	External	
ASSOCIATIONS	1st Hundred	2nd Hundred		60 Metronome	100 Metronome
Grouping	26	21	16	4	12
Predicative relationship	14	14	2	4	2
Causal relationship	2	1	–	–	2
Co-existence	20	10	10	2	–
Identity	1	7	4	8	–
Linguistic-motor forms	36	36	54	20	38
Word-completion	1	1	6	8	2
Sound	–	8	6	34	38
Rhyme	–	1	–	6	–
Indirect	–	–	–	4	–
Meaningless	–	–	2	4	6
Failures	–	–	–	–	–
Repetition of stimulus-word	–	–	–	6	–
Egocentric reaction	1	–	–	–	–
Perseveration	1	–	2	6	4
Repetition of reaction	5	8	2	0	6
Same grammatical form	67	58	64	56	54
Same number of syllables	43	41	56	60	42
Alliteration	10	12	12	42	48
Consonance	12	15	16	52	52
Same ending	10	6	10	14	6
Internal associations	42	36	18	8	16
External associations	57	53	68	30	38
Sound reactions	1	10	12	48	40
Number of associations	100	100	50	50	50

41

certainly be no question here of psychological fatigue which, as Aschaffenburg has shown, brings about an increase of sound associations. The preceding psychic effort is much too slight for that. On the other hand, the relaxing of interest could very well be identified with lassitude in Kraepelin's[2] sense.

116   The columns after those giving figures for normal conditions describe the changes of association under the influence of artificially distracted attention. From a purely dynamic point of view one could say that the "associative energy" (Ranschburg[3]) was to such an extent diverted to another area that only a fraction of it is still available for the reaction. Thus a correspondingly poor or easy (that is, strongly canalized) association is given, because the stimulation of ready and accustomed cerebral mechanisms requires a smaller amount of energy than the canalization of relatively new and unaccustomed connections. From this point of view, the increase of linguistic-motor forms by 18 per cent in internal distraction can easily be understood;[4] but to understand the origin of the numerous sound reactions in external distraction is more difficult. Aschaffenburg believes that it is possible to hold motor excitation responsible.[5] This exists in mania, exhaustion,[6] and alcoholic intoxication. But it has been proved that flight of ideas, or modes of association similar to flight of ideas, can also occur without

2 *Psychol. Arb.*, I, p. 53. Kraepelin distinguishes between "lassitude" [*Müdigkeit*] and "fatigue" [*Ermüdung*]. Lassitude he regards as a sort of warning, a subjective feeling which, however, usually but not always develops before real fatigue.

3 Ranschburg and Hajós, *Beiträge zur Psychologie des hysterischen Geisteszustandes* (1897).

4 Aschaffenburg, I, p. 239. At the time of the formation of the external association linguistic habit predominates, while later, on reflection, a secondary tendency to co-ordinate develops.

5 "The facilitation of motor-impulses must be considered the essential factor responsible for the number of sound reactions exceeding the norm" (Aschaffenburg, II, p. 69; see also the work of Smith, Fürer, and Rüdin on the effects of alcohol, in Kraepelin's *Psychol. Arb.*). [For Rüdin, see Bibliography. Smith and Fürer did not contribute to *Psychol. Arb.*, though Rüdin and others cited their work on this subject.]

6 The expression "exhaustion" merely denotes a higher degree of impairment of mental and physical energy (Aschaffenburg, II, p. 47).

motor excitation, e.g., in epilepsy (Heilbronner[7]), catatonia, and manic stupor.[8]

117   In our experiment, motor excitation is as good as excluded. (The act of writing, which could be interpreted as "motor excitation," is excluded in internal distraction, the results of which coincide with those of external distraction.) Thus no relationship between sound reactions and motor excitations can be demonstrated; rather do we see the origin of sound reactions in diminished attention. Distraction has primarily an inhibiting effect on the development of internal associations (of "high valency") and favours the formulation of external, i.e., more mechanical association-forms, hence sound reactions in large numbers. In further description of the experiment we shall have ample opportunity to point out shifts of association-form towards external, that is mechanical associations. We can say that, when the experiment was at all successful, these shifts only occasionally took place.

118   It is striking that, in this obvious tendency towards mechanical reaction, sound reactions too were clearly favoured. But in the present state of our experience sound reactions are not mechanical, they are apparently non-canalized associations. In our interpretation, sound reactions, which are on only a slightly higher level than mere repetition of words, are the most primitive of associations by similarity. After early childhood they are no longer used but, always called up by the act of speech, they predominate as soon as a disturbance impedes the activities of the next higher levels of association (slips of the tongue or mis-hearing). They are, because of their uselessness in the normal thought-process, repressed and usually exist outside consciousness.

119   We call the increase of linguistic-motor forms and sound reactions the blunting of the reaction. The attentive reaction, which takes place in the focus of consciousness, is not a sound reaction (unless this is expressly sought); but if one succeeds in directing attention to another activity, that is moving the

---

7 Heilbronner, "Über epileptische Manie nebst Bemerkungen über die Ideenflucht" (1903).

8 There are, incidentally, also pure manias which, particularly when subsiding, still show a definite flight of ideas in a completely steady state of motility.

psychic reaction outside the focus of consciousness, then all those associations occur that had been repressed from clearly conscious reactions. We shall deal later in detail with the significance of this hypothesis for the pathology of association.

120   With faulty attention the stimulus-concept is not raised to a level of complete clarity or, in other words, it remains on the periphery of consciousness and is apprehended only by virtue of its external appearance as sound. The cause of these defective perceptions lies in the weakness of their emotional tone which, in its turn, is dependent on the disturbances of attention. Every process of apperception of an acoustic stimulus begins at the level of pure sound perception. From each of these levels associations can be externalized if simultaneously the speech centres are ready to discharge. That this does not normally happen is due to the inhibiting effect of directed attention, that is the raising of the stimulus-threshold for all inferior and undirected forms of association.

121   In this case the high frequency of meaningless reactions, up to 6 per cent in external distraction, is noteworthy. They are partly due to strong perseverations, e.g.:

intention ⎯⎯ out of humour ("one notices the
                                                    intention" etc.)[9]
to rescue ⎯⎯ art (art of poetry)

strong ⎯⎯ mighty
hatred ⎯⎯ magnificent[10]

and partly to distraction due to the unaccustomed noise of the metronome, e.g.:

appearance   rhythm

122   This reaction shows to some extent how strong an effect the disturbing stimulus had on this subject. The intense lowering of attention also explains the unusually high number of sound reactions. The gradual predominance of acoustic and linguistic factors is also illustrated by the distinct rise of the figures in the columns for alliteration and consonance; there

[9] [The reference is to a well-known quotation from Goethe's *Torquato Tasso*, Act II, Sc. I: "Man merkt die Absicht und man ist verstimmt" ("One notices the intention and becomes out of humour").]

[10] [In German, a rhyme: *mächtig/prächtig*.]

is also a definite increase in the words of the same number of syllables. The increase of perseveration during distraction is not easy to explain; perhaps it can be attributed to the lack of association caused by distraction. It seems to us worth mentioning that the external distraction in this case is a progressive one. We have used the sounds to demonstrate the progression. We divided the two experiments of external disturbance each into three parts and counted the sound associations in each part.

123   The progression is as follows:

1st experiment: 5, 5, 7.
2nd experiment: 5, 6, 8.

124   *Subject 2.* The general character of the associations is objective. The external associations only slightly predominate over the internal. Internal distraction seems to have had the most intense effect in this case. Sound reactions increase continuously from the first hundred on. The group of verbal associations shows, in comparison with the former case, certain differences during distraction. The agreement in grammatical form shows a distinct increase, and the agreement of number of syllables also increases generally. Consonance and alliteration, however, decrease somewhat. We do not of course know the individual causes of these differences.

125   The relatively numerous failures are striking, most of them occurring in the first hundred. Of the four in the first hundred, three were in answer to emotionally potent stimulus-words. In the second hundred there is only one, but at the same time numerous predicates, in this case value judgments coming to the fore. This circumstance seems to indicate that failures are essentially emotional phenomena, emotional inhibitions, as it were; they disappear in the second hundred with the occurrence of facilitated and more familiar subjective judgments. As in the former case, there is a definite rise of perseveration.

126   We should like to point out that in this case the largest number of indirect associations coincides with the smallest number of sound reactions and, conversely, the largest number of sound reactions coincided with the smallest number of indirect reactions. This correlation is, as will appear later, probably not coincidental.

45

Subject 2. About 24 years of age, intelligent, well read

ASSOCIATIONS	NORMAL		DISTRACTION		
				External	
SPECIAL QUALITY	1st Hundred	2nd Hundred	Internal	60 Metronome	100 Metronome
Grouping	27	14	10	16	16
Predicative relationship	18	26	18	18	20
Causal relationship	1	3	–	2	–
Co-existence	24	16	11	22	8
Identity	2	1	4	18	12
Linguistic-motor forms	21	36	50	16	36
Word-completion	–	1	2	2	6
Sound	–	1	1	–	2
Rhyme	–	–	–	2	–
Indirect	3	1	2	2	–
Meaningless	–	–	–	–	–
Failures	4	1	1	2	–
Repetition of stimulus-word	–	–	1	–	–
Egocentric reaction	1	1	–	–	–
Perseveration	1	1	2	2	4
Repetition of reaction	–	4	–	2	–
Same grammatical form	55	47	63	76	64
Same number of syllables	31	24	29	36	40
Alliteration	12	15	10	2	6
Consonance	12	17	17	8	12
Same ending	4	9	14	6	8
Internal associations	46	43	28	36	36
External associations	47	53	65	56	56
Sound reactions	–	2	3	4	8
Number of associations	100	100	100	50	50

127   The nature of internal distraction (which, with this subject, was in general more successful than with the preceding one) deserves some discussion. We intentionally directed the subject's attention mainly to visual images, as in our experience these are the sensory phenomena that most frequently accompany the association experiment and in most subjects occur with great vividness. Much rarer, on the other hand, is the ability to observe and report this phenomenon accurately. For instance, the first subject gave some rather unsatisfactory information in this respect. The second subject, on the other hand, observed very acutely on the whole and was able to give clear information. The experiment is best illustrated by a few examples:

singing   opera (or concert) singing

Directly after grasping the stimulus-word, the subject sees a scene from *Tannhäuser* on a certain stage.

hearth   fire

sees a particular memory-image of a fireside scene at a house in London.

tile   roof

sees red roofs.

journey   itinerary

sees an English traveller.

apple   tree

sees a picture of Eve with the apple.

honour   sense (of)

sees the vivid memory-image of a scene from Sudermann's *Honour*.

sail   cloth

sees a sailing-boat.

deportment   rule

47

sees the vivid memory-image of her younger brother at a school for dancing and deportment.

modest   -y

sees the picture of a certain young girl.

plant   kingdom

sees a certain picture-book with pictures of plants.

sign   post

sees a crossroads.

peacefully   rest peacefully

sees a certain small kitten.

music   enjoyment

sees the interior of a certain concert-hall (vivid memory-image).

128   These examples show that the reactions are very simple, mainly linguistic-motor forms. The mental images are in a certain associative relationship with the reaction. According to the subject's account they occur directly with the reaction, if not before it. In our view the reactions are mostly mechanical side-associations which are stimulated on the way to a higher reaction. The stimulus-image did not reach the level of complete clarity as it lacked the necessary energy to emerge or (not to speak in Herbart's terms) remained in the periphery of the field of consciousness, inhibited by the clear visual image. The following examples show this inhibition of the reaction, together with complete clarity of the visual image:

praise   praise for the singer

The subject sees a certain teacher, who praises her.

manners   good manners

sees the picture of a Swiss country community—of an old "custom."

like   like will to like

sees the written sum: 2 × 2 = 4.

to stretch   catstretcher (*Katzenstrecker*)

48

sees a stretched rubber-band (*Katzenstrecker* is a popular nickname for a man from Lucerne).

tight   tight-fisted

sees a tight (narrow) lead-pipe.

stone   buck (*Stein/Bock*)

sees a collection of minerals.

change   time (*Wechsel/Zeit*)

sees a promissory note (*Wechsel*).

fashion   woman of fashion

sees an elegant youth.

dull   eyes

sees a dull, rainy landscape (constellated by the day of the experiment).

mirror   smooth

sees the window of a certain glazier's.

forward   march

sees a copy of the *Forward* (newspaper).

down   to cut

sees a low stool in a certain sitting-room.

129   In these reactions the connection between reaction and inner image is, as it were, completely broken. The reaction mostly comes quite mechanically from a lower level of the process of apperception, while the mental image mostly represents quite a different apperception of the stimulus-word.

130   Conversely, the visual image may be stimulated from a lower level of apperception, as the following examples show:

number   number, quantity (*Zahl, Menge*)

sees a newly extracted tooth (*Zahn*).

to will   you must (*wollen/du musst*)

sees a woolly (*wolliges*) sheepskin.

49

¹³¹   *Subject 3.* The character of the associations is objective. The external associations predominate, particularly the linguistic-motor forms. Both attempts at distraction were very successful, particularly internal distraction, which resulted in 29 per cent of sound reactions. A few reactions under internal distraction are of interest:

        lid   nid (senseless rhyme)

The subject sees a beermug with a lid.

        hall   throat (*Halle/Hals*)

sees a waiting-room in a certain station.

        fall   staff

sees a waterfall.

        stone   bone (*Stein/Bein*)

sees a picture of the little town of Stein on the Rhine.

¹³²   The fact that the number of internal associations remained nevertheless above the normal level in internal distraction, and in the first half of external distraction, can be attributed to the fact that the artificial lowering of attention was not uniform and continuous but decreased from time to time, whereupon normal reactions were given. The reactions obtained from the same subject in a state of great physical and mental fatigue give a more uniform picture of associative levelling-down. According to these findings, the state of fatigue has no other significance for this experiment than a uniform lowering of attention; its repercussion on the association is in no way different from the results of the distraction experiments. Nor is a difference discernible in the finer points of individual associations—which cannot be counted or measured—except in a very few reactions, the content of which is caused by the particular constellation of fatigue. As appears from our further observations on this subject and also from Aschaffenburg's investigations, no specific change, other than the blunting of the emotional response during the state of fatigue, can be demonstrated. The blunting of the reaction in fatigue can easily be accounted for by a decrease of attention. We also have every reason to assume

Subject 3. About 21 years of age, intelligent, well read

SPECIAL QUALITY	NORMAL		DISTRACTION			
ASSOCIATIONS			Internal	External		FATIGUE
	1st Hundred	2nd Hundred		60 Metronome	100 Metronome	
Grouping	8	9	19	14	14	4
Predicative relationship	16	22	13	22	4	1
Causal relationship	–	–	2	–	–	–
Co-existence	22	7	4	–	2	10
Identity	3	12	6	10	6	2
Linguistic-motor forms	46	44	26	32	54	40
Word-completion	1	2	5	10	10	–
Sound	–	–	15	6	6	1
Rhyme	3	1	9	–	–	25
Indirect	1	3	1	–	2	3
Meaningless	–	1	–	6	2	12
Failures	–	–	–	–	–	–
Repetition of stimulus-word	–	–	–	–	–	–
Egocentric reaction	–	1	–	–	–	–
Perseveration	1	2	1	2	–	–
Repetition of reaction	7	12	6	8	8	8
Same grammatical form	63	50	62	52	54	70
Same number of syllables	52	46	60	44	50	73
Alliteration	6	4	16	14	12	18
Consonance	24	7	35	18	30	47
Same ending	13	20	22	20	16	44
Internal associations	24	31	34	36	18	5
External associations	71	63	36	42	62	52
Sound reactions	4	3	29	16	16	26
Number of associations	100	100	100	50	50	100

that the blunting of the reaction in alcoholic intoxication and manic excitation (observed by Kraepelin's school) is nothing but a symptom of disturbed attention. The connection with motor excitation suggested by Aschaffenburg is in our view merely an indirect one: the motor excitation lowers the intensity of attention and therefore brings about a blunting of associations. The disturbance of attention by motor excitation is a matter of experience and in the named conditions has long been known as "distractibility." Since attention as an affective condition is also linked to certain somatic (that is, muscular) processes, the decrease of its stability can be attributed to motor excitation. Thus Aschaffenburg is not correct when he considers motor excitation as the direct cause of the blunting of the reaction; motor excitation is absent in a whole series of abnormally low reactions. But common to all these conditions is a disturbance of attention, which is probably always the immediate cause for all association types similar to flight of ideas.[11] The origin of disturbed attention is of course different in (i.e., specific to) each single process; it can equally well be based on motor excitation or on loss or decrease of kinesthetic feelings, on raising of the muscular stimulus-threshold, on mental excitement, or on psychological split (as in our experiments).

133   The great variability of intensity of attention makes all association experiments with alcohol and fatigue susceptible to an error extremely difficult to estimate, so that in the state of our present experience it is practically impossible to say anything positive about the extent of the disturbances of association through alcohol, etc. Judging from the percentage ratios of these fatigue experiments, the subject must have been in an absolutely psychotic state. According to Aschaffenburg's theory, a result with 5 per cent internal associations and 27 per cent sound reactions corresponds to a state of heavy intoxication or serious mania or a state of quite abnormal fatigue. The intensity of this blunting, however, can easily be explained by the fact that great but not abnormal fatigue was accompanied by marked drowsiness. The decrease of attention, with raising

11 Aschaffenburg errs when he says, for example, that Nordau's descriptions referred to hypomanics; they refer rather to the larger group of individuals incapable of concentration and showing blunt association-type.

of external stimulus-thresholds, peculiar to this condition is, in analogy with distraction experiments, to be considered as one of the main causes of the blunting.[12] The intensity of drowsiness is an unmeasurable quantity; how much drowsiness was present in the states of fatigue examined by Aschaffenburg?

134   Drowsiness is not merely a somatic, physiological, but also to a certain extent a psychological phenomenon, which may perhaps be described by the name "autohypnosis." It is primarily a psychological event that takes place in the area of consciousness. It is mainly stimulated by somatic sensations but can also be produced by pure suggestion. Exactly the same applies to the effect of alcohol. The effects of alcohol may be to a large extent, particularly in the beginning of narcosis, purely suggestive; this probably accounts for the fact that the effects of alcohol on different dispositions may be quite different. Can one exclude or calculate the suggestive effects of alcohol in the alcohol experiment? In our view this is not possible. Therefore great caution is advisable in psychological alcohol experiments. Accordingly, disturbance of attention in fatigue and alcohol experiments need not always have its roots in motor excitation, but could equally well be derived from suggestion.

135   Let us return to our experiment. The great prevalence of external association can be attributed to momentary decrease of attention. The cause of the blunt reaction can, however, lie deeper. It is not unthinkable that there are individuals who, because of a congenital or acquired anomaly, have a more superficial mode of association than others; this anomaly may possibly lie in the sphere of attention, in that fatigue appears much more quickly than in other people. The figures for the sister and mother of subject 3 are interesting in this respect as observations of family psychology. We give the tables here.

136   *Subject 4*, about 20 years of age, is the sister of subject 3. The associations have in general an objective character; the external ones predominate considerably, especially the linguistic-motor forms. Sound reactions also are numerous, so that the character of the normal state looks like the result of a distraction experiment. In the experiment of internal distraction there is an unexpected increase of internal associations as well

12 See below, experiment in drowsiness with subject 15 (educated men).

Subjects 4 and 5. Sister and mother of subject 3

ASSOCIATIONS	SUBJECT 4			SUBJECT 5	
	NORMAL		DISTRACTION	NORMAL	
SPECIAL QUALITY	1st Hundred	2nd Hundred	Internal	1st Hundred	2nd Hundred
Grouping	3	8	16	24	17
Predicative relationship	7	8	8	10	7
Causal relationship	–	–	1	1	0
Co-existence	8	6	3	8	8
Identity	2	4	1	6	13
Linguistic-motor forms	67	56	39	46	45
Word-completion	4	8	14	3	4
Sound	3	5	9	–	3
Rhyme	2	1	2	–	–
Indirect	2	3	5	1	2
Meaningless	1	–	1	1	1
Failures	1	–	–	–	–
Repetition of stimulus-word	–	1	1	–	–
Egocentric reaction	–	–	–	–	–
Perseverations	1	–	·2	1	2
Repetition of reaction	9	7	4	9	5
Same grammatical form	61	51	53	82	66
Same number of syllables	48	47	35	51	38
Alliteration	13	11	13	5	12
Consonance	14	19	24	16	17
Same ending	11	14	7	18	10
Internal associations	10	16	25	35	24
External associations	77	66	43	60	66
Sound reactions	9	14	25	3	7
Number of associations	100	100	100	100	100

as a clear increase of sound reactions. The superficiality displayed in the experiment under normal conditions is in our experience abnormal, thus we must assume a disturbance of attention in this state. The subject is a definite "motor type"; from other experiments performed with the subject it becomes apparent that motor perception predominates by far over the other senses.[13] Externally too the motor disposition is shown by great vivacity of movement and a strongly developed ability for motor expression. It must here be stressed that this active motility by far exceeds the limits of conscious innervation and is expressed in motor automatisms that are innervated by unconscious psychological complexes. Among the reactions of the normal state there are two linguistic automatisms that are very probably related to an unconscious complex. This complex is closely connected with the affect concerning a past engagement. Thus we have two probable reasons for the strikingly blunt reaction-type: the strong and abnormally independent motor tendency and a partially suppressed affect. The latter probably has the most significance for the blunting.

137 (It would be too much of a digression to examine the individual psychology of this case more closely. This will be done elsewhere.)

138 The increase of internal associations during distraction experiments is a phenomenon that we find again in subjects of different character[14] who under normal conditions also show an abnormally blunt type. We know no other explanation for the improvement of reaction-type in this case than that the attention, which under normal conditions is tied to the emotional complex, is released by the conditions of the experiment (new to the subject) and can therefore be used. Nevertheless, great fluctuation of attention occurred; this is indicated by the large number of sound reactions, together with the relatively numerous internal associations.[15]

---

[13] By that we do not mean that some sort of motor excitation is responsible for the blunt reaction type. In personalities of a motor type the motor factors perhaps play an independent role in the word-image combination in that they facilitate talking.

[14] Cf. subject 16 (educated men).

[15] Cf. subjects 15 and 16 (educated men).

139   A special peculiarity of this subject is the occasional occurrence of marked synesthesias (*audition colorée*), which influence the reaction. Examples under normal conditions:

to kiss (*küssen*)   yellow

ü is yellow for the subject.

misery (*Elend*)   something red

e is red.

indolent (*träge*)   blue

ä is blue.

140   Examples from the distraction experiment:

orgy   orgy

Subject sees a yellow mass.

pious   blessed

sees something yellow.

141   Strangely enough, the subject [3], who has the same reaction-type as subject 4, is also a definite "motor type" and also has very vivid synesthesias, which, as it happens, did not appear in the reactions.

142   The following phenomena from the distraction experiment are worth mentioning:

stork   -'s leg

Subject sees a church-tower.

to hinder   hammer-let (Hamlet)

sees a brake.

fall   bone (*Fall -z bein*, paper-knife)

sees a high wall from which one could fall.

red   wine

sees a red sphere.

barrel   -ter (*Fass -ter* [*Vater?*])

sees a certain cellar.

56

143   From the subject's account, the visual image fills consciousness completely and exclusively, the verbal reaction being
given almost involuntarily and touching consciousness only
quite superficially. The above examples show clearly and repeatedly the purely mechanical character of the verbal reaction.

144   *Subject 5* is the mother of subjects 3 and 4. Quantitatively
the reaction-type shows much similarity with that of subjects
3 and 4. The objective character of the reactions is qualitatively
also very similar. Particularly prominent in these three people
are the linguistic-motor forms. Characteristic of this family type
are sound reactions under normal conditions, which distinguishes this type from others. For comparison, we give the main
figures for these subjects under normal conditions:

	Internal Associations	External Associations	Sound Reactions
Mother	29.5%	62.0%	5.0%
Elder daughter	27.5%	67.0%	3.5%
Younger daughter	13.0%	71.5%	11.5%

145   We draw attention to the increasing degree of blunting in
the younger daughter. If the figures were all from the same
individual one could believe that it is a distraction experiment. Perhaps this relationship is accidental but perhaps it has
deeper psychological reasons. We refer to a similar observation
reported below. Ranschburg[16] found 11.8 per cent more internal associations in old than in young subjects.

146   *Subject 6.* Such external associations as are usually found
in the normal state predominate. The second hundred shows a
slight increase of external associations and a clear increase of
sound reactions. The quality of association deviates considerably from the types so far reported, reactions of strongly subjective character occurring with this subject. They are in part
highly charged value judgments, e.g.:

pupil	boring	school	beautiful
father	good	frog	nice
book	interesting	piano	horrible

147   On the other hand, it is the predicates that designate properties of things that are to a greater or lesser extent evident

16 Ranschburg and Balint, p. 689.

Subject 6. About 35 years of age, intelligent, very well read, poetic talent

ASSOCIATIONS	NORMAL		DISTRACTION		
				External	
SPECIAL QUALITY	1st Hundred	2nd Hundred	Internal	60 Metro-nome	100 Metro-nome
Grouping	9	14	8	8	6
Predicative relationship	32	14	30	24	36
Causal relationship	1	–	–	–	–
Co-existence	12	18	14	16	10
Identity	2	6	2	6	2
Linguistic-motor forms	39	39	40	34	42
Word-completion	–	1	–	2	–
Sound	–	4	–	4	2
Rhyme	4	2	–	2	2
Indirect	1	2	2	2	–
Meaningless	–	–	–	–	–
Failures	–	–	2	–	–
Repetition of stimulus-word	–	–	2	–	–
Egocentric reaction	10	4	6	8	4
Perseveration	–	–	–	2	4
Repetition of reaction	15	5	4	4	4
Same grammatical form	43	52	48	46	40
Same number of syllables	50	33	36	42	42
Alliteration	11	13	6	8	2
Consonance	26	28	12	12	10
Same ending	8	10	0	2	8
Internal associations	42	28	38	32	42
External associations	53	63	56	56	54
Sound reactions	4	7	–	8	4
Number of associations	100	100	50	50	50

to the senses. In the second hundred an increase of groupings from 9 to 14 and a decrease of predicative relations from 32 to 14 can be noticed; accordingly the quality of reactions is altered in so far as they assume a noticeably more objective character with a tendency to irrelevant clichés. The decrease of predicative relations is due to the shifting of subjective value judgments into the background. Thus the more subtle quality of the reactions also shows a markedly fading interest. The relaxation of attention is shown very clearly in the decrease of egocentric reactions from 10 to 4. From this result the distraction experiments must be considered a failure. Objectively this is also shown by the subject's being unable simultaneously to follow the beat of the metronome and to react; either the motion of writing ceased at the moment of reaction or the reaction-time lengthened to the next pause in the beat, when the reaction was given with renewed attention. The only disturbing influence was the perseveration phenomenon, which significantly only occurred with external distraction.

148   The almost undiminished personal interest at the time of external distraction is well illustrated by the relatively large number of egocentric reactions. We will refrain from judging how far the relatively strong verbal connection by consonance under normal conditions is caused by the constellations of active poetic application. Many reactions of this subject betray a strong visual predisposition. From the subject's own account every stimulus-concept presents itself as a quite definite picture. The entirely individual character of the reactions distinguishes this subject from others and differentiates her from the subjects so far discussed. It is interesting to learn whether this type is accidental or whether it is of familial origin. Happily we are in the position of being able to some extent to answer this question.

149   *Subject 7.* The number of internal associations considerably predominates over the external ones. The number of predicative relations is extremely great. Most of these consist of subjective value judgments, some of which are highly charged, e.g.:

to cook	laborious	to ride	dangerous
water	wonderful	prison	horrible
star	magnificent		

About 40 per cent of the reactions betray an egocentric direct wish or a defence.

150   *Subject 8.* The internal associations are more numerous than the external. This subject also showed a very subjective reaction-type, which appears particularly in the large number of predicative relations and especially in the numerous subjective value judgments. The number of egocentric reactions too is rather high.

151   From these figures and from the individual quality of the reactions, a clear familial relation emerges. Thus we can conclude with some probability that the subjective reaction-type of subject 6 is based not on coincidence but on familial disposition. It will be of interest to consider the quantitive aspects within this family; particularly whether, in the case of the youngest member, we can prove an analogous proportion in respect to the blunting phenomenon found in the family of subjects 3, 4, and 5. For this purpose we again collate the main figures of our subjects in a normal state.

Subject 7.   The mother of subject 6, over 50 years of age, educated

ASSOCIATIONS	NORMAL	ASSOCIATIONS	NORMAL
SPECIAL QUALITY	1st 100	SPECIAL QUALITY	1st 100
Grouping	9	Egocentric reaction	40
Predicative relationship	16	Perseveration	3
Causal relationship	8	Repetition of reaction	25
Co-existence	12	Same grammatical form	45
Identity	3	Same number of syllables	22
Linguistic-motor forms	4	Alliteration	–
		Consonance	9
Word-completion	–	Same ending	–
Sound	–		
Rhyme	–	Internal associations	78
Indirect	–	External associations	19
Meaningless	1		
Failures	–	Sound reactions	–
Repetition of stimulus-word	–		
		Number of associations	76

	Internal Associations	External Associations	Sound Reactions	Egocentric Reactions
Mother	75%	19%	0	40%
Elder daughter	56%	39%	1%	15%
Younger daughter	35%	58%	5.5%	7%

152 These figures show a complete analogy to what we find in subjects 3, 4, and 5. This too looks like a distraction experiment which goes as far as the reversal of the relation of internal to external associations. There is a corresponding increase of sound associations as well as a decrease of egocentric reactions which, as was shown in subject 6, express the degree of personal interest. This strange analogy between the two family types does appear to be more than mere coincidence. Unfortunately our material is not sufficient to elucidate these observations. A final statement and interpretation of this apparent fact must for the moment await an experiment at present being carried out based on specially collected material.

Subject 8. The elder sister of subject 6, about 39 years of age, educated

ASSOCIATIONS	NORMAL	ASSOCIATIONS	NORMAL
SPECIAL QUALITY	1st	SPECIAL QUALITY	1st
	100		100
Grouping	6	Egocentric reaction	15
Predicative relationship	49	Perseveration	–
Causal relationship	1	Repetition of reaction	14
Co-existence	18	Same grammatical form	29
Identity	1	Same number of syllables	33
Linguistic-motor forms	20	Alliteration	10
		Consonance	10
Word-completion	–	Same ending	1
Sound	–		
Rhyme	1	Internal associations	56
Indirect	1	External associations	39
Meaningless	1		
Failures	–	Sound reactions	1
Repetition of stimulus-word	–		
		Number of associations	78

153   The reaction-type of the last three subjects is characteristic and widespread. What distinguish it from other less definite types are the numerous predicates, among which is a considerable number of subjective value judgments. We call this type the predicate type. The following three subjects are further examples of it.

154   *Subject 9.* The predominance of predicative relationships is clear in all phases of the experiment. Internal distraction could not be carried out as the subject was not capable of dividing her attention. The experiment of external distraction failed completely as the subject, exactly like subject 6, could not carry out two actions at the same time and therefore behaved exactly like subject 6. Only in the larger numbers of verbal connection by number of syllables, alliteration, and consonance may a certain shift of reaction towards the mechanical side be noticed.

155   Three of the four failures under normal conditions are associated with emotionally charged stimulus-words *(unjust, rich, stupid)*.

156   The average predominance of internal association over external is noteworthy in an educated subject. The reaction-type is a mixed one and does not by any means show the strongly subjective character of subjects 6, 7, and 8.

157   *Subject 10.* The predicative relationships are on the average many times as numerous as the number of groupings. With reference to the failure in distraction, the same must be stated as for subjects 6 and 9. The reaction-type is, particularly in the first hundred under normal conditions, a somewhat subjective one, which incidentally is also expressed by the 9 per cent of egocentric reactions. Perseverations occur solely with distraction. As in subject 9, there is an increase in the number of syllables and consonances, which perhaps may be interpreted as slight disassociation. The large number of failures in all phases of the experiment is striking. Of the 14 failures under normal conditions, 10 coincide with emotionally charged stimulus-words *(must, unjust, violence, to threaten, to suffer, etc)*; in another two failures the subjective emotional charge of the stimulus-word is only probable. It must here be said that the subject is slightly hysterical in so far as she has somnambulant dreams. We attribute the large number of failures to this

Subject 9. About 20 years of age, well read, fairly intelligent

SPECIAL QUALITY	NORMAL		DISTRACTION	
ASSOCIATIONS	1st Hundred	2nd Hundred	External 60 Metro-nome	External 100 Metro-nome
Grouping	4	19	18	22
Predicative relationship	37	37	38	34
Causal relationship	5	2	2	–
Co-existence	26	14	14	14
Identity	1	3	4	12
Linguistic-motor forms	23	23	20	18
Word-completion	–	–	2	–
Sound	–	–	–	–
Rhyme	–	–	–	–
Indirect	–	–	–	–
Meaningless	–	–	–	–
Failures	2	2	2	–
Repetition of stimulus-word	–	–	–	–
Egocentric reaction	3	4	–	–
Perseveration	2	1	–	–
Repetition of reaction	13	10	6	4
Same grammatical form	29	33	20	46
Same number of syllables	38	34	56	54
Alliteration	10	6	8	16
Consonance	15	12	10	20
Same ending	3	8	8	16
Internal associations	46	58	58	56
External associations	52	40	38	44
Sound reactions	–	–	2	–
Number of associations	100	100	50	50

63

Subject 10. About 20 years of age, intelligent, very well read

ASSOCIATIONS	NORMAL		DISTRACTION		
			External		
SPECIAL QUALITY	1st Hundred	2nd Hundred	60 Metronome	100 Metronome	FATIGUE
Grouping	8	16	6	10	12
Predicative relationship	31	17	38	34	30
Causal relationship	1	–	–	–	–
Co-existence	14	13	10	4	12
Identity	3	11	18	14	6
Linguistic-motor forms	31	35	18	20	30
Word-completion	–	–	–	–	1
Sound	1	–	–	4	1
Rhyme	–	–	2	–	1
Indirect	1	1	–	–	2
Meaningless	–	–	–	4	2
Failures	8	6	6	10	3
Repetition of stimulus-word	–	–	2	–	1
Egocentric reaction	9	2	–	4	3
Perseveration	–	–	4	2	2
Repetition of reaction	16	5	18	14	18
Same grammatical form	48	51	44	42	48
Same number of syllables	36	33	46	40	41
Alliteration	10	3	8	10	8
Consonance	7	9	14	12	13
Same ending	5	8	18	16	18
Internal associations	40	33	44	44	42
External associations	48	59	46	38	48
Sound reactions	1	–	2	4	2
Number of associations	100	100	50	50	100

Subject 11. Mother of the previous subject, about 56 years of age, very intelligent, educated, well-read

ASSOCIATIONS	NORMAL		ASSOCIATIONS	NORMAL	
SPECIAL QUALITY	1st Hundred	2nd Hundred	SPECIAL QUALITY	1st Hundred	2nd Hundred
Grouping	5	4	Egocentric reaction	6	5
Predicative relationship	56	35	Perseveration	1	–
Causal relationship	2	–	Repetition of reaction	5	4
Co-existence	4	4	Same grammatical form	27	34
Identity	–	1	Same number of syllables	37	41
Linguistic-motor forms	28	50	Alliteration	11	3
			Consonance	8	14
Word-completion	3	4	Same ending	1	10
Sound	–	–			
Rhyme	–	–	Internal associations	63	39
Indirect	1	–	External associations	32	55
Meaningless	–	–			
Failures	–	1	Sound reactions	3	4
Repetition of stimulus-word	–	–			
			Number of reactions	96	96

abnormality. We shall present the proof of this hypothesis in a publication about association anomalies in hysteria which will appear later.[17]

[158]   *Subject 11* is an outstanding predicate type of subjective character with numerous value judgments. A marked slackening in the second hundred is striking; this may be attributed to obvious and objectively established boredom. Thus the second hundred does not correspond to normal conditions but rather to a distraction experiment. Nevertheless, if we compare the

[17] In his experiments on normal people Aschaffenburg had only one subject who had a strikingly large number of failures; he was a dreamy, vague, poetic young man (IV, p. 243). [The textual allusion is to "Association, Dream, and Hysterical Symptom," infra.]

reaction-type of this subject with that of the daughter, subject 10, we find the same phenomenon as before, that is that the daughter's reaction-type is a blunter one than that of the mother.

	Internal Association	External Association
Mother	51%	43.5%
Daughter	36%	53.5%

159   We take this opportunity to repeat that in spite of this agreement the phenomenon may be pure coincidence and therefore urgently requires retesting.

160   We also give the figures for three further subjects. *Subject 12*, a North German lady. The large number of current phrases is particularly striking. Internal distraction failed. External distraction shows a definite disturbance of attention. The reaction type is objective.

161   *Subject 13.* Very diffident, hence the large number of repetitions of the stimulus-word. Only distraction by metronome-beat of 100 was to any degree successful. The writing movements were, in accordance with what has been said before, very awkward.

162   *Subject 14.* We give figures for this subject only for the sake of completeness. The reaction-type is an objective one. Internal distraction was only partially successful. Its effect is uncertain as, because of the omission of the second hundred of normal reactions, we have no information on the degree of variation in normal people. The second hundred could not be obtained for external reasons.

Summary of the Group of Educated Women

163   Unfortunately the material collected in this group is quantitatively somewhat uneven. On the other hand, the linguistic background is very similar, only one out of the fourteen subjects coming from North Germany and all the others being Swiss, whose colloquial language is the Swiss dialect. Their level of education is in general very high, two of the subjects having University education. Six subjects know one or two foreign languages. Ten subjects are relatively well read. Dis-

Subject 12. About 40 years of age, very intelligent, well-read

ASSOCIATIONS	NORMAL		DISTRACTION		
				External	
SPECIAL QUALITY	1st Hundred	2nd Hundred	Internal	60 Metronome	100 Metronome
Grouping	23	12	15	12	2
Predicative relationship	1	16	19	6	8
Causal relationship	1	1	–	–	–
Co-existence	34	18	18	22	6
Identity	7	6	9	4	10
Linguistic-motor forms	34	56	34	52	70
Word-completion	–	–	–	–	–
Sound	–	–	–	–	–
Rhyme	–	1	1	2	2
Indirect	–	–	–	–	–
Meaningless	–	–	–	–	–
Failures	–	–	4	–	2
Repetition of stimulus-word	–	–	–	–	–
Egocentric reaction	–	–	–	–	–
Perseveration	1	–	–	2	–
Repetition of reaction	6	5	5	–	2
Same grammatical form	57	92	64	82	56
Same number of syllables	50	52	57	56	38
Alliteration	5	4	10	–	4
Consonance	16	18	12	20	12
Same ending	25	16	12	18	20
Internal associations	25	19	34	18	10
External associations	75	80	61	78	86
Sound reactions	–	1	1	2	2
Number of associations	100	100	100	50	50

Subject 13. About 22 years of age, intelligent, all-round culture

ASSOCIATIONS	NORMAL		DISTRACTION	
			External	
SPECIAL QUALITY	1st Hundred	2nd Hundred	60 Metronome	100 Metronome
Grouping	11	21	22	10
Predicative relationship	18	19	20	14
Causal relationship	5	1	2	–
Co-existence	10	10	16	20
Identity	3	12	16	16
Linguistic-motor forms	46	31	14	34
Word-completion	–	1	–	–
Sound	–	–	–	–
Rhyme	–	1	–	–
Indirect	–	–	–	–
Meaningless	–	–	–	–
Failures	6	–	6	–
Repetition of stimulus-word	–	4	4	6
Egocentric reaction	–	–	–	–
Perseveration	–	–	–	–
Repetition of reaction	9	11	4	2
Same grammatical form	61	60	56	68
Same number of syllables	43	43	42	42
Alliteration	8	3	8	6
Consonance	10	14	8	14
Same ending	11	12	18	16
Internal associations	34	41	44	24
External associations	59	53	46	70
Sound reactions	–	2	–	–
Number of associations	100	100	50	50

68

Subject 14. About 22 years of age, fairly intelligent, cultured

ASSOCIATIONS	NORMAL	DISTRACTION
SPECIAL QUALITY	1st Hundred	Internal
Grouping	29	9
Predicative relationship	1	10
Causal relationship	–	1
Co-existence	31	12
Identity	2	12
Linguistic-motor forms	34	51
Word-completion	–	1
Sound	2	–
Rhyme	1	2
Indirect	–	–
Meaningless	–	–
Failures	–	2
Repetition of stimulus-word	–	–
Egocentric reaction	–	–
Perseveration	–	–
Repetition of reaction	14	1
Same grammatical form	95	69
Same number of syllables	59	40
Alliteration	10	9
Consonance	15	22
Same ending	24	7
Internal associations	30	20
External associations	67	75
Sound reactions	3	3
Number of associations	100	100

traction experiments were carried out with ten subjects; of these in five cases external and internal distraction, in two cases only internal and in three cases only external was carried out. External distraction was definitely successful in four cases, internal in three. One case of internal and one of external distraction were partially successful.

164   Distraction failed in four cases, of which three are definite predicate types. (All predicate types who took part in the distraction experiments at all showed a much smaller distraction phenomenon than the other subjects.) Of the six subjects over 30 years of age, three showed an average predominance of internal association over external; of the eight subjects under 30 years of age, only one subject showed a predominance of internal association over external.

II. EDUCATED MEN

Nine subjects with 3,793 associations

165   *Subject 15.* Reactions were obtained from this subject in four different states of disturbed attention: in the states of internal and external distraction, fatigue, and morning drowsiness on waking. The reaction-type is a very blunt one, as the ratio between internal and external associations shows, 15 : 78 and 29 : 65. The reactions show a very objective, almost entirely verbal character. The distraction experiments do not have much influence on the ratio between internal and external associations; on the other hand, the progression of sound reactions illustrates the increasing disturbance of attention, which reaches its maximum in the second external distraction experiment. Fatigue, which admittedly in this case was not very great, produced no change in type. The state of drowsiness caused a disturbance of attention which far surpassed the effect of the second external distraction. The subject experiences intense morning drowsiness after mental work at night, and it is difficult to wake him up completely. These reactions were obtained while the subject lay in bed and was only partially awake. The subject had been warned beforehand. The two experiments were carried out on two different days with an interval of about a week. As the figures show, the type is an

*Subject 15.** 28 years of age, intelligent, very well educated*

SPECIAL QUALITY	NORMAL		DISTRACTION	External		FATIGUE	DROWSINESS	
	1st Hundred	2nd Hundred	Internal	1st Part	2nd Part		1st Part	2nd Part
Grouping	9	13	4	10	12	10.2	2	–
Predicative relationship	6	16	19	10	4	10.2	5	2
Causal relationship	–	–	–	–	–	–	–	1
Co-existence	18	5	6	8	14	14.1	14	6
Identity	6	8	5	10	2	2.5	5	2
Linguistic-motor forms	54	52	56	46	54	53.8	40	51
Word-completion	1	–	8	4	12	2.5	2	2
Sound	–	–	2	6	2	–	4	5
Rhyme	4	4	1	2	8	2.5	20	21
Indirect	2	2	1	2	4	–	2	2
Meaningless	–	–	–	2	–	3.8	–	–
Failures	–	–	–	–	–	–	–	–
Repetition of stimulus-word	–	–	–	–	–	–	–	–
Egocentric reaction	1	–	3	–	–	–	–	–
Perseveration	–	–	2	2	–	2	4	–
Repetition of reaction	5	5	2	6	2	6	9	2
Same grammatical form	73	47	47	54	46	63	59	60
Same number of syllables	53	45	49	46	42	44	61	58
Alliteration	7	6	5	10	4	4	17	9
Consonance	15	23	16	24	20	5	32	36
Same ending	19	15	9	18	18	14	33	36
Internal associations	15	29	23	20	16	20.4	7	3
External associations	78	65	67	64	60	70.4	59	59
Sound reactions	5	4	11	12	22	5	27	32
Number of associations	100	100	100	50	50	78	78	78

* [To facilitate reference, all the cases are numbered serially in this paper. Originally, those in each category were numbered separately.]

excessively blunt one. Sound reactions are extraordinarily numerous, particularly the rhymes. The figures for verbal connection are very high. This reaction-type shows the reaction to the most primitive linguistic mechanisms in, as it were, complete isolation. Fatigue is entirely excluded in these experiments; there is merely a decrease of active attention normal towards the end of sleep. As far as we know, attention is completely extinguished in sleep. If one succeeded in obtaining a reaction from a sleeping (but not somnambulant) subject, sound reactions would be the only result. In our view absolute undeviating attention directed inwards would have the same result. We are in the happy position of being able to report on a case that proves this to be so.

166   The subject N. was deeply disturbed by violent affects. Outwardly the main symptom was an almost complete lack of ability to concentrate. She kept the cause of her affects secret. In the experiment, to which she submitted out of scientific interest, she produced, apart from a few inexplicable (senseless) reactions, mainly sound and rhyme reactions.

167   We should like to compare this case with a distraction experiment spread out over several days. Attention is completely bound up with the inner, emotionally charged complex,[18] from which she cannot detach herself for comparatively unimportant incidents. Her attention is thus abnormally low for anything that does not concern the complex. We cannot of course judge how far this withdrawal is conscious. As the subject related, at the beginning of the experiment certain strongly charged ideas belonging to the complex were in her mind, which she constantly tried to suppress, because she feared they might betray themselves in the reaction. From the second third of the experiment onwards, only the feeling-tone of the complex persisted in consciousness, without these accompanying vivid ideas. The next things to occur to the subject were only sounds. The

---

18 By "emotionally charged complex" we mean the sum of ideas referring to a particular feeling-toned event. We shall always use the term "complex" in this sense in what follows. [In the present volume, "emotionally charged" is the translation adopted for German *affektbetonte* and, as a rule, "feeling-toned" for *gefühlsbetonte*. Cf. vol. 1, par. 168, n. 2a, and vol. 3, "Psychology of Dementia Praecox," pars. 77 ff. (ch. 2).]

stimulus-words only made an impact by the sound and never by the sense.

168 These observations prove most clearly the dependence of sound reactions, particularly those of the blunt reaction type, on disturbance of attention. Now, how can we explain the normally blunt reaction-type? The subject was psychologically trained and took the greatest interest in the experiment. The blunt reaction-type would seem to be connected with the fact that many educated subjects regard the experiment as simply verbal; they see the experiment against a verbal background and thus they try to respond to the stimulus-word by the first word to occur, without considering the meaning of the stimulus-word. They do so because it seems obvious to them that an isolated stimulus-word cannot have any special significance. This is how we explain the great predominance of verbal and sound associations. All those subjects who let themselves be influenced by the meaning rather than by the mere word tend to form internal associations. The meaning that different people give to the stimulus-word will vary. In our experience there are two main types of people: (1) The subject tries to do justice to the meaning as objectively as possible; therefore in his reaction he produces some general or special association of objective significance; the reaction is usually a co-ordinating relationship. (2) The subject endeavours to designate in a telling way the object named by the stimulus-word, which he vividly pictures. To state something about the stimulus-word, the subject uses the predicate. The reaction is therefore in most cases a predicative relationship.

169 On these grounds the blunt reaction-type of certain educated subjects should not be considered as the result of some disturbance of attention but as an "attitude phenomenon" (Bleuler). By the term "attitude phenomenon" we understand with Bleuler the emergence of an apparently abnormal reaction type through intentional preference for a certain mode of reaction. The mode is not, however, as must be stressed, chosen arbitrarily but motivated by the particular psychology of the subject. The more intense the attitude to the sound-effect of the stimulus-word, the blunter the reaction-type must become, for, by specially directed attention, the subject will stress

and put in the foreground all the more primitive associations that are repressed in the normal act of speech. Thus a very paradoxical picture can be created by the numerical presentation of the results of the experiment; we can understand it only on the grounds we have given. The following case will illustrate this.

170   *Subject 16.* Here we find again a strikingly blunt reaction-type in the experiment under normal conditions, which is illustrated particularly by the large number of sound reactions. The blunting is considerably increased in the experiment with internal distraction; on the other hand, in the experiment with external distraction a striking "improvement" of reaction appears, the number of internal associations far exceeding that for the experiment under normal conditions. The "improvement" is quite clearly demonstrated by the decrease and eventual disappearance of the sound reactions.

171   This particular result is unique in our experiments and needs discussion. We have already mentioned the present subject in discussing subject 4 of the group of educated women, who presented a similar picture; we then assumed that suppressed affect was the cause of the blunt reaction-type. In this connection the very satisfying findings presented above in the discussion of subject 15 of the group of educated men should also be mentioned. The recent very strong affect that took complete possession of this subject was the direct cause of the preponderance of sound reactions. The affect in this case was repressed, inasmuch as it did not manifest itself directly in the reaction but only indirectly through a splitting of attention. One must assume a similar psychological situation also for subject 4 of the group of educated women and so explain the blunt type. The fact that subject 4 of the group of educated women and subject 16 in the group of educated men are of the same type is perhaps fortuitous.

172   Affect is probably completely out of the question in subject 16. We must therefore look for another cause for the blunt type: we find it in the attitude phenomenon. Subject 16 is thoroughly trained psychologically and at the same time has extraordinary powers of concentration. The subject had from the first directed his attention towards the sound of the stimulus-

Subject 16. *47 years of age, intelligent, very well educated*

SPECIAL QUALITY	NORMAL		DISTRACTION			
ASSOCIATIONS	1st Hundred	2nd Hundred	Internal	External		FATIGUE
				1st Part	2nd Part	
Grouping	16	15	12	20	20	10.2
Predicative relationship	6	5	6	12	2	8
Causal relationship	–	–	–	4	2	–
Co-existence	4	6	8	14	8	5
Identity	6	8	2	10	10	6
Linguistic-motor forms	51	45	38	28	58	38
Word-completion	2	1	–	–	–	2
Sound	8	10	24	6	–	24
Rhyme	1	3	–	–	–	2
Indirect	6	6	10	4	–	1
Meaningless	–	1	–	–	–	–
Failures	–	–	–	–	–	–
Repetition of stimulus-word	–	–	–	2	–	–
Egocentric reaction	–	–	–	–	–	5
Perseveration	1	1	–	–	–	–
Repetition of reaction	3	13	8	4	6	10
Same grammatical form	75	63	62	70	74	58
Same number of syllables	48	37	42	48	56	41
Alliteration	25	22	38	16	6	28
Consonance	25	23	38	24	16	23
Same ending	14	12	10	10	12	10
Internal associations	22	20	18	36	24	18
External associations	61	59	48	52	76	49
Sound reactions	11	14	24	6	–	28
Number of associations	100	100	50	50	50	78

75

word and consequently reproduced the first association to occur. These can only be primitive verbal connections and sounds, if our presuppositions on associations closest to the perception of the stimulus-word are at all correct. In this way the abnormally blunt type in the experiment under normal conditions can be explained without difficulty.

173   The blunting increases in the internal distraction experiments. The subject carried out this experiment in a model way; concentration on the D (distraction) phenomenon was excellent, as was the reporting of it. We therefore have no reason, in this case, not to assume distraction of attention. Thus the blunt type of reaction in this experiment is to be attributed to decrease of attention. It springs from a root different from the one in the experiment under normal conditions; consequently it is not an attitude-phenomenon.

174   External distraction has a disturbing effect on the attention of most subjects and therefore causes blunting. In the present case the effect appears to be the opposite. The normal state of this case is characterized by the attitude phenomenon; attention is directed exclusively to the linguistic aspect. Now this attitude is disturbed by external distraction and the subject now has a different relation to the stimulus-word; i.e., the exclusive observation of the sound is disturbed and thus the production of the nearest primitive association is prevented. If the associations that are always repressed under normal conditions sink back into repression, then the next ones to follow must be the associations conditioned by the meaning of the stimulus-word; i.e., the number of sound-reactions must fall and the number of internal associations must rise. That is the case here.

175   The figures for fatigue show a remarkable agreement with those for internal distraction. Judging from external demeanour one could diagnose quite severe fatigue. This was actually not the case. The fatigue was by no means abnormally severe but merely a relatively slight evening fatigue which, according to the subject's account, did not noticeably influence the reaction.

176   Here again we have an attitude phenomenon and met a disturbance of attention. That the attitude was apparently more intense in this state can perhaps be deduced from the fact that the subject, who is a "motor" type, is when slightly fatigued liable to motor excitation. Speech motility of course also plays

76

a part in general motor excitation, the speech mechanism very easily responding to the appropriate stimulus. This circumstance may have coincided in this case with the special attitude, resulting in a greater number of purely mechanical connections.

177   As can be expected of such a type, the personal and subjective elements in the quality of the reactions gradually recede, with few exceptions.

178   *Subject 17.* The reaction-type is fairly blunt. In internal associations predicates are particularly prominent and have an almost exclusively objective character. As the number of egocentric reactions shows, relatively few subjective aspects appear. But as predicate types always present emotionally charged constellations, there is here, too, an emotionally charged complex noticeable in the reactions. The experiment was carried out on a very hot day: among the repetitions, there is *snow* twice and *to*

Subject 17.   About 26 years of age, intelligent

ASSOCIATIONS	NORMAL		ASSOCIATIONS	NORMAL	
SPECIAL QUALITY	1st Hundred	2nd Hundred	SPECIAL QUALITY	1st Hundred	2nd Hundred
Grouping	9	9	Egocentric reaction	3	3
Predicative relationship	23	26	Perseveration	5	–
Causal relationship	–	–	Repetition of reaction	9	5
Co-existence	21	5	Same grammatical form	44	49
Identity	–	10	Same number of syllables	44	46
Linguistic-motor forms	41	41	Alliteration	6	4
			Consonance	14	9
Word-completion	2	4	Same ending	2	13
Sound	–	–			
Rhyme	–	2	Internal associations	32	35
Indirect	2	2	External associations	62	56
Meaningless	–	–			
Failures	2	1	Sound reactions	2	6
Repetition of stimulus-word	–	–	Number of reactions	100	100

sweat twice. Apart from these there are the following perseverations:

1. stove	warm	4. water	to bathe
2. to walk	hot	5. to dance	to sweat
3. (–	–)		

179   *Subject 18.* The subject, a doctor, 36 years old, felt indisposed during the experiment under normal conditions. The experiment with external distraction could not be carried out because of illness. The hundred associations carried out in "fatigue" were obtained after an eventful night without sleep.

180   Internal distraction and fatigue show a striking agreement: a most definite decrease of internal associations, increase in external and particularly in sound associations and word-completion, an increase in the "same number of syllables" group, while the figures for the same grammatical form remained on the whole uninfluenced. In the first hundred in the experiment under normal conditions, there is a preponderance of internal over external associations (47 : 43); in the second hundred the relationship is reversed (30 : 59). The constant increase of word-completion and sound reactions in the experiment with internal distraction is nicely demonstrated if they are counted separately in each third of the hundred associations. We find:

1st third: 2 word-completions, 6 sound reactions
2nd third: 5 word-completions, 7 sound reactions
3rd third: 9 word-completions, 9 sound reactions

181   The predicates are already on the decrease in the second hundred of the experiment under normal conditions, even more so with internal distraction; they disappear completely in fatigue. Rhymes do not become prominent till the fatigue experiment; we only find two under internal distraction and none in the experiment under normal conditions.

CONSTELLATIONS AND COMPLEXES

182   In subject 18 we meet a relatively large number of associations that can be explained only by reference to individual experiences from the recent past or present, e.g., *ring / garden*: at the time of the experiment a gold ring had been found in the garden of the establishment where the subject worked and its owner had not been found.

78

Subject 18.   36 years of age

ASSOCIATIONS	NORMAL			
SPECIAL QUALITY	1st Hundred	2nd Hundred	INTERNAL DISTRACTION	FATIGUE
Grouping	24	14	7	4
Predicative relationship	23	13	11	–
Causal relationship	–	3	–	–
Co-existence	15	12	5	9
Identity	–	8	–	–
Linguistic-motor forms	28	39	31	20
Word-completion	1	–	16	16
Sound	2	4	20	27
Rhyme	–	–	2	8
Indirect	7	6	7	8
Meaningless	–	1	1	1
Failures	–	–	–	–
Repetition of stimulus-word	–	–	–	–
Egocentric reaction	1	1	–	–
Perseveration	3	–	1	2
Repetition of reaction	2	–	–	–
Same grammatical form	42	57	45	47
Same number of syllables	33	30	47	53
Alliteration	15	22	32	26
Consonance	18	27	41	39
Same ending	6	11	6	21
Internal associations	47	30	18	4
External associations	43	59	36	29
Sound reactions	3	4	38	58
Number of associations	100	100	100	100

183   Or *clothes / Stapfer*. A patient by the name of Stapfer, who was in the care of this particular colleague, worried him greatly because, for example, he ordered clothes and afterwards always found so much to criticize in them that he finally would not wear the garment; there then followed much unpleasantness with the tailor and other suppliers.

184   Or *pencil / Kohinoor*. Our colleague had at the time of the experiment just learned about the useful properties of this brand of pencil.

185   Or *murderer / Kaufmann*. Our colleague had at this time to give an opinion of a defendant by the name of Kaufmann, who had committed murder when intoxicated.

186   This type of association is caused by definite constellations (Ziehen), referring to relatively new, subjective, possibly emotionally charged experiences.[19]

187   In some subjects (e.g., subjects 25 and 27, uneducated women) we find none at all or only very few. Such individuals react throughout entirely objectively and betray practically nothing personal in the associations. For example, they associate *river / stream; school-boy / girl; table / floor; lamp / oil; mountain / valley; to kiss / to laugh; to plunder / to catch; to beat / to bite; prison / punishment*; etc.

188   Admittedly other subjects also make objective associations; from time to time there are among them associations which, in spite of their objectivity, allow conclusions about the subject, although they do not in the least betray his inner personality. It will not be difficult, for instance, to recognize the male nurse from the following compilation of associations (subject 35, uneducated men): *to fetch / to run; to stink / foul air; to inform / report; prison / asylum; ill / melancholic; errand / to run; freedom / convalescence; consciousness / to drink* or *sobriety*, etc.

189   Nevertheless the constellation plays only a very indirect role in these associations.

190   Then there are subjects—that is to say, associations—in which not the momentary constellations but the individual experiences predominate (e.g., subject 19, educated men):

19 We know, of course, that no reaction is fortuitous, but that each one, even the most objective, is caused by definite constellations. It makes, however, a great difference whether, e.g., *murderer* is associated with *Meier* and thus points to a

Lake (See)	*Untersee* (the subject had from time to time been to that lake)
father	*grandfather* (the subject still has a grandfather)
mountain	*Glärnisch* (the subject had been to that mountain once, without the journey having had any special meaning for him)
hair	*hair-lotion* (the subject occasionally prepares a hair-lotion in the dispensary for the patients)
sweet (Süss)	*Süsskind*[20] (proper name of someone not at all important to the subject)
potato	*tobacco fields* (fortuitous memory of a journey from Basel to Heidelberg)
coffee	*Brazil* (the subject had several times drunk Brazilian coffee)

191   These are mainly subjective reminiscences. Going a step further, we encounter the constellations *sensu strictiori* that we first mentioned when discussing subject 18 in the group of educated men. Individuals with many constellations usually also have many reminiscences (e.g., subjects 18 and 19, educated men).

192   A separate group of constellations arises in some individuals through the influence of the immediate surroundings in which the experiment is carried out. The reaction-words *carpet, flowers, ink-pot, calendar, books, pen-holder, landscape, telephone, wallpaper, curtain, mirror, sofa*, etc., usually refer to objects in the consulting-room even if they are associated with a quite suitable stimulus-word. The subject does not necessarily need to see the objects but only to know that they are in the room (see subject 25, uneducated women).

193   From pathology—in normal, imbecilic, hysterical stupidity—quite pronounced cases of this type of association are known to us.[21]

194   If the stimulus-word evokes a subjective emotionally stressed

---

definite murderer, or *murderer* is associated with *criminal* which expresses a general thought. This difference we stress by using the designation "constellation."

20 [*Süsskind*, literally 'sweet child.']

21 See Jung, "On Simulated Insanity."

image with the corresponding reaction then we get a special type of constellation-association—namely, the egocentric (as in Part I). In subject 4 [educated women] we find only a few, e.g., *piano / horrible* (the subject had to put up with the tinkling of her not exactly musical neighbour). Or *to be lazy / glorious*; the egocentricity of this reaction is readily understandable for a busy person who is looking forward to approaching holidays.

195   In some cases an egocentric reaction can be directly replaced by a missing reaction, a failure (see definition in Part I). It is not true that there is no reaction at all, but through a conscious or unconscious inhibition the reaction-word does not get as far as being spoken. This is probably not the origin of all failures, but certainly of the majority.

196   Girls, for example, fail with stimulus-words bordering on sexual themes, e.g., *to love, to kiss, to stroke, to choose, fidelity,* etc. Often it does not actually come to a "failure" but the association *to love / brother* takes a relatively long reaction-time, so that the experimenter after some experience soon discovers who is concealed behind the innocent-seeming brother.

197   The associations *wedding / unhappiness, to kiss / never,* and others of subject 19, educated men, have an analogous significance; the subject was at that time in a state of "suspense and anxious longing."[22]

198   Now it is possible that an emotionally charged complex of ideas becomes so predominant in an individual and has such a profound influence that it forms a large number of constellations, failures, and reactions with long reaction-time, all referring to this complex of ideas. Subjects 19, 20, 21, and 22 of the group of educated men will give us an opportunity to return to this special form of constellation; the majority of complexes operative in the association experiments relate to direct or transposed sexuality. In the work on the associations of hysterics we shall return to the effect of the complex.

199   In subject 18 of this group, we can show, besides many reminiscences, fifteen constellations in the first hundred under normal conditions, four in the second hundred, one under internal distraction, and twelve in fatigue. In the experiment un-

22 [Well-known phrase, *Hangen und Bangen,* from one of Schiller's poems.]

der normal conditions it is often the names of definite people, e.g., *clothes / Stapfer; keeper / Baum* (Baum is the name of a particular keeper); *tooth (Zahn) / Göschenen* (the subject had a discussion in Göschenen about the poet Zahn).

200   The constellation also expresses itself through proper names with subject 19 of this group. When the constellations are on the increase owing to fatigue (e.g., subject 18, educated men) they nearly always consist of the reaction in the form of a proper name; the reaction is associated to the stimulus-word also through similarity of sound (e.g., the internal connection of *clothes / Stapfer* in contrast to the purely sound connection *Stahl* [*steel*] / *Stapfer*).

201   *Subject 19.* Physician, 25 years old. Fatigue was defined as the condition of the subject at ten o'clock in the evening after a full working day.

202   The ratio between internal and external associations is not unambiguous in the different experiments. The maximum of external associations, 61 per cent, is found in fatigue but it is only a little larger than the figure in the first hundred under normal conditions, 57 per cent. This maximum of external associations corresponds to a minimum of sound reactions.

203   Internal distraction proves stronger than external. The first fifty associations with external distraction were obtained with a metronome beat of 60, the second fifty with a beat of 100, and the last eighty-five associations with a beat of 108. Internal distraction corresponds to a maximum in the columns for sound reactions, same number of syllables, same grammatical form, alliteration, and consonance.

204   In external distraction the sound associations decrease progressively and the indirect associations rise progressively, a proportion that we shall often meet again in distraction experiments. In the last third of the experiments with internal distraction the subject became uninterested, as if hypnoidal. At this point the number and intensity of visual images decreased, while the sound associations increased, as follows:

1st third: 3 sound associations
2nd third: 6 sound associations
3rd third: 18 sound associations

83

Subject 19. Physician, 25 years of age

ASSOCIATIONS	NORMAL		DISTRACTION				
				External			
SPECIAL QUALITY	1st Hundred	2nd Hundred	Internal	60	100	108	FATIGUE
				Metronome beats			
Grouping	19	27	11	20	20	–	20
Predicative relationship	9	20	10	12	6	10	13
Causal relationship	–	1	2	–	–	2	1
Co-existence	11	13	8	2	2	6	5
Identity	5	10	7	–	2	12	6
Linguistic-motor forms	41	17	30	34	32	40	50
Word-completion	3	–	–	–	2	1	1
Sound	6	6	27	20	14	5	1
Rhyme	–	–	1	–	–	1	–
Indirect	6	5	6	12	12	18	–
Meaningless	–	1	1	–	10	–	1
Failures	–	–	–	–	–	–	–
Repetition of stimulus-word	–	–	–	–	–	–	–
Egocentric reaction	–	–	2	2	8	–	–
Perseveration	–	4	–	2	2	–	1
Repetition of reaction	3	2	3	4	8	21	8
Same grammatical form	60	59	66	52	52	50	50
Same number of syllables	28	27	50	46	46	36	37
Alliteration	14	14	38	36	18	15	8
Consonance	30	23	43	28	30	20	20
Same ending	11	9	11	4	4	9	6
Internal associations	28	48	23	32	26	12	34
External associations	57	40	45	36	36	58	61
Sound reactions	9	6	28	20	16	7	2
Number of associations	100	100	100	50	50	85	78

84

205   The number of perseverations fluctuates within the normal limits. We give as example:

fidelity ⟋⎯ perjury
once ⎯⟍ merry *(fidel)*

The origin of this perseveration is obvious. *Fidel* is on the one hand a sound association of *fidèle*, the latter being a translation of "faithful." Here is another example:

fruit   Thurgau
false   Falk (falcon)

The family gets its fruit from Thurgau, from a Mr. Falk. Falk is a sound association to the second stimulus-word and in co-existence with the first. And, for instance,

to love ⎯⎤ Stern (star)
son ⎯⎦ Isaac

Stern is the name of a young Jewish lady. Isaac, the son of Abraham, is a fairly frequent though not a current association. The association to Stern is internal.

Alt   Uchtspringe
Freiheit (freedom)   at the Altmann

Alt is, as is well known, the director in Uchtspringe. Freiheit is the name of a peak near the Altmann, in the Säntis area.[23] Thus we have here a perseveration of purely external nature.

206   With internal distraction we find in our subject an example of persistent perseveration of visual images appearing with the reaction. The reaction-words are associated with the stimulus-word only by sound:

		Visual image
malt (*Malz*)	painter (*Maler*)	brewery
omnipotence (*Allmacht*)	Halma [a game]	a barrel of malt
spring (*Quelle*)	the house at the fountain	in a district where there was always a strong smell of malt, the subject had often seen malt-carts in his youth

23 [Dr. Konrad Alt (1861–1922) was director of a mental hospital at Uchtspringe, Saxony, renowned for its advanced methods. The Säntis and the Altmann are high mountains in northeastern Switzerland.]

207   After the first reaction, *malt* / *painter* (*Maler*), the subject could not repeat his own reaction-word; he had forgotten it. While forming associations his attention was directed much more to visual associations than to verbal reaction. For similar reasons we find this forgetting of the stimulus or reaction-word much more frequently in pathological cases of emotional stupidity and hysteria.

COMPLEX-PHENOMENA AND THE UNCONSCIOUS

208   Going through the associations of our subject, only the experienced observer would notice the complex-phenomena which are very important in normal subjects as a basis of comparison with pathological ones, where complexes play a large role. Unfortunately reaction-times were not taken in the material of subject 19 now being used.

209   The material used here is derived not only from experiments on subject 19 used previously in our work but also from some earlier ones. What we recorded was the following (starred: not used in this work):

On Sept. 17	78 associations without fatigue*
Dec. 27	78 associations without fatigue*
Dec. 27	a further 78 associations in fatigue
Feb. 22 (foll. year)	156 associations in fatigue*
Aug. 19	200 associations without fatigue
Aug. 19	100 associations with internal distraction
Aug. 25	185 associations with external distraction

210   The subject had, during the time of the experiments, formed an attachment to a young woman. To make the experiments understandable it must also be mentioned that the young man had not yet outgrown adolescent internal conflict, and as he had had a strict Christian upbringing, his inclination for a Jewish girl worried him a great deal. Let us call her Alice Stern: we shall be keeping as near the truth as is necessary for the experiment. In the experiment on September 17 we find the following complex-constellations:

1. wedding	misfortune
2. come	come with me
3. to suffer	oh heavens—yes!
4. misery	who has not spent miserable nights?

5. to kiss	never
6. game	sweet games will I play with you
7. sofa	a particular chaise-longue (in the drawing-room of the young woman)
8. to love	is useless
9. fidelity	sweetheart
10. wreath	bridal wreath (thought of with the appropriate melody)[24]
11. hope	Thou shalt in life (quotation, continuing "be with us loving and comforting")

211   Numbers 1, 5, and 8 are disguised wishes, although the external form is a negation. Numbers 2, 4, 6, 10, and 11 are quotations or lines from songs; number 6 is the continuation of number 2, a quotation from the *Erlkönig*.

212   It is most noteworthy that in the other seventy-eight associations only one other quotation occurs, namely

to be compelled   "no man can be compelled to be compelled"[25]

and quotations are very rare in the associations of this subject. Thus the complex makes use of a mode of reaction that is not usual in this subject: in fact, it is characteristic that the subject had only (to his shame, it might be said) salvaged from the *Erlkönig* this small fragment, "Come with me, sweet games will I play with you" into conscious memory.[26] Of the *Jungfernkranz* (bridal wreath), too, he only knows the very small fragment of the text, "We shall weave a bridal wreath for you," although he knows the whole tune. We shall return later, in the work on hysterical associations, to the frequently quite unconscious and automatic emergence of tunes and quotations, often only in fragments. (Cf. a similar phenomenon in subject 26, uneducated women.)

213   In the first experiment of December 27 the subject formed among others these associations:

1. it	"It, it, it, and it. It is a hard end"
2. you	yes . . . I

---

[24] [The song "Wir winden dir den Jungfernkranz," from Weber's opera *Der Freischütz*.]

[25] [In German, *müssen / "kein Mensch muss müssen."* The quotation is from Lessing's *Nathan der Weise*.]

[26] [In the original, he misquotes even this fragment.]

3. parting   is painful
4. star *(Stern)*   hm!
5. game   amusement (with long reaction-time)
6. heart   (the subject asks to be allowed not to say
the reaction; it would have been Stern)

²¹⁴   The associations 1, 2, 3, 4, and 6 are self-explanatory after what has already been said. In 5 the long reaction-time, occurring suddenly, is suspicious.

²¹⁵   From the experiment of December 27 in fatigue, the following associations taken in their context are striking:

1. to kiss   yesterday
2. to love   yesterday
3. already *(schon)*   yesterday (the stimulus-word *tears* [*Tränen*] had preceded it; the subject thought he heard *schön* [beautiful]; we might have here a perseveration of the umlaut)
4. miracle   yesterday
5. to pray   yesterday

²¹⁶   The reaction-times were usually quite short. The subject had the feeling that the reactions had taken him unawares. In the whole experiment no other reaction was repeated, except *kraut* twice (with *potato* and *sauer*). In the other experiments, too, repetitions are rare.

²¹⁷   All the stimulus-words quoted belong to those with a close connection with the complex "Stern." The stimulus-word *already (schon)* was understood as *beautiful (schön)*, preceded by *tears (Tränen)*. As we recall, examples 4 and 5 especially were reactions at that time most closely connected with the complex (religion!). *To kiss* and *yesterday* are not to be regarded as a recollection; their relationship was not of this nature. It cannot be said with any certainty whether the unconscious had permitted itself to use the reaction *gestern (yesterday)* symbolically on account of its second syllable, or whether this word has any connection with the fact that this experiment took place immediately after the Christmas holidays, during which the subject had been tremendously pleased by a small present from the young woman. But the fact that this word, and this word only, is so often repeated in the experiment as a reaction to

88

the complex stimulus-words is most striking. It replaces the quotations of the previous experiment (in this experiment there is not a single one).

218   The experiment of February 22 of the following year took place in fatigue. The following associations are worthy of mention:

song   Lore (a complex quotation; "Of all the girls, etc., I
            like Lore best"; the vowel *o* occurs in the bisyllabic
            real first name of the young woman; the two names
            are very similar in sound)
sacrifice — dog (*Hund*) (apparently senseless reaction)
wedding — ram (*Hammel*)

—a perseveration of the reaction. In the combination *sacrifice /
ram / wedding*, the complex certainly played a part; in this connection the perseveration in the experiment under normal conditions of August 19 is comprehensible:

{ to love — *Stern* (star)
    son — Isaac!

219   One association is senseless: *rich / yesterday*; probably *yesterday* occurs as an association produced in embarrassment which has become stereotyped; it occurs again in this experiment in *a people / yesterday*. Here too one can only conjecture; perhaps the concept "Jews" is the link. The association *game / parents* can be explained as indirect; the link, which was unconscious, is the quotation: "My dear child, come away with me, beautiful games, etc." the significance of which we learned above. The following associations also occur:

inn	the Star (*Stern*; the subject was aware of the complex here)	to part	hurt
		to cut	hurts
	complex here)	to stroke	hurts
to kiss	together	to beat	hurts
to love	roses	to sing	hurts

220   The first four associations belong to the complex, the following are probably only stereotyped repetitions of "parting hurts." Here too the repetition must still be considered as the effect of the complex.

221   Otherwise only a few repetitions occur.

89

222   In the distraction experiments there is no manifestation of the complex.

223   *Subject 20.* In the second half of the experiment under normal conditions,

(1) the internal associations increase from 49 per cent to 54 per cent, while the external decrease;

(2) the sound reactions increase from 2 per cent to 6 per cent;

(3) the perseverations from 6 per cent to 8 per cent;

(4) the egocentric reactions from 14 per cent to 27 per cent;

(5) the constellations from 56 per cent to 73 per cent;

(6) the repetitions from 6 per cent to 15 per cent.

224   The following are well above average in number: Internal associations,

Subject 20. Science teacher, 25 years of age

ASSOCIATIONS	NORMAL		ASSOCIATIONS	NORMAL	
SPECIAL QUALITY	1st Hundred	2nd Hundred	SPECIAL QUALITY	1st Hundred	2nd Hundred
Grouping	19	21	Egocentric reaction	14	27
Predicative relationship	28	32	Perseveration	6	8
Causal relationship	2	1	Repetition of reaction	6	15
Co-existence	15	2	Same grammatical form	46	26
Identity	–	–	Same number of syllables	28	15
Linguistic-motor forms	20	19	Alliteration	5	6
			Consonance	8	14
Word-completion	2	5	Same ending	1	–
Sound	–	1			
Rhyme	–	–	Internal associations	49	54
Indirect	–	–	External associations	35	21
Meaningless	1	5			
Failures	10	11	Sound reactions	2	6
Repetition of stimulus-word	–	–	Number of associations	78	78

perseverations,
egocentric associations,
failures,
and the predicates (v. infra, the section on averages).

225   The linguistic-motor reactions are roughly equal in both halves; there are no indirect associations.

226   The figures given above indicate that the subject reacts very subjectively and that by analogy a complex can be presumed in addition. The high number of constellations (56 per cent and 73 per cent) makes this very probable. On analysis, they predominantly refer to *school* and *bride*. The subject is an enthusiastic teacher; on the other hand the complex *bride, wedding,* etc., plays a preponderant role in his reactions, particularly in the second half, where the subjective phenomena are in any case more numerous.

227   In the first half:
26 per cent of the reactions refer to school, 21 per cent to the bride complex.
In the second half:
21 per cent of the reactions refer to school, 24 per cent to the bride complex.

228   In addition, two to three failures in the first half and the majority of failures in the second half refer to the bride complex, e.g., the failures after the stimulus-words *to stroke, ill, to suffer, to kiss.*

229   Apart from this, the complex is expressed less deviously than in the preceding subject; it is less repressed and does not fall back on song-quotations as with the former subject. Incidentally, *school* and *bride* are closely connected in subject 20, as he cherished the dream that he would soon be married and his wife would assume an important position in the institute.

230   Among the thirteen repetitions in the first half, the name of the institute occurs four times, an important event at the school twice, the name of the fiancée three times. In the second half, the name of the fiancée occurs seven times in the reactions, the word *child* twice, at which the subject thought of his future parenthood. The other repetitions mostly concern school matters; three times the subject was annoyed at the seemingly nonsensical stimulus-word and each time reacted angrily with "Rubbish!"

91

231   The perseverations, with two exceptions, concern school and family affairs.

232   Finally, a few examples of these complex-associations:

grandmother	S. will be (S. is the name of his fiancée)
cross	I as a teacher, according to S.
⌠ to come	written to S.
⌡ year	will marry (in two years)
⌊ Sunday	S. comes
⌠ to kiss	(subject will not react)
⌡ naturally	(subject will not react)
to love	S.
tears	she cried (S.)
⌠ fidelity	S.
⌡ once	S.
⌠ hope	that we can marry
⌡ small	child (!)
⌠ to pray	shall I never (image of praying child)
⌡ dear	child
⌐ where?	in bed
⌊ old	S.
ring	at betrothal
to stroke	(will not react at first) S.
child	my future (one)
⌠ sweet	a brand of chocolate, received from S.
⌡ to ride	M—, home of fiancée, where she used to ride
⌐ friendly	S.'s family
⌊ three	members of the family (there are three in S.'s family)

233   The bracketed stimulus-words followed each other immediately in the experiment.

234   With the increase of the subjective emotional content in the course of the experiment the value of the individual reactions also increases, as the figures show.

235   *Subject 21.*[27] In the second hundred reactions of the experiment under normal conditions we find a maximum of co-ordinations, predicative relations, of internal associations generally, while the external associations diminish greatly. This maximum also covers the perseverations and egocentric associations.

[27] The reactions of this subject are given in detail in the section on Calculations of Averages, Complex-Constellation Type, pars. 429ff.

Subject 21. *Physician, 23 years of age*

SPECIAL QUALITY	NORMAL		DISTRACTION		
ASSOCIATIONS	1st Hundred	2nd Hundred	Internal	External 60 Metronome	100 Metronome
Grouping	19	20	7	12	8
Predicative relationship	16	42	26	20	14
Causal relationship	–	–	3	2	–
Co-existence	24	5	10	30	22
Identity	5	3	5	10	4
Linguistic-motor forms	29	23	22	12	38
Word-completion	–	–	–	–	–
Sound	2	3	18	4	6
Rhyme	–	1	–	–	–
Indirect	2	1	3	2	6
Meaningless	3	2	6	8	–
Failures	–	–	–	–	–
Repetition of stimulus-word	–	–	–	–	–
Egocentric reaction	4	19	2	–	2
Perseveration	4	40	5	4	10
Repetition of reaction	8	8	8	4	4
Same grammatical form	58	26	32	62	42
Same number of syllables	34	22	35	50	52
Alliteration	12	8	31	12	10
Consonance	18	13	33	16	8
Same ending	6	5	2	–	–
Internal associations	35	62	36	34	22
External associations	58	31	37	52	64
Sound reactions	2	4	18	4	16
Number of associations	100	100	100	50	50

93

236   In comparison with the average figures for educated men, the predicates in the second hundred, the total of internal associations generally, as well as the perseverations and egocentric reactions, are high above average, in the following ratio:

Predicates	42 : 19.7
Internal associations generally	62 : 36.7
Perseverations	40 : 2.4
Egocentric reactions	19 : 2.8

while the remaining figures deviate little from the average. With the fifteenth stimulus-word of the second hundred (*to kiss*) the complex-reactions begin, at first still interspersed with others; then the complex persists through twenty-six associations, then again with interruptions, disappearing again towards the end of the second hundred. Thus altogether we find a maximum of 50 per cent of complex-constellations in the second hundred of the experiment under normal conditions; 13 per cent in the first hundred; under internal distraction 5, under external 8. We have already found an increase of complex-reactions in the second hundred of the experiment under normal conditions with subject 20, educated men. The appearance of the complex, in this case conjured up by an appropriate stimulus-word *to kiss*, causes a big increase of internal associations, probably due to the intense stimulation of attention. That the manifestation of the complex corresponds to an increase of internal associations is a proof that our classification is to some extent valid and natural. The stronger the emotional stress of the stimulus-word is for the individual and the more attention is devoted to that stimulus-word, the more the number of internal associations rises. This phenomenon is the exact opposite of the distraction phenomenon. Attention is improved because of the invasion of an emotional complex, which absorbs the whole personality, because the attention is directed more to the significance of the stimulus-word.

237   If attention is distracted from the experiment not by external distraction but by an emotionally charged complex, as for example in subject 18 quoted above (experiment after sleepless, eventful night) who was under the influence of strong emotion, then we see the opposite of the phenomena that we have just described in subject 21: internal associations decrease

and the result is very similar to an experiment with internal or external distraction.

238   Thus in the second hundred, strong emotionally charged complexes were more manifest and perseverated more; there is, in contrast to the phenomenon usually appearing in the second hundred, an increase instead of a decrease of internal association, predicates, etc. That there are, among the stimulus-words of the second hundred, in the experiment under normal conditions, rather more words that stimulate slightly emotionally charged ideas is of no consequence in this case or in that of subject 20 of this group, because the complex manifests itself even with stimulus-words that are seemingly of no special significance.

239   It is noteworthy that in complex-constellations the reactions readily come in the form of sentences, in other associations only rarely.

240   In distraction the complex no longer plays a role. In internal distraction we find a maximum of sound reactions (18), which is somewhat above the average for educated men.

241   In the first group of external distraction experiments we find in the reactions a maximum of "same grammatical form" (62) and "same number of syllables" (50); in internal distraction, on the other hand, a maximum of alliterations (31) and consonance (33 per cent).

242   *Subject 22.*

Internal associations. Decrease in the second hundred of the experiment under normal conditions, which is much more marked under distraction.

External associations. Increase in the second hundred and under distraction. Most predicates decrease mainly in the second hundred, as do the constellations.

Linguistic-motor forms. Increase in the second hundred and in the second half of the distraction experiments; there we find a maximum of linguistic-motor forms.

Repetitions and failures. Most frequent in the second hundred of the experiment under normal conditions; in addition, under distraction there is an increase of same grammatical form, same number of syllables, alliteration, consonance, and same ending.

243   In the second part of the distraction experiments there is an

Subject 22. *Chemist, about 24 years of age*

ASSOCIATIONS	NORMAL		DISTRACTION	
			External	
SPECIAL QUALITY	1st Hundred	2nd Hundred	60 Metronome	100 Metronome
Grouping	21	18	24	16
Predicative relationship	20	14	2	10
Causal relationship	2	2	–	2
Co-existence	18	11	16	16
Identity	5	9	24	10
Linguistic-motor forms	26	32	28	44
Word-completion	–	–	2	–
Sound	2	2	4	–
Rhyme	1	–	–	–
Indirect	2	1	–	2
Meaningless	1	1	–	–
Failures	2	9	–	–
Repetition of stimulus-word	–	1	–	–
Egocentric reaction	3	5	2	2
Perseveration	2	1	–	4
Repetition of reaction	11	12	8	2
Same grammatical form	37	54	86	70
Same number of syllables	35	34	58	42
Alliteration	7	5	8	8
Consonance	7	11	24	12
Same ending	9	8	24	12
Internal associations	43	34	26	28
External associations	49	52	68	70
Sound reactions	3	2	6	–
Number of associations	100	100	50	50

improvement of reaction (perhaps due to getting used to distraction); slight increase of internal associations and predicates, absence of sound reactions, slight increase of constellations, slight decrease of same grammatical form and of same number of syllables, consonance, and same ending; on the other hand, increase of linguistic-motor forms and thereby of external associations. Perseverations also occur here most frequently.

244   The constellations are nearly all conditioned by love or the subject's profession. There occur:

In the 1st hundred, normal conditions	44%
In the 2nd hundred, normal conditions	20%
In the 1st half of distraction	6%
In the 2nd half of distraction	14%

245   The following perseverations, caused by a complex, are worthy of note:

1. ⎰lady   of the heart
   ⎱shoulder   blade
    to twine   entwine (the subject pictures an erotic situation)

2. ⎰square (*Platz*)   Town Hall
   ⎱lawn   *Platz* (this perseveration is not fortuitous either; a definite story, with erotic significance for the subject, is linked with the Town Hall square)

246   Failures appear in two forms in subject 22: sometimes the verbal reaction fails and in its place there is a vivid visual image, for example, or a vivid emotionally charged sensation, which the subject subsequently describes.

247   In the other group there are inhibitions because certain erotic memories emerge.

248   Under distraction no failures occur. The egocentric reactions predominate in the experiment under normal conditions and refer mainly to erotic subjects.

249   Of the repeated reaction-words only *bright, good,* and *beautiful* occur more than twice.

250   *The complex.* The erotic complex rules a large number of reactions—a total of thirty in the experiment under normal

97

conditions, and ten in the second half under distraction (15 per cent under normal conditions and 20 per cent in the second half under distraction are demonstrable). In the first half, where distraction is more complete, we find none. The complex is hardly suppressed; on the contrary, it is manifest.

251 The progressive decrease of sound reactions in the course of the external distraction experiments and the increase of indirect associations is in keeping with our assumptions. (See "Averages.")

252 *Subject 23.* The figures show a very slight distraction-phenomenon. The proportion of internal and external associations changes very little in the distraction experiment, so that the variation in the results of the two experiments in fatigue are greater than between normal conditions and distraction. On the other hand the sound associations increase under distraction, as with subject 19 of this group; in both there are fewer sound reactions in fatigue.

253 The associations in fatigue were obtained from both subjects under very similar conditions (normal fatigue after a doctor's working day, 10 o'clock in the evening), while a sleepless night, with heavy psychic demands due to emotion, preceded the associations in fatigue of subject 18 of this group. Here we find in fatigue an increase of sound reactions.

254 The negligible difference caused by distraction may in subject 23 be connected with the fact that the number of internal associations is already fairly low in the experiment under normal conditions (24, that is 26 per cent instead of 36.7 per cent, as in the average of educated men) and the number of external ones fairly high (72, that is 69 per cent instead of 52.7 per cent, the average of educated men). The number of internal associations in the experiment under normal conditions is roughly the same as the average number of internal associations under distraction (in educated men).

255 The effect of fatigue is visible in the first fatigue experiment but not in the second.

256 The figures for alliteration and consonance in distraction have perceptibly risen, as with subjects 18 and 22 of this group.

257 The number of repetitions is throughout above the mean; there are relatively many words that are repeated twice but

98

Subject 23. *Physician, 25 years of age*

ASSOCIATIONS SPECIAL QUALITY	NORMAL		DISTRACTION	External		FATIGUE	
	1st Hundred	2nd Hundred	Internal	60 Metronome	100 Metronome	1st Experiment	2nd Experiment
Grouping	9	9	11	12	8	13	13
Predicative relationship	14	17	18	16	16	6	20
Causal relationship	1	–	–	–	–	–	1
Co-existence	24	7	–	8	14	7	12
Identity	5	19	8	2	10	9	5
Linguistic-motor forms	43	43	55	56	42	61	49
Word-completion	–	–	2	–	–	–	–
Sound	–	3	4	6	2	1	–
Rhyme	1	–	–	–	–	–	–
Indirect	2	1	–	–	4	1	–
Meaningless	1	–	2	–	4	1	–
Failures	–	–	–	–	–	–	–
Repetition of stimulus-word	–	–	–	–	–	–	–
Egocentric reaction	3	3	–	–	–	–	–
Perseveration	5	1	2	2	–	1	4
Repetition of reaction	16	15	22	12	10	18	18
Same grammatical form	57	51	47	42	50	67	59
Same number of syllables	42	42	45	32	28	45	48
Alliteration	8	6	20	22	28	20	11
Consonance	14	10	28	26	38	21	14
Same ending	12	10	12	10	14	12	10
Internal associations	24	26	29	28	24	19	34
External associations	72	69	63	66	66	77	66
Sound reactions	1	3	6	6	2	1	–
Number of associations	100	100	100	50	50	156	156

only very few that are often repeated. In almost all experiments we find *pleasant, unpleasant, gladly, unwillingly, friendly,* and similar words among the repetitions. We shall not examine the individual cases of repetition and perseveration any further here, because they do not point towards such obviously emotionally charged ideas as in the earlier cases; nevertheless, these do not entirely lack this background.

258   The constellations are few and far between. Here too we find a decrease of sound associations at the same time as an increase of indirect associations in the second part of external distraction.

GENERAL REMARKS ON THE GROUP OF EDUCATED MEN

259   We had at our disposal nine subjects, whose ages ranged from 23 to 47, with altogether 3,793 associations. With five subjects, the experiments were carried out with internal as well as external distraction; in one case only with internal distraction, and in one case only with external distraction; in two cases no distraction experiment took place. With five subjects, associations in fatigue were also worked over, with one subject associations in a state of drowsiness. All the subjects in this group have had academic education. Six of them are physicians, one a medical student, one a grammar-school teacher, and one a chemist. All are German-Swiss.

260   Only one subject is of the predicative type (No. 17). Unfortunately we could not carry out a distraction experiment on him.

261   The experiment with internal distraction was successful in four cases; the sharp increase of sound reactions is most characteristic, the decrease of internal with the increase of external associations is less prominent. In one case (16) the result was unexpected, in another (23) there was no definite result; the subject had a minimum of internal and a maximum of external associations already in the experiment under normal conditions.

262   External distraction was clearly successful in two cases; in two cases the success was very moderate, in one case (23), on the other hand, no definite effect was noted. In general the effect of internal distraction is more intense than that of external. These particular subjects always succeeded in fulfilling the experimental conditions for internal distraction.

263   The associations obtained in fatigue give a result similar to
that of distraction in three out of the five cases. In one case (18)
it is particularly clear; but it is possible that perhaps fatigue
was not, or not solely, responsible for that, as the subject had
had a particularly exciting experience during the sleepless
night and probably was still very much distracted by it during
the experiment.

264   The association experiment in drowsiness with subject 15
also gave a result similar to that of a distraction experiment.

265   In four subjects (19, 20, 21, 22) we find in the course of the
experiment, particularly under normal conditions, extensive
complex phenomena. In the first three (19, 20, 21), we see that
the internal associations increase in the second hundred of the
experiment under normal conditions and the external associations decrease, i.e., the opposite of what one would expect. At
the same time we find an increase in the complex-constellations. In the distraction experiment the complex-constellations usually decrease or disappear.

266   The subject need not be conscious of the complex phenomena and they often do not emerge till the association results are statistically worked over and grouped. Thus, lesser
complex-phenomena may also be found in subjects without
this distinct complex-type, e.g., in subject 18 (see below, the
examples of association-types given in detail) or in subject 16,
where in plotting a curve of reaction-times, several emotionally
charged associations from long ago appeared. Practically every
lengthening of reaction-time, even within quite normal limits
(of which the subject is not aware), signifies, as far as we know
at present, that the particular stimulus-word has touched upon
a feeling-toned complex. We shall describe these findings in
a later communication.

III. UNEDUCATED WOMEN
Eight subjects with 2,400 associations[28]

267   *Subject 24.* The associations of this subject are given in detail among the examples of association types (see below). As in

28 For technical reasons the experiment with internal distraction could not be
carried out with any of the uneducated subjects.

Subject 24. Nurse, 18 years of age, Swiss, secondary-school education

ASSOCIATIONS	NORMAL		DISTRACTION	
			External	
SPECIAL QUALITY	1st Hundred	2nd Hundred	60 Metronome	100 Metronome
Grouping	23	20	16	14
Predicative relationship	23	37	20	22
Causal relationship	2	1	–	–
Co-existence	28	14	38	30
Identity	1	5	2	2
Linguistic-motor forms	23	23	14	30
Word-completion	–	–	–	–
Sound	–	–	6	2
Rhyme	–	–	–	–
Indirect	–	–	2	2
Meaningless	–	–	–	–
Failures	–	–	–	–
Repetition of stimulus-word	–	–	–	–
Egocentric reaction	3	–	–	–
Perseveration	1	–	4	4
Repetition of reaction	11	9	14	2
Same grammatical form	60	53	68	58
Same number of syllables	36	44	48	46
Alliteration	16	7	4	12
Consonance	15	11	12	8
Same ending	5	6	10	8
Internal associations	48	58	36	36
External associations	52	42	54	62
Sound reactions	–	–	6	2
Number of associations	100	100	50	50

uneducated subjects generally, we find relatively more internal reactions and fewer linguistic-motor forms than in educated subjects. The increase of internal associations, particularly of predicates in the second hundred of the experiment under normal conditions, may be attributed to the predominance of personal participation after the subject had grown used to the experiment. We have already met this phenomenon several times.

268   Although distraction was successful, it was not exactly striking. External associations increased, sound and indirect associations, which are quite absent under normal conditions, occurred. Strikingly enough, perseverations are also more numerous.

269   Distraction had little effect, for several reasons: the subject has relatively many predicative reactions without actually belonging to the predicative type; the latter, however, is distinguished by a weaker distraction-phenomenon. The subject often found it difficult to divide her attention and to react simultaneously to the metronome and the stimulus-word. Secondly, the experiments with uneducated women gave us the impression that these found dividing their attention more difficult than did educated subjects. They are usually completely absorbed by the experiment and work with quite concentrated attention. The stronger the means of distraction, the more desperate their effort. Thirdly, we know that in this case the experiment had a very strong psychic effect on the subject. Emotions relating to the subject's complex, some of which were only recently assuaged, came to the fore and strongly affected the reaction. The experiment was a revival of a complex that had become somewhat latent. That is why we find a large number of obvious complex-reactions even in the distraction experiment, which as a rule is rarely the case.

270   The complex-phenomena require a short explanatory case-history. The subject had a country background and became a nurse at seventeen, after brooding at home for a year upon the unhappy termination of a love-affair. Her irascible father did not want to know anything of the relationship and once there was a scene during which he cursed her because she had dared to contradict him. Facial burns, accompanied by great terror, and a tedious illness had revived this psychic pain through

brooding shortly before the associations were taken. The association experiment gave rise to a further exacerbation of this unhappy memory; the effect persisted for some time, a proof of how intense a reagent these experiments are, particularly with uneducated subjects, and with how strong an affinity an emotionally charged complex attracts and uses for itself as large a number of stimulus-words or stimulus-concepts as possible. Now, six months after the experiment, the subject has a more objective attitude towards the complex which, however, still strongly affects her. While then, in her explanation, she emphasized that she was bound to be unhappy because of her father's curse, she now no longer conceals the deeper erotic connections when she has to comment on her reactions. It is striking how vividly she still remembers every reaction she then gave.

271   The number of demonstrable complex-constellations is (in percentages):

	1st half	2nd half
Under normal conditions	15	21
With distraction	16	14

272   As already stated, we only rarely find complex-constellations under distraction and hardly ever to this extent. Naturally this interferes severely with distraction. The maximum of complex-constellations in the second hundred under normal conditions is, as in other cases, explicable by a difference of attitude, through becoming familiar with the experiment.

273   Perhaps in order to be less obvious, perhaps because it takes less effort, the complex expresses intimate feelings by clichés such as quotations, words of songs, titles of stories, and such like. Quotations are frequently masks. We use them in everyday life, too, in this sense. One sings certain songs in certain moods, often because one does not want to express the thoughts that underlie the moods; so they become masked. Or the song, the quotation, is used to exaggerate a rudimentary feeling, perhaps to awake a spark of feeling by this exaggeration; one need only think of patriotic songs and poems to celebrate birthdays, special occasions, and festivals. Examples:

come   to the meadow

The quotation comes from the story of the lazy school-boy who wants to tempt the hard-working one to play truant; the lazy one later becomes a tramp, the steady, hard-working school-boy a respected teacher. For the subject the quotation has a quite different background. In any case it is not without reason that the meadow occurs twice as a reaction in the experiment under normal conditions. In the orchard of her parents' house there is a beautiful tree surrounded by grass; here she often used to dream and, as she watched trains coming and going on the nearby railway-line, she would make fantastic travel plans. After the unhappy end of her love-affair the subject had a wish-fulfilment dream: she was lying next to her beloved in the grass. She still thinks of this dream with pleasure. To the stimulus-word *dream* she immediately reacts with *pleasure* and her eyes shine at the memory of that wish-dream. Further quotations:

> at home   it's nice

refers to a song, the meaning of which is clear. Further:

> once   I was happy

The subject once heard a wicked, stupid catatonic woman sing:

> Once I was so happy,
> But now no more,
> Love, the magician, deceived me full sore.

In the next three associations she remains caught up in the complex:

once	I was happy
wonder	of love
blood	of expiation (thinks of her father's curse)
wreath	death (for months she thought of dying; she intentionally ate almost nothing for weeks so that she might become ill, and lost a lot of weight in the process. After the experiment, which revived the complex again—particularly after a visit home that she made soon afterwards—she started to eat very little even with us and to lose weight till the matter was discovered and the folly of her behaviour made clear to her).

105

274   On other occasions the subject quotes the titles of stories, the content of which refers to her complex, e.g.:

seven   brothers

"The Seven Brothers" is the title of a story in which devoted brother-love is rewarded.[29] The association immediately following is:

ill   my brother

275   The quotations, six in all, occur only in the experiment under normal conditions (as with subject 19, educated men) and all evidently refer to the complex.

276   We have already quoted two examples where the complex entraps the subject in an idea. Others occur, e.g., this perseveration:

friendly ⌐ friendship
three   ⌐ friends

The subject has an intense need for friendship; but there have always been disappointments—her best friend married another girl.

277   Another example, from the experiment under distraction:

meadow   the orchard
to bring   the apples

278   We have here a direct perseveration not of the reaction but of the image of the underlying situation. We shall in the course of the work include these forms also in the concept of perseveration. The connection between meadow and orchard is clear to us at once from what has been said above (meadow!). The "apples" of course come from the same orchard.

279   Of the four (8 per cent) perseverations in the distraction experiment, there is only one that probably refers to the complex.

280   *Repetitions.* In the experiment under normal conditions, seven reaction-words occur several times (two to five times); at least thirteen of these seventeen words belong to the com-

---

[29] After the breaking off of her romance, her brother was the only person in whom the subject confided.

plex. In the distraction experiments (one hundred reactions) there are altogether eight reaction-words that occur several times (two to three times). The ratio expressed as a percentage is also roughly the same as under normal conditions ($2 \times 8 = 16$). Of those, four (8 per cent) definitely refer to the complex.

281 It is striking how often *human being* appears as a reaction; eight times in three hundred associations (normal conditions and distraction). There are seven reactions that certainly belong to the complex. *Human being* sometimes refers to a quite definite person, sometimes to the subject herself.

282 Similarly we find the reaction *the person* several times used as a general term, with quite concrete meaning in reference to the complex, e.g.:

propriety the person
bad   the person

283 The subject is thinking of a quite definite person, her friend, who plays an important part in the complex. She is not morally faultless—has, for instance, an illegitimate child. By the reaction *human being* she often means this same friend, who in her more frivolous life had more luck in love than the more serious subject, e.g.:

⎰indolent the human being
⎱virtue   of human beings

In this example there was even a perseveration of the same reaction-word, from which can be gathered how strong is the emotional charge of this idea.

284 We often find the definite article used in the reaction as a disguise of the complex-constellation. Our subject, for example, used the article 26 times in the reactions under normal conditions; seventeen of these reactions definitely refer to the complex. The connection is less striking under distraction.

285 We find the phenomenon again in other subjects. To illustrate the complex-reactions here are some relevant examples:

decent   the person (see above)
to be careful the person
bad   the person

107

to pray	the pious one (referring to herself; she prayed a great deal when most unhappy)
⎰wonder[30]	of love (referring to herself, also to expiation)
⎱blood	of expiation (she feels guilty towards her father; there is a perseveration of the external form of the reaction here)
omen	of punishment (in the same way this reaction would be quite nonsensical grammatically and can only be explained by the assumption that we are probably dealing with the after-effect of the previous reaction form. This reaction is separated by several from the one before)
normal	the human being (a quite definite one)
meadow	the orchard ⎱ (for explanations of these
to bring	apples ⎰ associations see above)
mild	the father
clever	the snake (quite definite people)
⎰willing	the school-boy ⎤ in these associations the subject
⎱order	the industrious ⎬ was particularly thinking of the
	worker ⎦ friend of her youth
angry	the human being (means her father)

and so on.

286   In the distraction experiment the subject did not understand several stimulus-words, namely: *hatred, love, repentance, fall, pleasant, penny, glass, to hammer, entrance, ears, to inhibit.*

287   It soon transpired on analysis that the subject could not, or would not, understand the first series of quoted stimulus-words, owing to the half-conscious, half-unconscious effect of her complex. According to her, all these stimulus-words touched most intimately upon the complex that she was trying to suppress.

288   The stimulus-words of the second series were really not understood because of the acoustic disturbance of the metronome. The subject thus found a further method here of hiding her complex in an apparently unobtrusive way; it is adapted to the situation, for, as the second series of stimulus-words (which do not touch upon the complex) proves, it is easy not to understand stimulus-words, or to understand them wrongly, in

[30] The braces to the left of the stimulus-words indicate that these immediately succeeded each other.

108

the constant noise of the metronome beats of the distraction experiment (to compensate for this, another stimulus-word was introduced into the experiment).

289   This not wanting to understand corresponds to a repression of the complex that was to a greater or lesser extent conscious. There is no difference in principle from the cases (hysteria!) where not reacting or falsely reacting occurs involuntarily.

290   Under complex-reactions we have a large group; that of masked complex-reactions. In our subject the masking, so far as we could discern it, was achieved by the following means:

1. By quotations (songs, book-titles, quotations from texts).

2. By the use of unobtrusive general concepts with a quite special meaning with reference to the sense of the complex.

3. By the addition of the article. The reaction thus receives an apparently even more objective appearance; it then appears like the practised reply of an elementary-school child.

4. By misunderstanding the stimulus-words that allude to the complex.

291   Finally it must be reported that abnormally long reaction-times frequently occur in the complex-reactions; unfortunately, however, no systematic measurements were taken with this subject, so that we cannot develop this point further in the case before us.

292   *Subject 25.* In the first place, the high figures for grouping and co-existence are striking, both under normal conditions and under distraction. Some of them are far above the mean values. On the other hand, the figure for predicative and linguistic-motor reactions is relatively small and below the mean, particularly in the case of the predicative reactions. The explanation of these figures is probably the extraordinarily objective, steady mode of reaction, which is apparently little disturbed by complexes.

293   A few reactions with a rather long reaction-time are to be noted. In our experience reactions with a time of more than 5.0 seconds are generally suspect of referring to emotionally charged constellations.

294   In this subject we find twelve associations with a reaction-time of more than five seconds under normal conditions, in the distraction experiment only three.

109

Subject 25. Nurse, 22 years of age, South German, intelligent but not educated

ASSOCIATIONS	NORMAL		DISTRACTION	
			External	
SPECIAL QUALITY	1st Hundred	2nd Hundred	60 Metro-nome	100 Metro-nome
Grouping	33	34	18	22
Predicative relationship	3	9	2	4
Causal relationship	–	1	4	2
Co-existence	36	25	28	34
Identity	6	11	24	18
Linguistic-motor forms	15	16	20	18
Word-completion	–	–	–	–
Sound	–	1	2	–
Rhyme	–	3	2	2
Indirect	4	–	–	–
Meaningless	3	–	–	–
Failures	–	–	–	–
Repetition of stimulus-word	–	–	–	–
Egocentric reaction	–	1	–	–
Perseveration	–	–	–	–
Repetition of reaction	5	8	–	–
Same grammatical form	91	78	92	88
Same number of syllables	67	56	58	48
Alliteration	8	7	2	2
Consonance	7	18	22	14
Same ending	22	19	22	16
Internal associations	36	44	24	28
External associations	57	52	72	70
Sound reactions	–	4	4	2
Number of associations	100	100	50	50

295   In the following examples with lengthened reaction-time, the lengthening is presumably to be interpreted as the effect of an erotic complex:

wedding	miss	6.8[31]
to kiss	to laugh	6.0
to love	gladly	5.6
male nurse	wardrobe	8.0
dream	basket	6.4
ripe	fruit	6.6
to bless	to receive	5.8

296   The subject usually reacts strongly to allusions of an erotic nature and also blushes easily. She admits herself that she was embarrassed at answering to the first three stimulus-words. She also found it awkward to say the word *nurse* which first occurred to her as an answer to the stimulus-word *male nurse*, obviously because she immediately thought of erotic relations. She searched in her surroundings and named the first object she saw in the room: *wardrobe.*

297   At the stimulus-word *dream,* an erotic thought prevented her from reacting. Instead of giving a reaction according to sense, the subject again let herself be distracted by externals, happened to see the waste-paper basket, and said *basket.* Thus a senseless reaction was given as a result of the complex. The reactions *ripe / fruit (Obst)* (the subject first thought of "fruit" [*Frucht*]) and *to bless / to receive* are obviously again examples of the same sexual embarrassment.[32]

298   Distraction by surrounding objects is, as far as we know from our experience in psychopathology, a phenomenon that must be interpreted in both cases as the effect of emotion.[33] In embarrassment or bewilderment, which are caused when the stimulus-word conjures up emotionally charged ideas that the subject consciously or unconsciously tries to repress, the subject lets herself be completely distracted by externals and verbally reacts by simply naming an object from her surroundings.

[31] Reactions of between one and two seconds are considered normal. [All reaction-time data in this paper are in seconds.]

[32] [German *Obst* is the equivalent of English 'fruit' in a collective sense. *Frucht* is the term for particular fruit but is also used in the phrase "the fruit of the womb."]

[33] Cf. "emotional stupidity": Jung, "On Simulated Insanity."

We find this phenomenon very marked in certain hysterics, for example.

299   Of the sixteen reaction-words, from the experiment under normal conditions, that are repeated we call special attention to: *diligent* five times, *good* three times, *well-behaved* twice, *right* twice. The others are divided among very varied ideas. One can more or less see from these the strict morals of the subject. It is characteristic that these indications of subjectivity disappear under distraction.

300   In classifying, it was rather difficult always to draw the dividing line with certainty between grouping and co-existence.

301   Finally, it can be said of the subject that she belongs to an objective reaction-type that is very little influenced by constellations, and which we find again in subject 27 of this group.

302   The following reactions might illustrate this general objective reaction-type of the subject.

soft	hard	to rinse	to wash	fidelity	obedience
youth	age	building	wall	to plunder	to catch
sorrow	worry	sleeve	dress	freedom	solitude
window	glass	park	garden	regret	fear
false	right	glass	iron	stork	dove
sweet	sour	couch	chair	bike	car
wide	narrow	to paint	to varnish		
honey	bee	star	moon		

303   The unusually high number of reactions with the same grammatical form runs parallel to the many groupings and co-existences and confirms what has just been stated.

304   Distraction is very obvious. There is a decrease of internal, an increase of external associations. We only find sound reactions in the second hundred of the experiment under normal conditions and under distraction; on the other hand, direct associations only in the first hundred, so that our assumed rule of reciprocity between indirect and sound associations would again be correct here.[34]

305   It must, incidentally, be mentioned that the subject carried the experiments out with great enthusiasm and also made a great effort under distraction to do justice to the higher demands by devoting all her attention to the experiment.

[34] See below, Calculations of Averages, par. 405 (6).

306   *Subject 26.* The subject has a rather obvious tendency to make rhymes, which increased in the second half of the distraction experiment.

307   The usual distraction phenomenon did not appear, although the subject does not belong to the predicate type. Marking the beats was done with great irregularity. The predicates increase under distraction; the external associations, particularly the linguistic-motor reactions, decrease; only the sound reactions increase constantly.

308   Constellations are found mostly in the second hundred of the experiment under normal conditions and in the first half of the distraction experiment. The latter fact shows that the distraction experiment was after all partially successful; for, with the exception of subject 24 of this group, where the distraction experiment was equally unsatisfactory, the constellations disappeared almost completely under distraction in the other subjects.

309   We here describe individual examples: To the stimulus-word *lamp*, the subject did not react till 20.0 seconds later with *oil-lamp*. She had just before had the pleasant dream that instead of the 9 o'clock meal, which she rarely took, she was getting a new lamp in her room, which she wanted very much.

310   window   glass   10.0 (thought of *vitrine* in between)

The subject thought of a large shop with beautiful glass cases. She had for some time been the private nurse of the wife of the owner of such a shop and was very attached to her former patient. The subject had learned the French expression *vitrine* for "glass case" from the sister of this patient. One can see how a particular thought occurring at the time is responsible for an apparently insignificant expression.

311   to strike   6 o'clock   2.0

The subject had carried out night duty in a ward, always having to get up at 6 o'clock in the evening.

312   to paint   *peintre*   6.8

This reaction, with a lengthened reaction-time, refers to a year's stay in French Switzerland. The subject, then a young girl, was admired by a painter; he was also very keen to paint

113

Subject 26. Nurse, 21 years of age, Swiss, secondary-school education

ASSOCIATIONS	NORMAL		DISTRACTION	
			External	
SPECIAL QUALITY	1st Hundred	2nd Hundred	60 Metro-nome	100 Metro-nome
Grouping	20	16	22	8
Predicative relationship	5	11	16	18
Causal relationship	1	1	2	–
Co-existence	24	10	18	8
Identity	4	6	10	14
Linguistic-motor forms	43	47	24	36
Word-completion	1	1	–	2
Sound	–	–	2	2
Rhyme	1	2	2	8
Indirect	–	5	2	2
Meaningless	–	–	2	2
Failures	1	1	–	–
Repetition of stimulus-word	–	–	–	–
Egocentric reaction	1	–	–	2
Perseveration	2	2	2	–
Repetition of reaction	6	5	8	4
Same grammatical form	75	50	76	60
Same number of syllables	48	39	56	46
Alliteration	9	8	6	2
Consonance	13	9	18	16
Same ending	13	11	12	20
Internal associations	26	28	40	26
External associations	71	63	52	58
Sound reactions	2	3	4	12
Number of associations	100	100	50	50

114

her. In the reaction-word *peintre* there is, besides a masking of the constellation by a quite blunt association, a further constellation, in that the subject in this instance uses, together with the reminiscence of an erotic experience in French Switzerland, a French word. In the distraction experiment she produces the reaction

| painter | *peintre* | 13.0 |

with the same constellation. The characteristically long reaction-times in both places are worthy of note.

313   In rapid succession the following reactions occur:

| wedding | tomorrow | 2.2 |
| come | tomorrow | 1.4 |

This repetition is not a coincidence. The subject was celebrating her saint's day the day after the experiment under normal conditions took place. She was happy, for she wanted to go out, and she had been invited out for this day and would be receiving all the congratulations at home; among these she was also expecting a letter from her sweetheart.

314   Further, we find the reactions:

| rich | in love | 2.0 |
| poor | in virtue | 2.2 |

The first is a quotation from Ernst Zahn's novel *Albin Indergand* (1901). It refers to a love-story and has the significance of a complex quotation for the subject, like the one we discussed in subject 19 in the group of educated men and subject 24 (uneducated women). The second is an analogous but original form. The subject was thinking of another nurse with whom she had had an argument the day before on the subject of "love," in which the other had maintained a much less idealistic attitude to the question than had the subject. The stimulus-word *poor* has become associated with the previous stimulus-word *rich* and the emotionally charged reaction connected with it, whereupon she became conscious of the contrast between her "ideal of love" and that of the other nurse. By *poor in virtue* she means the other nurse.

315   The same thought gave rise to the following quotation:

| to despise | you think | 2.2 |

115

The quotation is word for word as follows:

Perhaps you believed
I should hate life,
[Flee to the deserts,
Because all dream buds
Had not bloomed?] (Goethe, *Prometheus*)

The subject knows only the first two lines of this quotation, she had quite forgotten the part in brackets. At this, the subject vividly thought of the other nurse and her low views on the subject of "love." One sees from this how closely related expressions and quotations of this sort become associated with feeling-toned complexes, helping to create the infinitely copious unconscious verbal material used by feeling-toned complexes, which makes possible, for example, the poet's countless variations on one single thought.

316   A further quotation:

finally   does not last for ever   5.6

again refers to her love-complex. The reaction-time is strikingly long. The subject was thinking of the "brother of a woman friend," who turned out to be her sweetheart; she was anxiously awaiting news of whether he had accepted a certain post abroad, wishing he would not go.

317   At the stimulus-word *to kiss* the subject reacted in a tone of surprise: "*To kiss*—yes—I cannot tell you that; we have just been talking about something." She meant the discussion with the other nurse, who said that kissing was something dirty. To the stimulus-word *time* the subject reacted:

time   according to   2.0

The next reaction but one was

to reign   according to . . .   3.8

318   At *to reign* an older nurse who was in charge of the whole department came to her mind. A trifling incident of about that time made the subject think: "She regiments us in everything." The stimulus-word *to reign* released this thought, which the subject could not utter; in its place appears the reaction-word *according to* used almost immediately before, which had a

116

meaning when used with *time* but with *to reign* at the most only a remote one. Thus the gap in the reaction produced by the affect is filled by a reaction-word already used. A similar phenomenon was already observed in subject 19 in the group of educated men, who in an experiment under fatigue always reacted with *yesterday* to a series of stimulus-words that touched upon the complex.

319   The reaction

to love	in need of	4.0

is accompanied by a sudden change of facial expression. This phenomenon refers to her love-complex and is important for us because we find similar reaction-phenomena (changed facial expression, sudden lowering of voice) in the pathology of associations, where emotionally important complexes are concerned.

320   At

to choose	advice	3.2

the subject thought that one must be very careful in one's choice of a husband; she thought that one ought to have good advice when having to make one's choice.

321   A quotation, the reaction

hope	does not let one sink	1.8

is based on a recent letter which the young man from Western Switzerland (*le peintre*) had written to her a short while before, and from which it transpired that he had not yet given up hope of winning her.

322   On the reaction

love (*lieb*)	empty (*leer*)	3.0

the subject put an unusual inflection; it refers to her own love-life and must be put by the side of the reaction:

to love	in need of	4.0

with a change of facial expression.

323   The reaction

lazy	why	1.8

is again a quotation. The text on which it is based runs as follows:

> The girl came to the spider
> And the spider said: Why so late?
> I have been spinning threads for three hours
> See how finely and delicately they are twisted!

The content of these lines is summarized by the stimulus-word *lazy*. Also the reaction is determined by sound in the stimulus-words *spät* (late) and *gedreht* (twisted). An obvious condensation (Freud) of the situation and apparent form into the word *träge* (lazy) has occurred in the subconscious; this is already proved by the fact that the reaction-time is quite short and therefore there can be no question of a conscious search for quotations. One also sees that the subconscious or unconscious likes to associate quotations or complexes, often in such a way that fragments of quotations and songs which happen to have been picked up, and the continuation of which the subject does not know, are directly connected with the complex. In our present case, for example, the subject does not know the poem by heart.

324   We still have to prove that behind this quotation there lies a feeling-toned thought.

325   The verse, taken from a school poem, corresponds to the feeling-toned situation at the time. The subject was then, as already mentioned, on night duty in a ward. She slept during the day. In the morning she was relieved by the nurse who was on day duty in the same ward; she had several times in the last few days been annoyed that this nurse relieved her so late; we find the expression of this in this reaction.

326   Behind the seemingly insignificant, quite impersonal reaction:

> something   important   1.2

is concealed the thought of the saint's day on the morrow.

327   To the stimulus-word *to woo* there was no reaction. The cause of this is once more the conversation with the other nurse about love. She recounted that she had permitted herself the joke of writing to an obscure marriage bureau, whereupon a

widower had been recommended to her by this bureau as a good match. This idea displeased the subject very much.

328   To the stimulus-word *doing* the subject reacts *and not doing* (10 secs.). Behind this superficial reaction the thought of the argument about love is once more concealed.

329   When a complex is hidden behind quotations or superficial reactions of this sort, the reaction-time is usually short. While in the so-called failures attention is quite absorbed by the complex that is to be suppressed (that is, hidden from consciousness or from the experimenter) here a division of attention takes place. One part is devoted to the verbal reaction and this then bears a very superficial (linguistic-motor, sound) character; the other part is occupied by the emotionally charged idea. This part is frequently repressed and does not clearly emerge to consciousness. This interpretation is also confirmed by the frequent observation that such quotations and superficial reactions are produced with the most indifferent expression in the world although the observer, for example, knows that they refer to a strong emotionally charged complex and are conditioned by it.

330   The main part of the emotionally charged complex becomes split off and repressed. At the same time the chain of ideas unfolding in consciousness contains as representative of the complex only a quotation, for instance; this appears after a short reaction-time and indicates to the expert that under this cover an important complex is exerting its influence in the subconscious.

331   In other cases, where the affect is already shown in the quality of the reaction (intonation, expression), this split does not take place; the reaction becomes more difficult and the reaction-time lengthened (see the example *to love / in need of*; 4.0).

332   In the distraction experiment we find in subject 26, in the group of uneducated women, among the few reaction-words (*bicycle, Zurich, clear, sad*) that are repeated several times, two in which a complex is probably the cause of the repetition.

333   About the reactions

> bike   wheel   tram   bicycle

the subject afterwards explained that her sweetheart cycled a lot, which immediately came to her mind when she heard the stimulus-words. The reactions

fire	Zurich	station	Zurich

remind her that in the discussion about love she had defended the town of Zurich and its inhabitants against the other nurse. The reactions

moved	sad
mild	sad

are connected with incidents in her family. In the reactions

sin	world	0.8
remorse	death	1.2

a recent accident was on her mind, in which a patient managed to drink some Lysol from an instrument dish. There were no serious consequences but the incident had happened in the ward in which the subject was on duty and had left her with a very unpleasant impression and a great feeling of guilt; hence also the perseveration in the above reactions.

334   *Subject 27.* The result of the experiment has the greatest similarity with that of subject 25 of this group. Admittedly the distraction phenomenon is not so marked (the subject gave her whole attention to both experiments). Reactions from the sound group are completely absent and the number of linguistic-motor forms is very small. The co-existences show high figures. The predicates are few, egocentric reactions absent, which indicates a very objective grasp of the stimulus-words. The figures for the same grammatical form of the stimulus-word and reaction are strikingly high, as in case 25 of this group. Thus our subject also belongs to the same quite objective reaction-type without demonstrable constellations. Many associations have lengthened reaction-times, without our having a retrospective explanation for it. We do not possess a more detailed analysis.

335   *Subject 28.* The predicates are relatively few (in the experiment under normal conditions, for example, only 8.5 per cent instead of 20.4 per cent, the average for uneducated women). The groupings, too, are below average in the experiments

Subjects 27 and 28. Nurses, 23 and 28 years of age, Swiss, elementary-school education

ASSOCIATIONS	SUBJECT 27				SUBJECT 28			
	NORMAL		DISTRACTION		NORMAL		DISTRACTION	
			External				External	
SPECIAL QUALITY	1st Hundred	2nd Hundred	1st Half	2nd Half	1st Hundred	2nd Hundred	1st Half	2nd Half
Grouping	46	46	54	26	21	32	14	16
Predicative relationship	4	2	–	6	9	8	4	6
Causal relationship	1	3	–	–	1	1	–	–
Co-existence	30	15	18	32	32	15	14	12
Identity	4	13	16	18	6	8	12	8
Linguistic-motor forms	14	18	12	18	30	32	50	48
Word-completion	–	–	–	–	–	–	–	–
Sound	–	–	–	–	–	2	2	8
Rhyme	–	–	–	–	–	–	2	–
Indirect	1	2	–	–	–	–	–	2
Meaningless	–	1	–	–	–	1	–	–
Failures	–	–	–	–	1	1	2	–
Repetition of stimulus-word	–	–	–	–	–	–	–	–
Egocentric reaction	–	–	–	–	–	–	–	–
Perseveration	–	1	–	–	–	–	–	2
Repetition of reaction	8	5	6	4	10	9	0	2
Same grammatical form	85	86	96	90	76	69	68	70
Same number of syllables	60	53	58	56	54	43	48	42
Alliteration	11	6	8	2	16	19	28	28
Consonance	15	7	10	8	14	21	30	36
Same ending	25	17	12	24	17	14	12	22
Internal associations	51	51	54	32	31	41	18	22
External associations	48	46	46	68	68	55	76	68
Sound reactions	–	–	–	–	–	2	4	8
Number of associations	100	100	50	50	100	100	50	50

under normal conditions and under distraction; the linguistic-motor reactions, on the other hand, are above average for uneducated women (the latter is 24 per cent under normal conditions and 28.8 per cent under external distraction). On the whole, we are confronted by a case with relatively few internal and many external associations.

336   Although, or rather because, the general reaction-type appears somewhat superficial, the distraction experiment was successful, considering that uneducated women with many predicatives are usually more difficult to distract. Even if the external associations are no more numerous in the second part of the distraction experiment than in the first hundred under normal conditions, the internal associations have definitely decreased, while the sound reactions have increased.

337   In the second hundred under normal conditions we have an increase of internal associations. At the same time, we find (as so often) an increase of constellations, which are probably, as many cases show, the cause of this shift. (The fact that among the stimulus-words of the second hundred there are more than in the first hundred of the kind likely to awaken emotionally charged concepts may have an influence here.) In the first hundred under normal conditions six constellations, in the second hundred under normal conditions ten, in the distraction experiment two can be demonstrated. In the distraction experiment they are much less frequent. We have here almost exclusively complex-constellations.

338   The complex is linked to a romance with an unhappy ending. The subject was disloyally deserted by her lover after a long relationship.

339   The long reaction-times (mostly more than five seconds) are almost exclusively confined to these complex-constellations. Examples:

male nurse	hospital orderly	11.4	(the lover was a
heart	stomach	6.4	male nurse)
to stroke	to love	5.6	
to part	to go	5.6	
dear	angry	8.8	
freedom	imprisoned	6.0	
to despise	respected	18.4	
band	to tear up	5.2	
false	falseness	7.2	

340   The subject did not really want to give an account of the few remaining constellations and long reaction-times, which cannot easily be recognized as belonging to the complex; they are therefore all the more suspect.

341   Here again we see the specific way in which the complex is manifested, i.e., the lengthened reaction-times. (This does not mean that these do not also occur in other cases, e.g., with rather difficult, unfamiliar stimulus-words.)

342   We have already found lengthened reaction-times as complex-phenomena (subjects 26 and 27 of this group); here they are almost exclusively complex-characteristics. There is a transition to the so-called "failures," where there is no verbal reaction at all.

343   The repetition of reaction-words is almost exclusively limited to the experiment under normal conditions and concerns sixteen different words; the majority of them designate things from the everyday life of a nurse.

344   *Subject 29.* A glance at the ratio of the predicate to the groupings tells us that the subject must be classed as a predicate type. In keeping with the rule for the predicate type we find no clear effect of distraction. Sound reactions and indirect associations only occur in the first part of distraction. Egocentric reactions are well represented and evenly distributed. The highest number of internal and the smallest number of external associations occur again in the second hundred of the experiment under normal conditions. There we also see a maximum of failures (7), which are nearly all caused by a complex. Unfortunately the subject never gave us an exact explanation and her retiring character induced us not to insist on one. The subject only confessed that memories of particular events in her family were largely behind the failures and the lengthened reaction-times. In a few instances unusual stimulus-words were responsible.

345   *Subject 30.* Distraction was clearly successful; it is mainly characterized by a decrease of groupings and increase of linguistic-motor forms; the number of predicates, although fairly numerous, is somewhat more stable. The largest number of perseverations occurs under distraction, particularly in the second hundred of the distraction experiment. There are no egocentric reactions. From the type of reactions it is not clear

Subjects 29 and 30. Nurses, 18 and 27 years of age, Swiss, elementary school education

ASSOCIATIONS	SUBJECT 29				SUBJECT 30			
	NORMAL		DISTRACTION		NORMAL		DISTRACTION	
			External				External	
SPECIAL QUALITY	1st Hundred	2nd Hundred	1st Half	2nd Half	1st Hundred	2nd Hundred	1st Half	2nd Half
Grouping	22	19	14	12	19	30	4	8
Predicative relationship	27	45	50	48	32	32	36	16
Causal relationship	1	1	–	–	2	1	–	–
Co-existence	31	14	16	12	26	12	10	6
Identity	2	3	6	10	2	4	6	2
Linguistic-motor forms	16	11	18	18	18	18	36	66
Word-completion	–	–	–	–	–	–	–	–
Sound	–	–	2	–	–	–	–	2
Rhyme	–	–	–	–	–	–	–	–
Indirect	–	–	4	–	–	–	–	–
Meaningless	–	–	–	–	–	–	4	–
Failures	1	7	–	–	1	3	–	–
Repetition of stimulus-word	–	–	–	–	–	–	4	–
Egocentric reaction	3	2	2	2	–	–	–	–
Perseveration	7	1	2	–	2	–	8	14
Repetition of reaction	13	11	14	6	14	9	18	4
Same grammatical form	50	29	28	32	31	35	38	60
Same number of syllables	37	24	48	52	53	43	20	14
Alliteration	6	3	6	6	13	9	28	30
Consonance	9	5	12	6	15	12	34	30
Same ending	–	2	2	4	6	11	20	28
Internal associations	50	65	64	60	53	63	40	24
External associations	49	28	30	40	46	34	52	74
Sound reactions	–	–	2	–	–	–	–	2
Number of associations	100	100	50	50	100	100	50	50

whether constellations or complexes play a part in the associations of the subject or not. It is easier to draw some conclusions from the reaction-times occurring, for example, after provocative stimulus-words, e.g.,

to kiss	morning kiss	8.4
to remember	letter	11.0
bad	(failure)	
rascal	without means	12.6

346   But we lack a detailed psychological analysis in this case. In the distraction experiment, repetitions of the form of the reaction occur; mainly we find reactions in the form of a whole sentence, e.g.,

sin	man sins
repentance	man repents
love	people love
strong	man is strong
hatred	people hate, etc.

347   Strikingly long reaction-times do not occur here; whether the repetition of form, particularly the reoccurrence of the word *man*, indicates similar complex-phenomena to those we found in subject 24 of this group cannot be established.

348   Seen from outside the associations of our subject make a very objective impression, without many subjective constellations. The rather variable and often strikingly long reaction-times, however, indicate that, behind the apparently objective reactions, complex-constellations are probably to be found after all. For practical reasons it was not possible in all cases to carry out a thorough psychological analysis, as could fortunately be done with a number of subjects.

349   *Subject 31.* The reactions are characterized by the great predominance of predicates, which make up the majority of the large number of internal associations. There is a definite inclination towards value judgments, which, however, do not have an expressly subjective (egocentric) character. The reactions betray a strong involvement with the experiment and with the meaning of the stimulus-word. In this way, in spite of a certain reticence and reserve, the more intimate content does emerge rather clearly. The subject is a very capable and practical housemaid, very religious. Occasionally she thinks of

Subject 31.   Maid, about 27 years of age, Swiss, elementary school education, fairly intelligent

ASSOCIATIONS	NORMAL		DISTRACTION	
			External	
SPECIAL QUALITY	1st Hundred	2nd Hundred	1st Half	2nd Half
Grouping	10	13	10	20
Predicative relationship	48	32	37	32
Causal relationship	–	–	–	2
Co-existence	11	4	14	4
Identity	2	5	2	2
Linguistic-motor forms	23	42	25	32
Word-completion	–	2	2	2
Sound	–	–	–	2
Rhyme	–	–	2	–
Indirect	–	–	2	–
Meaningless	–	–	–	–
Failures	6	1	6	4
Repetition of stimulus-word	–	–	–	–
Egocentric reaction	–	–	2	–
Perseveration	–	1	–	–
Repetition of reaction	15	15	8	2
Same grammatical form	38	38	34	40
Same number of syllables	42	36	44	54
Alliteration	3	11	6	8
Consonance	11	15	10	8
Same ending	6	8	4	6
Internal associations	58	45	47	54
External associations	36	51	41	38
Sound reactions	–	2	4	4
Number of associations	100	100	50	50

126

marriage. In the reactions under normal conditions the following reactions are repeated:

practical	twice	good	3 times
house	twice	beautiful	4 times
room	twice	wonderful	3 times
church	twice	man (husband)	3 times
God	twice	child	5 times

350 Shortly before the associations were obtained the subject was attacked by a large dog, which greatly frightened her.

351 The reaction *dog* was repeated four times. Once the subject showed a strong perseveration with the image of the dog.

$\begin{cases} \text{to growl} \\ \text{knot} \end{cases}$ dog
the knots (lumps) on the paws of the dog

352 The reaction *wolf* is also repeated twice. To the stimulus-word *cunning* the subject reacts with *wolf*, volunteering that actually *fox* had occurred to her first. These reactions and repetitions clearly show feeling-toned complexes and therefore a strong personal participation.

353 The distraction experiment, which incidentally was carried out very inadequately, had no effect at all. Thus we have here the same behaviour as in the predicate types described above.

354 The failures, numerous with this subject, are distributed as follows: Of the seven failures under normal conditions, five concern emotionally charged stimulus-words such as *heart, custom, flatterer, faithful, rich, revenge,* etc. In the two series of experiments under distraction, the failures (ten in the one and five in the other) concern 8 per cent of emotionally charged stimulus-words in the one and 4 per cent in the other—a further proof that the majority of failures can be attributed to emotional causes.

SUMMARY

355 In the group of uneducated women we have eight subjects, with ages ranging from 18 to 28, and altogether 2,400 associations. From each subject we have two hundred associations under normal conditions and one hundred under external distraction.

356 Most of the subjects are fairly intelligent. More than half

have attended secondary as well as primary schools. Seven subjects usually speak the Swiss dialect, only one speaks a South German dialect, which is more like standard German. Seven subjects are nurses, one is a maid. Two subjects react as predicate types; with neither was the distraction experiment successful. With a third subject, who gave a good number of predicates without actually belonging to the predicate type, the distraction experiment also failed; partly, no doubt, because the subject, in order not to let her attention be distracted, did not always make the strokes to the beat of the metronome at the stimulus-words. The distraction experiment was only partly successful with a subject with many groupings and no constellations. She almost doubled her effort in the distraction experiment, in order to pay attention to the stimulus-words as well as to the metronome beats.

357   With the remaining four subjects the distraction experiment was successful, although in general these subjects also strained their powers in the distraction experiment and made considerably more effort than in the experiment under normal conditions, because they found it more difficult than the educated subjects to divide their attention. On the whole the uneducated women were the group least able to divide their attention. The sound associations play a much smaller role as distraction phenomena than in the groups of educated subjects. Two subjects are of a purely objective type with few predicates, practically no constellations and strikingly many reaction-words with the same number of syllables as the stimulus-word. In two other subjects (24 and 26), complex-phenomena in various forms are predominant. In three subjects an increase of internal and a decrease of external associations can be observed in the second hundred of the experiment under normal conditions; it usually appeared that the complex-phenomena were also more obvious in the second hundred under normal conditions, while they diminish in number under distraction. In the marked cases, e.g., subject 24, the manifestation of the complex in the second hundred of the experiment under normal conditions is certainly not dependent on the increase of emotionally charged stimulus-words. It also appears with stimulus-words that for other people do not have this property at all.

IV. UNEDUCATED MEN

358   In the group of uneducated men we tabulate only a summary for the first six cases; the columns omitted are of no special interest. For the group of linguistic-motor forms, we have obtained the following mean values, from which none of the six subjects deviates significantly: experiment under normal conditions, first hundred 27, second hundred 30; external distraction, first half 22, second half 34. Definite complex-constellations are hardly demonstrable, and in almost all cases detailed analyses are lacking.

359   *Subject 32.* The external associations predominate over the internal but not to the same degree as in the educated subjects. The effect of distraction is clear: in the second hundred of the experiment under normal conditions we see the number of internal associations fall and the external ones rise somewhat. The figures for failures and egocentric reactions (4, 8, 6, 4) are strikingly high; they exceed the mean for these reaction-forms. In the absence of a more detailed analysis it is not really possible to find the significance of the failures in each association. There are practically no definite constellation-associations; neither do the reaction-times—apart from the few failures—betray any complex-constellation. They vary within narrow limits, 0.6 to 2.6 seconds.

360   *Subject 33.* Predominance of external associations, as in the preceding case. In the second hundred of the experiment under normal conditions, an increase of internal and decrease of external associations appears. We have been able to explain this phenomenon where we met it in other groups up to now, almost without exception, by the fact that the feeling-toned association-complexes emerge more clearly. Probably this is the case here too; yet the constellation-associations are here not very obvious and we possess only a fragmentary analysis. The sum of reaction-times in the second hundred is greater than in the first; the longer reaction-times are more numerous. In the second hundred there occurs significantly the reaction *family / alone,* 4.4 secs., the longest reaction-time that occurs with this subject.

361   The young man is engaged to a nurse. A series of reactions

with somewhat longer reaction-times are probably determined by this thought-complex.

362 We find the most marked distraction phenomena in the first part of the distraction experiment, where we also find six sound associations.

363 We find indications of constellations in our subject in single reactions referring to military service.

pupil	soldier
faithful	soldier
row	rank

Others refer, with fairly great probability, to his engagement and his fiancée:

dear	to trust	1.6
hope	at last	1.6
wreath	ring	3.2
fidelity	to let go	2.4
everywhere	alone	?
family	alone	4.4
to part	to come together	1.6

364 These reaction-times, which are rather long in relation to the other associations, support this interpretation. We find practically no quotations or the like in this or in the preceding subject.

365 *Subject 34.* The distraction experiment was not very successful; nevertheless it must be taken into consideration that the use of associations belonging to the sound and residual groups is more frequent in the distraction experiment than under normal conditions; the egocentric reactions disappeared in the distraction experiment, a phenomenon that may be regarded more or less as the effect of distraction. No constellation- and complex-associations are manifest.

366 *Subject 35.* The subject can just be included in the predicate type. A certain effect of distraction can nevertheless be noted. We see the internal associations decrease noticeably in our table and a definite increase of external associations only in the second part of the distraction experiment; on the other hand there is a maximum of sound reactions in the first part of the distraction experiment. Perseverations and egocentric reactions are completely absent. No constellation-associations are

Subjects 32–37. Male nurses: (32) 40 years of age, Swiss, elementary-school education, fairly well read; (33) about 25, South German, elementary-school education; (34) 54, secondary-school education, intelligent, rather neurasthenic; (35) 37, elementary-school education; (36) 30; (37) 36, secondary-school education

ASSOCIATIONS	SUBJECT 32 NORMAL		SUBJECT 32 DISTRACTION		SUBJECT 33 NORMAL		SUBJECT 33 DISTRACTION		SUBJECT 34 NORMAL		SUBJECT 34 DISTRACTION	
SPECIAL QUALITY	1st Hundred	2nd Hundred	External 1st Half	External 2nd Half	1st Hundred	2nd Hundred	External 1st Half	External 2nd Half	1st Hundred	2nd Hundred	External 1st Half	External 2nd Half
Grouping	34	12	16	16	32	37	24	20	5	22	10	12
Predicate	12	28	18	10	1	4	2	8	17	16	12	30
Internal associations	49	41	34	26	33	42	26	28	23	38	22	42
External associations	50	51	62	60	64	53	64	66	75	59	56	48
Sound reactions	–	–	–	–	2	1	6	–	–	1	4	2
Remaining group	1	8	2	14	1	4	4	6	2	2	18	8
Number of associations	100	100	50	50	100	100	50	50	100	100	50	50

ASSOCIATIONS	SUBJECT 35				SUBJECT 36				SUBJECT 37			
Grouping	15	15	22	10	32	16	18	12	46	27	30	22
Predicate	31	28	20	16	3	5	–	2	9	11	6	10
Internal associations	49	46	44	26	35	21	18	14	56	40	38	32
External associations	48	48	46	68	63	78	68	80	40	56	56	58
Sound reactions	1	1	4	–	1	1	8	4	1	1	–	2
Remaining group	2	5	6	6	1	–	6	2	3	3	6	8
Number of associations	100	100	50	50	100	100	50	50	100	100	50	50

evident. We quoted this case (one of the preceding cases from this group could also have been taken) in our discussion on constellations and complexes (see subject 18, educated men) as an example for those cases in which we find the first constellations and/or subjective reminiscences.

367   *Subject 36.* The internal associations diminish in number in this case as in the first few cases of this group. The predicates especially are very few. Define effects of distraction: the internal associations decrease both in the second hundred of the experiment under normal conditions and in the distraction experiment, particularly in the second part. Sound reactions, rhymes, and indirect and senseless reactions are numerous in the distraction experiment, particularly in the first part. In the second part they diminish again somewhat, but on the other hand the decrease of internal and increase of external associations is most marked. The figures for the same grammatical form are, as in the next case and in nos. 25 and 27 in the group of uneducated women, strikingly high (86 in the first hundred under normal conditions, 44 in the second hundred; 88 in each of the two halves of the distraction experiment). In keeping with this finding, egocentric associations are absent and the constellation-associations completely recede into the background and cannot be clearly recognized, as in the cases quoted.

368   In the second part of the distraction experiment there appears a certain amount of repetition, probably in embarrassment and as a distraction phenomenon:

17.[35]	door	castle (or lock)
55.	hall	castle hall
57.	bridge	castle bridge (drawbridge)
69.	shield	castle shield (or lockplate)
81.	cellar	cellar-door
87.	corridor	door

369   *Subject 37.* Among the fairly abundant internal associations there are mainly groupings, while the predicates are not particularly numerous. The linguistic-motor forms are relatively few. A glance at the ratio of internal to external associations shows at once that the distraction experiment was successful;

[35] The numbers refer to the order of the stimulus-words on the form; they are given only to show at what intervals these repetitions occur.

in fact the numbers obtained in the second hundred of the experiment under normal conditions foreshadowed it.

370 Our subject is like subject 36 of this group, and subjects 27 and 25 of the group of uneducated women, in the marked prominence of groupings and the figures for the same grammatical form, the decrease of predicative relationships and the almost complete absence of egocentric reactions and constellation-associations. We have here an objective balanced reaction-type.

371 This case is distinguished from the others by the predominance of subordinations and definitions within the groupings, while the other three subjects mentioned previously produced more actual co-ordinations.

Stimulus-word	Subject 25	Subject 27	Subject 36	Subject 37
	(Uneducated women)		(Uneducated men)	
Sunday	Tuesday	Monday	Monday	holiday
schoolboy	girl	teacher	teacher	boy
head	foot	arm	neck	part of human being
ink	pen	pen	pencil	writing material
bread	meat	cheese	flour	food
lamp	oil	candle	light	object in a room
tree	chair (?)	bush	bush	plant
wood	coal	coal	coal	fuel
slate-pencil	pen	pen	blackboard	school implement
fruit	plum	apple	vegetable	fruits
helmet	glove	sword	cuirassier	head-covering

372 *Subject 38.* The subject may perhaps be included in the predicate types, although the predicates do not predominate greatly in the second hundred. Strikingly many co-existences. No reactions in the sound group. In the residual group the number of failures is noteworthy. The maximum (five) occurs in the second hundred of the experiment under normal conditions. The sudden occurrence of 6 per cent of repetitions of the stimulus-word in the second part of the distraction experiment is surprising. We also find 2 per cent of perseverations there. In the second hundred of the experiment under normal conditions the number of internal associations rises and that of external associations falls, as we have already found several

Subject 38. *17 years of age, technical-school boy, fairly intelligent, nervous*

ASSOCIATIONS	NORMAL		DISTRACTION	
			External	
SPECIAL QUALITY	1st Hundred	2nd Hundred	60 Metronome	100 Metronome
Grouping	13	22	26	12
Predicative relationship	35	26	12	14
Causal relationship	–	1	–	–
Co-existence	26	10	22	12
Identity	3	2	14	8
Linguistic-motor forms	22	34	22	44
Word-completion	–	–	–	–
Sound	–	–	–	–
Rhyme	–	–	–	–
Indirect	–	–	–	–
Meaningless	–	–	–	–
Failures	1	5	4	4
Repetition of stimulus-word	–	–	–	6
Egocentric reaction	2	–	–	–
Perseveration	–	–	–	2
Repetition of reaction	12	5	–	–
Same grammatical form	44	48	82	64
Same number of syllables	32	30	40	40
Alliteration	12	15	12	16
Consonance	17	18	26	22
Same ending	2	13	10	14
Internal associations	48	49	38	26
External associations	51	46	58	64
Sound reactions	–	–	–	–
Number of associations	100	100	50	50

times in connection with the emergence of complex-constellations. In spite of the predicate type, the distraction experiment was successful. The number of internal associations decreased and that of external associations increased more and more. The predicates in particular diminish noticeably in the distraction experiment.

373   The exact figure for new constellations cannot be given; nevertheless a series of constellations exists, besides an enormous quantity of reminiscences from subjects taught at a grammar school. Individual associations with very long reaction-times are striking, e.g.:

exercise-book	squared	7.4
book	interesting	10.1
obstinate	the enemy	17.2
to stroke	*caresser* (French)	6.4
evil	devil	10.4
wicked	devil	28.0
to come	the yellow peril	8.4
to kiss	Oberon	6.8
to love	mother	13.0
dear	mother	9.0
strange	a poem	11.0
to disgust	dirty	6.8

374   In the distraction experiment the reactions with strikingly long reaction-times are very few. Probably a more detailed analysis would have found one or more complexes behind these reactions. Eroticism, school, and fear of a small operation were probably the decisive reasons for the lengthening of the reaction-times.

SUMMARY

375   In the group of uneducated men we have seven subjects and 2,086 associations. All subjects are fairly intelligent but with the exception of subject 37, who has received a secondary-school education, and subject 38, who is attending a technical school, they have all only had elementary-school education. Four subjects are German Swiss, speaking the ordinary dialect; one subject is South German but has long been resident in Switzerland, and the Swiss dialect therefore came quite naturally to him. Only one subject speaks the Swabian dialect, which

approximates more closely to standard German. One subject, the technical school boy, speaks standard German at home.

376   Two subjects may be considered to be predicate types; as in most subjects of this type, distraction was not really successful in the first case, but it was in the second. With one subject, who produced relatively few internal and many external associations in the experiment under normal conditions, distraction was also not very successful. In all other subjects the effect of distraction was obvious (in all subjects of this group only external distraction was used).

377   Sound associations as signs of distraction never occur to the same extent as with the educated subjects.

378   Two subjects (36 and 37 of this group) belong to a type having very many groupings, few predicates, and many reactions with the same grammatical form; they are distinguished at the same time by the paucity of egocentric reactions and constellations. We also meet this type in the group of uneducated women (subjects 25 and 27). For the rest, the whole group of uneducated men is distinguished by the fact that constellations and complexes are few in number and can only be guessed at; this does not mean, however, that, within narrow limits, the fluctuations of the reaction-times do not betray the workings of complexes. Quotations and similar reactions suggesting a complex were found only rarely in this group, an exception being the youngest of the group, the technical school boy. He reacted with many subjective reminiscences and a number of constellations, which may in part be interpreted as complex-constellations.

379   In subjects 33, 34, and 38 we find an increase of internal associations in the second hundred of the experiment under normal conditions. Whether this can always be explained by the effects of complexes cannot be ascertained with certainty in all cases.

380   In general the uneducated men are distinguished from the uneducated women in our experiments in that subjectivity and feelings are less prominent. This difference hardly exists in the educated subjects. Among the educated men there are as many subjective types who react strongly with feeling as there are among the women; the educated men have more feminine characteristics in this respect than the uneducated.

381   Finally, it may be permissible to point out once more that an overwhelming number of the complexes we have discovered in our subjects are erotic. In view of the great part played by love and sexuality in human life, this is not surprising.

B. CALCULATIONS OF AVERAGES

I. Experiment under Normal Conditions

382   Having discussed the individual subjects, we still have to study the interrelations of the groups of reactions. In the individuals the proportions of these is markedly variable, as a glance at the previous tables shows. Besides the individual causes, one of the main reasons for these variations is the intensity of concentration, the effect of which we have already mentioned several times. The fact that some individuals tend to react with internal associations and others with external ones is primarily a question of attention. Everyone gifted with speech has all the different qualities of association at his command: which quality of association he expresses depends in the main only on the degree of attention devoted to the stimulus-word. Where our distraction experiment was successful— that is, where the conditions of the experiment were carried out in the way intended by the experimenter—the identical unequivocal phenomenon appeared: the external associations and sound reactions increased at the expense of internal associations. The type of reaction shifted towards the accustomed and canalized and thus to the mechanical, concrete and verbal connections. With increasing distraction the effect of the "law of frequency" increases, ideas that are often spatially or temporally related being evoked. The less an idea is focussed upon, the more the valency of associated, mainly linguistic, elements increases, the threshold is lowered and these elements are therefore produced again.

383   We do not wish to discuss here the different psychological theories of attention. We regard attention as a state occurring in association-complexes and ultimately characterized by muscular tension, which provides the psychophysical basis for the complex. The stabilizing of the idea in the field of consciousness seems to be the aim of the physical echo. It is probably through the somatic connection that the idea, or the "feeling"

137

replacing it, is kept in focus. It becomes a "directional idea" (or a "directional feeling"). From it result two types of effect:

(1) ideas promoting all associated ideas, particularly those associated with direction,

(2) ideas inhibiting all ideas not associated, particularly those not associated with direction.

384   If the intensity of concentration is raised for a non-associated idea, then the directional idea is correspondingly shifted from focus, i.e., it loses intensity. Its impact decreases correspondingly: thus the difference in the threshold value of all other associations becomes smaller. The directional selection becomes more difficult and is increasingly subject to the effect of the law of frequency, i.e., all those associations which, through practice and habit, form the largest component of consciousness come to the fore. The law of frequency now assumes the role previously played by the directional idea. As regards our experiment, this means that ideas already automatized and condensed in language assist the subject in his effort to comprehend the meaning of the stimulus-word and to work it over.

385   In the act of apperception and the further working on the stimulus-word, all these purely linguistic connections are suppressed, so that in part they manifest themselves only very faintly and vaguely and in part they remain completely unconscious. If the linguistic connections enter the field of consciousness, the higher associations are pushed into the background; some of them faintly reverberate and some remain unconscious (according to Wundt "unnoticed"). (It is possible that they are not even formed, but this is difficult to prove.) In linguistic mechanisms, however, the process has not yet reached its lowest level; mere repetition of the sound reaction is suppressed during the mechanical linguistic reaction. If, by further lowering of attention, we remove the linguistic mechanisms, which in most cases still possess some meaning, the sound reactions come to the fore; these represent the lowest level of linguistic reaction and therefore remain constantly below the threshold of consciousness in everyday life. In the process of development of the child's speech, sound reactions, as is well known, still play a fairly important part; later they are increasingly suppressed and usually enter into the uncon-

scious, from which they can under normal conditions be brought up only with a certain effort.

386   We have deliberately discussed only the effect of distraction on linguistic functions. We note in addition that the law of frequency also applies to the selection of internal images. It struck us how often old childish memories cropped up, even with quite everyday objects, in the state of internal distraction (N.B. decidedly more frequently than in the normal state).

387   In the individual accounts we pointed out the similarity between the distraction phenomenon and manic reaction. The reactions under distraction are in no way different from manic reactions as found by Aschaffenburg and observed by us in many manic associations. Liepmann,[36] who in a recently published monograph explains *flight of ideas* as a result of a disturbance of attention, reached a similar view to ours. Considerations such as Liepmann makes in his work have for some time pointed directions in our experimental work. The results of our experiments confirm Liepmann's views. As regards the psychological mechanism of flight of ideas, our views are completely in agreement with Liepmann. We therefore refer to his monograph.

388   Aschaffenburg has introduced us to another reaction-type similar to the manic, the fatigue type. Other investigations, carried out under Kraepelin's direction, report analogous results under the influence of alcohol. Aschaffenburg considers, as is well known, motor excitation responsible for the occurrence of sound reactions. An obvious objection to this interpretation is that the conditions described are to a high degree characterized by disturbance of attention. It has been proved by our experiments that sound reactions are, one might say exclusively, caused by disturbance of attention. The motor excitation is a probably inessential side-effect which, at the most, could be the cause of the disturbance of attention. The latter seems to be the case in fatigue and alcoholism. In manic flight of ideas another factor must certainly also be considered as a cause of disturbance of attention, the specific excitation, the psychological nature of which is still quite obscure to us.

[36] Liepmann, *Über Ideenflucht, Begriffsbestimmung und psychologische Analyse* (1904).

Disturbance of attention due to motor excitation in fatigue and alcoholism could in our view be interpreted thus: the physical correlates of the attention phenomenon, the muscular tensions, become under the influence of motor excitation shorter and more variable. The psychophysical basis of accentuated ideas thus reaches a degree of instability that is represented psychically as a weakness of the directional idea. According to Liepmann's principles, from this weakness of the directional idea flight of ideas must result, which in the association experiment appears as sound reactions, etc. It is possible that in acoustic linguistic experiments motor excitation, which is of course also transmitted to the linguistic-motor system, furthers the release of the mechanical reaction; but it is never its sole cause.

389   From this we may expect the occurrence of a blunt reaction-type or a sound reaction wherever there is a disturbance of attention; conversely we may suspect a disturbance of attention where sound reactions occur.

390   This fact appears to us of great diagnostic value; it is, moreover, an essential condition for the understanding of the reactions generally.

391   Because of the relatively great variations in the individual figures, a general survey of our figures is difficult; we have therefore compiled tables in which the arithmetical means of certain groups have been calculated in percentages to make comparison easier. We realize that a calculation of averages from figures of such diversity is a somewhat hazardous undertaking. Even if the quantitative relation of the individual groups to each other is somewhat variable, we are nevertheless convinced that at least the main figures, that is, those for internal and external associations and for sound reactions, do present a true picture of the mode of reaction. The quantitative interrelation of certain special groups, e.g., particularly of co-existences, is partly subject to certain sources of error that are caused by the selection of stimulus-words. It is certainly clear that, where nouns only are used, reactions show ratios rather different from those brought about by mixed stimulus-words. Nevertheless our relative figures retain their value, as all subjects were given the same set of stimulus-words.

392   We have classified our material according to different cri-

teria; first of all the question of the relation of educated to uneducated subjects interested us. Aschaffenburg has found, as is
well known, a relatively strong predominance of external over
internal associations in his educated subjects. On the other
hand, Ranschburg and Balint have found a marked predominance of internal associations in uneducated subjects. See here-
with Tables A and B for the first and second hundred of normal
associations.

393   Our uneducated subjects were almost all male and female
nurses of the hospital. We must now confess that this selection
of uneducated subjects is not a particularly good one, for among
the nursing staff there are many individuals who are above the
low average level of education. It might be better to substitute
the term "half-educated" for "uneducated." The level of education and intelligence of the male subjects is in general somewhat above that of the female subjects.

394   The female subjects show a relatively high number of internal associations; strangely enough the number of internal
associations rises considerably in the second half of the experiment, the predicates particularly showing an increase. In addition there is an increase in the residual group and in the sound
reactions. There is probably a connection between the increase
of predicates and of linguistic-motor forms and the decrease of
correspondence of grammatical forms. The figures for linguistic connections are very high.

395   The male subjects show in general a blunter reaction-type
than the female subjects. The second hundred does not differ
significantly from the first, only the figures for indirect associations and for consonances show a rather striking increase.

396   The increase of failures in the second hundred of both
groups may perhaps be attributed to the unfortunate coincidence that the number of feeling-toned stimulus-words is somewhat greater in the second hundred than in the first. As we have
seen, the failures mainly coincide with feeling-toned stimulus-
words. It is noteworthy that the men produce a larger number
of egocentric reactions than the women, as well as a definitely
smaller number of predicates.

397   The egocentric reactions, i.e., the influence of personal
wishes and values, is probably connected with the number of
perseverations; this is somewhat higher for the women than for

A. The First and Second Hundred of Normal Associations: Uneducated

	WOMEN		MEN	
SPECIAL QUALITY	1st Hundred	2nd Hundred	1st Hundred	2nd Hundred
Grouping	24.2 ⎫	26.2 ⎫	25.2 ⎫	21.5 ⎫
Predicative relationship	18.8 ⎬44.0	22.0 ⎬49.3	15.4 ⎬41.7	16.8 ⎬39.4
Causal relationship	1.0 ⎭	1.1 ⎭	1.1 ⎭	1.1 ⎭
Co-existence	27.2 ⎫	13.6 ⎫	21.7 ⎫	13.0 ⎫
Identity	3.3 ⎬52.8	6.8 ⎬46.1	7.8 ⎬55.7	12.2 ⎬55.7
Linguistic-motor forms	22.3 ⎭	25.7 ⎭	26.2 ⎭	30.5 ⎭
Word-completion	0.2 ⎫	0.0 ⎫	– ⎫	– ⎫
Sound	– ⎬0.3	0.3 ⎬1.4	0.7 ⎬0.7	0.5 ⎬0.6
Rhyme	0.1 ⎭	0.6 ⎭	– ⎭	0.1 ⎭
Indirect	0.6 ⎫	0.8 ⎫	0.5 ⎫	1.2 ⎫
Meaningless	0.3 ⎪	0.2 ⎪	0.1 ⎪	0.2 ⎪
Failures	1.2 ⎬2.1	1.6 ⎬2.6	0.8 ⎬1.4	2.2 ⎬3.6
Repetition of stimulus-word	– ⎭	– ⎭	– ⎭	– ⎭
Egocentric reactions	0.8	0.8	2.0	1.5
Perseveration	1.5	0.6	1.0	0.4
Repetition of reaction	10.2	8.8	14.1	10.5
Same grammatical form	63.2	54.7	60.1	58.4
Same number of syllables	49.9	42.2	41.1	37.0
Alliteration	10.2	8.7	9.0	9.0
Consonance	12.3	12.2	11.1	14.0
Same ending	11.7	11.0	16.4	16.2
Number of associations	800	800	700	700
Number of subjects	8		7	

the men but alters in accordance with the decrease of egocentric judgments, a finding that will be confirmed in the future. We attribute this to the fact that it is mainly feeling-toned reactions that have a tendency towards perseveration, as we have already frequently pointed out in the individual accounts.

398   With the educated subjects, in the first place one is struck by the generally blunter reaction-type. The subjects are nearly

B. The First and Second Hundred of Normal Associations: Educated

SPECIAL QUALITY	WOMEN		MEN	
	1st Hundred	2nd Hundred	1st Hundred	2nd Hundred
Grouping	13.4 ⎫	14.0 ⎫	16.1 ⎫	16.5 ⎫
Predicative relationship	21.8 ⎬36.9	18.6 ⎬33.2	17.3 ⎬34.0	22.2 ⎬39.5
Causal relationship	1.7 ⎭	0.6 ⎭	0.6 ⎭	0.8 ⎭
Co-existence	16.5 ⎫	11.2 ⎫	18.2 ⎫	7.5 ⎫
Identity	2.7 ⎬57.2	6.7 ⎬58.9	3.2 ⎬56.6	8.3 ⎬49.0
Linguistic-motor forms	38.0 ⎭	41.0 ⎭	35.2 ⎭	33.2 ⎭
Word-completion	1.0 ⎫	2.0 ⎫	1.1 ⎫	1.1 ⎫
Sound	0.3 ⎬2.1	1.9 ⎬4.5	1.5 ⎬3.3	2.3 ⎬4.0
Rhyme	0.8 ⎭	0.6 ⎭	0.7 ⎭	0.6 ⎭
Indirect	0.9 ⎫	1.0 ⎫	2.8 ⎫	2.2 ⎫
Meaningless	0.1	0.1	0.7	1.2
Failures	1.9 ⎬2.9	0.9 ⎬2.4	1.7 ⎬5.2	2.6 ⎬6.1
Repetition of stimulus-word	– ⎭	0.4 ⎭	– ⎭	0.1 ⎭
Egocentric reactions	2.7	1.5	3.6	2.6
Perseveration	0.8	0.5	3.1	1.8
Repetition of reaction	8.0	6.5	7.5	7.6
Same grammatical form	53.9	54.0	52.1	46.1
Same number of syllables	43.9	39.2	37.0	32.6
Alliteration	9.0	7.8	9.2	8.8
Consonance	14.6	15.2	15.1	16.2
Same ending	9.8	11.3	8.2	8.8
Number of associations	1100	1100	800	800
Number of subjects	11		8	

all highly educated people: the women too, with few exceptions, are of a high level of education.

399   The difference between male and female subjects is not considerable in the first three groups, with the exception of a slight preponderance of internal associations in the men (in which groupings particularly play a part). On the other hand, considerable differences appear in the residual group, in which

the high figures for indirect associations in the men are particularly striking, being more than twice those of the women. The average of sound reactions in the men is somewhat higher than in the women. The inverse relationship of indirect association and sound reactions, which was previously suspected, is indicated here too:

	WOMEN		MEN	
	1st hundred	2nd hundred	1st hundred	2nd hundred
Sound reactions	2.9	2.4	5.2	6.1
Indirect association	0.9	1.0	2.8	2.2

We shall discuss this phenomenon in the discussion of distraction averages.

400   Here also the egocentric reactions of the men exceed those of the women. The number of perseverations corresponds to that of egocentric reactions, as in the uneducated subjects—a further proof of the largely affective nature of perseverations (N.B. only in the experiments under normal conditions).

401   The difference between educated and uneducated subjects can be best made clear by putting the average figures of both groups side by side (Table C).

402   The educated subjects show a clearly blunter reaction-type than the uneducated. The difference is best expressed by stating: In contrast to the uneducated subjects the educated subjects show a distraction phenomenon.

403   If we suppose the figures for the uneducated subjects are those of a subject under normal conditions, then the figures for the educated subjects bear the same relation to them as those of a distraction experiment. The sound reactions and the figures for the residual group are proportionately increased, as we have repeatedly seen in the individual accounts.

404   What is the origin of this difference? One cannot assume that the educated subjects in effect think more "bluntly" than the uneducated; that would be nonsense. One can merely assume that in the experiment they thought more "bluntly" than the uneducated subjects. This appears to us really to be the case, and it seems that from this the explanation of the reaction-type can be deduced.

C. Averages for Educated and Uneducated Subjects

SPECIAL QUALITY	EDUCATED		UNEDUCATED	
Grouping	15.0		24.2	
Predicative relationship	19.3	35.8	18.2	43.4
Causal relationship	0.9		1.0	
Co-existence	13.3		18.8	
Identity	5.2	55.3	7.5	52.4
Linguistic-motor forms	36.8		26.1	
Word-completion	1.3		0.1	
Sound	1.5	3.4	0.3	0.5
Rhyme	0.6		0.4	
Indirect	1.7		0.7	
Meaningless	0.5		0.1	
Failures	1.7	4.0	1.4	2.2
Repetition of stimulus-word	0.1		–	
Egocentric reaction	2.4		1.1	
Perseveration	1.5		0.8	
Repetition of reaction	7.3		10.9	
Same grammatical form	51.5		59.2	
Same number of syllables	38.2		42.5	
Alliteration	8.7		9.3	
Consonance	10.2		12.3	
Same ending	9.5		13.8	
Number of associations	3800		3000	
Number of subjects	19		15	

405   As proof for this assumption the following points may be considered:

(1) The agreement in grammatical form and number of syllables of the stimulus-word and reaction is clearly higher in the uneducated subjects. This fact seems to indicate that the uneducated subject sticks more closely to the stimulus-word or is more influenced by it than the educated subject.

(2) The number of meaningless reactions is considerably smaller in the uneducated subject. He has better control over himself or he pays more attention to his reaction.

(3) The uneducated subject surpasses the educated mainly in the number of groupings: i.e., he makes a greater effort to do justice to the meaning of the stimulus-word than the educated subject does.

(4) The uneducated subject surpasses the educated in the number of co-existences, which are mainly made up of spatial concepts, i.e., the uneducated subject makes an effort to imagine clearly the object named by the stimulus-word, and he naturally must associate that which is co-existent with it. The educated subject, on the other hand, has fewer co-existences, as he limits himself to connecting linguistic forms.

(5) The uneducated subject has roughly half as many egocentric reactions as the educated. This fact indicates that he lets himself go much less and exposes undisguised subjective wishes and valuations much less. He makes an effort to achieve as objective as possible an interpretation of the stimulus-word.

(6) One of the main proofs is the almost sevenfold greater number of sound reactions in educated subjects. In this laziness is most clearly revealed. The subject who is intensely attentive produces practically no sound associations.[37]

406   For these reasons we regard it as proved that the difference between educated and uneducated reaction-types, as far as it is expressed in these figures, is merely a functional one and only has the significance of an attention phenomenon.

407   If we may estimate the degree of attention from the figures for sound reactions, the residual group and the linguistic-motor forms, then the uneducated women achieve the highest degree of attention and the educated men the lowest. This fact becomes evident if we examine the groups divided according to sex with respect to these points of view.

408   What is the origin of this difference of attention[38] between educated and uneducated subjects? Various factors must be considered:

(1) The uneducated subject is unused to an experiment of this kind. Naturally, it seems stranger and more difficult to him than to the educated subject, who is much more capable of understanding the significance of the experiment and who must

---

37 With the exception, of course, of people with specific dispositions.
38 By this we mean a difference of attention only in the quantitative sense, not by any means a qualitative difference.

from the first feel more at home than the uneducated in an intellectual activity. The stimulation of the uneducated subject by the experiment is therefore greater and more general, which is why more effort is made in reacting.

(2) Words without any sentence connection are called out to the subject. Under normal circumstances, if one calls anything out to someone it is, as a rule, a command or a question. The uneducated subject, in contrast to the educated, is not used to dealing with individual words outside the sentence connection, particularly if he has never learned a foreign language from books. Thus the stimulus-word contains something strange for the uneducated subject. Under the influence of habit he interprets it instinctively as a question, with the intensity of attention necessary for producing an appropriate answer. The stimulus-word is mostly something to the uneducated subject for which he constructs for himself some interrogative connection, to which he then replies.[39]

(3) The uneducated subject knows words only, so to speak, related to a sentence, particularly when they appear as an auditory phenomenon. In the context of a sentence the words always have a meaning; the uneducated subject therefore knows the word less as mere "word" or verbal sign but much more as meaning. Therefore the uneducated subject grasps the semantic value of a single word only in a fictitious sentence-context, while to the educated the stimulus-word usually remains merely "word" without specific semantic value.[40]

409 Summarizing, we can say that the uneducated subject shows, in keeping with his lower degree of education, a narrower interpretation of the experiment, particularly of the stimulus-word called out to him, than the educated subject whose approach to the matter is much cooler and more businesslike. In other words: the uneducated subject shows a certain tendency

[39] One can say that in general the more uneducated and unintelligent a subject is, the more he interprets the stimulus-word as a question. This is shown most clearly in idiots, who, with few exceptions, always interpret the stimulus-word as a question and then give a definition or an explanation of it in the reaction.
[40] Incidentally, educated subjects have the same experience with words of a language that they have never read in print or writing. When stimulus-words are called out in dialect, the educated subjects sometimes have difficulty in understanding the words, because they are used to hearing dialect words only in a sentence-connection.

to assimilate the stimulus-word in the form of a question, because it is most usual for called-out verbal sounds to have the connotation of questions.

410   This attitude to the stimulus-word becomes more evident in certain pathological cases, where the association experiment is nothing but a 2 × 200 sentence-long conversation on a feeling-toned theme. From these observations one can readily deduce that the uneducated subject pays greater attention because the meaning of the stimulus-word influences him more than it does the educated subject.

411   The difference between educated and uneducated subjects is in the contrast of their interpretations of the stimulus-word. This principle of differentiation allows us to discern two groups, even if vaguely delineated. This distinction, however, is such a general one that it does not take into account other essential differences in the reaction-types. We have therefore made an effort to find other more subtle principles of classification. We asked ourselves whether there are other general factors that influence the reaction, apart from the attention phenomenon.

412   One principal factor is the individual character. The difference in interpretation discussed above is an intellectual or associative disposition, which may be the same in individuals of widely varying character. As regards characters, the state of affairs is different. From our experiments two easily recognizable types emerge:

(1) A type in whose reactions subjective, often feeling-toned experiences are used.

(2) A type whose reactions show an objective, impersonal tone.

413   The former type exhibits reminiscences of a personal kind that often show a very strong feeling-tone. The latter type couples words with words and concepts with concepts, but the personal plays a quite subordinate role in the reaction. This type can be called objective.

414   The first type can be divided into three groups.

(a) The stimulus-image emanating from the stimulus-word acts principally through its feeling-tone. Usually the feeling-tone of the stimulus-image excites a whole complex of memories belonging to it. The reaction then is inherent in the constellation of this complex. In practice a subject of this type, at least in an extreme case, can easily be distinguished from the others. We call this type the complex-constellation type.

(β) The image evoked by the stimulus-word is a personal memory usually taken from everyday life. The reaction contains this image or is at least distinctly constellated by it. We call this type the simple constellation type.[41]

(γ) The image evoked by the stimulus-word acts through one or other of its associated attributes (partly the sensory aspects of the image, partly feeling-tones). Presumably the stimulus-image appears in strong relief; now one, now another characteristic comes to the fore and thus, in conjunction with other features, determines the reaction; thus it usually contains a predicate of the object designated by the stimulus-word. We call this type the predicate type.

415   The common factor in the types described under (α), (β), and (γ), as opposed to the objective type (2), is a marked stress of that part of the reaction that is individual, personal, and independent of the stimulus-word. Thus we can say that the difference between type 1 and type 2 is the egocentricity of attitude.

416   The points presented make clear the general psychological laws that rule our experiment. This does not by any means reveal all the roots from which complications in the reactions originate.

417   As regards the egocentric attitude, we have tacitly presupposed that the reaction is a more or less clear symbol of internal processes. As long as we know that the subject is speaking freely we can let this assumption prevail *cum grano salis*. The picture of reactions, however, changes at once when the egocentric attitude conduces to feeling-toned complexes, which the subject does not wish to betray.[42] This occurs particularly in the

[41] We stress here once more that by this classification we intend to mark only the clear and obvious differences in the mode of reaction. We know very well that basically every subject belongs in fact to, for example, the complex-constellation type, as no reaction is fortuitous but irrevocably conditioned by the psychological past of the subject. What we wish to clarify by our classification is the degree of subjective dependence in so far as it is clearly expressed in the reactions.

[42] This not-wanting-to-betray is, as we have become convinced from numerous experiments, by no means always a conscious not-wanting but quite often an

complex-constellation type. For instance, the stimulus-word raises the complex of an unhappy love that is being kept as secret as possible. If the subject reacted according to his internal images, then he would exteriorize that part of the complex in the reaction through which it could be betrayed. The concealing of an emotion is always characterized by a quite particular attitude, a particular state of feeling. Without conscious censure, the emerging part of the complex is suppressed by the feeling of being directed not to betray, which is present in consciousness and from which specially attuned inhibitions arise. Of course the process of suppression may take place at a considerably more conscious level (or more unconscious, as in hysteria!). Instead of the suppressed complex-image another association fitting in with the feeling of being directed is put in its place and exteriorized.

418   Thus the true inner association is concealed and the secret kept. It may be extraordinarily difficult for the experimenter, who does not enjoy the complete confidence of the subject, to decide in certain cases whether anything was concealed or not. The decision may perhaps be impossible with people who are capable of controlling themselves to a high degree. In most cases, however, the subjects betray themselves after a short time. According to the laws discussed previously, there must be certain phenomena that betray the suppressed complex. We shall here disregard the lengthening of reaction-time,[43] which occurs with great regularity.

419   The suppression is betrayed:

(1) By an unusual and suspicious phrasing of the reaction that cannot be explained by the stimulus-word alone, but the peculiar character of which is bound to have been constellated by an X. Occasionally this X can be deduced directly from the peculiarly forced character of the reaction. Such reactions frequently occur in the form of sentences.

(2) By the attention phenomenon. A subject who interprets the stimulus-word as a question and therefore produces a series of highly potent associations suddenly, in the absence of ex-

---

unconscious inhibition, which in most cases also causes a lengthening of the reaction-time.

[43] A later paper will report on the variation of the reaction-times. [See infra.]

ternal disturbance, reacts with a sound or some other strikingly superficial association. This result is suspicious; an internal disturbance or an internal distraction must have occurred. The subject may give no information. With a similar stimulus-word the phenomenon is repeated. We are now practically sure that there is something behind this. This suspicion has never proved unjustified. A complex has suddenly emerged, has attracted some of the attention to itself; meanwhile the reaction is produced and, owing to the disturbance of attention, it can be only a superficial one.

(3) By a failure. The emerging complex absorbs all attention so that the reaction either is forgotten or, owing to the absence of all associations, cannot take place.

(4) By perseveration. In this case the critical reaction may be quite unobtrusive but the subsequent one has an abnormal character, in which the preceding reaction takes over the role of the constellation X. The perseverating factor is the emotion stimulated by the preceding association.[44]

(5) By assimilation of the stimulus-word. The stimulus-word is interpreted for no apparent reason in a particular, rare sense or is misunderstood in a striking way according to a feeling-toned conscious idea.[45]

420   The above points are the main criteria of a concealed complex.[46]

421   We have purposely devoted so much attention to the dis-

---

[44] A subject whose inner life is strongly affected by an unpleasant financial matter reacts within normal time to *ill* with *poor* and in the following reaction, *Stolz* ('pride') / *Bolz* ('arrow'), with lengthened reaction-time. For no obvious reason the association is a senseless rhyme. Sound associations and rhymes occur in this subject only at "critical" points. *Poor* has a quite special emotional significance for this subject; attention remains attached to the constellated complex, which results in a disturbance of the succeeding reaction because of internal distraction.

[45] The subject already quoted in the preceding footnote reacts to *pity* with *poor ones* (*poor* has a particular feeling-tone). The succeeding association is *yellow* (*gelb*) / *much*. It is another perseveration of the financial complex, *gelb* being immediately assimilated as *Geld* (money), although the subject has long been familiar with all the stimulus-words on our list.

[46] In some subjects the repetitions also have a certain significance as the indirect expression of the complex. (We have pointed this out several times in the relevant section.) Certain words that are more or less closely associated with the complex, or that indirectly replace it, are frequently repeated.

cussion of these subtler psychological phenomena because the affective processes, the traces of which we pursued with the greatest possible care in normal reactions, play the most prominent role in the pathological reactions, as we shall show in detail later. What might perhaps be put to one side as a subtlety in a normal reaction will be revealed as the most significant factor in a pathological reaction. For the present we place great value on the realization that the reactions are an extraordinarily sensitive test for affective processes in particular and the individual response of the subject in general.

422   To illustrate our discussion we present associations of the six main types [1 (a), (b); 2 (a), (b-i), (b-ii), (c)].

1. OBJECTIVE TYPE

423   (a) Reactions of a subject whose attitude is essentially objective. At the same time the interpretation of the stimulus-word as a question is in the background. There is a tendency merely to put words next to each other, partly in accordance with the law of similarity, partly according to current verbal connections (subject 15, educated men).

Christmas	Easter	ring	finger
Sunday	Monday	tooth	time
winter	spring	window	frame
lake (or sea)	ocean	frog	leg
pupil	teacher	sweet	sour
father	mother	to ride	to travel
table	leg	friendly	painful
head	scarf	to cut	knife
ink	pen	crown	realm
needle	holder	rough	-ian (ruffian)
bread	to earn	prison	detention
lamp	shade	to part	to avoid
tree	clearing	(scheiden)	(meiden)
mountain	green	ill	weak
dream	froth (Schaum)	air	song
(Traum)		potato	to salt
exercise-book	knife	to be lazy	armchair
paper	cutter	coffee	to drink
book	to read	sacrifice	to bring
school	to attend	wedding	feast
to sing	to write	grandmother	father

bad	naughty	dark	light
to clap	hands	heart (*Herz*)	pain (*Schmerz*)
year	month	bird	nest
to threaten	fist	white	black
long	narrow	game	card
rich	poor	Kaiser	Wilhelm
suffering	joy	moon	light
eye	tooth	to beat	to throw
youth	game	to light	house
inn	{ At the Sign of the Bloody Bone	star	shooting
		to stroke	cat
		grand	magnificent
family	scandal	child	dog
misery	sorrow	sofa	to lie
to pay attention	to note	wild	animal
		tears	to shed
fist (*Faust*)	Goethe	loyalty	German
people	rebellion	once (*einmal*)	never (*keinmal*)
murderer	blood	wonder	of wonders
everywhere	I am at home	blood	vengeance
to calculate	to measure	wreath	athlete
to kiss	mouth	to choose	choice
ripe	fruit	right	might
bond	of love	to have to	no man must have to[48]
ground	found		
play	of waves	hope	does not let one perish
journey	to Canossa		
to quarrel	fight	small (*klein*)	my (*mein*)
blue	red	unjust	faithlessness
flower	calyx	world (*Welt*)	pain (*Schmerz*)
cherry	stone	strange	unknown
institution	male nurse	slate-pencil	to write
piano	to play	to growl	dog
oven	town[47]	knob	-stick
to walk	to go	fruit	to eat
to cook	to eat	false	fox
water	to drink	helmet	ornament
to dance	music	hay	straw
cat	mouse	cleanly	painfully
dozen	by the (dozen)	(*reinlich*)	(*peinlich*)

[47] [*Oven* stands for the German *Ofen*, the German name of Buda, the sister town of Pest (Hungary). *Ofen* really means 'oven.']
[48] [Cf. supra, par. 212, n. 15.]

to surmise	W (name of acquaintance who formulated a certain hypothesis)	trap (*Falle*)	rope (*Strick*) (*Fallstrick,* 'snare')
		to be revolted	gruesome
		resin	to stick
head	blood and wounds	neck	to wring
		steep	mountain
at home	it's nice	swing	to swing
hedge	rose	to fetch	to bring
indolent	lazy	skull	formation
vinegar	sour	to use	to be able to
hot	cold	stamp	*timbre*

424   The subject is a doctor, as several technical medical terms, such as *needle-holder* and *skull-formation*, indicate. We do not include those reactions constellated by the profession in the "constellations" in the narrower sense in which we interpret these. Such reactions are not subjective; they belong not only to the individual, but more or less to a whole profession. The only subjective constellation is *to surmise* / *W*.

425   (b) Reactions of a subject whose approach is objective and to whom the meaning of the stimulus-word is much more important than to the preceding subject. The tendency is to give as correct a reaction as possible (subject 27, group of uneducated women):

table	chair	to sing	to rejoice
head	arm	hoop	ring
ink	pen	tooth	mouth
needle	thread	window	floor
bread	cheese	frog	stork
lamp	candle	flower	grass
tree	bush	cherry	peach
mountain	valley	institution	school
hair	thread	piano	violin
wood	coal	fern	rose-bush
salt	flour	to walk	to jump
dream	sleep	water	wine
exercise-book	book	to dance	to sing
paper	material	dozen	ten
book	newspaper	heart	warm
school	church	bird	cat

to swim	to go	people	household
game	to sing		(*family* is
Kaiser	king		implied)
moon	stars	murderer	robber
to beat	to bite	everywhere	here
obstinate	gentle	to kiss	to flatter
to light	to extinguish	bad	good
star	sun	ripe	bitter (*sweet*
to stroke	to beat		is implied)
great	wonderful	band	material
child	woman	ground	floor
to ride	to travel	walk	to jump
friendly	cross	to quarrel	to make it up
file	hammer	sofa	chair
crown	helmet	to love	to hate
to paint	oil	wild	tame
thanks	you're welcome	tears	to laugh
rough	fine	to spare	better
to stink	to taste	wonder	nature
prison	dungeon	blood	human being
to separate	to join	wreath	flowers
ill	healthy	to choose	to meet
potato	bread	right	wrong
trap	to catch	force	voluntary
to disgust	to taste	revenge	peace
to be lazy	to work	hope	joy
coffee	milk	to pray	to believe
victim	saviour	freedom	imprisoned
wedding	funeral	world	nation
angry	satisfied	strange	at home
soldier	civilian	to growl	to bite
to clap	to sing	knot	rope
to threaten	to beat	false	true
behaviour	polite	helmet	sword
to fall	level	plate	tray
to suffer	healthy	hay	grass
youth	age	pure	clean
inn	hotel	to surmise	to doubt
family	husband	head	arm
to pay attention	to hear	at home	away
		vinegar	wine
fist	hand	resin	pitch
		swing	to throw

426   The subject is a nurse from our hospital. Subjective factors are entirely absent from the reactions. Her manner is extraordinarily objective and calm. In contrast to the preceding subject it must be noted that here the meaning of the stimulus-word is the decisive factor, which is expressed in many contrasting ways.

2. EGOCENTRIC ATTITUDE

(a) Simple-constellation type

427   Reactions of a subject in whose reactions numerous subjective experiences are used. The attitude is egocentric in so far as subjective memories prevail (subject 18, educated men).

father	anxious (the subject is the father of a new-born child)	to sing	Miss B. (name of a singer who was at the hospital just at that time)
head	round		
ink	sour (*red/litmus* is implied)	ring	hospital gardens (a ring was at that time found in the garden of the hospital)
bread	bread-factory		
lamp	smells		
tree	F. (name of an acquaintance connected with a certain experience)	tooth (*Zahn*)	Göschenen (the writer, Zahn, lives in Göschenen)
mountain (*Berg*)	Ütliberg	window	opening
		frog	tree-frog
hair	falling out	flower	rose
salt	Rheinfelden (where there are salt works)	cherry	juicy
		hospital	R. (a certain hospital for feeble-minded children)
wood	ebony		
dream	R. (name of a colleague who was occupied with dream-analyses at this time)	male nurse	B. (name of a particular nurse)
		fern	tape-worm
paper	fraud (paper in the sense of documents in evidence about a case of fraud)	oven	Pest[49]
		to be obliged to	Lessing (a famous quotation from Lessing is implied)
book	letter (*Buch-stabe*, 'letter of the alphabet')	revenge	thirst
		hope	pregnancy (this constellation is explained by earlier comments)
pencil	Kohinoor (the subject uses this brand)		
school	S. (name of the place where the subject went to school)	small (*Klein*)	male nurse (Klein is the name of a nurse)
		to pray	church

49 [See n. 47.]

liberty	statue (the subject had been in America and particularly admired New York)	row	M. (name of someone who had made a joke referring to the word "row")
unjust	to imprison (constellation from daily intercourse with querulous patients)	to walk	L. (name of patient who often went for walks)
to be lazy	wonderful	to cook	cooking lessons
coffee	Mocha	water	supply
sacrifice	L. (name of an ailing painter who had a predilection for painting sacrificial scenes)	to dance	concert-hall (the hall in which the dances at the hospital are held)
wedding	without alcohol (the subject is a teetotaller)	dark	room (the subject is an enthusiastic amateur photographer)
grand-mother	dead	heart	failure
wicked	R. (name of a patient with a moral defect)	bird	paws (*claws* is to be interpolated)
to need	B. (name of a colleague)	to swim	L. (name of a patient who often used the swimming pool)
year	and day	white (*Weiss*)	malaria (a patient named Weiss suffered from malaria)
to threaten	threatener (*Drohweber*, nickname of a patient who frequently uttered threats)	game	Halma (which was at that time played in the wards)
sour (*sauer*)	dough (*Teig*) (*Sauerteig*, 'dough')	thirteen	shorthand (*to write* is to be interpolated; the subject was keenly occupied with short-hand)
youth	Munich (newspaper *Youth*)		
family	day		
sorrow	sorrowful		
to pay attention	association-experiment (momentary constellation)	sofa	cushion
nature	R. (name of a patient)	thousand	Basel (a student friend of subject from Basel went under the name of "Tausig," the dialect form of *tausend* (thousand). The stimulus-word was of course called out in standard German but assimilated in the dialect form by the subject)
folk	*Folk-Psychology* by Wundt (a work that had recently been ordered by the hospital)		
murderer	G. (name of a murderer who was just then in the hospital for examination)		
everywhere (*überall*)	superman (*Übermensch*)	to love	ball
to calculate	slide-rule	son	sonny (the subject is the father of a new-born son)

wild	dentist ("Wild" is the name of a dentist)	at home (*daheim*)	newspaper (called *Daheim*)
tears	vale	vinegar	home-made
war	turmoil	trap	mousetrap
faithful	little dog	throat	epiglottis
once	shorthand again (see above)	to strike	(name of a doctor who had been struck by a patient)
miracle	Lourdes		
blood	English (in England the word must not be said)	star	C. (Stern, 'star,' is the name of a patient in Ward C)
right	and duty	to stroke	kitten
ground	and soil	grand	Grossman (name of
game (*Spiel*)	thing (*Zeug*) (*Spielzeug*, 'toy')	(*grossartig*)	patient who was included merely as a
arm	W. (name of a patient who had injured his arm)	sweet	sound-association) bananas (cf. the reaction *wood/ebony*. The
blue	Grotto in Capri		subject had recently
strange	stranger		given some lectures on
to growl	bulldog		travels in Africa)
knot	East Swiss (memory of his student years)	friendly	H. (name of an acquaintance)
fruit	to steal	to float	S. (name of a famous
false	trap		airman)
helmet	house (Helmhaus, a public building in Zurich)	skull rough (*rau*)	occiput A.1 (Rau is the name of a patient in Ward
misery	hunger		A.1)
hay (*heu*)	Heustrich (name of a spa)	to report prison	male nurse police-barracks (the
raspberry	park (the raspberries in the hospital garden)	to separate ill	police in Zurich) sulphuric acid diabetes

428   This type is characterized by the emergence of numerous subjective experiences, mostly of recent origin and belonging for the most part to the field of everyday activities. It goes without saying that, in spite of the objective character of the constellations, some also occur that belong to a feeling-toned complex. These are, however, relatively rare in comparison with the others and are in some cases well concealed. The recently experienced joy of fatherhood has an after-effect in several reactions: *father / anxious, hope / pregnancy, son / sonny*. This feeling-toned diminutive seems to us echoed in the somewhat striking reactions: *to stroke / kitten, fidelity / little dog*.

(b) Complex-constellation type

429   (i) Reactions of a subject in whose reactions a feeling-toned complex appears quite openly. The meaning of the stimulus-word is brought into relation with the complex (subject 21, educated men).

wood	pile	friendly	very nice
dream	studies (simple	crown	queen
	constellation)	rough	table
exercise-	pen	to stink	pooh!
book		shrill	hurt
paper	line	to separate	W. (name of a mental
pencil	big		patient whose marriage
school	bank		ended in divorce)
to sing	choir	potato	broth
ring	on the finger	to be lazy	nice
tooth	teeth	cross	I am not
window	frame	come	with me to the
frog	hops		theatre X (a certain
flower	stem[50]		theatre)
hospital	big	year	1904
piano	I cannot play	family	V. (subject's own
male	B. (name of a certain		family)
nurse	male nurse)	to take	I should
stove	wood	care	
to walk	a long way	finally	it will end
to dance	hotel F. (a certain ho-	folk	worth much
	tel where there was	slate-	she is a teacher
	dancing)	pencil	
dark	room	to growl	poodle
heart	red	knob	knob-stick
bird	feathers	false	blonde (a "lady," who
to swim	movement		is false and blonde, to
game	children		be interpolated)
Kaiser	Wilhelm	helmet	fire brigade
to hit	to beat	clothes	woman's skirt
to set	S. (name of an	softly	she comes along
fire to	incendiary)	gallantly	up the stairs
star	Miss Stern (an actual	plate	on the table
(*Stern*)	person)	misery	she cries
grand	ah!	hay	in it lies a farmer
child	children	raspberry	in the wood
dark red	again ah!	at home	in D. (home of the
to ride	riding track		sweetheart)

50 [The German word *Blumenstock* (literally, 'flowerstick') is mainly used for a tree-shaped potted plant such as a fuchsia.]

murderer	in C (a certain insane murderer in Ward C in the hospital)	wonder (miracle)	would have to happen
everywhere	K. is (the name of a mobile catatonic)	blood	she is anaemic
		wreath	on the coffin
to calculate	I cannot	to choose	another
		to part	I need not
to kiss	again and again ⎤	right	she is not
	wonderful ⎥ complex	to have to	I do not have to
natural	wonderful ⎬ of a	force	I do not use on her
bad	no ⎥ romance	revenge	oh no!
time	not now ⎥ recently	hope	I do not know
ripe	I am for it ⎦ terminated	small	oh no!
row	soldiers	to pray	perhaps
ground	and soil	dear	she was to me
game	child	wool	a woman's dress
poor	poor as a beggar	old	perhaps
to quarrel	oh rot!	freedom	she could have
sofa	is soft to sit on	unjust	I was not
to love	ah!	world	wide
son	son and father (the subject had had unpleasant quarrels with his family on account of his romance)	strange	that she is now
		hedge	fence
		lazy	sometimes (i.e., sometimes she is lazy)
		to woo	a woman
		hot	love
wild	mother (*wild* = angry; *wild* is here assimilated into the complex in the special sense of the dialect expression)	conscious-ness	yes, in the focus of consciousness
		vinegar	sour
		trap	into it
		to disgust	yes, so-so
tears	she has now (that is, the abandoned sweetheart)	riot	there is therefore none
		resin (*Harz*)	hair (*Haare*)
protection	I cannot offer her	to dress up	yes, fine and gallant
war	if there only were		
faith	I have not kept	omen	bad
once	and never again		

430   A strong feeling-toned complex is characteristic of this mode of reaction. The stimulus-word is assimilated as a question; the experiment therefore bears the imprint of a conversation in which the subject has only a rather dim awareness of the current situation. This explains the somewhat abnormal character of a conversation of this type. The mode of reaction can be explained by a very strong psychological sensitivity. The relatively numerous interjections and the egocentric references, not only within the complex, also point towards this. The sub-

ject's egocentricity emerges clearly throughout. He is mentally entirely sound and would at other times probably have presented a much more objective type. The abnormal character of the reaction is to be attributed merely to the temporary but prevailing emotion. One could generalize and say that this abnormal state, caused by the affect, is the prototype of the hysterical reaction.

431   (ii) Subject 24 of the group of uneducated women is a good example of a complex appearing in a disguised form. We refer to the associations already given in detail in the relevant section.

(c) Predicate type

432   Reactions of a subject who judges the object of the stimulus-word from a personal point of view (subject 7, educated women).

lake	beautiful nature	moon	beautiful
schoolboy	diligent	to beat	unnecessary
father	something wonderful, good, holy	to light	an art, till one managed it
needle	work	to sing	beautiful
bread	best food	ring	something silly
lamp	work	tooth	glad not to have any more
tree	something beautiful		
mountain	terrible, climbing is nicer	frog	something unnecessary
		flower	joy
hair	head-dress	cherry	good fruit
salt	strengthens food	hospital	narrow
wood	fire	piano	mainly laborious
dream	many experiences	male nurse	respect
exercise-book	much work for the children	fern	beautiful wood
paper	blessed, because we write on it	stove	lovely in cold winter
		to walk	one sometimes must
book	joy	to cook	laborious
school	joy	water	lovely
dozen	straight, order	to dance	gladly when one is young
dark	horrible		
heart	beats	cat	sneak
bird	lovely, to fly	star	magnificent
to swim	lovely	grand	pompous
white	hard, bright	child	gift of God
game	to enjoy	sweet	pleasant
thirteen	clumsy	to ride	dangerous

friendly	duty	to stink	sometimes, alley
crown	unnecessary	shrill	to hurt
rough	weather	ill	to hurt

433 The characteristic of this mode of reaction is an unusually strong personal participation, which leads to a constant evaluation of the object, usually with reference to herself.

II. Sex Differences in the Experiment under Normal Conditions

434 We have considered our individual figures from the point of view of the sex difference and calculated their averages (see Table D).

D. Sex Differences in the Experiment under Normal Conditions

SPECIAL QUALITY	MEN		WOMEN	
Grouping	19.8		19.4	
Predicative relationship	17.9	38.6	20.3	40.7
Causal relationship	0.9		1.0	
Co-existence	15.0		17.1	
Identity	7.8	54.0	4.8	53.6
Linguistic-motor forms	31.2		31.7	
Word-completion	0.5		0.9	
Sound	1.2	2.0	0.6	2.0
Rhyme	0.3		0.5	
Indirect	1.6		0.8	
Meaningless	0.5		0.1	
Failures	1.8	3.9	1.4	2.4
Repetition of stimulus-word	0		0.1	
Egocentric reaction	2.2		1.3	
Perseveration	1.5		0.8	
Repetition of reaction	9.9		8.2	
Same grammatical form	54.3		56.4	
Same number of syllables	37.0		43.7	
Alliteration	9.1		8.9	
Consonance	14.0		13.5	
Same ending	12.4		10.9	
Total associations	3000.0		3800.0	

435   In considering the figures, one is struck by the slightness of the difference between the two sexes. With few exceptions the figures essentially tally; in any case, the definite numerical differences that separate the group of educated from the uneducated are absent. In the men the type is somewhat blunter than in the women; the men have rather more sound associations, also more indirect associations; these phenomena may be connected with the blunter type. The larger number of egocentric reactions and perseverations seems, according to earlier investigations, to depend on the men's more uninhibited behaviour. The difference in the figures for coincidence of grammatical form and number of syllables is analogous to the corresponding difference between educated and uneducated subjects, and may be attributed to the fact that in our male subjects, particularly in the uneducated ones, the level of education is higher than in the corresponding women subjects. From the figures of the experiment under normal conditions nothing typical of feminine psychology emerges, which does not mean that no differences exist. Our method of investigation is obviously far too crude to discover subtle differences of this sort.

III. Averages of the Distraction Experiments

436   We give in Tables E and F a compilation of the average figures from the distraction experiments. To facilitate comparison we are putting the average for experiments under normal conditions alongside.

437   The figures for the distraction experiments show a progressively blunter type of reaction than those obtained under normal conditions. The main difference is quite unequivocal. The internal associations decrease under distraction as opposed to the external associations and sound reactions, both of which increase.

438   Looking at the figures for internal associations, we see that the women in this group have higher figures than the men. The lowest figures are for men. The objection that the women start with a higher number of internal associations under normal conditions applies only to uneducated women. Educated women show a somewhat blunter reaction-type, under normal conditions, than educated men. The fact that the number of

E-1. Averages in the Distraction Experiments: Uneducated Women

SPECIAL QUALITY	NORMAL	EXTERNAL DISTRACTION	
		60 Met.	100 Met.
Grouping	25.2 ⎱	19.0 ⎱	15.7 ⎱
Predicative relationship	20.4 ⎬46.6	20.6 ⎬40.3	19.0 ⎬35.2
Causal relationship	1.0 ⎰	0.7 ⎰	0.5 ⎰
Co-existence	20.4 ⎱	18.2 ⎱	18.5 ⎱
Identity	5.0 ⎬49.4	9.7 ⎬52.2	9.2 ⎬61.0
Linguistic-motor forms	24.0 ⎰	24.3 ⎰	33.3 ⎰
Word-completion	0.3 ⎱	0.2 ⎱	0.5 ⎱
Sound	0.1 ⎬ 0.7	1.7 ⎬ 2.9	2.0 ⎬ 3.7
Rhyme	0.3 ⎰	1.0 ⎰	1.2 ⎰
Indirect	0.7 ⎱	1.2 ⎱	0.7 ⎱
Meaningless	0.2	0.7	0.2
Failures	1.4 ⎬ 2.3	1.0 ⎬ 3.4	0.5 ⎬ 1.4
Repetition of stimulus-word	0 ⎰	0.5 ⎰	0 ⎰
Egocentric reaction	0.5	0.5	0.5
Perseveration	1.0	2.0	2.5
Repetition of reaction	9.5	8.5	3.0
Same grammatical form	58.9	62.5	62.2
Same number of syllables	46.0	47.5	44.7
Alliteration	8.4	11.0	11.2
Consonance	12.2	18.5	15.7
Same ending	11.3	11.7	16.0
Total ⎰ Associations	1600	400	400
⎱ Subjects	8	8	8

internal associations does not fall as low in women as in men means that the women were less adaptable to the purposes of the experiment than were the men. Comparing the minus differences of the internal associations clearly shows the smaller interest of the women.

439 The remaining differences are unfortunately not equally apparent, as they are divided into three groups, the content of which is of varying psychological valency. Therefore the number of internal associations is the best simple measure of the degree of distraction. The differences for the men show a cer-

E-2. Averages in the Distraction Experiments: Uneducated Men

SPECIAL QUALITY	NORMAL	EXTERNAL DISTRACTION	
		60 Met.	100 Met.
Grouping	23.3 ⎫	20.8 ⎫	14.8 ⎫
Predicative relationship	16.1 ⎬ 40.5	10.0 ⎬ 30.8	12.8 ⎬ 27.6
Causal relationship	1.1 ⎭	0 ⎭	0 ⎭
Co-existence	17.3 ⎫	19.1 ⎫	12.5 ⎫
Identity	10.0 ⎬ 55.6	17.4 ⎬ 58.5	15.1 ⎬ 63.3
Linguistic-motor forms	28.3 ⎭	22.0 ⎭	35.7 ⎭
Word-completion	0 ⎫	0 ⎫	0 ⎫
Sound	0.6 ⎬ 0.6	1.4 ⎬ 3.1	0.8 ⎬ 1.0
Rhyme	0 ⎭	1.7 ⎭	0.2 ⎭
Indirect	0.8 ⎫	3.4 ⎫	1.4 ⎫
Meaningless	0.1 ⎪	1.1 ⎪	2.0 ⎪
Failures	1.5 ⎬ 2.4	1.4 ⎬ 6.4	2.2 ⎬ 7.6
Repetition of stimulus-word	0 ⎭	0.5 ⎭	2.0 ⎭
Egocentric reaction	1.7	0	0
Perseveration	0.7	0.5	0
Repetition of reaction	12.3	5.1	4.0
Same grammatical form	59.5	67.7	64.5
Same number of syllables	39.0	45.7	48.2
Alliteration	9.2	8.0	12.4
Consonance	12.5	23.4	18.8
Same ending	16.3	14.3	18.2
Total ⎰ Associations	1400	350	350
⎱ Subjects	7	7	7

tain agreement, while the minus difference of uneducated women is greater than that of educated women, which would indicate better adaptation of the uneducated women to the experiment.

	EDUCATED		UNEDUCATED
	Internal Distraction	External Distraction	External Distraction
Women	−5.5	−2.8	−8.8
Men	−12.3	−11.8	−11.3

Minus difference of internal associations

F-1. Averages in the Distraction Experiments: Educated Women

SPECIAL QUALITY	NORMAL	INTERNAL DISTRACTION	EXTERNAL DISTRACTION 60 Met.	100 Met.
Grouping	13.7⎫	14.0⎫	11.7⎫	11.5⎫
Predicative relationship	20.2⎬35.0	15.0⎬29.5	21.2⎬33.6	19.0⎬30.7
Causal relationship	1.1⎭	0.5⎭	0.7⎭	0.7⎭
Co-existence	13.8⎫	10.0⎫	12.7⎫	8.0⎫
Identity	4.7⎬58.0	4.3⎬44.8	10.5⎬48.9	9.0⎬56.0
Linguistic-motor forms	39.5⎭	30.5⎭	25.7⎭	39.0⎭
Word-completion	1.5⎫	4.5⎫	3.0⎫	2.2⎫
Sound	1.1⎬3.3	5.1⎬11.6	5.5⎬10.2	6.5⎬9.2
Rhyme	0.7⎭	2.0⎭	1.7⎭	0.5⎭
Indirect	0.9⎫	1.6⎫	1.0⎫	0.2⎫
Meaningless	0.1⎪	0.5⎪	1.2	1.5⎪
Failures	1.4⎬2.6	1.1⎬3.8	2.0⎬5.7	1.5⎬3.9
Repetition of stimulus-word	0.2⎭	0.6⎭	1.5⎭	0.7⎭
Egocentric reaction	2.1	1.0	1.2	1.0
Perseveration	0.6	1.0	2.2	1.7
Repetition of reaction	7.2	3.5	6.5	5.0
Same grammatical form	53.9	59.0	54.0	53.0
Same number of syllables	41.5	45.5	47.7	43.5
Alliteration	8.4	11.1	11.7	12.5
Consonance	14.9	19.3	19.0	20.6
Same ending	10.5	11.8	11.7	13.0
Total ⎰ Associations	2200	500	400	400
⎱ Subjects	11	6	8	8

440   Admittedly the plus differences in the group of sound reactions again show a more significant increase in educated women than in uneducated:

	Uneducated women	Educated women
Plus difference of sound reactions	2.6	8.3 and 6.4

441   The cause of this contradiction might be that the educated women's attitude to the experiment was considerably more variable than that of the uneducated female subjects. Both

F-2. Averages in the Distraction Experiments: Educated Men

SPECIAL QUALITY	NORMAL	INTERNAL DISTRACTION	EXTERNAL DISTRACTION	
			60 Met.	100 Met.
Grouping	16.3 ⎫	8.6 ⎫	15.6 ⎫	10.8 ⎫
Predicative relationship	19.7 ⎬ 36.7	15.0 ⎬ 24.4	12.0 ⎬ 28.0	10.4 ⎬ 21.8
Causal relationship	0.7 ⎭	0.8 ⎭	0.4 ⎭	0.6 ⎭
Co-existence	12.8 ⎫	6.1 ⎫	12.8 ⎫	12.0 ⎫
Identity	5.7 ⎬ 52.7	4.5 ⎬ 49.2	9.2 ⎬ 57.2	6.6 ⎬ 61.4
Linguistic-motor forms	34.2 ⎭	38.6 ⎭	35.2 ⎭	42.8 ⎭
Word-completion	1.1 ⎫	4.3 ⎫	1.2 ⎫	2.6 ⎫
Sound	1.9 ⎬ 3.6	15.8 ⎬ 20.7	8.0 ⎬ 9.6	3.8 ⎬ 8.2
Rhyme	0.6 ⎭	0.6 ⎭	0.4 ⎭	1.8 ⎭
Indirect	2.5 ⎫	4.5 ⎫	3.2 ⎫	6.2 ⎫
Meaningless	0.9 ⎪	1.6 ⎪	2.0 ⎪	1.8 ⎪
Failures	2.1 ⎬ 5.5	0 ⎬ 6.1	0 ⎬ 5.2	0 ⎬ 8.0
Repetition of stimulus-word	0 ⎭	0 ⎭	0 ⎭	0 ⎭
Egocentric reaction	2.8	1.1	0.8	1.6
Perseveration	2.4	1.6	2.0	3.0
Repetition of reaction	7.5	3.8	6.8	6.2
Same grammatical form	49.1	50.5	59.2	51.8
Same number of syllables	35.0	44.6	46.4	41.0
Alliteration	9.0	27.3	17.6	13.2
Consonance	15.6	33.3	23.6	20.6
Same ending	8.5	8.3	11.2	10.0
Total ⎰ Associations	1600	550	250	435
⎱ Subjects	8	6	5	5

groups carry out the instructions of the experiment, the making of strokes and the simultaneous reaction, with somewhat more difficulty than the men. If one compares, for example, the differences of educated men and women in the internal distraction experiment, one is immediately struck by the more complete effect of distraction in the men. The only essential difference between the two female groups is perhaps that educated women are capable at least at times of dividing their attention.

167

442   It seems to us now that we have here a certain difference in the mode of reaction of men and women, a difference that can be determined quantitatively. As, however, with the limited material, sources of error are not excluded, we offer these observations for further discussion.

443   The figures in the individual groups of the scheme show certain variations that need discussion. While the co-ordinations decrease fairly evenly with distraction, the predicates under distraction present a somewhat different aspect in men and in women.

	EDUCATED	UNEDUCATED
	External Distraction	External Distraction
Women	−0.2	−0.6
Men	−8.5	−4.7

Minus difference of the predicates

444   The table shows that under distraction the predicates decrease to a lesser degree in women than in men. Here let us remember that in the discussion of the predicate type we stated the hypothesis of the primary, sensory vividness of the stimulus images, which invites predicates. This psychological peculiarity shows itself, of course, in a state of attempted division of attention; this will hinder the experiment in that, in the absence of active concentration, the primarily vivid images absorb the interest and thereby bar or impede the division of attention as planned in the experiment. We shall see this phenomenon quite clearly in the result of the distraction experiment of the predicate type, to which we are referring. There are relatively very many predicate types among the women, which is probably the reason for the apparent prevalence of the predicate. In contrast to the decrease of internal associations there is an increase of external associations, in so far as this is not influenced by a stronger rise of sound reactions. The three groups do not participate equally in the increase of external associations. We even notice that the number of coexistences shows rather a tendency to decrease. We tabulate the differences again here:

UNEDUCATED		EDUCATED	
Women	Men	Women	Men
−2.0	−1.5	−3.4	−0.4

Difference between normal experiment and distraction
with reference to coexistences

445   They are all, contrary to expectation, minus differences. This shows that the coexistences cannot be held responsible for the increase of external associations. Remembering the discussion where we explained that coexistences frequently arose owing to the effort of vividly imagining the object of the stimulus-word, then the decrease under distraction is comprehensible; coexistence is to some extent a step towards internal association and therefore plays a part in its decrease.

446   The groups of identities and linguistic-motor forms in general show a rise—which is, however, affected by a big increase of sound reactions, causing, for example, in the group of educated women particularly, a decrease of the two groups. We explain these variations by the irregularity of distraction often mentioned. The quantitatively infrequent occurrence of word-completion in uneducated subjects is striking. We believe that inadequate verbal facility is responsible for this, particularly lack of practice in standard German. Experiments with uneducated Germans, viz., North Germans, might produce different figures. Sound associations are decidedly more frequent in educated subjects than in uneducated.

447   The indirect associations behave strangely. We have already indicated an inverse relationship of their increase with sound associations. In our averages one is first struck by a dependence on the degree of distraction.

	UNEDUCATED		EDUCATED	
	Women	Men	Women	Men
Normal conditions	0.7	0.8	0.9	2.5
Distraction	0.9	2.4	0.9	4.6

448   These figures show that uneducated subjects produce fewer indirect associations on the average under normal conditions than do the educated and that women produce fewer than men. Under distraction the women's aversion to indirect associations is shown even more clearly. While a quite definite increase is shown in the men, the average figure for educated women under normal conditions remains the same, and in uneducated women only a quite insignificant increase occurs. Thus, in this respect, a significant difference between the sexes must exist, the nature of which is at present unknown to us. The nature of indirect associations, discussed above (predominantly sound reactions as intermediate links), makes a

169

dependence on distraction readily comprehensible. Thus with the increase of sound reactions we could expect an increase also of indirect associations. For the sake of clarity we briefly repeat the relevant figures here:

	UNEDUCATED				EDUCATED			
	Women		Men		Women		Men	
	S.R.	Ind.	S.R.	Ind.	S.R.	Ind.	S.R.	Ind.
Normal conditions	0.7	0.7	0.6	0.8	3.3	0.9	3.6	2.5
External distraction I	2.9	1.2	3.1	3.4	10.2	1.0	9.6	3.2
External distraction II	3.7	0.7	1.0	1.4	9.2	0.2	8.2	6.2
Internal Distraction (educated subject only)	—	—	—	—	11.6	1.6	20.7	4.5

449   Although the simultaneous increase of sound reactions and indirect associations under distraction, already mentioned above, is indicated in general in these figures, the parallelism of the two groups is in places somewhat unbelievable. If a parallel between the two groups really exists, one would expect that the maxima of indirect associations would sometimes coincide with the maxima of sound reactions. This is by no means the case. In considering, in the figures for the distraction experiments, the maxima of indirect associations, we see that the maxima only coincide in two cases. No corresponding increases of indirect associations coincide with the maxima of sound reactions. Thus no clear and simple connection in the form of a direct proportion exists. Neither do these figures provide easily recognizable clues to an inverted relationship. Only the group of educated men shows a co-incidence of a striking maximum of indirect associations with the minimum of sound reactions, which is nevertheless a noteworthy fact. In the female groups we see the indirect associations strikingly lagging behind the sound reactions. In the educated men a distinct increase of sound reactions, from 3.6 per cent under normal conditions to 20.7 per cent under distraction, corresponds to an increase of only 2 per cent of indirect associations, while their maximum coincides, as already stated, with

170

a minimum of sound reactions. This aspect of the indirect associations seems to indicate a certain interdependence of the two groups; we see this as an increased occurrence of indirect associations affecting mainly the group of sound reactions. Taking the group of sound reactions in relation to indirect associations, we get the following picture:

	UNEDUCATED				EDUCATED			
	Women		Men		Women		Men	
	S.R.	Ind.	S.R.	Ind.	S.R.	Ind.	S.R.	Ind.
External distraction I	1.7	1.2	1.4	3.4	5.5	1.0	8.0	3.2
External distraction II	2.0	0.7	0.8	1.4	6.5	0.2	3.8	6.2

450   The pure sound associations show, with one exception, inverse relation between the two groups. The choice of sound associations for the purpose of the demonstration is not arbitrary, since they form the main part of the whole sound group; at the same time they are the associations that are suppressed under normal conditions (this does not apply to all rhymes, for example). It is just this fact, that the pure sound associations are repressed under normal conditions, that has the greatest significance for the explanation of the inverse relation. The unspoken and mostly quite unconscious intermediate links between indirect associations are in the majority of cases sound associations. Under normal conditions sound associations are continually opposed by inhibitions, as they are, as a rule, quite inexpedient in respect to the process of association and are therefore excluded. There will always be a certain tendency to suppress the sounds; the slighter the distraction of attention the stronger this tendency will be, but the greater the distraction is, the weaker it will be. With increasing distraction the reaction will be more and more influenced by sound, till finally only a sound is associated. Between the influence of sound and the sound association there comes a point where, although the sound association cannot conquer the inhibition it encounters, it does exclusively affect the sense of the following reaction by interrupting the connection between stimulus-word and reaction; it is immaterial whether the subconscious sound association is formed centripetally or centrifugally. The mediating

171

sound association, which almost reaches the threshold of reaction, leads to the formation of the indirect association. Of course the intermediate links need not necessarily always be sound associations; they need only invite enough inhibition to remain just below the threshold of reaction. Thus we interpret the indirect association as a symptom of repression of inferior associations, which almost reach the threshold of reaction.[51] Using this interpretation the apparently inverse relation of sound association and indirect association can be easily understood: if the sound association predominates, one can conclude from this that the inhibition of sounds has not occurred; therefore repression and consequently indirect association are also prevented. If the number of sound associations decreases it is a sign that inhibition is increasing, thus providing the conditions for the occurrence of indirect associations. The indirect associations are therefore a transitional phenomenon which reaches an optimum at a certain degree of distraction. This also explains the increase apparently in proportion with the sound reaction and the subsequent decrease in inverse proportion after the critical point has been reached.[52]

451   Claparède, who has worked on the question of indirect associations from another angle, believes that it is the "résultat du concours de plusieurs associations intermédiaires, chacune trop faible pour être consciente."[53] From the results of experiment we are in complete agreement with this interpretation. The tendency to form a meaningful association, which derives from the stimulus-concept, inhibits sound associations. Both

[51] We note that the description of indirect associations at present deserves no greater value than that of a working hypothesis. We willingly offer our figures and our interpretations for further discussion in the hope that several research workers in cooperation might succeed in solving this question satisfactorily.

[52] The occurrence of indirect associations under the influence of a distraction of attention has long been known from another source. The tangential naming of pictures in alcoholic delirium (Bonhöffer), in epileptic mania (Heilbronner), in certain catatonic and hysterial conditions, etc., is nothing but indirect association which is formed not, as in our experiment, through shift via sound similarity but through a shift via image similarity. Thus, in this case, it is a supplementary phenomenon of flight of ideas in the visual sphere and corresponds at all points to the phenomena we have shown in the acoustic-verbal sphere. [For Bonhöffer and Heilbronner, see Bibliography.]

[53] Cf. Claparède, L'Association des idées (1903), p. 140; and idem, "Association médiate dans l'évocation volontaire" (1904).

are too weak, however, to produce a reaction. If the sound association, not linked in meaning with the stimulus image, predominates, then the indirect association comes into being; otherwise it is a reaction that, although strongly influenced by sound, is nevertheless meaningful. Piéron's[54] interpretation, which states that the third link of the indirect association has greater interest for the individual than the intermediate link, does not fit in with the results of our experiment. Nevertheless there is something attractive about Piéron's view and it is valid for all those cases where the external stimulus is unconsciously assimilated as a strongly charged complex, dominant in the subject's consciousness. (We shall discuss this further possibility of an indirect association in a later paper.) Piéron's view does not fit in with a vast number of the indirect associations of everyday life. From many examples we mention only one very instructive observation from our own experience.[55] One of the present authors was smoking a cigar; suddenly it occurred to him that he had no more matches on him. He had a longish train journey before him and had put a good Havana cigar in his pocket in order to smoke it on the way. He now thought he would have to light the cigar from the one he was finishing. With that, the narrator was satisfied and dropped the train of thought. For about one minute, he looked out of the window at the landscape, which he observed attentively; suddenly he noticed himself saying involuntarily and quite softly: "Bunau-Varilla." Bunau-Varilla is the name of a well-known Panamanian agitator in Paris. The observer had read the name several days before in the *Matin*. As this name appeared to him to be without any connection with the contents of consciousness, he immediately directed his attention to the name and observed what occurred to him in the process (Freud's method of spontaneous association). Immediately *Varinas* occurred to him, then *Manila*, almost simultaneously also *cigarillo*, and with it a vague feeling of a South American atmosphere; the next clear link was the Havana cigar and with it the memory that this cigar had provided the content of the penultimate thought-cycle. The intermediate links, *Varinas* and *Manila*,

[54] H. Piéron, "L'Association médiate" (1903).
[55] [Cf. "The Psychology of Dementia Praecox," par. 110, where the example is given with slight differences.]

are brands of tobacco, both of which had the tone of some-thing Spanish for the narrator; *cigarillo* is the Spanish word for cigarette; the observer had smoked cigarillos with Manila tobacco in a Spanish colony but not in South America. Never-theless there was a faint "South American" echo about *cigarillo*. While the observer was looking out of the window he had not the slightest feeling of such a train of thought, his attention was completely concentrated on the landscape. The unconscious train of thought leading to the formation of "Bunau-Varilla" was: *Havana cigar / cigarillo* with Spanish-South American background / a travel memory with *Manila-cigarillo* / Spanish-American brand of tobacco *Varinas* / (*Varinas* and *Manila* con-densed by dream-mechanism into) *Varilla / Bunau-Varilla*. A sufficient reason for the subconscious pursuance of the thought of the cigar was that the observer had prepared himself not to miss lighting the Havana cigar from the end of the cigar still alight. According to Piéron, "Bunau-Varilla" would have to be the emotionally charged final link desired by the ob-server. This is what in fact it is not; it is merely a product of condensation formed by the competition between several very weak intermediate links (according to Claparède's interpreta-tion). The mechanism is a linguistic-motor automatism such as occurs not infrequently in normal subjects (in certain hyster-ical subjects, it is true, far more often). The subconscious as-sociation-process takes place through similarities of image and sound; in fact all associations taking place in the subconscious, i.e., outside the range of attention, do so (with the exception of certain somnambulant processes). In connection with Jeru-salem's[56] communication Wundt[57] calls the intermediate link "unnoticed" in contrast to "unconscious," in which we can perceive not material objection but merely a verbal quibble. It is not surprising that Scripture[58] obtains doubtful results in his experiments on indirect associations, and Smith[59] and

[56] Jerusalem, "Ein Beispiel von Assoziation durch unbewusste Mittelglieder" (1892).

[57] Wundt, "Sind die Mittelglieder einer mittelbaren Assoziation bewusst oder unbewusst?" (1892).

[58] Scripture, "Über den assoziativen Verlauf der Vorstellungen" (1889).

[59] William Smith, *Zur Frage der mittelbaren Assoziation* (1894).

Münsterberg[60] obtained no results, because their experiments were set in a way that did not favour the production of indirect associations. The best indirect associations are provided by careful self-observation in everyday life.[61] Indirect verbal associations originate, as our experiment shows, mainly in distraction experiments.

452   Meaningless reactions show, as is to be expected, an increase under distraction.

453   The failures, the mainly emotive nature of which has already been frequently stressed in the individual descriptions, are conspicuously absent in the group of educated men under distraction. For the rest they present a constant pattern. We shall return to this group in the discussion of the average of the predicate type.

454   A state of affairs similar to that of meaningless reactions obtains in the repetition of the stimulus-word; it too increases under distraction.

455   We have combined the four last-mentioned groups to form the so-called residual group, with the original purpose of collecting the abnormal subsidiary phenomena of the association experiment into this group. From the number of this group we then hoped to obtain a certain co-efficient of the emotional state into which the subject was brought by the experiment. The decision to include the indirect associations also in this group was based on the assumption, in itself not improbable, that in indirect associations, because of their provenance from sound-shifts, we really have experiments that have failed. Naturally we interpreted the meaningless reactions, as well as the last two groups, as experiments that failed. In this interpre-

[60] Münsterberg, *Beiträge zur experimentellen Psychologie*, IV (1892), p. 9. Münsterberg states emphatically: "Indirect associations through unconscious intermediate links do not exist." All that can be said is that there were none in his experiments.

[61] There are several good examples of indirect associations in Cordes, "Experimentelle Untersuchungen über Assoziationen" (1899), pp. 70, 71, 75. The supposition that the intermediate links of indirect associations are unconscious is for Cordes "a theoretical construction which it will never be possible to prove empirically, for unconscious psychic phenomena cannot be experienced." The author would in any case modify this apodictic statement if he were at all acquainted with the results of hypnotism.

tation we were supported by certain experiences in the patho-logical field—that is, the association phenomena in emotional stupidity,[62] where the figures for this group rise considerably. It is true that the results of our experiments do not confirm the original assumption of the emotional nature of indirect associ-ations. This does not hold in the other three groups. The na-ture of the emotion, however, must be defined more precisely for these three groups. Meaningless reactions and repeated stimulus-words originate according to our experience as a rule from stupefaction, which is produced by the way the experiment is set, while the majority of failures are based on emotion evoked through the awakening of feeling-toned com-plexes. Stupefaction, caused by the way the experiment is set, can in that case be completely excluded. The inclusion of failures in the residual group is therefore arguable. We have therefore substituted the non-committal designation "residual group" for "emotion group," the name we originally chose for this group. The summation of the figures for these groups was undertaken for clarity of arrangement, with full realiza-tion of its provisional and inadequate nature. Everyone who has done experimental work, particularly with such involved material, knows that one must pay dearly for one's experience and that one knows afterwards what one should have known before.

456   The distribution under distraction of egocentric reactions (which to some extent represent a pointer to feeling-toned reactions) is best demonstrated by a tabulated survey of the differences from the results under normal conditions.

	UNEDUCATED		EDUCATED	
	Women	Men	Women	Men
No. of egocentric reactions under normal conditions	+0.5	+1.7	+2.1	+2.8
Difference under distraction	0.0	−1.7	−1.0	−1.6

457   These differences show that according to our material the minus differences of the men are greater than those of the women; thus that, although women do not betray greater ego-centricity under normal conditions than men, they maintain it more firmly under distraction than men do.

[62] See Jung, "On Simulated Insanity."

176

458   With respect to perseverations, we have already several times proved a certain dependence on strong feeling-tones. As regards its frequent increase under distraction, we assumed the cause to be lack of association with distracted attention. Obviously various complicated conditions are involved here which we cannot separate beforehand. The following table of differences from normal conditions shows the effect of distraction on perseverations.

UNEDUCATED		EDUCATED	
Women	Men	Women	Men
+1.2	−0.4	+1.1	−0.2

459   From these figures it appears that in men perseverations decrease under distraction, while in women they increase.

460   The number of egocentric reactions gives us a rough measure of how many feeling-toned references to the ego occur among the reactions;[63] the number of perseverations indicates something similar to us, but in a less direct form.

461   As stated above, in women there is less effect of distraction on the reaction. From this one may conclude that female attention with respect to our experiment has proved less easy to divide. The smaller change in the number of egocentric reactions in women may be connected with this. If the number of egocentric reactions shows only a slight tendency to decrease, a similar tendency is to be expected in perseverations. These increase, however. We explain this by the fact that in the associationless vacuum artificially created by distraction feeling-toned contents of consciousness can persist more easily than otherwise. Why women in particular should have the tendency to perseverate under distraction we do not know. Perhaps it is connected with more intense feelings?

462   That attention cannot easily be divided in women may be based on the following causes:

(1) We have already indicated that various individuals (predicate types) presumably have fundamentally much more vivid inner images than others. By "more vivid images," we mean such as have combined in themselves a greater intensity of attention or, in other words, such as appear simultaneously

[63] In women by no means all egocentric references emerge freely, for the simple reason that the experimenters are men.

177

with many other associations evoked by them. The larger an association-complex is, the more the "ego-complex" is also involved. It is therefore understandable that with the vividness of the inner images, not only does the number of internal predicates increase but also the number of subjective value judgments generally—that is, of egocentric reactions.

(2) The vividness of the inner image is by no means always a primary involuntary phenomenon but can also be an artificial one; the attention is purposely directed to it or, in other words, numerous new associations accompany an image that appears with few collateral associations. This process is stimulated by the image that appears; it is actually realized through another association-complex, which at the time fills consciousness. The vividness of the inner image is thus in one case primary and involuntary, in the other case secondary and willed. The latter form is then under the influence of another intellectual phenomenon present at the time.

(3) If the inner images are basically very vivid and plastic, i.e., if they occur from the first together with many collateral associations, they must always have a quite definite effect on attention and therefore make more difficult or hinder its division, according to the degree of vividness. This is, as we shall see, the case with the predicate type.

(4) If the inner images are under the influence of an already existing association-complex, artificially vivid or plastic, it then depends on the stability of this complex whether the dividing of attention will be possible or not.

(5) We have no reason to assume that the inner images are in general fundamentally more vivid in women than in men (otherwise all women would probably belong to the predicate type.) We have, however, reason to assume, as we have already demonstrated above, that the reactions of uneducated subjects, particularly of uneducated women, are based on a (quasi) intentionally produced vividness of the stimulus-image. The association-complex responsible for this is the special view that uneducated people take of the association experiment. As, under the influence of this dominating image, they interpret the stimulus-word mainly from the point of view of meaning, they must apply more attention to stimulus-image, thus necessarily yielding less to distraction, as our figures show. That it is par-

ticularly the uneducated women who yield least to distraction agrees with the fact that they are the most strongly under the influence of this particular interpretation of the experiment. That educated women also show a tendency to yield less than men to distraction cannot also be attributed to this particular interpretation of the experiment but must be related to the fact, already mentioned, that among our educated female subjects there are relatively many predicate types, who show practically no distraction phenomenon at all. We therefore give in Table G the average figures of the educated women who are not predicate types.

G. Educated Women excluding Predicate Types

SPECIAL QUALITY	NORMAL		EXTERNAL DISTRACTION	
			60 Metronome	100 Metronome
Grouping	15.2		13.5	10.8
Predicative relationship	14.0 }30.2		14.0 }28.3	9.6 }20.8
Causal relationship	1.0		0.8	0.4
Co-existence	15.3		12.4	7.2
Identity	4.8 }62.6		11.2 }50.4	8.8 }62.8
Linguistic-motor forms	42.5		26.8	46.8
Word-completion	1.5		4.0	3.6
Sound	1.4 } 3.7		8.0 }14.0	9.2 }13.2
Rhyme	0.8		2.0	0.4
Indirect	1.0		1.2	1.6
Meaningless	0.1		2.0	0
Failures	0.9 } 2.4		1.6 } 5.0	0.4 } 3.2
Repetition of stimulus-word	0.4		0.2	1.2
Egocentric reaction	0.3		0.4	1.6
Perseveration	0.7		2.4	0
Repetition of reaction	6.9		4.8	3.6
Same grammatical form	41.8		63.2	42.4
Same number of syllables	60.1		47.6	57.2
Alliteration	8.5		13.2	15.2
Consonance	14.7		21.2	24.0
Same ending	12.6		15.2	13.2
Total { Associations	1200		250	250
Total { Subjects	6		5	5

463 From the figures of this table it immediately appears that it is not the case that the women's attention is less easily divided than the men's, but that it was the predicate type that strongly affected the average for educated women. Our figures show a definite distraction phenomenon that in no way lags behind that of the men.

464 Repetitions of the same reactions decrease with distraction; the reasons for this are easy to understand.

465 The numbers of verbal connections rise under distraction, thus expressing quantitatively the influence on the reaction in terms of external and mechanical factors. It is noteworthy that in uneducated subjects there is under normal conditions not only a greater agreement of grammatical form than in educated subjects but that the distraction experiment increases this even more intensely than in educated subjects, although in uneducated subjects the distraction phenomenon is less distinct. The following differences[64] clearly demonstrate this:

	Women	Men
Uneducated	+3.4	+6.6
Educated	+1.4	+4.7

466 The figure for the agreement of grammatical form does not only begin at a higher level in uneducated subjects but under distraction rises still higher than the corresponding figure for educated subjects. The reason for this probably lies in the fact that educated subjects have numerous current phrases at their command even under distraction.

467 The figures for agreement in number of syllables, aliteration, consonance, etc., need not be commented on.

468 The almost general decrease of figures for verbal connections in the second part of distraction is connected with the decrease of sound reactions. This change can be attributed to habituation, when the factors of very intense distraction gradually recede.

IV. Average of the Predicate Type under Normal Conditions and under Distraction

469 Tables H and I give the average figures for all those subjects whom we call "predicate types." We have included in this

[64] Difference between the figure for identical grammatical form under normal conditions and the average number of distraction experiments.

180

type all those subjects in whom the internal associations predominate over the group of linguistic-motor forms; the number of predicates is on an average more than twice the number of co-ordinations. Among the subjects used for the calculation of averages there are seven women and two men.[65]

470   We have placed the average of all other types next to the predicate type for comparison. The difference is striking. The predicate type shows no change worthy of mention under distraction: the predicate type does not show divided attention, while all the other types show themselves accessible to disturbing stimuli, at least to some extent. This fact is extraordinarily strange.

471   As we have already indicated, we assume that the individuals belonging to the predicate type have basically more vivid images on which attention is already involuntarily fixed in the moment of their emergence (contrary to deliberately produced vividness). We have noticed in our material that among the reactions of the predicate type there are, besides numerous value judgments, also strikingly many predicates designating sensory properties of the object of the stimulus-word, particularly visual ones. Individual subjects reported at once that they sometimes received quite definite plastic images.[66] We based the theory of the predicate type on this observation.

472   An inner image is vivid if the associations immediately connected with it spring to mind. The nearest associations upon the image of a concrete object are the sensory aspects: the visual, the acoustic, the tactile, and the motor. A vivid image can be said to be in the state of being concentrated upon.[67] The more vivid an image is, the stronger are the inhibitions emerging from it against everything not associated with it; the attention will therefore be all the less prone to be divided. That the distraction phenomenon is virtually absent in the predicate type we regard as proof of the correctness of our

[65] From the predicate-type class, containing three sub-groups, only one subject was used for calculation.
[66] These plastic images correspond roughly to Ziehen's individual images. We purposely did not ask about them during the experiment, to avoid directing attention to them by this suggestion. In many individuals only a slight effort of attention is needed to produce plastic images immediately. In this case only the vague and general verbal images are suppressed, which can happen half unconsciously with appropriate suggestion, particularly with unpractised subjects.
[67] That is, it concentrates attention upon itself.

H. Averages of Predicate Types

		EXTERNAL DISTRACTION	
SPECIAL QUALITY	NORMAL	60 Met.	100 Met.
Grouping	12.5 ⎤	14.8 ⎤	13.1 ⎤
Predicative relationship	32.1 ⎬45.7	31.2 ⎬46.5	30.5 ⎬43.8
Causal relationship	1.1 ⎦	0.5 ⎦	0.2 ⎦
Co-existence	13.5 ⎤	13.7 ⎤	11.7 ⎤
Identity	4.1 ⎬48.6	8.0 ⎬44.9	8.5 ⎬49.3
Linguistic-motor forms	31.0 ⎦	23.2 ⎦	29.1 ⎦
Word-completion	0.8 ⎤	0.8 ⎤	0.2 ⎤
Sound	0.3 ⎬ 1.5	1.4 ⎬ 3.0	1.1 ⎬ 1.5
Rhyme	0.4 ⎦	0.8 ⎦	0.2 ⎦
Indirect	0.8 ⎤	1.7 ⎤	0.2 ⎤
Meaningless	0 ⎟	0.2 ⎟	1.1 ⎟
Failures	2.4 ⎬ 3.2	2.5 ⎬ 4.6	2.5 ⎬ 4.6
Repetition of stimulus-word	0 ⎦	0.2 ⎦	0.8 ⎦
Egocentric reaction	3.6	1.7	1.4
Perseveration	0.8	1.1	1.1
Repetition of reaction	9.9	8.0	4.8
Same grammatical form	40.7	43.1	45.4
Same number of syllables	37.3	44.0	47.4
Alliteration	7.9	8.8	10.8
Consonance	12.9	15.4	14.2
Same ending	6.7	7.7	11.1
Total { Associations	1792	350	350
Total { Subjects	9	7	7

interpretation. The predicate type cannot divide his attention because his fundamentally vivid inner images make so much demand on his attention that inferior associations (which make up the distraction phenomenon) do not occur at all.

473   By means of our hypothesis all the peculiarities of the predicate type can now be explained.

(1) The large number of predicates. The subjects name a particularly striking characteristic of the inner image and

I. Averages of Non-Predicate Types

SPECIAL QUALITY	NORMAL	EXTERNAL DISTRACTION	
		60 Met.	100 Met.
Grouping	21.5 ⎫	18.0 ⎫	14.3 ⎫
Predicative relationship	13.5 ⎬ 36.0	11.3 ⎬ 29.9	10.8 ⎬ 25.4
Causal relationship	1.0 ⎭	0.6 ⎭	0.3 ⎭
Co-existence	17.2 ⎫	16.0 ⎫	12.2 ⎫
Identity	7.3 ⎬ 58.2	13.2 ⎬ 57.2	10.8 ⎬ 62.8
Linguistic-motor forms	33.7 ⎭	28.0 ⎭	39.8 ⎭
Word-completion	0.8 ⎫	1.3 ⎫	1.7 ⎫
Sound	1.1 ⎬ 2.5	4.7 ⎬ 7.5	4.2 ⎬ 7.0
Rhyme	0.6 ⎭	1.5 ⎭	1.1 ⎭
Indirect	1.5 ⎫	2.2 ⎫	1.9 ⎫
Meaningless	0.3 ⎪	1.2 ⎪	1.3 ⎪
Failures	1.0 ⎬ 2.9	0.8 ⎬ 5.1	0.8 ⎬ 4.7
Repetition of stimulus-word	0.1 ⎭	0.9 ⎭	0.7 ⎭
Egocentric reaction	1.0	0.6	0.7
Perseveration	0.9	1.8	1.9
Repetition of reaction	8.5	6.5	4.0
Same grammatical form	62.1	66.9	63.8
Same number of syllables	42.9	47.3	43.5
Alliteration	9.4	12.4	14.1
Consonance	14.4	22.4	20.8
Same ending	14.0	15.4	16.6
Total { Associations	4586	1000	1085
Total { Subjects	23	20	20

naturally use the predicate for this purpose. The large number of internal associations is mainly to be attributed to the number of predicates. The ratio of internal to external associations reminds us of that in uneducated subjects. The common factor, however, is only the degree of attention applied. The predicates are also retained under distraction, which we regard as clear proof of the involuntary nature of the plasticity of the image.

(2) The large number of egocentric reactions. The more vivid the image is, or the greater is the complex of associations present in consciousness, at any given moment, the more it is bound to stimulate and absorb into itself the associations making up the consciousness of the personality, in order by this synthesis to remain conscious. Thus a whole series of personal references must be added to the emerging complex of associations, which are then designated as particularly striking properties of the images and so become reactions. This is how egocentric reactions originate.

(3) The relatively large number of failures. These occur as a rule in reactions to the stimulation of a strong feeling-toned complex, which grips the attention so firmly that no further reaction can take place. It is quite feasible that in the predicate type more feeling-toned complexes are stimulated than in other types as a result of the more vivid images. It follows as an essential consequence of our assumptions that under distraction the failures show a tendency to increase. A certain amount of attention may be left over from what is fixed to the image, but if this is needed for an activity (marking the metronome-beats), then none is left for reacting; no decrease in the number of failures can result from this.

474   From the figures for the distraction experiment it emerges that the predicate type is not a fortuitous momentary attitude but constitutes an important psychological characteristic, which also obtains under different conditions.[68]

V. The Influence of the Grammatical Form of the Stimulus-word on the Reaction

475   As can easily be appreciated, the choice of stimulus-word with all its different properties is of some consequence. There is a whole series of stimulus-words that have predictable reactions. Thus, for instance, there is a large number of designations for concrete objects with which coexistent images are regularly associated, quite apart from many stimulus-words that call forth stereotyped word-connections, e.g., *to part / hurts; to part / to avoid; blood / red.* For the quantitative

---

[68] By this we mean, of course, merely our experimental conditions. Under the influence of fatigue or alcohol the predicates would probably decrease; this, however, remains to be investigated.

ratios it is of considerable importance whether the stimulus-word is a noun, adjective, or verb. A main factor will then be the frequency of the particular word-form. From a random selection in books one can say that language uses on average twice as many nouns as adjectives or verbs. Thus a noun used as a stimulus-word will, in accordance with the law of frequency, be "answered" more easily than all other word-forms. On the other hand, the lower frequency of verb and adjective will cause rather more difficulty in reaction, quite apart from the fact that, to most subjects, an adjective or a verb in the infinitive, standing outside the context of a sentence, appears more peculiar than a noun, particularly one that is the name of a concrete object, about which something can be said. We have made a comparative examination of this from the material of the experiments under normal conditions and have found the following average figures:

REACTIONS TO VERBS

	Noun	Adjective	Verb	ASSOCIATIONS		Sound
				Internal	External	
Educated men	63.2	15.8	20.6	48.4	41.6	7.4
Uneducated men	32.7	21.7	45.5	49.6	47.4	1.1
Educated women	45.7	19.4	34.7	55.5	39.2	4.5
Uneducated women	52.8	14.4	32.6	69.0	29.6	0.3
Predicate type	54.8	26.2	18.9	62.8	33.4	2.7
Non-predicate type	46.7	15.0	38.1	52.4	41.8	4.2

REACTIONS TO ADJECTIVES

	Noun	Adjective	Verb	ASSOCIATIONS		Sound
				Internal	External	
Educated men	53.1	43.6	2.9	43.5	45.0	8.0
Uneducated men	32.4	64.8	2.7	44.8	51.0	3.4
Educated women	39.1	52.6	7.4	43.3	45.4	3.1
Uneducated women	49.4	47.3	3.0	60.8	37.3	1.1
Predicate type	64.0	29.7	5.2	64.2	28.2	1.9
Non-predicate type	35.5	59.9	4.4	42.8	51.0	4.3

476 The number of agreements in grammatical form quoted among the individual figures shows that the stimulus-word and reaction do not by any means always agree in grammatical form. The above table shows the average figures, calculated as percentages, for the best-characterized group of our subjects.

185

We decided against giving the individual figures, to avoid a confusing accumulation. Also, the average figures show most clearly the characteristic variations with which we are essentially concerned.

477   It is striking that in the verb groups, with one exception, the reactions to verbs were mainly nouns; only the group of uneducated men reacted mainly to verbs with verbs. The educated men reacted mostly with nouns. These (strangely enough) have most in common with the uneducated women, while the educated women are closest to the uneducated men. It is clear from the beginning that the verbal law of frequency has great influence on the preference for this or that mode of reaction. It is therefore quite understandable that educated men, who in any case have a very blunt reaction type, should prefer the readier noun to the rarer verb; it is not so easily understandable that uneducated women should react in an apparently similar way and this needs detailed investigation.

478   While, according to our observations, educated men usually append nouns to verbs, uneducated men make an effort to do justice to the meaning of the stimulus-word by reacting with a similar verb. A similar effort on the part of the educated women is somewhat less clear. This mode of reaction, the psychology of which we have discussed in detail, is conditioned, as is well known, by the effort to react mainly in accordance with the meaning of the stimulus-word. We have previously seen that uneducated women lead in this respect. Accordingly one would expect that uneducated women would react with an ever higher number of verbs than uneducated men. It must, however, be remembered at this point that the uneducated women's level of education is the lowest, that thus their verbal education and facility is also the lowest; consequently, reacting to verbs will be most difficult for this group, as verbs are even rarer for them than for the other groups.[69] They are therefore dependent on nouns that can most easily be combined with verbs. The uneducated women's effort to produce a meaningful reaction determines the choice of a noun that is not merely joined to the verb but expresses, wherever possible, something significant about the meaning of the verb.

[69] The fact that the majority of the subjects are Swiss, and therefore working under the more difficult linguistic conditions, must be remembered here.

479   We have therefore carried out a further investigation to test this interpretation and to learn how great is the number of internal associations that are reactions to verbs. With these figures we are in a position to prove our interpretation. We have therefore placed next to the figures giving the preferred word-forms the figures showing the quality of the associations given in reaction to verbs. We give the appropriate figures once more together with those for the experiment under normal conditions for the groups mainly under consideration here.

EDUCATED MEN		
	Internal Associations	External Associations	Sound Reactions
Normal conditions	36.7	52.7	3.6
Reactions to verbs	48.4	41.6	7.4
Plus difference	11.7		

480   This table shows that the reaction-type when stimulus-words are verbs is considerably blunter than for the list of stimulus-words mainly composed of nouns. Thus it has been proved numerically that for educated men too there exist far fewer canalized connections between verb and verb than between noun and any of the three other parts of speech. Comparing the appropriate figures for uneducated women with these, we find confirmed our assertion that the nouns preferred by this group possess a higher quality.

UNEDUCATED WOMEN		
	Internal Associations	External Associations	Sound Reactions
Normal conditions	46.6	49.4	0.7
Reactions to verbs	69.0	29.6	0.3
Plus difference	22.4		

481   It becomes apparent from these figures that the vast majority of associations in reaction to verbs are highly significant and appropriate to the meaning of the stimulus-word. The sound reactions in the two groups quoted are also remarkable.

Their larger proportion under normal conditions in educated men shows how slight is the influence of the meaning of the stimulus-word. Conversely the decrease of the corresponding figures for uneducated women is characteristic of the increased influence of the meaning of the verbs. From the ratios of these figures it is permissible to conclude that, on account of their lower frequency and consequently the greater difficulty of reacting, the influence of verbs on attention is greater than that of nouns.

482 The adjectives show, as a glance at the table demonstrates, a reaction analogous to verbs, except that in general they have rather less influence on the reaction-type. It may therefore be assumed that the reaction to adjectives generally encounters little difficulty.

483 The predicate type reacts to verbs predominantly with nouns, while on the average all non-predicate types react to verbs with twice as many verbs as the predicate type.[70] We examine again the quality of the associations with which the predicate type reacts to verbs:

	PREDICATE TYPE			NON-PREDICATE TYPE		
	Int. Assn.	Ext. Assn.	S.R.	Int. Assn.	Ext. Assn.	S.R.
Normal conditions	45.7	48.6	1.5	36.6	58.2	2.5
Reactions to verbs	62.8	33.4	2.7	52.4	41.8	4.2
Plus difference	17.4			16.4		

484 As the plus differences show, the influence of the verbs is roughly the same in both cases; no plus difference of internal associations surpassing that found in the non-predicate type corresponds to the numerous nouns in the predicate type. Thus we have no reason to suppose that in the predicate type the verb has a greater influence on the attention, that is, that it presents greater difficulties in reaction. The predicate type shows no difference of attention in relation to the verb but only the difference that educated subjects in general display, namely, that they prefer the noun on account of its greater

[70] It must be noted here that of all the eleven predicate types used in these calculations only two are uneducated and of these only one is a woman.

familiarity. This is because in our predicate types the majority are educated subjects.

485   The reaction of predicate types to adjectives is in contrast to our earlier findings. As the figures in the tables show, in the four groups first dealt with more adjectives are given as reactions to adjectives than verbs to verbs. In the predicate type, which is mainly distinguished by attributes in adjective nouns are given greater preference (as opposed to non-predicate form, the difference is only 10.8 per cent. On the other hand, types)—namely, 28.5 per cent more. This preference for nouns is caused by the predicate type's effort to react mainly in the form of attributes and not only, as our figures show, by reacting with a predicate but also, conversely, by discovering a noun for an adjectival stimulus-word.[71] Let us now examine the proportions with reference to the quality of adjectival reactions.

	PREDICATE TYPE			NON-PREDICATE TYPE		
	Int. Assn.	Ext. Assn.	S.R.	Int. Assn.	Ext. Assn.	S.R.
Normal conditions	45.7	48.6	1.5	36.0	58.2	2.5
Reactions to adjectives	64.2	28.2	3.9	42.8	51.0	4.3
Plus difference	18.5			6.8		

486   As these figures show, the large number of nouns in the predicate type is connected with a rise of internal associations. Thus we do not in this case have a mere juxtaposition of familiar nouns but constructions that, owing to the particular mental attitude of the subject, are matched to the stimulus-word. This although, in view of the figures for the other groups, the juxtaposition of a similar adjective seems easier for them. The latter is clearly demonstrated by the small plus difference of internal associations in the adjectival reactions of the non-predicate type.

487   It also becomes clear from the figures for adjectival reactions that the predicate attitude is by no means fortuitous but

71 This can be explained from the psychology of the predicate type. The subjects of this type are distinguished by their particularly vivid images. Therefore, they always see the adjective as the property of a definite object, which they then name in their reactions.

corresponds to a quite definite psychological disposition, which is maintained even when other modes of reaction would be much easier than the predicate form.

SUMMARY

488   The associations show normal variation, principally under the influence of:

(1) Attention
(2) Education
(3) The individual characteristics of the subject

489   (a) Decrease of attention owing to any internal or external factors causes a blunting of the reaction type, i.e., the internal or fully valent associations recede in favour of external associations or sound associations.

(b) Distraction of attention according to our experimental design caused, apart from the above-mentioned changes, an increase of indirect associations which must therefore be interpreted as distraction phenomena and can be derived as internal links from the competition of two weakly stressed (less valent) associations.

(c) Educated subjects have a blunter reaction-type on the average than uneducated. The difference can essentially be explained by a difference in the interpretation of the stimulus-word.

(d) No essential differences emerged in the degree of division of attention by distraction between educated and uneducated subjects.

(e) The most considerable variations in associations are conditioned by individual differences.

490   (1) As regards the effect of sex on the mode of reaction under normal conditions no clear differences emerge from the average figures. Only in the distraction experiment does the peculiarity of female subjects show, in that they possess less ability to divide attention than male subjects.

(2) The individual variations can be classified into the following types:

I. *Objective type.* The stimulus-word is taken objectively, that is:

(*a*) mainly according to its objective meaning; the reaction is matched to the sense of the stimulus-word as much as possible and linked by meaning to the stimulus-word.

(*β*) mainly as verbal stimulus; the reaction is in part matched purely verbally, in part it merely marks the juxtaposing of a canalized association, in which the meaning relationship rather recedes into the background.

II. *Egocentric attitude.* The stimulus-word is taken subjectively (egocentrically).

(*a*) *Constellation type.* The personal elements used in the reaction belong to one or more emotionally charged complexes, there being two possibilities:

(*aa*) The complex-constellations are spoken without concealment.

(*ββ*) The complex-constellations appear in veiled form as a result of a not always conscious repression.[72]

(*β*) *Predicate type.* This type has presumably the psychological peculiarity of particularly vivid (plastic) inner images, by which its particular mode of reaction may be explained. This type also shows at best an abnormally low ability to divide attention, which is expressed in the distraction experiment by an, on the average, almost complete lack of blunting phenomenon.

491   As a general result important for pathology, it emerges that the blunting of reaction-type in fatigue, alcoholic intoxication, and mania may be attributed primarily to a disturbance of attention. The observations on the affective side of associations (effects of feeling-toned complexes) might be of importance for the experimental investigation of pathological feeling changes and their consequences.

---

[72] We use the term "repression" in the sense of Breuer and Freud, to whose work *Studies on Hysteria* we are indebted for valuable stimulus for our work.

492   Finally we may be permitted to express our sincerest thanks to our esteemed director, Professor Bleuler, for valuable encouragement. We are also particularly grateful to Mrs. Jung for active help in the repeated revision of the extensive material.

EXPLANATION OF GRAPHS

493   In the accompanying graphs the arithmetical means of internal associations, external associations, sound reactions, and reactions in the residual group of different groups are presented. The averages shown are:

I: internal associations   S: sound reactions
E: external associations   R: reactions in the residual group

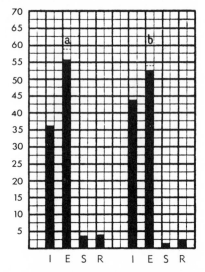

Graph I. Averages from Experiments under Normal Conditions
(a) Educated Subjects: 23 subjects, 3,800 associations
(b) Uneducated Subjects: 18 subjects, 3,000 associations

494   Graph I. The educated subjects have fewer internal, more external and more sound associations under normal conditions than the uneducated subjects.

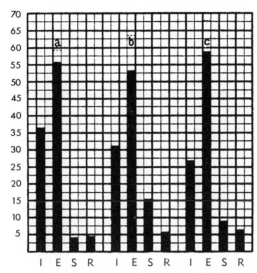

*Graph II. Averages from Experiments with Educated Subjects
under External Distraction*

   (a) Normal conditions (Graph I, a): 23 subjects, 3,800
      associations

   (b) Distraction experiment with 60 metronome-beats
      per minute: 13 subjects, 650 associations

   (c) Distraction experiment with 100 metronome-beats
      per minute: 13 subjects, 835 associations

495   *Graph II.* A definite, regular decrease of internal associations from *a* to *c* is found, i.e., according to the intensity of the
method of distraction. Secondly, an increase of sound reactions
in both distraction experiments emerges from the graph. The
result of distraction consists in general of an increase of external associations plus an increase of sound reactions. This
sum (E + S) is indicated in places by adding to column E a
dotted column equal to the height of S. This column (E + S)
increases regularly from *a* to *c*. The decrease of I and the increase of (E + S) under distraction demonstrates clearly the
effect of distraction. S*b* and S*c* are both bigger than S*a*. The
reactions in the residual group increase from *a* to *c*.

193

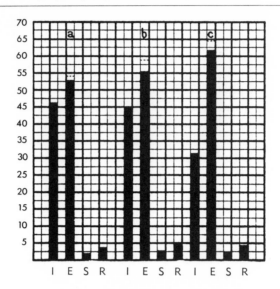

70
65
60
55
50
45
40
35
30
25
20
15
10
5

I E S R   I E S R   I E S R

Graph III. Averages from Experiments with Uneducated Subjects under External Distraction

(a) Normal conditions (Graph I, b): 15 subjects, 3,000 associations

(b) Distraction experiment, 60 metronome-beats: 15 subjects, 750 associations

(c) Distraction experiment, 100 metronome-beats: 15 subjects, 750 associations

496   *Graph III.* The picture, apart from the different starting point, is similar to the distraction experiment with educated subjects:

Gradual decrease of internal associations from *a* to *c*;

Gradual increase of external associations plus sound reactions from *a* to *c*. R increases under distraction, S only a little, the sound reactions generally play a much smaller part than in educated subjects.

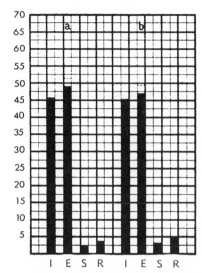

Graph IV. Averages from Experiments with Subjects of the Predicate Type (Educated and Uneducated)

(a) Normal conditions: 9 subjects, 1,792 associations
(b) Distraction experiments (60 and 100 metronome-beats taken together): 7 subjects, 700 associations

497 *Graph IV.* While in educated subjects the ratio of I : E is 2 : 3, and in uneducated subjects I : E is 5 : 6, here it is 1 : 1.1. S is smaller than in educated subjects but greater than in uneducated under normal conditions. In group R the ratio is inverted. Strikingly enough, in contrast to the preceding pictures, this ratio hardly changes under distraction. There is only a minimal decrease of I and a very small increase of (E + S). R has increased a little.

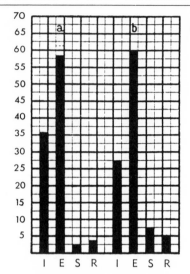

I   E   S   R   I   E   S   R

*Graph V. Averages of all Experiments in the Remaining Subjects
(Non-predicate Types)*
(a) Normal conditions
(b) Distraction experiment

498   *Graph V.* The picture is a striking contrast to the picture
in graph IV. Under normal conditions the ratio I : (E + S)
equals 10 : 17, approximately 2 : 3; in the distraction experiment 10 : 24, approximately 2 : 5. S increases considerably, R
less.

196

AN ANALYSIS OF THE ASSOCIATIONS
OF AN EPILEPTIC[1]

499   Epilepsy is one of the few mental diseases of which the symptomatology is particularly well known and delimited by innumerable clinical and systematic inquiries. Psychiatry has shown that in the epileptic, besides the symptoms of the fit, there is usually a mental degeneration that can be claimed to be specific and therefore of diagnostic value. Here are the principal traits of those epileptics who show degeneration according to the recognized textbooks of psychiatry:

1. *Intellect.* Mental debility, slowness of mental reactions, fussiness, restriction and impoverishment of ideas combined with poor and stereotyped vocabulary, frequently abnormal preponderance of fantasy.

2. *Emotional disposition*: Irritability, moodiness, strong egocentricity, exaggeration of all feelings, particularly religious ones.

500   These attributes comprise what is known as the epileptic character, which, once established, has to be considered a permanent formation. Transitory accentuations of one or the other trait are quite likely, radiating like ripples from occasional fits. It is occasionally possible to make the diagnosis with sufficient certainty by recognizing the epileptic character, even if fits are not known to have occurred. Such cases, however, are on the whole rare. Very frequently the epileptic character is not very obvious, particularly if the fits are infrequent. It would therefore, for practical purposes, be most valuable to find a method of concise formulation of the epileptic degeneration.

501   Repeated attempts to investigate the permanent epileptic changes by means of experimental methods have recently been

---

1 [First published as "Analyse der Assoziationen eines Epileptikers," *Journal für Psychologie und Neurologie*, V (1905):2, 73–90. Republished in *Diagnostische Assoziationsstudien*, Vol. I, pp. 175–92 (III. Beitrag). Translated by M. D. Eder in *Studies in Word-Association*, pp. 206–26. See supra, par. 1, n.1.]

made: thus Colucci[2] and Breukink[3] tested by means of the ergo-graph; Sommer[4] and his pupil Fuhrmann[5] in particular turned their attention towards associations in epileptics. We consider the latter research as particularly suited for a precise formulation of epileptic degeneration.

502   Fuhrmann reports on an investigation into the associations of two epileptics. The first concerns a patient who was taken ill in his tenth year. The author found that predicates in particular occurred repeatedly and that egocentricity played a prominent part. Not all reactions could be regarded as "associations"; there were also verbal reactions, the content and form of which had no inherent connection with the stimulus-word. Fuhrmann calls these reactions "unconscious." They appear mainly at the beginning of the test sequence (according to the table given by Fuhrmann). Test sequence I starts with the following reactions:

1. bright	faith	5. red	parents
2. dark	health	6. yellow	father
3. white	arm	7. green	chair
4. black	blue	8. blue	arm

503   Fuhrmann does not attempt any interpretation. Kraepelin[6] mentioned this observation in the latest edition of his textbook, where he states:

[It seemed] as if these ideas, only released but not produced by the experiment, emerged from permanent general trains of thought. Their contents were mainly related to the illness or else to the patient's personal circumstances. We may well assume that the frequency of such associations, determined by inner conditions, not by external stimulation, is particularly facilitated by the mental slowness of epileptics, which prevents them from associating quickly and easily with the stimulus-word, as normal people do.

2 "L'Allenamento ergografico nei normali e negli Epilettici" (1902).
3 "Über Ermüdungskurven bei Gesunden und bei einigen Neurosen und Psychosen" (1904).
4 *Lehrbuch der psychopathologischen Untersuchungsmethoden* (1899).
5 *Analyse des Vorstellungsmaterials bei epileptischen Schwachsinn* (1902).
6 *Psychiatrie: Ein Lehrbuch für Studierende und Ärzte* (7th edn., 1904), II, p. 626. [The passage is not included in the abstracted translation by Diefendorf (1907).]

504   In 1903 I demonstrated the frequent occurrence of such meaningless connections in an imbecile in a state of emotional stupidity in my paper "On Simulated Insanity." Wehrlin[7] recently expressly referred to these facts, supported by evidence, in his research on associations of imbeciles and idiots. According to our experience these meaningless reactions always occur when the patient is in a state of emotional stupidity, which can, of course, occur in quite a number of mental abnormalities. These "unconscious" reactions are therefore not at all specific for epilepsy.

505   Let us return to Fuhrmann's paper. In the first case a repetition of the experiment with the same stimulus-words was carried out after about a month.

506   The second case concerns a patient who had been ill since he was sixteen. Here the experiment was repeated four times within eight months, and a considerable restriction of the extent of the associations, a striking monotony in the reactions, could be observed. Basing his opinion on the associations of two female idiots, Fuhrmann considers that there is a "marked" difference between epilepsy and idiocy, in that general concepts have no meaning for idiots. Wehrlin's investigation shows that the idiot is aware of general concepts but these are extremely primitive. Thus the difference may be more subtle than Fuhrmann appears to assume.

507   Riklin, in his notable paper on "Relieving Epileptic Amnesias by Hypnosis,"[8] reports on several association experiments with epileptics. This author deals more with the qualitative aspect of the reactions and arrives at a variety of important findings.

508   He finds a clinging to the content of a reaction and to the same grammatical form, strong egocentricity, personal constellations, a frequent emotional charge in the content of the reaction, and a paucity of ideas.

509   These peculiarities are to a great extent nothing but reflections of the epileptic character. Riklin states that it is possible to read the signs of epileptic degeneration from a sequence of associations. In scrutinizing Riklin's observations, however, it

[7] "The Associations of Imbeciles and Idiots" (1904).
[8] "Hebung epileptischer Amnesien durch Hypnose" (1902).

has to be pointed out that: (1) Perseveration of the grammatical form need by no means always be an epileptic symptom. Wehrlin's paper shows very marked perseveration of grammatical form in imbeciles and idiots. (2) Perseveration of the content occurs also in normal subjects, as I have shown, together with Riklin, in the first contribution of the Diagnostic Association Studies.[9] Egocentricity and personal constellation too happen in the normal and in the feeble-minded, as well as feeling-toned reaction-contents. The paucity of ideas is, of course, not characteristic for epilepsy, but for mental deficiency generally, and in a certain sense also for emotional stupidity, where it assumes the special form of "associative vacuum."

510   In epilepsy therefore it is a question of the quantity of these symptoms in any given case. It will also have to be considered whether they may perhaps have a more specific quality. I have made it my task to clarify these issues and to attempt to separate what is specific for epileptic associations from the various types of the normal and from congenital mental deficiency. Such an investigation has, of course, to be based on extensive material. The Swiss Asylum for Epileptics in Zurich, with its large numbers of patients, offered a favourable opportunity.

511   The material comes mainly from this institution, where it was collected by the Medical Superintendent, Dr. Ulrich; some of it came from the Burghölzli Asylum for the Insane. The total number of experimental subjects was 158, the total number of associations 18,277. This extensive material allowed us to form some ideas about associations in epileptics; for this reason Dr. Ulrich and I began a methodical inquiry into this subject which contains so much of interest. In order to comprehend the essence of the abnormalities of epileptic association as fully as possible, I classified the material as follows:

512   First, I excluded those cases who were not congenitally mentally defective and those who only contracted epilepsy after leaving school, i.e., after puberty.

513   By doing this I discarded the cases, so frequent among epileptics, that are complicated by congenital mental deficiency. According to Wehrlin's paper, it seems that imbeciles have a rather characteristic type of association which is mainly marked

---

9 "The Associations of Normal Subjects," supra.

by the tendency to "define" the stimulus-word. The first records of epileptics showed us association types which from the very beginning revealed the greatest similarity to the imbecile type. In cases of epilepsy complicated by imbecility or by mental degeneration in early youth, the similarity was even greater. In order to find the specific epileptic, it was necessary to eliminate the cases we have mentioned.

514   For practical reasons the field of inquiry was further divided; in this paper I am analyzing the reactions of a typical case as fully as possible, and in a forthcoming publication Dr. Ulrich is going to discuss the variants of the epileptic types of association.

515   Before dealing with the observations themselves, I must make a few remarks about the technique of obtaining the associations.

516   The preparation of the subjects for the experiment is by no means unimportant. One has to consider that as a rule people have no idea what the experiment demands of them; therefore they easily get bewildered. If they become markedly so, this has a distinct influence on the result, as I have repeatedly seen. We therefore introduce the experiment in each case with an instruction: the subject is told that some random word is going to be called out, to which he or she has to answer as quickly as possible with the word or idea that comes to mind without reflection. The instruction is illustrated by a practical example in which the experimenter gives a reasonably complete list of the possible associations. In this way the subject is enabled to select freely from this list the reaction that appeals to him most. The unbiased subject will, of course, choose the type of reaction that is characteristic of him. We take special care that the subject does not make a special effort to respond, if possible, with one word only. If this is, nevertheless, the case, then the characteristic form of the response becomes completely obscured and the reaction-time is considerably shortened. In women it is often necessary to subdue a nascent emotion by talking casually about the experiment. I usually do this by presenting the experiment as a kind of game.

517   For these experiments a new list of stimulus-words was used. I chose two hundred words; 75 of them denote concrete ideas, 25 denote abstract ideas, 50 of them are adjectives, and

50 are verbs. The sequence is as follows: noun–adjective, noun–verb. They are as mixed as possible so that related stimulus-words do not occur in immediate sequence. No attention was paid to the number of syllables. The stimulus-words were taken from widely varied fields of everyday life, unusual words being avoided as much as possible. Intentionally a number of emotionally charged ideas were interspersed, such as love, to kiss, bliss, friendly, etc., because a particular significance is attached to these words. The reaction-times were checked by a 1/5-second stop-watch.

518   I have chosen the following case from our material:

M. Joseph. Toolmaker, born 1863, widowed, no children. 19 convictions. No family history of illness admitted. Good at school, completed a three-year apprenticeship with a locksmith. Good testimonials. No major illness during early years, particularly no sign of epilepsy. Married in 1888. In 1893 his wife contracted a psychosis and died soon after in a lunatic asylum. After his wife was taken ill, the formerly stable and industrious patient began wandering about all over Europe. He left every place of employment after a short time, took to drink, travelled aimlessly about, even in forests. During this period there were frequent collisions with the police, mainly for theft. The patient claims amnesia for most of them. In 1893–94 he was three times in lunatic asylums for violent *mania transitoria*. In 1896 he fractured his skull. In 1896–98 he was again in various lunatic asylums for delirium. In 1898 one-sided twitching, occurring in fits, was noticed. At that time a relatively lucid delirium, with plastic and very stable visions, was observed, and the patient described it with much emotion. The end of 1904 was spent by the patient aimlessly in the mountains eating only poor food. Following a drinking bout, he stole a bicycle. After the theft he wandered aimlessly about and then came into the hands of the police. He was brought in here for observation, which revealed:

Mental deficiency in an epileptic character. Frequent short lapses of consciousness with aura: "Sees black dots, five to six in a row, which are always moving up and down; head feels as if in a clamp or pressed together by screws; chest feels as if a drop were trickling down inside it; there is buzzing in the ears, then fear overcomes him as if he had done something wrong, or he has pains in the back that rise to the head; he has the feeling that he wants to tear everything up, or it is as if a railway engine suddenly rushed towards him." After this aura he gets giddy, everything is spinning around him and he loses consciousness. The lapses of consciousness were also observed during conversation and particularly while playing cards. Intolerance of alcohol to a high degree.

519   The associations in this case seemed to me in various respects rather typical for epilepsy, although not all the characteristic symptoms appear in them. This is because each case has its peculiarities, so that here too rather an important role is played by the individual differences between the various reaction-types.

		Secs.
1. coal	hard coal	7.2
2. moderate	eating little	12.0
3. song	to sing, to sing a song	6.2
4. to assume	I assume, what do I assume? several things	23.2
5. pain	because I am ill	4.2
6. rotten	if an apple is rotten, a plant, everything can get rotten	5.8
7. moon	that is the moon in the sky, here we have the moon	3.4
8. to laugh	man laughs	4.2
9. coffee	one drinks it, drinks it every day	4.0
10. wide	this is the width of a distance (accompanied by an explanatory gesture)	6.2
11. air	this is the air, nature's air, healthy or unhealthy, fresh air is fresh air	2.2
12. to carry (to wear)[10]	I carry (or wear) something, a burden or fine clothes	5.0

520   These first twelve reactions already allow some conclusions. Above all it is striking that the subject reacts not with *one* word but usually with whole sentences. This fact has a certain significance. In my experience, which is supported by the material of more than thirty thousand normal associations, healthy people as a rule tend to react with one word (N.B. after being instructed as explained above). There are exceptions when even educated people may prefer the form of a sentence; Riklin and

---

[10] [German *tragen* has both these meanings. All reaction-time data in this paper are in seconds.]

I quoted such an example in our paper on the associations of healthy people. That subject belongs to the "complex-constellation type," i.e., to that reaction-type whose associations are at the time of the experiment under the influence of an affect-charged complex of ideas.[11] In such cases one recognizes at once the peculiar constellations from the contents of the associations. I refer to this quotation. Among healthy people there is also a type who likes to react with two or more words, though not actually in sentence-form:

521   *The Predicate Type.*[12] People belonging to this type tend mainly to judge and evaluate the object described by the stimulus-word. This is, of course, done in predicate form; thus the tendency is quite obvious and the use of several words sufficiently explained. Certainly neither of these types can be confused with the reactions that now concern us.

522   In the pathological field, however, the sentence form is so frequent and occurs so widely that one can hardly recognize in it anything pathognomonic.

523   An observation (which I cannot, it is true, support at present by figures) has to be mentioned: uneducated mental patients appear to tend more to form sentences than educated ones. Should this observation become confirmed, it would not be difficult to combine it with the fact that uneducated people are more concerned with the meaning of the stimulus-word than are educated ones, as has already repeatedly been stressed in previous papers. Uneducated people at a very low level, who tend to "answer" with something that is as "fitting" as possible and to explain the stimulus-word as well as possible, need more words for it than educated ones, who merely juxtapose words. This tendency to explain becomes most obvious in idiots and imbeciles, who very frequently form whole sentences.[13] Our subject shows a preference for sentences which, in the absence

---

[11] See "The Associations of Normal Subjects," par. 429, supra. This case concerns a love-affair that ended unhappily and, moreover, with distressing circumstances that fully explain the strong affect.

[12] Ibid., par. 432.

[13] A further reason that, in Bleuler's view, facilitates the occurrence of sentences in mental defectives is that it is difficult for them not only to understand a word outside the context of a sentence, but even to think words outside a sentence context.

of sufficient data, is difficult to understand; it may therefore be inferred that we are faced with some abnormality.

524 Before dealing with the contents of the reactions we must pay some attention to the reaction-times. These are abnormally long. (The average reaction-time of uneducated subjects is 2.0 secs.) This does not permit us to draw any conclusions at present, because there is no syndrome in which the reaction-time could not be prolonged. As is well known, Aschaffenburg found somewhat extended reaction-times also in manic patients. It may, in any case, not be advisable to investigate the reaction-times found in the association experiment, isolated from the analysis of the association contents, because they depend to a high degree on the momentary contents of consciousness.

525 Let us now consider the quality of the associations. We notice at once that the subject focuses on the meaning of the stimulus-word; there is an outspoken tendency to clarify and characterize the object denoted by the stimulus-word. Wehrlin described this tendency as particularly characteristic for congenital mental deficiency. Perhaps, however, the strong tendency to explain occurs in every variety of mental defect, and it may be assumed that the feeble-minded converge in some respects towards the congenital mental defective, even if the causes of the two conditions are entirely different. The tendency to explain is so obvious in our case that here too we can without difficulty demonstrate the kind of explanation found by Wehrlin among imbeciles. Reactions such as these can be regarded as "tautological clarifications":

to assume	I assume
to carry	I carry something
air	this is the air

526 These can be taken as explanation by "examples":

moderate	eating little
rotten	if an apple is rotten
wide	this is the width of a distance (with explanatory gesture)

527 These indicate the main quality or activity:

| to laugh | man laughs |
| coffee | one drinks it |

205

528   From this we can see no more than a very marked conformity with the explanatory tendency of imbeciles. Moreover, one can even say that the subject is taking pains not to be misunderstood in this respect. Thus he is adding something that confirms and elaborates the explanation in places where there is some doubt whether it is a superficial familiar word-connection, such as in *song / to sing, coffee / one drinks it.*

song	to sing, to *sing a song*
coffee	one drinks it, *drinks it every day*

(Similarly in 4, 11, 12.) These examples show that the subject needs to accentuate his tendency to explain.

529   Out of the twelve reactions cited, which show a tendency to explain, we find three containing the word "I." Such reactions belong to the egocentric type. There are egocentric reactions in the normal as well, particularly in subjects with an "egocentric attitude."[14] This attitude can express itself in three different ways:

1. The subject reacts with a number of personal reminiscences.

2. The subject is under the influence of an emotionally charged complex of ideas. He relates almost every stimulus-word to himself (i.e., to the complex) and responds to it as if it were a question concerning the complex (a prototype of paranoia, therefore!).

3. The subject belongs to the predicate type and evaluates the content of the stimulus-word from the personal angle.

530   In these three types the subject puts himself occasionally into the foreground. Apart from this, egocentric reactions occur as a rule somewhat more frequently in the educated than in the uneducated, but mainly when the subjects are at their ease. For uneducated men we found an average of 1.7 per cent egocentric reactions, for uneducated women only 0.5 per cent. All the more remarkable is the strong predominance of egocentricity here. The cause of it could in the first place be ascribed to mental deficiency. Imbeciles use personal reminiscences relatively often because, owing to their narrow horizon, they have no others available. Wehrlin has given good examples of this.

14 See "The Associations of Normal Subjects," par. 427.

Figures found in our material obtained from imbeciles have shown a fluctuation of the numbers for egocentric reactions between 0 and 2.7 per cent. Among fifteen imbeciles there are no more than nine who show egocentric reactions. It must, however, be mentioned that in Wehrlin's material[15] there is an imbecile who is distinguished by the fact of having produced no less than 26.5 per cent egocentric reactions. This is quite an unusual result, for special reasons. This imbecile is also different from the other subjects in that he has not an actual tendency to explain, but with each stimulus-word he forms a "schoolroom-type" sentence which often begins with "I"; e.g.,

fall[16]	I fall down	to run	I run swiftly
to loathe	I loathe rotten fish	advice	I ask father's advice
head	I have a head	reward	I deserved the reward

531   The examples show that, as Wehrlin has already mentioned, this imbecile is mainly trying to formulate correct "schoolroom" sentences, saying "I" in places in which other imbeciles say "one" or "the man." The description "egocentric" can therefore be applied to this case only with some qualification. As already mentioned, this case is an exception and does not alter the fact that as a rule imbeciles avoid the ego-reference. Egocentric reactions in imbeciles are not much in evidence; on the contrary, the subjects prefer the expressions "one," "someone," etc., in order to avoid the "I"-form. Hysteria, too, which has numerous ego-references, prefers the less suspect "one."

532   Our case, with his outspoken tendency to explain, also shows a prominence of egocentric reactions, such as we do not find in imbeciles with the same tendency to explain. One can object that R.12, *to carry / I carry something*, is a "schoolroom" sentence. But one cannot make this objection to 5, *pain / because I am ill.*

533   It is strange enough to see the strong egocentric aspect in imbecility; it is even stranger to observe the peculiar way in which the subject words his explanation.

534   I have already pointed out that in a way the subject accentu-

15 Case 13 of Wehrlin's paper.
16 [German *Falle*: "fall" was substituted for the correct translation, "trap," which would not have made sense in this example.]
207

ates his tendency to explain by repeating his reactions in a confirmatory way, finally adding an attribute. But the subject goes even further; he is not satisfied with a simple reaction, but it evidently gives him special satisfaction to make his explanation more complete.

535   In R.4, *to assume / I assume, what do I assume?* Several *things*, one can virtually see how he is trying to bring something more descriptive into it. He gets into an entirely abnormal excitement with R.11, *air / this is the air, nature's air, healthy or unhealthy, fresh air is fresh air.*

536   The urge to completeness leads to pleonasm in R.10, *wide / this is the width of a distance* (with explanatory gesture). (See also 6, 7, 12.)

537   In the reactions 11, *fresh air*, and 12, *fine clothes*, the attributes seem to give quite a special emphasis. The effort with which the subject reacts suggests some inadequacy because this display of words goes far beyond what would be necessary to cover the stimulus-word. This fact at once gives the impression of an unnecessary and exaggerated tendency to elaborate. Precisely this trait is absent in the imbecile; he is satisfied with a not too long reaction that appears to him reasonably suitable, but which frequently does not get beyond the most primitive indications and quite undeveloped concepts. Our subject, however, has a strong inclination to accumulate and to elaborate the reactions, occasionally far beyond what is necessary.

538   The twelve reactions quoted give us reason to suspect feeblemindedness which is specifically tinged by a strong tendency towards egocentricity and elaboration.

539   Let us now see our patient's further reactions:

13. plate   dinnerplate—dinnerplate—for dining

The reaction is repeated with emphasis as if in confirmation. As it is not enough, it is further defined; an unnecessary reiteration. Quite similarly constructed, but even more specific, is

| 14. tired | I am tired—yes, tired—the body is tired | 3.0 |
| 15. intention | I have the intention—to invent a machine—to draw—to provide— to live properly | 13.0 |

This reaction too is overdone. It contains two explanations by

208

means of definite examples, one of which is a personal constellation (the subject is a toolmaker) and three times qualified.

16. to fly	the bird flies	4.8
17. eye	the eye sees	2.8
18. strong	am strong, that is strong	4.6

Again a clumsy ego-reference followed by a confirmatory but unnecessary sentence.

| 19. fruit | this is a fruit, a *tree*-fruit | 7.0 |

The tendency to confirm and complete leads here to the formation of a new word *tree-fruit* (see also below on this reaction).

| 20. to create | to work hard means to create | 3.6 |

To work has an emotionally charged attribute.

| 21. sail | a sail is a sailing boat on the water | 6.8 |

Note the repeated return of the stimulus-word in the reaction. Up to now there were no more than three associations in all in which the stimulus-word did not recur in some form.

| 22. modest | yes, man is modest when he has learned something | 9.0 |

Yes is an expression standing for a feeling that is about to take the shape of ideas and words (see R.14). Wherever strong feelings, either easily aroused or very intense, are involved (as in hysteria and certain organic brain-lesions), *yes* and *no* are frequent. The content of this association points to a train of thought hardly to be found in someone born mentally defective.

23. floor	floor of the room	3.8
24. to whistle	I whistle	3.2
25. purpose	for what purpose? For what purpose are you doing this?	5.6

The reaction is particularly striking because of the repetition of the stimulus-word. Here again we can see that the subject understands the stimulus-word as a question.[17]

| 26. hot | it's too warm, too hot | 2.0 |

Up to now, hardly one of the reactions shows as well as this one the subject's tendency to confirm and complete the reaction

---

[17] Cf. "The Associations of Normal Subjects," par. 408 (2).

with emphasis. It is as if the subject is each time trying to clarify the meaning of his reaction with special vigour. This emphatic underlining shows up well in the accentuation *too warm, too hot.*

27. resin	fir resin, the resin grows on the fir-tree, on the pine-tree	3.8
28. to arouse	I arouse—I arouse my friend, he is asleep	8.4

Both reactions are again characterized by great completeness, especially the latter, where the subject even completes the picture by *he is asleep.*

29. apple	there are various apples	6.6

This reaction can be found extremely frequently in exactly the same form in imbeciles.

30. wicked	one says, who is wicked? so-and-so is wicked, that is a wicked person	6.0
31. case	a brief-case	3.0
32. to drink	I drink lemonade	3.0
33. bed	sleeping—I have the bed for	3.0
34. worthy	that person is worthy to whom him honour is due *(sic)*	9.4

This reaction has linguistically miscarried. Epileptic mental deficiency seems to have in common with congenital mental deficiency that the patient is clumsy and arbitrary in the handling of the language. In imbeciles we find many faulty formulations of sentences and also clumsy neologisms. However, in the association experiment one must not simply ascribe linguistic clumsiness to mental deficiency, since there may also be momentary emotional disturbances that interfere with the linguistic expression. We shall come back to this later.

35. danger	I am in danger, in danger of life	4.2
36. to visit	I visit a patient	4.8

The latter reaction may again be an ego-reference.

37. locksmith	I am a locksmith, an artisan	2.8
38. high	the steeple is usually high	4.8
39. hatchet	the hatchet is an axe	3.4
40. to mix	don't mix yourself up in other people's affairs	6.2

This reaction very much resembles a common phrase. It is the first in this case. As is well known, just such reactions are very common in normal subjects.

| 41. path | that is a footpath, a field-path | 3.2 |
| 42. round | it is a sphere, otherwise it is not a sphere, if it is not round | 3.8 |

A reaction very typical of the pedantic fussiness of the subject.[18]

| 43. blood | every man has, every animal only good or bad, that is the difference | 3.4 |

In this long-winded reaction we again find similar evaluations to those in R.11. There it was *healthy or unhealthy air*, here it is *good or bad blood*. The constellation common to both is apparently the question of health, which is important for the patient. R.5 and R.36 also refer to this complex. The strong predominance of the illness-complex in the associations of the epileptic has also been stressed by Fuhrmann.

44. to let	I let lodgings	6.0
45. cautious	Man, be cautious	4.8
46. merry	I am merry, I am gay	3.6

[18] Such reactions differ distinctly from certain reactions that can occasionally be obtained from loquacious imbeciles. I quote the following as examples of this type:

Sunday	consists of a day when one does nothing, when one goes to church
mountain	a high mountain, with houses or without houses
salt	something to salt with. One salts meat
exercise-book	is made of paper. One makes a newspaper of it
ring	on the finger—jewelry—chain
attendant	someone who attends in hospitals, institutions, almshouses
piano	where music is, on the top floor where the organ is, the Misses have played it, next to it (even tells a story of an organ-player)
to swim	in the lake, in the water, in the Rhine, one needs swimming trunks
to cook	necessary for the meal, soup, flour, meat, pots and pans, casserole
star	parts of the sky, system of planets, sun, moon, and stars

In these associations the emphasis and confirmations of the epileptic are absent; they do not express the emotional moment so well. They are more enumerations, which frequently appear like flights of ideas; the train of thought progresses and does not stick anxiously to the stimulus-word.

47. market	the annual fair, that is a market, the fair at Basel only recently took place	7.0
48. to forget	I have forgotten something	5.0
49. drum	the kettle-drum is a drum	3.2
50. free	I am free—I am free, I am a free citizen, it would be nice if only it were true	4.0

In this reaction, apart from the repeated emphasis on *free*, the egocentric relation, clothed in the evaluation *nice*, is noticeable.

51. carriage	a carriage, a team of horses	4.4
52. to eat	I am eating, I am eating a stew	2.4
53. insolence	if a person—there are people who are insolent, insolent in their speech, insolent behaviour	6.8
54. fast	the engine runs fast (probably a constellation arising from his daily work)	3.8
55. fireplace	is a chimney, a factory chimney	2.4
56. to enjoy	I enjoy an evening entertainment, I enjoy pleasure	4.0
57. parson	is a clergyman, a pastor that ought to be a righteous man	2.2

To the reaction, which would be quite sufficient in itself, a feeling-toned evaluation is attached. It resembles R.15: *intention to live properly*. Are these perhaps indications of a tendency in the epileptic to moralize?

58. easy	what is not easy is difficult	5.0
59. neck	is the neck (points at his neck) every man has a neck	2.8
60. to wish	I wish you luck in the New Year	3.0
61. stone	a marble stone, there are various stones, stone is a product of nature[19]	4.6

Imbeciles too are inclined to use abstract nouns of foreign origin (substance, material, article, etc.), which, however, they frequently use in a truly grotesque way.

62. distinguished	the educated man is distinguished	6.2
63. hose	the rubber hose is a hose	4.0
64. to love	I love my neighbour as myself	5.0

19 [German *Naturalie*, which is felt to be a foreign word.]

This reaction seems to me characteristic for the epileptic: Biblical form, strong emotional charge, and egocentricity. For comparison I assembled the reactions to *to love* of ten imbeciles chosen at random:

1. friendly	6. I love father
2. to be angry	7. if one loves one another
3. fiancé	8. if two are fond of each other
4. if one loves someone	9. if one likes someone
5. pleasant	10. if one loves someone

With one exception (6), the imbeciles react very impersonally and in a considerably less colourful way than the epileptic.

65. tile	there are grooved tiles in Basel	
66. mild	is mild weather, is mild, is warm	2.8

540   It is hardly necessary to pile up any more examples. The further associations of this case contain nothing fundamentally new.

541   Some more general clarifications may be useful. It must first be mentioned that the subject made gestures with most reactions (which were indicated each time by a tick on the association form). The gesture expressed, wherever possible, confirmation and completion. Secondly, the stimulus-words were repeated in 30 per cent of the reactions. As I shall demonstrate in a later paper, "The Reaction-time Ratio in the Association Experiment," the repetition of the stimulus-word in the normal subject is not accidental but has deep reasons, like all the so-called disturbances occurring in the experiment. Apart from these rare cases in normal subjects, in which the stimulus-word is each time quickly repeated in a low voice because of a general self-consciousness, this disturbance mainly occurs only at those points where an emotional charge from the previous reaction perseverates and hinders the following associations. In hysterics I have also seen that the complex-constellating stimulus-word tends to be repeated in a questioning tone.[20] These observations teach us that those places where repetitions of the

[20] Certain stimulus-words can touch off a feeling-toned complex of ideas that is very important for the individual. This results in certain disturbances of the association which we have described as "complex-characteristics," such as: abnormally long reaction-times, repetition of the stimulus-word, abnormal wording of the critical or of the following reaction.

stimulus-word occur are not at all unimportant in normal subjects. For epilepsy, however, other mechanisms may also have
to be considered. In this case the first four stimulus-words were
repeated, the fourth, *to assume,* even three times. Then there
was nothing repeated until the fifteenth, *intention.*[21] At the
beginning a general self-consciousness is likely. In *assume* perhaps the "difficulty" of the word can have played a part; the
same applies to *intention.* Both, moreover, have extraordinarily long reaction-times (23.2 and 13.0 secs.) which exceed by far
those of other reactions. Perhaps then the repetition of the
stimulus-word is not simply to be explained by the "difficulty"
of the word, but could have been brought about by a perseverating emotional charge. The preceding reaction is *I am tired—
yes, tired—the body is tired*: 3.0; the following reaction-time
is 13.0.

542   Apart from the content, the word *yes* already points to the
existence of a stronger feeling-tone. The subsequent repetition
of the stimulus-word appears in 19, *fruit.* The reaction preceding this is *am strong, that is strong*: 4.6 (fR-T 7.0).[22] 21, *sail*
is repeated. Preceding reaction: *to work hard means to create*:
3.6 (fR-T 6.8). 22, *modest* is repeated. Preceding reaction:
a sail is a sailing boat on the water: 6.8 (fR-T 9.0).

543   Here we have two stimulus-word repetitions immediately
following one another, whereby the reaction-times progressively increase: 3.6—6.8—9.0.

544   The reaction to *sail* is a linguistic mishap (in my investigations into reaction-times, linguistic slips have proved to be complex-characteristics). At the near end of the scale is *to work
hard,* an emotionally charged, probably egocentric reaction.
The third reaction (22) is *yes, man is modest when he has
learned something.* It is not difficult to see here a relation in
the content to *to work hard.* The assumption that the emotional charge of *to work hard* has perseverated behind the
linguistically disturbed reaction and constellated R.22 is therefore not unlikely.

545   47, *market* is repeated. Preceding reaction: *I am merry, I
am gay*: 3.6 (fR-T 7.0). 51, *carriage* is repeated. Preceding

[21] *Intention* is in any case a very insidious word for certain people.
[22] [fR-T = reaction-time of the following association.'

reaction: *I am free—I am a free citizen, it would be nice, if only it were true*: 4.0 (fR-T 4.4).

546   With the exception of the first four reactions most of the other repetitions of stimulus-words coincide with reactions that immediately follow egocentric associations. The reaction-time in these cases is mostly abnormally prolonged. To avoid being unduly long-winded I shall not bring any further evidence for this fact; I can, however, give an assurance that, with only very few exceptions, all the other repetitions of stimulus-words took place near strong emotional charges.

547   In several reactions a certain linguistic awkwardness was noticed. One is tempted, in analogy with imbecility, to make the epileptic mental defect responsible for these faulty formations. We know, however, another source for slips of the tongue: namely, the strong emotional charge of a complex aroused by the stimulus-word. In my communication on reaction-time in association experiments I shall quote a number of examples from which it can be seen how reactions are influenced in normal subjects by an emotionally charged complex. Apparently quite casual slips of the tongue, which the subject himself hardly notices, prove to be meaningfully determined products of the mixture of two competing ideas.[23] Before therefore ascribing the linguistic mishaps to mental defect it is advisable to investigate whether perhaps the mechanism discovered in the normal subject is here too the cause of the incorrect sentence or word-construction. Amongst the associations quoted here, there are three linguistically incorrect ones. I am pairing each of these three associations with the immediately preceding ones (the incorrect construction is given in italics):

18. strong	am vigorous, that is, strong	4.6
19. fruit	(stimulus-word repeated) this is a fruit, a *tree-fruit*	7.0
20. to create	to work hard means to create	3.6
21. sail	(stimulus-word repeated) *a sail is a sailing boat* on the water	6.8
33. bed	sleeping—I have the bed for	3.0
34. worthy	(stimulus-word repeated) that person is worthy *to whom him honour is due*	9.4

23 Cf. also Freud's observations in *The Psychopathology of Everyday Life.*

215

548   These three faulty constructions have in common:

1. The stimulus-word of the faulty association was each time repeated.

2. Every one of the incorrect reactions has a reaction-time not only higher than that of the preceding reaction but prolonged beyond the average of the others.[24]

3. Two of the incorrect associations follow emotionally charged reactions: for the third this is at least probable according to the content and the analogy with similar cases.

549   These observations give us so many starting points for an explanation that we may hardly assume mental deficiency to be the cause of the incorrect constructions.

550   From these observations we can see that a specific epileptic mechanism can be found neither in the numerous repetitions of the stimulus-word, nor in the faulty constructions of the sentences. It is, however, debatable whether anything specifically epileptic can be seen in the intensity of these otherwise normal processes. Here perhaps the reaction-times, a valuable aid for judging emotional processes, can give us some information.

551   All time-averages given here are "probable means."[25] The time measurements for the subject give 4.2 seconds as a general probable mean (uneducated normal person: 2.0 secs.). The general reaction-time is thus more than twice as long as that of corresponding normal subjects. This mean, however, is only a "gross" figure; it is composed of several unequal magnitudes. As I shall show in my later publication, reactions complicated by feelings are usually prolonged. If therefore there are many such reactions the general mean, may under certain circumstances be strongly influenced. If we now eliminate all those reactions that, according to the criteria already given, are remarkable because of their feeling-toned egocentric contents and also those reactions that immediately follow these, then we obtain 3.8 secs. as a probable mean for all the assumedly un-

24 I find in normal subjects that reactions constellated by a conscious or unconscious complex often show abnormally long reaction-times; in some cases the emotional charge can even involve the following reaction, for which the reaction-time also becomes extended.

25 See Aschaffenburg, "Experimentelle Studien über Assoziationen" (1896 ff.). (For the calculation, see my later paper on reaction-times.)

complicated reactions, while the probable mean for those eliminated is 4.8 secs.

552   Thus the feeling-tone makes a difference of 1.0 sec. This
state of affairs is not very different from that of the normal. As
we have seen in several examples, there is frequently a considerable difference between the times of feeling-toned associations and those of the reactions immediately following them.
We therefore investigate separately the time of these two groups.
As a mean for the reactions containing a feeling-toned idea we
have 3.6 secs., a figure 0.2 secs. lower than the mean for associations not feeling-toned; for the associations immediately following those that are feeling-toned, however, there is a mean
of 5.8 secs. This unusually high mean, which exceeds that for
the uncomplicated reactions by not less than 2.0 sec., expresses
the important fact that the feeling-tone inhibiting the reactions
perseverates from the critical reaction and exerts its main
influence on the following reaction. Thus the effect of the
feeling-tone inhibiting the reaction cannot as a rule be demonstrated in the critical reaction but only in the following
reaction. One must therefore assume that in this case the feeling-tone does not properly set in until after the critical reaction, increases very gradually, and then decreases slowly, still
inhibiting the following reaction. This state of affairs appears
the more remarkable when we remember that the experimenter has to write down the reaction, to read the stop-watch,
and to call out the next stimulus-word, and that the writing
down of the reaction, which may be rather long, takes most of
the time. I also tried to make similar observations about the
associations of normal subjects. For this purpose I took the
associations of a case of whom I possess a most detailed analysis,
so that I was fully informed as to all complex-constellated associations. The probable mean of all associations not complicated
by feelings is 1.2 secs. The mean of the feeling-toned reactions
is 1.6 secs. The mean of the reactions immediately following
the feeling-toned ones is 1.2 secs. This equals the mean of the
uncomplicated reactions. If, therefore, in the mentally normal
subject the complex-arousing stimulus-word is followed by a
reaction-time on average 0.4 secs. longer than that of the immediately following or irrelevant stimulus-word, this only
means that in the normal subject the feeling-tone sets in much

faster and subsides again incomparably faster than in our epileptic; thus the average reaction-time of the following association is unimpaired in the normal subject, whereas in our epileptic, as we have seen, the reaction-time for the following critical association is unusually prolonged.

553   This important and interesting peculiarity appears to be of a pathological nature; how far it is typical for epilepsy has to be learned from the further study of our vast material.

554   There seems to be something characteristic for our case in this phenomenon, because one can also assume the existence of such an enormous emotional process from the quality of the associations. I have repeatedly pointed out the fact that the subject frequently emphasized his reactions with his voice as well as also sometimes with words giving expression to some feeling (e.g., *hot* / *it's too warm, too hot; tired* / *I am tired—yes, tired —the body is tired*; etc.). This peculiar form of reaction also seems to indicate that the feeling-tone sets in slowly and increases slowly, in this way releasing even more associations in a similar direction. It is most likely that the feeling-tone in the epileptic is of greater intensity than in the normal subject, which again is bound to prolong the feeling-tone. It is, however, difficult to say whether the epileptic's feeling-tone is necessarily abnormally prolonged.[26]

555   In my analytic investigations into the reaction-times of normal subjects I was able to demonstrate the existence of one or more feeling-toned complexes of ideas that constellate a large number of the associations. I have already pointed out that in our epileptic also there exists a complex that constellates many of the associations. It is the complex of the illness. The following associations may be related to this complex:

5. pain	because I am ill	4.2 (fR-T 5.8)
14. tired	I am tired—yes, tired—	
	the body is tired	3.0 (fR-T 13.0 Rr)[27]

[26] This suggestion would also explain the epileptic perseveration in terms of the abnormality of the feeling-tone. It is, however, not unthinkable that the epileptic idea is abnormal in that it lasts longer than in the normal subject, and therefore produces a number of associations that still belong to the initial idea. Under these circumstances one could certainly expect relatively numerous perseverations of the contents. There is, however, none present in this case.

[27] Rr = repetition of the stimulus-word in the following reaction.

18. strong	am vigorous, that is, strong	4.6 (fR-T 7.0 Rr)
43. blood	every man has, every animal only good or bad, that is the difference	3.4 (fR-T 6.0 Rr)
46. merry	I am merry, I am gay	3.6 (fR-T 7.0 Rr)

A more remote constellation might be:

11. air	this is the air—healthy or unhealthy	2.2 (fR-T 5.0)
36. to visit	I visit a patient	4.8

The reaction following is:

37. locksmith	I am a locksmith, an artisan	2.8

556   Because of his illness the patient was hospitalized, a fact that made a great impression on him. He feared especially that he might never be discharged, nor be able to work and earn his living any longer. He was also homesick. The following reactions perhaps refer to this aspect of the complex:

20. to create	to work hard means to create	3.6 (fR-T 6.8 Rr)
35. danger	I am in danger, in danger of life	4.2 (fR-T 4.8)
50. free	I am free—I am free, I am a free citizen, it would be nice if only it were true	4.0 (fR-T 4.4 Rr)
60. to wish	I wish you luck in the New Year	3.0 (fR-T 4.6 Rr)

Regarding this last reaction, it must be added that the associations were taken before Christmas—at a time, therefore, when sensitive patients suffer twice as much from hospitalization.

557   These few examples may suffice to show that quite a number of associations are constellated by a feeling-toned complex. This state of affairs in itself is not at all abnormal, since the associations of normal people are also often constellated by such complexes.

SUMMARY

558   I. In common with the associations of normal persons:
(a) The patient adapts himself to the meaning of the stimulus-word in the same way as uneducated subjects. Therefore there are no superficial word associations.

219

(*b*) The associations are partly constellated by an illness-complex.

II. In common with the associations of imbeciles:
(*a*) The adaptation to the meaning of the stimulus-word is so intense that a great number of associations has to be understood as "explanation" in the sense of Wehrlin's paper.
(*b*) The associations are in sentence-form.
(*c*) The reaction-times are considerably prolonged, compared with the normal.
(*d*) The stimulus-word is frequently repeated.

III. Peculiarities compared with normal and imbecile subjects:
(*a*) The "explanations" have an extraordinarily clumsy and involved character which is manifest particularly in the confirmation and amplification of the reaction (tendency to completion). The stimulus-word is frequently repeated in the reaction.
(*b*) The form of the reaction is not stereotyped, apart from the egocentric form that occurs particularly often (31%).
(*c*) Frequent emotional references appear rather bluntly (religious, moralizing, etc.).
(*d*) The reaction-times show the greatest variation only after the critical reaction. The abnormally long times are therefore not to be found with particularly difficult words, but in places determined by a perseverating emotional charge. This permits the conclusion that the feeling-tone probably sets in later and lasts longer and is stronger in the epileptic than in the normal subject.

559   In conclusion I beg to remark that the value of my analysis lies only in the case-material and that therefore I do not dare to draw any general conclusion from it. There are many forms of epilepsy that may have quite different psychological characteristics. Perhaps the fact that my case is complicated by a fracture of the skull sets it apart.

THE REACTION-TIME RATIO IN THE
ASSOCIATION EXPERIMENT[1]

560   As the subject of the present investigation I have chosen the ratio of the time-interval between calling out the stimulus-word and the patient's verbal reaction. I am calling this period simply the *reaction-time*, knowing that it is a matter of a compound whole that can be divided, not only deductively but also empirically, into numerous components. I am not going to attempt an analysis of this kind for it could only be a matter of hypotheses that would have to be supported, quite unjustifiably, by anatomical data. The components of our reaction-time are known to us only in part, and careful examination must necessarily show them to be tremendously complicated, as we can see from the following summary given by Claparède:[2]

1. Transmission of sound to the ear of the recipient.
2. Neural conduction to the auditory centre.
3. Word-recognition (primary identification).
4. Word-comprehension (secondary identification).
5. Evocation of the associated image, i.e., pure association.
6. Naming of the idea evoked.
7. Excitation of the motor speech-apparatus or the motor-centre of the hand when measurement is made by means of a Morse telegraph key.
8. Neural conduction to the muscle.

561   A purely superficial examination of these eight factors shows that only a few of the most important processes are

---

1 [Originally published as "Über das Verhalten der Reaktionszeit beim Assoziationsexperimente," *Journal für Psychologie und Neurologie*, VI (1905): ½, 1–36; republished separately the same year as Jung's *Habilitationsschrift*, i.e., treatise submitted for recognition as lecturer in psychiatry at the University of Zurich. Republished in *Diagnostische Assoziationsstudien*, Vol. I, pp. 193–228 (IV. Beitrag). Translated by M. D. Eder as "Reaction-time in Association Experiments," *Studies in Word-Association*, pp. 227–65. See supra, par. 1, n.1.]

[In this study, the symbol σ = a millisecond, or 1/1000th of a second.]

2 *L'Association des idées* (1903), p. 275. The construction of the schema follows Ziehen, "Die Ideenassoziation des Kindes" (1900), p. 14.

stressed. The innumerable possibilities of intra-cerebral process are by no means exhausted in this summary.

562 So far as we know these components, they are of very short duration, even the longest of them should not exceed 50 σ (Ziehen). Some of these components might, in normal circumstances, be of fairly constant duration, as for instance the time of the neural conduction, of the excitation of the centres, etc. In any case, their variations will occur only within relatively narrow limits. The variation of the identification periods, however, are greater, and the longest of all are the actual association-time and that of the verbal formulation of the reaction. Thus, in the association experiment, the latter factors will be of the greatest importance.

563 Anyone conversant with the association experiment knows how wide are the limits within which reaction-times vary. In our experience times of up to six seconds are by no means rare, even with quite normal subjects. The great variability of the times gives us the necessary lead for establishing a *method of measurement*. So long as we have inadequate knowledge of the causes of the variations, small differences cannot tell us anything; we do not therefore need a complicated experimental set-up in order to measure the intervals in one-thousandths of seconds, for we can safely ignore small differences so long as the causes of the greater variations are still hidden. Quite apart from the fact that the complicated methods of exact time-measurement do not reveal more than measurements taken with a 1/5-second stop-watch, there are weighty arguments against the use of complicated apparatus like labial keys[2a] and megaphones or of dark-room methods. Considering that Mayer and Orth[3] even thought it necessary that the eyes should be closed throughout the experiment, to avoid distracting sensations, surely the apparatus mentioned do not contribute anything to the simplification of the experiment or the prevention of disturbing influences. In any case, inexperienced subjects should not be used in experiments of this kind if one is not to

2a [Labial keys are electrical contacts fastened to the subject's lips; they close an electrical circuit that is interrupted each time the subject opens his mouth and thus mark the moment when the reaction is uttered—C. A. M.]

3 "Zur qualitativen Untersuchung der Assoziationen" (1901).

risk gross distraction. Finally, in the case of psychotics exact measurements are impossible.

564   For this reason, measurement with a 1/5-second stop-watch not only appears entirely satisfactory, but has been proved adequate by several other writers in numerous experiments. Mayer and Orth worked with a 1/5-second stop-watch, so did Thumb and Marbe,[4] Wreschner,[5] Sommer, and others. Claparède[6] holds that this is adequate in all experiments regarding successive associations. Besides the fact that the watch is easy to handle, a further special advantage is that the second hand disturbs the experiment as little as possible, a factor which is particularly valuable in experiments with uneducated subjects, who are easily upset.

565   Considering the great differences in the times, it means little that the times measured are all somewhat too long. All of us who have worked with a stop-watch know too that it functions with only limited precision, since the stopping mechanism does not always hold the second-hand at the exact place it was at when the button was pressed. There are also certain variations in the personal equation that can influence the measurement. In spite of numerous imponderables, we can still, at least in my experience, assume that the measurements are accurate to approximately 1/5 second, i.e., 200 σ. This small disadvantage has not so far had any adverse effect on our experiments.

566   The material that forms the basis of this investigation consists of time-measurements that were taken by Riklin and myself[7] during association experiments with normal subjects. Out of 38 cases, whose associations we have already discussed, reaction-times were taken in 26. In about half the cases Riklin did the timing. The personal differential in the measurements of the two experimenters can, as we have established by means of control experiments, be determined at less than 1/5 second and can, therefore, be considered unimportant.

---

[4] *Experimentelle Untersuchungen über die psychologischen Grundlagen der sprachlichen Analogiebildung* (1901).

[5] "Eine experimentelle Studie über die Assoziation in einem Falle von Idiotie" (1900).

[6] Op. cit., p. 261.   [7] "The Associations of Normal Subjects," supra.

567   Here are the number and analysis of the measurements:

1. 7 uneducated women	1,201 reaction-times	
2. 7 uneducated men	1,007	" "
3. 6 educated women	948	" "
4. 6 educated men	988	" "
26 subjects	4,144 reaction-times	

A. The Average Duration of an Association

568   In his studies of associations, Aschaffenburg says: "The fact that the difference between duration of the association of normal subjects and that of others, which lies between 1,200 and 1,400 σ, can be as much as 50 per cent is of the greatest importance. This brings home to us how little value can be attributed to the absolute duration."[8]

569   Aschaffenburg bases this opinion on the observation that the reaction-time is subject to very considerable individual variations. Correspondingly, the data recording the average duration of association contained in the literature show wide discrepancies. Féré,[9] for instance, found an average of 700 σ in men, 830 σ in women. Galton[10] gives 1.3 seconds as the average, and Trautscholdt's[11] figures range between 1,154 and 896 σ.

570   These examples should suffice to show how little agreement there is between the various writers. The differences can be reduced to the following points:

(1) The methods of measurement differ according to the apparatus used and other experimental conditions.

(2) The degree of practice of the subject is variable.

(3) The methods of computing the mean vary. In practice, only two methods of computation are in use:

a. The arithmetical mean.

b. The probable mean (Kraepelin).

571   In view of the fact that excessively long reaction-times frequently occur in the association experiment, the application of the arithmetical mean does not appear advisable in that by

[8] "Experimentelle Studien über Assoziationen" (1896), p. 272.
[9] The Pathology of the Emotions (orig. 1892).
[10] "Psychometric Experiments" (1897).
[11] "Experimentelle Untersuchungen über die Assoziation der Vorstellungen" (1883).

224

this method the high values influence the otherwise quite low average values in a most disturbing and possibly quite misleading manner. This can be avoided by using the method of the probable mean, which consists in arranging the figures in the order of their numerical value and taking that nearest the middle. By this means the influence of excessively high values is eliminated. In by far the largest number of cases the probable mean is for this reason lower than the arithmetical mean. For example, three of my subjects show the following values:

Probable mean	1.8	2.0	1.6
Arithmetical mean	2.8	3.0	3.6

As the example shows, such differences can influence the general mean to a considerable extent. It is therefore not a matter of indifference which method of calculation is used. Ziehen's "representative value," which demands fairly intricate calculations, should, for this reason, not meet with much approval, although it does make possible a very just appraisal of the individual figures. Finally, the highest value depends on external contingencies, and can be used only in certain conditions.

572 For these reasons, the probable mean appears to be the method with the most to recommend it for quickly deriving averages from large numbers of figures.

(4) The number of subjects used by the early writers on this subject was mostly too limited, and their selection too one-sided.

573 My endeavours have not been directed towards discovering absolute means, but merely approximate figures which can, to a certain extent, give us the levels of the values of normal subjects from varying social strata. As I believe that the association experiment, carried out in approximately the way it has been practised in this clinic for several years past, will play an important role in the future diagnosis of mental illness, it seems to me to be most important to find general normal mean-values which can form a firm basis for the assessment of pathological values.

574 The general mean-value of the duration of an association seems to be 1.8 seconds. This figure was arrived at in the following way: First of all, the probable mean for each of the twenty-six subjects was calculated, and then the arithmetical mean was derived from the individual values. This method was

chosen because twenty-six subjects represent a very modest number, and it would be unjust to exclude the individual values from the calculation through the application of the probable mean.

575   This mean shows a fairly long duration of the reaction-time; it it considerably higher than the values given in the literature. The causes of this lengthening can be attributed to the following:

(1) The points mentioned above (measurement with a stopwatch, unpractised subjects, who in part come from lower social strata).

(2) The majority of the subjects are Swiss, the significance of which in our acoustic/linguistic experiments has already been emphasized in our previous contribution, which the reader may refer to.[12]

576   The varying data show what the interpretation of the values depends on. The variability of the mean is most easily demonstrated by classifying the subjects according to certain simple criteria and comparing the figures of the individual groups.

B. *Sex and Reaction-time*

577   As already mentioned, Féré has given longer times for women than for men. This result is confirmed by our figures:

men	1.6 secs.
women	2.6 secs.

These values indicate that women reacted considerably more slowly in our association experiments. It must be pointed out in criticism of this result, however, that the educated women among the subjects approach the educational level of the educated men, whereas, on the other hand, the cultural level of the uneducated women is inferior to that of the uneducated men. As may be known from Ranschburg's[13] and our own earlier investigations,[14] uneducated subjects, and especially the women among them, produce much higher figures than educated subjects, and give a considerably higher percentage of

---

12 "The Associations of Normal Subjects," supra, par. 10.
13 Ranschburg and Balint, "Über quantitative und qualitative Veränderungen geistiger Vorgänge im hohen Greisenalter" (1900).
14 "The Associations of Normal Subjects," supra, pars. 436ff.

internal associations, while purely linguistic associations are very much less prominent. According to Ziehen's[15] observations on children, associations by means of internal connections (semantic relationships) are distinguished by the longer reaction-times, whereas verbal associations need the shortest times. This fact stressed by Ziehen, was denied by Aschaffenburg,[16] since he finds on the basis of his observations "that no form of association is characterized by especially notable differences of duration." The figures given by Aschaffenburg can, it is true, not be interpreted in any other way, but they can perhaps be explained by his one-sided selection of subjects. Ziehen's claim that "images that are related to each other externally, such as, for instance, rhyming words" are reproduced more quickly, is in full accord with everyday experience.

578   This point, too, should be taken into account in explaining the longer association-times of women. Whether this explanation is sufficient, further consideration will tell. In any case, we must investigate the influence of education before discussing a possible sex difference in the reaction-times.

C. Educational Level and Reaction-time

	Educated Subjects		Uneducated Subjects	
579	Men	1.3 secs.	1.8 (1.6)[17] secs.	
	Women	1.7 "	2.2 "	
	Average	1.5 "	2.0 (1.9) "	

580   Our previous investigations demonstrated that uneducated subjects produce more internal associations than the educated. The ratio of internal to external associations is 43 : 53 per cent with uneducated and 36 : 59 per cent with educated subjects. One is therefore tempted to connect the differences in the reaction-times with these ratios and to state: the smaller number of internal associations with educated subjects corresponds to the shorter reaction-time, and vice versa, the greater number of internal associations with uneducated subjects corresponds to the longer reaction-time.

15 "Die Ideenassoziation des Kindes."
16 "Experimentelle Studien über Assoziationen."
17 Among the uneducated male subjects there is a young man of a slightly hysterical disposition, whose mental soundness we may have overestimated. His probable mean is no less than 3.4 seconds (an abnormally high value!). If this doubtful subject is left out, then the mean for men is only 1.6 seconds.

581   However plausible this hypothesis may appear, particularly in view of Ziehen's statements, consideration of the figures of the different sexes does show, however, that the position is not so simple. On closer consideration of the educational levels of the subjects, it must be expressly mentioned that the educational difference between the educated and the uneducated is incomparably greater than that between educated men and women, so that it is quite incomprehensible why the time-difference of 0.4 seconds is the same between educated men and women as between educated and uneducated subjects. Moreover, the reaction-time of 1.7 seconds for educated women, as against 1.3 for educated men, does not correspond at all to the percentage-ratio of internal and external associations; for the educated women show 35 : 61 per cent and the men only 36 : 56 per cent. Similarly, the time-difference of 0.4 and 0.6 seconds respectively between uneducated men and women in no way corresponds to the difference in educational level between the two sexes in the uneducated group. In both cases there remains a time-difference against the female which in no way corresponds to any variation in educational level. If we take the time-difference of the two groups of men on the one hand and of women on the other, the difference in educational standards is a sufficient explanation, as has already been very clearly shown in the ratio of the association-qualities one to another. The observations of Wreschner[18] and Wehrlin[19] also lend support to this assumption, as they have demonstrated a general slowing down of associational activity in cases of pathological deficiency in intelligence and education (congenital feeble-mindedness). Wehrlin demonstrates an increased incidence of internal associations along with longer reaction-times.

582   Whereas the uneducated women produce slightly more internal associations than the men, the position with regard to educated men and women is actually the reverse, in that the educated women have fewer internal associations than the men; nonetheless, there is a time-difference between the sexes that is greater than that between the educated and uneducated. As we have seen, we can account for this neither by a greater number of internal associations, nor by the small difference in educa-

18 "Eine experimentelle Studie über die Assoziation in einem Falle von Idiotie" (1900).
19 "The Associations of Imbeciles and Idiots" (orig. 1904).

tion. Here a new factor seems to be at work, presumably the difference of sex.

583   The justification of this hypothesis will be dealt with below. Before we approach this task, however, we must investigate the influence that the individual stimulus-word has on the reaction.

D. *The Influence of the Stimulus-word on the Reaction-time*

584   The preceding investigations into association-times have been principally concerned with the connection between the quality of the association (i.e., the reaction) and its duration. Trautscholdt attempted to establish certain connections and claims, among other things, that verbal associations take the shortest time. Ziehen's and Aschaffenburg's observations have already been mentioned. We must now find out whether the influence on the reaction-time of the two components of the association—the stimulus-word and the reaction—cannot be examined separately. Only an extensive material can be expected to yield definite information. For this reason I have already attempted, with Riklin, to demonstrate the influence of the stimulus-word on the quality of the reaction. Here certain regular occurrences appeared, namely:

585   (1) The grammatical form of the stimulus-word has a considerable influence on the form of the reaction, and the form of the reaction is indeed determined by it; the subject tends to clothe the reaction in the grammatical form of the stimulus-word.[20] Individual figures showing this tendency vary greatly. My stimulus-words, which consist of 60 per cent nouns, 18 per cent adjectives, and 21 per cent verbs (the various parts of speech are well mixed up in order to avoid a continuation of one form of reaction), have given these results:

586   Individual figures of grammatical agreement vary between 26 per cent and 95 per cent. The average figure for educated subjects is 51 per cent and for the uneducated 59 per cent. Thus the uneducated show a somewhat clearer tendency to

---

[20] Münsterberg, Kraepelin, and Aschaffenburg have all dealt with this question. Kraepelin found that, in about 90% of cases, where the stimulus-word was given in the form of a noun, the reaction was also given as a noun; Aschaffenburg, testing 16 subjects, found the same result in 81%. It may be remarked that he used only nouns as stimulus-words, on principle. This fact induces the subjects to indulge in perseverating with the same reaction-form; that is why these figures have only limited value. By "grammatical form" I understand merely noun, adjective, or verb.

allow themselves to be influenced by the form of the stimulus-word. (This holds good not only for the grammatical form but also for the number of syllables and alliteration!)

587   (2) The tendency to agreement in grammatical form is limited by the influence of the law of frequency. In speech, adjectives and verbs occur only about half as often as nouns.[21] The noun, therefore, has a higher frequency-value, so that the probability of the reproduction of a noun is greater than that of an adjective or verb.

588   In our experiments noun stimuli were followed, on an average, by 73 per cent nouns (Aschaffenburg: 81 per cent). As verbs and adjectives have a lower frequency-value, their influence on the form of the reaction will be correspondingly less. Our experience confirms this supposition: verb stimuli were followed, on an average, by 33 per cent verbs. The number of nouns is on an average 49 per cent, it has thus been lowered through the tendency to agreement in grammatical form. A somewhat stronger influence is exerted by adjective stimuli, which are followed by 52 per cent adjectives. The number of nouns was reduced to a mean of 44 per cent through adjective stimuli. From these facts it appears that the frequency of nouns can be reduced, on the average by about half, by using verbs and adjectives as stimulus-words.

589   (3) From our earlier investigations[22] it appears that the quality of the association is influenced to quite an extent by the grammatical form of the stimulus-word. Whereas, for example, with uneducated women the ratio of internal to external associations is 1 : 1.06, the ratio of associations which follow adjectives in particular is 1 : 0.62 and that of associations following verbs is 1 : 0.43. The number of internal associations to verbs and adjectives thus increases considerably. The same phenomenon is also found in educated subjects, but in a smaller degree. The increase in internal associations seems to be accounted for by the fact that, by virtue of the lower frequency-value of verbs and adjectives, fewer common word-sequences exist with these than with nouns. For this reason associations following verbs and adjectives are much less canalized and

21 I have counted them in newspapers and in interview articles and have found approximately the same proportion.
22 "The Associations of Normal Subjects," supra. pars. 475ff.

require a greater concentration, as a result of which, of course, semantic relationships emerge more readily than superficial and more external connections.

590 Thus we can see that more internal associations follow verbs and adjectives than follow nouns; according to observations made by Ziehen, who has found higher time-values for semantic relationships, it is to be expected that on the average verbs and adjectives should be followed by higher time-values than nouns. As, however, nouns refer to images that are to be evaluated differently, and that can to a great extent influence the reaction-time, they have been classified as concrete and abstract. One further reason was that uneducated subjects especially are easily startled by abstract terms.

591 The probable mean-times for all subjects are as follows:

Concrete nouns	1.67 secs.
Abstract nouns	1.95 "
Adjectives	1.70 "
Verbs	1.90 "

These figures correspond to our expectations: reactions to verbs and adjectives show a longer time than those to concrete nouns. The longest time of all is taken for abstract terms, which was also to be expected.

592 This picture becomes more interesting when the subjects are divided into groups.

Probable Mean of the Reaction-times
to Concrete Nouns etc. as Stimulus-words

	UNEDUCATED		EDUCATED	
	Women	Men	Women	Men
Concrete nouns	2.0	1.7	1.6	1.4
Abstract nouns	2.8	1.9	1.8	1.3
Adjectives	2.2	1.7	1.7	1.2
Verbs	2.4	2.0	1.9	1.3

593 The table[23] shows that uneducated people have longer reaction-times than educated ones. The longest time occurs for abstract ideas with uneducated women, whereas with educated men these words need an even shorter time than concrete ideas. It is striking that, in contrast to all other subjects, educated

23 The individual values on which this table is based vary between 1.0 and 4.4 seconds.

men have the longest reaction-time in response to concrete ideas. This fact is significant in so far as it shows that the influence of the stimulus-word on the duration of the association does not consist merely of those elements just mentioned. If we compare the figures of this group with the values that Aschaffenburg has found with similar subjects, it appears that the figures found by using a stop-watch are similar to those obtained by labial key and chronoscope.[24]

E. *The Influence of the Reaction-word on the Reaction-time*

594   In the above discussion we have explained how the reaction-time is affected by the stimulus-word's being a noun, adjective, or verb. We must now find out what happens to the reaction-time when the reaction-word is a noun, adjective, or verb.

595   The probable mean-times of all subjects are as follows:

concrete nouns as reaction-words				1.81 secs.
abstract	”	”	”	1.98 ”
adjectives	”	”	”	1.65 ”
verbs	”	”	”	1.66 ”

596   If we compare this table with the earlier one, which gave the mean-times for the corresponding stimulus-words, it appears that in both cases abstract terms produce the longest intervals (1.95 and 1.98 seconds); if the reaction-word is a concrete one a longer time is taken than that produced by a concrete stimulus-word (S. 1.67; R. 1.81 seconds). This difference might be due to the fact that there are many current word-compounds containing nouns, whereas noun following noun signifies an inner relation, or at least an association by co-existence (which, by the way, in uneducated subjects appears as an internal association; cf. our earlier investigations).[25] Under the heading "concrete nouns as reaction-words" numerous internal associations are crowded together, which is probably the cause of the long reaction-time. The opposite can be seen with verbs and adjectives as reaction-words. Their average val-

---

[24] One could easily pose a whole series of questions on this theme; for instance, what is the reaction-time when verb is followed by verb and noun by noun? how does this vary between different subjects? and so on. This, however, would lead us too far afield.

[25] "The Associations of Normal Subjects," supra, par. 445.

ues are less, compared with those on the earlier table (1.70, 1.90 : 1.65, 1.66) because under these headings, particularly in that of verbs, current word-compounds abound.

597   The probable mean-values of the individual classes of subject are these:

Probable Mean-times for Concrete Nouns etc.
as Reaction-words[26]

	UNEDUCATED		EDUCATED	
	Women	Men	Women	Men
Concrete nouns	2.2	1.85	1.7	1.5
Abstract nouns	2.7	2.0	2.0	1.4
Adjectives	2.0	1.7	1.7	1.2
Verbs	1.9	1.7	1.8	1.3

598   These relatively lower values for adjectives and verbs are shown here in all four groups. Here, as in the previous table, the uneducated women again show the highest figures. The relatively high figures for concrete nouns are striking. The fact already mentioned in the previous section, that cultured men take their longest time to react with concrete nouns, is also in evidence here. An explanation of this is perhaps to be found in the circumstance that in this group very many semantic relationships (causing delay) occur.

F. *The Influence of the Quality of the Association on the Reaction-time*

599   As we have seen, Aschaffenburg's investigations into the influence of the quality of the association on the reaction-time did not lead to unequivocal results; Ziehen's success, already mentioned, is therefore all the more encouraging. I too have conducted some research on this subject in which I have confined myself to the three principal groups of our earlier classification: internal, external, and sound reactions. This has produced the following average figures:

	UNEDUCATED		EDUCATED	
	Women	Men	Women	Men
Internal associations	2.8	1.9	2.1	1.6
External "	1.9	1.7	1.8	1.3
Sound reactions	2.6	2.4	2.0	1.8

[26] The individual mean-values on which this table is based vary between 1.0 and 4.0 seconds.

600   There is a distinct difference between the reaction-times for internal and external associations in that external associations take up decidedly less time. A different picture is presented by sound reactions, where one would expect the shortest times, as sound reactions quite rightly are to be regarded as the lowest and least valuable form of association, and for that reason could be produced in the shortest time. In practice, however, the situation is obviously not as simple as one would surmise in theory. As I have so often observed, the most superficial sound reactions very often take a very long time. As a rule, in my experience, sound reactions are usually abnormal reactions and their formation is mostly attributable to some kind of distracting influence; of what kind this disturbance usually is, the following chapter will show.

G. *Prolonged Reaction-time*

601   To demarcate the concept of a "prolonged" reaction-time, I call any time prolonged that takes longer than the probable mean for the subject concerned. Thus, if the average for the individual subject is 2.5 seconds, then 3 seconds is overlong.

602   Let us first recapitulate what is so far known of the causes that (of course, only in our experiments) lengthen reaction-times:

(1) Certain grammatical forms of the stimulus and reaction-words.

(2) Semantic relationship between stimulus- and reaction-words.

(3) The rarity or difficulty of the stimulus-word (abstractions!).

(4) Ziehen[27] states the remarkable fact that (in contrast to generic reactions) individual associations prolong the reaction-time.

(5) Mayer and Orth[28] in their experimental studies on associations found that the reaction-time was lengthened when the active will intervenes between stimulus-word and reaction. If between the stimulus-word and the reaction an emotionally charged conscious content occurred, the reaction-time was on the average considerably prolonged, as compared to those of

[27] "Die Ideenassoziation des Kindes."
[28] "Zur qualitativen Untersuchung der Assoziationen."

all the other reactions. Contents charged with unpleasure[29] have an especially delaying effect.

(6) In our earlier investigations[30] on the associations of normal subjects, we pointed out that abnormally long reaction-times occur particularly when the stimulus-word touches on a feeling-toned complex, i.e., a mass of images held together by a particular affect. So we were able not only to confirm the observations of Mayer and Orth, but also to demonstrate in various cases that: (*i*) The cause of several, or even very many, long reaction-times is generally the complex, and (*ii*) of what type the complex is.

603   It appears to us to be of the utmost importance that prolonged reaction-times can indicate the presence of feeling-toned complexes. So here we may perhaps have a means of discovering by a short and simple examination certain things that are individually extraordinarily important—namely, those complexes that are distinctive features in the psychology of the personality. This would also be of great assistance in pathology, since in this way we could find—in cases of hysteria, for example—valuable pointers to the pathogenic complexes of images of which the hysterical patient is not always aware.

604   To clarify matters more fully, I have, with the help of educated subjects who are also reasonably introspective, made a thorough analysis of individual associations, to which I should now like to refer.

605   *Subject No. 1:* a married woman who placed herself at my disposal in a most co-operative manner and gave me all the information I could possibly need. I am reporting on the experiment as fully as I can so that the reader may picture it as completely as possible.

The probable mean reaction-time for this experiment was 1.0 second.

1. head	-scarf	1.0
2. green	grass	0.8
3. water	-fall	1.0
4. to pierce	to cut	0.8
5. angel	-heart	0.8

---

[29] Ziehen first drew our attention to the fact that in cases of prolonged reaction-time a "relatively strong emotional charge" often occurred. Op. cit., 2nd contrib., p. 36.

[30] "The Associations of Normal Subjects," supra.

Up to this point the reactions followed without the slightest emotional charge, quite smoothly and impassively. R.5 is striking; the subject can for the moment give no justification or explanation of how she came to -*heart*, which she feels is a word-compound. Suddenly through her mind flashes "Engelhard," a name that had always been familiar to her. This is therefore an indirect association of the type known as displacement by sound similarity. We now come to the question of why this indirect association should have occurred so suddenly. As a result of our earlier investigations,[31] we find that under certain circumstances indirect associations are more often found with a state of disturbed attention. It may therefore be assumed that the distraction of the subject's attention can produce indirect associations. The subject repudiates any disturbance coming from without. Nor is she aware of any inner disturbance. When consciousness cannot furnish any data, an unconscious excitation may still have disturbed the reaction. The stimulus-word *angel*, however, was for this subject not emotionally hinged. As we know from earlier investigations, a preceding emotionally charged association can leave a trace in the unconscious and unconsciously constellate[32] the reaction, particularly when the preceding association had a strong feeling-tone. R.4, *to cut*, had evoked in the subject some slight anxiety, the image of blood,[33] etc. The subject is pregnant and now and again has feelings of anxious anticipation. Whether the image *blood* had determined the reaction *heart* I shall not try to decide.

The feeling-tone of *to cut* was according to the subject so slight and secondary that the connection did not strike her. It was for this reason that the extension of the reaction-time usual in similar situations failed to occur.

6. long	short	0.8
7. ship	sailing	0.8
8. to plough	field	1.0
9. wool	silk	1.0
10. friendly	charming	1.2
11. table	chair	1.2
12. to carry	to lift	1.2
13. state	to make	1.2
14. insolent	snobbish	1.2 *(trotzig/protzig)*

[31] Ibid., par. 449.
[32] On perseveration, cf. Müller and Pilzecker, "Experimentelle Beiträge zur Lehre von Gedächtnis" (1900).
[33] Cf. R.143, *blood*, infra.

236

(This rhyme is a constellation. The subject recalls that she once read it on one of my association-forms.)

15. to dance	to leap	0.8
16. lake	sea	0.8
17. ill	well	1.2
18. proud	fiery	1.2

The last two reactions show some (albeit slight) feeling-tone.

19. to cook	to learn	0.8
20. ink	black	1.0
21. evil	good	0.8
22. needle	thread	1.0
23. to swim	to learn	0.8

Here R.19 recurs with the same short reaction-time. The subject admits that she has not learned much about cooking and had never learned to swim at all well.

24. journey	Berlin	1.2

Constellation of a journey some months previously, the date of which, by the way, approximately coincides with the start of her pregnancy.

25. blue	heaven	0.8
26. bread	to eat	1.2
27. to threaten	fist	1.2
28. lamp	green	1.4

Here we find the first rather long time. The subject had hardly noticed her hesitation, nor had she been aware of any particular feeling-tone. The previous stimulus-word, *to threaten*, does, however, have something insidious to many subjects. If we think of the feeling of anxious anticipation mentioned earlier, we perhaps have a clue to the elucidation of this extended reaction-time; it is perhaps a perseveration. The feeling-tone in such cases need not appear with the previous reaction. In our experience, affective processes always take longer than purely associative processes, both to appear on the surface and to take their course. The feeling-tone lingers on, as can be observed in certain hysterics.

The reaction *green* is a constellation from her *domestic* life (lamp-shade).

29. rich	poor	1.0
30. tree	green	0.8

Here we have the same reaction as 28 with a very short interval, a phenomenon that may be accounted for by the fact that associative processes that have just come into consciousness tend to return, i.e., can very easily be repeated.[34]

Our earlier investigations[35] have also taught us that repetitions of a reaction are frequently based on a particular feeling-tone, in that the repeated words are associated with a feeling-toned complex. The feeling-tone pervading such a word is the mechanism that evokes it again and again in appropriate circumstances.

31.	to sing	can	2.4

A very superficial reaction, similar to *to learn* with *to cook* and *to swim*, with a strikingly long reaction-time. The subject is very musical, but has always regretted that she cannot sing, and indeed this has hurt her more than, for instance, her not being able to swim.

32.	sympathy	to have	1.0
33.	yellow	gold	1.0
34.	mountain	to climb	1.0
35.	to play	children	1.0
36.	salt	salty	1.4

In this reaction the subject comes up against a certain inhibition for the first time, whereas all the earlier reactions had followed easily. The subject explained that at first she did not understand the word *salt* at all and had had to make a deliberate effort to grasp it. In spite of the prolonged reaction-time and the exertion of attention, a very superficial reaction followed, which is determined to a considerable degree by sound. The subject cannot explain this disturbance. Let us look again at the previous reaction, *children*; this belongs quite clearly to the pregnancy-complex; the feeling-tone has persisted and caused the disturbance.

37.	new	old	1.0
38.	custom	habit	1.0
39.	to ride	to travel	1.0
40.	wall	-maps	1.0
41.	stupid	clever	1.0
42.	exercise-book	book	1.0
43.	to despise	*mépriser*	1.8

Once again a longer reaction-time and, also, a striking rendering of

---

[34] Cf. Müller and Pilzecker, op. cit.
[35] "The Associations of Normal Subjects," supra, pars. 350ff.

the reaction into French. The reaction is also very superficial and adds nothing new to the idea referred to by the stimulus-word.

To despise is, for the subject, accompanied by an unpleasant feeling-tone. Immediately after the reaction it occurred to her that she was momentarily afraid that her pregnancy might by its various effects cause her to lose her husband's regard. Then she immediately remembered a married couple who had at first been ideally happy and then had become estranged: the couple in Zola's novel *Vérité*. Hence the reaction's being in French.

These reminiscences, needless to say, were not conscious at the time of the reaction.

44. tooth	time[36]	1.0
45. correct	false	1.0
46. nation	faithful	1.4

Again a longer time with a slightly unpleasant feeling-tone. She thinks that some song contains the phrase "a faithful people," but has a feeling that there is something about it personally unpleasant to her.

The preceding reaction, which has no perceptible feeling-tone, is *false*; *loyal* is the opposite. This observation suffices to bring the subject to the correct explanation: the reaction *false* had stimulated her pregnancy-complex, and in particular her fear of her husband's estrangement.

47. to stink	to be scented	1.0
48. book	to read	1.0
49. unjust	just	0.8
50. frog	leg	1.2
51. to part	to avoid	0.8
52. hunger	thirst	0.8
53. white	black	1.0
54. ring	finger	1.0
55. to watch	to listen	1.0
56. pine	forest	1.0
57. dull	fine (weather)	1.0
58. plum	pear	1.0
59. to meet	sure	1.0
60. law	to keep	1.2
61. dear	man	1.2
62. glass	clear	1.0

[36] [This association derives from the German phrase "der Zahn der Zeit" = "the tooth (i.e., ravages) of time."]

The strong sound association of *clear* is probably also due to the previous reaction.

63. to argue	to quarrel	1.2
64. goat	bleats	1.2
65. big	little	0.8
66. potato	field	1.0
67. to paint	painter	1.0
68. part	piece	1.0
69. old	young	1.0
70. flower	red	0.6 *(Blume/rot)*

This notably short reaction-time is explained by the subject by the fact that the first syllable of the stimulus-word *Blu-me* had already caused that of *Blu-t* (blood); cf. 4 and 143. Here we have a kind of *assimilation* of the stimulus-word to the strong pregnancy-complex.

71. to beat	to stab	1.0
72. box	-bed	1.0
73. bright	brighter	1.4 *(hell/heller)*
74. family	father	1.4

These four reactions are interesting. It will be remembered that with 4 *to pierce/to cut* we came across the pregnancy-complex for the first time. Without the subject having had any idea that this reaction was important, we here have *to pierce* following immediately on the *Blu-me/Blut* association. The following R.72 also came quite smoothly without any feeling at all. The reaction itself is, however, striking. The subject, who occasionally visited our asylum, meant the deep beds used there—the so-called box-beds. She was somewhat puzzled by this explanation, because the expression "box-bed" was not particularly familiar to her. Following this somewhat unusual association, we have a sound association of relatively long duration, thus a phenomenon that we have already indicated earlier to be indicative of a complex. "Heller" (brighter) is the name of a person who was once important—though indirectly—to the subject. Quite probably no strongly emotional memories are connected with this name. There was only a very slight hesitation, implying a subjective feeling. For this reason, the supposition that the sound reaction is connected with the strange previous reaction does not seem to be entirely groundless. The reaction *bed* is later repeated with the clear impression of a word-combination in 199—*bone-bed (Knochen-bett)*, a meaningless combination inexplicable to the subject; if we consider a change of sound in view of her pregnancy-complex, the

association could be very significant—*Wochen-bett* (childbed).[36a]
If we take this hypothesis as a basis, the above series is explained in
the clearest way; again we have the pregnancy-complex with blood,
operation, childbed; the feeling-tone here becomes obviously stronger
and disturbs the following reaction (perhaps *bright* cannot be assimilated to the complex!); finally, we have *father*.

75. to wash	washerwoman	1.0
76. cow	stupid	0.8
77. strange	-ness	1.0
78. fortune	fortunate	0.6
79. to tell	mother	1.4
80. propriety	Ge-	1.2 *(Ge-)*
(*Anstand*)	usage	2.0 *(Sitte)*

R.78 is very short, which is rather striking in a stimulus-word that
could easily have stirred up the complex. The following reaction,
therefore, takes proportionately longer, 1.4 seconds, which up to
now has been symptomatic of a complex. The reaction *mother*
explains the prolonged time. R.80 is disturbed, not surprisingly, as
the complex was so obviously touched; only after 2 seconds do we
get the reaction *usage*, after the *Ge-* prefix first. In this the feeling-
tone of *mother* still perseverates in the subject. The subject cannot
find any connection between *propriety* and *Ge-*. Above all she cannot think what word she wanted to start with *Ge-*. We are thus
dependent only on suppositions. With 79 the pregnancy-complex
appeared again quite clearly. We have already seen on several occasions that it is characterized mainly by feelings of *anxiety* and
apprehension. We have also already seen that the first syllable of a
stimulus-word is assimilated to the complex (*bloom/blood*); is the
first syllable of *Anstand* (propriety) = *Anst*, assimilated as *Angst*
(fear) and then *Ge-* = *Geburt* (birth)? This hypothesis immediately
struck the subject as near the truth. This construction may well
appear to many to be made in the manner of the augurs; I would
not record it here if I had not come across many analogous phenomena in both healthy and sick subjects.

81. narrow	-minded	0.6
82. brother	sister	0.8
83. to damage	to avoid	1.2 *(schaden/*
		meiden)

36a [Cf. "The Psychology of Dementia Praecox," par. 110, where the same association is rendered in translation as *mild / bed*; *child / bed*.]

This is very reminiscent of 51, *scheiden/meiden* (to part/to avoid). Has *schaden* perhaps been repressed by the complex as too unpleasant and been assimilated as *scheiden*? Repressive assimilations of this nature frequently occur in hysterics. The subject is quite unable to explain this.

84. stork	to bring	3.4

This abnormal time is quite clearly caused by the complex.

85. false	cat	1.0
86. fear	to have	1.0
87. kiss	me	1.2

The emphasis on the ego in R.87 could perhaps also be determined by the critical reaction to 86.

88. conflagration	fire	1.2
89. dirty	yellow	1.0
90. door	closed	0.8
91. to choose	choice	1.2
92. hay	grass	1.0
93. still	quiet	0.8
94. scorn	derision	1.0
95. to sleep	to stay awake	1.0
96. month	May	1.0
97. coloured	blue	1.2
98. dog	cat	1.0
99. to talk	speak	1.0
100. coal	dust	1.0
101. moderate	drinking	1.0
102. lid	eye-	1.0
103. to suppose	to believe	1.2
104. ache	heart	0.8 *(Schmerz/Herz)*

This rhyme, which has a relatively short reaction-time, is stated by the subject to be a mere catch-phrase.

105. lazy	sluggish	1.0
106. moon	-calf	1.0
107. to laugh	to cry	1.0
108. coffee	to drink	1.0
109. wide	narrow	1.0
110. air	thick	1.0
111. to carry	to lift	1.0
112. plate	round	0.8

R.110 is somewhat unusual; it seems as if the constellation *wide/ narrow* has had a particularly powerful influence. Does it perhaps echo through to R.112?

The next following reactions are entirely objective in character— neither the subject nor the observer noticed anything special about them. The times are never more than 1.2 seconds. We shall therefore pass them over.

143. blood	red	0.6	
144. to let (a house)	to let	1.2	
	to avoid	2.0	
145. caution	leniency	1.0	*(Vorsicht/ Nachsicht)*

R.143 is very quick. This is the well known reaction which already occurred at 70 *(Blume)*. It is followed by a longer time and a repetition of the stimulus-word—the only one in the whole series. R.145 is likewise superficial, not even meaningful but only linked in form and sound.

Because they are of no importance I am omitting the subsequent associations.

162. distinguished	noble	1.2	
163. tube	sly	0.8	*(Schlauch/ schlau)*

The subject explained that at the time of the second of these two reactions she still felt the persistent influence of *distinguished*. The lady had previously been in rather better financial circumstances and occasionally feels this loss.

172. to turn	round	1.4

The cause of this longer time is obscure if *round* does not have the supposed emotional influence mentioned above. The subject has no explanation to offer.

175. trust	me	1.4

Here again we have the fear of the estrangement of her husband— associated with her complex.

190. to bring	something	1.2
191. inn	The Stork	1.0

What *something* represents is clear from the subsequent reaction.

195. mirror	shining	1.4
198. to punish	prison	1.4

Neither of these long reaction-times can be satisfactorily explained. The subject told us that on 195 first the image *glatt* (smooth) occurred to her but this became *glänzend* (shining). It is hard to say why *glatt* should have been suppressed.

Apart from the fact that she had been aware of a slight hesitation, the subject had no explanation for R.198. Even if we cannot think of a plausible explanation, we may, in the light of previous experience, be fairly sure that some kind of feeling-toned complex is at the root of it. As a later example will show, it does not need to be anything actual, but can be an old reminiscence that has apparently vanished a long time ago.

199. bone	-bed	1.0	*(Knochen/-bett)*

Compare the remarks on 72. The interesting point in this case is that the subject had not the faintest suspicion about the significance of the association.

The following associations should be mentioned:

164. to love	faithful	1.0
167. bill (of exchange)	false	1.0
181. duty	faithful	0.8
187. snake	deceitful	0.8

45 had *false* as reaction in 1.0 seconds, 46 *faithful* in 1.4. These words, for which the subject obviously has a predilection, appear to recur with gradually decreasing reaction-times.[37] It is also interesting that apparently words representing a complex tend to occur automatically in places where the meaning no longer warrants it; this is not the case here, but we have demonstrated it in an earlier investigation.[38]

606   The analysis of the reactions of this subject have shown that times of over 1.2 seconds, with the exception of a few reactions quoted above, can be attributed to the influence of a feeling-toned complex, for two reasons.

(1) The association through which the complex is constellated has a prolonged reaction-time.

(2) The association immediately following that through which the complex has been constellated has an extended reaction-time owing to the reverberation of the feeling-tone.

[37] In a case of this kind, more exact timing would be desirable.
[38] "The Association of Normal Subjects," supra, pars. 211f.

607　　Apart from those with longer reaction-times, there are numerous other associations with complex-constellations. In general, reactions with a powerful feeling-tone and a distinct indication of a complex show longer reaction-times. The meaning of the association is grasped with a fair consistency only when a very strong and differentiated feeling-tone, or a very characteristic form of the reaction, brings one complex into consciousness. In the reactions given, this only occurred once, with *stork / to bring*. In all other reactions the feeling-tone, or the special form of the reaction, provided merely pointers to the subsequent identification of the complex.

608　　At the time, only the aspect of the complex appearing in the reaction was available to consciousness. From these facts it becomes evident that consciousness plays only a minor role in the process of association.

609　　All our thinking and acting, the vast bulk of which appears to us to be conscious, actually consist of all those little bits that are finely determined by innumerable impulses completely outside consciousness. To our ego-consciousness the association-process seems to be its own work, subject to its judgment, free will, and concentration; in reality, however, as our experiment beautifully shows, ego-consciousness is merely the marionette that dances on the stage, moved by a concealed mechanism.[39]

610　　An analysis of this series of tests shows the influence of the complex on association. Although, as people are fond of saying, associations are made at one's own discretion and the subject can say whatever he wishes, nevertheless he does not in fact say what he wishes but is *compelled* to betray precisely what he feels most sure of concealing. The reactions, therefore, are by no means random thoughts but simply symptomatic acts,[40] directed by a psychic factor that can behave like an independent being. The feeling-toned complex, for the time being split off from consciousness, exercises an influence that constantly and successfully competes with the intentions of the ego-complex; in spite of the rejecting and repressing attitude of the ego-complex, it brings about subjective and treacherous reactions and arouses associations the meaning of which is utterly

[39] From this we can also gather that those who equate psyche with consciousness actually take *partem pro toto*.
[40] Cf. Freud, *The Psychopathology of Everyday Life* (orig. 1904).

unexpected by the ego-complex. Thus we find a series of intimate secrets divulged in the associations of our subject, and it is not only complexes referring to her actual situation, but the most important complexes, which form the content of her joys and sorrows. At the time of the test we find the most powerful complex to be the psychic equivalent of pregnancy, round which revolve her anxious anticipation and her love for her husband, coupled with slightly jealous fears. This complex is of an erotic nature, and still active; it is therefore understandably in the foreground. Not less than 18 per cent of the associations can safely be related to this.[41] Besides this we find some other complexes, of considerably lower intensity: loss of former prosperity, some deficiencies felt to be disagreeable (singing, swimming, cooking), and finally an erotic complex dating back many years to her youth, which could be shown to be the cause of only a single association. (Unfortunately I have had to leave this one out, out of respect for the subject herself.) The probable mean of this subject was 1.0 second. 30.5 per cent of reactions exceeded this mean, 20.5 per cent took 1.2 seconds. Of these, 32 per cent could clearly be attributed to the influence of a complex. 6 per cent of reactions took 1.4 seconds, 75 per cent of which were certainly conditioned by the complex. 3 per cent were in excess of 1.4 seconds and all of these were certainly due to the influence of a known complex.

611   *Subject No. 2*: an educated man of middle age. His reaction-type is as objective and superficial as that of Subject No. 1. I shall, therefore, confine myself to giving only his critical reactions. The subject is a physician and often takes part in our experiments, which he follows with interest.

The probable mean of the series of tests is 1.2 seconds.

1. head	part	1.4
2. green	blue	1.0
3. water	to clean	2.6

The stimulus-word immediately aroused an unpleasant feeling-tone suggesting something sexual, coupled with a sense of inhibition. Immediately after his reaction, the subject clearly recognized that *water* had been understood in the sense of *urine*.

| 4. to pierce | to strike | 1.0 |
| 5. angel | pure | 1.0 |

[41] Only 4% of the associations can safely be related to other complexes.

6. long	large	1.2
7. ship	large	1.0

Here we have a distinct perseveration. With *large*, R.6, there was at first a clearly sexual feeling-tone, followed by the second reaction and immediately afterwards the reason for this was clearly recognized. It concerned a recollection: the subject had heard from us that certain women patients frequently associate sexual implications to the word "long."

8. to plough	to turn up the soil	1.0	
9. wool	sheep	1.2	
10. friendly	..., busy	1.2	*(tötig, tätig)*
11. table	fish	0.8	*(Tisch/Fisch)*

R.10 is clearly disturbed. We have here a slip of the tongue.[42] The subject immediately corrected himself with *tätig*. At this stage he felt a vaguely unpleasant sensation, somewhat like an inner restlessness, which persisted during the following reaction. Hence the unmotivated rhyme. *Freundlich/tätig* (friendly/busy) is striking, and the subject is unable to explain it. The slip of the tongue that produced *tötig* instead of *tätig* gave the impression that the reaction should really have been *böse* (bad). But even this reaction was incomprehensible to him (for the probable explanation, see below, 86).

15. stem	long	1.2	
16. to dance	to steam	1.8	*(tanzen/ dampfen)*
17. lake	large	1.2	

In R.15 we once again have *long* with its sexual tone and almost simultaneously the reminiscence mentioned above. R.16 is due to similarity of sound and has an abnormally long reaction-time. The sexual tone of R.15 is persisting, with an admixture of irritation, and brings about the repetition of the earlier association *long, large*.

18. ill	poor	1.2	
19. pride	bolt	1.6	*(Stolz/Bolz)*

Poor is accompanied by a vague feeling of dislike, but there is no particular image connected with this. *Pride* is felt to be even less pleasant and we had here a feeling of rejection and restraint. The meaningless rhyme and the prolonged time are doubly determined. The subject has financial worries that have been troubling him for

---

42 [*Tötig*, not actually a word, suggests *töten*, 'to kill.']

some time. He had been accused frequently, particularly in the past, of pride. This reproach, converging with the business of the money, forms a particularly painful contrast. This connection was of course only realized after the reaction was given.

20. to cook	well	1.0	
21. ink	to come	1.4	(*Tinte/ kommen*)

The association is the phrase "in die Tinte kommen" (to get into hot water); it has an unpleasant tinge and is related by the subject to the money business. There is also an immediate recollection of an erotic complex, dating back several years, which has associations of unpleasure.

24. to swim	well	1.2
25. journey	gay	1.6

Numerous indistinct recollections of travelling with predominantly pleasant associations.

26. blue	lake	1.2
27. bread	daily	2.0

Bread excites a slightly unpleasant feeling—the impression is almost like that of *poor* and there is an accompanying feeling of restriction. Later this is seen to have a clear connection with his financial worries.

28. to threaten	evil	1.4

A very unpleasant tone, connected subsequently with the memory of the erotic complex already mentioned and a feeling of guilt.

29. lamp	shade	1.2
30. rich	poor	1.4

Poor again has the suggestion of unpleasure and again recalls the money business.

31. tree	trunk	1.2
32. to sing	to spring	1.8

Tree again evokes the sexual tone of *long*, for the reasons given above, coupled with irritation; to this is to be related the rhyme and the long reaction-time.

33. sympathy	the poor	1.4	
34. yellow	much	1.2	(*gelb/viel*)

The poor again arouses the money-complex, this time with very distinct feeling-tone. *Gelb* (yellow) is at once assimilated as *Geld* (money), in spite of the stimulus-word being correctly understood. The money-complex has forestalled the ego-complex by means of the revealing *much*.

36. to play	ball	1.2	
37. salt	dripping	1.4	(*Salz/Schmalz*)

The association *to play/ball*, which in itself is quite innocuous, immediately acquires an erotic feeling-tone, since the word *ball* changed in meaning to *dance*. Here the erotic complex reappeared; hence the rhyme and longer reaction-time in the following association. Needless to say that at the instant of the reaction the trend of thought broadly outlined here was not conscious, but only indicated by fleeting feelings. The awakening of the associated images occurs as a rule afterwards, when the subject's attention is especially directed to the feeling-tones that appear in their place.

38. new	old	1.2	(*neu/alt*)

The *a* in *alt* was conspicuously prolonged, giving rise to the suggestion that perhaps the reaction should have been *arm* (poor) but it came out as *alt* (old). The money-complex had recently become more acute.

39. morality	immorality	1.8

A slight hesitation—a vague suggestion of guilt in the enunciation of *immorality*. The erotic complex once again.

40. to ride	to drive	1.4
41. wall	place	1.8
42. stupid	clumsy	2.0

The subject can offer no explanation for R.41; he feels as though it should be "no place in the sun." A somewhat painful tone to R.42 leads straight to the money-complex with the clear recognition that *to drive* is conditioned by the complex, although the feeling-tone peculiar to the complex has emerged only with R.42. The reaction *place* belongs to the money-complex rather than to *wall*. R.42 also makes the erotic complex vibrate slightly.

43. exercise-book	book	1.4	
44. to despise	to respect	1.2	
45. tooth	money	1.4	(*Zahn/Geld*)

To respect seems to have struck very close to the money-complex because *Zahn* (tooth), in spite of correct interpretation, is assimilated as *zahlen* (to pay), hence *money*. Here again, we have the money-complex forestalling the ego-complex.

46. correct	incorrect	1.2
47. people	poor	1.8

Again the delayed reaction with the money-complex.

60. to hit	marksman	1.2
61. law	not set	4.8

At 61 there is an inexplicable feeling of restraint which for a long time does not permit of any reaction, and then finally a disturbed, meaningless reaction which seems as if it may perhaps be a defensive expression. Later a whole series of painful memories came to mind all of which dealt with actions that, like the erotic complex, did not conform to the laws of morality.

The following reaction

62. dear	good	2.0

is also under the influence of these memories of past immorality.

69. part	part of the body	1.8

Here again we have the sexual constellation, as in R.6 and 15.

76. to wash	filth[43]	1.6

A slight feeling of guilt and penitence. Later, the erotic complex. For the coarse mode of expression, see 90.

78. strange	newcomer	2.0

First the feeling that the reaction would be *poor*, but then the re-action *Neuling* (newcomer) predetermined by 38 (*neu/alt* [*arm*]). Of course the reaction followed without any conscious awareness of this constellation. *Strange* has again hit the money-complex. One can see how this complex sends out its *poor* at every opportunity.

79. fortune	misfortune	1.4

is predetermined by the preceding reaction.

80. to tell	mother	1.2
81. propriety	not proper	3.6
82. narrow	narrow-minded	1.8

[43] [*Dreck*, which also means excrement.]

R.80 followed without any particular feeling-tone. On the other hand *propriety* immediately called up inhibitions with unpleasant feeling, which clearly persisted throughout the following association. Afterwards memories of various scenes from childhood which are clearly constellated by *mother*. It was a matter of a few impressive moments when his mother in rightful anger had maintained that he was not a decent person and never would be. One scene was particularly clear when the subject in his teens had behaved coarsely and indecently towards a lady. This memory led again immediately to the erotic complex and here the subject had something similar to reproach himself with. It must therefore be this complex that is concealed at the root of this long reaction-time, and of the various screen-memories (Freud).

| 86. false | evil | 1.4 |

Here we have *evil* repeated for the third time. (In the entire series it occurs six times and *good* or *well* five.) *Evil* always brings with it the feeling of guilt that is peculiar to the erotic complex. As you can see, this word, together with *good*, has a similar tendency to increase in frequency, as *poor* does for the money-complex. (*Poor* occurs four times in a manifest and three times in a repressed form.) The first time *evil* appeared was in 10, but at that stage it was obviously repressed, as there are strong inhibitions against the erotic complex in the subject's present emotional life.

| 89. fire | sea | 1.8 *(Brand/Meer)* |

The stimulus was correctly understood, but changed immediately into *Brandung* (surf); hence the association of *sea*, with a somewhat longer reaction-time. *Brand* (fire) was therefore assimilated. The previous association does not constellate this assimilation. *Brand*, however, has an unpleasant tone and this is associated in his mind immediately with the meaning of acute alcoholism and, together with the latter, the memory of his having once been in that state, which aroused painful feelings. This time the ego-complex has forestalled the old but still active memory, which has assimilated the stimulus-word in a convenient sense and has thereby drawn a veil over the painful memory, i.e., has hidden it from consciousness. This mechanism (the censor in the Freudian sense)[44] plays a very prominent role in hysteria. It must be emphasized that it is not at all a function of consciousness but an automatic mechanism that regulates what may or may not come into the conscious mind.

| 90. dirty | filthy *(dreckig)* | 1.4 |

[44] Cf. *The Interpretation of Dreams* (orig. 1900).

The coarse wording of this reaction is determined by the moral feeling of repugnance that is tied up with the erotic complex.

> 91. door   to show   1.4

This reaction too, negative and dismissive as it is, is determined by the same feeling.

> 92. to elect   *Maire* (mayor)   2.2

With *to elect* we meet a new complex. This is a matter of hopes of promotion, of *mehr* (i.e., more) from several points of view. It is at the same time the hope of holding a leading, no longer a subordinate, position. Thus the determination of *Maire* is not purely a matter of sound, but also of sense in a symbolic form. The right reaction would have been *manager*. This word, however, is associated with the secret wish and for that reason is subject to the inhibition that suppresses the wish itself. Thus instead of the correct reaction we have an image associated with it that is outwardly determined by the word *mehr* (more), which itself is characteristic of the momentary mood. This process has great similarities to the hysterical talking at cross purposes of the Ganser syndrome,[45] or perhaps even more to the associating at cross purposes of dementia praecox, in which this kind of metaphor is particularly common. Analogous phenomena occur relatively frequently in everyday life— I mean the word-and-melody automatisms. The following good example was given me by a lady I know. She told me that for some days the name *Taganrog* had been, as it were, on the tip of her tongue but she had not the remotest idea where it came from. I asked her about her emotional experiences and repressed wishes of the recent past. After some hesitation she told me that she very much wanted a housecoat (*Morgenrock*) but that her husband had not shown the desired interest. *Morgen-rock : Tag-an-rog*—you can see that the two words are related partially through meaning and partially through sound. The appearance of the Russian name could be attributed to the fact that the lady had met someone from Taganrog at about the same time.[46] Vast numbers of similar combinations can very easily be demonstrated, if one were to take the trouble of getting to the bottom of all the tunes one hums or whistles to oneself or hears from others. A colleague on his hospital rounds caught a fleeting glimpse of a nurse who was allegedly preg-

---

[45] Riklin, "Zur Psychologie hysterischer Dämmerzustände und des Ganser'schen Symptoms" (1904).

[46] A similar word-automatism (Bunau-Varilla) is reported in "The Associations of Normal Subjects," *supra*, par. 451.

nant and caught himself a moment or so later in the act of whistling the tune of: "Es waren zwei Königskinder, die hatten einander so lieb" (There were two royal children, who loved each other so, etc.), although his conscious mind was occupied with something completely different. Another colleague betrayed to me the sad end of a love-affair by a succession of melody automatisms.

One can see from these examples roughly the course taken by thought processes when they lack conscious awareness. Each association occurring in consciousness evokes as it were an echo of similarities and analogies that fades out through all stages of similarity of sound. The best examples are furnished by dreams.

| 95. mockery | scorn | 1.4 |
| 99. dog | dead | 1.6 |

This reaction amazed the subject. He could not understand how he could have arrived at this unusual association. The somewhat long time taken suggests a feeling-tone; this is at first described by the subject as indistinct, and then later as sad. The cue *sad* then reminds him of the incident at the root of this feeling. Some twenty years previously he had had to have a dog he was very fond of destroyed. This loss had been *sad* to him for some considerable time.

| 102. moderate | immoderate | 1.6 |

The longish time of this superficial reaction is explained by its connection with R.89 (*Brand*).

| 104. to suppose | to believe | 2.0 |

Suppose is a suggestive word as a stimulus and there are few subjects who do not feel affected by it. In this case it hit the erotic complex.

| 105. pain | scorn | 1.2 |
| 108. to laugh | to chatter | 2.8 (*lachen/ schwatzen*) |

The *sch* of the reaction *schwatzen* was rather prolonged. First for a moment *schmerzen* (pain) came to mind momentarily though clearly, hence the length of time. *Schmerzen* was at once involuntarily suppressed. The feeling-tone expressed had a tinge of grief. The subject admits having an almost morbid sensitivity to mockery. 95: *mockery/scorn*, 105: *pain/scorn*, and 108: *laugh/pain*, are now closely linked. The determination of *schwatzen* is on the one hand alliteration and on the other semantic relationship: *über Einen schwatzen* (to gossip about someone).

| 120. to create | to operate | 2.0 |

Here we have the complex of his professional life which produces the lengthened reaction-time.

127. resin	tree	2.0	(*Harz/Baum*)

First, a feeling occurred as if the association was *hart/arm* (hard/poor), in which *arm* was almost spoken out loud. This is a reappearance of the money-complex.

Also the following reaction:

128. to wake	to awaken	1.6

is therefore still very superficial, with relatively long time.

130. bad	evil	0.8	
131. briefcase	wood	0.8	(*Mappe/Holz*)

The subject takes *Mappe* in the sense of a briefcase in which he usually fetches (*holen*) money. The reaction *Holz* (wood) is quite meaningless and the subject was amazed at first until he remembered the meaning that he had attributed to *Mappe*. *Holz* conceals *holen*, which obviously belongs to the repressed money-complex.

148. forget	-fulness	2.0	
149. drum	beat	1.2	
150. free	-dom	1.2	
151. wagon	-barricade	3.0	(*Wagen/-burg*)

148 has a very unpleasant feeling-tone. Nothing particular was reported about 149 and 150, but at 151 there is a strong but inexplicable inhibition. *To forget* awakens the memory of an event several years ago, when he broke with a faithless friend. 149 is an echo of the song "Der treue Kamerad" (The faithful comrade): "Die Trommel schlug zum Streite/Er ging an meiner Seite, etc." (The drum beat for the battle, He walked by my side). 150 hints at the break. 151: *wagon* appears to have been assimilated only with difficulty. The compound *Wagen-burg* is strange, but became intelligible through the subject's remark that the place where he first recognized the friend's false-heartedness was Augs*burg*. All these data were at the time of the reaction unconscious. The complex betrayed itself at first only by the slightly unpleasant but otherwise indefinable feeling shown in 148. The connection of this series was only established later.

153. impudence	confounded	2.0
154. quick	-ness	0.6

R.153 belongs to the same mood as the reactions given above. (N.B. The analysis of these was undertaken only on completion of the entire series.) This mood is the anger about the insolence of the false friend. This strong feeling-tone seems to have persisted as far as 154.

167. change	of time	1.8

The stimulus-word has again hit the money-complex—hence the long reaction-time.

184. deaf	to fly	2.6 (taub/fliegen)

The subject has assimilated *taub* (deaf) as *Taube* (dove) although he did understand the stimulus-word correctly. (He is familiar with the stimulus-words and has experimented with them himself on various occasions.) The reaction-time is very long. *Deaf* hits on a fear-complex of limited range. He suffers from recurrent catarrh of the Eustachian tubes and his hearing in one ear has therefore deteriorated. He connects this fact with the fear, often exaggerated, of becoming totally deaf. *Deaf* thus has too unpleasant a tone and is therefore quickly suppressed.

190. to bring	money	1.2
191. vocabulary[47]	to fetch	2.2

The last reaction is senseless, but can be explained as a perseveration of the money-complex stimulated by *to bring*.

195. mirror	soul	1.8
196. full	filth	1.4
197. understand- ing	good	1.6
198. to punish	for evil	2.2
200. beautiful	good	1.6

R.195 for some unknown reason is somewhat inhibited. Perhaps "mirror of the soul" already presaged the ethical tone of the following reaction. With *full* it is quite clear: "the soul is full of filth." This coarse expression again reveals the revulsion already mentioned (90). The following reaction, *good*, is loosely connected with its stimulus-word and is repeated at the next opportunity (200). Each time it represents the erotic complex.

R.198 is clearly influenced by the complex.

612   In contrast to the case of the previous subject, we have here a whole series of feeling-toned complexes, which are interconnected only slightly or not at all. Whereas with the female

47 [*Wortschaft*, not an actual word; apparently a mistake for *Wortschatz*, 'vocabulary.']

subject (No. 1) the sexual complex (pregnancy) with its various branches (fear, jealousy, etc.) is predominant, with the male subject (No. 2) the sexual complexes play a less important part. From personal respect for the subject I cannot give all the reactions. It is easy enough to demonstrate, however:

1. Sexual complexes:
An erotic complex, belonging to the past, now over and done with, which is expressed almost exclusively in ethical feeling-constellations (revulsion, remorse).

An actual erotic complex, expressed merely through erotic feeling-constellations (not reported).

At least three sexually charged ideas, independent of each other.

2. The money-complex.

3. Ambition—with at least four secondary memory-complexes.

4. Personal sensitivity—with at least three secondary memory-complexes.

5. Friendship.

6. Two feeling-toned reminiscences, independent of each other (dead dog, deafness).

613   Thus we have about ten complexes, independent of each other, that are touched on in the series of experiments. Subject No. 2 is a few years older than No. 1. In the latter case, as was mentioned, 18 per cent of the associations were to be attributed to the sexual complex, whereas only 4 per cent came under the influence of other emotions. On the other hand, with subject No. 2, 53 per cent of the associations can be related to the influences of complexes. This great number of constellations does not in any way indicate that the analysis was taken further, or that subject No. 2 gave fuller information than No. 1, but it is also to be recognized objectively that subject No. 2 (at least at the time of the experiment) was more emotional than No. 1. We recognize this from the numerous disturbed reactions and the striking assimilations and repressions.[48]

48 Cf. also the "complex-characteristics" in our earlier investigation: "The Associations of Normal Subjects," supra, par. 417.

614   Of the 53 per cent of the associations mentioned, only 10 per cent can be attributed directly to the sexual complex, namely the actual erotic complex, 11.5 per cent to the money-complex, 2.5 per cent to ambition, 4.5 per cent to personal sensitivity, 3 per cent to the broken friendship; to the erotic complex of the past, which is only betrayed by feelings of revulsion and remorse, 9 per cent can be related, and 12.5 per cent are connected to about six smaller, more or less separate emotional complexes. Thus with the male subject the sexual complex as such is very much in the background against the many other influences (10 : 43).

615   This case shows us even more than the preceding one just how much of the individual personality is contained in the associations. The experiment provides data about a whole series of highly important psychological contents; it gives us as it were a cross-section of the actual personality from a psychological point of view.

616   *Subject No. 3:* a youngish educated man.[49] I am limiting myself in this case entirely to the critical associations and am reporting on it mainly to show again what in principle emerged in the two preceding cases. The probable mean time for this subject is 1.6 seconds.

1. head	neck	1.2
2. green	mouse	0.8
3. water	green	1.0

What strikes one in this series is the peculiar reaction *mouse* and the perseveration of *green*. *Neck* is a reverberation from the day before the experiment when the subject had seen a film about the death of Marie Antoinette. The subject is not sure where *mouse* comes from, he only has the feeling that it is a slip of the tongue and supposes it should have been *neck (Hals)* or *house.*

4. to pierce	to fence	1.2
5. angel	house	1.6

Here we have, with a long reaction-time, the reaction *house* assumed in 2, and now the memory comes back. The subject's grandfather had often in times past sung the song "Es geht durch alle Lande—ein Engel still" (A silent angel walks through every land,

49 [This case is also discussed in "The Psychological Diagnosis of Evidence," infra.]

etc.). Just as frequently he would sing: "Mein Häuschen steht im Grünen" (My little house stands in the greenwood, etc.).

A series of feeling-toned images, only some of which are pleasant, are associated with these songs. Hence the perseveration of *green* and the slip of the tongue *mouse*.

13. state	church	1.8

This reaction is somewhat hesitant since *church* represents the sizeable complex of a rather strong religious attitude.

16. to dance	not	1.8

This reaction really is "I cannot dance," to which a very unpleasant feeling is connected, for the subject has experienced a disappointment in love, which a friend who could dance well has been spared.

18. ill	not	1.6

Here again a stimulus-word is felt to apply to himself: he is *not ill* from despair over the unfortunate ending of the romance.

22. angry	friendly	1.8
23. needle	nail	1.2 (*Nadel/Nagel*)

Angry arouses the feeling of jealous animosity that the subject feels towards a certain rival. The sound association that follows is conditioned by the perseveration of this feeling-tone.

30. rich	rather	2.8
31. tree	branches	1.6

R.30 refers to the match that did not materialize, hence the long reaction-time. The next reaction is still somewhat long and has a rather stilted and artificial character; it also seemed to the subject to have a rather ironic tone which holds for the following reactions, too:

32. to sing	beautiful	1.4
33. pity	absolutely not	1.8

by which he means that he does not deserve any pity because everyone forges his own fate.

44. detest	rascals	5.0 (*Kerle*)
47. people	religion	1.6
48. to stink	abominable	1.0
50. unfair	atrocious	1.8

R.44, *rascals*, means the Jews. The lady concerned is Jewish. *People* again arouses the image *Jews* but this is repressed. *Religion* comes in in its place because the religion of his beloved had aroused scruples in the religious-minded subject. The following feeling-toned reactions refer to the complex rather than to the stimulus-words. (Similarly in subject No. 2 a coarse reaction betrayed the affect.)

54. white	snow	1.8

A feeling of "having finished" or "death"; refers to the love-complex.

61. law	absolute	1.4

Here we again have the reaction of R.33 expressing the same feeling: "it is the law, it must be so."

62. dear	beautiful	1.2
66. tall	fine	1.2

Both reactions have an ironical flavour and relate to the complex.

74. wild	animal	1.8

Wild (dial., "angry") he applies to himself on account of the complex.

75. family	house	1.0

House seems to represent the complex of all family memories. (Also in *to cook/house*.) Here we have a relatively short reaction-time.

79. luck	game	1.8

Clearly refers to the love-complex.

80. to tell	to talk	1.6 *(erzählen/talk)*

The reaction is in English. We have already seen that French reactions are suspect; this English one too refers to the complex. The subject at first wanted to tell the story of his disappointment to his brother, who lives in America, but then decided against this. Hence the English form.

83. brother	sister	2.0 *(Bruder/sister)*

Again an English form with a long reaction-time! *Brother* has probably subconsciously awakened the image of the earlier reaction. *Sister* comes because his sister at that time was on the point of leaving for a French boarding-school in the same way as his brother had left some time earlier for America. This analogy has condensed itself into *sister*.

| 88. to kiss | absolutely | 1.6 |

Absolutely is the key-word to the love-complex.

| 91. door | mouse | 1.6 |

The slip of the tongue of R.2 reappears, probably to mask *house*, which stands for the complex.

| 92. choose | Kaposi[50] |

Actually the word *caprice* came up momentarily as the reaction, but was immediately suppressed and altered into *Kaposi*. *Caprice* was the choice of the lady in question. *Kaposi* is only an example of similarity in sound and is constellated by a conversation of a few days earlier in which Kaposi was mentioned.

| 105. pain | kissing | 1.0 |
| 106. lazy | sow | 1.4 |

The coarser expression of the last reaction is caused by the feeling of anger perseverating from R.105.

| 115. intention | kissing | 1.8 (*Absicht/ küssen*) |

Absicht he immediately assimilated as *absolut*, which refers to the complex; he then reacted as if this were the meaning of the stimulus-word.

125. purpose	absolutely	
	none	1.2
126. hot	yes	2.2
134. worthy	daft	2.0
135. danger	glad	1.4
136. high	no, low	2.8
140. to mix	blood	2.0
143. blood	to mix	1.4

These reactions are all sometimes more, sometimes less clearly constellated by the love-complex, and in this naturally the constellating factor was not a clear image, but only a certain not very distinct mood.

| 144. to let | family | 1.6 |

[50] [Famous Viennese dermatologist (1837–1902).]

For a moment *house* loomed up but was repressed and replaced by the somewhat striking reaction *family*. This is association 75, which is again suddenly taken up to mask the word *house*, which represents the complex.

145. caution   intention   2.0 (*Vorsicht/*
                                                          Absicht)

Here clearly *absolut* came first but was inhibited and masked by *Absicht* through a sound association—perhaps association also contributed.

160. to wish   absolutely not   1.8

617   I shall not add any more examples; they do not in principle add anything new, only confirm what we have already established with the previous cases.

618   The love-complex is clearly in the foreground with this subject. At least 52 per cent of the associations can be referred to it with certainty. The family-complex can be demonstrated in 11 per cent of the associations. Now and again there is evidence in 7 per cent of the associations of a complex of ambitious strivings. Numerous individual feeling-toned reminiscences can be demonstrated in 27 per cent of the associations. The general probable mean time in this case is 1.6 seconds. 31 per cent of the reaction-times exceed this mean. 17 per cent amount to 1.8 seconds. Of these 85 per cent are certainly constellated by a complex, whereas in 15 per cent this influence is doubtful or not demonstrated. 4.5 per cent of the associations took 2.0 seconds. 89 per cent of these can with certainty be traced back to the influence of a complex, whereas this influence is uncertain in 11 per cent. 9 per cent of the associations took over 2.0 seconds. All these can be attributed to the influence of a complex.

619   It is unnecessary to add more examples, for one would constantly have to repeat oneself. As far as our experience goes, the complex-phenomena are the same with all subjects. Only the type of complex, naturally, varies with sex and educational level.[51]

51 The concept of *repression*, which I use on many occasions in my analyses, requires a brief explanation. In Freud's works this concept (which in any case the meaning of the word itself indicates) has the character of an active function, frequently a function of consciousness. In hysteria one may, however, get the

620   The perseveration of a feeling-tone deserves attention. As is well known, perseveration plays a particularly important part in the pathology of the process of association. Investigations made with normal subjects might be of some help in elucidating the nature of morbid perseveration. In our experiments the perseveration of a feeling-tone occurred so often that we were able to express it statistically to a certain extent. For example, subject No. 2 showed 32 reaction-times of over 1.6 seconds, of which 16 were themselves followed by longer reaction-times. In 10 cases, only the subsequent reaction was prolonged, in 3 the two following, and once in each case the three, four, and five subsequent reaction-times were prolonged. As can be seen from this survey, we quite often observe a discontinuous decrease in the reaction-times. I have seen a quite similar but even clearer discontinuous decrease in some cases of hysteria and dementia praecox, and mostly at points suspect of complex.

621   To summarize:

(1) From the figures given, it follows that relatively long reaction-times are almost without exception caused by the intervention of a strong feeling-tone.

(2) Strong feeling-tones as a rule belong to extensive and personally important complexes.

(3) The reaction can be an association belonging to a complex of this nature and take its feeling-tone from this complex, though the complex need not be conscious. The *constellation* (Ziehen) of an association is mostly unconscious (or not-conscious); the constellating complex here plays the part of a quasi-independent entity—a "second consciousness."

(4) The feeling-tone can unconsciously also influence the next reaction, in which several phenomena are to be observed:

---

impression that *repression* equals deliberate forgetting. With normal subjects it might, however, be a more passive "sliding into the background"; at least here repression seems to be something unconscious, to which we can only indirectly attribute the character of something willed or something *wished*. If, nevertheless, I speak of repressing or, better, concealing, this can be taken as a metaphor from the psychology of the conscious. Essentially it comes to the same thing because objectively it does not matter one way or the other whether a psychic process is conscious or unconscious. (Cf. Bleuler, "Versuch einer naturwissenschaftlichen Betrachtung der psychologischen Grundbegriffe" (1894).)

(a) The reaction influenced by a perseverating feeling-tone has a prolonged reaction-time.

(b) The reaction is still an association belonging to the group of images of the preceding complex.

(c) The reaction is abnormal in character: it can (i) be disturbed through a slip of the tongue or through repetition of the stimulus-word; (ii) be abnormally superficial (sound reactions).

(5) The feeling-tones in question are mostly unpleasant.

(6) The characteristics of an unconsciously constellating complex are: long reaction-time, unusual reaction, failures, perseveration, stereotyped repetition of the stimulus-word ("complex-representative"), translation into foreign language, strong language, quotations, slips of the tongue, assimilation of the stimulus-word (possibly also misunderstanding of the stimulus-word).

(7) Erotic complexes seem to play a particularly significant part.[52]

H. *The Quantitative Ratio of Prolonged Reaction-times in a Greater Number of Subjects*

A. STIMULUS-WORD AND PROLONGED REACTION-TIME

622 It would be interesting to learn whether the rules we have discovered in the analyses given above can be applied to a greater number of subjects about whom we have not adequate information. Practical experience teaches us that there are very few people who can pursue their own psychological processes in their subtlest details. Hence a very narrow limit is imposed on subjective analysis. The results given above should, however, make it possible, objectively, to penetrate into the complexes hidden in the associations and at least to demonstrate that rules gained from subjective analysis probably have a general validity. Hence I have investigated, in a comparative manner, the kind of words that are usually followed by prolonged

---

[52] I must observe that the analysis of the associations of an uneducated subject would take a very different and more complicated form. As explained by Riklin and myself, the uneducated subject is inclined to concentrate on the meaning of the stimulus-word; for this reason his reaction-times are longer and it would be difficult to decide to what extent feelings or attitudes account for these.

reaction-time. Eleven subjects provided my material; of these, nine were uneducated and two educated.

623   I. Five subjects reacted with prolonged times to the following stimulus-words:

needle	false	⎰[despise: 7 subjects]⁵⁴
⎰hair⁵³	to court	⎱inn
⎱salt	⎰to disgust	to remember
⎰[tooth: 3 subjects]⁵⁴	⎱uproar	ripe
⎱window	resin	
fern	pyramid	
hope	to hit	
strange	to threaten	

624   It is not surprising that stimulus-words such as *fern, uproar, resin,* and *pyramid* cause a lengthening in the reaction-time, for they are rather rare words and uneducated people do not have at their disposal ready-made associations to them. But this cannot be said of the words *needle, hair, to hit, ripe,* etc., for these on the contrary are words that occur very frequently in everyday language. The reasons why these words should cause long reaction-times can only be found by means of the above analyses; in most cases they are words that readily arouse emotional associations for they already have in themselves a certain feeling-value, as for example: *hope, false, to hit, to threaten, to remember, ripe,* etc., for women *hair,* too, should have an emotional value. The words *salt, window, uproar, inn,* have no striking emotional value, but in the original series they follow stimulus-words that evoke feeling; and for this reason, as has many times been shown, come into the orbit of a perseverating feeling-tone. *Hair* and *tooth* can cause long reaction-times, particularly with women, whereas *to disgust* and *to despise* generally stimulate feeling. *Needle* does not in fact follow a stimulus-word arousing feeling; in this case, however, another factor might play a part. This word (*Nadel* in the German original) is pronounced differently in dialect: the vowel *a* is pronounced nearer to an *o* and the ending is transposed into *-dlé*. On the other hand, in the dialect the *a* in the word *Nabel* (navel) is

---

53 The stimulus-words bracketed together followed immediately on each other in the test series.

54 The stimulus-word in square brackets is given because it seems more likely to arouse a complex than *window* or *inn.*

pronounced exactly as in academic German and likewise the ending is unchanged. *Nabel* is the only dialect word that sounds at all like *Nadel* in academic German. For this reason inevitably this word must be evoked in the Swiss-German subject when *Nadel* is called out. As we have seen, it does not necessarily come into consciousness at the time: the inhibition connected with this word can nevertheless influence the association occurring in consciousness. That this is no idle speculation is borne out by the similar case of the word *book*, with which seven out of eleven subjects took prolonged times. *Book* (*Buch* in German) is pronounced in the dialect as *Buoch*. The dialect word *Buch*, however, means *Bauch* (belly), which is a very unpleasant stimulus-word. In experiments on psychotics it has frequently occurred that *Buch* has been immediately understood as *Bauch* and the corresponding reaction followed.

625   11. Six out of eleven subjects reacted with prolonged times to the following stimulus-words:

dream	damage	impetus
paper	to spare	premonition
book	dreadful	to stink
frog	gentle	to forge
nurse (male)	{ to surmise: 8 subjects	to caress
right	{ of age	family

Of age, impetus, and *premonition* can be considered "difficult" words in which the rarity probably prevails over any possible feeling-value.

626   Since *paper* is a very common word it is difficult to say just what is its capacity to arouse emotion. *Nurse* (*male*) is effective because it is in constellation with uneducated subjects who are all male or female nurses in our hospital. The meaning of the word *gentle* (*leise* in German) became clear to me when a South German male nurse reacted with *big* (*gross*): he had in fact in the meantime suppressed the association *Läuse / klein* (lice / small). What matters here is the sound similarity as in the case of *book*. It is striking that so many long reaction-times should occur with the word *frog*. With one exception, the subjects giving these long times were all women. The man who had a long reaction-time could give the reason: *frog* had struck the emotional complex associated with a new-born son.

Possibly in the subconscious of a woman, too, the frog's likeness to a small, naked wriggling baby can arouse feeling; so a sexual complex would be touched on which could well be present in every woman, even if only unconsciously.

627   The feeling-value of the other stimulus-words is clear and requires no further explanation.

628   III. Seven out of eleven subjects reacted to the following stimulus-words with prolonged reaction-times:

$$\left\{\begin{array}{l}\text{freedom}\\\text{unjust}\\\text{world}\\\text{loyalty}\end{array}\right.\qquad\begin{array}{l}\text{to disgust}\\\text{to despise}\\\text{to pay attention}\\\text{to kiss}\end{array}$$
consciousness

Only *consciousness* could be rated as "difficult." The stimulus-words *freedom, unjust,* and *to pay attention* presumably produce long reaction-times in the nursing staff, which can easily be understood. *World* may well have prolonged times so frequently because it is placed between two words that arouse emotions.

629   IV. Eight to ten out of eleven subjects had long reaction-times to the following stimulus-words:

heart   to surmise
violence   {to kiss: 7 subjects
wonder   {natural: 9 "

It is not so much the relative rarity of the word *to surmise* that is important, but its capacity to arouse complexes. *Miracle* often seems to excite religious complexes associated with inhibitions. *Natural* is influenced by the immediately preceding erotic-sexual stimulant *to kiss* and is therefore very embarrassing for both sexes. *Violence* attracts the maximum of prolonged reaction-times. This is perhaps mainly due to the fact that all the subjects are closely connected with the mental hospital.

630   From this account we can see that the difficulty or rarity of a stimulus-word can certainly influence the reaction-time; but in the vast majority of cases the stimulus-words that produce long reaction-times are characterized by a high feeling-value. Thus the principal cause of prolonged reaction-times. This objective statistical examination shows the principal cause of

prolonged reaction-times to be the emotional effect of the stimulus-word.

631   I have tried to estimate roughly the quantitative values for the four series given above, and have compiled them in the following summary:

Out of 200 stimulus-words, 48 aroused prolonged reaction-times in 5 or more out of 11 subjects.

17 stimulus-words produced prolonged reaction-times in 5 subjects. Of these 76% referred to affective images.

17 stimulus-words produced prolonged reaction-times in 6 subjects. Of these 76% referred to affective images.

9 stimulus-words produced prolonged reaction-times in 7 subjects. Of these 89% referred to affective images.

5 stimulus-words produced prolonged reaction-times in 8 to 10 subjects. Of these 90% referred to affective images.

632   On the average, therefore, approximately 83 per cent of the stimulus-words producing prolonged reaction-times have affective value, whereas only about 17 per cent have a delaying influence through their intrinsic difficulty. Of the stimulus-words arousing affects, at least 28 per cent have a mainly erotic-sexual affective value.

B. INCIDENCE OF PROLONGED REACTION-TIMES WITH INDIVIDUAL SUBJECTS

633   It follows from the explanations given above that emotional processes are of the greatest significance in the origin or formation of abnormally long reaction-times. As we know from everyday experience, it is in the sphere of the emotions that the greatest individual differences exist. For this reason, it should be worthwhile investigating what is the numerical proportion of abnormally long times with the different subjects. For this investigation, I used the material given by twenty-six subjects. (Uneducated: seven women and seven men. Educated: six women and six men. Thus a total of over 4,000 individual data.)

634   As already mentioned, all those reaction-times that exceeded the individual probable mean times were considered to be prolonged. True, we came upon a series of reactions showing neither a particularly long duration nor obvious complex-influence. On the other hand, if we raise the upper individual

limit for normal times, we are thrown on to the arithmetical mean in which the prolonged times are taken into account. This limit is then individually far too high, for which reason no characteristic figures can be obtained in this way. I therefore decided to select the individual probable mean as the upper limit, first, because the abnormally long times are not taken into account in this (the probable mean is as a rule lower than the arithmetical mean) and, secondly, because (according to the analysis of subject No. 1) of those times exceeding the probable mean by only 0.2 seconds, almost a third are clearly influenced by feeling-toned complexes, whereas all the very long times depend entirely on the effect of complexes. In this way we encounter almost all the prolonged reaction-times produced by affects. As is clear from several examples, there is a certain proportion between the intensity of the affect and the length of the reaction-time. Hence one can deduce, *cum grano salis*, very intensive affects from very long reaction-times. By means of the arithmetical mean the prolonged reaction-times are taken abundantly into account in a calculation of averages. For the four groups mentioned I am giving the figures for the probable and arithmetical means, the percentages of prolonged reaction-times, and the difference between the two means.

		Probable Mean	Arithmetical Mean	Difference	% of Prolonged Reaction-times
Uneducated	Women	2.2	2.9	0.7	49.2
	Men	1.8	2.4	0.6	40.9
Educated	Women	1.7	2.2	0.5	42.4
	Men	1.3	1.7	0.4	41.8

635   The four columns in this table all say approximately the same thing in different forms, namely that the uneducated women, as well as having the highest probable mean, also have the greatest number of prolonged reaction-times. The differences between probable and arithmetical mean times are most instructive: the group of educated men has a smaller difference than the other three groups. This figure states that the prolonged reaction-times of educated men are on average shorter than those of the other groups, that consequently the emotional inhibitions in all the other subjects—for this is the

main point, not the difference in educational levels—even if they do not always occur more frequently, are still more fundamental and abundant than those of the educated men. From this I see that the experimenter, who is in every respect on the same level as the group of educated men, as far as the other groups are concerned is of the opposite sex or a superior or both. This seems to me sufficient reason for the prevalence of emotional inhibitions in the other subjects.

636   In stating the influences of the emotions on the length of reaction-times, I have ventured into a sphere so complicated, and therefore so subject to great individual variations, that there is no point in giving the individual figures on which the above table is based. Only untenable hypotheses could be based on the differences.

GENERAL RECAPITULATION

637   A. In time-measurements, using a stop-watch, made with both educated and uneducated subjects, the average reaction-time came out at 1.8 seconds.

B. The times of male subjects (1.6 seconds) are on average shorter than those of female subjects (2.9 seconds).

C. Similarly, the times of educated subjects (1.5 seconds) are, on average, shorter than those of the uneducated (2.0 seconds).

D. The quality of the stimulus-word exerts a certain influence on the reaction-time. The average shortest times follow concrete nouns (1.67 seconds), the longest follow abstract nouns and verbs (1.95 and 1.90 seconds). Educated men form an exception to this rule in that with them it is usually the concrete nouns that are followed by the longest times.

E. The quality of the reaction also seems to have a certain influence on the length of the reaction-time. The longest times occur with abstract nouns (1.98 seconds), the shortest with adjectives and verbs (1.65 and 1.66 seconds). Concrete nouns (1.81 seconds) are in the middle. Educated men here again are the exception in that their longest time occurs with concrete nouns.

F. The quality of the association has a distinct influence on the reaction-time. Internal associations command a longer reaction-time than external ones. Sound reactions generally show

269

relatively long times because they are abnormal and owe their appearance to certain disturbances occasioned by inner distractions.

G. Those reaction-times that exceed the probable mean are for the most part caused by the eruption of intense emotions associated with individually important complex-images. The subject is mostly unaware of the reason for the prolonged reaction-time. Hence, too, long reaction-times can serve as a means of uncovering emotionally charged complexes, both conscious and unconscious. (Important in hysteria!)

H. Prolonged reaction-times tend to follow certain stimulus-words. About 83 per cent of these are mainly characterized by their affective value, whereas only about 17 per cent cause prolonged reaction-times on account of their difficulty or rarity.

638   Very frequently the dying away of the feeling-tone is shown and it extends to the subsequent reactions which are thereby disturbed (perseveration).

BIBLIOGRAPHY

Aschaffenburg: "Experimentelle Studien über Assoziationen" in Kraepelin, *Psychologische Arbeiten*, I (1896), II (1899), IV (1904).

Bechterew: "Über zeitliche Verhältnisse der psychischen Prozesse bei in Hypnose befindlichen Personen" (1892).

Idem: "Über die Geschwindigkeitsveränderungen der psychischen Prozesse zu verschiedenen Tageszeiten" (1893).

Cattell: "Psychometrische Untersuchungen" in Wundt, *Philosophisches Studien*, III (1885).

Claparède: *L'Association des idées* (1903).

Idem and Israïlovitch: "Influence du tabac sur l'association des idées" (1902).

Féré: *The Pathology of the Emotions* (1899; orig., 1892).

Freud: *The Interpretation of Dreams* '(orig., 1900).

Idem: *The Psychopathology of Everyday Life* (orig., 1904).

Galton: "Psychometric Experiments" (1897).

Jung and Riklin: "The Associations of Normal Subjects" (orig., 1904).

Kraepelin: *Experimentelle Studien über Assoziationen* (1883).

Idem: "Über den Einfluss der Übung auf die Dauer von Assoziationen" (1889).

Idem: *Über die Beeinflussung einfacher psychischer Vorgänge durch einige Arzneimittel* (1892).

Mayer and Orth: "Zur qualitativen Untersuchung der Assoziationen" (1901).

Müller and Pilzecker: "Experimentelle Beiträge zur Lehre vom Gedächtnis" (1900).

Münsterberg: "Die Assoziation sukzessiver Vorstellungen" (1890). Idem: *Beiträge zur experimentellen Psychologie* (1889–92).

Ranschburg and Balint: "Über quantitative und qualitative Veränderungen geistiger Vorgänge im hohen Greisenalter" (1900).

Riklin: "Zur Psychologie hysterischer Dämmerzustände und des Ganser'schen Symptoms" (1904).

Sommer: *Lehrbuch der psychopathologischen Untersuchungsmethoden* (1899).

Thumb and Marbe: *Experimentelle Untersuchungen über die psychologischen Grundlagen der sprachlichen Analogiebildung* (1901).

Trautscholdt: "Experimentelle Untersuchungen über die Assoziation der Vorstellungen" in Wundt, *Philosophische Studien*, I (1883).

Walitsky: "Contribution à l'étude des mensurations psychométriques des aliénés" (1889).

Wehrlin: "The Associations of Imbeciles and Idiots" (orig., 1904).

Wreschner: "Eine experimentelle Studie über die Assoziation in einem Falle von Idiotie" (1900).

Ziehen: *Introduction to Physiological Psychology* (1892; orig., 1891).

Idem: "Die Ideenassoziation des Kindes" (1898–1900).

EXPERIMENTAL OBSERVATIONS ON THE
FACULTY OF MEMORY[1]

639   We have often observed in our association experiments
with hysterical patients that the patient would not react for a
long time to stimulus-words that were obviously related to his
complex, and then would suddenly ask, "What was the word
you said?" Closer interrogation revealed that the patient had
forgotten the word of which he had just been reminded. We
immediately recognized that this striking disturbance of memory was identical with the type of *forgetting* described by
Freud, i.e., the "not wanting to remember" unpleasant impressions. The phenomenon that we observed is a particular
case of a general tendency to repress and then forget the unpleasant image. (Cf. Freud's papers.[2])

640   It is to the credit of Freud, and partly also of Breuer—as
is probably well known—that they have amply demonstrated
this fact (forgetting equated with repression) in hysterical patients. The validity of this can be doubted only by someone
who has not himself tested Freudian psychoanalysis. In more
recent works[3] Freud has demonstrated that the same mechanisms of repression are at work in the normal dream and in
trivial incidents of everyday life (parapraxes in speaking, reading, etc.). In our experimental investigations we have also succeeded in demonstrating the repressed complex in such associations as are produced by calling out a stimulus-word. The
laying bare of a repressed complex is of immense practical
importance, e.g., in hysteria. Every hysterical patient has a

---

1 [First published as "Experimentelle Beobachtungen über das Erinnerungsvermögen," *Zentralblatt für Nervenheilkunde und Psychiatrie* (Leipzig), XXVIII
(1905; n.s. XVI):196 (Sept.), 653–66. It was not included in the first volume of
Diagnostische Assoziationsstudien, whose contents Jung referred to in the opening sentence, and it is here first republished.]
2 Freud, "The Neuro-Psychoses of Defence" (orig. 1894), "The Psychical Mechanism of Forgetfulness" (1898), "Screen Memories" (1899), *The Psychopathology
of Everyday Life* (orig. 1904).
3 Freud, *The Interpretation of Dreams* (1900).

repressed complex of causal significance. It is therefore essential for treatment that the complex be identified, unless one wants to forego such important psychotherapeutic aids. As Freud has shown, however, the inhibitions repressing the complex are so strong that the images concerned are very often split off from consciousness. It was to overcome this barrier that Freud invented his ingenious method of *free association*. This method is, however, extremely time-consuming and its use presupposes certain qualities in both the patient and the doctor. The same inhibitions are betrayed in our own method of association. A tabulation of the stimulus-words that have brought up inhibitions shows quite clearly into which category the repressed complex may fall, and from this one can obtain valuable pointers to supplementary questions. To get a clearer idea of the type of complex one can then intersperse additional pertinent stimulus-words. The art of the method, which is never easy to use, lies in distinguishing the reactions connected with a complex from the irrelevant ones. I have therefore compiled a series of so-called *complex-characteristics*.[4] In principle the complex-characteristics are the same for normal and pathological associations. Furthermore, to lay bare the complex is of far-reaching significance in applying our experiments to the field of criminal psychology. Hans Gross and his pupils have shown this, stimulated by our experiments.[5] The complex in this case is the fact of a crime: the stimulus-words are the designations of things associated with the mental picture of the crime.

641   The observations mentioned in our first paragraph became the point of departure for a new method that points to those associations attributable to complexes. The *reproduction method*, as I should like to call it, can be described as follows: After completing an association test (usually one hundred words), we try to find out whether the subject remembers how he reacted to individual stimulus-words. We simply repeat the experiment, always allowing the patient enough time to recall

4 See my "The Reaction-time Ratio in the Association Experiment," supra.
5 Hans Gross, "Zur psychologischen Tatbestandsdiagnostik" (1905); Wertheimer and Klein, "Psychologische Tatbestandsdiagnostik" (1904); Alfred Gross, "Zur psychologischen Tatbestandsdiagnostik als kriminalistisches Hilfsmittel" (1905); Stern, "Psychologische Tatbestandsdiagnostik" (1905); Hans Gross, "Zur Frage des Wahrnemungsproblems" (1905).

his previous reactions. In this reproduction method certain regular characteristics come to light, which I should now like to outline briefly. In these experiments my leading idea was to find out whether failures of memory were accidental or whether a system behind them could be revealed. I have carried out this experiment on mentally healthy people and on patients, and have, at least in principle, always found the same phenomena. (Organic disturbances of memory are of course excepted.) As this article is only concerned with establishing and describing this phenomenon, I have selected as examples two pathological cases in which the phenomenon in question is quite pronounced.

642   CASE No. I

A 32-year-old professional musician who was undergoing psychoanalytical treatment because of vague anxiety-states and a compulsive fear of not being able to give solo performances. Two years previously he had become engaged, but the engagement soon broke up owing to moodiness and quarrelling. The young woman was of an implacable, quarrelsome, and jealous nature. This led to violent rows and finally to the breaking off of the engagement when the patient made the mistake of writing picture postcards to another girl. During the nights following these quarrels the patient could not sleep, and it was then that the first nervous symptoms appeared. About a year previously he had had a secret affair with a lady of a rich and distinguished family, but this had soon been broken off. In January of that year the patient became engaged to a rather unintelligent girl who was, however, already three months pregnant by another man, which the patient did not then know. The numerous excitements brought on by these circumstances aggravated his nervous condition to such an extent that he had to seek medical advice. It should also be mentioned that he had led a very dissolute life between the ages of 18 and 25, as a result of which his physical strength had allegedly been greatly impaired.

Association and Reproduction Test

643   The results of the two tests are set side by side. Those associations that were either not reproduced or wrongly reproduced are shown in italic type.[6]

6 [In the German version, the items of this list were not numbered. They have now been numbered to facilitate comparison with the list for Case No. II. The list for Case No. I omits, perhaps inadvertently, 51, *frog*.]

Stimulus-word	Re-action	Re-action-time (secs.)	Repro-duction	Remarks
1. *head*	*empty*	3.2	to see	Complex underlying the illness.
2. *green*	*lawn*	2.2	colour, tree	Probably perseverating feeling-tone.
3. *water*	*to drown*	2.2	deep	The patient had had thoughts of suicide as a result of his illness.
4. *to stab*	*dead*	1.8	unpleasant	—
5. angel	beautiful	8.0		Here the feeling-tone of the previous reaction has probably perseverated. Word not at first understood. Erotic reminiscences easily aroused by this word.
6. long	table	2.8	—	—
7. *ship*	*crew*	3.0	to travel, to drown	Suicide by drowning.
8. to plough	peasant	2.0	—	—
9. wool	sheep	2.0	—	—
10. friendly	very	2.8	—	Affair with the lady.
11. desk	high	3.6	—	Prolonged reaction-time due to perseverating feeling-tone.
12. *to ask*	*difficult*	3.2	to put	Same complex.
13. state	beautiful	2.4	—	—
14. obstinate	very	2.0	—	1st fiancée.
15. stalk	green	2.2	—	—
16. to dance	good	2.2	—	—
17. lake	stormy	2.0	—	—
18. ill	unpleasant	8.8	—	Illness.
19. conceit	very	2.8	—	Relations with the lady.
20. to cook	good	2.0	—	—
21. ink	black	1.8	—	—
22. wicked	very	4.8	—	1st fiancée.
23. pin	prick	1.4	—	—
24. *to swim*	*not*	2.8	good	Suicide.
25. *journey*	*difficult*	2.4	long	Perseverating feeling-tone.
26. blue	colour	2.0	—	—

Stimulus-word	Re-action	Re-action-time (secs.)	Repro-duction	Remarks
27. bread	to taste	2.8	—	—
28. to threaten	me	10.4	—	Fear of the future: suicide.
29. *lamp*	*good*	2.2	to burn	Perseverating feeling-tone.
30. rich	pleasant	3.4	—	The lady.
31. *tree*	*green*	2.0	high	Perseverating feeling-tone.
32. *to sing*	*beautiful*	1.4	good	(ditto)
33. *sympathy*	*pleasant*	4.6	to have	Ostensibly the illness-complex, but probably something else as well which is not divulged.
34. *yellow*	*material*	5.4	colour	Not at first understood.
35. mountain	high	1.2	—	—
36. to play	children	2.4	—	—
37. salt	bitter	1.8	—	—
38. *new*	*material*	2.4	dress	?
39. *habits*	*good*	3.0	bad	Early life: adulterous relationship with the lady.
40. to ride	pleasant	3.6	—	—
41. wall	white	2.2	—	—
42. *stupid*	*cattle*	4.8	very	2nd fiancée.
43. *notebook*	*blue*	2.2	to write	Perseverating feeling-tone.
44. *to despise*	*him*	3.4	me	Early life: erotic complexes.
45. tooth	sharp	2.2	long	Perseverating feeling-tone.
46. correct	to write	3.8	—	Correspondence behind 1st fiancée's back.
47. people	Swiss	2.4	—	—
48. to stink	dung	2.0	—	—
49. *book*	*beautiful*	3.6	good	Perhaps not at first understood. Otherwise?
50. *unjust*	*judge*	2.0	very	The reaction *very* might indicate a connection with one of the erotic complexes.

276

Stimulus-word	Re-action	Re-action-time (secs.)	Repro-duction	Remarks
52. to separate	acid (noun)	6.0	—	Not at first understood. Relationship with the lady.
53. hunger	pang	2.0	—	—
54. white	lamb	2.2	—	—
55. *cattle*	*to slaughter*	4.4	to kill	Memories of quarrels with 1st fiancée.
56. to pay attention	very	2.0	—	Perseverating tone.
57. pencil	long	2.0	—	—
58. sultry	weather	4.8	—	—
59. plum	blue	1.8	—	—
60. *to hit*	*target*	2.0	marksman	Rendezvous with the lady.
61. law	to despise	2.6	—	The lady is married.
62. dear	she	2.6	—	The lady.
63. glass	transparent	2.0	—	—
64. *to quarrel*	*unpleasant*	2.2	violent	1st fiancée.
65. goat	pasture	3.8	—	Perseverating tone. Stimulus-word was repeated by the patient.
66. *big*	*man*	2.4	child	?
67. potato	to eat	1.8	—	—
68. *to paint*	*wall*	3.2	beautiful	?
69. *part*	*whole*	3.0	?	Suggestion of "sexual parts."
70. *old*	*coin*	7.4	man	As a result of previous word the fear of impotence is aroused.
71. flower	smells	1.6	—	—
72. *to fight*	*stick*	2.0	violent	Quarrel with 1st fiancée.
73. *box*	*to put in*	3.4	?	Perseverating tone.
74. wild	horse	1.6	—	—
75. family	to have	2.6	—	2nd fiancée.
76. to wash	face	1.8	—	—
77. *cow*	*to slaughter*	2.6	to kill	Memories of rows with 1st fiancée.
78. strange	to me	2.0	—	1st fiancée.
79. luck	to have	1.6	—	—
80. to tell	story	1.6	—	—
81. *poise*	*good*	2.0	habit	Early life: the lady.
82. narrow	boot	1.8	—	—

Stimulus-word	Re-action	Re-action-time (secs.)	Repro-duction	Remarks
83. brother	sister	1.2	—	—
84. *damage*	*to have*	1.6	to do	Impotence.
85. stork	long	1.0	—	—
86. *false*	*to write*	5.8	to speak	Correspondence behind 1st fiancée's back.
87. fear	to have	1.2	—	—
88. to kiss	her	2.0	—	The lady.
89. fire	house	4.0	—	Word not understood, perseverating tone.
90. dirty	street	1.2	—	—
91. *door*	*house*	2.0	high	?
92. to elect	electorate	2.0	—	—
93. hay	sweet-smelling	1.4	—	—
94. still	water	2.4	—	Suicide.
95. *scorn*	*pleasant*	1.6	unpleasant	Perseverating tone.
96. *to sleep*	*very*	2.2	deep	(ditto)
97. month	January	4.6	—	Cf. R.3; stimulus-word at first not understood. January is the critical month.
98. coloured	cloth	1.6	—	—
99. *dog*	*snappish*	2.4	to snap	Quarrel with 1st fiancée.
100. to speak	sensitive	1.8	—	—

⁶⁴⁴   In these associations several clearly feeling-toned complexes are evoked. Their symptoms are mainly a delayed reaction and its influence on the following reactions. I will not proceed further with this analysis as it might lead too far.[7]

⁶⁴⁵   The remarks given with the reactions should enable the reader to get his bearings. Those points where the analysis showed an association constellated by a complex have been noted. If we now look over the whole experiment we can see that, with very few exceptions, the incorrect reproductions to the repeated stimulus-words are those that are directly constellated by a feeling-toned complex or those that immediately

[7] The complex phenomena are comprehensively presented in my "The Reaction-time Ratio in the Association Experiment"; see supra.

follow a critical one, and therefore fall within the area of the perseverating feeling-tone. In many places the perseveration can be quite easily recognized by the prolonged reaction-time or by the form and content of the reaction. Out of 38 incorrect reproductions there are only five in which analysis could not demonstrate any kind of complex-constellation. Nevertheless, the prolonged reaction-times usually found in such places indicate a feeling-tone.

646 Analysis is exceptionally difficult and time-consuming in the case of half-educated and uneducated people; in fact, it often proves almost impossible to reach any depth because of lack of co-operation. Also, with patients from an out-patients' clinic, you may easily meet people who have every reason to keep their secrets. Apart from these exceptions, which need not be considered, it becomes quite clear that the forgetting does not apply to the irrelevant reactions, but to the significant complex-reactions. Should this be generally confirmed, we should have found a method, in this reproduction process, of objectively revealing complexes from the reactions. But this method can also be theoretically valuable in that it shows us a way to investigate the much discussed connection between feeling-tone and memory.

647 Before we go further into these questions, I should like to refer to a second case.

648   CASE No. II

An educated young man, 22 years old, excitable and sensitive, sanguine, morally unsound, not particularly intelligent. He is well known to the writer and has also given sufficient information about the complexes broached by the associations.

Complex I: The patient is very excitable and extraordinarily sensitive. This characteristic brings him into frequent conflict with his environment. One of these conflicts has led him to a mental hospital. The patient had a good friend who once made a joke of sketching him with ass's ears, and produced this caricature in the presence of ladies. The patient took him to task about this, but the perpetrator denied having done it, whereupon the patient slapped his face and challenged him to a duel with sabres.

His relationship with his family is strained.

Complex II: Numerous love-affairs. The patient had been given a diamond pin by one amorous lady, which he wore in his tie, and had recently lost a stone from this, which annoyed him a great deal.

One of these relationships is with a Greek woman. In the year he has just completed in the cavalry he led a wild and dissolute life.

Complex III: The patient recently wanted to become engaged to a woman of means, but it came to nothing.

Complex IV: The patient has decided to study agriculture, which seems to keep him occupied for the time being, and he is also enthusiastic about rowing and other sports.

649   I am giving full details of the associations in this case. The method of analysis is the same as that I have already demonstrated in the work on the reaction-times. I have marked with the appropriate number all the places where the analysis certainly or in all probability shows a complex. Those associations to which the reactions were either not remembered or wrongly remembered in the reproduction test are shown in the table, as on the previous occasion.

Stimulus-word	Re-action	Re-action-time (secs.)	1st Repro-duction	2nd Repro-duction	Remarks
1. *head*	*hat*	2.8	—	cover	Stupidity complex (ass's ears) and th supposition, owin to stay in mental hospital, that he i mentally ill.
2. green	colour	1.4	—	—	—
3. *water*	*to row*	2.6	?	—	IV.
4. to stab	spear	2.8	—	—	I. Sabre duel.
5. angel	heaven	1.8	—	—	—
6. long	—	—	—	—	I. Not understood, reaction omitted.
7. ship	-building	1.0	—	—	—
8. to plough	field	2.2	—	—	} IV.
9. wool	sheep	1.2	—	—	
10. friendly	Mr. Z.	2.4	—	—	Acquaintance at the hospital.
11. desk	bank	2.2	—	—	—
12. *to ask*	*answer*	3.6	?	—	III.
13. *state*	*Switzerland*	3.8	—	institu-tion	Preceding R.12 ref to complex III. Owing to the per severating feeling tone the reprodu tion is disturbed.

Stimulus-word	Re-action	Re-action-time (secs.)	1st Repro-duction	2nd Repro-duction	Remarks
14. obstinate	wench	4.8	—	—	"The Obstinate Wench," popular song. The stimulus-word *to ask* has touched complex III. How much the feeling-tone rever-berates can be gathered from the way the reaction-times increase and from the content of R.14.
15. stalk	flower	1.8	—	—	—
16. to dance	ladies	3.8	—	—	II.
17. lake	Zurich	2.0	—	—	IV.
18. *ill*	*medicine*	4.2	—	to be	I. Complex of hos-pitalization, obser-vation of his mental state.
19. conceit	Mr. S.	1.8	—	—	I. Acquaintance in the hospital.
20. to cook	kitchen	2.0	—	—	—
21. ink	to write	1.6	—	—	—
22. *wicked*	*Mr. C.*	3.0	to be	—	I.
23. *pin*	*tie*	3.2	cravat	tie-pin	II.
24. to swim	water	2.0	—	—	IV.
25. journey	adventure	3.8	—	—	II.
26. blue	colour	2.4	—	—	—
27. bread	corn	2.8	—	—	V.
28. *to threaten*	*angry*	3.0	—	someone	I. Duel complex.
29. lamp	light	2.0	—	—	—
30. *rich*	*money*	3.4	—	to be	III.
31. *tree*	*leaves*	3.0	leaf	—	—
32. to sing	music	2.8	—	—	Here the critical reaction is obvious-ly *rich/money*, after which the reaction-times decrease in proportion. The re-action after the critical one is uncertain
33. sympathy	to have	2.6	—	—	—

Stimulus-word	Re-action	Re-action-time (secs.)	1st Repro-duction	2nd Repro-duction	Remarks
34. yellow	colour	2.8	—	—	—
35. *mountain*	*climbing*	1.8	—	tour	—
36. to play	tennis	3.0	—	—	IV.
37. salt	sea	4.2	—	—	—
38. new	-Greek	6.2	—	—	II.
39. habits	& customs	2.2	—	—	—
40. to ride	horse	1.8	—	—	II.
41. wall	papered	3.4	—	—	—
42. *stupid*	*Mr. B.*	6.4	to be	—	I. Similar to R.22, same complex.
43. notebook	to write	2.2	—	—	—
44. to despise	Mr. H.	2.8	—	—	I. Acquaintance in the hospital. With this man the patient had had a similar experience to that given in complex I.
45. tooth	to pull	2.4	—	—	—
46. *correct*	*answer*	8.0	right and proper	—	I. Connected with the denial in complex I.
47. people	race	2.0	—	—	—
48. to stink	carbolic	3.6	—	—	I. The hospital.
49. book	to read	1.6	—	—	—
50. unjust	Russia	3.0	—	—	—
51. frog	leg	1.6	—	—	—
52. *to separate*	*marriage*	6.0	?	—	III.
53. hunger	to eat	4.0	—	—	—
54. white	colour	3.4	—	—	—
55. cattle	cattle-breeding	2.6	—	—	IV. Here again the timing shows a regular decrease after the critical reaction.
56. *to pay at-tention*	*lecture*	6.2	—	question	IV.
57. pencil	to write	4.2	—	—	—
58. sultry	sky	7.6	—	—	I. Stay in hospital
59. plum	stone-fruit	3.0	—	—	IV.
60. to hit	to shoot	2.6	—	—	I.
61. *law*	*state insti-tutions*	6.2	?	—	I.
62. dear	beloved	7.4	—	—	II or III.
63. glass	water	2.2	—	—	—

Stimulus-word	Re-action	Re-action-time (secs.)	1st Repro-duction	2nd Repro-duction	Remarks
64. to quarrel	difference	4.8	—	—	I.
65. goat	farming	2.8	—	—	IV.
66. *big*	*Germany*	11.2	?	tree, pine	Refers to himself as he is exceptionally tall.
67. potato	farming	2.8	—	—	IV.
68. to paint	pictures	2.4	—	—	—
69. part	to have	4.6	—	—	III. He had hoped to become a partner in his prospective father-in-law's business.
70. old	to become	1.8	—	—	—
71. *flower*	*blossom*	3.4	—	{ stem, to bloom, leaves	IV.
72. to fight	sabres	4.0	—	—	I.
73. box	lid	2.8	—	—	—
74. *wild*	*to become*	3.2	—	to be	I. Wild, evil.
75. family	parents	4.6	—	—	I.
76. to wash	soap	3.6	—	—	—
77. cow	farming	4.4	—	—	IV.
78. strange	to be	4.0	—	—	—
79. luck	lucky	2.2	—	—	—
80. to tell	story	1.6	—	—	—
81. *poise*	*to have*	3.0	—	& customs	I.
82. *narrow*	*a flat*	5.0	room	—	I. Stay in hospital.
83. brother	siblings	4.4	—	—	I.
84. *damage*	*to inflict*	2.8	{ to have, to suffer	{ to have, to suffer, to endure, to inflict	I. Refers to excesses in drunkenness.
85. stork	bird	4.0	—	—	Word not at first understood.
86. false	envy	4.8	—	to be	—
87. fear	to have	3.8	—	—	—
88. to kiss	pleasant	3.4	—	—	II.
89. fire	brigade	6.4	—	—	—
90. dirty	street— instantly	6.8	—	—	Marked increase in times from R.88 onwards. Cf. below.
91. door	to open	1.6	—	—	—
92. to elect	election	3.2	—	—	—
93. hay	haymaking	3.2	—	—	IV.
94. still	at night	3.6	—	—	II.

Stimulus-word	Re-action	Re-action time (secs.)	1st Repro-duction	2nd Repro-duction	Remarks
95. scorn	& derision	1.8	—	—	At first did not understand the word.
96. to sleep	at night	2.0	—	—	II.
97. month	12 months in a year	3.2	—	—	—
98. coloured	flowers	8.2	—	—	—
99. dog	Great Dane	2.4	—	—	—
100. to speak	foreign language	5.0	?	—	II. The Greek woman.

Note to test: Reactions 94–98 are influenced by a complex that requires some elucidation. These reactions show various intense complex-characteristics. Obviously the complex is hidden by the words at night. From the first reproduction onwards, there is a marked increase in the reaction-time. I suggested to the patient that this might be due to a more recent love affair, but he did not admit it. There is a similar increase in the time taken after 88, to kiss/pleasant, and it is difficult to understand why 56, to pay attention/lecture, should take as long as 6.2 seconds. Complex-characteristics in reactions to words such as to kiss, to sleep, still, to pay attention, gave rise to the suspicion that the patient had begun an affair behind our back.

On the day following these tests we intercepted a letter addressed to the patient. This was from a girl whom he had met when he was allowed to go out on parole, and suggested how they could keep their relationship secret and how they could arrange a rendezvous.

650   In this series of associations there are obvious complexes expressed in the usual way. Out of one hundred reactions there are only 13 in which memory failed. When we now examine where these 13 unrepeated reactions occur, we see that 12 of them are found at points constellated by a complex;[7a] one follows immediately on a complex-reaction. We may therefore suppose that the disturbance of memory is connected with the complex, or with its feeling-tone. As I have shown earlier,[8] strong emotions, especially feelings of unpleasure, are expressed in abnormally long reaction-times.

651   The arithmetical mean time of all correctly repeated reactions is 3.0 seconds. The mean of those not repeated is 5.0 seconds. Thus the times taken for those reactions not repeated

7a [Jung is apparently referring to the first column of reproductions, in which there are actually 12, not 13, incorrect reproductions. There are 14 in the second column.]

8 "The Reaction-time Ratio in the Association Experiment."

are significantly longer than those of the others, which gives us an objective confirmation of our supposition that there is a connection between the disturbance of memory and the strong feeling-tone of the reaction.

652   The first reproduction test followed immediately after the initial test of one hundred reactions. I had the test repeated again on the following day, and the results are shown in the column headed "2nd Reproduction."

653   Of the hundred reactions, 14 were incorrectly reproduced on the second occasion. (The second reproduction was assumed to be correct if it was the same as the first reproduction, when the initial reaction had been incorrectly remembered.)

654   Eleven of the fourteen incorrect reproductions concern reactions that had been correctly reproduced the first time but that, because of their content or the length of time taken, appeared to suggest the presence of a complex. Only three were wrongly remembered on the second reproduction. We can thus see that the amnestic blockages have developed further in the same direction as in the first reproduction test, and give rise to a series of reactions that also belong to the complexes. For practical purposes it would seem to be advisable to leave some time between the first test and the reproduction tests.

655   In my experience the amnestic blockages occur just as frequently with critical reactions as with those immediately following. These two cases represent the usual behaviour. But there are even more island-like amnesias, particularly, as it seems, in hysteria, where the feeling-tones are of great intensity and can extend over many subsequent reactions. Thus, I recently found in the case of a 23-year-old hysterical woman, who had only 13 per cent incorrect reproductions, the following interesting chain of reactions:

1. water	—		(no reaction)
2. to sting	bee	1.8	
3. *angel*	*-court*[9]	21.0	In the repeat the patient believed she had not given any reaction, as with No. 1.
4. *long*	*knife*	9.0	
5. *ship*	*steamer*	7.0	
6. *to plough*	*field*	4.2	R. garden

[9] [German *Engel/-hof*; in Switzerland, a name sometimes given to a farm or house.]

656   The stimulus-word *water* had awakened the memory of a
suicide-attempt, as was subsequently shown through psychoanalysis. With *angel* the image of death and the hereafter immediately appeared, this time with persisting feeling-tone that
hindered the subsequent reactions in a way shown by the decrease in reaction-times. All four reactions showed themselves
to be amnestically blocked.

657   The theory of our phenomenon is closely related to the
teaching of Freud, whose psychological depth and fertility are
still not sufficiently appreciated, in particular by psychiatrists.
Freud says in effect that forgetting is frequently caused by the
feeling of unpleasure associated with the forgotten image, i.e.,
one is inclined to forget what is unpleasant and what is associated with the unpleasant.[10] The process underlying this forgetting is the repression of the affect of unpleasure which one
can observe every day in hysterical cases. "Systematic" forgetting plays, as I have shown,[11] an important part in the origins
of the so-called Ganser's twilight state. Up to now only Riklin[12]
has taken up my suggestion and developed it with any result.
These investigations fully confirm the correctness of Freud's
teachings on this point. That just the essential matter (i.e., the
repressed complex charged with unpleasure) is forgotten is the
obstacle in psychoanalysis that is often the most difficult to
overcome. One usually comes up against amnesia ("I don't
know," "I have forgotten," etc.) where the important matter
lies. The amnestic blockages in our experiment are nothing
but hysterical amnesias. They also have in common with hysterical amnesia that not only what is significant is forgotten,
but also related ideas which happen to coincide with the perseverating unpleasure.

658   The reaction-words that are so easily forgotten seem like
excuses; they play a similar role to that of Freud's "screen
memories." When, for example, a hysterical young girl takes
an agonizingly long time to react to *to kiss* with *sister's kiss*

---

[10] Cf. Pick, "Zur Psychologie des Vergessens bei Geistes- und Nervenkranken"
(1905).
[11] "A Case of Hysterical Stupor in a Prisoner in Detention"; "On Simulated
Insanity." [For Sigbert Ganser, see *Psychiatric Studies*, index, s.v.]
[12] Riklin, "Zur Psychologie hysterischer Dämmerzustände und des Ganser'schen
Symptom" (1904).

and afterwards has forgotten how she did react, it is understood without further ado that *sister's kiss* was only an evasion, which must conceal an important erotic complex. Such reactions are reminiscent of simulation (naturally, unconscious) and resemble the "screen memories" with which hysterical subjects conceal events that are of causal importance.[13] Another reason for the speedy forgetting of these reactions is their superficiality; for these words can just as well be replaced by a number of different words of an equally superficial kind. The deceptive nature of such reactions is one aspect of the well-known general impression that has so often caused hysterical subjects to be accused of conscious pretence. It should, however, be pointed out that very often the complex hidden by such an evasion is completely cut off from consciousness, since in fact hysterical subjects can *very often* only under hypnosis be shown what lies behind the suspect reaction.

659   As the experiment shows, the incorrect reproduction has the value of a complex-characteristic. (I do not know whether irrelevant reactions are also forgotten.) It can have a positive value through its content since, as a second association to the stimulus-word and the repressed complex, it can be very useful in analysis. The same is, of course, true in research on criminal psychology. I should like to point out that, as in the association test, so also in the reproduction method, the repressed complex can betray itself in the reaction even though it is unconscious; it does so when it is split off from consciousness, as is often the case in hysterical patients. So far as I can see, where repressed complexes are concerned the same phenomenon occurs with normal, hysterical, and catatonic subjects; in normal cases there is a brief embarrassment or momentary blockage, in hysterical cases there is the well-known arbitrary amnesia, and in catatonic cases there is a complete barrier. The psychological mechanism, however, is the same.

13 Cf. Riklin, "Analytische Untersuchungen der Symptome und Assoziationen eines Falles von Hysterie (Lina H.)" (1905).

PSYCHOANALYSIS AND
ASSOCIATION EXPERIMENTS[1]

660   It is not easy to say in a few words what is the essence of Freud's theory of hysteria and of the psychoanalytic method. Freud's terminology and conceptions are still in the making—luckily, if I may say so, because, in spite of the amazing progress that, thanks to Freud's contributions, insight into hysteria has made in recent years, neither Freud nor we, his followers, have gained full knowledge of it. It is therefore not surprising that Freud in his most recent publication on hysteria[2] has for the most part abandoned the terminology that he had laid down in the *Studies on Hysteria*, and substituted for it a number of different and more fitting expressions. One must understand Freud's terms not as always sharply defined scientific concepts but more as opportune coinages from his rich vocabulary. Anyone writing about Freud should therefore not argue with him about words but rather keep the essential meaning in mind.

661   Freud sees hysteria as caused by and manifesting a series of psychic traumas, culminating at last in a sexual trauma in the prepubertal period. The so-called psychogenic character of hysteria was, of course, already known before Freud. (We have to thank Möbius[3] in particular for a concise definition of the term "psychogenic.") It was known that hysteria stems from ideas marked by the strength of their affect. But it was only Freud who showed us what lines the psychological process follows. He found that the hysterical symptom is essentially a symbol for (fundamentally sexual) ideas that are not present in consciousness but are repressed by strong inhibitions. The repression occurs because these crucial ideas are so charged with painful affects as to make them incompatible with ego-consciousness.

1 [First published in "Psychoanalyse und Assoziationsexperiment," *Journal für Psychologie und Neurologie*, VII (1906): 1-2, 1-24. Republished in *Diagnostische Assoziationsstudien*, Vol. I, pp. 258–81 (VI. Beitrag). Translated by M. D. Eder in *Studies in Word-Association*, pp. 297–321. See supra, par. 1, n. 1.]

2 "Fragment of an Analysis of a Case of Hysteria" (orig. 1905).

3 [Paul Julius Möbius (1853–1907), German neurologist who influenced Freud.]

662   The psychoanalytic method is inseparably linked with this conception. It acknowledges the concept of repressed and therefore unconscious ideas. If we inquire from patients about the cause of their illness, we always obtain incorrect or at least incomplete information. If we had been able to get proper information as in other (physical) diseases, we should already have known a long time ago of the psychogenic nature of hysteria. But this is just the trick of hysteria, that it represses or forgets the real cause, the psychic trauma, and substitutes for it superficial "cover" causes. We often hear from hysterics that their illness stems from a cold, from overwork, from real organic disturbances, etc. And so many doctors are fooled again and again. Others turn to the opposite extreme and allege that all hysterics are liars. So they entirely misunderstand the psychological etiology of hysteria, which actually exists only because ideas incompatible with ego-consciousness have been repressed and can therefore not be reproduced. By means of Freud's psychoanalytic method the barriers between ego-consciousness and repressed ideas are bypassed. This method consists mainly in the patient simply telling spontaneously everything that comes into his mind (Freud called this "free association"). An elaborate description of this method can be found in Freud's book *The Interpretation of Dreams*. Although it is theoretically *a priori* certain that all human ideas are determined, in a most wonderful way, by psychological laws, it is still easy to conceive that an inexperienced person would get lost in the maze of ideas and would finally be hopelessly caught in a blind alley. It is and will remain one of the main objections against the general acceptability of Freud's method that the prerequisite for the practice of psychoanalysis is psychological sensitivity as well as technique, i.e., characteristics that cannot be taken for granted in every physician or psychologist. Then there is a particular way of thinking required for psychoanalysis, which aims at bringing symbols to light. This attitude, however, can only be acquired by constant application. It is a way of thinking that is innate in a poet but is carefully avoided in scientific thought, which is said to be characterized by clear-cut ideas. Thinking in symbols demands from us a new attitude, similar to starting to think in flights of ideas. These seem to be the reasons why Freud's method has only exceptionally been understood and even more rarely

practised, so that there are actually only a few authors who appreciate Freud, theoretically or practically (Löwenfeld, Vogt, Bleuler, Warda, Störring, Riklin, Otto Gross, Hellpach).[4]

663 Freud's psychoanalysis is, in spite of the many valuable experiences given to us by its author, still a rather difficult art, since a beginner easily loses courage and orientation when faced with the innumerable obstacles it entails. We lack the security of a framework that would enable us to seek out essential data. Having to search haphazardly in treatment is often tantamount to realizing that one has no idea at what point to tackle the problem.

664 The association experiment has helped us to overcome these first and most important difficulties. As I have shown, particularly in my paper "The Reaction-time Ratio in the Association Experiment,"[5] complexes of ideas referred to as emotionally charged are shown up in the experiment by characteristic disturbances, and their presence and quality can be inferred precisely from these disturbances. This fact is known to be the basis of the "psychological diagnosis of evidence" inaugurated by Wertheimer and Klein,[6] Hans Gross,[7] and Alfred Gross,[8] an apparently not unpromising method of diagnosing from the associations the complex underlying a crime. Everybody, of course, has one or more complexes that manifest themselves in some way in associations. The background of our consciousness (or the unconscious) consists of such complexes. The whole material that can be remembered is grouped around these. They form higher psychic units analogous with the ego-complex.[9] They constellate our whole thinking and acting, therefore also our associations. With the association experiment we always combine a second, which we call the reproduction test.[10] This test consists in making the subject state how he

4 [For Jung's reviews of books by Leopold Löwenfeld and Willy Hellpach, see Vol. 18, *Miscellany*.]

5 See supra, pars. 602 ff.

6 Wertheimer, "Experimentelle Untersuchungen zur Tatbestandsdiagnostik" (1905). Wertheimer and Klein, "Psychologische Tatbestandsdiagnostik" (1904).

7 "Zur psychologischen Tatbestandsdiagnostik" (1905).

8 "Die Assoziationsmethode in Strafprozess" (1906). Grabowsky, "Psychologische Tatbestandsdiagnostik" (1905).

9 Bleuler, "Versuch einer naturwissenschaftlichen Betrachtung der psychologischen Grundbegriffe" (1894) and "Consciousness and Association" (orig. 1905).

10 Jung, "Experimental Observations on the Faculty of Memory," supra.

responded to each stimulus-word in the first test. Where memory fails we usually find a constellation through a complex. The reproduction technique also allows a more detailed description of the complex-disturbances.

665   Every psychogenic neurosis contains a complex that differs from normal complexes by unusually strong emotional charges, and for this reason has such a constellating power that it fetters the whole individual. The complex, therefore, is the *causa morbi* (a certain disposition is, of course, presupposed!). From the associations we can often quickly recognize the nature of the complex, thereby gaining important starting points for causal therapy. A by-product, not to be underestimated, is the increased scientific insight that we obtain into the origin and intrinsic structure of psychogenic neuroses. The essence of these insights has, of course, already been given us long since by Freud, but here he is far too advanced for the understanding of his time. I may therefore be allowed to try to open up new avenues to Freud's body of knowledge. In the papers of the Diagnostic Association Studies published so far, Freud's principles have already been repeatedly used to explain various points. In the present paper I propose to illustrate the connection of psychoanalysis with the association experiment by means of practical examples. I am choosing a common case of obsessional neurosis which I treated in June 1905.

666   Miss. E. came to me for hypnotic treatment of insomnia, which she had had for four months. Besides sleeplessness, she complained of an inner restlessness and excitement, irritability towards her family, impatience and difficulty in getting on with people. Miss E. is 37 years old, a teacher, educated and intelligent, has always been "nervous," has a mentally defective younger sister; father was an alcoholic. Present condition: well nourished, no physical abnormality detectable. Patient makes numerous conspicuously restless and twitching movements. When talking she rarely looks at the doctor, mostly speaks past him, out of the window. Occasionally she turns even further round, often laughs unintentionally, frequently makes a shrugging movement with the shoulder, as if shaking off something repulsive, simultaneously stretching the abdomen forward in a peculiar way.

Her history is very incomplete and vague. One learns that she had been a governess abroad, and was not then ill. The illness started only in recent years and developed gradually to the present climax. She had been treated by various doctors without any success. She now wanted to try hypnosis, but she had to say at once that she was firmly convinced hypnosis would not be successful. Her illness was incurable and she was sure to go mad. She had in any case repeatedly thought that she was not normal, she must already be mad. Here it was obvious that the patient was apparently talking around something that she either did not want to or could not say. On urgent questioning she declared at last, with many defensive movements and persistent blushing, that she certainly could not sleep, because each time she started going off to sleep the thought came that she certainly would not be able to sleep, she would never be able to sleep until she was dead; then she promptly woke up again and could not sleep any more for the rest of the night. Each time she felt tired and again wanted to sleep, a tremendous fear that she would never again be able to sleep until she was mad or dead woke her up afresh. She had a great struggle to bring herself to this explanation, making numerous defensive gestures, which almost gave the impression that she had something sexually indecent to tell and was ashamed of it. Here again the abdominal movements became noticeable. She repeatedly giggled in a coy way. As this gave an inadequate picture of her condition, I was led to ask whether there were any other ideas that tormented her during her sleeplessness. "No, I don't remember anything else—everything is mixed up—oh, there are thousands of things going through my head." She could not, however, produce any of them, made defensive gestures and suddenly said: In any case, she often had such silly thoughts that they actually overcame her and she could not get rid of them whatever efforts she made. She regretted that she could not tell me these thoughts, because she was afraid that I might also be overtaken by such obsessional ideas. Once before she had told a priest and a doctor about some of her thoughts, and she had always had the compulsive idea that she must have infected those people with them, so that they too had obsessional ideas. She had certainly already infected me. I reassured her; I had already heard many such ideas and it had not done me the slightest harm. After this statement she confessed, again with those peculiar defensive gestures, that besides the idea that she had infected the priest and the doctor with obsessional ideas she was tortured by the thought that a woman neighbour who had recently died had, on her account, died without the last sacrament and was having to suffer all the tortures of hell. She had had this idea only since the death; before that she had for several years had the idea that a boy whom she had brought up had afterwards died from the beatings that she had occasionally given him. The fear had tortured her so much that she had twice been obliged to write to the pupil's family to ask how he was. Each time she had done it in quite a casual manner. The good news that she had received on each occasion had calmed her down for the time being, but a few days later the fear was upon her again. This idea had now vanished, but instead she had to blame herself for the death without extreme unction of the neighbour. Her common sense told her that these ideas are nonsense (she said this with a very uncertain voice), but perhaps it was not (she quickly added). Thus she did not correct it completely, but was apparently entirely dominated by the obsessional idea.

The anamnesis did not reveal any sexual abnormalities; i.e., anything that might refer to sexual processes was immediately rejected.

An attempt at hypnosis was frustrated because she could not keep her eyes fixed on anything. In order not to compromise this method from the very beginning by useless trials, I decided first to obtain some information about the psychic material underlying the condition. I therefore carried out the association experiment with her.

1. THE ASSOCIATION EXPERIMENT

667 Here is the whole test:[11]

Stimulus-word	Reaction	Reaction-time (secs.)	Reproduction
1. head	thoughts	2.2	hair
2. green	grass	1.8	+
3. water	drinker, to drink	2.4	glass
4. to prick	needle	3.6	+
5. angel r.	heaven	2.6	+
6. long r.	short	4.0	+
7. ship	sea	1.4	+

668   I cannot give a complete analysis of the associations. In answer to all questions the patient confined herself to saying that nothing special had come to her mind at the critical points. It was thus impossible to find the determinant of the reactions by means of subjective analysis. The objective result of the experiment was, however, sufficient to diagnose the complex, at least in outline, independent of the information given by the patient. I should like to explain in as much detail as possible how I came to this diagnosis.

11 The incorrectly reproduced associations are in italics. + = correct reproduction. r. = here the patient repeated the stimulus-word quickly in the reaction. One frequently meets this phenomenon in and after complex-reactions.

669   In anticipation, I should mention that the probable mean (Kraepelin) of all the reaction-times of the experiment is 2.4 seconds. This mean is definitely too high for an intelligent and educated person. The mean obtained for twelve educated subjects is 1.5 secs. Since it is mainly emotional influences that prolong the reaction-time,[12] we may infer, from this high figure, a rather strong emotionality in the patient. The reader is asked to keep in mind this figure of 2.4 secs. during the following discussion of the reactions.

670   1, *head / thoughts*, is wrongly reproduced. The complex of the illness may have had an influence here.

671   3, *water / drinker, to drink*, shows a verbal deviation: *drinker* has been corrected to *to drink*. The father was a heavy drinker. The three following reaction-times are all longer than 2.4 secs.; furthermore, there are two stimulus-word repetitions. From *drinker* a perseverating emotional charge may be assumed.[13]

672   5, *angel / heaven*, may have recalled the obsessional idea of the neighbour who died without the sacrament.

8. to plough	to sow	2.2	+
9. *wool*	*to spin*	3.4	—[14]
10. *friendly*	*loving*	3.6	*good*
11. *table*	*woman*	4.6	—
12. to ask	to reply	2.4	+
13. state	church	2.2	+
14. *sulky*	*brave*	1.8	*friendly*
15. stalk	flower	1.8	+

673   What disturbance prolonged the reaction time of *wool* I cannot say. Experience shows that *friendly* (10) very easily produces erotic reminiscences. The remarkable *table / woman* (11), which the patient cannot explain, seems to point to the erotic significance of R. 10. Sensitive people, as all neurotics are, always take stimulus-words personally. It is therefore easy to assume that the patient would like to be the "loving, good woman." That the word *friendly* has a certain tendency to be reproduced becomes apparent from its reappearance in 14.

---

[12] Cf. Jung, "The Reaction-Time Ratio in the Association Experiment," etc.
[13] I cannot deal here with the justification of these inferences. See ibid.
[14] — = not reproduced.

(Feeling-toned ideas have, of course, a stronger tendency to be reproduced than others.)

16. to dance	to jump	1.8	+
17. lake r.	water	2.4	+
18. ill	healthy	2.0	+
19. pride	haughty	5.0	+
20. to cook	to roast	2.0	+
21. ink	pot	2.0	+
22. *wicked*	*good*	3.0	−
23. needle	prick	2.2	+
24. to swim	water	2.0	+
25. journey	railway	2.2	+
26. blue	red	1.8	+
27. bread	knife	2.0	+
28. *to threaten*	*naughty*	8.0	−

674 *To dance* (16) tends to arouse erotic reminiscences. This assumption is not unjustified here because the following reaction is disturbed.

675 *Ill* (18) and *pride* (19) may easily have been taken personally. *Pride* shows distinct complex-characteristics, *wicked* (22) and *to threaten* (28) obviously aroused feelings too. The response *naughty* to *to threaten* sounds like an association to a child's idea. Has a schoolgirl's reminiscence perhaps been aroused here? *To threaten* can in any case arouse many feeling-toned associations. People with lively complexes are usually somehow afraid of the future. One can therefore often see that they relate *to threaten* to the threatening uncertainty of their future. Naturally, there are often underlying concrete associations as well. One must not forget that a word like *threaten* is seldom used; owing to this "difficulty" it has a somewhat exciting influence; this does not necessarily mean that a complex underlies it. It seems to me wiser, however, to consider the influence of a complex than of a "difficulty." (Cf. Freud's analyses!)

29. lamp	light	1.8	+
30. rich	poor	1.8	+
31. tree	green	1.2	+
32. to sing	to dance	2.0	+
33. pity	poor	2.0	+
34. *yellow*	*flower*	4.2	*green*

35. mountain r.	work[15]	2.8	+
36. to play	children	2.2	to dance
37. salt	bread	2.8	+
38. new	old	1.6	+

676   *To dance* (16), mentioned in the previous sequence, returns here twice, thus revealing a clear tendency to be reproduced, in accordance with its not inconsiderable emotional charge. In this way frequent repetitions can give away a great deal. A gentleman whom I had asked to be a subject for the experiment was convinced he would not give away any complexes. On the way to me he worked out what he would answer to my stimulus-words; it occurred to him at once that he would say "Paris," a word that seemed to him to have absolutely no personal meaning. True enough, he repeated "Paris" many times during the experiment, declaring this word to be absolutely fortuitous. Six months later he confessed to me that at the time of the test he had still been under the impression of an event that had strongly affected him and which had occurred in Paris. At that time, however, he had thought that Paris had no significance at all for him. I have no reason to doubt this man's truthfulness. *Yellow* (34) certainly had a personal effect, judging from the surrounding complex-disturbances. The patient has a sallow elderly complexion. Women are very sensitive to such things, particularly if an erotic complex is present.

677   That *children* (36) is not reproduced but replaced by another erotic term seems to be worth mentioning.

39. *habit* r.	*nasty or bad*	12.2	*vicious habit*
40. to ride r.	to drive	2.4	+
41. *wall*	*room*	3.0	–
42. *silly* r.	*clever*	2.8	–
43. exercise-book	book	3.0	+
44. to scorn	*disdain*	15.2	*to despise*
45. tooth	abscess	1.4	+

678   In this sequence we meet several serious complex-disturbances. With *habit* (39) and *to scorn* (44), the patient made defensive movements and stamped her foot. An "ugly" or "bad" habit can easily be interpreted in a sexual sense: e.g.,

15 [The association in German seems to have been suggested by *Bergwerk*, 'mine.']

masturbation is a "nasty" habit, a "vicious habit." People indulging in such "vicious habits" are "scorned."

679   *Silly* (42) may be personal or may still belong to the range of the emotional charge perseverating from *habit*. Here her gestures by no means contradict a sexual complex. *Habit* could in some circumstances also mean "the drink habit" and thus have aroused the complex of the drunkard father.

46. *correct* r.	*I should always like to say just the opposite*	7.6	*incorrect*
47. people r.	father	6.0	+
48. to stink	fragrance	4.8	+
49. *book* r.	*pen*	4.4	*exercise-book*
50. *unfair* r.	*sense*	3.6	*fair*
51. frog	green	2.4	+
52. to separate	marriage	2.2	+
53. hunger	thirst	1.4	+
54. white	black	1.8	+

680   If the patient, as we assume, takes the stimulus-words personally and has an erotic complex as indicated, then it is understandable that to *correct* (46) "she would always like to say the opposite," as this fits her behaviour; it also fits the father's dipsomania. Ideas that are determined twice or more do not exclude each other; according to Freud they are even the rule.

681   That *people* (47) is associated with *father* is striking. The reaction seems to be within the field of the emotional charge of *correct*. This could lead to the conclusion that there is some connection, unclear up to now, between her self-reproaches and *father*. (This connection will become clear later on.)

682   What sort of interference acted on *book / pen* (49) is not easy to say. *Book*, pronounced as it is spelled [*Buch*], means "belly" [*Bauch*] in the Swiss dialect. In a sexual complex such an assimilation could easily occur. I have seen it repeatedly in other subjects.

683   The consistent decrease of the reaction-times from *correct*, 7.6 secs., however, indicates a serious complex-interference that begins with this stimulus-word and gradually decreases during the next seven reactions. *Unfair* (50) seems to have been taken personally, and this fits well with her self-recrimination.

55. cattle r.	cow	4.2	+
56. to attend	disobedient	4.0	+
57. *pencil*	*to sharpen*	3.0	*pointed*
58. dull	weather	1.8	+
59. plum	tree	3.8	+
60. to meet	certain	1.4	+
61. law	state	2.8	+
62. *dear*	*good*	4.0	*child*
63. glass	wa-water	1.6	+
64. *to quarrel*	*argument*	2.4	*discord*
65. *goat*	*milk*	2.0	*to milk*

684   I have no explanation for the disturbance at 55, *cattle*. *Disobedient* (56) reminds one of the previous *naughty*, which may be related to the pupil already mentioned. The disturbance of the following unrelated reaction indicates the perseverating emotional charge. R.59, *plum / tree*, does not seem to have passed by smoothly, judging by the length of the reaction-time. The word here used for *plum* is not an everyday word; it is, however, unlikely that for this reason it takes an educated subject such a long time to react. (Wehrlin's idiots have average figures varying between 3.0 secs. and 37 secs. Therefore 3.8 seems far too long for an educated person.) The German *Pflaume* (plum) is, like Swiss *Zwetschge* (plum), a popular sex-symbol in our colloquial language.

685   *Dear* (62) can easily indicate an erotic complex. At *glass* (63) the complex of the dipsomaniac father apparently comes to the surface again with the strong emotional charge attached to it (hence the disturbance of the two following reactions).

66. large	small	2.6	+
67. potato r.	floury	6.0	+
68. to grind	mill	2.0	+
69. part r.	small	11.6	+
70. *old*	*ugly*	3.0	*young, unattractive*
71. *flower*	*beautiful*	2.0	*scent*
72. *to beat*	*rod*	2.8	—
73. cupboard	table	2.8	+

686   *Large* (66) is as a rule taken personally. The patient is very short. With an erotic complex, she is, as we have already seen,

298

bound to be much concerned with her body. This might explain the disturbance of the following reaction.

687   For *part* (69), the reaction-time is very much extended. It is usual to interpret "part" as "genital." Here the strong emotional charge is characteristic for this association. It is not surprising under this constellation that *old* (70) is given a personal erotic meaning. How strongly emphasized in this patient is the question of physical beauty and her own ageing can be seen from the perseveration *beautiful* (71). *To beat / rod* (72) can again have been specially constellated by the obsessional idea that she had caused her pupil's death.

74. wild	child	2.4	+
75. family	large	2.4	+
76. to wash r.	to clean	3.0	+
77. cow	to milk	1.8	+
78. stranger	nostalgia	14.8	+
79. happiness r.	unhappiness	3.0	+
80. to tell	story	1.6	+

688   The minor disturbance at 76, *to wash,* can be explained by the preceding erotic concepts *child* and *family*. *Stranger* (78) apparently aroused a personal association, to be explained later on.

81. propriety	intellect	4.6	+
82. narrow r.	small	3.2	+
83. brother	sister	1.0	+
84. damage r.	neighbour	4.0	+
85. stork r.	church	2.4	+
86. false r.	unfaithful	3.0	+
87. fear	anxiety	2.4	+
88. to kiss	mouth	2.2	+
89. fire	blaze	1.8	+
90. dirty	sticky	2.2	+
91. door	fold	1.6	+

689   The sound association of 81, *propriety / intellect (Anstand / Verstand)* is most striking. Let us remember the disturbances produced by *habit*! There we suspected the "vicious habit" of masturbation. Here too this complex could have been aroused. In this case *intellect* is not fortuitous. According to a

popular belief masturbation destroys the reason, the "intellect." One has also to bear in mind the patient's bemoaning that she is afraid of losing her reason.

690   *Narrow / small* (82) is still under the influence of the preceding reaction: *small* probably belongs to the body-complex in view of its being repeated (66); *narrow* may, under the constellation of the preceding association, refer to the *introitus vaginae* and therefore be connected with *small*, which indicates her figure; the ominous "part" too is *small* (this assumption will be confirmed). *Damage* (84) is probably taken personally; *neighbour* fits neatly. She has done immense damage to the neighbour by being guilty of her dying unabsolved. Under the sexual constellation, however, "damage" can also have been taken personally; one does personal and mental damage to oneself by masturbation (see above). The neighbour then provides a cover (see Freud's similar conclusions). Behind the neighbour the patient herself may be hidden. That an emotional charge interfered here becomes apparent from the following disturbances. At 86, *false / unfaithful,* a definite erotic reminiscence can easily have come to the surface in an elderly spinster.

92. to choose r.	teacher	4.4	+	
93. hay	straw	1.8	+	
94. *still*	*stool*	13.0	*child*	
95. mockery	scorn	1.4	+	
96. to sleep r.	to wake	3.4	+	
97. month	year	1.6	+	
98. coloured	gaudy	2.4	+	
99. dog	cat	1.2	+	
100. to talk	to be silent	1.4	—	

691   To *to choose* (92) women like to associate the thought of marriage.

692   The patient's father was a teacher. She is a teacher. It would be easy to assume that she has marriage with a teacher in mind. The father-complex may, however, also have to be considered here (see below). *Still / stool* (94) is a striking sound association. The explanation is given by the erotically charged term *child.* A child can be "still"; but the dead are also still (obsessive idea: she has caused the pupil's death by ill-treating him). Behind this there may be erotic connections, associated

with German "stillen" (to suckle). (Cf. 49, *book*, and subsequent comment.) The same word (*stillen*) can be used for quieting a child or quieting sexual desire. *To sleep* (96) has many erotic associations. The patient cannot sleep, for instance; sleeplessness in younger people, however, is often the expression of lack of sexual satisfaction (Freud). Anyone inexperienced in the field of pathological association psychology will probably shake his head at the above suppositions; he will perhaps see in them not just hypotheses but sheer phantasms. The judgment on them will perhaps be the same as on Freud's *Interpretation of Dreams.*

693 Let us next summarize the result of the association and reproduction test. As I have already said, the patient did not give any information about herself; I am therefore entirely dependent on the objective data of the test and on my experience.

694 The probable mean of the reaction-times is 2.4 secs. Forty-four per cent of the reaction-times exceed 2.4 secs. Amongst these are figures of up to 15.2 secs., pointing to the dominance of emotion or, in other words, a considerable lack of control of the psychic material.

695 In the analysis we indicated the existence of various complexes. The erotic complex appears to play a dominant role. Here I give a tabulated survey of the complex-reactions. The following examples should be understood as related to an erotic complex:[16]

10. friendly	loving	3.6	good
11. table	woman	4.6	—
12.		2.4	
13.		2.2	
14.		1.8	
16. to dance	to jump	1.8	+
17. lake r.	water	2.4	+
34. yellow	flower	4.2	green
35. mountain r.	work[17]	2.8	+
36.		2.2	

[16] In order to set the complex-disturbances in relief, I am adding all the perseveration phenomena and also the gradually decreasing times of the subsequent reactions.
[17] [See supra, n. 15.]

39. *habit* r.	*nasty or bad*	12.2	*vicious habit*
40. to ride r.	to drive	2.4	+
41. *wall*	*room*	3.0	—
44. *to scorn*	*disdain*	15.2	*to despise*
45.		1.4	
59. plum	tree	3.8	+
62. *dear*	*good*	4.0	*child*
66. large	small	2.6	+
67. potato r.	floury	6.0	+
68.		2.0	
69. part r.	small	11.6	—
70. *old*	*ugly*	3.0	*young, un-attractive*
71. *flower*	*beautiful*	2.0	*scent*
72. *to beat*	*rod*	2.8	—
73.		2.8	
74. wild	child	2.4	+
75. family	large	2.4	+
76. to wash r.	to clean	3.0	+
81. propriety	intellect	4.6	+
82. narrow r.	small	3.2	+
83.		1.0	
86. false r.	unfaithful	3.0	+
87.		2.4	
88.		2.2	
89.		1.8	
92. to choose r.	teacher	4.4	+
93.		1.8	
94. *still*	*stool*	13.0	*child*
95.		1.4	
96. to sleep r.	to wake	3.4	+
97.		1.6	

696   These associations, which presumably have a sexual background and which show all the characteristic complex-disturbances, could be interpreted as follows:

697   The patient feels herself to be old and ugly, is very sensitive about her sallow complexion, above all pays anxious attention to her body; in particular she does not like being so small. Presumably she has a great desire to get married; she would certainly be a loving wife to her husband and she would like to have children. Behind these not very suspicious erotic symptoms, however, there seems to lie a sexual complex that the

patient has every reason to repress. There are signs that allow the conclusion that she pays more than usual attention to her genitals. In a well brought-up and educated woman this can only refer to masturbation; masturbation, however, in the wider sense of a perverse self-satisfaction.

698   Masturbation is one of the most frequent sources of self-reproach[18] and self-criticism. This complex, or, better, this aspect of the sexual complex, is also indicated by the following associations:

14. *sulky*	*brave*	1.8	*friendly*
19. pride	haughty	5.0	+
22. *wicked*	*good*	3.0	—
23.		2.2	
24.		2.0	
42. *silly* r.	*clever*	2.8	—
43. exercise-book	book	3.0	+
46. *correct* r.	*I should always like to say just the opposite*	7.6	*incorrect*
47. people r.	father	6.0	+
48. to stink	fragrance	4.8	+
49. *book* r.	*pen*	4.4	*exercise-book*
50. *unfair* r.	*sense*	3.6	*fair*
51.		2.4	
52.		2.2	
53.		1.4	

699   To the complex of the alcoholic father can be related:

3. *water*	*drinker, to drink*	2.4	*glass*
4.		3.6	
63. glass	wa-water	1.6	+
64. *to quarrel*	*argument*	2.4	*discord*
65. *goat*	*milk*	2.0	*to milk*

700   From this tabulation it can be seen that the sexual complex is well in the foreground. Although, as I have already mentioned, a direct confirmation of this interpretation was not to be had from the patient, I took the complex-diagnosis as confirmed for the reasons I have just given.

---

18 The reproaches are originally restricted to the sexual complex but, according to our experience, are soon applied to a wider field.

701   I told her therefore that I was sure her obsessional ideas were nothing but excuses and shiftings, that in reality she was tortured by sexual ideas.

702   The patient denied this explanation with affect and sincere conviction. Had I not been convinced through the association experiment of the existence of a particularly marked sexual complex, my certainty would probably have been shaken. I appealed to her intelligence and truthfulness: she assured me that if she knew of anything of the kind she would tell me, because she well knew it would be silly to conceal such thoughts from the doctor. She had thought of getting married, "as everyone else did, but not more." After this I let the patient go and asked her to come again in two days' time.

2. PSYCHOANALYSIS

703   For psychoanalysis the patient's mental condition is important, but still more important is the mental condition of the doctor. Here probably lies the secret of why Freud's psychoanalysis is disregarded by the world of science. He who approaches a case with anything but absolute conviction is soon lost in the snares and traps laid by the complex of hysterical illness at whatever point he hopes to take hold of it. One has to know from the very beginning that everything in the hysteric is trying to prevent an exploration of the complex. Where necessary, not only the patient's interest and his regard for the doctor fail, but also his thinking, memory, and finally even his language. But precisely these peculiar defence-mechanisms give the complex away.

704   Just as hesitating, faulty reproduction and all the other characteristic disturbances always occur in the association experiment whenever the complex is touched on, so in the analysis difficulties always arise whenever one gets close to the complex. In order to bypass these difficulties, Freud, as is well known, induces "free associations." It is a very simple method and one has only to practice it for some little time to become reasonably familiar with it. In this case I carried out psychoanalysis strictly on Freud's lines. I made the patient take an easy-chair and sat down behind her, so as not to confuse her. Then I asked her to tell me calmly everything that came into her mind, no matter what it was about. The patient laughed;

surely one could not say every piece of nonsense that came into one's mind. But I adhered to my request. Then she tried several times to say something, suppressed it, however, each time with the excuse that it was silly—I would laugh at her and think she was an ungrateful person who could only offer banalities. I did nothing but encourage her to continue to talk and eventually the patient produced the following sentences: "I think I shall never get well—now you are sure to laugh— but I am convinced that I shall never get well—you cannot hypnotize me—you will no more cure me than any other doctor has—it will only get worse, because now I have to reproach myself that with my nonsense I am only unnecessarily wasting your time." This idea was not quite unjustified because the patient always blurted out the sentences after long intervals, so that it took us almost half an hour to come to this meagre result. She continued: "I am thinking now of my people at home, how hard they work and how they need me; while I am here, good for nothing but my silly ideas—you too will certainly become infected by them—now I am thinking that I cannot sleep, that last night I took 1 g. of Veronal, although you have forbidden it—I am sure I shall never be able to sleep. How can you expect to cure me?—What do you want me to tell you? [Here a certain restlessness became noticeable.] But I cannot tell you every piece of nonsense that comes into my head. [Increasing restlessness, shrugging of the shoulders, makes stamping movements with her foot now and then, shakes herself as if in great indignation.] No, this is nonsense—I don't know of anything else now—really, I don't know of anything else. [Very restless, wriggles and turns in her chair, makes defensive movements by shaking her thorax to and fro and makes elbow movements as if pushing something away.] At last she jumps up and wants to go, she cannot think of anything else at all! With gentle force I make her sit down in the chair and remind her that as she has come to me to be cured, she must follow my directions. After a long debate on the use and purpose of my method, she at last consents to stay and continue, but soon the movements of indignation and defence are resumed, she literally wriggles in the chair; occasionally she straightens herself with a forcible movement, as if she had come to a decision after the greatest struggle with herself. At last she says meekly: "Oh, something silly came into my head—you are sure to laugh—but you must not tell anybody else—it is really nothing—it is something quite simple—no, I can't tell you, never—it has nothing at all to do with my illness—I am only wasting your time with it—really, it doesn't mean anything at all—have I really got to tell it? Do you really insist on it? Oh, well, I may as well tell you, then I shall be rid of it. Well,— once I was in France—no, it's impossible, and if I have to sit in this chair for another four weeks [with sudden determination] well, I was a governess in France—there was also a maid-servant—no, no, I cannot tell it—no, there was a gardener— for goodness sake, what will you think of me? This is really sheer torture—I have certainly never thought of such a thing!"

705   Between these painful ejaculations the following story at last emerged with innumerable stoppages and many interruptions, during which she asserted that this was the first and last session with me.

706   Her employer also had a gardener, who once said to her that he would like to sleep with her. While saying this he tried to kiss her, but the patient pushed him away. When she went to bed that evening she listened at the door and wondered what it would be like if he did come to sleep with her; then a frantic fear overtook her that he might really come. Once in bed she was still compelled to think of what it would be like if he came, then reproached herself anew for thinking such things. The thought of what it would be like to sleep with the gardener did not, however, leave her, although she was again and again shocked at finding herself capable of such thoughts. In this mental turmoil she was unable to get to sleep until the morning.

707   The first session took no less than an hour and a half. Its result was a sexual history! What was particularly interesting to me was its quite spontaneous appearance with the same gestures that I had immediately noticed in the patient at the first consultation. These tic-like phenomena had a very close and easily understandable connection with the repressed sexual matters! I arranged the following session for two days later, which was at once accepted, the patient looking very relieved and not saying another word about leaving.

306

708   On the day of the appointment I was busy with some urgent work when the patient came and therefore sent her a message, asking her to come in the evening instead. She, however, sent the reply that she could not possibly wait, she had to speak to me urgently. I thought something special had happened and went to her. I found her in great distress: she had not slept at all, not a minute, she had had to take drugs again, etc. I asked her whether she had been brooding again over her obsessional ideas: "No, something much worse; now I have my head full of that nonsense that I told you about last time. Now I can think only of these stories and therefore cannot close an eye; because of them I toss and turn all night long and cannot get rid of these thoughts for a minute. I have definitely got to talk to you now; it gives me no peace." She went on to tell me that last time she had gone home very much relieved and calmed down, almost in a gay mood, and had hoped she would now at last be able to sleep, but then a story came into her mind that she should have told me last time, but which she had thought was not really of any importance. She had determined now not to "act so silly" as last time, but freely to tell everything she thought of. Then the confession would soon be over. So I resumed the analysis, hoping it would go off smoothly without the endless preliminaries of the time before. I was, however, completely mistaken. The patient repeated the interjections of the first session almost verbatim. After an hour and a half of mental torture I brought the following story to light: In the same house where the patient was a governess, there was also a maid[19] who had a lover, with whom she had sexual intercourse. This girl had also had sexual intercourse with the gardener. The patient often discussed sexual topics with her and in particular the sex life of master and mistress. The patient and the maid even investigated their beds for sperm stains and other signs of sexual intercourse! Every time, after such amusements, the patient suffered the severest self-reproaches on her indecency and spent sleepless nights, during which she turned and tossed about because of torturing reproaches and voluptuous fantasies.

19 Cf. the reference to this maid in the first session.

709   When, after tiresome resistance, the story was out at last, the patient declared: now she had come to the end, this was all, nothing else came to her mind now. If only she could sleep; the telling of these stories did not help at all.

710   Two days later she came to the third session and said: After the previous session she had been rather quiet again, but as soon as she was in bed at night another new story had come to her mind which had tortured her incessantly, with the obsessive reproach that again she had not told me everything in the session. She was sure now that today she could tell me the story quickly, without the continuous resistance as in the first two sessions. The third one, however, proceeded exactly in the same way as the two previous ones: incessant interjections, excuses, etc. Particularly conspicuous was the tendency to present the matter as perfectly natural, as if there was nothing to it. It was about a second maid who was in service with the same employer. The master had a valet who pursued the girl. He did not, however, succeed in seducing her. At last, one evening, when there was a party in the house, he managed to entice the girl into the garden. The couple was, however, surprised by the mistress at the critical moment. At this the youth is said to have exclaimed: What a pity, he was just ready! The patient heard this story from the first maid. At first she made out not to have the slightest interest in the story, as if she found it downright repulsive. This, however, had been a lie, because in fact she had had the greatest interest in it; she had several times tried to bring the maid back to this topic in order to hear every detail. At night she had hardly been able to sleep from curiosity, and had incessantly had to ask herself the questions: What did the two want in the garden? In what posture could they have been found by the mistress? What had the youth been ready for? What would have happened if the mistress had not come? Although she knew the answers perfectly well, she could not stop asking herself these questions over and over again. At last she was compelled to think over persistently what she would have done in such a situation. This excitement lasted for several days.

711   We have mentioned being struck by her matter-of-fact presentation of the story. She said, for instance, very reluctantly that the lad was after the maid. From the reluctance it could be

308

expected that something rather unpleasant was to come, but she continued as follows in an indifferent tone: "The lad was just in love with the girl. This is nothing unusual? This happens often?—oh, now there is something again—no, that I cannot—" etc. While telling the story she always tried from time to time to belittle and talk herself out of her belief in the importance of an event by inserting such generalizing rhetorical questions.

712   From now on, during the whole period of the analysis (three weeks), the original obsessional ideas were absent; their place had been taken by sexual ideas. The memories underlying the obsessional ideas that had already been dealt with constantly tormented the patient. She was so obsessed by these sexual reminiscences that she was never able to find peace until she had told the story again. She expressed great amazement at this change; the stories came like beads on a string, as if they had been experienced yesterday. Things occurred to her of which she had previously been quite unconscious but which she now again recalled (Freud's hypermnesia). Of course, these admissions have to be taken with the same reserve as the familiar "I don't know." The patient may quite well have ardently cultivated all her sexual ideas without remembering them, and spun them out right up to the moment when she had to speak about them objectively. In her stories one can often see immediately what is to come from her gestures, while she still repeatedly asserts that she certainly does not remember anything more. Her everyday person and her sexual person are just two different complexes, two different aspects of consciousness that do not want to or must not know anything of one another. The split of the personality here is, however, only hinted at (as in every vigorous complex, the peculiarity of which is a striving for autonomy). But it is only a step to the classic examples of split personality, all of which are, of course, produced by the mechanisms demonstrated by Freud.[20]

713   With these three sessions a certain conclusion was reached, in so far as one could not avoid relating the obsessional idea that she had caused the death of her former pupil to the self-reproaches connected with the sexual stories. This apparently

[20] Cf. Jung, "On the Psychology and Pathology of So-called Occult Phenomena" (1902).

was also felt by the patient when she spontaneously mentioned that many years had already passed since these events, and the thought that she had caused the pupil's death had long ceased to torment her. Probably for the purpose of escaping from the unbearable sexual ideas, she transferred the guilt from this field to that of her educational methods. The mechanism, which is well known, is this: if one has continually to reproach oneself in one sphere, one tries to compensate for these deficiencies in another sphere, as if the same deficiencies were present there as well; this is particularly obvious in masturbators (compulsive brooding, cleanliness, and orderliness). It therefore seems to be not incidental that precisely these stories, underlying a past obsessional idea, were told first. Since there were in present consciousness no obsessional ideas directly supported by these stories, there were no special resistances present. Hence, the stories were relatively immaterial.

714   I refrain from presenting the subsequent sessions in detail; they all followed the pattern already described. No admonition, no pointing out the absurdity of her stereotyped resistance, could make the patient talk more quickly and spontaneously. Every new session was a new torture, and at almost every one the patient declared that this was the last. Usually during the following night, however, there came new material that tormented her.

715   The reminiscences of her time as governess were succeeded by a series of unsavoury stories that had served as a topic for conversation with the neighbour for whose death without the sacraments the patient reproached herself. The neighbour was a person about whose dubious past a number of rumours were current. The patient, who is a very decent girl and comes from a respectable family, known to me, had in her own view a dubious past herself and reproached herself for it. Therefore it is not surprising, psychologically, that she was immediately attracted by the interesting neighbour. There the *chronique scandaleuse* of the day used to be discussed, and in this connection the patient had quite a number of obscene stories and jokes to tell me, which I need not repeat here. For this also she reproached herself. When the neighbour quickly succumbed to an illness, the patient transferred the reproaches, which actually were about her sexual curiosity, to the death of the

neighbour, who had died without absolution because the patient had during her visits enticed her to sinful conversations. The type of reminiscence and of reasoning seems to suggest that this obsessional idea is simply a new version of the earlier obsession about the death of the pupil. The religious obsession took her first to the priest and then to the doctor. She felt that she had infected both of them with her obsessions. She had therefore done something similar to what she had done to the neighbour whom she had destroyed simply by being what she was, as she had originally also destroyed the pupil. Underlying all this is the general idea that she is a horrible creature who infects everything with her depravity.

716 During the following sessions the patient dealt mainly with a series of stories that she had recently discussed with a girl friend. The friend has an office job in a big shop. There she hears quite a number of juicy things from the men, each of which she retails to the patient while they are still warm. On one occasion the friend said she intended to have sexual intercourse just simply to see what it was like. This thought mightily excited the patient; she told herself incessantly that she too would like to have it. This, however, was sufficient reason for renewed self-reproaches. From this incident onwards there was an increasingly clear trend towards referring sexual subjects to herself; during almost every session obscene jokes and the like had to be told again. From the ideas referring to herself there came first all the reminiscences of former love-affairs and longings for affection. The recounting of these on the whole rather harmless events went off fairly smoothly. Only one incident had a stronger emotional charge. She was in love with a young man about whom she knew very little and thought he was going to marry her. Later, however, he left her without a goodbye and she never heard from him again. For a long time she kept on waiting for him and always hoped he would write to her. To this refers 78, *stranger / nostalgia*,[21] 14.8 secs. As already mentioned, the patient could not then explain the significance of this reaction. While the old love stories were told without any major difficulties, once this phase had passed

[21] [German *fremd/Heimweh*; "fremd" is an adjective the literal translation of which ('strange') would be misleading. The noun had therefore to be used, although not strictly apposite.]

resistance set in. The patient definitely wanted to leave, she had no more to tell. I told her that I had not heard anything about her earlier youth. She thought she would soon be finished with that, there was not much to tell about her youth. She had hardly finished this sentence when she was compelled to repeat several times her vehement tic-like defensive gestures, an unmistakable sign that much more very important material could be expected. With the greatest resistance and the most painful contortions she told in a jerky manner of a book that she had found at home, when she was ten years old, the title of which was *The Way to Happy Matrimony*. She asserted that she had no longer any idea what was in it. But as I continued to be relentless, recollections recurred after a while, and it turned out that the patient still remembered every detail, frequently even the wording. She gave a detailed account of the first sexual intercourse and its complications; the academic description without any personal reference seemed to me peculiar and unusual. I suspected that something must be concealed behind this façade. It was not long before the patient related that at the age of fourteen she had found in her elder brother's pocket a small book in which was reprinted a letter. The letter was written by a young wife to an intimate friend and discussed the secrets of the wedding night in a very obscene and lascivious manner. Apparently I was on the right track, as this story showed. The patient's next recollection concerned erotic dreams that she had had only quite recently. The dreams were outspoken ejaculation dreams and represented sexual intercourse undisguised. This was followed by the confession of having several times tried to hold the dream-image and to masturbate. Then it turned out that masturbation had also occasionally been practised before this. With the masturbation was linked a persistent thinking about her own genitals; she is compelled to wonder whether she "is properly built," whether perhaps she has not a too narrow introitus; she also has to investigate this state of affairs with the finger. She frequently has to look at her naked body in the mirror, etc. She has a long series of fantasies on sexual intercourse, she is compelled especially to imagine in every detail how she would behave during the first intercourse, etc. In this connection she also confesses to feeling a strong libido (which at the beginning she

312

had emphatically denied). She would very much like to get married, and therefore attaches sexual fantasies to most of the men she meets. She also imagines herself in the leading part of all the sex stories she has collected. Thus she tells, for instance, of a naïve young acquaintance, a girl who, on a trip in a crowded railway compartment, had to sit on her teacher's lap. The girl afterwards laughingly related that the teacher never forgot his role, he even carried a ruler in his trousers pocket. About this story the patient thinks that she too would enjoy it if a teacher took her on his lap, but she would know what the ruler in the trousers pocket meant. (The previously not-completely explained reaction [92] *to choose / teacher* may have been constellated partly by this story.)

717   With great reluctance she also admits that at the age of fourteen she had once laid herself upon her younger sister "as if she had been a man." At last, in one of the latest sessions, came the narration of an event which in every respect had the significance of Freud's youth trauma. At the age of seven or eight she had repeatedly listened to the sexual intercourse of her father and mother. Once she noticed that her mother struggled and did not at all want to let the father come to her again. For a long time after that she could not face her parents any more. Then her mother became pregnant and gave birth to her younger sister. She bitterly hated the little sister from the very beginning, and only much later was she able to over-come a deep aversion to the child. It is, of course, not quite unlikely that the patient imagined herself as one of the acting persons in this story and that she adopted the role of the mother. This very plausible connection easily explains the strong emotional charge in all associations to the father.

718   Of course, the psychic trauma of such an observation be-comes a complex with a very strong emotional charge in a child's mind, which is bound to constellate the thinking and acting for years to come. This was, in a classic way, the case with this patient. It gave a quite definite direction to her sexual function.[22] This becomes obvious from the analysis of her re-pressed material; it is always chiefly connected with digging

---

22 With this one can also compare the fact that many sexually perverted per-sons (fetishists) have acquired their abnormality through an incidental sexual event (see Krafft-Ebing, *Psychopathia Sexualis*).

out and imagining situations of sexual intercourse. Surprisingly, in spite of her sexually extraordinarily lively fantasy, she never became deeply involved with men and anxiously repulsed every attempt at seduction. But instead she was attracted, with an almost magical force, to doubtful females and dirty topics of conversation which, at her level of education and intelligence, one would not have expected. The two last sessions were particularly instructive in this respect. She produced the choicest selection of most repulsive obscenities that she had occasionally heard in the street. What these obscenities, the narration of which I must be spared, had in common were various abnormalities of sexual intercourse (e.g., too wide, or too narrow introitus, sexual intercourse of a little hunchback with a huge fat woman, etc.). The number and the extreme vulgarity of these jokes appeared to me almost incredible for such an educated and decent lady. The phenomenon, however, is explained by the early perverted direction of the sexual function, which is mainly concerned with finding out unclean sexual practices, i.e., the symbolic repetition of eavesdropping on sexual intercourse. This complex, caused by listening to the sexual act, has throughout her life determined a multitude of sexual actions and associations with their peculiar manifestations. This, for instance, is the reason why the patient performs a sort of sexual intercourse with her little sister, why her listening at the door to hear whether the gardener is coming still haunts her, why she has to carry out the disgusting job of examining her employers' bed, why she has to seek the company of morally dubious people, etc. Her defensive movements and the peculiar pushing forward of the abdomen also show how the effect of the complex spreads in all directions. It is worth noting, too, that she appears at each session in a different dress.

719   Using the sexual function in this way is bound to be incompatible with her otherwise gently disposed character; a rejection and repression of sexuality as absurd as it is repulsive must have taken place, because it is impossible that an educated and sensitive woman can combine these obscenities with the other contents of her mind. These things can only be tolerated when repressed. But they do exist, they actually have a separate ex-

istence, they form a state within the state, they constitute a personality within the personality. Expressed in other words, there are two mental attitudes present, kept apart by strong emotional barriers. The one must not and cannot know anything of the other. This explains the peculiar disturbances of reproduction that counteract the analysis. The ethically superior mind has not the associations of the other at its disposal; she must therefore think she has forgotten these ideas and that she has never known such things. I am therefore inclined to accept that the patient was really convinced that nothing more came into her head, that it was not a lie when she asserted with the greatest persistence that she had no more to say.

720   But even if a complex is still so far repressed, it must yet have a constellating influence on the contents of normal consciousness, for even the deepest split of consciousness does not reach the indivisible basis of the personality. Thus the repression must leave a certain imprint on the conscious processes; the normal consciousness must somehow explain away the emotional condition that a repressed complex leaves behind. What is simpler, therefore, than to produce an idea compatible with normal consciousness as an explanation for the persistently self-reproachful and discontented mood? To explain away the pangs of conscience related to the sins of the governess phase, the patient displaces her self-reproach on to her method of teaching, which she feels must have led to a disastrous result; otherwise she would not persistently experience the feeling of self-reproach when she recalls incidents of that time. As we have already seen, the origin of this obsession acts as a pattern for the obsessional guilt about the neighbour's dying unabsolved. The accumulation of obsessive ideas about the doctor and the priest has its good reason in the fact that these people were not at all indifferent to her sexuality, as the patient admitted to me. By having a sexual effect on her they become in a way accomplices in her wickedness; she therefore expects them to feel equally guilty.

721   After this analysis we can understand the role, still unclear in the associations, that the father plays in her erotic complex. In general the analysis supports to the widest extent the hypotheses suggested by the associations. The associations actually

served as signposts among the maze of ever-changing fantasies that at every stage threatened to put the analyst on the wrong track.

722 The analysis was carried out every other day for three weeks and lasted one and a half to two hours at a time. Although at the end of the three weeks the patient had neither achieved proper sleep nor peace of mind, I discharged her and heard no more of her until the end of November. During the last days of November 1905 she suddenly came to see me and presented herself as cured. After the termination of the treatment she had still been very agitated for about four weeks. Sometimes she was tortured at night by her sexual images, sometimes again by obsessional ideas. In particular the obsession about the neighbour frequently recurred and did not give her any peace until she went to the daughter of the dead woman to make her tell her about the death scene for the nth time. When the daughter told her again, as usual, that the mother had died peacefully, the patient suddenly became convinced that the woman had after all received the last sacraments. With this all obsessional ideas suddenly disappeared. Sleep returned and was only occasionally somewhat disturbed by sexual images.

723 What had brought about this happy ending of the treatment?

724 It is obvious that the daughter's story, which the patient had heard many times without any effect, was nothing but the vehicle for the final removal of the obsession. The actual turn for the better occurred at the beginning of the treatment, when the sexual images replaced the obsessional ideas. The confession of her sinful thoughts may have given considerable relief to the patient. But it seems unlikely that the cure can be ascribed entirely to their verbal expression or to the "abreaction." Pathological ideas can be definitely submerged only by a strong effort. People with obsessions and compulsions are weak; they are unable to keep their ideas in check. Treatment to increase their energy is therefore best for them. The best energy-cure, however, is to force the patients, with a certain ruthlessness, to unearth and expose to the light the images that consciousness finds intolerable. Not only is this a severe challenge for the patient's energy but also his consciousness begins to accept the existence of ideas hitherto repressed.

316

725   The split-off contents of the mind are destroyed by being released from repression through an effort of the will. So they lose a great deal of their authority and therefore of their horror, and simultaneously the patient regains the feeling of being master of his ideas. I therefore put the emphasis on arousing and strengthening of the will and not on mere "abreacting," as Freud originally did.

726   It appears, from some recent publications, that Freud's theory of obsessional neurosis is still consistently ignored. It therefore gives me great satisfaction to draw attention to Freud's theories—at the risk of also becoming a victim of persistent amnesia.

SUMMARY

727   1. The complex that is brought to light through the associations offered by patients with psychogenic neuroses constitutes the *causa morbi*, apart from any predisposition.

2. The associations may therefore be a valuable aid in finding the pathogenic complex, and may thus be useful for facilitating and shortening Freud's psychoanalysis.

3. The associations supply us with an experimental insight into the psychological foundation of neurotic symptoms: hysteria and obsessive phenomena stem from a complex. The physical and psychic symptoms are nothing but symbolic manifestations of the pathogenic complexes.

THE PSYCHOLOGICAL DIAGNOSIS OF
EVIDENCE[1]

I

728   It is a matter of common knowledge that the evidence of witnesses, that most unpredictable element in legal proceedings, has recently become the object of experimental research. Perhaps the most credit belongs to William Stern, whose extensive "Contributions to the Psychology of Evidence"[2] is a real treasure-house from both the theoretical and the practical points of view. The aim of these papers is obvious; the ultimate goal is a general improvement in human memory, the utter unreliability of which is not apparent without experiment. The reports of Stern's experiments on legal evidence have gradually found their way to most of the major universities and have thus become widely known. It is therefore probably not necessary to deal with them in detail in this paper. In Stern's school the main object of investigation is the reliability of evidence; it uses the technique of the examining magistrate for the purposes of experiment. The question, however, with which we shall deal here, though not less important from the legal point of view,

---

1 [First published as "Die psychologische Diagnose des Tatbestandes," *Schweizerische Zeitschrift für Strafrecht* (Bern), XVIII (1905), 369–408, and again in *Juristische-psychiatrische Grenzfragen* (Halle), IV (1906): 2, 3–47; republished as a pamphlet the same year under the same auspices, and again in 1941 by Rascher, Zurich and Leipzig.

[For a preliminary report of the case described in Part II (pars. 770ff.) see "On the Psychological Diagnosis of Facts," *Psychiatric Studies*, Vol. 1 of the *Collected Works*. Jung wrote that report on the actual evening of the day during which he had conducted the test herein described more fully.

[While *Tatbestandes* means 'facts,' as translated in the title of the preliminary report, it may mean 'evidence' in a forensic context. Cf. Freud's "Tatbestandsdiagnostik und Psychoanalyse," translated in the Standard Edn., IX, as "Psycho-analysis and the Establishment of the Facts in Legal Proceedings" (main title) and as "Psycho-analysis and Legal Evidence" (page headings).]

2 [I.e., the series *Beiträge zur Psychologie der Aussage*, which Stern published in Leipzig.]

is at the same time of medical and psychological significance; it concerns the "diagnosis" of a criminal case by study of the psychological make-up of the witness.

729   This new field of research is best explained by proceeding in an historical fashion; the problem is thus most easily understood even by the layman in psychology.

730   Wilhelm Wundt, stimulated by Galton,[3] introduced into German psychology a simple experiment which we propose to call the "association experiment." The experiment consists essentially in the experimenter calling out some random word to the subject, in reply to which the subject has as quickly as possible to say the first word that comes into his or her head. A large number of repetitions of this procedure yields a series of pairs of words which one can call *associations*.[4] The word called out is known as the *stimulus-word*, the reply as the *reaction*. As can easily be seen, this experiment, which appears so academic, was of course originally used only for psychological purposes far remote from any practical use. The main interest lay in the logical relation of word-pairs. There were also questions on how far back one could trace the associations, and whether they had already developed in the subject at an early age or not until later in life. The first relevant German paper, by Trautscholdt, on "Experimental Investigations into the Associations of Ideas,"[5] deals exclusively with this topic. Later investigations by others of the Wundt school, such as those described in the papers by Scripture[6] and Cordes,[7] were also concerned with purely theoretical questions. The experiment produced positive results and gained practical importance only when the psychiatrists took the matter in hand. This progress is connected with three well-known names: Kraepelin, Sommer, and Ziehen. These three research workers proceeded almost independently from one another and each of them in his own way. Kraepelin, who belonged to the school of Wundt, dealt first with certain theoretical questions, with which we are

3 "Psychometric Experiments" (1897).
4 Strictly speaking, these are of course not associations, only remote verbal reflections of the purely psychological process of association.
5 "Experimentelle Untersuchungen über die Assoziationen der Vorstellungen" (1883).
6 "Über den assoziativen Verlauf der Vorstellungen" (1889).
7 "Experimentelle Untersuchungen über Assoziationen" (1899).

319

not concerned here. Ziehen made a special study of the results of the experiments with children. Sommer used the findings as an aid to psychiatric diagnostics.[8] This summary shows the manifold aspects of this simple experiment. As every layman would imagine, the possibilities of reaction to stimulus-words are apparently innumerable. It was therefore a great achievement to be able to prove that certain restricting laws are in operation.

731   This proof is the result of the excellent study by Aschaffenburg,[9] a pupil of Kraepelin. He was able to show by means of experiments, as interesting as they were laborious, that mental and physical fatigue exert a definite influence on associations, as can be clearly demonstrated by statistics. It became apparent that under the influence of fatigue there was in particular an increase in what are called *sound associations*[10] (e.g., *dish / fish, red / bread, wood / good*). Aschaffenburg took this important fact as a starting-point, and he then showed that similar associations occurred in a mental disease, namely in *mania*. The question of the common psychological cause of the same phenomenon in these heterogeneous psychic states remained for the time being obscure. In 1901 Bleuler inaugurated research into associations at the Psychiatric Clinic in Zurich. These investigations led in 1904 to the discovery that sound associations are due to disturbances in attention.[11] A second result was that the content of the reactions was not *merely coincidental* but *inevitable*; i.e., what came into the minds of the subjects was not meaningless and incidental material but was determined according to a law by the individual content of the subject's ideas. This may be illustrated by the following example.

732   One of my subjects was a young man who had had an unpleasant dispute with his family a short time before the experiment. He wanted to marry a girl of whom his parents did not approve. As an obedient son he had to give her up, hard though it was for him. These events dominated his interests

---

[8] For further details, see "The Psychopathological Significance of the Association Experiment," *infra*.

[9] "Experimentelle Studien über Assoziationen" (1896–1904).

[10] On the clinical side, Heinrich Schüle (1886; pp. 84, 191) has drawn attention to the "predominance of assonances" in cerebral exhaustion.

[11] Jung and Riklin, "The Associations of Normal Subjects," *supra*.

at the time of the experiment. It is therefore not surprising that numerous reactions were influenced by the recollection of this experience, as the examples show.

Stimulus-word	Reaction
to kiss	again and again
bad	no
time	not now
mature	am I
to love	ah!
son	father and son
wild	mother (wild=furious)
tears	she now has
protection	I cannot offer to her
war	yes, if only there were
faith	I did not keep
once	and never again
miracle	would have to happen
blood	she is anaemic
choose	another one
to part	I need not
right	she has none
fond	I was, of her
wool	a woman's dress
unfair	I was not
stranger	yes, now she is

733   On rereading these reactions it can be seen at once that their contents are not meaningless and that these are not random choices out of the thousands of possible reactions, but just those that indicate the ideas occupying the foreground of the individual interest. It is, as already mentioned, the story of an unhappy love-affair. Such a recollection, which is composed of a large number of component ideas, is called a *complex of ideas*. The cement that holds the complex together is the *feeling-tone* common to all the individual ideas, in this case unhappiness. We are therefore speaking of a *feeling-toned complex of ideas*,[12] or simply of a *complex*. In our case the complex has the effect that the subject does not react by arbitrary or random connections of words but derives most of his reactions

---

12 This term is a pleonasm, because there are no complexes of ideas other than emotionally charged ones. The stronger the complex is, the more vivid an emotional tone one has to infer.

from the complex. The influence of the complex on thinking and behaviour is called a *constellation*.[13]

734   The reactions of our subject are thus *constellated by a complex.*

735   Does this behaviour work according to a law, and are the reactions in all subjects constellated by complexes?

736   There is no one who has no complexes, just as there is no one who is without emotions. Yet human beings differ immensely in the strength of their emotions. In accordance with the intensity of their emotions people's thinking and behaviour are constellated by their complexes, and so are their associations. One is bound to ask, with some surprise, whether revealing or concealing one's complexes is not a matter for individual decision. By no means everyone will disclose his secrets so openly and without embarrassment as this young man did. True, this young man was an exception; he had confidence in the experimenter and said everything just as it came into his head. By no means everyone behaves like this; on the contrary, many are strictly on their guard not to say anything that might be compromising. Others are more casual and just fit one word to another without thinking of any deeper connections. Does a complex constellate the association even in a case where one is not thinking of anything in particular and certainly not of one's secrets? Theoretically, the question has definitely to be answered in the affirmative, because nobody can do anything that is impersonal; there is certainly no psychic manifestation that has not an individual character. Practically, however, it is not so easy to answer the following question: Is it also possible to demonstrate the constellation by complexes in associations in which the subject either does not want to give himself away or is not thinking of anything in particular?[14]

737   In spite of having formulated the appropriate questions, psychology has up to now been unable to prove anything of individual significance in the associations. It was our experiments that first succeeded in finding the approach to this goal.

[13] The concept in this case originates with Ziehen, *Introduction to Physiological Psychology* (orig. 1891). Freud's "symptomatic behaviour" means the same thing.
[14] "The Reaction-time Ratio in the Association Experiment," supra.

738   As already mentioned, not every subject reacts as openly as the case described above; as a rule the associations are at first sight quite impenetrable and sound impersonal and safe, like those that follow here.

to dance	not	to sing	beautiful
ill	not	pity	not at all
angry	friendly	detest	rascals
needle	nail	people	religion
rich	rather	stink	abominable
tree	branches	unfair	atrocious

739   These associations appear to have an impersonal character and are thus very different from those quoted earlier. This might therefore lead to the assumption that they are nothing but casual, entirely incidental word-connections. On questioning the subject, however, we learn that this is by no means the case. It is not accidental that the subject responds to *to dance* with *not*, but it corresponds to a quite special individual situation. The man who was my subject could not dance, a fact that annoyed him, particularly because a friend was very good at dancing and thus won the love of a very "eligible" girl. My subject also wanted to marry an "eligible" girl, but did not succeed, and this angered him even more than not being able to dance. It worried him so much that he nearly became *ill* with it, but he did *not* really become ill in spite of his despair. The girl is *rather rich*. He does *not at all* deserve any *pity* for his lack of success because everybody has to work for his fortune. And because the lady who turned him down was Jewish, he came to *detest* the rascals (i.e., the Jews). Since the Jewish *people* have a different *religion* from his, the problem of religion is of course also particularly important for him. Towards the end his anger breaks through more plainly with the expostulations *abominable* and *atrocious*.

740   Thus here too we find the complex and its constellation quite distinct. Up to now we have relied entirely on the statements of the subject. But now let us look more closely into the contents of the reactions.

741   It is definitely striking that the reactions to *to dance* and *ill* are *not,* just as remarkable as that the subject says *rascals*

in answer to *detest,* and *not at all* to *pity.* Surely one could at these points think of much more innocent and objective connections which seem to be nearer at hand, e.g.,

to dance	music, dance-hall, ball, etc.
ill	disease, doctor, etc.
detest	respect, contempt, etc.
pity	for the poor, the sick, or compassion, etc.

742   The unusual content of the reaction therefore already allows us to infer a constellation by complex. So it is, for instance, striking if an elegant young man reacts to *goat, potato, cow,* each time by *agriculture.* The explanation is that he is a student of *agriculture* in his first term. I could easily pile up examples, but this is not necessary; for even without them it is feasible to conclude from the unusual content of a reaction that there is a constellating complex. This can be done even without getting information from the subject afterwards. If, for instance, a marriageable girl responds to *to kiss* with *sister's kiss,* it is not difficult to guess what is meant by that.

743   But this does not exhaust the possibilities of suspecting and proving the influence of a complex, even without later information. Besides the content of the reaction, we have another very fine criterion for the complex-constellation; this is the *reaction-time.* We always measure the time elapsing between pronouncing the stimulus-word and the reaction with a 1/5-second stopwatch. As might be expected, these times vary in an apparently random fashion. Closer inspection, however, soon shows that very long reaction-times nearly always occur in quite definite places. The following example shows which are the critical spots:

		(secs.)
head	hair	1.4
green	lawn	1.6
water	*deep*	5.0
to stab	knife	1.6
long	table	1.2
ship	*sinking*	3.4
to ask	to reply	1.6
wool	to knit	1.6
sulky	friendly	1.4

lake	*water*	4.0
ill	healthy	1.8
ink	black	1.2
to swim	*to be able to*	3.8

744   In this example most of the figures vary between 1.2 and 1.8 seconds. But besides these there are four unusually long times, ranging from 3.4 to 5.0 seconds. If we ask the subject now why he hesitates at these points, we learn that once in a moment of despair he had seriously contemplated suicide by drowning. The stimulus-words *water, ship, lake,* and *to swim* stimulated this complex. During the short interval between stimulus-word and reaction something unpleasant (the complex) had crossed the subject's mind, and the result was a slight hesitation. The same phenomenon is noticeable in everyday conversation when we ask someone something that is unpleasant either to us or to the other person; we dither a little and hesitate over the question or with the answer. The hesitation here is quite involuntary and a kind of reflex. It is noteworthy that the same hesitation also occurs at the moment of the reaction, when we are quite unaware of the complex-releasing effect of the stimulus-word. Hundreds of cases have taught us this. From this we see that the stimulus-word can also release complexes of which we are not aware at the moment, which may even be separated from consciousness by amnesia, such as is very often the case in hysteria. By measuring the reaction-times we therefore have another means of detecting complex-constellations, even without co-operation from the subject.

745   There is also a third method of finding a complex, which is called the *reproduction method.*[15]

746   We usually record a series of a hundred responses from the subject whose complex we wish to investigate. When this series is complete, we ask the subject to repeat his reaction to every single stimulus-word. Here memory often fails. Then we go into the question of whether the points where incorrect or incomplete reproductions are given are random or determined. For the sake of simplicity we give here the previous example again.

15 "Experimental Observations on the Faculty of Memory," supra.

stimulus-word	reaction	reproduction[16]
head	hair	+
green	lawn	+
water	*deep*	*to swim*
to stab	knife	+
long	table	+
ship	*sinking*	*steamer*
to ask	to reply	+
wool	to knit	+
sulky	friendly	+
lake	*water*	*blue*
ill	healthy	+
ink	black	+
to swim	*to be able to*	*water*

747   The reproduction fails for *water, ship, lake,* and to *swim,* i.e., for the same stimulus-words for which long reaction-times had originally been recorded. This shows that memory fails in the places where there is a complex in operation. We do not want to deal here with the interesting theory concerning these disturbances; this has already been done in the paper mentioned above. It should merely be remembered that memory is seriously deranged by an affect, as nobody knows better than an examining magistrate. Let us summarize briefly: We can demonstrate the complex-constellation objectively by the unusual or in any way striking content of the reaction, by the prolongation of the reaction-time, and by incorrect reproduction.

748   If we apply these three criteria to the associations, we soon find, however, that the matter is not as simple as it looks, because we see that, though these criteria apply to certain associations, they make no sense at all in, for instance, the following cases:

to stab	knife	1.6	+
angel	pure	1.2	+
long	trunk	2.8	tree
ship	man	1.2	+
to plough	field	1.4	+
wool	sheep	1.6	+
friendly	lovely	1.6	+
table	leg	4.0	chair

[16] The plus sign means that the reproduction was correct. Incorrect reproductions are given.

326

to ask	answer	1.6	+
the State	form (shape)	6.2	Switzerland
white	black	1.2	+
pencil	pen	1.0	+
lovable	dear	1.4	+
glass	to love	4.6	to drink

749   If we apply our three criteria to these associations we find *long, table, the State, glass* to be the critical stimulus-words. This grouping does not tell us anything and does not lead to any hypothesis. But could it not be that the complex is not yet fully aroused by the stimulus-word, but makes its appearances only with the reaction? In this case the reaction following the critical reaction would be mainly affected. Let us apply this to our example and consider the stimulus-words preceding the apparently critical reactions. They are *angel, friendly, to ask, lovable.*

750   Whereas we had questioned the subject, a young man, on the previous stimulus-words in vain, his face brightened up when we offered him the new ones. He had just become secretly engaged; the beloved had answered his question with a friendly "yes." In this case, therefore, the post-critical reaction is also constellated by the complex. This very common process is called *perseveration.* That perseveration can also strongly influence the contents of a reaction is shown by the example:

lovable ⎯⎯⎯⎯⎯⎯⎯ dear
glass ⎯⎯⎯⎯⎯⎯⎯ to love

751   I have chosen a rather simple example to demonstrate what is from the practical point of view an important variety of the complex-constellations. As a rule the situation is much more complicated, inasmuch as all the possible factors are present together. In people whose emotions are easily roused (hysterics) the complex-constellation can even extend over a whole series of ensuing reactions. A hysterical female patient who had attempted suicide, for instance, reacted as follows:

1. water	(failure)[17]	—	+
2. to sting	bee	1.8	+
3. angel	inn	21.0	(did not react at all, as after *water*)

[17] "Failure" means that the subject could not think of anything at all here.

4. long	knife	9.0	(as 3)
5. ship	steam	7.0	(as 3)
6. to plough	field	4.2	garden

752   From the seventh reaction on there were again normal re-action-times and correct reproductions. In this example we can observe various features. The subject does not know in the least how to react to *water*. The reaction-time extends as it were to infinity. Ultimately, of course, she would come to some sort of a reaction, but to a forced one, which is of no use. We therefore never wait longer than about 30 seconds. What prevented the patient from reacting was the unpleasant recollection of the suicide attempt which cropped up here. In *angel / inn* the reaction-time is extremely long, because *angel* reminds her at once of the suicide attempt again, of dying and the next world, and this time with such an intensity that the emotional tone of the complex lasts over the next three reactions. The gradual subsiding of the emotional tone from reaction 3 on can clearly be seen in the reaction-times.

753   We have discussed here the most important disturbances that the complex produces in association and reproduction, and have now to deal with the question of how much of these theoretical findings can profitably be used for practical purposes.

754   In the first place, we have gained with this experiment a most valuable tool for psychology. With it we can demonstrate the existence of certain complexes of individual significance for our subjects, a fact that is bound to become of great theoretical importance. Secondly, the experiment is important for psychiatric practice in that, especially in hysteria, in which as a rule the whole mental life is disturbed, it provides us with the most valuable indications for finding the pathogenic factor, since in hysteria a complex is always at work.[18] The experiment serves us equally well in the elucidation of another mental disorder, *dementia praecox*.

755   The latest application of our experiment was suggested by Wertheimer and Klein,[19] two pupils of the well-known crim-

---

[18] See in particular Riklin, "Analytische Untersuchungen der Symptome und Assoziationen eines Falles von Hysterie" (1905).
[19] "Psychologische Tatbestandsdiagnostik" (1904). [For further comment on this work, see infra, Appendix, no. 5, n. 2.]

inal psychologist Hans Gross. This is its application to the delinquent—the exploration of the complex underlying a crime. Just as any subject who submits to the experiment unconsciously gives himself away, as we have shown, so the criminal, who has knowledge of certain facts, is bound to do the same. This, it is hoped, will make it possible to prove by experiment whether or not a person has any knowledge of certain facts. As everyone will appreciate, this question is of enormous practical importance.

756 While the paper by Wertheimer and Klein mentioned above made only general suggestions about this, Wertheimer has dealt in another paper[20] with relevant experiments carried out in Külpe's laboratory at Würzburg. The experiment was set up as follows.

757 The subject was shown a picture, the contents of which he had to commit to memory (e.g., a picture of a religious service in the chapel of a crypt). The stimulus-words were in some cases chosen from the picture (names of objects shown or otherwise obvious associations with it), but in other cases irrelevant words with no recognizable relation to the picture were used. These stimulus-words were called out to a number of subjects. The reaction-times were recorded with exact instruments (megaphone and chronoscope). The subjects had previously been instructed not to give themselves away, i.e., not to give any associations revealing that they had seen the picture. The results are in keeping with our previous exposition. The stimulus-words arousing the complex (relating to the picture) yielded an unusually large number of *long* reaction-times, and in these cases the reactions also gave a strange impression; there was something deliberate about them. It also often happened that the complex-characteristics appeared in reactions to irrelevant stimulus-words. In these cases a stimulus-word relating to the complex had appeared immediately before. Wertheimer was also able to confirm that the more emotional involvement there was, the more marked were the reaction-times and the qualitative and perseverative phenomena.

758 Since the Wertheimer-Klein publication similar experiments

[20] "Experimentelle Untersuchungen zur Tatbestandsdiagnostik" (1905).

which provided similar results have been carried out by Hans Gross[21] and by Dr. Alfred Gross[22] of Prague. What underlay these experiments was the knowledge or lack of knowledge of a certain room and its furniture. Alfred Gross has discussed very clearly the general aspect of the problem,[23] especially with regard to its juridical application.

759   I should like to mention first, among the critical comments, that by William Stern:

The problem is certainly very interesting from a purely psychological point of view, and the suggested procedure is to be welcomed as a remarkable extension of our methods of approach, but it seems to me that there is a powerful objection to the practical forensic application of the method. In court there is no really sharp distinction between those people in whose minds the facts of the case are present and those in whom they are completely absent, since nearly everyone who has to do with a case in a law court, whether as the defendant or as a witness, knows either what he is accused of or why he is being interrogated, no matter whether he was actually in any way involved. Even the mind of someone falsely accused is, from the very first examination by the magistrate, continuously burdened with ideas concerning the matter. Every suggestion must call to consciousness the ideas with which he is preoccupied, just as if he were guilty, and must also evoke emotional reactions which in their manifestations, even as part of an experiment, can hardly be distinguished from those of guilt; it is well known that blushing, which so often occurs as a result of baseless accusations, has before now been interpreted as a symptom of guilt. Is there not a similar great danger in the psychological experiments suggested by Wertheimer and Klein?[24]

760   I feel obliged to support this objection fully, and should in particular like to stress that the innocent as well as the guilty has the greatest interest in reacting so as to show to the best advantage. The guilty man is afraid to give himself away, and the innocent to put himself in the wrong, by reacting in an awkward manner. The critical reactions will therefore in both

[21] "Zur psychologischen Tatbestandsdiagnostik" (1905) and "Zur Frage des Wahrnehmungsproblems" (1905).
[22] "Zur psychologischen Tatbestandsdiagnostik als kriminalistisches Hilfsmittel" (1905–6).
[23] "Die Assoziationsmethode im Strafprozess" (1906), p. 19.
[24] "Psychologische Tatbestandsdiagnostik" (1905–6), p. 145.

cases be accompanied by strong emotional tone, which interferes in a characteristic way with the associations. This might make it difficult to distinguish between guilty and innocent. We shall come back to this question in more detail in the second part of the paper.

761   In a recent publication Stern discussed my paper "The Reaction-time Ratio in the Association Experiment," in which I gave a detailed analysis of the experiment. Stern considers it of doubtful value to let the subjects explain the associations afterwards, as I made them do. I am ready to admit that the method is in any case difficult and dangerous. For this reason I chose as subjects for the analysis three people whose life and psychological make-up were known to me, and who were themselves psychologically experienced, especially in the observation of association. One could not ask everyone for an explanation of his associations, because they are not casual things but the most intimate and affective ones, on which even an honest self-criticism may fail to function. A certain special experience in the experimenter and also a fair knowledge of certain aspects of psychopathology are necessary with subjects who are not used to psychological experiments. These are the principles of Sigmund Freud's ingenious psychoanalysis.[25] Only when one has completely assimilated Freud's method is one able with any certainty to consider associations from a psychoanalytical point of view. It has to be conceded to Stern that an inexperienced experimenter can easily make the gravest mistakes with this delicate material. In any case, even Freud has been accused of interpreting into a subject's statement more than is in it. To this reproach, however, it must be said that very likely everyone would respond with a canalized association rather than a spontaneously created association when asked what comes to mind in connection with a certain idea; this, of course, applies also to any retrospective elucidation.

762   In his discussion of Wertheimer's suggestion Kraus[26] puts forward the idea that the method has not been sufficiently tried out. I would draw Kraus's attention to the fact that a number of papers were published from the Psychiatric Clinic of Zurich

[25] Breuer and Freud, *Studies on Hysteria* (orig. 1895); Freud, *The Interpretation of Dreams* (orig. 1900).
[26] "Psychologische Tatbestandsdiagnostik" (1905).

University which discuss the method in considerable detail.[27] That the method lends itself to the discovery of complexes seems to me beyond doubt. When it comes, however, to applying the method to someone giving evidence, one cannot be too careful. Therefore I agree with Kraus when he foresees great difficulties in applying the experiment in judicial procedure.

763   Kraus continues: "But I must ask, can the examiner claim the right to base any judgment on the inextricably entangled web of my associations?"

764   The author may forgive me if behind this question I suspect insufficient appreciation of the problem of association. A careful study of the existing literature would have taught him that the "web of the associations" is precisely not "inextricably entangled." If it were we should be at our wit's end, and we could refrain *a priori* from searching for laws among the infinite number of chance events. The experiment is simply based on the fact that there actually are laws determining the possibilities which *more and more* exclude the unaccountable.

765   If we know these laws, then we also know the intimate association-processes of the subject, whether he likes it or not. Kraus thinks one would have for that purpose to have "that rare gift for psychoanalysis of which Freud brings amazing evidence in his remarkable papers." Freud is certainly a man of genius, but his psychoanalysis is, in its principles at least, not an inimitable art, but a transferable and teachable method, the practice of which is greatly helped by the association experiment, as can perhaps be seen from the papers published from our Clinic.[28]

766   I repeat what I have already said elsewhere: The truth of this experiment is not obvious, it has to be tested; only someone who has used it repeatedly can judge it. Modern science should no longer recognize judgment *ex cathedra*. Everybody

[27] Bleuler, "Upon the Significance of Association Experiments"; Jung and Riklin, "The Association of Normal Subjects," supra; Wehrlin, "The Associations of Imbeciles and Idiots"; Jung, "An Analysis of the Associations of an Epileptic," supra; also, Riklin, "Die diagnostische Bedeutung des Assoziationsversuches bei Hysterischen" (1904) and "Analytische Untersuchungen der Symptome und Assoziationen eines Falles von Hysterie" (1905).

[28] Alfred Gross replied in detail to Kraus's deliberations in "Zur psychologischen Tatbestandsdiagnostik" (1905).

derided and criticized Freud's psychoanalysis,[29] because they had neither applied nor even understood the method, and yet it ranks among the greatest achievements of modern psychology.

767   Weygandt,[30] too, thinks that there is still a long way to go before it will be possible to use the method in forensic procedure. He also thinks it desirable that the experiments should continue, especially with uneducated subjects. Weygandt further draws attention to the fact that the criminal probably does not observe the scene of the crime so closely that stimulus-words for the tests can simply be taken from the objects situated there. It is also likely that the emotional tone necessary for interfering with the association is precisely what the habitual criminal lacks.

768   These objections must be unreservedly acknowledged.

II

769   The practical application of the association method is best illustrated by a case on which I was consulted in my capacity as a doctor. Here is the history of the case.[31]

770   One evening in September 1905 an elderly gentleman came to see me. He was evidently agitated and asked for a consultation on an important matter. He told me that he lived with a young man of eighteen, his protégé. For several weeks he had noticed that on a number of occasions larger or smaller amounts of money had been missing from the strongbox. Although he was somewhat absent-minded and not particularly careful in money matters, he was quite sure that there was a deficit of at least 100 francs. He reported the matter at once to the police, but there was no evidence at all against anyone. Recently there had been some changes among the servants; it was thus possible that one of the maids had taken the money. Now it had also occurred to him that his protégé might have stolen from him. If he knew that the young man was the thief, he would do whatever he could to prevent the police getting to know of it; in that case he would rather deal quietly with it himself in

[29] See n. 25, supra.
[30] "Zur psychologischen Tatbestandsdiagnostik" (1905).
[31] For a preliminary report of the case, see "On the Psychological Diagnosis of Facts," *Coll. Works*, Vol. 1.

order to avoid embarrassment for the family of his protégé, who were highly respectable. For the purpose of coming to a decision in this awkward dilemma he wanted me to hypnotize the young man and question him, while under hypnosis, as to whether he was the culprit or not. I rejected this suggestion because such an undertaking is not only technically most difficult but also fruitless. But I suggested the association experiment. Fortunately the young man had intended once before to consult me because of some minor nervous complaints. Thus the guardian was able to send him to me under the pretext of a consultation. Before long the young man turned up and consented to the experiment.

Experimental Procedure

771   In order to stimulate the complex as strongly as possible, I prepared a sheet of stimulus-words in which I distributed thirty-seven words relevant to the possible facts of the matter. The guardian had informed me that the money was always kept hidden in a drawer amongst shirts and ties beneath a small board. The drawer was in a chest and was kept locked. It was possible that it had been opened with a master key. In the same room there was also a trunk in which money was occasionally kept. A linen-cupboard also stood near the chest of drawers. The suspect youth had recently bought a watch and given some small presents to his sister. He might have got the money from the theft; his guardian, however, did not know, because he hardly ever bothered about his protégé's finances. There were no other significant features in the room where the thefts had taken place. As critical stimulus-words I chose: *to give a present, watch, to give, drawer, sister, burglary, writing case, sin,*[32] *to threaten, key, to steal, board, to look for, to lock up, master key, to hide, thief, to find, wrong, shirt, to watch, tie, trunk, to hit, to catch, police, to moan* [accuse],[33] *chest of drawers, arm* [poor],[34] *to arrest, jail, false,*[35] *anxiety, linen-cupboard, to punish, month,*[36] *criminal.* These thirty-seven stimulus-words touching the complex were distributed amongst sixty-three "irrele-

---

[32] The delinquent comes from a religious family.
[33] [German *klagen* has both meanings.]
[34] [German *arm* or *Arm* has both meanings.]
[35] *False* means that he has stolen from his benefactor.
[36] So many months in jail.

vant" stimulus-words, special care having been taken so that an irrelevant stimulus-word was frequently put immediately following a critical one. This was done because of the fact that the emotional charge often perseverates into the post-critical reaction. In this way it could be hoped that the complex-constellation would emerge fairly clearly. I am now going to describe the experiment as it took place. Between the sections I shall insert explanatory remarks. At the end I shall give a statistical survey to bring the experiment to life. The association experiment was complemented by a reproduction test.

772   I should like to point out that the probable mean[37] of the reaction-times in this case, in which the subject belongs to the educated class, is 2.0 seconds. Excessively long reaction-times therefore are those above 2.0.

1. head	nose	2.0	+
2. green	blue	1.2	+
3. water	air	1.6	blue
4. to stab	painful	2.0	+
5. murder	manslaughter	1.4	+
6. long	short	1.8	+
7. five	six	1.4	+

These reaction-times show no peculiarities as yet, though one might perhaps mention the incorrect reproduction for *water* as suspect, suggesting a complex-constellation. It is, of course, impossible to explain every minute complex-interference by means of an obviously incomplete analysis carried out in retrospect, as in this case.

8. *to give a present*[38]	gen–*generous*[39]	2.0	to give
9. wool	. cloth	1.4	+

The reaction to the first complex-stimulus-word fulfils the above criteria for interference by the influence of a complex.

[37] The method of the "probable mean" (Kraepelin) consists in putting the numbers into a sequence according to their magnitude and then simply taking the middle number. As to the advantages of this method, cf. Jung, "The Reaction-time Ratio in the Association Experiment," supra.

[38] The intentionally inserted stimulus-words relating to the complex are italicized in each case.

[39] The words indicating the complex are also italicized. [In this case, the reaction was stammered: German *frei-freigebig*, 'free-freely giving.']

The reaction itself is characterized by a slip of the tongue. The reaction-time is not short and the reproduction is incorrect. No after-affect on the following association.

10. *watch*	mechanism	2.2	+
11. table	leg	1.8	wood

The second complex-stimulus-word *watch* produces a foreign word[40] as a reaction, which is somewhat unusual. The reaction-time is excessive.[41] The post-critical reaction is incorrectly reproduced, so that a perseverating emotional charge may be suspected.

12. *to give*	*to steal*	2.6	+
13. chair	-leg	2.0	+
14. sulky	morose	2.8	+

In 12, the complex is openly expressed with an excessive reaction-time. The post-critical reaction-times are rather long. The reproduction is not disturbed.

15. *drawer*	wood	1.6	+
16. *sister*	brother	1.8	+
17. lake	water	1.4	+
18. ill	well	2.0	—[42]

Here no obvious complex-influence on the two critical stimulus-words is apparent. The missing reproduction for *ill* may be due to something other than the theft-complex.

19. *burglary*	*theft*	1.8	+
20. to cook	—	—	—
21. ink	paper	2.6	+

Here we have all the criteria of the complex-constellation. The perseveration was so strong that it led to a failure, an absence of the post-critical reaction. The reaction-time for 21 is still very long.

22. evil	good	2.0	+
23. *writing-case*	paper	2.0	+
24. to swim	good—don't know	2.0	freely, doing well

[40] [Orig. *Mechanismus*, not a German word.]
[41] Cf. "The Reaction-time Ratio in the Association Experiment."
[42] The minus sign indicates that the reaction could not be remembered.

The critical stimulus-word interfered again with the post-critical reaction and its reproduction by means of a perseverating emotional charge.

25. *sin*	disgrace	1.8	+
26. blue	black	1.4	+
27. bread	water	1.6	+
28. *to threaten*	—	—	—
29. *key*	lo–hole	2.6	+
30. rich	poor	1.2	+

Sin obviously did not, or not appreciably, arouse the complex. *To threaten*, however, is followed by the failure to react characteristic of emotion and by lack of reproduction. This powerful effect of the stimulus-word may perhaps also be ascribed to the fact that 27 already contains the expression of a complex-constellation: bread and water = jail. In 29 the disturbance is very obvious; the reaction is disturbed by a slip of the tongue, and the reaction-time is excessive.

31. tree	green	1.2	+
32. *to steal*	*to take*	2.4	+
33. *board*	wood	2.8	+
34. yellow	black	2.2	+

To take does not contradict the complex. I do not know whether the long reaction-time following *board* stems from this complex-word or by perseveration from *to steal*. The reaction-time after *yellow* is, however, still excessive, which might indicate some slight perseveration from *board*.

35. mountain	high	1.8	+
36. *to look for*	*to find*	1.6	+
37. salt	—	—	+
38. new	old	2.0	+

The characteristic perseveration, with inhibition of the following reaction, originates with *to look for*. *To find* does not contradict the complex; on the contrary.

39. *to lock up*	*to imprison*	2.6	to release
40. *to ride*	river	2.0	+

The critical stimulus-word distinctly influences not only the expression of the complex, but also leads to a mishearing of the subsequent stimulus-word; as shown also in the reproduction (*riding*: *reiten* = Rhein). Mishearing of the stimulus-word is a not infrequent phenomenon in a complex-constellation.

41. *master key*	*key*	1.6	+
42. stupid	intelligent	3.0	+

Key, as an associative response to the complex, must not, of course, be overvalued. The prolonged reaction-time in R.42 is more telling.

43. exercise-book	book	1.8	+
44. *to hide*	*to find*	2.0	+
45. tooth	painful	1.4	+

To find is a frequent association to *to hide*, so it must not be too highly valued as a complex-association. It looks as if *to hide* has only just touched the complex. The response to *to look for* was also *to find* (36). Such comparisons are useful, even if they do not reveal very much. Occasionally, however, they are valuable if one is trying to detect an unknown complex.

46. right	false	2.2	+
47. *thief*	*burglar*	4.6	criminal
48. *to find*	*to steal*	2.6	to look for
49. book	—	—	statute-book

With *thief*, serious complex-disturbances set in which I need not elaborate.

50. *wrong*	right	1.2	+
51. frog	water	2.2	tadpole
52. to separate	tadpole	2.6	+

Strong perseveration appears to be connected with *wrong*. But it is more likely that this disturbed sequence is still under the influence of R.47ff, as can often be seen in strong emotion. If one watches the subject during the experiment, one can frequently see facial expressions at complex-points that at once reveal the strong emotional charge. This was the case here. From 47 on the subject became restless, gave embarrassed titters, moved his chair to and fro, rubbed his hands or hid them in his pockets. This shows that the disturbances in the associations, as well as other symptoms, are only expressions of the total effect.

338

53. hunger	thirst	1.4	+
54. *shirt*	white	2.0	cloth
55. child	small	1.8	+

Shirt seems to have made a hit.

56. *to watch*	*to miss*	1.8	*s–conceal*[42a]

The influence of the complex is here particularly obvious in the reproduction. The slip of the tongue *s* could be an anticipation of con*ceal*, or should *s* have become *steal?*

57. *necktie*	cloth	1.6	+
58. dim	dark	1.6	+
59. *trunk*	to pack[43]		+
60. *to hit*	*to miss*	1.8	certain
61. statute	-book	1.8	+
62. lovable	faithful	1.8	+
63. *to catch*	*to miss*	2.4	to get hold of
64. to quarrel	to love	3.4	—

From this series we see the part that *to miss* plays. It occurs only in response to complex-stimulus-words, when it is in each case incorrectly reproduced. It seems to be one of those cover-words that not infrequently appear in this experiment. What is hidden beneath it seems to be the thief's fear of a surprise. The words relating to the locality of the incident, *tie, trunk,* appear to be of little influence.

65. *police*	*thief*	3.6	+
66. large	small	1.6	+
67. *to moan [accuse]*	to sigh	1.6	+
68. to paint	beautiful	3.8	+
69. *chest of drawers*[44]	comfortable	2.8	+
70. old	new	1.2	+

Police is a direct hit; *to moan* has its after-effect. *Chest of drawers* is translated [see n. 44] after a long reaction-time; the hit has thus been parried.

[42a] [German: *aufpassen/verfehlen* . . . *st–verstecken,* with *stehlen* conjectured.]

[43] Unfortunately the reaction-time could not be assessed here because of a breakdown of the stop-watch.

[44] [German *Kommode,* and the original reaction *bequem* has the same meaning, 'comfortable,' as *kommode.*]

71. flower	heath	2.0	+
72. arm [poor]	leg	1.6	+
73. wardrobe	cupboard	2.0	+
74. wild	brook	2.0	+
75. family	sister	2.2	+
76. to wash	clean	1.8	+
77. cow	bull	1.8	+
78. strange	to watch	2.2	+

In this sequence *poor* (cause of the theft?) has no arousing effect. The choice of *sister*, however, for family, which had not been intended to be a complex-word, does not seem to be co-incidence. *To watch* as an association to *strange* is odd; is there perhaps the faint thought behind it that someone must have watched and reported him, so that now even a stranger (my-self) knows of the deed? Of course, the suspicion is not proof; one has, however, to keep such trains of thought in mind in the interpretation.

79. to arrest	thief	3.4	+
80. story-telling	fairy-tale	2.0	+
81. manners	custom	1.8	+
82. narrow	broad	1.8	+

To arrest was a direct hit; then there was a slowly declining charge (reaction-times!).

83. brother	sister	1.4	+
84. jail	prison	4.2	+
85. stork	child	2.2	+
86. false (cannot understand the stimulus-word at first, then)	rich	4.0	+

Rich is a peculiar reaction to *false*; if, however, a subject has stolen a considerable sum from his benefactor, then the response is no longer quite incomprehensible.

| 87. anxiety | silly | 2.4 | — |
| 88. beer | wine | 1.6 | + |

It was easy for the subject to persuade himself that his anxiety about giving himself away with the experiment was silly.

89. fire	shot	2.0	+
90. dirty	clean	1.4	+
91. door	trap-	1.6	+
92. *linen-cupboard*	wood	3.0	+
93. hay	grass	1.6	+

Linen-cupboard appears, to draw conclusions from the long reaction-time, not to be quite without meaning.

94. quiet	calm	2.0	+
95. mocking	irony	1.6	+
96. *to punish*	*to release*	2.4	+

An obvious complex-constellation.

97. *month*	week	1.8	+
98. coloured	green	6.2	+

Month, under the constellation of punishment, had obviously a strong affect.

99. *criminal*	*thief*	2.2	murderer
100. to talk	to be silent	2.6	to speak

773   The total result of this experiment appeared so convincing to me that I told the subject point-blank that he was a thief. The young man who, up to now, had shown an embarrassed smiling face, turned suddenly pale and protested his innocence with great excitement. I then pointed out to him several points in the experiment that seemed to me particularly convincing. Thereupon he suddenly burst into tears and confessed.

774   Thus the experiment was a complete success.

775   This success, however, has to be examined critically. Above all, one has to keep in mind that the thief is not a hard-boiled habitual criminal but a sensitive young man who is also apparently tortured by his bad conscience (the complex). His complex had high emotional charges, which clearly affected the associations and in this way made the diagnosis of the theft possible. Had he had weaker emotional charges, the disturbances would also have been less, and the diagnosis would have been that much more difficult. Another circumstance that helped was that the culprit reacted in the manner of educated people, with single words and relatively short reaction-

times. Had he been uneducated, or even somewhat mentally defective, he would have preferred to respond with sentences or definitions, which are also always connected with rather long reaction-times. In this association-type[45] the subjects deliberate the reaction and formulate it as "suitably" as possible, which is apt to put the complex-constellations in the background.

776   Not only the success of the method, however, but also the method itself has to be critically examined, inasmuch as we are not yet at all sure whether the critical stimulus-words cannot cause disturbances in innocent persons as well. The stimulus-words are partly such that even without a special complex they can arouse emotions or touch other complexes as well. There are also some words among them that are not in current use and that therefore have few ready connections in the language. Lastly, not all the rather long reaction-times are necessarily due to the influence of a complex, since they can just as well be caused by the rarity of the stimulus-word.[46]

777   The rarity and complexity of the stimulus-words are, of course, also affect-arousing, in so far as they demand more attention. Many people also become inhibited because of the fear of appearing foolish, particularly uneducated women, who, in any case, get very easily embarrassed. It may therefore, *a priori*, be assumed that complex-characteristics may appear at moments when emotions have been aroused purely because of these difficulties. Then, a case is easily imaginable in which, by means of intended complex-stimulus-words, complex-symptoms are produced that are not, however, related to the suspected or expected complex but to a similar one that incidentally interferes with the one for which we are looking. Such a case can give rise to the most serious misinterpretations. Finally, disturbances can be produced by one group only of the complex-stimulus-words, so that one remains in doubt whether the subject is guilty or innocent. This can also occur if another complex interferes with the expected one.

778   In the face of these difficulties it has to be plainly admitted

[45] See Wehrlin, "The Associations of Imbeciles and Idiots."
[46] In this respect there are characteristic differences between words, e.g., the probable mean for concrete nouns is 1.67 secs., for general concepts 1.95 secs., adjectives 1.70 secs., verbs 1.90 secs. See "The Reaction-time Ratio in the Association Experiment."

that one hundred stimulus-words are definitely too small a sample to confirm beyond doubt the existence of a complex and to exclude the influence of interfering complexes. In our case, the attempt succeeded that one time because the situation was simple; another time, however, it could easily fail. The obstacles that arise in these experiments are shown by the controls that I set up to check the list of stimulus-words specially chosen for the case of theft. [See pp. 344, 346.]

779 I took as subjects two educated young men with whom I was closely acquainted. The one whom I am going to describe as the Informed knew the significance of the experiment carried out on him; the other was completely unaware of it. I am calling the latter the Uninvolved. The experiment was carried out on both of them in exactly the same way as on the Culprit. I must point out that for every subject one has always to think in terms of *his* probable mean-time.

Mean-time of:	Secs.
Culprit	2.0
Informed	1.4
Uninvolved	1.8

On the whole, the differences in these figures have an individual significance only.

780 For the sake of brevity I have to restrict myself to discussing only the critical reactions, and just indicating the complexes of the controls.

8. *to give a present* passes smoothly for the Uninvolved; the post-critical reaction-time of the Informed is prolonged beyond the mean.

10. *watch* produces a failure in the Uninvolved, thus a complex-symptom. This subject is at present going through an unpleasant *waiting period* which seems to him to last very long (therefore the extended reaction-time for *long*). *Watch* arouses the same idea in him. The time for the Informed is also somewhat above the mean. The post-critical reactions are incorrectly reproduced by both controls as well as by the Culprit; therefore, the influence of a complex is likely. We can see that here all three of them are suspect. The analysis shows us, however, that for the Uninvolved the feeling-tone of the waiting time is very strong so that perseveration may be assumed. For

343

Stimulus-Word	CULPRIT Reaction	R-T	Rep.	INFORMED Reaction	R-T	Rep.	UNINVOLVED Reaction	R-T	Rep.
1. head	nose	2.0	+	neck	1.0	+	feet	1.0	+
2. green	blue	1.2	+	blue	0.8	+	yellow	0.8	+
3. water	air	1.6	blue	ship	1.0	+	sky	1.0	+
4. to stab	painful	2.0	+	knife	1.4	+	parade	2.2	+
5. murder	manslaughter	1.4	+	deed	1.0	+	death	1.2	+
6. long	short	1.8	+	short	0.8	+	short	2.2	wide
7. five	six	1.4	+	six	0.8	+	seven	1.4	+
8. *to give a present*	gen–*generous*	2.0	to give	to give	1.2	+	to give	1.4	+
9. wool	cloth	1.4	+	dress	2.0	+	sheep	1.6	+
10. *watch*	mechanism	2.2	+	hand	1.6	+	—	—	+
11. table	leg	1.8	wood	bench	1.0	chair	chair	1.2	bed
12. *to give*	*to steal*	2.6	+	to take	1.4	+	to give a present	1.4	+
13. chair	-leg	2.0	+	table	1.0	+	seat	2.4	leg
14. sulky	morose	2.8	+	good-natured	1.8	+	cheeky	1.6	+
15. *drawer*	wood	1.6	+	table	1.8	+	*chest of drawers*	1.2	+
16. *sister*	brother	1.8	+	brother	0.8	+	brother	1.4	+
17. lake	water	1.4	+	water	1.2	+	river	1.8	sky
18. ill	well	2.0	—	healthy	1.0	+	healthy	1.4	+
19. *burglary*	*theft*	1.8	+	*theft*	1.4	+	*thief*	2.0	+
20. to cook	—	—	—	gas	1.0	+	to eat	1.4	+
21. ink	paper	2.6	+	paper	1.8	+	pen	2.6	to wri
22. evil	good	2.0	+	good	1.0	+	good	1.4	+
23. *writing-case*	paper	2.0	+	paper	1.8	+	envelope	2.6	+
24. to swim	good, don't know	2.0	freely, doing well	water	1.8	+	to dive	1.2	+
25. *sin*	disgrace	1.8	+	deed	2.8	+	pardon	2.2	+
26. blue	black	1.4	+	green	1.4	+	Zurich	1.6	water
27. bread	water	1.6	+	envy	1.2	to bake	corn	1.8	to eat
28. *to threaten*	—	—	+	hand	0.8	+	murder	2.6	crime
29. *key*	lo–hole	2.6	+	room	1.2	drawer	*burglary*	1.8	+
30. rich	poor	1.2	+	poor	0.8	+	poor	1.6	+
31. tree	green	1.2	+	shrub	1.2	+	fruits	1.4	fruit
32. to steal	*to take*	2.4	+	carpet	3.0	to take	*to punish*	1.8	thief
33. *board*	wood	2.8	+	wood	1.6	+	carpenter	1.8	table
34. yellow	black	2.8	+	green	2.8	+	Uri	2.8	+
35. mountain	high	1.8	+	valley	1.2	+	peak	2.0	valley
36. *to look for*	*to find*	1.6	+	*to find*	0.8	+	*to find*	1.0	+
37. salt	—	—	+	pepper	0.8	+	pepper	1.6	+
38. new	old	2.0	+	old	0.8	+	old	1.2	+
39. *to lock up*	to *imprison*	2.6	to release	money	3.2	key	*caught*	1.6	+
40. to ride	river	2.0	+	to drive	1.2	+	to fall	3.2	+
41. *master key*	*key*	1.6	+	*key*	1.6	+	*thief*	2.0	+
42. stupid	intelligent	3.0	+	clever	1.0	+	intelligent	1.0	—
43. *exercise-book*	book	1.8	+	pen	1.0	+	pupil	2.8	+
44. *to hide*	*to find*	2.0	+	to play	1.2	+	to find	1.2	+
45. tooth	painful	1.4	+	wild*	1.6	+	dentist	1.8	+
46. right	false	2.2	+	wrong†	0.8	+	false	1.8	+
47. *thief*	*burglar*	4.6	criminal	*to steal*	1.4	+	*burglary*	1.6	+
48. *to find*	*to steal*	2.6	to look for	*to look for*	1.0	+	a find	2.4	to loo for

* [Orig. *Zahn/zahm*, which gives a resemblance, and *wild*, 'wild', is the opposite of *zahm*, 'tame'.]   † [In the sense of 'incorrect'.]

the Informed, on the other hand, setting up house plays a prominent role at present: he has lately been intensely occupied with the question of furniture. The feeling-toned background for the furniture-complex is his fiancée.

12. *to give* passes smoothly for the controls. For the Uninvolved, however, the post-critical reaction is disturbed. We learn that he depends on someone else's favour (*to give a present*) during this waiting period, which is very unpleasant for him.

15. *drawer* produces the reaction *chest of drawers* in the Uninvolved, which one might actually have expected from the Culprit. The association of *drawer* and *chest of drawers* just happens to be a very common association by contiguity which would not mean very much even for the Culprit. One could, however, easily be misled by it.

16–32. These sequences are very instructive. 16. *sister* releases the same response from all of them, but the Culprit has the longest reaction-time.

19. The reaction to *burglary* is very "suspicious," particularly in the Uninvolved. It is not known to me that he has ever stolen anything, nor has he admitted any such offence. Even if he carried such guilt within him, his reaction is *de facto* worthless with regard to the complex in question, although the assumption would be tempting. The strong after-effect on the subsequent reaction is, however, absent in the controls.

23. *writing-case* produces disproportionately long reaction-times in the controls. Therefore the utmost caution is indicated here. The analysis could not trace the influence of a complex in the controls. Perhaps the "difficulty" of the word was mainly responsible.

25. *sin* hits the controls harder than it does the Culprit.

28. *to threaten* has a special effect on the Uninvolved, but not nearly as much as on the Culprit.

29. *key.* The reactions of the controls contain straightforward complex-words.

32. *to steal* reveals strong complex-influence in the controls. In the Informed it is a jocular reminiscence of the furniture-complex; in the Uninvolved the interference stems mainly from his reaction *to punish*, originating from the fact that he

Stimulus-Word	CULPRIT			INFORMED			UNINVOLVED		
	Reaction	R-T	Rep.	Reaction	R-T	Rep.	Reaction	R-T	Rep.
49. book	—	—	statute-book	cover	1.2	+	to read	1.6	pupil
50. *wrong*	right	1.2	+	right (noun)	0.8	+	right (noun)	1.8	+
51. frog	water	2.2	tadpole	leg	1.4	+	toad	2.0	+
52. to separate	tadpole	2.6	+	to know	1.2	+	to combine	1.8	+
53. hunger	thirst	1.4	+	thirst	0.8	+	thirst	1.2	+
54. *shirt*	white	2.0	cloth	waistcoat	1.8	+	to dress	1.8	+
55. child	small	1.8	+	small	2.0	+	mother	1.6	stork
56. *to watch*	*to miss*	1.8	de-hide	to attend	1.4	+	to retain	5.0	+
57. *necktie*	cloth	1.6	+	bow	1.2	+	collar	2.0	+
58. dim	dark	1.6	+	clear	1.4	+	bright	1.4	+
59. *trunk*	to pack	—	+	*key*	1.4	+	to lock	1.4	+
60. *to hit*	*to miss*	1.8	certain	*to find*	1.4	+	to shoot	1.4	+
61. statute	-book	1.8	+	law	1.2	+	crime	3.0	+
62. lovable	faithful	1.8	+	dear	0.8	+	hatred	1.0	+
63. *to catch*	*to miss*	2.4	to get hold of	chance	2.2	+	*thief*	3.0	+
64. to quarrel	to love	3.4	—	to argue	1.8	+	to fight	1.4	+
65. *police*	*thief*	3.6	+	soldier	1.4	+	crime	3.8	offence
66. large	small	1.6	+	small	0.4	+	king	1.8	+
67. *to moan* [accuse]	to sigh	1.6	+	to weep	1.8	—	law court	2.0	judge
68. to paint	beautiful	3.8	+	colour	1.6	+	artist	2.0	+
69. *chest of drawers*	comfortable	2.8	+	drawer	1.8	+	furniture	3.8	+
70. old	new	1.2	+	young	0.8	+	young	1.6	+
71. flower	heath	2.0	+	blossom	1.0	+	garden	2.0	+
72. *arm* [poor]	leg	1.6	+	rich	0.8	+	rich	1.4	+
73. wardrobe	cupboard	2.0	+	cover	1.0	+	clothing	4.0	furnitur
74. wild	brook	2.0	+	tame	1.0	+	lion	2.2	+
75. family	*sister*	2.2	+	party	2.2	+	house	3.0	+
76. to wash	clean	1.8	+	to comb	1.0	+	to comb	1.6	+
77. cow	bull	1.8	+	ox	1.0	+	milk	1.4	+
78. strange*	*to watch*	2.2	+	native	1.4	+	native	1.8	+
79. *to arrest*	*thief*	3.4	+	*thief*	1.6	+	criminal	1.8	+
80. story-telling	fairy-tale	2.0	+	story	1.0	+	story	1.2	+
81. manners	custom	1.8	+	custom	1.4	+	insolence	1.8	+
82. narrow	broad	1.6	+	wide	1.2	+	broad	1.2	+
83. brother	*sister*	1.4	+	sister	1.0	+	sister	1.6	+
84. *jail*	*prison*	4.2	+	*freedom*	1.2	thief	*criminal*	2.8	thief
85. stork	child	2.2	+	child	1.4	+	child	1.6	+
86. *false*	*rich*	4.0	+	true	1.4	+	honest	1.8	+
87. *anxiety*	silly	2.4	+	grief	1.2	+	distress	1.4	+
88. beer	wine	1.6	+	wine	1.2	+	wine	1.6	+
89. fire	shot	2.0	+	tavern	1.6	+	heat	1.8	+
90. dirty	clean	1.4	+	cleanly	1.0	+	neat	1.2	+
91. door	trap-	1.6	+	hinge	1.2	+	house	1.6	+
92. *linen-cupboard*	wood	3.0	+	does not know the word			furniture	1.8	+
93. hay	grass	1.6	+	straw	1.0	+	straw	1.2	+
94. quiet	calm	2.0	+	calm	1.2	+	calm	1.2	+
95. mocking	irony	1.6	+	ridicule	1.0	+	gay	5.2	disgrace
96. *to punish*	*to release*	2.4	+	just	1.6	+	*offence*	2.2	criminal
97. *month*	week	1.8	+	January	1.2	+	year	1.8	+
98. coloured	green	6.2	+	multi-coloured	1.2	+	water	4.2	+
99. *criminal*	*thief*	2.2	murderer	*punishment*	1.4	+	*guilty*	3.8	murdere
100. to talk	to be silent	2.6	to speak	to reply	1.0	+	to speak	1.2	+

* [The German text misprints *Freund*, 'friend', here, though it gave *fremd*, 'strange', in the original list.]

considers the loss of his job, which he had suffered, as a punishment.

With these examples it can be most impressively shown what unexpected difficulties the use of the test would have to face, even though it can theoretically be taken as certain that disturbances in associations are as a rule related to emotions and emotions to complexes; which complexes, however? This is the great question.

33. The strongest reaction to *board* is from the Culprit, although the contents of the reaction do not give anything away. The incorrect reproduction of the Uninvolved, however, is again disturbing. It is the result of the perseveration of R.32.

36. The most striking effect of *to look for* is on the Culprit (perseveration!).

39. *to lock up* produces very suspicious reactions. In the controls other complexes again interfere; in the Informed it is the furniture-complex, this time in obvious connection with the question of the money needed for new furniture. For the Uninvolved it is again the complex about his unsatisfactory social position, which I cannot discuss here in greater detail. It is, however, remarkable that at this point the controls utter words indicative of complexes; the perseveration in the Uninvolved also corresponds to this.

41. *master key* acts in the same way, distinguishable from the Culprit's reaction only by lack of perseveration.

44. The action of *to hide* is also not distinguishable. There is interference by complexes in the controls as well.

47. *thief* has definitely the strongest effect on the Culprit, although the reactions of the controls are also complex-words.

48. Again, *to find* releases a feeling-toned reminiscence in the Uninvolved which confuses the result.

50. *wrong* and 54. *shirt* are uncertain.

56. *to watch* releases a complex (a love-affair) in the Uninvolved, thus distorting the result.

57. *necktie* and 59. *trunk* are uncertain.

60. *to hit* has the strongest effect on the Culprit.

63. *to catch out* and 65. *police* act in a very suspicious way, particularly in the Uninvolved; the complex of a secret love-affair interferes here.

67. *to moan* [*accuse*] is uncertain.

347

In 69. *chest of drawers*, the controls react with *drawer* and *furniture* more adequately than the Culprit with *comfortable*. Yet this reaction can easily be understood as a diversion, as a means of masking the complex. In strongly charged complexes, e.g., in hysteria, such diversions are the rule.

72. One might expect a similar result with *arm* [*poor*] / *leg*.

79. *to arrest* and 84. *jail* release the strongest reaction in the Culprit.

86. *false* and 87. *anxiety* act most strongly on the Culprit.

92. *linen-cupboard*, 96. *to punish*, and 97. *month* are uncertain. The Uninvolved has for *month* the complex of the waiting-period, hence the strong perseveration.

99. The effect of *criminal* is not clear.

781   The result of the control-experiments is depressing: Obvious complex-symptoms can be seen at the critical points, not only in the Informed but remarkably often also in the Uninvolved, who really should have no theft symptoms at all. As it happened, however, he had two dominant complexes that could also be aroused by the stimulus-words pertaining to the theft complex. This brings home to us a fundamental weakness of the experiment: this is the multiplicity of meanings that the stimulus-words can have. One can hardly imagine how many associations, both concrete and symbolical, such words can arouse. Even for the sole purpose of narrowing the range of these possibilities, wide practical experience is required. We can come somewhat nearer to this goal by compiling as many stimulus-words as possible and by taking those that are as specialized as possible as critical stimuli. A test with only one hundred reactions is definitely inadequate.

782   But, one is bound to ask with amazement, how could I dare to accuse the young man of the theft in view of such an uncertain state of affairs? Above all it must be stressed that, in addition to the practical test, there exists something that cannot be put on paper: namely those imponderables of human contact, those innumerable and immeasurable facial expressions which, to a large extent, we do not even consciously perceive, which affect only our unconscious, but which are most powerfully convincing. Apart from this indescribable quality that belongs to the experiment *in vivo* there is, however, some

more tangible evidence that can be considered convincing: above all, there is the total result which, however, does not appear in the tables and which becomes obvious only by using statistical methods. Let us first consider the average of the reaction-times.

783   For certain reasons, which I cannot enlarge on here, we take the arithmetical mean.[47]

Mean for . . . stimulus-words	Culprit	Informed	Uninvolved
neutral	1.9	1.0	1.9
critical	2.8	1.5	2.5
post-critical	3.8	1.4	1.8

784   Reduced to the level of the mean value of the Culprit's neutral reactions, the picture is as shown in Graph A (p. 350).

785   From Graph A it can be seen that the Culprit is quite different from the controls in that his mean for post-critical reactions is excessively high and even greatly surpasses the mean of the critical reactions. That means, psychologically speaking, that the Culprit's emotions during the critical reactions were much stronger than those of the controls and therefore perseverated with greater intensity. Although the critical mean value of the Informed nearly corresponds to that of the Culprit, the post-critical mean value falls below this level, just because in the Informed the emotions connected with the complex are missing. For him it is nothing but a complex of ideas concerning the experiment. This is even more obvious in the Uninvolved, for whom, as we have seen, the theft-complex is not in question and there is only a complex that occasionally interferes at the same stimulus-words. Actually, the critical mean of the Uninvolved should not have exceeded the neutral mean at all. That this does happen, however, stems from the fact that critical and post-critical stimulus-words together comprise not less than 65 per cent of all the stimulus-words. For this reason alone the critical stimulus-words are very likely to arouse the unconnected complexes.

786   This graph also shows how the mere knowledge of the

[47] The reasons are given in detail in "The Reaction-time Ratio in the Association Experiment."

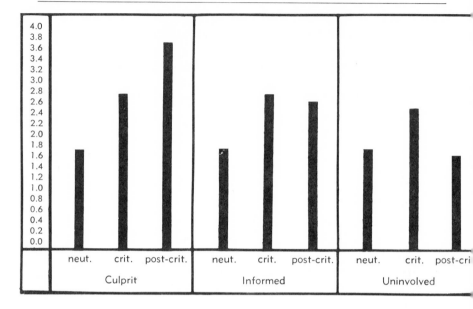

Graph A: Mean Values of Reaction-Times

complex can compromise the result.[48] In spite of all difficulties, however, the graph shows considerable material indicting the Culprit.

787   As we have seen, incorrect reproductions are also among the complex-symptoms. The Culprit reproduced 20 per cent of the reactions incorrectly, the Informed 5 per cent, the Uninvolved 21 per cent [see Graph B].

788   As Graph B shows, the Culprit made mistakes in not less than 90 per cent of the reproductions of the critical and post-critical responses, the Informed in 80 per cent, and the Uninvolved in 71 per cent.

789   Here again we see the strongest weight of evidence in the Culprit, although the figures for the controls are also unexpectedly high.

[48] We have here, however, to consider that the reduction of the Informed to the level of the Culprit is not a quite unobjectionable procedure, because the times can only be extended upwards and not downwards. Finally, it is also characteristic that the innocent can act quickly, that is, without hesitation.

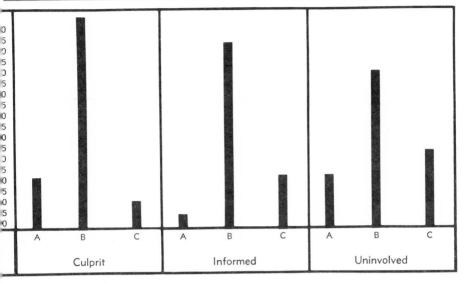

A = Total of incorrect reprods. in % of total reprods.
B = Incorrect reprods. (%) for critical and
      post-critical reactions.
C = Incorrect reprods. (%) for neutral reactions.

Graph B: Incorrect Reproductions

790   The question of how often there are reactions to critical
stimulus-words that may indicate the complex is an interesting
one. According to Wertheimer's data we could expect significant findings. Here we must take into account that any grouping from this point of view is extremely arbitrary. In the graphs
I have always emphasized the critical reactions by the type. As
can be seen, I have proceeded in a very generous way. This is
one source of error: another is the fact mentioned above that
the reaction may, contrary to expectation, conceal the complex
instead of revealing it. For the Culprit, there are 49 per cent
indications of complexes in critical and post-critical reactions,
for the Informed 32 per cent, and for the Uninvolved 46 per
cent. True, the figure for the Culprit is the highest, but this
does not prove very much.

791   The circumstance that the scene of the crime was somewhat
commonplace presented a great difficulty in the experiment; it
need not always be so. On the contrary, the scene could in another case be of such a special kind that there would inevitably

351

be a large number of complex-stimulus-words which would appear harmless to the Uninvolved, while the Culprit would continually avoid complex-constellations; as our experience shows, that cannot happen without characteristic disturbances. So much can already be seen from Gross's and Wertheimer's experiments.

792   In summarizing, I must point out that the Culprit is distinguished only by the quantitative aspects of his complex-symptoms, and that this lends support to the diagnosis of the theft. Had the association method not become a most valuable diagnostic aid for psychopathology, making it possible to get access to pathological complexes, and had we not acquired a certain experience in carrying it out, I would not have ventured on that bold diagnosis. It was, however, the analogies with psychopathology that convinced me. I cannot therefore blame anyone who is not equally convinced. Far be it from me to dash cold water on the interesting and undoubtedly promising efforts and expectations of success in the psychological diagnosis of the criminal case; I am not sorry, however, with this case, to have been put in the position of giving a warning against undue optimism. I am giving it in the interest of this incomparably fine psychological method of investigation, which could easily be brought into discredit by drastic failures. The association method is a delicate tool which, up to now, is suitable for use only by experts, and one has on countless occasions to pay dearly for one's mistakes if one is not very experienced. Thus, as the method stands at present, one must not expect too much of it; it has, however, possibilities all of which can hardly be foreseen. The present article is meant not only as a warning but also as an encouragement to practise the association method, which is one of the most fruitful in all psychology.[49]

49 [The last sentence was omitted in the 1906 version.]

ASSOCIATION, DREAM, AND
HYSTERICAL SYMPTOM[1]

I. The Associations

793   I should like to support and clarify the views on the nature of anomalies of association in hysteria expressed in two others of these Studies[2] by presenting further investigations. The subject of this research is the following case:

A 24-year-old girl of fair intelligence and average education, physically healthy. The mother suffers from osteomalacia, which has completely crippled her. Otherwise nothing of hereditary relevance can be established. The patient is the youngest child, the only daughter, and has four elder brothers. Healthy up to school age. Very sensitive at school but made good progress. During the second year at school, twitching of the right arm began which soon made writing impossible; then the twitches became generalized until at last a hysterical chorea developed. The patient even became the focus of a small epidemic of chorea among the pupils. The chorea manifested itself in tic-like attacks, said to have lasted 1–2 minutes each. The patient threshed about and stamped, and occasionally screamed as well. There was no disturbance of consciousness during the attacks, which occurred 15–20 times a day. Menstruation set in at the age of 15 years. With the first period the attacks of chorea ceased quite suddenly (two years before this, the parents had consulted a specialist, who had said that the attacks would stop with menstruation). During the same week, however, dull sensations in the head set in, always towards evening. The sensations gradually assumed the character of heat, which got considerably worse during

1 [Originally published as "Assoziation, Traum und hysterisches Symptom," *Journal für Psychologie und Neurologie*, VIII (1906): 1–2, 25–60. Republished in *Diagnostische Assoziationsstudien*, Vol. II (1909), 31–66 (VIII. Beitrag). Translated by M. D. Eder as "Association, Dream, and Hysterical Symptoms," *Studies in Word-Association*, pp. 354–95. See supra, par. 1, n. 1.]
2 Jung, "Psychoanalysis and Association Experiments," supra; Riklin, "Cases Illustrating the Phenomena of Association in Hysteria" (1906).

each period. The complaint increased with the years. At last the heat-sensations began at about 10 o'clock in the morning and gradually increased until they became unbearable. During the last three years the complaint became so bad that the patient was tortured by heat sensations in the head almost all day long. Innumerable attempts at cure by every conceivable method had no success at all. In the morning the patient was occasionally still able to help a little with the housework. From 10 o'clock on she walked restlessly about, persistently complaining about her head. Gradually she became afraid of other people and shunned all social contacts. During the summer she spent the hot weather in the cellar. In the winter she could not stand a heated room. Patient consulted me during the summer of 1905. This was followed by rapid deterioration. She was afraid of going mad, and had hallucinations of white and black figures at night. Was incessantly trying to be admitted to this institution. Was admitted in the autumn of 1905.

Condition: Well-nourished, graceful person. Expression of suffering which appears to be aimed at arousing sympathy; listless behaviour without any energy at all, which is also expressed by a spidery, sloping handwriting. Incessantly complains of heat sensations in the head. Complaints uttered in a whining tone of voice. The patient describes her sensations as follows: "My whole head is blocked up to the neck and quite hot, I must have a temperature of 104° in the head, it is quite tense as if choking; my throat is hot, dry, and parched, and I feel strangled. The feeling of dryness and heat at the back of my throat is terrible. It is always worse after a meal. At the same time my body is quite cold, my hands blue, my feet like ice. It seems to me if I could only once bleed properly from the *nose* I would feel easier. I keep imagining myself *bleeding from the nose and mouth*, a whole wash-basin full; I keep imagining *big clots of blood. I am also always dreaming of blood.* Often I dream I am wading in blood, the whole room is full of blood or *blood is gushing out of my nose, mouth, eyes, and ears.* Just as often I dream of *fire*; then everything is *ablaze*."

When going off to sleep she often imagines she sees a black man who stretches his black hand towards her and clutches her arm. Occasionally she also dimly sees white female apparitions.

Since January 1905 menstruation has ceased, there is severe constipation; flatulence, alleged to have persisted for several months, which makes the abdomen protrude noticeably. The patient finds sitting unbearable, therefore remains standing or walks up and down the room. Profound loathing of meat, avoids everything that

354

makes her hot. She has only to hear steam being let into the radiators and she feels worse. She washes in cold water several times a day and practises gymnastics in her room. These activities are very important for her. In a strange contrast to this are her aversion and dread of regular work, which she thinks is very bad for her condition. She shows a pathological love of orderliness and cleanliness (formerly, she says, she had for a time a compulsion to touch, so much so that she constantly had to touch all the objects in the room while walking about). The patient has no insight at all into the psychological nature of her complaint but is firmly convinced of an organic change in the head; she cannot, however, help laughing when explaining that one of her doctors took her for a case of Graves's disease. She has, of course, no idea of the causes of her illness, as little as the doctors who had hitherto treated her.

794   There can hardly be any doubt that this is a case of hysteria. The long duration of the illness and the lack of alteration in the syndrome, not quite usual in hysteria—i.e., the unchanging character of the main symptoms—point to a deep-seated paralysis of psychic energy and a complete subjugation of the personality by the illness. The patient has been ill for seventeen years. In considering the peculiarity of the case one must take into account the fact that there has been a continuous development from the "St. Vitus's dance" (choreatic tic) into the present condition. It cannot be assumed that the chorea was cured, but everything speaks for the fact that under the influence of the first period it was simply replaced by another manifestation of the basic illness. Her completely childish and asthenic personality shows all the characteristics of the infantile Meige-Feindel tic.[3]

795   For the sake of clarity I am now going to describe the association experiments that I carried out with the patient. The patient had treatment from October 1, 1905, to December 21, 1905. The experiments were made during this period. The treatment resulted in a certain success, which had considerable influence on the experiment. The tests were carried out each time in a room that had been only moderately heated ($13°C. = 55.4°F.$), because the patient could not stand more than about $11°C. = 51°F.$ for any length of time.

3 [See Meige and Feindel, *Tics and Their Treatment* (orig. 1902).]

Test I

June 23, 10 a.m.   With reproduction test.

Stimulus-word	Reaction	Reaction-time (in ⅕-secs.)	Repro-duction
1. head	-ache	6	
2. green	-pip	33	
3. water	–	–	
4. to sting	bee	9	
5. angel (Engel)	-court (-hof)[3a]	105	–
6. long	knife	65	–
7. ship	steamship	35	–
8. to plough	field	21	garden
9. wool	to knit	75	
10. friendly	-ness	11	
11. table	-leg	30	
12. to question	–	–	
13. state	–	–	
14. stubborn	stubborn person	40	
15. stalk	flower-stalk	11	
16. to dance	dance-floor	10	
17. lake	Lake Zurich	29	
18. sick	–	–	
19. pride	conceit	19	
20. to cook	cookery school	13	
21. ink	ink-pot	9	
22. bad	badness	39	
23. pin	pincushion	10	
24. to swim	swimming-school	45	
25. travel	travelling-rug	60	
26. blue	Blue Street	35	
27. bread	breadless (unemployed)	20	
28. to threaten	punishment	60	to punish
29. lamp	lampshade	11	
30. rich	riches	21	
31. tree	fruit-tree	23	
32. to sing	singsong	16	
33. pity	regret	35	

[3a] [See supra, par. 655, n. 9.]

356

Stimulus-word	Reaction	Reaction-time (in ⅕-secs.)	Repro-duction
34. yellow	yolk	26	
35. mountain	Mount Utli	23	
36. to play	chess	16	
37. salt	salt-cellar	12	
38. new	Neumünster	15	
39. morals	morality	46	
40. to ride	riding-school	18	
41. *wall*	wallpaper	12	–
42. *silly*	silliness	45	–
43. exercise-book (*Heft*)	school-book (*Schulheft*)	15	
44. to despise	–	–	
45. *tooth*	eye-tooth	15	–
46. *right*	to make right	25	–
47. people	People's Press	23	
48. *to stink*	jackdaw	50	–
49. book	school-book	15	
50. unjust	–	–	
51. frog	tree-frog	25	
52. to separate (*Scheiden*)	divorce (*Ehescheidung*)	32	
53. hunger	to eat	19	
54. white	snow	18	
55. cattle	herd of cattle	32	
56. to attend	attention	30	
57. pencil	pencil-holder	31	
58. dull	–	–	
59. plum	plum jam	66	
60. to hit	–	–	
61. law	–	–	
62. love	unloving	15	
63. glass	water-glass	8	
64. *to argue*	to quarrel	23	–
65. goat	goat's milk	12	
66. grand	grandeur	15	
67. potato	potato-flour	20	
68. to paint	oil-painting	21	
69. part	part-payment	26	

Stimulus-word	Reaction	Reaction-time (in ⅕-secs.)	Repro-duction
70. old (*alt*)	Altstetten	49	
71. flower	bunch of flowers	51	
72. *to strike*	hammer-stroke	30	–
73. cupboard	linen-cupboard	21	
74. wild	wild duck	21	
75. family	family dinner	26	
76. to wash	–	–	
77. cow	cow's milk	10	
78. guest	guest-book	30	
79. luck	good luck	53	
80. to tell	tale	15	
81. manners	training in manners	55	
82. narrow	–	–	
83. brother	–	–	
84. shame (*Schade*)	shame-joy (*Schadenfreude*)	10	
85. stork	stork's nest	26	
86. false	falsehood	37	
87. anxiety	feeling of anxiety	20	
88. to kiss	sister's kiss	65	
89. fire	great fire	28	
90. dirty	–	–	
91. door	lock	21	
92. to elect	election for the Co-op	55	
93. hay	hay-cart	19	
94. still	rest	39	
95. *ridicule*	ridiculous price	10	ridiculously cheap
96. to sleep	sleeplessness	17	
97. month	monthly meeting	15	
98. coloured	–	–	
99. dog	faithful dog	15	
100. to talk (*reden*)	consultation (*Sprechstunde*)	67	

796   This test was given during the consultation. Let us first look at the associations from the statistical angle. I am limiting myself to the classification into internal and external associations, sound reactions, failures, and indirect associations.[4] This rough classification suffices for our purposes. The patient produced:

Internal associations	16%
External associations	60
Sound reactions	9
Failures	14
Indirect associations	1
Incorrect reproductions	14

797   External associations form an exceptionally large majority. The patient, though not unintelligent, lacks higher education (she has only had an elementary education and was often absent from school). A glance at the reactions shows that the external associations consist mainly of combinations of motor verbal patterns, of word compounds. Besides these we also find quite a number of word complements (sound reactions). The large number of failures is striking. If we compare the figures with the average figures for educated women:[5]

Average for Educated Women

Internal associations	35.0
External associations	58.0
Sound reactions	3.3
Failures	1.4

we see that the patient's figures show a much more superficial mode of association; they approximate to the figures of the distraction experiment. Average of the distraction experiment with 100 metronome beats per minute:

Educated Women excluding the Predicate Type

Internal associations	20.8
External associations	62.8
Sound reactions	13.2
Failures	0.4

[4] Cf. "The Associations of Normal Subjects," supra, pars. 20ff.
[5] Ibid., Table F.

359

798   Thus one might think that the attention was distracted during the experiment. This leads to the question of the cause of the distraction, i.e., what was it that had a disturbing influence? No external causes could be found. Therefore the possibility of a psychological interference must be considered. We need not go far in our search, because the patient is already full of a subject that makes every interest in her environment fade, namely, the complex of ideas regarding her illness. All her attention is riveted to her symptoms and only a small remnant is available for the association experiment; hence the superficial reaction-type. She is so much absorbed by her illness that she hardly allows the meaning of the stimulus-word to reach her; in most cases she is quite satisfied simply to grasp the outer form of the word and her intellectual effort is confined to finding a commonplace association to the stimulus-word. She listens with only "half an ear" and lets the stimulus-words, as it were, slip away from her. She cannot bring herself to devote her attention to the experiment; this is apparently not interesting enough compared with the complex. The small amount of self-control sometimes dwindles to nothing (failures), and this actually often happens wherever a commonplace combination of words is not ready on the tip of her tongue; this also often occurs when the stimulus-word has aroused emotionally charged associations, as we shall see later. As soon as she realizes that the reaction is not at her fingertips, she completely refrains from forcing one. Here the experiment reveals the meaning of the clinically conspicuous aboulia, which, as usual, consists in the fact that the whole interest is absorbed by the complex, i.e., by the hysterogenic complex underlying the manifest illness, so that nothing remains for the environment.[6]

799   The probable mean of the reaction-times of the experiment is 5.2 seconds; it is thus very high. We believe that such prolonged intervals are due to certain emotional inhibitions.

800   As in the case reported in "Psychoanalysis and Association Experiments," an analysis of the patient was impossible because she appeared quite indifferent and did not want to deal with any questions that did not concern her symptoms. The repres-

---

[6] A similar case of diversion phenomenon is reported supra, pars. 170ff., where, however, quite a recent affect formed the cause of the interference.

sion, i.e., the inhibition arising from the pathogenic complex, was at that time still too strong.

801 After the consultation during which this test was taken, the patient went home again. As already mentioned, the illness grew rapidly worse. Three months later she was admitted to this hospital.

Test II

October 5, 5 p.m.

1. head	headache	1.6
2. green	–	–
3. water	water-works	2.8
4. to sting	stinging-nettle	2.4
5. angel	–	–
6. long	long-winded	2.2
7. ship	–	–
8. to plough	–	–
9. wool	cotton-wool	2.2
10. friendly	friendliness	3.0
11. table	table-mate	2.2
12. to question	question-mark	6.6
13. state	–	–
14. stubborn (*trotzig*)	stubborn person (*Trotzkopf*)	3.2
15. stalk	flower-stalk	6.0
16. to dance	dance-floor	4.0
17. water	water-lily	9.0
18. sick	sickly	3.4
19. pride	–	–
20. to cook	–	–
21. ink	ink-blotter	4.6
22. bad	badly	–
23. pin	pincushion	2.4
24. to swim	swimming-pool	4.0
25. travel	–	–
26. blue	–	–
27. bread	–	–
28. to threaten	–	–

802 The patient gave up completely at No. 28, declaring she could not stand any more. She could not be induced to stay in the consulting room any longer. Therefore it was not possible to make a reproduction test. An analysis was equally

361

impossible. Nevertheless a number of points emerge from the result. Above all, one is again struck by the peculiar character of the associations: there is nothing but word combinations and there are numerous failures. Expressed in percentages there are:

Tests	I	II
Internal associations	16%	0%
External associations	60	46.4
Sound reactions	9	14.2
Failures	14	39.2
Indirect associations	1	0

803   This is quite an unusual picture. The patient's behaviour during the test was characteristic. She held her head in both hands, and from time to time she sighed because of the unbearable heat in her head, caused by the heated room (55°F.! The patient is unaware that she experiences 55° as pleasantly cool in summer, while she finds the same temperature unbearable in winter. The operative factor in the air temperature is the mere concept!) During the test she obviously was completely absorbed by the complex. It is not surprising therefore that she could not spare any attention for the tedious experiment. Thus we have a distraction phenomenon again, but in a considerably higher degree than in Test 1. The deterioration of her condition decidedly increased the distraction of her attention; i.e., her attention is, even more than previously, directed towards the complex, so that she participates less in the experiment. To direct the attention towards the experiment is obviously very strenuous for her, so that she is already tired after 28 reactions and has to abandon the test. Her available energy has been reduced to a minimum. This is already shown in the enormous number of failures, which have almost tripled compared with the first test. She again fails at stimulus-words that do not immediately arouse a commonplace combination of words. But not all failures can simply be due to the lack of commonplace word combination (e.g., for *to cook* there are the common combinations *cooking-stove, cookery*, etc.; for *state* there are *statecraft, state-house*, etc.; for *travel, travelling bag*, etc.). Nor can all the long reaction-times be accounted for by verbal difficulties (e.g., *water*, with 9.0 secs., with which there are many common combinations). We must also consider the

possibility of these disturbances being caused by affects that may be due to unconscious inhibitions arising from the pathogenic complex underlying the illness.

804   The probable time-mean of the test is 5.2 seconds (the failures taken as 20.0 secs., though usually we waited up to 30 secs.). The probable mean is therefore very high.

Test III

October 9, 5 p.m.   With reproduction test.

1. lamp	lamp-chimney	1.8	
2. rich	riches	1.8	
3. tree	tree-trunk	1.4	
4. *to sing*	*singsong*	3.2	*operetta*
5. *pity*	–	–	*pitiful*
6. yellow	golden-yellow	3.2	
7. mountain	mountain range	4.8	
8. *to play*	operetta	6.6	*ball*
(spielen)	*(Singspiel)*		*(Spielball)*
9. salt	salt-cellar	6.8	
10. new	new moon	3.0	
11. *morals*	–	–	*morality*
12. to ride	riding-school	3.0	
13. wall	wall-painting	4.6	
14. silly	silliness	4.0	
15. exercise-book	school-book	2.2	
(Heft)	*(Schulheft)*		
16. *to despise*	–	–	*despicable*
17. tooth	toothache	2.0	
18. right	–	–	
19. people *(Volk)*	fair *(Volksfest)*	2.0	
20. to stink	–	–	
21. book	school-book	3.8	
22. unjust	–	–	
23. frog	tree-frog	2.4	
24. *to separate*	–	–	*divorce*
(scheiden)			*(Ehescheid-ung)*
25. hunger	hunger-pangs	5.0	
26. white	snow-white	2.0	
27. cattle	herd of cattle	4.1	
28. to attend	attention	2.4	
29. pencil	pencil-holder	6.6	
30. dull	–	–	

| 31. plum | – | – |
| 32. to hit | – | – |

805 This test shows some changes compared with the previous ones. The result expressed in percentages is as follows:

Tests	II	III
Internal associations	0.0%	3.1%
External associations	46.4	59.3
Sound-reactions	14.2	6.2
Failures	39.2	31.2
Incorrect reproductions	–	18.7

806 Here we have one more distraction-experiment. The probable time-mean is

Test I	Test II	Test III
5.2 secs.	5.2 secs.	4.6 secs.

807 Compared with the second test there is some shortening of the reaction-time, which is probably to be explained mainly by the relative reduction in the failures. This result may perhaps permit the conclusion that the patient had pulled herself together a little. This seems also to express itself in the fact that in spite of the early failure in the association test she was willing to do the reproduction test. This test also went four reactions further than the previous one (28, 32). The number of sound reactions has not inconsiderably decreased, to the benefit of the external and internal associations. This also allows us to infer some improvement in her concentration.

Test IV

October 17, 5 p.m.   With reproduction test.

1. law	against the law	5.0
2. love	unloving	3.0
3. glass	glass-cupboard	2.0
4. to argue	–	–
5. goat	goat's milk	2.8
6. grand	grand city	4.8
7. potato	potato-field	5.6
8. to paint	painter's studio	5.4
9. part	partner	3.0
10. old	old town	9.6
11. flower	flowerlet	2.4
12. to strike	–	–

364

13. cupboard	linen-cupboard	5.6
14. wild	–	–
15. family	family dinner	4.0
16. to wash	–	–
17. cow	cow's milk	3.2
18. guest	guest-book	3.4
19. luck	good luck	2.8
20. to tell	–	–
21. manners	training in manners	2.8
22. narrow	–	–
23. brother	–	–
24. shame (*Schade*)	shame-joy (*Schadenfreude*)	3.6
25. stork (stimulus-word first misunderstood—then failure)		
26. false	falsehood	8.2
27. anxiety	feeling of anxiety	3.0
28. to kiss	sister's kiss	4.0
29. fire	fire-blackened	6.8
30. dirty	dirty marks	7.0
31. door	trap-door	4.8
32. to choose	–	–
33. hay	–	–
34. still	–	–

808   This test was carried out at a time when the patient was not so well (one of those fluctuations that are not unusual in the course of hysteria). The test certainly again looks like a distraction experiment. Apart from one exception (*to kiss / sister's kiss*) the patient so to speak never bothers with the meaning of the stimulus-word but contents herself with the perception of the outer word-form. There were no mistakes in reproduction. The test yielded two reactions more than the previous one (32, 34). In percentages:

Tests	II	III	IV
Internal associations	0.0%	3.1%	2.9%
External associations	46.4	59.3	58.8
Sound reactions	14.2	6.2	5.8
Failures	39.2	31.2	32.3
Incorrect reproductions	–	18.7	0

365

The probable time-mean is:

Tests	II	III	IV
	5.2	4.6	5.4
	secs.	secs.	secs.

⁸⁰⁹ Thus we again have an increase in the reaction-time, which we may ascribe to the unfavourable attitude of the patient at that moment. The lack of incorrect reproductions may, in view of the small number of reactions, be accidental, but it is also possible that this time the patient remembered the reactions in order not to make any mistakes with the reproduction later on.

Test V

November 9, 5 p.m.   With reproduction test.

1. ridiculous	–		–
2. *to sleep*	rest	1.8	*tired*
3. *month*	–	–	*time*
4. coloured	Negro	6.3	
5. dog	domestic animal	3.4	
6. to talk	to tell a story	4.8	
7. coal	to iron	4.0	
8. moderate	–	–	
9. song	tune	3.6	
10. to assume	facts	10.0	
11. *pain*	ill	5.2	*illness*
12. lazy	to work	5.4	
13. moon	–	–	
14. to laugh	merry	–	
15. coffee	breakfast	2.2	
16. wide	measure	3.6	
17. air	warm	5.0	
18. to frighten	anxiety	7.6	
19. plate	to eat	7.0	
20. *tired*	*to sleep*	4.4	*bed*
21. *intention*	*to damage*	7.4	?
22. to fly	–	–	
23. eye	–	–	
24. strong	vigorous	2.6	
25. fruit	–	–	
26. *to be busy*	*industrious*	3.0	*to work*
27. sail	ship	7.0	

366

28. modest	content	6.4	
29. ground (does not understand stimulus-word at first)	land	10.0	
30. to whistle	sound	6.4	
31. purpose	cause	3.4	
32. *hot*	yes, yes, in here	4.0	*light*
33. hand	limb	3.0	
34. *to wake*	*awake*	3.0	*to get up*
35. apple	don't know *Affeltrangen* (*place*)	13.6	
36. naughty	–	–	
37. mouth	teeth	7.2	
38. to drink	liquid	4.4	
39. *bed*	*tired*	7.2	*to sleep*
40. *pretty*	*beautiful*	4.0	*?*
41. *danger*	–	–	*terrible*
42. to visit	–	–	
43. *worker*	*occupation*	6.4	*to be occupied*
44. high	mountain	4.6	
45. axe	wood	9.4	
46. to remember	to watch	2.0	
47. path	a walk	5.0	
48. round	sphere	2.4	
49. *blood*	–	–	*red*
50. devoted	–	–	
51. precaution	to watch	–	
52. *funny*	*story*	4.8	*to laugh*
53. market	to shop	3.0	
54. *to forget*	*thought*	5.4	*story*
55. drum	noise	5.0	
56. free	free-spoken	6.6	
57. carriage	to ride	3.2	
58. to eat	appetite	5.0	
59. insolence	–	–	
60. fast	to walk	2.4	
61. chimney	smoke	2.6	
62. enjoy	pleasure	3.2	
63. parson	sermon	2.4	
64. light	weight	3.6	
65. neck	slim	7.0	

66. to wish	present	5.6	
67. stone	hard	8.8	
68. noble	rich	5.4	
69. hose	rubber	2.6	
70. to love	beautiful	9.4	?
71. tile	roof	3.4	
72. mild	temperature	4.8	
73. *greed*	craving for money	6.4	
74. to search	–	–	
75. blanket	–	–	
76. good	–	–	
77. leaf	–	–	
78. to torture	illness	6.0	
79. station	to go on a journey	4.8	

810   This test shows quite a different association type compared with the previous tests. It is as if the patient had suddenly found a different attitude.[7] The percentages are as follows:

Tests	II	III	IV	V
Internal associations	0%	3.1%	2.9%	56.9%
External associations	46.4	59.3	58.8	18.9
Sound reactions	14.2	6.2	5.8	1.2
Failures	39.2	31.2	32.3	21.5
Indirect associations	0	0	0	1.2
Incorrect reproductions	–	18.7	0	21.3

811   Looking at the association tests, the results of which we have given here in figures, we see that the patient's reactions have assumed a normal character. She now goes into the meaning of the stimulus-word and thus produces a preponderance of internal associations.[8]

812   The abnormal component parts have rather diminished, so that, for instance, the number of sound reactions does not exceed the normal mean. Only the number of failures is still abnormally high; it has, however, considerably decreased compared with the earlier tests. The patient's perseverance has increased remarkably, in that this test lasts longer by 45 reactions

[7] This is not actually the case, however, because already in Test I the patient showed the beginnings of a less superficial association type.

[8] Thus the patient now shows a reaction-type that we not infrequently see in uneducated people: a great many internal associations, few external ones, and very few sound reactions.

368

than the previous one. The time-mean is 5.4 seconds, as in the previous test. The reaction-time is thus still very long.

813   This test was carried out three weeks after the previous one. In the meantime the treatment had clearly improved the patient's condition. Therefore one may ascribe the improvement of the association type also to this fact. In the previous tests we mainly stressed the lack of entering into the meaning of the stimulus-word, the absolute preponderance of external associations, the enormous number of failures, and the rapid onset of fatigue as pathological signs and as an abnormal domination of the patient's interest by the complex. The improvement in the condition is thus particularly expressed, from the psychological point of view, in the fact that the patient again takes a more or less sufficient though quickly tiring interest in objective processes. The treatment is resolving her possession by the complex. Her personality is gradually being freed from the tyranny of the illness and is again able to assimilate objective material, in other words to adapt itself again to the environment. As stigmata of hysteria the following are, however, still present: the enormous number of failures; the long reaction-times and other complex-characteristics, i.e., signs of a pathological emotionality, which is, as we know, the psychological foundation of hysteria.

Test VI

December 1, 5 p.m.   With reproduction test.

814   The test comprised one hundred reactions. It was concluded not because of the patient's fatigue, but because I considered one hundred reactions enough to analyze. I shall describe and discuss the test in individual sections.

815   I should like to remark at the outset that the probable time-mean of this test is 5.2 seconds. It is thus not lower than the preceding ones. In spite of this apparent similarity, however, the temporal aspects are in their averages entirely different from those in the previous tests. For the purpose of discussing these relations I am splitting each test up into sequences of six to ten reactions, and for each sequence I have calculated the arithmetic time-means.[9] I have arranged the means thus obtained in curves below.

9 The failures were calculated at 20 secs. each.

Test I. The curve fluctuates very much. Near the beginning there is a line of relatively short times which, after various fluctuations, rises higher and higher. Towards the end there are very strong increases in reaction-times which, however, are again somewhat shortened, but do not reach the initial level. The curve gives the impression that the patient has noticed the excessive times and therefore pulled herself together for a few reactions. Test I was carried out during the consultation. As reported in the case-history, the condition afterwards rapidly deteriorated. This deterioration shows in the curve of . . .

Test II. Here the curve starts rather high, and after pulling itself together for a short time it rapidly collapses.

In *Test III* the curve begins low. The patient had (as she told me at the time) made a resolution to take great pains this time to answer quickly. The carefully gathered energy, however, does not last; the reaction-times increase progressively until they become very high. The observation of this weakness probably induced the patient to a little spurt at the end which, however, exhausts the remains of her energy.

Test IV. The curve starts a little higher than last time (the patient was, as we mentioned before, indisposed psychologically at the time of this test). Here too there is a steady increase in the reaction-times.

Tests I–IV mainly yielded external associations and failures. We can already see from the curves that this mode of association is linked with rapidly increasing reaction-times.

Test V. Here the curve begins very high (perhaps to be explained by the fact that the patient was still discouraged by the previous tests and therefore had some resistance against the experiment). It decreases quickly, however, and then, after a stronger fluctuation stays near the centre, though rising slightly. Then there is a more noticeable and longer-lasting final spurt, which, however, ends in a quick and steady increase of the reaction-times. The final spurt has completely exhausted the patient's energy.

Test VI. In this last test (after two months' treatment) the curve begins at a medium height and then falls quickly to a very low level, which is fairly well maintained during the whole test without any appreciable fluctuations and only towards the end shows a tendency to rise. Test V shows, at least in its middle parts, a tendency towards steadiness, which is finally reached in Test VI. Tests V and VI are, however, those that show a normal mode of association. Thus the normal type appears to go with the tendency to steadiness in the reaction-times. At the same time a very low level is reached and maintained in Test VI.

I should like to mention that the one hundred stimulus-words given in Test I were used a second time in Tests II–IV and a third time in Test VI. As the curves show, repetition of the tests had no noticeable effect in reducing the reaction-times. Tests II–IV made one rather suspect the contrary. According to Kraepelin's findings, a relatively rapid shortening of the reaction-time is actually to be expected because of a fixation of the reactions. In Test VI, however, there are not only no fixations but entirely different reactions (in accordance with the new attitude that had first appeared in Test V).

816   As has repeatedly been indicated in the discussion of the curves, the increased reaction-times are linked with a strong tendency towards fatigue, i.e., with a complete inability to detach the attention from the syndrome. The patient has great difficulty in directing her attention to anything but her illness for any length of time; because of the exertion she tires very quickly. The curves representing the time-extensions are therefore also curves representing weakness of energy. This immediately becomes obvious when we turn them over and read them from right to left. Then they look like the *work-graphs* of an easily tiring neurotic (will-fatigue!). In particular we notice the facilitation and the increased reaction-times in curves I, V, and VI, the final spurt in curves I, III, and V. In curves I and VI the progressive fatigue is clearly marked. This shows that in certain cases the association experiment also gives information on energy and fatigue.

Analysis of the Associations Obtained in Test VI

I am setting the associations of Test VI side by side with those of Tests I–V for the purpose of analytical comparison (time in seconds):

Tests		I		II–IV (V)		VI	
1. head	-ache	1.2		headache	1.6	pa–head-pains	1.8
2. green	-pip	6.6		–		forest	3.2
3. water	–			water-works	2.8	deep	1.4
4. to sting	bee	1.8		stinging-nettle	2.4	bee	2.8
5. *angel*	-court	21.0	[?][10]	–		–	
6. *long*	knife	9.0	[?]	long-winded	2.2	road	5.0
7. *ship*	steamship	7.0	[?]	–		ocean	4.0
8. *to plough*	field	4.2	[garden]	–		to demand/ to give	7.4

[10] Failure or incorrectness of reproduction is indicated in square brackets.

371

9. wool	to knit	15.0	cotton-wool	2.2	(stimulus-word not understood) to knit	10.2
10. *friendly*	-ness	2.2	friendliness	3.0	–	[people]
11. table	(does not at first understand stimulus word, then:) -leg	6.0	table-mate	2.2	room	9.0

1: *head*, of course, arouses the complex in that the patient has localized the main symptoms in the head. Although the times are not long, we find a disturbance by a slip of the tongue in Test VI instead. The two previous reactions have the superficial character that we not infrequently find in complex-reactions and that are meant to make light of the complex.

3: *water* appears still to belong to the field of the perseverating feeling-tone.

5: *angel* shows complex-characteristics. The patient is not religious but still childlike. She has often during recent months had thoughts of dying; she even had one evening hallucination of the "black bone-man" stretching out his hand towards her. This is reason enough for the complex-interference. We have, however, to go even deeper. The patient has an intimate and confidential relation to her mother. The two women are moreover tied together through severe illness. The mother suffers from osteomalacia and is totally crippled. The mother is for the daughter not only an example in a moral respect but perhaps also a foreboding of her own fate. The fear of having to expect a fate similar to that of the mother may not be very far from the patient. Lastly, one has to remember the fact that young girls and hysterics talk of *dying* when they want *to love*.

The disturbances last from *angel* to 8. In Test I there was even an amnesic island.[11]

In 8, another stimulus-word was substituted in Test VI to make the complex more precise: *to demand* is followed by 7.4 seconds, the next stimulus-word *wool* is misunderstood, with 10.2 secs. With *to demand* I get the patient to produce further ideas:

The patient literally says: "I thought you (the author) demanded too much of me, it is *too much* if you are always wanting me to get well." It seemed to me that the patient was somehow "skipping over

[11] Cf. "Experimental Observations on the Faculty of Memory," supra.

372

it," although in hysterics the thought of the doctor who carries out the treatment tends to be associated with strong emotional charges.[12] Therefore I simply said: *"The* demand." The patient starts slightly, saying: "I don't know what you mean—I really cannot think what you can still want of me." Then she suddenly bursts out into loud laughter, blushes, and says no more. The progress of this analytical detail is as follows: First the patient accuses me of demanding too much of her, then there are the familiar negativistic excuses and lastly, behind laughter, a strong emotionally charged thought which may not be difficult to guess. The laughter is diagnostically important: it often indicates in psychoanalysis that a complex has been touched. It is obvious that no one but the patient *demands anything* that is *too much.* Freud says: "Many of my neurotic patients who are under psychoanalytic treatment are in the habit of confirming the fact by a laugh when I have succeeded in giving a faithful picture of their hidden unconscious to their conscious perception; and they laugh even when the content of what is unveiled would by no means justify this. This is subject, of course, to their having arrived close enough to the unconscious material to grasp it after the doctor has detected it and presented it to them."[13]

10, *friendly* seems to be critical in Test II, but not in Tests I and VI.

Analysis: First there are strong inhibitions ("I don't know anything," etc.). Then "I was thinking of you, sir. You were not nice to me last time." This reminiscence refers to a definite incident, when the patient had transposed her bad temper on to me and alleged afterwards that I had been in a nasty mood ("transitivism" in affect). This idea seems enough to explain the disturbance. I indicated before that the patient transposed the "demanding too much" on to me, she also fits me out with *her* bad temper and accuses me of being unfriendly to her. She thus *demands* that I should be friendly to her, and if I am as usual I am not friendly enough, for she still complains of my unfriendliness. So she wants even more friendliness from me; that allows me to conclude that the patient is erotically not indifferent to me. Of course, I cannot give in to this demand. Thus the patient demands too much. She only acquired this aspect of the complex while she was here. The complex disturbances may therefore increase at *friendly.*

[12] Transference [*Transposition*] to the doctor; see Freud, "Fragment of an Analysis of a Case of Hysteria" (orig. 1905).
[13] *Jokes and Their Relation to the Unconscious* (orig. 1905), p. 170.

Tests	I		II–IV		VI	
12. to question	–		question-mark	6.6	answer	5.8
13. state	–		–		state-house	11.6
14. stubborn (trotzig)	stubborn person (Trotzkopf)	8.0	stubborn person	3.2	character	6.0
15. stalk	flower-stalk	2.2	flower-stalk	6.0	flower-stalk	10.6
16. to dance	dance-floor	2.0	dance-floor	4.0	ball	5.4
17. lake (water)	Lake Zurich	5.8	water-lily	9.0	deep	7.2
18. sick	–		sickly	3.4	hospital	6.2 ve
19. pride	conceit	3.8	–		yearning/ nostalgia	7.4
20. to cook	cookery school	2.6	–		kitchen	3.6
21. ink	ink-pot	1.8	ink-blotter	4.6	to write	2.0

In 12, *to question*, obvious complex-disturbances are aroused that involve the subsequent reaction as well.

Analysis: "I thought the Doctor was asking me a lot, I know absolutely nothing more—I certainly don't know anything else." The patient said this with emphasis and an angry ill-humoured face, which was in striking contrast to her usual politeness and submissiveness; then she suddenly burst out into loud laughter, which she tried to suppress by expressing anger: "Oh, what a strain!"—"This is impossible!"—"I have never thought of that!," because she did not think of the special and, for a young girl, so immensely important meaning of the word *question* at the moment of the reaction. She thinks this meaning has only now occurred to her; "of course, she never thinks of such a thing otherwise." Thus we have here a further indication of the presence of an erotic complex.

16: *stubborn* is very suitable to bring out a reference to the ego. Particularly if the reaction to it is *character* or *quality* or *misbehaviour*, we may suspect the subject of the experiment behind it. With *character* the reference to the ego becomes obvious, hence probably also the stronger disturbances, compared with the previous reactions.

Analysis: "People are often stubborn—for instance, I was, too, when I was a child. Once I was rather stubborn and did not want to go to school any more—I was twelve years old then, I think. From then on I did not go to school."

It is known that the patient could no longer go to school because of her St. Vitus's dance; now she interprets this illness as misbe-

374

haviour, and here she even says she did not go to school any more out of *stubbornness*. But if we ask her in another context why she no longer went to school, then she says she was very ill at that time. For the moment we must be satisfied with this information. The twelfth year of life has, however, another significance which is infinitely more important, as we shall see later on.

Like *stubborn/stubborn person*, 16, *to dance/dance-floor* skips over the deeper meaning. Only the reaction *ball*, which goes more thoroughly into the meaning of the stimulus-word, brings about a distinct complex-disturbance. *Dance-floor*[14] is something that is abhorrent to the circles to which the patient belongs, while *ball* is actually the legitimate opportunity to start erotic relationships. The patient is compelled to laugh when she is asked for associations to *ball*; she therefore may well have erotic ideas.

In 19, *yearning* was given as a stimulus-word in Test VI.

Analysis: The patient declares stubbornly and with obvious resistance that absolutely nothing but *nostalgia* comes to her mind in response to *yearning*. I insisted something would occur to her. To this, suddenly loud laughter, which is at once angrily suppressed: "Oh no, now that spoils it for me—this is boring!" We had the same reaction to *demand*. There is probably a strongly repressed erotic desire.

Tests	I		II–IV		VI	
. bad	badness	7.8	badly	3.8	*disobedient*	7.6 [child]
. pin	pincushion	2.0	pincushion	2.4	*child/work*	7.8 [dear]
. to swim	swimming-school	9.0	swimming-pool	4.0	public baths	6.4
. *travel*	travelling-rug	12.0 ?	–		railway	4.8
. blue	Blue Street	7.0	–		colour	1.8
. bread	breadless (unemployed)	4.0	–		baker	2.0
. *to threaten*	(does not understand stimulus-word)				to expect/visit	3.6
	punishment	12.0	(to punish)			

Here ends Test II

14 [German *Tanzboden*, lit. 'dance-floor,' has the sense of a low-class dance-hall.]

Test III

29. lamp	lampshade	2.2	lamp-chimney	1.8	light	4.0
30. rich	riches	4.2	riches	1.8	money	6.8
31. tree	fruit-tree	4.6	tree-trunk	1.4	garden	3.6
32. to sing	singsong	3.2	singsong	5.2	concert	5.2

22: *bad* is taken personally; *disobedient* seems to express the complex best.

Analysis: "I was bad to you the other day—years ago too I was often bad—and disobedient at school, etc."

23: The association *child/work* is peculiar and cannot be explained by the patient. The reproduction yields the more suitable association *dear*. Preceding is the school-complex, which is most closely connected with the concept of *work*. I should like to remind the reader that the stimulus-words *to work* and *worker* in Test V produced complex-disturbances. Moreover, the patient always stresses that she is not "lazy," she would like to do the right kind of work; she also complained of certain relatives who said of her that all she was suffering from was "laziness." The stimulus-word *child* is a word which, as a rule, has a critical effect in the erotic complexes of women.

There are complex-characteristics in 25: *travel*.

Analysis: "Oh, I am thinking of a nice journey to Italy that I should like to do one day"—long interval. With great embarrassment: "Honeymoons are spent in Italy, too."

28, Test VI: *to expect*.

Analysis: "I don't expect anything—absolutely nothing—yes, health—and—," loud laughter again which the patient tries angrily to suppress. Thus the same reaction again as to *demand* and *yearning*.

30: *rich*.

Analysis: "I should like to be rich, then I could stay here a long time for treatment"; then there are strong inhibitions that bar any further ideas. For the patient "to stay a long time for treatment" equals "to remain for a long time in a personal relationship to the doctor."

Tests	I		II–IV		VI
33. *pity*	regret	7.0	–	[pitying]	–
34. yellow	yolk	4.8	golden-yellow	3.2	canary-bird	5
35. mountain	Mount Utli	4.6	mountain-range	4.8	mountain-range	10.

o play	chess	3.2	operetta	6.6	[ball]	ball	6.8	
alt	salt-cellar	2.4	salt-cellar	6.8		to cook	2.2	
ew	Neumünster	3.0	new moon	3.8		house	7.0	
norals	morality	9.2	–		[morality]	*hope/happy*	8.2	[joy]
o ride	riding-school	3.6	riding-school	3.0		path	1.8	
vall	wallpaper	2.4 ?	wall-painting	4.6		room	5.2	
illy	silliness	9.0	silliness	4.0		se–sensible	7.2	
xercise -book (Heft)	school-book (*Schulheft*)	3.0	school -book	2.2		copy-book (*Schreibheft*)	5.2	

R.33: *pity.*

Analysis: "I cannot imagine at all what *pity* might have to do with me—oh, perhaps with my illness—people ought to pity me."

I give here only one example of the inhibitions the patient had about this word: in fact, the resistance lasted much longer and also showed itself in a suffering facial expression. The tendency to arouse pity is of great significance in the history of the patient's illness. Through her illness she achieved not having to go to school any more. Later on she was the "pitied" centre of the whole family. The patient must have some, though dim, awareness of this role; it may perhaps be the origin of the strong resistance.

35: *mountain.*

Analysis: Does not want to know anything about it, she has nothing to do with mountains, this is no concern of hers. She has also never been on a mountain, although she would like to go once to the Alps, but this is, of course, impossible because of her illness, and then she cannot even travel by rail, she cannot stand it.

The patient speaks quite negatively, as if a mountain-trip was of no importance to her. A few days before the test I made a trip into the mountains, after which the patient was unhappy because I had not taken her with me; she had never seen the mountains close to. She completely repressed this incident, without actually any obvious reason, unless "travelling" was of a certain complex-significance. She has all sorts of erotic fantasy relations to the doctor. A journey with the "erotic symptom figure" is a metaphor for a "honeymoon." This is probably the reason why this event was sexually repressed.

38: *new.*

Analysis: The patient has become an intimate friend of a lady who moved into a *new house*, to which the patient takes a peculiar liking. She envies the lady particularly for the way she runs her house. "I shouldn't mind something like that." This interest seems to be symptomatic. The analysis meets with great resistances ("one often moves into a new house—we at home also have a new apartment," etc.). I now ask pointedly: "When does one move into a new house?" This rather general question causes the patient great embarrassment, she blushes and confesses: "When one gets married." Thus she has assimilated the "new house" to her erotic complex.

39. (Test VI): *hope*. The analysis at once produces lasting giggles and that says enough. The laughter here is, however, very inadequate. R.23, *child* also produced a disturbance. We shall come back to this complex at 69.

42: *silly*. The analysis yields self-reproaches about the time when the patient left school for good (12th year of her age). She reproaches herself for not having learned enough because of lack of energy, and for being therefore "silly."

Tests	I		II–IV		VI	
44. *to despise*	–		–	[despicable]	people	7.
45. *tooth*	eye-tooth	3.0 ?	toothache	2.0	mouth	3.
46. *right*	to make right	5.0 ?	–		to check (up on)	6
47. people (*Volk*)	People's Press (*Volksblatt*)	4.6	fair (*Volksfest*)	4.0	crowd	5.
48. *to stink*	jackdaw	10.0 ?	–		to die/cemetery	3.
49. book	school-book	3.0	school-book	3.8	to read	2.
50. unjust	–		–		wedding/church	3.
51. frog	tree-frog	5.0	tree-frog	2.4	green	2.
52. *to separate* (*scheiden*)	divorce (*Ehescheidung*)	6.4	–	[divorce]	divorce	4.
53. hunger	to eat	3.8	hunger-pangs	5.0	dog/to bark	6.
54. white	snow	3.6	snow-white	2.0	snow	3.
55. cattle	herd of cattle	6.4	herd of cattle	4.2	herd of cattle	9.

44: *to despise*.

Analysis: The patient always feels slighted; she felt her incomplete education as something for which she must be despised; people also despised her for her illness, which they interpreted as laziness. Is there perhaps anything else in her illness that makes her particularly despicable? We know that sexual self-reproaches tend to be connected with this.

46: *right* also shows disturbances. The analysis yields only gen-

378

eralities that are difficult to interpret. Is there perhaps anything in her activities that is not or was not "right"?

53 (Test VI): *dog* has a very long reaction-time (6.8 secs.).

Analysis: The patient has dreamed of dogs, which probably have an erotic significance (see below!).

Tests	I		II–IV		VI	
56. to attend	attention	6.0	attention	2.4	attention	2.8
57. pencil	pencil-holder	6.2	pencil-holder	6.6	black	5.0
58. dull	–		–		weather	2.0
59. plum	plum jam	8.3	–		cat/domestic animal	8.0
60. to hit	–		–		marksman	3.6

End of Test III

Test IV

61. law	–		against the law	5.0	against the law	5.4
62. love	unloving	3.0	unloving	3.0	child	2.0
63. glass	water-glass	1.6	glass-cupboard	2.0	bottle	8.0
64. *to argue*	*to quarrel*	4.6 ?	–		discord	7.8
65. goat	goat's milk	2.4	goat's milk	2.8	fire/house	3.8
66. grand	grandeur	3.0	grand city	4.8	ocean	11.0
67. potato	potato-flour	4.0	potato-field	5.6	dish (food)	6.8

57: *pencil.*

Analysis: The patient thinks of those tests when I sat opposite her and, while she did addition, occasionally made marks with a blue pencil in her exercise-book.[14a] Nothing else occurs to her after this idea. These tests took place shortly before Test VI. It may thus only be a reminiscence which, however, must somehow be constellated. One might perhaps suspect a masturbation-complex or another sexual fantasy. During the whole time of the treatment I avoided the topic of sex as much as possible, and only towards the end did I come to speak of it. If, therefore, a masturbation or other physical sexual complex was present, it was not aroused during the treatment (i.e., by Test VI), and thus could become more or less dormant,

14a [This apparently refers to a performance or calculation test, devised by Kraepelin, and still in use at the Burghölzli. The patient has to add pairs of digits and write the sum down in an exercise-book, in which the experimenter enters a mark at each minute in order to indicate the patient's rate of performance. Dr. C. A. Meier has kindly supplied this information.]

particularly when it was not being activated. Tests I–IV took place at the beginning of the treatment, when the complexes were still very active. Test VI was not carried out until the third month. This might explain the lack of complex-characteristics in this part of Test VI. In Test I the after-effect may last up to R.61.

In R.62, the more obvious hint, *child*, has a stronger perseverating effect than the former superficial *unloving*.

Tests	I		II–IV		VI	
68. to paint	oil-painting	4.2	painter's studio	5.4	picture	2.
69. part	part-payment	5.2	partner	3.0	birth/difficult	4
70. old (*alt*)	Alt-stetten	9.8	old town	6.6	old man	3.
71. flower	bunch of flowers	10.2	flowerlet	2.4	garden	5.
72. *to strike*	hammer-stroke	6.0	–		to sit/tired	2.
73. cupboard	linen-cupboard	4.2	linen-cupboard	5.6	room	7.
74. wild	wild duck	4.2	–		lion	3.
75. family	family dinner	5.2	family dinner	4.0	large	5.
76. to wash	–		–		kitchen	6.
77. cow	cow's milk	2.0	cow's milk	3.2	man/pater-familias	8.
78. guest	guest-book	6.0	guest-book	3.4	spare room	5.
79. luck	good luck	10.6	good luck	2.8	joy	5.
80. to tell	story	3.0	–		story	3.

69 (Test VI): *birth/difficult.*

Analysis: "My mother had difficult labours; she has told me that her illness was caused by childbearing" (let us remember here 23, *child/dear*, and 39, *hope/happy*). Although R.69 does not show any external complex-characteristic that is especially conspicuous, it contains a clear description of the complex. The mother's fate is bound to be a warning to the daughter, because it is easy for her to be afraid that if she gets married she might also become a victim of osteomalacia. It would not be surprising then if the sexual fantasies carried rather gloomy emotional charges and therefore could be maintained only under a certain mental reservation, i.e., in the repression, because then there would not be any pleasurable expectation attached, but a strong feeling of unpleasure. This realization came perhaps rather early and had its share in the construction of the syndrome.

76: *to wash* with its conspicuous disturbances can have been constellated by *family* or by her obsessive cleanliness (see also the analyses of the dreams!).

77: That there is something attached to *family* becomes obvious in *man/paterfamilias*, 8.8 secs.

Tests	I		II–IV		VI	
. manners	training in manners	11.0	training in manners	2.8	morals	2.4
. narrow	–		–		space	3.6
. brother	–		–		siblings	7.8
. shame (*Schade*)	shame-joy (*Schaden-freude*)	2.0	shame-joy	3.6	loss	8.2
. stork	stork's nest	5.2	(does not understand stimulus-word) then	–	to fly	7.4
. false	falsehood	7.4	falsehood	8.2	people	3.2
. anxiety	feeling of anxiety	4.0	feeling of anxiety	3.0	trembling	4.2
. to kiss	sister's kiss	13.0	sister's kiss	4.0	sister's kiss	3.8
. fire	great fire	5.6	fire-blackened	6.8	house	8.8
. dirty	–		dirty marks	7.0	street	1.8
. door	lock	4.2	trap-door	4.8	lock	2.0
. to elect	election for the Co-op	11.0	–		–	
. hay	hay-cart	3.8	–		barn	2.2
. still	rest	7.8	–		quiet	6.8

End of Test IV

Test V

Tests	I		II–IV		VI	
. ridicule	ridiculous price	2.0	–		to laugh	2.8
. to sleep	sleeplessness	3.4	rest	1.8 [tired]	night	6.8
. month	monthly meeting	3.0	–	[time]	long	6.4
. coloured	–		Negro	6.8	painter	2.6
. dog	faithful dog	3.0	domestic animal	3.4	river/wide	3.0
. to talk (*reden*)	consultation (*Sprechstunde*)	13.4	to tell a story	4.8	people	6.2

81: *manners* tends to stimulate sexual complexes.

In 85, with *stork*, there are marked disturbances that can be related to the stimulus-word (the erotic meaning of which is of course well known) as well as to the preceding *accident*.

88: *to kiss* is rather harmlessly disguised by *sister's kiss* and clearly shows the naïve compulsion to repress (similarly *stork/to fly*). But perhaps *sister's kiss* has a very deep meaning that I could not have suspected at the time of the test (see the dream-analyses!).

89: *fire* shows long reaction-times throughout. *Fire* is one of the expressions by means of which the patient describes the head-symptoms. The response *house* is constellated by the dreams of fire in which she often sees houses ablaze.

92: *to elect* produces the utterly forced reply *election for the Co-op*.

Analysis: "One can elect (choose) a number of things, for instance a town councillor or anyone else"—(resistance, then giggling and embarrassment). We have already long known what a young girl associates with "choosing"; it is actually a "co-operative choice," namely, someone who co-operates for life. This probably explains the disturbances that follow, because this is the "burning" question *par excellence*.

97: *month* often excites the image of the period in a woman, which in our case has a special significance. Hence the complex-disturbance.

Summary of the Analysis

817   The association experiment and the analytical investigation into its results have given us insight into numerous trains of thought which, however, are still only vaguely differentiated. The analysis had to struggle with special difficulties because very few reactions in the three series appear normal. There is an abundance of complex-characteristics, which is further experimental evidence of how much the patient is overpowered by her complexes; we can almost say that not she but her complexes have the last word. The analysis not only met with great difficulties in getting at the critical reactions, because of the numerous complex-characteristics, but its task is made much more complicated by having to try to elicit further thoughts from the patient. Frequently the patient stops after only a few generalities and her laughter betrays that something is flashing through her mind. Interpretations that the patient can confirm are rare. She is so much under the influence of the complex that, if she were asked to evaluate its emotional significance, she would not be able to do so and would not know whether

it is important or not. We depend therefore almost entirely on conjectures, which, however, permit certain conclusions.

818   I have picked out only certain complex-constellations, although there are quite a number of others present. The associations produced in these are, however, only of secondary importance, so that I omitted their analysis for the sake of brevity.

819   There are a good many associations that show complex-characteristics throughout all three series and which therefore have to be understood as constant complex-constellations. In the majority of these cases a rather uniform interpretation is possible. Thus, for instance, it cannot be doubted that erotic ideas play an important part; they allow us here and there to recognize references to the doctor. In the second place comes the illness-complex. These two complexes, apparently independent of one another, have some aspects, however, in which they meet.

820   In analogy to the illness of the patient is the illness of the mother which, in its turn, touches the sexual complex of the daughter (*birth / difficult*, etc.). There are also certain signs that it is perhaps a physical sexual complex. Lastly, there is also a school complex present.

821   With these statements a number of threads has been provided that may lead us through the maze of the patient's thoughts. Because of her lack of self-control and her helplessness in the face of her complexes, however, the patient brings us into a precarious position in which we have to look for other means of finding confirmation of our assumptions.

822   Nature has an apparatus that makes an extract of the complexes and brings them to consciousness in an unrecognizable and therefore harmless form: this is the *dream*. As I thought I had found only the general idea with the association experiment, I collected the patient's dreams. From the beginning nothing but stereotyped blood and fire dreams were related, and these only in a vague form. One had of course to be prepared to obtain material from the past, only after it had been carefully sifted. Everything that was too obvious had been obliterated by strong inhibitions. Also, during the observation the patient dreamed very little, i.e., she remembered only a few dreams. Unfortunately, therefore, the material is not as plentiful as one could wish.

II. THE DREAMS

823   During the early months of the treatment I often inquired about her dreams. They were said to be infrequent; now and then the patient said she had again dreamed of *fire*, or of *blood*: "The whole room was full of fire or blood." Now and then she dreamed that blood was spurting from all the openings in her head, or she dreamed the same of another patient whom, in the dream, she saw in her room. The patient did not mention anything of any other dreams. The blood and fire dreams seemed to me to be stereotyped expressions of the dream-life, as the heat-sensations were of the waking life, which first of all symbolically represented the patient's phraseology (she had too much blood in her head, the blood was too hot; she had a temperature of 104°, she ought to be able to bleed properly once, everything in her head was like fire, everything was parched and charred, etc.). In the second place, the stereotyped dreams are, as always, symbolical expressions of the complex, which we have not yet clearly defined. For the therapeutic purpose of setting her against these dreams, which were often accompanied by anxiety, and for the theoretical purpose of learning whether she would abandon the dream-stereotypes and substitute something else for them, I said to the patient casually: "Blood is red, red means love, fire is red and hot, surely you know the song: No fire, no coal can burn as hot, etc. Fire, too, means love."

824   This interpretation made a strong impression on the patient. She burst out laughing with marked embarrassment. So she responded with feeling to my interpretation. My naïve interpretation of the dreams was based on the assumption that the dream symbolism would be simple and childish, in accordance with the patient's mentality. The interpretation took place in the middle of November. In the second half of November the following dreams occurred:

825   FIRST DREAM (Nov. 27). *"The room is full of cats, which are making a terrific noise."* During the dream, strong anxiety with anger. Details were denied. The above rather general statement had to stand.

826   The analysis was carried out in the same way as with the associations; I made her produce the first ideas that came to

384

mind, avoiding all suggestive remarks and pressing only if the patient appeared to succumb to a stronger inhibition. (The decrease of energy at the approach of a complex, the failure to respond in critical places, etc. are the same.) I should like to point out that in all the coming analyses the result is mentioned beforehand each time, while the material follows in small print. Anyone who is interested in the result only can skip the material.

827   *Result of the analysis*: The patient lived for eleven years in a place where she was frequently disturbed by caterwauling. This noise is known to be caused by mating fights. Behind the manifest dream-content is concealed the idea of sexual intercourse.

Material. Ideas relating to cats: The patient: "During recent nights there were now and then cats in the garden outside my room. I can't think of anything else—nothing at all (note the strong negations which are forerunners of an intensive inhibition. I insist)— I can think of absolutely nothing—yes, we had a lovely Angora cat once upon a time; unfortunately it was stolen." It is definitely peculiar that such a simple reminiscence should be subjected to such strong inhibitions; one has therefore to assume that this reminiscence has yet another aspect of personal significance. I therefore make her continue to associate: "(sounding angry) There are many cats that jump through our garden, yellow, black, white ones—I don't know what you want—(becomes very indignant, as if she were being forced to do something disgusting)—really, I can't think of anything else." This very decisive refusal has to be cut short; so I ask: "Were you disturbed by caterwauling at night?" "Never; it was actually quite impossible, because where I sleep at home one cannot hear the cats at all—as I said, I was never disturbed by cats—(in a casual tone, as if by the way) Oh, I remember that when I was ten or eleven, no, twelve years old (!), we lived in a place where there were always very many cats. They often made such a terrific noise at night that one thought the house would fall down. There were often about sixteen cats; they made this infernal row almost every night."

I asked: "How long did you live in this place?"—"Eleven years, i.e., from my 12th to my 23rd year." The patient is now 24! So she lived for eleven years, and actually until the year before, in a place where she was disturbed by caterwauling. As we have seen, the inhibition on the reminiscences about cats is so excessively strong that it leads to the greatest contradictions. It has to be pointed out that the patient's tone, which was usually very courteous and unassuming, became irritable and aggressive during the analysis; a manifestation quite unusual for her. Simultaneously her face more and more assumed an expression of suffering; she thus showed the same expression that otherwise belongs to the illness-complex. Now I asked her whether she knew the meaning of the nightly caterwauling, which she indignantly denied; I probed but received a vehement denial. A 24-year-old girl of average intelligence who has had a cat of her own, and apart from this had ample opportunity to learn about the behaviour of cats, must surely know what the nightly gatherings mean. When she is hysterical, she perhaps does not know it with her *ego-complex* but surely with her *sexual complex*.[15] Now I explained to the patient that the caterwauling meant *mating*. This was followed by visible excitement; the patient did not answer, blushed and looked out of the window. With reference to the dreams, I told her that cats had a symbolical meaning; she would be given the interpretation later. If one dreams of cats or *dogs*, this always means something definite. On the following days the patient repeatedly asked for the meaning of the dream, which interested her.

828   SECOND DREAM (Nov. 30). *"The whole room is full of mice, which are jumping all over the place and are making a great noise. The mice have an unusual appearance; they have bigger heads than ordinary mice, somewhat like rats, but they have big black ears; they also have peculiar glowing hot eyes."*

829   *Result of the analysis*: The mice conceal the reminiscence of two dogs (male and female) that the patient often saw playing together. The patient has already observed how dogs jump at each other. She has also seen the dog stand up against a maid. This again is about mating.

Material: Superficially we notice in this dream that on the whole the situation of the last dream is repeated, only the cats have been replaced by mice which, however, do not seem to be proper mice. The "glowing hot" eyes seem to be a fragment of the fire dreams. I put the text of the dream to the patient again; she has nothing to add.

Associations to the mice: "I particularly noticed that all the mice jumped out of little wooden huts—(this essential piece of description had apparently been kept under an inhibition and therefore could not be produced until now).—The huts looked like dog-kennels."

[15] See Bleuler's theoretical discussions in "Consciousness and Association" (orig. 1905).

Here we seem to be on a new track, because dogs do not appear in the dream. It is true that in the last analysis I drew the patient's attention to dogs. The idea "dog" seems to be indicated indirectly in the dream (i.e., it is repressed). I therefore take "dog-kennel" as the starting point of the analysis.

Ideas relative to *dog-kennel*: "Surely, there are many dog-kennels —(indignant) I don't know what you mean—there was nobody near us who had a dog—but one can see such dog-kennels everywhere— in gardens and courtyards—I cannot understand how you could suspect anything here—whatever could be behind it! For instance, *just behind our house there was a garden with a dog-kennel in it.* There were two dogs, two black ones, I think setters—perhaps a dog and a bitch; but the bitch was immediately removed—they often played together—they tore paper or pushed sticks about—or barked." Then comes a complete resistance with vehement indignation; she does not want to hear anything more about the dogs. After much persuasion it comes out at last that she often saw the dog stand up against the maid when she went into the garden. That the dog mounted the bitch is vehemently denied. But we know already that there are certain things that the patient cannot say, because the inhibitions are far too strong. It can with the greatest probability be assumed that she has seen it; this can be conjectured not only from the way she tells the story, but also from the whole situation. I say: "But one can often see dogs jump on each other's backs!" "Yes, I have often seen that in the street, but these two dogs did not do it." I asked her what the jumping meant: she explained it was a game, she did not know any other meaning. She said the last sentence in an irritated voice. We have to make the same comment here as on the previous dream: it is inconceivable that she does not know the meaning. Here, however, we must again remember the influence of the sexual complex on the conscious perceptions of the ego.

The dream may be reconstructed in the following way:

The mice are cover-figures which, however, are penetrated by the elements of the cat dream at several points. *Mouse* is a current association to *cat*, the two words can thus substitute for each other in the dream (or in a state of reduced concentration!).[16]

The mice are as noisy as the cats were, also they are in the room and in greater number. The mice have larger heads; thus they are

---

[16] We have shown that in a state of diversion of attention the indirect associations increase in such a way that a very frequent association replaces either the stimulus-word or the reaction, so that it appears as if the stimulus-word must have been misheard or that the patient reacted by a slip of the tongue. "The Associations of Normal Subjects."

not really mice, but larger animals. They have large black ears, like the black setters which also have big black ears. The mice jump out of kennels. The analysis points to a very ambiguous situation, the interpretation of which should not be difficult; it is *mating* again, as in the previous dream. That the dog jumps up on the servant seems to be a subtle indication as to what sort of person the thought of sexual intercourse refers to. This indication was missing in the first dream. Perhaps one may express the hypothesis that the first analysis stimulated the patient's sexual complex, so that her own person appeared in the next dream. I would also point out that as, in the earlier blood and fire dreams, the entire room was always full of blood or fire, the room is now full of cats and mice. The analysis took place on December 1, after the third dream, which follows. I did not inform the patient of the analysis of the second dream, so that when she had the third dream she had no insight about the content of the second dream.

830   THIRD DREAM (Dec. 1). *"She goes into a shop in the town to buy something. A big black dog that is very hungry comes along and jumps up on her, as if she could give him something to eat."*

831   *Result of the analysis*: In this dream the patient clearly takes the place of the maid of the previous dream, thereby revealing that the *idea of mating* refers to her.

Material: The manifest form of the dream betrays the content in line with the analysis of the preceding dream.

The patient is now in the situation of the maid; this clearly throws light on the critical point which remained unexplained in yesterday's dream, yet in the form that the patient could not understand on the previous day. Had she understood this symbol, it would probably not have been used—like the cats, the significance of which had been explained to her. Associations to the "dog jumping up": First there are generalities as usual, excuses and blockages which I am not going to reproduce, so as not to go into too much detail. At last she again thinks of the scene with the maid and the dog. Our first thought when considering the dream was of course this scene, but it was different for the patient. She has to search for it at great length, as if it were a reminiscence that had long since faded away and been forgotten. This is because at first she has to push aside all the resistances attached to this recollection. We are free from such resistances. The same thing happens to her in the dream-analysis as happened in the association experiment, when she always had the same blockages at critical points, even after two or

388

more repetitions, although one would actually expect that a reaction produced with so much effort would be more enduring than
one without any special significance.

On the same day I carried out the analysis of her main symptoms
(see below). During the following night she had a dream:

832   FOURTH DREAM (Dec. 2). *"She is standing in the corridor of
the Department and sees a tall black man coming along. He
is leading someone down the corridor, but she does not see
whether this person is a man or a woman."*

833   *Result of the analysis*: The black dog becomes the black
man, the scene is transferred to the Hospital. The black man
is the disease-producing sexual complex that brought the patient to the mental hospital. She is trying to gratify her desire
for love by falling in love with the doctor, but it is not to the
purpose, since the doctor is already married.

Material: The manifest form of the dream reminds us of the dog
scene, except that the big black dog has now become a big black
man. The maid of the dog scene (the patient herself) has become
blurred (the patient does not know whether it is a man or a woman).
The patient herself does not appear to take any further part in the
dream; we therefore have to look for her in a dream-figure, and may
well presume that she is the indistinct figure.

Associations to the "black man": "The man comes from the front
door, as if taking someone to the Department. He is dressed like a
judge of a Vehmic court[17] (whom she had once seen at the theatre);
he looks like a ghost, "like the black man whom I used to see when
going off to sleep." I asked her whether it had frightened her: "No,
I was not frightened of him—yet I was. I even wanted to retreat
into a room out of fright, but a nurse called out: 'Stop, this is forbidden! This room is already occupied.' " There is apparently an
inhibition attached to "fright." We have now traced the "black
man" of the *dream* back to the "black man" of the *vision*. The
vision shows the man stretching out his hand to catch hold of
her; this frightens her very much. The vision is a stereotyped com-
plex-expression, like the blood and fire dreams; it is thus a rather
rigid psychic product which it is not easy for the analyst to tackle.
In fact, the analysis comes up against strong barriers here which the
patient cannot break down. We therefore have to resort to conjecture. The black man who approaches her to catch hold of her
is analogous to the hungry black dog that jumps up on her. The

17 [A medieval tribunal that sat in secret.]

dog has a strong sexual background, which probably also belongs to the black man. The vision originated at a climax of the illness, when the patient was often thinking of death and was afraid she might even die as a result of her illness. As we indicated in the analysis of the associations, thoughts about death do not by any means exclude the sexual background; on the contrary, they can take the place of sexuality. As we have seen from the analysis of the associations and the analyses of the dreams so far, the patient is completely pervaded by a sexual complex. It is therefore most likely that the idea of intercourse is enacted in this dream as well. But let us leave this aspect for the time being and observe more closely the behaviour of the black man. At the height of the illness she is afraid she will die. Symbolically expressed: death is stretching his hand towards her, i.e., the illness will take her and lead her into the grave. The black man of the dream is leading an indistinct figure, who might represent the patient, into the mental hospital, and moreover to the same department where the patient is in actual fact. Thus the illness has not taken the patient to the grave but to the lunatic asylum.

The black man derives from the sexual dog, and the illness from the sexual complex.

To elucidate this sentence I beg to remind the reader of all the statements so far made: in the associations the clear and intensive activity of a sexual complex becomes obvious; in the dreams we found up to now nothing but metaphors for the sexual complex. At first there are the stereotyped blood and fire dreams, which are of a naïve symbolism. They say: "My blood is hot, I have strong sexual feelings of love." The dreams speak of sexual intercourse. Her illness is clearly connected with menstruation. That much is also acceptable to the patient, that the illness has a connection with the first period. Everything we were able to find out so far speaks for the sexual origin of the illness. What the patient is yearning for is doubtless The Man. She wants the man but has the illness; as long as she is ill she cannot get married. Does she want to be ill? We know the will-to-be-ill of hysterics. They escape into illness for some reason; they want to be ill. This is a truth that almost forces itself on the observer. From the asthenic personality of the patient who, for no other obvious reason, breaks down in the simple association experiment, which does not require any effort, I could not help getting the impression that she did not make any effort whatsoever to react normally, i.e., to be healthy; on the contrary, she behaved in such a way that one could not help seeing how ill she was and how little interest she had in being healthy.

She needs the illness as an obstacle to prevent her getting married. So she has the choice between illness and man, therefore the choice between the joys of sexual love and the care and attention given to the sick child, which also has its advantages for a naïve female mentality. I had explained to her the previous day that she wanted to be ill because she was afraid of getting married and being healthy. The dream is the answer to it. I had already told her dozens of times: "You are escaping into the illness again; you must not do that, it is forbidden." I said this to her each time she wanted to avoid telling me something unpleasant and disguised it by a headache and heat sensations. What does the dream say?

"But a nurse called: Stop, this is forbidden!" the nurse (thus my proxy) calls out in these words when the patient wants to take refuge in a room from fear of the black man (this part of the dream is, as its form shows, further protected by a special inhibition, so that it is produced only during the analysis). The fear of the sexual future and all its consequences is too great for the patient to decide to abandon her illness. She prefers to be ill, as she has been up to now, i.e., in actual fact to be nursed and pampered by her mother.

The dream, however, does not end with the presentation of this train of thought; it says, moreover, that the patient cannot retreat into the room, for it is already occupied. As the analysis shows, we assume that to take refuge in a room is a symbol for escaping into the illness, that therefore "room" means "illness." The patient is, however, in possession of her illness already, it therefore cannot be occupied by anyone else. But let us remember that "illness" is ambiguous. Her illness is the sexual complex, i.e., the repressed sexual feelings. The prohibition thus also says: It is forbidden to have sexual feelings, because something in the sexuality is already "occupied." Because of lack of time I had to interrupt the analysis at this point and to postpone it to the next day, when I intended to ask for information about which room it had been in the dream. On the following day I asked the patient at once which room it had been. She promptly replied: "Room No. 7." In order not to spoil anything, I asked the patient for the dreams of the previous night, before I began the analysis. She had dreamt again:

834   FIFTH DREAM (Dec. 3). *"I was outside and stood next to Miss L. We both saw that a house was on fire. Suddenly a white figure emerged from behind the house; we both got scared and exclaimed simultaneously: 'Lord Jesus!'"*

835   *Result of the analysis*: Here the black man has turned into

a white figure; the burning house is the sexual complex. Miss L. is a patient who has a crush on the author. She was, like the patient, taken ill because of an erotic complex. The patient therefore expresses through this person that she has fallen in love with the author. Thus the patient substituted the tender relationship with her mother, which is damaging to her energy, by the erotic relation to the doctor.

Material: The form of the dream shows us that because of the dream interpretation the black man had to assume another disguise and changed to the white apparition which, however, played the same frightening role. The situation too is similar in that, as the patient starts to do something, she is suddenly prevented. In the burning house we suspect the *heat* of sexual feelings. A pointer for the analysis is, by analogy with previous ones, that part of the last dream that was not completed at yesterday's analysis; namely *Room No. 7*. Room No. 7 is occupied by Miss L., a patient of the same age as our patient. This gives us a new point of vantage regarding the previous dreams. In that dream the patient thought something like this: "I go into Miss L.'s room, I do the same as Miss L." Particularly characteristic of Miss L., however, is the fact that she is in love with the writer—hopelessly, as the writer is already married. The patient therefore finds the "room" occupied in two senses: (1) Miss L. is already in love with the writer; therefore there is nothing left for her. (2) The writer is married; this precludes any tender emotion from the very start. In today's dream the idea of yesterday's is elaborated in more detail. In the dream the patient always does what Miss L. is doing. Thus she also watches the burning house. Therefore she also has a hot yearning or a burning love. The patient also knows that Miss L. was taken ill because of an unhappy love-affair. Here is a further very stimulating analogy! Therefore they both see how the white apparition, alias the black man, alias the illness, suddenly appears behind the fire of love and frightens them both, as love has made them both ill. Miss L. suffered from sudden depressive agitations, during which she behaved in an utterly despairing and senseless manner. The patient always was amazed at this and frequently stated with satisfaction that *she* was after all not so ill as to have to behave like that. I had also often told her (our patient) that if she had let herself go, she would have become even worse. Thus the patient could easily think, with her mild jealousy of Miss L., that Miss L. had let herself go more and therefore had become more severely ill. This is how "Room No. 7" was further determined. This point had not been explored in the former analysis; therefore we meet it again later on.

The content of this dream again throws light on that of the previous one in a peculiar way: The fear of the black man (sexual future) makes her escape into illness, which is, however, forbidden. Therefore the patient looks for a new way out: she does the same as Miss L., she falls in love with the doctor who can appreciate the complex and is a sexually harmless man; thus the dream finds a fortunate compromise. It replaces the love-giving but illness-producing mother by the healing but also sexually significant man. But there is a snag; the patient is poor and cannot stay at the clinic much longer, because she has not enough money. Miss L., however, is very rich and can stay as long as she likes. Miss L. then can take her place and "occupy" the room.

This manoeuvre also led nowhere and therefore the idea behind it remained active.

When I tactfully explained the content of these dreams to the patient she made a sad disappointed face—apparently the explanation was too blunt—and said in a suffering tone: "Oh, if my mother knew the things that are dragged out of me here!"

This reaction is noteworthy, since her mother would probably be indifferent to shades of feeling in her daughter. The answer, however, excellently depicts the cooling down and turning away of the patient's infantile sexual need for tenderness from the doctor and her reinsurance with the mother's love, a clear indication that the compromise is not tenable and the patient cannot separate herself from her childlike relation to the mother.

836   SIXTH DREAM (Dec. 6). *"My father is here and I am showing him the Institution by going through all the departments with him."*

837   *Result of the analysis*: The patient fulfils the wish to stay longer in treatment with the author, which she hopes will cure her.

Material: The patient states that this is only a fragment of a longer series of dreams which, however, she cannot remember. Even analysis cannot produce what is missing. It is not difficult to understand the dream; it represents an uncompleted piece of yesterday's dream. The patient behaves in this dream as if the Institution is more or less her home. I had asked her occasionally whether her father never came to visit her, to which the patient said that she thought she was here for such a short time that it was not worthwhile for her father to make the journey. In the dream apparently a situation has arisen in which the visit was worthwhile all the same. So the patient can stay here for a very long time (as she actually wants to do). Besides which, the dream shows the patient in an unexpected position of authority. She has the master key which opens all the departments for her; this leads to the conclusion that she is enjoying the quite special confidence of the doctor. What this confidential relation to the doctor means is not difficult to guess.

838   SEVENTH DREAM (Dec. 6, during the same night as the previous one). *"I am at home, Mother is sitting at the dinner table, you, Sir, opposite to her, and you are eating. Between Mother and you there is an empty chair. I want to sit down on this chair and eat too. But Mother has a hot flat-iron which she pushes towards me and that makes me get hot in the head. I tell Mother to put the iron away; she makes me feel hot with it so that I cannot eat. I too would like to eat with you both. At this you get up and shout at me that there is no need at all for me to eat now, I can just as well eat later."*

839   *Result of the analysis:* The patient desires a sexual relationship with the author, for she hopes that in this way she may get free of the influence of the mother which contributes to her illness. But the author is married, so that this wish cannot be fulfilled. She must therefore remain ill.

Material: This dream too shows a transparent symbolism; we can interpret it without any difficulty with the help of the pointers in Dream IV. We have seen that in Dream IV the patient starts to make a compromise between the infantile relationship to the mother and the sexual relationship to the man. Here the author clearly takes the role of the "man." The animal symbolism had already been dropped in the latest dreams, as it had been dealt with and become too transparent. So she has to create other coitus symbols. The dream begins with the patient being at home. This is the main question now which she puts to me daily: "How will it work out at home? I am always afraid it will go wrong again at home!" What is dangerous at home is mainly the mother, who as the careful nurse of her youngest child and image has apparently contributed her share to the patient's hysteria. Thus at home the question again arises: "Shall I continue with the role of the sick child that needs nursing, or shall I, in accordance with the doctor's advice, entrust myself bravely to the sexual future?" She therefore stands between

394

doctor and mother. The author is eating, she wants to eat with them, i.e., to do the same as the author. In what way can she do the same as the author? There is only one possibility, and that is the one that has already repeatedly been deliberated: to marry. She would like to sit in the chair next to the author, she would therefore like to sit beside him; this means nothing but that she relates to me in the sense of "husband." Does "to eat" therefore mean the marital function? We know Freud's principle of the displacement from below upwards. What happens to the mouth (in the dream, in hysteria, in schizophrenia) happens to the genitals. If one eats, one puts something into the mouth.

(A patient in the early stage of dementia once expressed her wish-delirium by saying that the man she desired as her bridegroom fed her with a spoon, which made her pregnant and she had a child.) So she wishes to enter into a sexual relationship with the doctor. But the mother makes her feel hot with the flat-iron, so she cannot sit down at the table, i.e., the mother brings back her illness (heat sensations in the head) and thus prevents her marriage. The fear that she may become worse again when she gets home is reflected here. Up to now the author has played a passive role, so that actually nobody but the mother stopped her from giving her love to the doctor. But now the author gets up and rejects her bluntly by forbidding her to "share the meal," i.e., to attach sexual thoughts to him, and at the same time comforts her by referring her to the future, when she can get married. This passage refers to a talk that I had with the patient a few days before, in which I carefully indicated that the question of getting married would not be so difficult later on, once she was well again. From this content it appears that the patient is again concerned with the dream-situation of the occupied room, with some variation, but this is connected with the obviously deep impression made on her by my previous analysis, in which I ruthlessly destroyed her illusions. Through this refusal she sees herself thrown back on the mother, and with the mother she becomes ill, because the mother does not want her to get married (see below). I have hardly concluded the analysis with the patient, when she says, quite out of context: "I am reminded of a dream that I used to have very often. I always used to dream of worms, reddish and whitish ones, the floor and the whole room were full of them (just like the blood, the fire, the cats, etc.). Very often, too, it was as if a colossal worm was being drawn out of my mouth." This dream in this context can be nothing but one of those penis dreams, so frequent in the normal as well as in the ill person (in dementia praecox, patients often have special neologisms for this such as

395

snakes, the stalk of a lily, staff of life, etc.). The *mouth* again indicates the displacement from below upwards.

It is therefore not unlikely that interference with marriage by the mother is the hysterogenous basic experience. Moreover, a sexual trauma has to be expected because of the lively eroticism of the patient. Therefore I told the patient that I was not satisfied, there must exist another experience which she had not yet told me, and which was of particular importance. Perhaps it would be revealed to me by her dreams. Perhaps this experience has also a connection with her cleanliness compulsion. Then for eight days the patient cannot recall any dream, although she knows she has had vivid ones. During this time I tried, as always, to get her interested in some activity and repeatedly discussed with her whether she did not know of any chance anywhere of earning a little money. After eight days had elapsed she again remembered a dream.

840   EIGHTH DREAM. *"I am at home and picking small coins up off the floor. I also find lovely stones, which I wash. I put the money and the stones on the kitchen-table and show them to my brothers."*

841   *Result of the analysis*: The patient thinks of going home, she has made several good resolutions and particularly thinks that she will find a substitute for the impossible relationship to the doctor in her family, especially in her brothers. The background of the dream, however, remains uninterpreted.

Material: In this dream she has realized her future earning of money. A new feature, however, is "the lovely stones" which she washes (cleanliness compulsion?). She shows her brothers what she has washed on the kitchen-table, which is perhaps reminiscent of the dinner-table? The analysis yielded nothing but generalities; the strongest resistances were put up against any deeper penetration. What are the brothers doing at the kitchen-table, are they perhaps replacing the doctor at the dinner-table? I could not solve this question.

842   NINTH DREAM (Dec. 12). *"I am going for a walk in Zurich, but it suddenly becomes the place where my home is. Outside a house I see a policeman standing, talking to a man whom I only see indistinctly. The policeman makes an extremely sad face and enters the house. Then suddenly Miss L. walks along the street with a terribly sad face. Then we are suddenly together in a room and are sitting at the dinner-table. Suddenly*

someone says that the house is on fire. Miss L. says: 'Now I am getting into bed.' I find this inconceivable and run out into the corridor, but there I am told there is no fire; it was therefore only a false alarm. Now I go in again and find myself at home in the kitchen with Mother, and two of my brothers are there too. A basket full of gorgeous apples is standing there. One of my brothers says: 'This also is something for me.'"

843 *Result of the analysis*: The patient, like Miss L., is disappointed in her hope of love which, however, she understands with regard to Miss L., whose less good qualities she scornfully stresses. So she goes home, where she again enters into a suspiciously intimate relationship with one of her brothers.

Material: The general situation of the dream is a similar one to that of the seventh dream. It is again about being together at the dinner- or kitchen-table. In the first part of the dream there is a policeman with a terribly sad face. Immediately afterwards and quite suddenly, Miss L. turns up with the same attribute. The policeman enters a house, and this is immediately followed by the patient eating with Miss L. in a room. Miss L. and the policeman are apparently equivalent. How and why has Miss L. changed into a policeman? I ask the patient for conspicuous characteristics of Miss L. The patient finds in particular that Miss L. has such peculiar manners that she is only half a woman, almost a man, and she is also very thin. We have a long thin sausage in Switzerland which is called something like "dried-up policeman."[18] This term is also used as a nickname for thin people. The patient thus indicates the less laudable aspects of Miss L. Why she does so is shown by the circumstance that the policeman speaks to a man whom the patient sees only indistinctly; if Miss L., however, speaks to a man, then in the dream it can be nobody but the author. It is therefore likely that the patient is again jealously stressing Miss L.'s feelings for the author, thence treating Miss L. very disdainfully. Then she sits with Miss L. at the dinner table. She is therefore in a sexual situation with her which, however, one must not think of as anything homosexual, as "dinner-table" in its sexual meaning has already been dealt with by the author; it would therefore be far too transparent. Here it probably only means: "I feel sexually as Miss L. does." The fire-alarm that follows also indicates this.

The patient goes outside to look. Miss L., however, goes to bed, i.e., becomes sick with love. To understand this, we must know that

18 [In German, *dürren Landjäger*.]

Miss L. always went to bed when she was excited. At the beginning of the dream the patient humiliates her rival, then when the sexual situation (fire-alarm) comes up, Miss L. actually becomes ill and therefore completely harmless. So the rival has been put out of the way. But the patient hears it is only a false alarm: this is the disappointment ("the room is occupied," "she cannot partake of the meal"). The author has spoiled her illusions, the transposition of her desire for love to the man has not succeeded, she therefore has to return to mother, where at least she finds an equivalent to the gratification of her need for love. Therefore the situation changes in the second part of the dream. The patient is suddenly at home with her mother in the kitchen instead of at the dinner-table. If only the relationship to the mother was concerned, there would be no need for the brothers. But two brothers are there as well and, as in the eighth dream, at the kitchen-table, but instead of the "lovely stones" a basket of "gorgeous apples" now stands there, and a brother says: "This also is something for me." The dinner-table scene of the seventh dream, as well as the dinner-table scene of this dream with Miss L., can hardly be interpreted in other than a sexual sense: now we have a similarly constructed picture in immediate succession to the sexual scene in that "dinner-table" has been replaced by "kitchen." In the first place the "gorgeous apples" look like the "lovely stones" on the kitchen-table, and secondly they are something edible (cf. Eve's apple). This is something for the brother, he gets some of it. We have to keep in mind: in the first part of the dream a sexual wish is destroyed for the patient; the second part can hardly refer merely to the mother, sex must somehow play its part here. I now make her produce ideas about the "apples": "I thought of the apples I saw at a fruiterer's[19] yesterday. I was there with Mrs. Jung." So she was there with my wife; this could be a clue. But now the analysis comes to a halt and no further progress can be made. So I make a fresh start with the brother: "This was my brother who lives in Italy: he has often invited me to go to Italy and visit him."

Remember here R.25, Test VI.

Travel: The patient associated at this point: "A nice journey to Italy—honeymoon." This would, however, be nothing to do with the brother, and yet the apples are meant for him too. I would like to add here another short dream which the patient had right at the beginning of the treatment. She dreamed that I came into the room and she said to me: *Unfortunately the nuts could not be gathered*

19 [The word used, *Sudfruchtengeschäft*, means a shop specializing in fruit from the South.]

398

yet, but she had a whole basket full of them at home. In this dream the patient offers the fruit to me, nuts. Nuts are as hard as stones, one has to open them to be able to eat them. Remember the "lovely stones," the "gorgeous apples," which she now allocates to the brothers. What her erotic expectation originally promised me is for the brother now, she has turned away from me.

I think that here it becomes obvious that there is something about the brother that goes beyond a sibling relation. The brother's significance for the sister becomes suspect (cf. *to kiss/sister's kiss*), and we cannot help having a strong feeling that here is something, sought for a long time, that would explain a lot, if we could be sure of it.[20] Some adventure of the time before puberty, in which the brother plays an impressive role, seems to be at the bottom here, a Freudian trauma. But the secret is well defended, and the analysis cannot gain access.

I told the patient quite casually of the content of the analysis, avoiding making any hints of a sexual nature. I wanted to avoid this because revealing the symbolism might make the next dream even more obscure. The inner development of the patient indicated in this dream, i.e., the turning away from the author, the abandoning of his point of view and the invalidating of his advice and teaching showed themselves (apart from an objective deterioration) in the significant fact that the patient now started again to dream of fire and blood; she "heard the *fire-alarm* every night."

The time of discharge now came nearer and nearer, and I hoped for a decisive dream, but the patient did not remember her dreams any more (except the fire dreams) apart from a single small fragment that did not tell us anything. On the morning of the day of her discharge I asked her, as usual, whether she had dreamt again. She said "Yes" but added quickly: "But I know already what the dream means, I noticed it at once. But I am not going to tell you; it is something from the past that I can only perhaps tell my mother." I implored her repeatedly, but in vain; she insisted it was of such a nature that she could only tell it to her mother. At last I said, then it must be a very unpleasant sexual story! The patient did not reply to that but looked out of the window. I could not venture to press the point any further.

Thus our dream-analysis and the analysis of the illness as a whole

---

[20] Here it should also be remembered that in the dream of the occupied room there was the call: "Stop, this is forbidden!" Perhaps my phrase made such an impression, because it was complex-stimulating and expressed something that was of great importance for the patient (if we assume that the complex here touched actually exists!).

remain incomplete, at a point which, however, appears clearly defined.

Summary of the Dream-Analyses

844   Although actually none of the analyses was as complete as we could wish, and in particular the last one breaks off at an important point, we have yet gained through them a number of valuable clues. Above all we see that the dreams completely confirm the complex revealed by the association tests. The associations point to an intensive sexual complex, and the dreams are about nothing but the theme of mating. This makes us realize that the complexes that constellate the associations of waking life also constellate the dreams. We have the same blockages that turn up in the association experiment, in the dream analysis too. The analysis of the dream-images revealed the sexual complex, its transposition to the author, the disappointment and the patient's reversion to the mother, and the resumption of a mysterious childhood relationship with the brother. The object of the next chapter is to show the sexual complex in the hysterical symptom and in the course of the illness.

III. THE HYSTERICAL SYMPTOM

845   It only remains now to apply our knowledge of the form and content of the sexual complex, gained in the two previous chapters, to the symptoms of the illness. Let us start with the "St. Vitus's dance."

846   According to the case history, as given by the patient, the St. Vitus's dance suddenly started one day for reasons unknown. All questions about the reason are answered in the negative, and it seems to be impossible to get at the cause, because it is unknown to the patient. But we already know very well the resistances that stand in the way of the production of all complex-ideas. Hysterics have access to their psychic material only in so far as it refers to insignificant ideas; but where the complex is involved they are powerless. The complex does not belong entirely to the hierarchy of ideas contained in ego-consciousness; because of its strong emotional charge it is more or less autonomous (as is, after all, any strong affect) and forces the association in its direction, even if the

ego-complex endeavours to think and act in its own interests. For this reason we cannot talk about "intimate" things with the same security and calm as of objective ones. The need to keep the "intimate" secret can become strengthened almost to the impossibility of producing it, as we have seen in the case described in "Psychoanalysis and Association Experiments." If, therefore, we want to get information on "intimate" matters, i.e., on the complex in a hysteria, we can get it only by detours. Freud made a method of the detour; it is psychoanalysis. First we liberate general cover-ideas which stand in some associative (often symbolical) relation to the idea of the complex, and so we gradually approach the complex from different aspects. The method is basically the same as that used by a skilled examiner for a nervous candidate. The candidate cannot answer the special and direct question, he is too agitated; so the examiner first gets him to answer a number of quite general and easy questions, the emotional charge of which is not too great, and then the required answer comes quite spontaneously. Similarly, if I at once ask the patient for the cause of her St. Vitus's dance, nothing will come of it; so first I make her answer harmless supplementary questions, and in this way learn the following:

She liked going to school, she also liked the teachers. Although she did not like all lessons equally she cannot, however, remember that she particularly disliked certain lessons, or that she particularly disliked certain teachers. She did not much like writing-lessons; she actually disliked this class. It was during the writing-lesson (in her second year at school) that her right hand first started twitching. Then the twitching became gradually stronger so that she could not write any more. She therefore had to miss the writing-lesson. Then the twitching started in the right leg too, so that soon she could no longer go to school at all. So the St. Vitus's dance gradually developed. She also remembers that she could not help crying "terribly" all the time and was afraid to go outside when it was raining, so that she frequently missed school for this reason as well. The St. Vitus's dance was sometimes more, sometimes less marked, so that sometimes she could go to school, sometimes stayed away. During her twelfth year, however, the illness became so violent that she had to give up school altogether.

847   I think it emerges clearly from this narration that the patient was an extremely spoilt child who used every opportunity

to keep herself away from school for the purpose of shirking the detested writing-lesson. The twitching in the arm conveniently began, which then ultimately served the purpose of making it completely impossible to go to school. The patient now also admits that she could have suppressed the twitching then if she had tried. *But it suited her to be ill.* The uncertainty with which the patient speaks of her feelings concerning her school reminiscences at the beginning of the analysis seems to me particularly instructive. First it seems to her that she liked going to school, then there are expressions of the feeling that it was after all not quite like that, and then comes the exact opposite, which coincides with the fact. This inconsistent way of presentation is actually a method of the patient (see the previous analyses). There is no indication that the patient is aware of the inconsistency at the moment; on the contrary, it seems that whatever she says at any given moment she absolutely believes. The school-complex, that well-known feature of all asthenic children, here leads to the formation of a hysterical symptom. The existence of an automatism understandably provides a suitable *locus minoris resistentiae*, from which further automatisms can develop if the situation demands it.

The day after this analysis the feeling-tones had changed again, the patient alleged she could not say she disliked going to school, she quite liked it. School never made much impression on her. She was much more occupied with other experiences, such as that once a schoolmistress had vehemently scolded her. So we have the same uncertainty and inconsistency here again.

848   During her twelfth year the St. Vitus's dance grew worse. The twelfth year seems (according to the analysis) also to be the year from the recollection of which the sexual cat dream emerged. During the twelfth year the first puberty feelings become apparent in many girls and they begin to be interested in sexual secrets. But her twelfth year has yet another significance for the patient. I made the patient associate to the complex of the mother; the result was as follows:

A lot comes to her mind here—(after a long pause)—because Mother is also ill, and yet is so content and cheerful; if only she could also be like that. Mother always said her osteomalacia came

402

from being married. But she had been taken ill 28 years ago; now the disease is curable, so the doctors say.

This remark made me ask: "Has this any significance for her?" None, she could not imagine at all what it might mean to her— she has never thought about it. I commented that the thought that she might have inherited a disposition to such an illness would be possible after all. She was never afraid of that, she would have got married in spite of it. I said that such a fear may perhaps have arisen in her at the time of the first period. "This is not possible, because my mother told me long before that, when I was *twelve years* old, that I must not get married, because then I would get the same illness."

849   We may conjecture from this remark that during her twelfth year discussions of far-reaching sexual importance took place, which must have made a strong impression on the patient's fantasy, judging from the strength of the resistance with which she tries to prevent the elucidation of this point. In any case, during the twelfth year we find one of the first components of the sexual complex. At the time of the first period she was faced with two complexes, one associated with a fully developed automatism, the other with the sexual feelings. The possibility of converting this decisive experience into a hysterical symptom is thus given, but not the necessity for it, because the impossibility of marriage appears by itself insufficient. We must also postulate the existence of an event that prepared the way for repressing the sexual complex, i.e., a sexual event of childhood. Here the sexual trauma, which the dreams seem to indicate, would fit in.

850   With menstruation a new form of existence sets in, the sexual one. It is therefore not surprising if the school-complex is replaced by the sexual complex, though only outwardly; as we have seen, it is still present in the associations, it is still an open wound which is above all sustained by self-reproaches. That the school-complex, i.e., the St. Vitus's dance, potentially still exists is expressed in the following way: The patient once had a particularly bad day. She described the heat sensations as intolerable; while she was speaking her right arm twitched from time to time, then the left one too. I drew her attention to these movements, then her legs also began to twitch slightly,

and she said: "I can only restrain myself with an effort from hitting out as I used to do. I feel the greatest temptation to do so!" We can see that the old automatisms are again ready to break through at any moment when her energy is completely exhausted (this confirms Janet's doctrine that each *abaissement du niveau mental* is accompanied by a flare-up of the automatisms). The onset of menstruation stimulates the development of the present complaints, heat sensations in the head and neck, a sensation as if all the blood is in the head, a temperature of 104°. Hands, feet, and body are cold. Simultaneously there are obsessive chains of ideas: she is constantly compelled to imagine that she is bleeding from the nose, from all apertures of the head, and that the clots that were discharged during the first period are in the head; she always wishes she could just once bleed enough from the head to fill a whole basin.

851 This strange symptom-complex without any doubt refers to the period: it is none other than a "displacement from below upwards" (Freud). The mechanism of displacement is operative in the patient; we have already found it in the dream-analyses in a form that can hardly be mistaken. The heat (blood and fire in the dream) is probably the sexual heat appearing with the period. For many months the period has ceased, after being rather irregular; besides this there is an obvious meteorism and a posture that makes the abdomen protrude even more. These are, according to Freud, symptoms of pseudo-pregnancy, an assumption that the psychological experience supports; where there is a complex of erotic expectancy in a young girl, the child plays a marked role in associations and dreams.[21] It will be remembered that this is in fact so in the associations of our patient. Furthermore, for the patient, pregnancy points to the danger of osteomalacia, which is bound to be strongly repressed. I am, however, unable to bring any positive evidence for Freud's conception.

852 The following symptomic acts probably also originate from the repression of the sexual feelings:

1. the constant craving to cool down;
2. the cold washes;
3. the horror of meat in any form;

[21] Cf., e.g., the sleep-walking fantasies of the case that I published in my study "On the Psychology and Pathology of So-called Occult Phenomena."

404

4. the inability to sit still;

5. a liking for indoor gymnastics while otherwise avoiding any physically strenuous occupations.

853   These symptomatic acts exactly correspond to the hygienic precepts against states of sexual excitement given in popular text-books.

854   Positive evidence for the repression of the sexual feelings is the consistent and obstinate evading of all sexual questions. As soon as the inquiry touches anything sexual, there is a barrier, and then one is usually held up by insurmountable obstacles. For theoretical reasons I made sure by appropriate questions that the patient was thoroughly informed about all the facts of sex, but she was unable to tell me where she knew all this from; she stubbornly denied having ever read anything about it or heard anything about it from anyone. She just knew it. Only towards the end of the treatment did the patient confess during the analysis, after protracted blocking, that a girl friend had enlightened her, when she was twelve years old. This too shows how strong the barriers are that guard the sexual secret.

855   I need not go any further into the visions; they have already found their interpretation during the dream-analyses.

856   The improvement moved at a slow pace, with frequent relapses. The energy visibly increased, so that the patient's vigour gradually extended to four and five o'clock in the after-noon (originally it had already been used up by 10 a.m.!). She was again able to read without any interruptions and to do some needlework. But the heat sensations remained, only their intensity seemed less, and during the third month of the treat-ment the patient stopped telling me about them. She only wondered why she recently has such frequent depressions, the cause of which she could not understand (originally when there was something unpleasant, she never mentioned depres-sion, only exaggerated heat sensations!). To my assistant, a lady doctor, however, the patient spoke of her heat sensations as before. After the dream of the dinner-table, when I had told her about her relationship with me, the earlier expressions were soon resumed, when talking to me as well. In the dream she heard the fire-alarm, and several times, particularly during the last week of her stay here, the black man, who had disap-peared after he had first been interpreted, came back too. The

dream-analyses show how this relapse can be explained. The patient was unable to reveal her innermost secret; the sexual compromise with myself had failed (apparently she could not find anything in me, apart from the sexual aspect, that would have been so valuable to her that she could have separated herself from her role as an invalid). As she was unable to separate herself from her secret, she had to cling to the heat sensations because of their repressive function, and so she came to resume the former symptoms and appropriate terminology, in this way demonstrating that my interpretations had been wrong; because she could not admit to herself that I was right, since that would have made the genuineness of her illness questionable.

857   About a month after the discharge her family doctor wrote to me that she was just as bad as before and that she now grumbled about the hospital and the doctor, with indications that the doctor had only tried to find opportunities to make morally dangerous conversation with her. Thus the sick personality, i.e., the sexual complex, entrenches itself behind aggressive defence-mechanisms; it discredits the moral personality of the doctor as much as possible, in order to invalidate the information supplied to the normal part of the mind. In this way the automatism of the illness secures itself a free road to unimpeded development, because each complex strives to live itself out unimpeded.

SUMMARY

858   The complex revealed in the associations is the root of the dreams and of the hysterical symptoms.

859   The interferences that the complex causes in the association experiment are none other than resistances in psychoanalysis, as described by Freud.

860   The mechanisms of repression are the same in the association experiment as in the dream and in the hysterical symptom.

861   The complex has an abnormal autonomy in hysteria and a tendency to an active separate existence, which reduces and replaces the constellating power of the ego-complex. In this way a new morbid personality is gradually created, the inclinations, judgments, and resolutions of which move only in the

direction of the will to be ill. This second personality devours what is left of the normal ego and forces it into the role of a secondary (oppressed) complex.

862 A purposive treatment of hysteria must therefore strengthen what has remained of the normal ego, and this is best achieved by introducing some new complex that liberates the ego from domination by the complex of the illness.

THE PSYCHOPATHOLOGICAL SIGNIFICANCE
OF THE ASSOCIATION EXPERIMENT[1]

⁸⁶³ Although there is more interest in psychology as a subject nowadays among non-psychologists than there was a few decades ago, nonetheless the relative youth of experimental psychology does mean that in this sphere little has as yet been clarified, and there is a good deal of controversy over many aspects of the subject. What is more, psychology is still a hybrid, inasmuch as the subject of experimental psychology is still in many institutions a very poor relation of philosophical psychology. The dogmatic nature of the latter is to blame for the manifold misunderstandings between the two kinds of psychologist. One wants to make psychology a creed, the other a science. Understandably these entirely divergent tendencies are in conflict with and hinder each other. This opposition makes itself felt most disagreeably in the field of nomenclature. The same words and concepts mean one thing with one writer and something quite different with another. So long as it is a matter of dogmas and axioms, which owe their existence to the *petitio* principle, one cannot hope for clarity, for each dogma entails a certain obscurity, as is well known. We are, therefore waiting for enlightenment from experimental psychology which, it is true, is still in its infancy yet can already look back on a rich harvest from the work in this field.

⁸⁶⁴ Psychopathology too has had to suffer for years from the same opposition. First, it had, with difficulty, to free itself from philosophical ideas, only to become subjected to rigid schematic anatomical notions which nowadays are still firmly fixed in many minds. It is only comparatively recently that we have the beginnings of an experimental psychopathology that has

---

¹ [First published as "Die psychopathologische Bedeutung des Assoziations-experimentes," *Archiv für Kriminalanthropologie und Kriminalistik* (Leipzig), XXII (1906): 2–3 (Feb. 15), 145–62. It was Jung's inaugural lecture, 21 October 1905, upon his appointment as lecturer in psychiatry at the University of Zurich.]

recovered from its birth-pangs. For this achievement we owe our gratitude to the alienists; first of all to the eminent psychiatrist Kraepelin, the pupil of Wilhelm Wundt, and secondly to the psychiatrist Sommer. Kraepelin has taken over a series of fundamental ideas and methods from Wundt's school and with these attempted to pave the way to an experimental science of the sick mind. Under his direction a large number of important papers[2] have been published that will provide a source of stimulating ideas and valuable methods for many years to come, even if the results of certain individual works are dubious or are, at least for the time being, of purely academic interest. The principal subjects of Kraepelin's research are mental ability, the influence of fatigue, drugs, and alcohol on simple psychic functions, fatigue and recovery, perception, etc.

865   This research is mostly concerned with the experimental demonstration of various influences on the mind of a normal person. The real value of Kraepelin's work, however, lies in opening up various new prospects in the field of psychopathology.

866   In addition to the papers on fatigue, Aschaffenburg's work on associations is particularly important in this context.[3]

867   Before we go any further into the content of Aschaffenburg's work, certain matters of a general nature must be discussed.

868   The ancients were already aware that the flow of our images and ideas is not entirely erratic; we find suggestions of laws of association in Plato and Aristotle,[4] the validity of which is still recognized today. The laws of simultaneity, sequence, similarity, and contrast are also the basis of Wundt's laws of association. Wherever in Nature there is a regular sequence of events the experiment can be applied. Thus experiments can also be made on the process of association, however complicated and difficult to follow this may be. After Galton's first tentative experiments,[5] Wundt and his group were the first to

---

[2] *Psychologische Arbeiten* (from 1896).
[3] "Experimentelle Studien über Assoziationen," ibid., I (1896), II (1899), IV (1904).
[4] A book that offers an excellent survey of the problem is Claparède, *L'Association des idées* (1903).
[5] "Psychometric Experiments" (1897).

make systematic investigations[6] into association processes. The method of the experiment is extraordinarily simple; the experimenter calls out a word to the subject, who then says what is immediately called to mind by the stimulus-word. The experiment is thus similar to any other in physiology in which we subject a living object to an adequate stimulus, as for example the application of electrical stimuli to various parts of the nervous system, light to the eye and acoustic stimuli to the ear. In the same way with the stimulus-word we are applying a psychical stimulus to the psychical organ. We introduce an image to the consciousness of the subject, and are given whatever further image is brought by this to his mind. We can thus quickly obtain a large number of connected images or associations. From the material thus obtained we can establish, by comparison with that from other subjects, that this or that particular stimulus will give a particular reaction. So we possess a means of investigating the law of association. The "law of association"! That sounds highly academic, and no one with knowledge of philosophy would hesitate to admit the possibility of such laws. However, the word "law" implies necessity and thus, applied to the experiment, it means that the stimulus-image must necessarily cause this or that particular association. The experiment would thus acquire the nature of something inexorable and causally inevitable. The subject must inevitably associate the appropriate image to a particular stimulus, just as the nervous system, when given a stimulus at one point, *ceteris paribus*, always causes contraction of the same muscle. If we recognize the necessity of laws of association, we must say that the subject has surrendered completely to the experiment because he must necessarily·have that thought which is associated with the particular stimulus. This involves the idea of determinism. Not everyone however, will go so far with us. There are still many educated people today who, on the ground of idealism and for other reasons, believe in the freedom of the will. Consequently these people must deny the necessity of the law of association, and resolve interconnection of ideas into a number of fortuitous events. They must assert that the experiment indicated is open to the wildest chance; that a person can not only say, but also think, whatever he wants to; that, from

6 Trautscholdt, "Experimentelle Untersuchungen über die Assoziation der Vorstellungen" (1883).

hundreds of things that occur to him, he can choose now one and now another according to his taste or present mood; that he is not obliged to think in terms of similarity or simultaneity, etc. These are the usual objections. The same objections are raised by serious-minded people to determinism. They maintain, in all seriousness, that man is capable of choosing from among his various motives before the act of will occurs. Does he also choose from among the motives of the motives, and the grandfathers and great-grandfathers of the motives? And what does he do with those motives which do not enter his conscious mind?[7] Or do the motives perhaps come to the surface from the transcendental sphere as an incomprehensible act of the Creator? If man wished to select from among his motives, he would have to spend years before he moved a finger in order to trace back to the mists of his childhood the entire series involved and consider all of them: he would never finish. In this process he would again and again be dependent on the results of all previous motives or *associations* to express himself with greater clarity. As you can see, it is *a priori* easy to refute the objection based on the principle of chance in psychical occurrences if the opposition is not intent on raising sophistical difficulties.

869   In principle, therefore, it must be accepted that association is a necessary sequence following certain laws. Hence an association experiment in which chance appears to have an absolutely free hand takes on the dignity and conclusiveness of any other scientific experiment. Chance, by definition, does not allow of any rules, but does permit necessary occurrences. A rule means a restriction, a limitation of the occurrence, which must empirically be capable of proof. In the same way, too, the multiplicity of possible associations, which to the layman appears inexhaustible, must empirically be limited to a certain extent.

870   This brings us back to Aschaffenburg's experiments.

871   The results of his investigation provide us with considerable insight into the vast difficulties of a huge subject. The most difficult of all is in fact the discovery of a law. From what points of view must the disconcerting profusion of thousands of associations be classified in order to obtain even a superficial impression of the whole? When one looks at the innumerable individual reactions one almost despairs of finding a

[7] The possibility of such motivations is proved by the post-hypnotic command.

foothold in the wild chaos. Wilhelm Wundt helped himself by means of certain logical principles of classification, based on the laws of simultaneity and similitude which have come down to us from classical times. Thus at least logical clues were obtained, although neither Wundt nor any of his pupils imagined that they could exhaust all the possibilities. Aschaffenburg and Kraepelin built further on the same foundations. They made one essential distinction: between internal and external associations. The following associations:

human being	boy
attack	defence
table	furniture

are internal associations, i.e., pairs in which the meaning or conceptual content of the words is the essential connecting link.

872   On the other hand, associations such as:

knife	trousers-pocket
water	fish
plant	pot

are external associations, i.e., the connecting link is not the intrinsic sense or meaning but an external contingency. One particular form of this external connection is the catch-phrase; as such phrases readily come to mind they are especially frequent in this experiment. For instance, the following associations, as purely verbal connections, are to be considered as external:

time	and tide
whisper	sweet nothings
stick	in-the-mud
die	is cast

873   Among external associations Aschaffenburg includes all current word-sequences.

874   Apart from the internal and external associations there is often also the case of a word merely suggesting another having a similar sound:

part	heart
cow	plough
rabbit	habit

These have been called sound associations.

875   In spite of the tremendous efforts made by various research workers, we have still not yet succeeded in finding a method of classification that is in principle entirely satisfactory. In any case, the present method suffices for solving many problems in association research.

876   One of Aschaffenburg's predecessors in the field of association research, the well-known psychologist Münsterberg[8] (now in America), believed he had found that the existence of three different intellectual types was proved by his experiments. He found that among a limited number of subjects there were some who reacted mainly in terms of super-ordination, others in terms of co-ordination, and others in terms of sub-ordination. Aschaffenburg, however, with a much more reliable method, found nothing of the kind.

877   The hope of finding categories governing association was thus premature. No regularity was to be detected *prima vista*. One subject would make many internal associations, another many external ones; one would make no sound reactions and another several. No one could account for the differences.

878   At this stage, however, Kraepelin and Aschaffenburg made one fundamentally important step forward. They altered the psychical condition of the subject in the most unequivocal manner; the subjects of the experiments were deliberately made as tired as possible in the following way: each of them would, after a full day's work at his usual profession, be given a series of association tests at intervals from eight o'clock in the evening to eight in the morning, the pauses being given to some other form of mental work. During the night the subjects were given nothing to eat.

879   By this means a state of intense fatigue was created.

880   One quite constant phenomenon now became evident in the associations of the various subjects; there was a decrease in the number of internal associations, and an increase in the external variety, and especially in the sound associations, i.e., associations with other words. Semantic connections grow weaker with increasing tiredness and are replaced by external

8 *Beiträge zur experimentellen Psychologie* (1889–92). [Hugo Münsterberg, professor of psychology at Harvard until his death in 1916, was an opponent of psychoanalysis.]

413

and superficial connecting links. It can thus be stated that the valency of associations decreases with increased tiredness.

881   Thus we have the first important rule about the faculty of association. Fatigue obliterates individual differences and drives the act of association in a particular direction. Besides this, Aschaffenburg also discovered that in one of his subjects who was suffering from a severe attack of influenza, the associations were similarly affected. So the special disposition of the brain caused by fever also has an adverse effect on the value of association tests in that mainly sound associations are produced.

882   These positive results, which far surpassed anything else that had hitherto been accomplished in the field of association research, provided Aschaffenburg with the link to the subject-matter of psychopathology. Clinical observations had long since established that in a certain mental illness, known as *mania*, a mode of association is prevalent that is similar to that found by Aschaffenburg in fatigue, i.e., the connections and sound associations were mainly superficial. The illness is characterized by a predominantly cheerful mood, distractability, and motor agitation, which are expressed in ceaseless compulsive activity. When we analyze the state of extreme fatigue, it is easy to find similar elements there. One has only to observe one's own state after a strenuous mountaineering expedition to be able to diagnose without difficulty an unaccountable superficial gaiety and a state of motor agitation, shown in countless irrelevant movements of the arms and legs. Sound associations, too, are easily seen in the jokes current among parties in mountaineering-club huts. Most of these are of the order of the pun, i.e., the onomatopoeic joke par excellence. Aschaffenburg believed that the common factor in these circumstances was *motor agitation*, and therefore attributed the cause of sound associations to this. In this, however, I think he was in error. In our hospital we have conducted systematic research[9] into associations for several years past and have obtained results that allowed of another interpretation. When a longish series of associations, say two hundred, is given to a subject, he will, without really becoming tired, soon find the process boring, and then he will not pay so much attention as at the beginning. For this reason we have separated the first hundred from the

9 Jung and Riklin, "The Associations of Normal Subjects," *supra.*

414

second in our classifications and have found that in all cases where the subject had become bored there is a clear decrease in internal associations and a proportionate increase in external and sound associations. This observation made us think that the cause of sound associations is not so much muscular stimulation, which is absent in normal boredom, but a lack of *attention*. We have been able to confirm this interpretation on the basis of numerous experiments in which the subject's attention has been methodically distracted.[10] Furthermore, we found an increase in the proportion of sound associations with subjects whose ability to concentrate had been weakened by a recent affect, with people in a somnolent state, and in addition with psychotics whenever their capacity for concentration is reduced. Kraepelin's school have also shown a levelling down of associations in cases of acute alcoholic poisoning. Aschaffenburg found the same thing in feverish patients. *It can therefore be said that the more the attention of the patient decreases, the more the external and sound associations increase.*

883 As you can already see from its numerous connections with altered psychical conditions, this empirically discovered law of association has, of course, great importance for the understanding of psychopathological states; in which, as is well known, one of the principle psychic functions, *the ability to concentrate*, is very frequently paralyzed or disturbed. In certain borderline cases between mental health and psychical disorder the experiment has already been of valuable service to us.

884 Our knowledge of factors governing association is, however, not exhausted with the statement that the seemingly unrestricted association depends to a large extent on the subject's attentiveness. Research into the associations of a large number of educated and uneducated subjects has enabled us to establish that *on average* the uneducated gave internal associations more often than the educated.[11] This apparent paradox can be explained as follows.

885 Educated people are used to dealing with words out of any context (as in grammatical studies, dictionaries, etc.). Thus

10 Ibid.

11 These findings confirm Ranschburg's statements. Cf. Ranschburg and Balint, "Über quantitative und qualitative Veränderungen geistiger Vorgänge im hohen Greisenalter" (1900).

when we call out a word to an educated man, it means no more to him than just a word. An uneducated person, on the other hand, is only accustomed to hear words in a sentence, where they always have a definite meaning. If we call a word out to an uneducated person, he always constructs something like a sentence round it. He understands the word as a question: hence the tendency of uneducated subjects to react with whole sentences or by the use of higher categories. Thus for instance the educated man will react to *table* with *table-cloth* to *chair* with *chair-leg*, whereas the uneducated man will react to the word *table* with *furniture*, and *chair* with *for sitting on*. The educated person finds it easy to grasp the experiment, while it costs the uneducated one an effort to do with words called out to him something different from what he is used to in his daily life. It therefore also happens that the uneducated are inclined to apply adjectives to themselves, particularly when they appear to express a judgment or anything of that kind, e.g., in the case of the word *stupid*. The degree of effort needed for concentration varies according to the subject's grasp of the experiment. This effort is obviously often greater in the uneducated than in the educated, and this naturally has some bearing on the valencies of the associations. With very uneducated and mentally defective[12] subjects, the reactions assume the character of definitions that frequently seem clumsy and comical, e.g.:

singing	consists of notes and hymn-books
strolling	when you go forward on your feet for a Sunday pint

886   From our approximately 150 normal subjects, who provided a stock of over 35,000 associations, it can be seen that there is not an infinite variety of modes of association, but only a limited number of types, which I do not propose to describe to you; it would lead us too far afield. I will mention only one type; there are people who from the very start react with an extraordinarily large number of predicates. One can make the objection that this particular incidence can be very easily attributed to chance. We have, however, been able to demon-

[12] Wehrlin, "The Associations of Imbeciles and Idiots" (1904).

strate that whole families associate in the same way, without any one member being aware of the reactions of the others. This fact indicates that the type cannot be accidental but must be due to causes that at present still escape our knowledge.[13]

887 As you can see, free choice does not play any part in the process of association. There are, however, certain rules: it depends on the momentary state of our attentiveness, our educational level, and the type of our family or other personal circumstances. You have perhaps already noticed that these three rules correspond to important criteria of personality; in other words, our personality (which, as is well known, one knows least of all) plays a decisive role in the determination of the whys and wherefores of our associations. *One associates according to what one is,* or, as the psychiatrist Weygandt not long ago appropriately said: "Tell me how you associate and I'll tell you who you are." This is no empty statement. I will briefly outline the evidence for it:

888 In the association experiment we measure time with a stop-watch to one-fifth of a second, from the moment the stimulus-word is called out to the moment the reaction is given. The interval of time taken we call the *reaction-time.* I will not bore you with an enumeration of the differing time-values. The assurance that the values fluctuate within a very wide range should suffice.

889 As in the classification of associations, one should not lose heart in one's attempt to evaluate seemingly fortuitous time-variations, since *a priori* one can hardly imagine that each of these variations has a particular significance. It is true that on closer examination we see that the internal associations, particularly reactions to abstract stimulus-words, on the whole require a longer time than the external associations. That, however, means very little—the differences are usually only fractions of seconds—beside the very much longer times that are often found with the simplest of associations. Here the time-differences can frequently be as much as twenty or thirty seconds without there being at first any indication of the reason

---

13 According to investigations made in this clinic, which have not yet been published. [Cf. infra, "The Family Constellation," and Fürst, "Statistical Investigations" (1907).]

417

for these variations. The subjects also cannot usually give any precise information about this. One gradually becomes accustomed to this chaos. We know from the research of Ziehen[14] and of Mayer and Orth[15] that it is particularly the associations that awaken memories of an unpleasant nature that take a long time. Thus, for example, A will take 0.8 seconds to react to *house* with *roof*: B gives the same reaction but takes 20 seconds. If we ask subject B whether, on hearing *house*, anything unpleasant crossed his mind, he tells us (for instance) that his house was recently burned down, which frightened him very much. Subject A, who had reacted in 0.8 seconds, has nothing special to report.

890   Here we have an idea charged with an unpleasant emotional tone associated with the stimulus-word and causing a lengthening of the reaction-time. Supposing that in this case B is a cultured person with the ability to analyze himself psychologically, and is prepared to offer up the knowledge of his deepest secrets, then we can pause after every reaction that takes longer than the average and ask what memory lies at the root of it.[16] We will assume further that the subject is able to give the desired explanation for each long reaction-time. When we have thus gone over one hundred reactions and analyzed them, we find that in many places where much time was taken it is not always fresh memories that are awakened but that one memory, e.g., that of a house that was burned down, caused a whole series of long reaction-times. This memory is reflected in the reactions to the following series of stimulus-words: *burn–fire–water–window–smoke–rescue–frightful–red*–etc.

891   These varying stimulus-words conjured up a certain scene, a particular picture from the mass of memories. The memory consists of a large number of single images; we therefore refer to it as a *complex-image*.[17] The complex of these images is held together by a particular *emotional tone*, that is, by the *affect of terror*, the vibrations of which can continue gently for weeks or months and keep the image of terror fresh and vivid for that length of time. During the day work and other interests pre-

[14] "Die Ideenassoziation des Kindes" (1898–1900).
[15] "Zur qualitativen Untersuchung der Assoziationen" (1901).
[16] Of course, we sometimes find long reaction-times that are due to other causes.
[17] Cf. Jung, "The Reaction-time Ratio in the Association Experiment," supra.

dominate, but from time to time these complexes make themselves felt through a faint and hardly recognizable unease or through slight feelings of anxiety, which seem to be unaccountable; at night they intrude into our dreams in a form the symbolism of which may be more or less pronounced.

892   There are other emotional complexes similar to the complex of the memory of the fire; one is concerned with losing large sums of money, and another with somewhat unfortunate family relationships. These three complexes all have the same effect on reactions; they cause longer reaction-times and certain other disturbances, all of which I cannot now enumerate.

893   If we spread out our psychological booty in front of the subject, he will be amazed that we have been able to build up, as it were, a precise inventory of his present psychological condition. In this way it appears that everything that occupies the mind of the subject is expressed in his associations. In any case, all the most important individual *complex-images* are met with. Our subject admits further that at the time of the reaction he hardly ever had the feeling that the stimulus-word had any connection with this or that memory. Only when we asked him did it occur to him how he had arrived at that particular reaction. Contrary to his expectations, the subject had as it were offered in his reactions a psychological snapshot of his mind.

894   We have been able to demonstrate fully this significant fact, the importance of which everyone psychologically oriented can easily gather, in hundreds of individual tests. It is, however, one of those not at all obvious facts that everyone doubts until he has convinced himself of its truth by conducting the experiment himself.

895   Thus we found a further and in my opinion the most important factor determining associations. We can see, from the fact that in the few seconds of the reaction we do not choose something fortuitous but unconsciously take an item from our memories, that our reactions, far from being the result of a free choice, are predetermined to the smallest detail by our complexes. The occurrences of everyday life are nothing but association experiments on a major scale; the things outside us are the stimulus-words to which we react according to what we are and have become, and never in any other way. No one

can get out of his own skin. We act as our psychological past, i.e., as our cerebral organization dictates. For this reason we are bound to expose ourselves in the association experiment in exactly the same way as we do in our handwriting.

896 You can see that in this strongly forged chain there is no gap where free choice or free will can break through. So you may believe me when I say that recognition of this fact is of great value in the investigation of mental illness.

897 Most cases of mental illness are, however, a matter of far-reaching change of personality. The association test at least paves the way for experimental research towards the discovery of the secrets of the sick mind.

898 Before we go into this new application of the association experiment, we must say a few words about the manifold difficulties that stand in the way of the experiment even with normal subjects.

899 We have been assuming that our subject is a man of excellent education, intellectually unbiased, and able to think objectively about his own feelings. In such a case, analysis will not be difficult. But if we were to take as subject a sensitive woman, who does not know us, the analysis would be considerably more difficult. Everyone is, above all, anxious to preserve certain secrets, particularly of a sexual nature, and will not disclose them at any price. It is here that from the very beginning the experimenter finds a significant and almost insurmountable obstacle in his endeavours to analyze. Then there are certain peculiarities of human consciousness that aid concealment and can make analysis extraordinarily difficult. I shall try to sketch these characteristics for you briefly.

900 We have all of us at one time or another experienced something really unpleasant, which has subsequently haunted us for a long time. The natural reaction to this was that we made an effort to forget this black spot, to repress it, in that we quite deliberately did not think about it. And eventually we succeeded in not thinking about it any more. We have forgotten. In associations, however, this black spot reveals itself, and the long reaction-times caused by it show that the vibrations of the former affect are still there. In analysis we have at first some trouble in thinking of the critical point, and the more unpleasant it was the longer it takes us to get back to it. All kinds

420

of other memories will come to mind first, but finally the old story will come up, and we can again feel slight vibrations of the old affect. Now there are people, lots of them, who cannot recollect the critical event at all; they have forgotten it. They have repressed the unpleasant experience so forcefully that it can no longer be revived. Very often, too, the inability to remember looks like a wish not to remember, i.e., the subject cannot will himself to think about it.[18]

901   Our question remains unanswered. Many experiments have been wrecked on this shoal. Nonetheless the situation is not hopeless. In the last resort one can hypnotize the subject, and then one sees why he could not think back. The critical incident is *so* unpleasant that one understands immediately why he did not wish to be reminded of it. In the more serious cases of hysteria this inability to remember is in fact the rule.[19] In these cases the complex is stronger than the conscious will and drives the subject in such a way that he cannot will himself to remember. The complex plays the part of a second and stronger personality, to which ego-consciousness is subjected. In these experiments we are shown the power of feeling-toned memories from which so many sensitive people suffer.

902   The inability to remember in its various forms is the principal obstacle to analysis. We shall not go into a series of lesser hindrances.

903   The objection may be made to analysis that one suggests something to the subject that is not in his mind. In my opinion, however, much too much has been attributed to suggestion. If suggestion were something better known and if so many superstitious meanings did not surround it, this could not then be maintained. It is quite impossible to suggest to a subject by means of a few well-oriented questions all his individual concrete experiences, with all the facets that they have in real life. A subject who lets himself have some experience suggested to him by a clumsy experimenter that he did not really have is a person who had previously had all sorts of phantasms in his mind. A psychologist, i.e., one experienced in the workings of the human mind, will not fall into this trap. He who under-

18 Jung, "Experimental Observations on the Faculty of Memory," supra.
19 On hysterical associations, cf. Riklin, "Analytische Untersuchungen der Symptome und Assoziationen eines Falles von Hysterie" (1905).

stands the experiment properly will no longer be afraid of the unknown quantity of suggestion.

904   So far as the content of complexes found among normal subjects is concerned, the subjects fall naturally into two groups: men and women.

905   To take the women first, their complexes are of a simpler nature and are usually easily recognizable. The woman's complex is, in essence, usually of an erotic nature (and I am using the word "erotic" in the noble literary sense as opposed to the medical). It is concerned with love, even in apparently intellectual women, and is often particularly intense in the latter, although it is only revealed in a negative way to the outside world. No woman who thinks scientifically will take amiss my revelation of this fact. It is as natural and undeniable as the physical sexual process, the existence of which is, it is true, kept secret but never denied. In unmarried women the complex is concerned with the remembrance of past erotic complexes or the expectation of future experiences. Among the secondary complexes, we find most frequently social questions, such as status and earning a living; in general these are clearly linked with the erotic expectation of the man, upon whose arrival the woman's social problem is usually resolved. In the third place come difficult family relations in the parents' home. Married women show complexes especially concerning pregnancy and children, then those connected with relations with the husband, and lastly social difficulties and domestic worries. Old erotic complexes strikingly often play a large part in the very great number of not quite happy marriages, in that they concern memories of previous lovers or at least hopes of this kind. It is mostly a case of the man she should really have chosen but did not marry.

906   In men the erotic complex is not nearly so much in the foreground as in women. It is perhaps on the same level as that of ambition, or striving for physical, intellectual, or financial power. Money usually plays the leading part. The differences between married and unmarried men are not great. In men's associations traces of the social battle show up much more clearly than in women's. Complexes in them are not nearly so easy to reduce to a common denominator as those in women,

which are almost all attributable to their erotic life. Nonetheless there are men too in whom the erotic complex is all-pervasive; the exception, however, proves the rule.

907 Recently Professor Gross and his pupils have emphasized that a complex can also concern crime, and that a criminal can in certain circumstances be unmasked by means of an association test. Laboratory tests designed to verify this assertion are now in progress. Not long ago for the first time, using this method, I succeeded in unmasking a person guilty of a considerable theft.[20]

908 These results achieved in the field of normality we have transferred to that of psychopathology, and here we have found feeling-toned complexes developed to a degree that amounts to caricature. Here I will first of all name the most common form of mental disorder: *hysteria*. Here the associations are often so much under the influence of a feeling-toned complex that the other parts of the personality hardly show up at all. The complexes themselves are of the same nature as in normal cases, except that the intensity of the emotional content is far greater than in the normal. As a rule, the times of critical reactions are much longer and the barriers to recollection much stronger than with normal subjects.

909 From this we can first of all conclude that the sensitivity (i.e., the excitability) of the emotions is greater in hysterical patients than in normal people. An integral part even of hysteria, however, is a complex of images linked with most powerful affect which, for some reason or other, is still reverberating in the patient and which his conscious mind finds unbearable; the *hysterical patient suffers from an affect that he has been unable to conquer.* The recognition of this is of the greatest importance in therapy.

910 You will now ask what is the relationship of this fact to the enormously complicated *symptomatology of hysteria.*[21] I will explain our view by giving two simple examples.

911 A hysterical girl suffers from time to time from a minor

20 Jung, "The Psychological Diagnosis of Evidence," supra.
21 On this question, see especially the works of Sigmund Freud, to whose far-seeing psychological understanding modern psychiatry will be *very much* indebted.

paralysis of the left arm. She is very worried about it and cannot give any adequate explanation for her symptom. From her associations we learn that there are troubles in the home and, in particular, that she is terrified of her father. By various means, which I unfortunately cannot describe to you now, we induced the patient to make the following confession:

912   She has a very unhappy relationship with her father, who is a coarse and irritable man. Each time she has had a scene with him the paralysis in her arm comes on. The first time it happened was after a particularly violent argument when her father finally seized her by the arm and forbade her the house.

913   Thus the symptom of paralysis is closely related to the complex shown in the associations. The complex is the intolerable thing that the patient is trying hard not to think about. She succeeds in freeing herself for days or hours at a time from its constant negative affect, but has instead acquired a hysterical symptom that she now makes responsible for all her dreary moods.

914   Another and simpler case concerns a young married woman who suffers temporarily from abasia, i.e., inability to walk. The associations revealed an unhappy marital relationship. The patient, however, did not want to go into the matter and denied absolutely that there was any connection between the abasia and her marriage. She attributed the onset of abasia to a chill. Under hypnosis, however, the matter became quite clear. The attacks of abasia came on each time immediately after brutal treatment by her husband. The first occasion was when she was fetched by this man, whom she did not love, for her wedding. She found she could no longer walk, and from that time onwards abasia had been the symbol of her suffering.

915   These two simple examples should suffice to make clear to you the connection between the symptoms of hysteria and the feeling-toned complex. In the depths of the mind of each hysterical patient we always find an old wound that still hurts or, in psychological terms, a feeling-toned complex.

916   Our association experiments have now also been able to demonstrate the same mechanism in cases of the next most prevalent group of mental illnesses, i.e., dementia praecox. In this too we are concerned with a complex buried in the depths

424

of the mind which, so far as we can see, causes many of the characteristic symptoms of this disease, in which admittedly we find ingredients lacking in hysteria.[22]

917   You may have gathered from these indications on the one hand how fruitful the application of the association experiment is for psychopathology, and on the other how universal is the significance of the feeling-toned complex.

[22] In order to avoid long-winded explanations in a lecture, I have expressed myself somewhat dogmatically. Dementia praecox unfortunately denotes a group of illnesses which have not yet been clearly defined clinically, and individual forms and descriptions can appear quite distinct from one another. Our experiments (whose results have not yet been published) show that the symptoms of this disease can be explained in a large number of cases as complex-phenomena. [See "The Psychology of Dementia Praecox" and other works in vol. 3, *Coll. Works.*]

DISTURBANCES OF REPRODUCTION IN THE
ASSOCIATION EXPERIMENT[1]

918   My reproduction method, which I introduced in a short communication in the *Zentralblatt für Nervenheilkunde und Psychiatrie* in 1905,[2] has recently been repeatedly criticized (by A. Gross, Heilbronner, and Isserlin[3]). Because of an undue amount of other work I am, to my regret, only now able to complete my unfinished paper by giving it the support of statistics. In 1905 I maintained the following:

919   If, after the completion of about one hundred associations, the subject is asked to repeat the original answers to the individual stimulus-words, memory will fail in several places, in such a way that the previous reaction is either not reproduced at all, is given incorrectly, is distorted, or only given after much delay. The analysis of the incorrectly reproduced associations showed that the majority of them were constellated by a "complex." Since most contemporary workers doing research in this field tend to attribute to Freud's psychoanalytical method no heuristic value at all, it is denied to me to take the shortest course and simply corroborate the above statement by means of analyses. To eliminate the subjective aspect of analysis, which is so much feared, I have no choice but to adduce as unobjectionable evidence the objective signs of complex-constellations, complex-characteristics, and their relation to incorrect reproduction. I found that, in associations that were recogniz-

1 [First published as "Über die Reproduktionsstörungen beim Assoziationsexperiment," *Journal für Psychologie und Neurologie*, IX (1907): 4, 188–97. Republished in *Diagnostische Assoziationsstudien*, Vol. II (1909), pp. 67–76 (IX. Beitrag). Translated by M. D. Eder in *Studies in Word-Association*, pp. 396–406. See supra, par. 1, n. 1.]

2 ["Experimental Observations on the Faculty of Memory," supra.]

3 Alfred Gross, "Kriminalpsychologische Tatbestandsforschung" (1907); Heilbronner, "Die Grundlagen der psychologischen Tatbestandsdiagnostik" (1907); Isserlin, "Über Jungs 'Psychologie der Dementia praecox,' etc." (1907).

able through complex-characteristics, a complex was responsible for the constellation, i.e., had "interfered" and brought about a disturbance. If these characteristics are really significant, i.e., if the analytical method has led to a correct result that could be verified, then the characteristics in general must stand in close relation to each other, i.e., they must tend to appear together in certain associations. This applies, for instance, to incorrect reproductions and prolonged reaction-times. If this is not the case and the complex-signs are indiscriminately scattered over the whole test, then the analysis has led to a wrong conclusion.

920   I further mentioned in my previous communication: (1) The incorrectly reproduced associations occasionally have an arithmetical time-mean that exceeds the general arithmetical mean (*one example*). (2) The incorrect reproductions apparently occur as frequently with the critical as with the post-critical reaction. (3) Occasionally there is a tendency to serial or to isolated disturbances in reproductions. (4) I looked for the theory of the phenomenon in the general characteristics of the complex. I then stressed one feature in particular, repression (Freud), because precisely this feature seemed to me best to explain the inhibition of the correct reproduction. The main characteristic of the complex is certainly its relative independence, which can manifest itself particularly in two directions: in increased emphasis and stability in consciousness, and in repression, i.e., resistance against reproduction while in the unconscious. Therefore the associations belonging to the complex lack the "disposability" of other less significant psychic material (this, by the way, happens only when the special complex is inhibited and must not come to the point of reproduction). The complex itself, of course, completely, even hypermnestically, controls its material. This reducing of the disturbance of reproduction to a more general psychological characteristic seems to me to explain something. Of course, the hypothesis does not apply to every case, for then one would first have to make sure that all interferences from outside (fortuitous ones) are completely excluded; my hypothesis applies only to the majority of cases, as well as only to the majority of complex-characteristics. (5) The complexes indicated

427

by the association experiment are usually charged with unease, which is why the exceptional condition of the complex during the experiment may well be described as "repression."

921   It is now my task to demonstrate exactly what my conception is based on, i.e., to prove that the disturbances in reproduction are complex-characteristics, and therefore as a rule appear together with other complex-characteristics. There cannot be a simple method of verification, because we have to consider that the reproduction-disturbance, like all other complex-characteristics, is not a necessary feature of the complex, and also that, like the other complex-characteristics, it is not exclusively tied to the critical reaction but can also occur with the one that follows. The complex-characteristic most frequently met with is the *reaction-time*.

Disturbance in Reproduction and Reaction-time

922   The most obvious method of comparison would be simply to compare the arithmetical mean of the times of the incorrectly reproduced associations with the arithmetical mean of all the times or of all the remaining times. But this method would only be to some extent reliable if the disturbance in reproduction coincided with the prolonged reaction-times. This, however, is not at all the case; the situation is much more complicated. The following quite varied cases occur:

1. Critical reaction with ⟨ prolonged reaction-time, reproduction-disturbance;

2. ⎰ Critical reaction with prolonged time,
    ⎱ Post-critical reaction with reproduction-disturbance;

3. ⎰ Critical reaction with reproduction-disturbance,
    ⎱ Post-critical reaction with prolonged reaction-time;

4. Post-critical reaction with ⟨ prolonged time, reproduction-disturbance;

5. Reproduction-disturbance of critical and post-critical reaction (twofold sequences of disturbance).

6. Reproduction-disturbance of critical reaction and of three and more successive reactions (threefold and fourfold sequences of disturbance).

428

923   These complicated relations have to be taken into account by the method. In a previous one of the Diagnostic Association Studies,[4] I used the probable mean to determine the prolonged reaction-times because of the fact that the arithmetical mean is as a rule disproportionally high owing to the undue influence of excessively long times, which obviously cannot be compensated for by excessively short times, since the reaction-time has unlimited variations only in the upper ranges. The probable mean therefore generally gives a much better picture of the average speed of reacting. What exceeds this average may as a rule be considered to be not quite normal. But the probable mean is only applicable for large series of numbers, otherwise it is too inaccurate, because it can be considerably altered by trivial chance-events. For small series of numbers we therefore have to use the arithmetical mean. So I have started with the probable mean of the whole test, first counting how many reaction-times of incorrectly reproduced associations exceed the probable mean, how many equal it, and how many do not reach it. If my previous assumptions are right, then one might expect to find the majority of reproduction-disturbances above the probable mean. Those reproduction-disturbances that fall on or below the probable mean can be due to perseveration and therefore may immediately follow a prolonged reaction-time; one has therefore in these cases to examine the reaction-time immediately preceding the disturbance. Actually the reaction-time immediately following should also be investigated, because the time-increase may not occur until afterwards. This, however, would lead us rather far afield. I have not embarked on this investigation hitherto, because it seemed to me that such cases are not very frequent. Let us first see how far we get with the two just mentioned. I should like to stress that since the methods just mentioned do not involve the subjective element, we can approach the task of verification with confidence.

924   The material I have chosen for my inquiry consists of twenty-eight cases, all of which were investigated some time ago and for purposes other than the verification of the present assumption. Not quite a third of the cases were investigated

4 "The Reaction-time Ratio in the Association Experiment," supra.

by me, the other two-thirds by various assistants, some of them several years ago. Among the subjects of the experiment only three are mentally sound, the others are neurotics and psychotics of the most varied kinds and of the most varied reaction-types. The material is therefore as heterogeneous as can be, offering the smallest chance of uniformity in the result. I have collected the results in the following table (all the times are given in 1/5 seconds):

Case and Diagnosis		Associations	Associations incorrectly repr. above/equal to/below the P.M.			I	II[5]
G.	Hebephrenia	100 P.M. 8.5 A.M. 9.0 I.R.[6] 35%	22	5	8	10.6	12.5
A.	Moral insanity	100 P.M. 12.0 A.M. 15.2 I.R. 45%	30	6	9	14.1	10.2
R.♀	Hebephrenia	100 P.M. 13.5 A.M. 20.6 I.R. 15%	11	—	4	—	11.7
P.	Paranoia	100 P.M. 11.0 A.M. 12.9 I.R. 22%	13	2	7	13.0	13.2
H.	Catatonia	100 P.M. 22.0 A.M. 30.3 I.R. 53%	33	1	19	25.0	31.0
G.♀	Hysteria & imbecility	50 P.M. 14.0 A.M. 17.0 I.R. 16%	6	—	2	—	16.0
W.♀	Dementia praecox	100 P.M. 10.5 A.M. 11.3 I.R. 53%	29	—	24	—	10.2

[5] The figures in these two columns give the arithmetical mean (A.M.) of the reaction-times of the associations immediately preceding the incorrectly reproduced ones: column I for the incorrectly reproduced associations with the probable mean (P.M.), column II for those below the probable mean.

[6] I.R. = incorrectly reproduced.

430

Case and Diagnosis	Associations	Associations incorrectly repr. above/equal to/below the P.M.			I	II
G. Organic mental defect	100 P.M. 47.0 A.M. 57.0 I.R. 67%	34	2	31	165.0	67.4
Z.♀ Dementia praecox	100 P.M. 10.0 A.M. 14.4 I.R. 51%	32	6	13	14.0	16.7
H.♀ Dementia praecox	100 P.M. 10.0 A.M. 11.5 I.R. 41%	22	5	14	9.0	10.3
V. Imbecility	100 P.M. 11.0 A.M. 11.1 I.R. 28%	16	5	7	10.2	16.1
E. Moral insanity	100 P.M. 15.0 A.M. 18.1 I.R. 30%	21	5	4	17.8	18.0
K.♀ Dementia praecox	100 P.M. 17.0 A.M. 21.8 I.R. 38%	23	—	15	—	24.4
K.♀ Dementia praecox	100 P.M. 5.0 A.M. 7.1 I.R. 25%	18	4	3	4.7	9.6
A. Paranoia	100 P.M. 13.5 A.M. 13.9 I.R. 14%	7	—	7	—	10.4
B. Psychopathy	113 P.M. 18.0 A.M. 19.5 I.R. 27.4%	16	2	13	19.0	17.6
S. Catatonia	100 P.M. 11.0 A.M. 14.3 I.R. 32%	24	3	5	11.6	16.6
H. Imbecility	104 P.M. 18.0 A.M. 30.4 I.R. 27.8%	14	4	11	56.7	24.4

Case and Diagnosis	Associations	Associations incorrectly repr. above/equal to/below the P.M.			I	II
S. Psychopathy	100					
	P.M. 12.0					
	A.M. 17.4	26	4	7	19.0	16.4
	I.R. 37%					
R. Dementia praecox	50					
	P.M. 32.0					
	A.M. 38.3	14	2	2	12.5	33.5
	I.R. 36%					
R.♀ Syphilis of the brain	100					
	P.M. 14.0					
	A.M. 17.3	23	3	20	12.6	15.3
	I.R. 46%					
S. Imbecility	100					
	P.M. 26.0					
	A.M. 37.5	13	—	8	—	55.8
	I.R. 21%					
J.♀ Normal	100					
	P.M. 7.0					
	A.M. 7.9	8	—	—	—	—
	I.R. 8%					
H. Alcoholism & imbecility	100					
	P.M. 10.5					
	A.M. 13.5	28	—	9	—	13.3
	I.R. 37%					
P. Normal	100					
	P.M. 7.0					
	A.M. 7.9	20	6	7	7.7	8.6
	I.R. 33%					
A. Normal	100					
	P.M. 7.0					
	A.M. 7.8	11	—	4	—	8.1
	I.R. 15%					
S. Moral insanity	100					
	P.M. 12.0					
	A.M. 13.9	27	2	11	9.0	13.3
	I.R. 40%					
W.♀ Neurasthenia	100					
	P.M. 15.0	21	1	9	9.0	16.8
	A.M. 17.2					
	I.R. 11%					

925   These figures lead to the conclusion that an average of 62.2 per cent of the incorrectly reproduced associations fall above the general probable mean of the reaction-times, 7.5 per cent

432

equal it, and 30.2 per cent lie below. This is as originally expected. An average of 33.0 per cent of the associations is incorrectly reproduced. The time-means of the last two columns have to be considered with the reserve mentioned above. They contain cases of quite different significance. As already stated, only the reaction-time immediately preceding the incorrect reproduction was considered, and this only in those cases in which the incorrect reproduction itself fell below the general time-mean. But it is quite possible that the incorrect reproduction is not the result of perseveration, but that the critical reaction has a short reaction-time, with the longer reaction-time following. In this event the result would be considerably distorted. Therefore we shall be faced with minimum figures. The time taken to give the incorrect reproductions discussed here exceeds, however, the probable mean by an average of 7.8 and the arithmetical mean by 4.1. The values on which this calculation is based vary, however, considerably. The series of numbers in the last column are not so varied and are richer in material, but the same considerations apply to them as to the figures of the last column but one. Here too we find that the reaction-time preceding these reproduction-disturbances exceeds the respective probable mean by 4.2 and the arithmetical mean by 0.4. Here we are reminded that the arithmetical mean tends to be disproportionally shifted upwards, as is anyhow sufficiently demonstrated by our figures. These figures are not contrary to expectation, but in my opinion confirm our assumption. If one considers how extremely complicated psychic processes are, and how difficult to control, especially in the field of associations, one is actually amazed at the relative regularity of the results, which cannot even be compromised by a schema that does not claim to be complete.

Series of Disturbance and Reaction-time

926   In my material, 63.9 per cent of all the incorrect reproductions are arranged in series. This fact shows that there is every reason to postulate a relationship between incorrect reproduction and complex, since the complex with its perseveration is a series-forming factor *par excellence* in the association experiment as well as in ordinary psychological life (which, according to the opinion of certain people, must not be related to

psychology). If this conclusion by analogy is right, then the series of disturbances must show the same complex-characteristics as the complex-sequences; hence, first of all prolonged reaction-times. In order not to amass unnecessary tables I omit giving figures for each subject. That there is enough material to calculate averages is evident from the above-mentioned percentage figure. The number of the incorrect reproductions underlying this calculation amounts to a little more than six hundred. We calculate the arithmetical mean for all the incorrectly reproduced associations following one another immediately and compare the mean with the probable mean and arithmetical mean for each subject. Sequences of

2 disturbances are on an average	7.7 above the	P.M.
2 " " " " "	3.6 " "	A.M.
3 " " " " "	9.6 " "	P.M.
3 " " " " "	6.3 " "	A.M.
4 " " " " "	11.6 " "	P.M.
4 " " " " "	6.4 " "	A.M.
5 and more " " " " "	6.7 " "	P.M.
5 and more " " " " "	2.4 " "	A.M.

927   We see an increase of the time-values up to the series of four disturbances, whereas for the series of five and more they are again lower. This result does not fit badly with the analytic consideration. Not infrequently we can see a strong complex perseverating through three and four disturbances, sometimes with uneven decrease of the reaction-times. The stronger is the complex aroused, the stronger, *cum grano salis*, will be the disturbances produced by it. In longer series, however, (which in any case are much less frequent), other factors that interfere with the experiment often appear.

928   We can summarize by saying: *In the main the disturbance in reproduction is correlated with a prolonged reaction-time; where it is not correlated with this, the preceding reaction-time tends to be prolonged in the majority of cases.* (The question of the reaction-time following is left open, because it is of secondary importance.)

929   One can apply another, perhaps even more instructive,

434

method to demonstrate the higher time-values of the disturbance-sequences. I have taken twenty-four cases with well-developed sequences from my material and arranged them in two categories as follows: First, those series that begin with a reaction-time longer than that of the immediately preceding associations, thus:

Association correctly repr.	Disturbances				Association correctly repr. at end of series
	I	II	III	IV	
9	10	8	6	6	7
10	82	15	—	—	11
6	92	15	8	—	8
12	35	16	16	—	14

etc.

930   In this way I have arranged one hundred and nineteen series of this category, added the individual columns, and divided by the numbers of figures in each column.

931   The second category concerns those series in which the disturbance begins with a reaction that is shorter than that of the immediately preceding correctly reproduced association. For the puipose of comparison I have also taken the reaction-time of the association preceding the one before the disturbance, no matter whether it has been correctly or incorrectly reproduced. Those complicated by "mistakes" were excluded from the calculation, although such sequences would have made my results even more impressive.

932   This category is therefore composed as follows:

Preceding association	Association correctly repr. with long R.T.	Disturbances			Association correctly repr. at end of series
		I	II	III	
14	17	8	21	—	10
12	15	13	55	12	13
8	40	12	20	—	9

etc.

933   This category consists of 56 sequences. A few sequences in which the correctly reproduced associations and the first disturbance of the series had the same reaction-time were equally

435

distributed among the two categories. The results are as follows (given in arithmetical means and in 1/5 seconds):

CATEGORY I Association correctly repr.	Disturbances					Association correctly repr. at end of series
	I	II	III	IV	V	
14.8	37.2	22.8	23.9	33.0	27.0	17.9

CATEGORY II Preceding association	Association correctly repr. with long R.T.	Disturbances			Association correctly repr. at end of series
		I	II	III[7]	
18.3	22.5	13.3	22.7	30.0	17.6

The average arithmetical time-mean of the 24 cases used here is 19.8. We see therefore that all our times, with *one* exception, lie considerably above this mean. The exception is found in those reproductions (Category II) which immediately follow a prolonged reaction-time.

Reproduction-disturbance and Probable Time-mean

934   If, as appears proved by the preceding investigation, the reproduction-disturbance occurs mainly in conjunction with prolonged times, one may venture the assumption that the number of disturbances with longer individual time-means generally increases. This seems, at least according to my (limited) material, to be actually the case. To a probable mean of

5–10: an average of 29.7 disturbed reproductions
10.5–15: ”   ”   ” 31.8   ”   ”
15.5–20: ”   ”   ” 31.8   ”   ”
20.5 and over: ”   ”   ” 44.2   ”   ”

To clarify this particular question, however, much more material is necessary.

Reproduction-disturbance and Complex-characteristics, excluding Prolonged Reaction-times

935   Besides prolonged reaction-times, I found the following to be complex-characteristics: reaction by two or more words if

[7] The fourth and subsequent disturbances are not given because they are based on too small a series of numbers (less than 20). But they all considerably exceed the general arithmetical mean, if only for the reason that the number and the series of disturbed reproductions tend to increase with the length of the reaction-time.

subject usually responds with one word, repetition of the stimulus-word, misunderstanding of the stimulus-word, mistakes, slips of the tongue, translation into a foreign language, reaction with some other unusual foreign word, insertion of "yes" or other exclamations before or after the reaction, any unusual contents of the reaction, perseveration as to content or form, etc. The evaluation of the originality of the content and opinion on the perseveration of content and form are subject to personal influences. Therefore I omit these two criteria from my investigation. I have only used the quite obvious perseveration of a reaction-word which reappears identically in the following reaction. I have selected from my material nineteen cases which are characterized by the fact that they mainly responded with only one word. I have counted how many of the above-mentioned complex-characteristics occur in the whole experiment and how many of these are incorrectly reproduced associations.

936   The following table contains the results of this investigation in individual figures:

Complex-characteristics for Associations Reproduced

	correctly	incorrectly
1.	0.08	0.16
2.	0.11	0.31
3.	0.03	0.27
4.	0.03	0.11
5.	0.15	0.20
6.	0.11	0.28
7.	0.37	0.40
8.	0.08	0.26
9.	0.06	0.16
10.	0.12	0.42
11.	0.27	0.39
12.	0.03	0.18
13.	0.06	0.15
14.	0.01	0.02
15.	0.06	0.33
16.	0.23	0.29
17.	0.04	0.15
18.	0.31	0.54
19.	0.18	0.29

937   If one considers that not all complex-reactions are necessarily reproduced incorrectly, and that the incorrectly reproduced associations comprise only one third of all the associations (in my material), then the result conveyed to us by the above table is still rather remarkable: we see that, in each case without exception, more complex-characteristics are produced with those associations that are going to be reproduced incorrectly later on. As a rule, they are recognizable beforehand. The incorrectly reproduced associations show on an average a little more than twice as many complex signs as those correctly reproduced.

SUMMARY

938   In my very heterogeneous material there is undoubtedly a relation between incorrect reproduction and prolonged reaction-time, and it shows itself in such a way that disturbances of reproduction chiefly occur with prolonged reaction-times but also partly following these. Furthermore, the association that is afterwards incorrectly reproduced has on average twice as many complex-signs as the correctly reproduced one (except for the over-long reaction-time, contents subjectively evaluated, and the correlated perseveration). From this it follows that the complex-characteristics tend to be grouped around certain associations. Without analyzing these one cannot see where the relationships between these greatly varying complex-characteristics originate.

THE ASSOCIATION METHOD[1]

939   *Ladies and Gentlemen*: When you honoured me with an invitation to lecture at Clark University, you expressed a wish that I should speak about my methods of work and especially about the psychology of childhood. I hope to accomplish this task in the following manner:

940   In my first lecture I shall tell you about the general points of view that enabled me to conceive my association method; in the second I shall discuss the significance of the family constellation; and in the third I shall go more fully into the psychology of the child.

941   I could easily confine myself exclusively to an exposition of my theoretical views, but I believe it will be better to illustrate my lectures with as many practical examples as possible. We shall therefore concern ourselves first with the association test, which has been of great value to me from both a practical and a theoretical point of view. The historical development of the

1 [The first of a series of lectures under the general title "The Association Method," delivered before the Department of Psychology in celebration of the twentieth anniversary of the opening of Clark University, Worcester, Massachusetts, September, 1909. The three lectures were translated by A. A. Brill and published in the *American Journal of Psychology*, XXI (1910), in a Clark University anniversary volume (1910; the same setting of type), and in *Collected Papers on Analytical Psychology* (London and New York, 1916; 2nd edn., 1917). For the second lecture, see "The Family Constellation," infra. The third lecture was the only one published in its original German version: see "Psychic Conflicts in a Child," *Coll. Works*, vol. 17, prefatory note.

[The original German version of the first two lectures was thought to have been lost, but recently Jung's holograph was found among his papers. While it has the appearance of a draft, it corresponds closely with the Brill translation. Both Freud and Jung lectured at Clark University in German; see Freud's "On the History of the Psycho-Analytic Movement," p. 31, and his "Five Lectures on Psycho-Analysis" (the Clark lectures), editor's note, p. 4. Both men received honorary doctorates of law at the Clark celebration, Freud's being in psychology and Jung's in "education and social hygiene."

[The present translation has been made from the holograph, in consultation with the Brill translation.]

association method and its use in psychology are both so well known to you that there is no need to enlarge upon them. In my practice I proceed by using the following set of words:[2]

1. head	34. yellow	67. carrot
2. green	35. mountain	68. to paint
3. water	36. to die	69. part
4. to sing	37. salt	70. old
5. death	38. new	71. flower
6. long	39. custom	72. to beat
7. ship	40. to pray	73. box
8. to pay	41. money	74. wild
9. window	42. stupid	75. family
10. friendly	43. exercise-book	76. to wash
11. table	44. to despise	77. cow
12. to ask	45. finger	78. friend
13. cold	46. dear	79. happiness
14. stem	47. bird	80. lie
15. to dance	48. to fall	81. deportment
16. village	49. book	82. narrow
17. lake	50. unjust	83. brother
18. sick	51. frog	84. to fear
19. pride	52. to part	85. stork
20. to cook	53. hunger	86. false
21. ink	54. white	87. anxiety
22. angry	55. child	88. to kiss
23. needle	56. to pay attention	89. bride
24. to swim	57. pencil	90. pure
25. journey	58. sad	91. door
26. blue	59. plum	92. to choose
27. lamp	60. to marry	93. hay
28. to sin	61. house	94. contented
29. bread	62. darling	95. ridicule
30. rich	63. glass	96. to sleep
31. tree	64. to quarrel	97. month
32. to prick	65. fur	98. nice
33. pity	66. big	99. woman
		100. to abuse

[2] [The holograph contains merely the direction "insert," and the list that follows here is from Brill, modified to conform to the present translation. It corresponds closely to a list that Jung customarily used in German, viz.:

1. Kopf	4. singen	7. Schiff
2. grün	5. Tod	8. zahlen
3. Wasser	6. lang	9. Fenster

440

942   This set of words has grown into its present form as a result of many years of experience. The words are chosen and to some extent arranged so as to touch upon almost all the complexes that commonly occur in practice. As the foregoing list shows, there is a regular mixture of the different grammatical features. For this there are definite reasons.

943   Before the experiment begins the subject of the test is given the following instruction: "Answer as quickly as possible with the first word that occurs to you." This instruction is so simple that it can easily be followed. The task itself, moreover, appears extremely easy, so that anyone might be expected to

10. freundlich	40. beten	70. alt
11. Tisch	41. Geld	71. Blume
12. fragen	42. dumm	72. schlagen
13. Dorf	43. Heft	73. Kasten
14. kalt	44. verachten	74. wild
15. Stengel	45. Finger	75. Familie
16. tanzen	46. teuer	76. waschen
17. See	47. Vogel	77. Kuh
18. krank	48. fallen	78. fremd
19. Stolz	49. Buch	79. Glück
20. kochen	50. ungerecht	80. lügen
21. Tinte	51. Frosch	81. Anstand
22. bös	52. scheiden	82. eng
23. Nadel	53. Hunger	83. Bruder
24. schwimmen	54. weiss	84. fürchten
25. Reise	55. Kind	85. Storch
26. blau	56. aufpassen	86. falsch
27. Lampe	57. Bleistift	87. Angst
28. sündigen	58. traurig	88. küssen
29. Brot	59. Pflaume	89. Braut
30. reich	60. heiraten	90. rein
31. Baum	61. Haus	91. Türe
32. stechen	62. lieb	92. wählen
33. Mitleid	63. Glas	93. Heu
34. gelb	64. streiten	94. zufrieden
35. Berg	65. Pelz	95. Spott
36. sterben	66. gross	96. schlafen
37. Salz	67. Rübe	97. Monat
38. neu	68. malen	98. hübsch
39. Sitte	69. Teil	99. Frau
		100. schimpfen

The lists on the following pages appeared in the holograph. The graphs did not appear, though referred to.]

accomplish it with the greatest ease and rapidity. But, contrary to expectation, people behave quite differently.

I. Example of a Normal Reaction-type

Stimulus-word	Reaction-time	Reaction	Reproduction
head	9	foot	part of the body
green	11	blouse	
water	14	clear	light
to sing	6	children	
death	11	do not like	
long	6	short	I, tall
ship	7	away	
to pay	6	bills	
window	9	room	
friendly	10	children	
table	9	chair	room
to ask	10	all sorts of things	
cold	7	warm	
stem	6	flower	
to dance	9	I . . .	like
lake	8	Zurich	
sick	8	sister [i.e., nurse]	
pride	6	people	
to cook	7	woman	
ink	5	black	
angry	10	children	people
needle	9	to prick	
to swim	10	healthy	
journey	9	England	I like, much
blue	10	pretty	I like
lamp	6	bright	
to sin	8	much	people
bread	10	good	I like, necessary
rich	9	beautiful	
tree	6	green	
to prick	9	needle	

II. Example of a Hysterical Reaction-type

Stimulus-word	Reaction-time	Reaction	Reproduction
needle	7	to sew	
to swim	9	water	
journey*†	35	movement, *voyager?*, to travel, ship	

* Stimulus-word misunderstood.   † Repetition of stimulus-word.

Stimulus-word	Reaction-time	Reaction	Reproduction
blue	10	colour	
lamp	7	to burn	
to sin	22	this idea is totally alien to me, I do not acknowledge it	
bread	10	to eat	
rich†	50	money—I don't know	possession
tree	6	nature	green
to prick	9	needle	
pity	12	feeling	
yellow	9	colour	
mountain	8	high	
to die	8	to rot	
salt	15	salty (laughs)—I don't know—NaCl	
new†	15	old—as the opposite	
custom	10	good—barbaric	
to pray	12	deity	
money	10	wealth	
stupid	12	narrow-minded—limited	
exercise-book	10	paper	
to despise	30	that is a complicated—too stupid	?
finger	8	hand—not only hand, also foot—limb—membre—extremity	?
dear	14	to pay (laughs)	
bird	8	to fly	
to fall†	30	tomber—I will say no more—what do you mean by to fall?	?
book	6	to read	
unjust	8	just	
frog	11	to croak	
to part	30	what does part mean?	?
hunger	10	to eat	
white	12	colour—all sorts of things—the light	
child†	10	little—I did not catch that—bébé	?
to pay attention	14	attentive	
pencil	8	to draw—all sorts of things can be drawn	

443

Stimulus-word	Reaction-time	Reaction	Reproduction
sad	9	to weep—this does not always happen	to be
plum	16	to eat a plum— to pick—What do you mean by it? Do you mean it symbolically?	fruit
to marry	27	what can you mean by that? *réunion*— bond	union, alliance

944　　The first thing that strikes us is the fact that many subjects show a marked prolongation of the reaction-time. This would seem to suggest intellectual difficulties—wrongly, however, for we are often dealing with very intelligent people with a good command of language. The factor responsible for this is connected with their feelings. In order to understand this, we must bear in mind that the association experiments investigate not just *one* component of the mind, since no psychological experiment can possibly be concerned with one isolated psychic function; no psychic occurrence is a thing in and by itself but rather the resultant of the entire psychological past. The association experiment, too, is not merely a method for the reproduction of separate word-pairs but a kind of pastime, a conversation between experimenter and subject. In a certain sense it is even more than this. Words are really a kind of shorthand version of actions, situations, and things. When I present the subject with a stimulus-word meaning an action, it is as if I presented him with the action itself and asked him, "How do you feel about it? What's your opinion of it? What would you do in such a situation?" If I were a magician, I should cause the situation corresponding to the stimulus-word to appear in reality and, placing the subject in the centre, I should then study his reactions. Undoubtedly the effect of my stimulus-words would be much more perfect. But as we are not magicians, we must content ourselves with the linguistic surrogates for reality; at the same time we must not forget that the stimulus-word will almost without exception conjure up its corresponding situation. All depends on how the subject reacts to this situation. The word *bride* or *bridegroom* will not evoke a simple reaction in a young girl; but the emerging strong

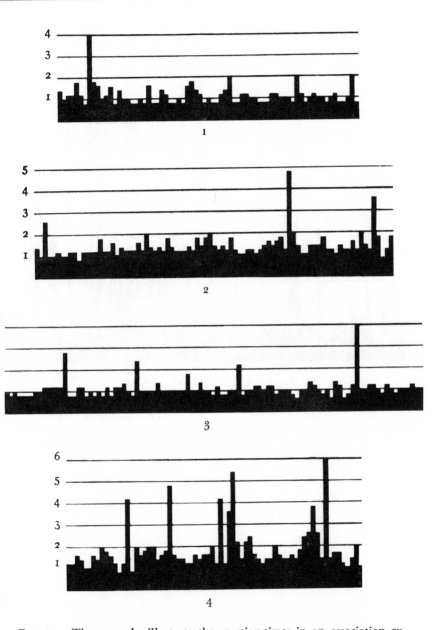

FIGS. 1–4. These graphs illustrate the reaction-times in an association experiment on four normal subjects. The height of each column indicates the length of the reaction-time

445

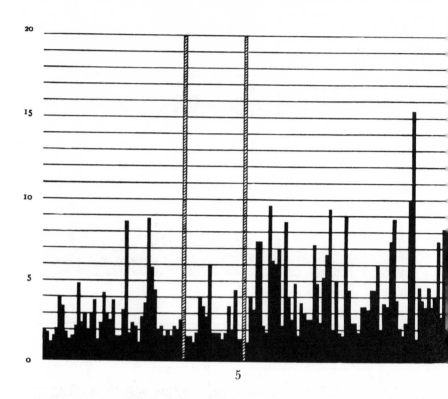

Figs. 5–7. These graphs show the profiles of the reaction-times in hysterical individuals. The lightly cross-hatched columns indicate places where the subject was unable to react (referred to as failures)

446

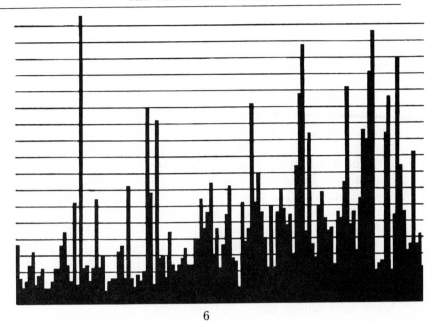

6

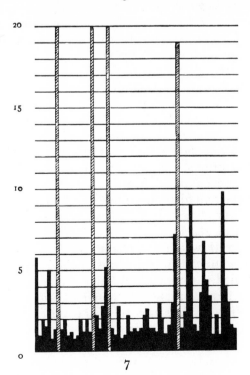

7

feeling tones will markedly influence the reaction and even more so if the experimenter is a man. So the subject is often unable to react quickly and smoothly to all stimulus-words. There are certain stimulus-words that denote actions, situations, or things about which the subject is also in reality unable to think quickly and with certainty, and this fact is demonstrated in the association experiments. The example I have just given shows an abundance of long reaction-times and other disturbances. In this case the reaction to the stimulus-words is obviously in some way inhibited—that is, the adaptation to the stimulus-words is disturbed. Stimulus-words are, however, nothing but part of the reality that impinges upon us; in a certain sense someone who shows such disturbances when confronted with stimulus-words is on the whole *inadequately adapted to reality*. Any disease springs from impaired adaptation; thus in our special case we are dealing with something morbid in the psyche, with something either temporarily or permanently pathological. That is, we are dealing with a psychoneurosis, with a functional disturbance of the mind.

945   This rule is, as we shall see later, not without its exceptions.

946   Let us now continue the discussion of the prolonged reaction-times. It often happens that the subject actually finds *no* answer to the stimulus-word. He fails to give any reaction and so for the moment abandons his agreement to follow the original instructions, showing himself incapable of adapting to the experiment. If this phenomenon occurs often in an experiment, it indicates that adaptation is seriously disturbed. I should like to remark that the reasons the subject gives for the refusal are utterly immaterial. Some find that too many ideas suddenly occur to them; others, that too few ideas enter their minds. In most cases, however, the difficulties experienced at first are so much of a deterrent that the subjects actually give up the reaction altogether. Example III shows a case of hysteria with many failures of reaction.

947   In example II we find a characteristic phenomenon: the subject is not content with the terms of the instruction; that is, he is not satisfied with *one* word but reacts with many. He apparently does more and better than the instruction requires, but in so doing he does not fulfil the terms of the instruction. Thus he reacts: *custom / good—barbaric; stupid /narrow-minded—limited*; all sorts of things.

448

III

Stimulus-word	Reaction-time	Reaction	Reproduction
to sing	9	beautiful	
death	15	terrifying	?
long*†	40	the time, the journey	?
ship†	—	—	
to pay	11	money	
window	10	big	high
friendly	50	a person	human
to cook	10	soup	
ink	9	black or blue	
angry	—	—	bad
needle	9	to sew	
lamp	14	bright	
to sin	—	—	
bread	15	for eating	
rich*†	40	good—comfortable	
yellow	18	paper	colour
mountain	10	high	
to die	15	awful	
salt†	25	salty	
new	—	—	good, beautiful
custom†	—	—	
to pray	—	—	
money†	35	to buy—one can	
exercise-book	16	to write	
to despise†	22	people	
finger†	—	—	
dear	12	thing	
bird	12	sings or flies	

* Stimulus-word misunderstood.   † Repetition of stimulus-word.

948   These examples show, first, that many more ideas are added to the reaction-word. The subject is unable to suppress these further ideas. In this way he also pursues a certain tendency that is more clearly expressed in the following reaction: *new / old—as the opposite.* The addition of *as the opposite* hints that the subject needs to add something explanatory or supplementary. This tendency is also shown in the following reaction: *finger / hand—not only hand, also foot—a limb—membre—extremity.*

949   Here we have a whole series of additions. It seems as if the reaction were not sufficient for the subject, as if something else

449

must always be added, as if what has already been said were incorrect or in some way incomplete. This feeling is what Janet calls the "sentiment d'incomplétude"; but this, however, does not explain anything. I am enlarging on this phenomenon because it is very common in neurotic individuals. It is not merely a trivial and incidental phenomenon in an experiment without significance, but rather an essential and universal phenomenon that plays a large part in the psychic life of neurotics.

950   By his desire to supplement, the subject betrays a tendency to give the experimenter more than he wants; he actually labours in his attempts to find further ideas so as eventually to find something entirely satisfactory. If we translate this elementary observation into the psychology of everyday life, it means that the subject has a tendency always to give to others more feeling than is demanded or expected. According to Freud, this is a sign of a reinforced object-libido, that is, it is a compensation for an inner discontent and lack of feeling. This elementary observation therefore points to one of the chief characteristics of hysterical patients, namely, the tendency to let themselves be carried away by everything, to fix their passion onto everything, and always to promise too much and hence keep only a few of their promises. Patients with this symptom are, in my experience, always rather disagreeable; at first they are enthusiastically enamoured of the physician, for a time going so far as blindly to accept everything he says; but they soon fall into an equally blind resistance to him, thus rendering any psychological influence absolutely impossible.

951   In this phenomenon we see the expression of a tendency to give more than the instruction asks for or expects. This tendency also betrays itself in other failures to follow the instruction:

to quarrel	angry—all sorts of things—I always quarrel at home
to marry	what can you mean by that? *réunion*—bond
plum	to eat a plum—to pick—what do you mean by it? do you mean it symbolically?
to sin	this idea is totally alien to me, I do not acknowledge it

450

952   These reactions show that the subject is not playing his part in the experiment. For the instruction is that he should answer only with the first word that occurs to him. But here it appears that the stimulus-words have an excessively strong effect, that they are taken absolutely *personally*, as if they were direct questions. The subject entirely forgets that he is faced with mere words presented in print. He looks for a personal meaning in them, tries to guess the meaning and defend himself against it, altogether forgetting the original instruction.

953   This elementary observation illustrates another common peculiarity of hysterical patients, namely, that of taking everything personally, of never being able to be objective and of allowing themselves to be carried away by momentary impressions; again the characteristic of the reinforced object-libido.

954   Yet another sign of difficulty in adaptation is the frequent *repetition of the stimulus-word*. The subjects repeat the stimulus-word as if they had not heard it distinctly or understood it. They repeat it just as we repeat an expected and difficult question so as to grasp it better and be able to answer it. This same tendency is shown in the experiment. The stimulus-words are repeated because they influence hysterical individuals as difficult personal questions do. In principle it is the same phenomenon as the additions to the reaction.

955   In many experiments we observe that the same reaction often occurs in response to the most varied stimulus-words. These words seem to tend especially to be repeated, and it is very interesting to find out what these words really mean to the subject. I have, for instance, observed a case in which the patient repeatedly reacted with the word *short* a great many times, often in places where it made no sense. The subject could not give the precise reason for repeating the word. From experience I knew that such predicatory words always refer either to the subject himself or to the person nearest to him. I assumed that he was referring to himself as "short" and in this way expressed something very painful to him. The subject was of very small stature. He was the youngest of four brothers; the others, in contrast to himself, were very tall. He was always the *child* in the family; he was nicknamed "Short" and was treated by all as the "little one." This resulted in a total loss of self-confidence. Although he was intelligent, and in spite of long

study, he could not make up his mind to sit for an examination; he finally became impotent, and sank into a psychosis in which, whenever he was alone, he took great pleasure in walking about his room on his toes in order to appear taller. The word *short*, therefore, stood to him for a great many painful experiences. This is usually the case with perseverated words; they always express something very important in the individual psychology of the subject.

956   The characteristics so far described do not occur at random in the experiment, but are found at very definite points, namely, where the stimulus-words touch upon emotionally charged complexes. This fact is the foundation of what is called the *diagnosis of evidence*, i.e., the art of detecting, by means of an association experiment, the real culprit among a number of people suspected of a crime. That this is possible I will demonstrate by a brief account of an actual case.[3]

957   On February 6, 1908, our matron informed me that one of the nurses had complained to her that on the previous afternoon she had been robbed. Here are the facts: The nurse had her money, which amounted to seventy francs, in a purse that she kept in her clothes-cupboard. The cupboard had two compartments; one belonged to the nurse who had been robbed and the other to the charge nurse. These two nurses slept in the same room (with the cupboard in it), together with a third nurse, who was an intimate friend of the charge nurse. The room was in a section of the hospital where normally six nurses were on duty and these could go into the room and use it if they wanted to. In view of this situation it was not surprising that the matron shrugged her shoulders when I asked her whom she suspected in the first place.

958   From further investigation it appeared that on the day of the theft the friend of the charge nurse had stayed in bed the whole morning because she did not feel very well. According to the evidence of the first nurse, the theft must have taken place during the afternoon. Among the other four nurses on whom suspicion might fall, there was one whose regular duty

---

[3] [The holograph here contains a direction to insert the experiment from the *Rivista di psicologia applicata*, i.e., "New Aspects of Criminal Psychology" (see infra, Appendix 2). Accordingly, pars. 957–983 here are translated from the Italian of that work, where the passage is omitted to avoid repetition.]

it was to clean the room, whereas the other three had no official business there, and it did not appear that any of them had been in the room, for whatever reason.

959   It was therefore very natural that the last three nurses were for the time being regarded as less suspect; I therefore first subjected the first three to the experiment.

960   From the particulars of the case I also knew that the cupboard was locked but that the key was near by and could easily be found; that on opening the cupboard the first thing visible was a fur stole, and that the purse was hidden in an inconspicuous place between the linen. The pocketbook was made of dark red leather and contained the following: one fifty-franc note, one twenty-franc piece, a few centimes, a little silver watch-chain, a seal for marking the crockery in the hospital, and a receipt from the Dosenbach shoe-shop in Zurich.

961   Apart from the nurse who had been robbed, and the culprit, only the charge nurse knew the exact particulars of the robbery, since the nurse who had been robbed thought at first that she had lost the money and asked the charge nurse to help her look for it. So the charge nurse was in a position to know the minutest detail of the case; this made the experiment particularly difficult because she was one of the most likely suspects. The conditions of the experiment were more favourable as far as the other nurses were concerned, since they did not know any of the particulars of the evidence and some of them did not even know that a robbery had been committed. As critical stimulus-words I chose the name of the nurse who had been robbed and also the following: *cupboard, door, open, key, yesterday, banknote, gold, 70, 50, 20, money, watch, purse, chain, silver, to conceal, fur, dark red, leather, centimes, seal, receipt, Dosenbach.* Besides these words which referred to the evidence proper, I also chose the following, which have a special affective value: *theft, to take, to rob, suspect, to accuse, court, police, to lie, to fear, to discover, to arrest, innocent.*

962   Against words of this last type it has been objected that they carry a strong emotional charge even for the innocent and that there is therefore no value in confronting people with them. We still, however, have to consider whether in an innocent person the affective charge has the same effect on the associations as it has in a guilty one, a question that cannot be

answered *ex cathedra* but only through experience. Until proof to the contrary is forthcoming I maintain that words of this class can also produce useful results.

963 I next distributed these critical stimulus-words among double the number of ordinary stimulus-words, so that for each critical word there were two ordinary ones. It is an advantage for the critical words to be followed by ordinary ones so that the influence of the former may stand out all the more clearly. One can, however, also let one critical word follow another when one wants to show up especially the importance of the second. I therefore put together *dark red* and *leather*, as well as *chain* and *silver*.

964 After these preparations I started the experiment on the three nurses. Since it is very difficult to present investigations of this kind in a foreign language I cannot give a full report on them here, but I shall content myself with giving an account of the general results and adding some examples. First, I subjected the friend of the charge nurse to the experiment; considering the circumstances, she seemed to be only slightly upset. Then I examined the charge nurse herself, who seemed to be possessed by a considerable agitation and who immediately after the experiment still had a pulse rate of 122 per minute. Lastly I dealt with the nurse who was responsible for cleaning the room where the theft had taken place. She was the calmest of them all; she was only slightly embarrassed and only in the course of the experiment did she realize that she was a possible suspect; towards the end of the experiment this manifestly disturbed her.

965 The outcome of the examination spoke very much against the charge nurse who, it seemed to me, showed a suspicious reserve—I would almost say impudence. With the precise idea of finding her guilty, I applied myself to the calculation of the results.

966 One can use all sorts of methods of computation, but they are not all equally good and equally exact. (One must always base one's judgment on calculation, because appearances are most deceptive!) The method most to be recommended is that of the probable mean of the reaction-times. It gives one a glimpse of the difficulties that the subject of the experiment has had to overcome in reacting.

454

967   The technique of this calculation is very simple: the probable mean is the number in the middle of the series of reaction-times. The reaction-times[4] are, for instance, arranged in the following manner: 5, 5, 5, 7, 7, 7, 7, *8*, 8, 9, 9, 9, 12, 13, 14; the middle number (8) is the probable mean of this series. I indicate the friend of the charge nurse by the letter A, the charge nurse by the letter B, and the third nurse by the letter C.

968   The probable means of the reaction-times are A, 10.0; B, 12.0; C, 13.5. From this result one cannot draw any conclusion.

969   The means of the reaction-times for the reactions without special significance, for the critical reactions, and for those immediately following ("post-critical"), calculated separately, are, however, of greater interest.

Probable Means of the Reaction-times

	A	B	C
Neutral reactions	10.0	11.0	12.0
Critical reactions	16.0	13.0	15.0
Post-critical reactions	10.0	11.0	13.0

970   Here is what results from this table: although A has the lowest mean of the reaction-time for neutral reactions, she has, in contrast to the other two subjects of the experiment, the longest reaction-time for the critical reactions.

971   The difference between the reaction-times for, let us say, neutral reactions and critical reactions is 6 for A, 2 for B, 3 for C; thus, about twice as high for A as for either of the others.

972   By calculations similar to those we have made for the reaction-times, we can work out how many complex-characteristics there are on an average for ordinary, critical, and other reactions.

Mean of the Complex-characteristics for All Reactions

	A	B	C
Neutral reactions	0.6	0.9	0.8
Critical reactions	1.3	0.9	1.2
Post-critical reactions	0.6	1.0	0.8

973   The difference between the neutral and the critical reactions is 0.7 for A, 0 for B, and 0.4 for C: A therefore leads.

[4] [The reaction-times are always given in fifths of a second.]

455

974   The next question concerns incorrect reproductions. The results of the computation are 34 per cent for A, 28 per cent for B, and 30 per cent for C. One can see that, in this connection also, A reaches the maximum value, and in this I seem to see a characteristic of A's guilt-complex. I cannot, however, set out here the reasons why I maintain that there is a connection between errors of memory and emotional complexes, since this would lead me beyond the scope of the present investigation. I therefore refer the reader to my paper "On Disturbances in Reproduction in the Association Experiment" [supra].

975   It often happens in the experiment that an association with a strong affective charge leaves behind it a perseveration, in the sense that not only the critical association itself but also two or three of the subsequent associations are incorrectly reproduced; it is therefore interesting to see what one finds if one arranges these associations in a series. The results of the computation are 64.7 per cent for A, 55.5 per cent for B, and 30.0 per cent for C.

976   Here again we find that A has the largest percentage. This may be partly due to the fact that A also has the largest number of incorrect reproductions: given the small number of reactions, it is obvious that the number of incorrect reproductions in a group increases in proportion to the total number of reactions. Even though this is probable, it can only happen to the same extent in experiments such as ours, in which B and C do not have a much smaller number of incorrect reproductions than A. It is significant that C, with her comparative lack of emotion during the experiment, has the minimum of incorrect reproductions in a series.

977   Since incorrect reproductions are also complex-characteristics, we need to find out how the incorrect reproductions of neutral reactions, critical reactions, and so on are distributed.

Incorrect Reproductions

	A	B	C
Neutral reactions	10.0	12.0	11.0
Critical reactions	19.0	9.0	12.0
Post-critical reactions	5.0	7.0	7.0

978   There is no need to add anything to emphasize the differences between neutral reactions and critical reactions in the different subjects: A leads in this respect also.

979   In this case, of course, the larger the number of critical reactions, the greater is the probability of a large number of incorrect reproductions. Supposing that the incorrect reproductions are distributed evenly and at random among all the reactions, then there will be a greater number for A (compared with B and C) as a reaction to critical words, since A has the largest number of incorrect reproductions. Admitting such a uniform distribution of incorrect reproductions, we can easily calculate how many of them belong to each single class of reaction.

Incorrect Reproductions

	TO BE EXPECTED			ACTUALLY OCCURRING		
	Neutral Reactions	Critical Reactions	Post-crit. Reactions	Neutral Reactions	Critical Reactions	Post-crit. Reactions
A	11.2	*12.5*	10.2	10.0	*19.0*	5.0
B	9.2	*10.3*	8.4	12.0	*9.0*	7.0
C	9.9	*11.1*	9.0	11.0	*12.0*	7.0

980   From this table it appears that the disturbances of reproduction of the critical reactions of A greatly exceed the expectation, whereas for C the figures are only 0.9 above expectation and for B the actual number is smaller.

981   All these data are pointers to show that in subject A the critical stimulus-words have acted with the greatest intensity so that the maximum suspicion falls on A. One could venture to declare this subject as the presumptive culprit: and on the same evening she made a full confession of the theft and thus confirmed the success of the experiment.

982   I maintain that a result so obtained is scientifically interesting and worthy of discussion. In experimental psychology there are many much less useful things than those with which we are dealing in this paper. Completely disregarding the theoretical interest, we have to take into account the not inconsiderable practical result: we have unmasked the culprit without the usual formalities, merely by taking the shortest route. What was possible in one or two cases should be possible in others, and it is well worth while to explore every conceivable way of making this method yield rapid and reliable results.[5]

5 [See the appendix, infra, pars. 1331ff., where the discussion of this case continues.]

983   This application of the experiment shows that it is possible to touch upon a concealed, indeed an unconscious, complex by means of a stimulus-word; and, conversely, we may quite certainly assume that behind a reaction showing complex-characteristics a complex is hidden, even though the subject may strongly deny it. One must get rid of the idea that people with a good education and some insight can always recognize and admit their own complexes. Every human mind contains much that is not admitted and hence, as such, unconscious; and no one can boast that he stands completely above his complexes. He who nevertheless maintains that he can is not aware of the spectacles upon his own nose.

*

984   It has long been believed that the association experiment enables one to distinguish certain *intellectual* types. This is by no means the case. The experiment does not give us any special insight into purely intellectual processes but rather into emotional ones. To be sure, we can establish certain types of reaction; they are not, however, based on intellectual peculiarities, but depend entirely on *emotional attitudes.* Educated subjects usually show trivial, well-canalized verbal associations, whereas the uneducated make more valuable, often more meaningful, associations. This behaviour would, from an intellectual point of view, be paradoxical. The associations, rich in content, offered by uneducated people are not really the products of a thinking rich in content but merely those of a particular emotional attitude. The whole thing is more important to the uneducated, his emotion is greater, and for that reason he pays more attention to the experiment than the educated person and his associations are therefore richer in content. Apart from those derived from a particular type of education, we have to consider four principal individual types:

1. An *objective type* with undisturbed reactions.

2. What is called a *complex type*, showing many disturbances in the experiment caused by the constellation of a complex.

3. What is called a *definition type*. This type always reacts with an explanation or a definition of the content of the stimulus-word, e.g.:

458

apple	a tree-fruit
table	a piece of furniture
to go for a walk	an activity
father	head of the family

985   This type is chiefly found among stupid people, and it is therefore common among imbeciles. It can also be found in people who are not really stupid but who do not wish *to be taken as stupid*. Thus, a young student, whose associations were recorded by an intelligent older woman student, reacted entirely with definitions. The subject was under the impression that he was undergoing an intelligence test, and therefore focussed principally on the meaning of the stimulus-words; his associations, therefore, looked like those of a half-wit. Not all half-wits, however, react with definitions; probably the only ones who react in this way are those who would like to appear cleverer than they are—that is, those to whom their stupidity is painful. I call this complex, which we often meet with, the "intelligence-complex."

986   This type often makes a strained and unnatural impression. They seem to be trying too hard:

anxiety	oppression of the heart
to kiss	love's release
to kiss	experience of friendship, etc.

These subjects want to be more than they are, they wish to exert more influence than they really have. Hence we see that people with an intelligence-complex are in general far from simple and free; that they are always somewhat unnatural and affected; that they show a predilection for complicated foreign words, high-sounding quotations, and other intellectual ornaments. It is in this sense that they want to influence their fellowmen, to impress others with their apparent education and intelligence, and thus to compensate for their painful feeling of stupidity.

987   4. The definition type is closely related to the *predicate type* or, more precisely, to the evaluating predicate-type. For example:

flower	beautiful	knife	dangerous
money	pleasant	death	ghastly
animal	ugly		

459

In the definition type it is the intellectual significance of the stimulus-word that is emphasized, but in the predicate type it is its *emotional* significance. There are predicate types who greatly exaggerate, whose reactions may be such as these:

piano	horrible
to sing	heavenly
mother	deeply loved
father	something good, noble, holy

988   In the definition type an absolutely *intellectual* attitude is manifested, or rather simulated, but here we have an attitude that is *full of feeling*. Yet, just as the definition type really means to conceal a lack of intelligence, so the exuberant *expression of feeling* conceals or overcompensates for a *deficiency of feeling*. This conclusion is illustrated in a very interesting way by the following discovery: Investigations of the influence of the family environment on association types reveal that young people seldom belong to the predicate type; in fact, the frequency of the predicate type increases with age. In women the increase of the evaluating predicate type begins a little after the fortieth year, and in men after the sixtieth. That is just the time when, owing to the decline of sexuality, considerable loss of feeling is in fact suffered.

989   If a subject shows a distinct predicate type, one may always infer that a marked deficiency of feeling is thereby compensated. One must not, however, conclude conversely that a deficiency of feeling must produce a predicate type, any more than that idiocy directly produces a definition type. A predicate type can also betray itself through external behaviour, as, for example, through marked affectation, enthusiastic exclamations, a certain genteel, refined demeanour, and the affected language so often observed in "society."

990   The complex type shows no particular tendency unless it be the effort to *conceal* complexes behind the disturbances of the experiment. The definition and predicate types betray a definite tendency to exert *some influence* on the experimenter. The definition-type tries to make an impact through his intelligence, whereas the predicate type displays his emotions. I need hardly add how important such observations are for the diagnosis of character.

991   Having finished an association experiment, I usually add

another experiment of a different kind, which I call *reproduction*. I repeat the same stimulus-words and ask the subjects whether they still remember their former reactions. In certain instances their memory fails and, as experience shows, such failures are brought about by stimulus-words that touch upon a feeling-toned complex, or by stimulus-words immediately following such critical words.

992   This phenomenon has been said to be paradoxical and contrary to all experience. For it is known that feeling-toned matters are better retained in memory than things of no special significance. This is certainly correct, but does not hold for the *linguistic* expression of a feeling-toned content. On the contrary, one very easily forgets what one has said under emotion, one is even apt to contradict oneself. Indeed, the efficacy of cross-examination in court depends on this fact. The reproduction-method therefore helps to emphasize the complex-stimulus still more. In normal people we usually find a limited number of incorrect reproductions, seldom more than 10 to 15 per cent, whereas in abnormal people, especially in hysteria, we often find from 20 to 40 per cent of incorrect reproductions. The uncertainty of reproduction is therefore in certain cases a measure of the emotivity of the subject.

993   Most neurotics show a pronounced tendency to hide their intimate affairs in impenetrable darkness, even from the doctor, so that he finds it very difficult to form an accurate picture of his patient's psychology. In such cases my orientation is greatly assisted by the association experiment. When the experiment is finished, I first look over the general trend of the reaction-times. I see a great many very prolonged times; this means that the patient can only adjust himself with considerable disturbance.

994   His psychological functions flow with marked internal friction, with resistances. Most neurotics react only with great and therefore very noticeable resistances; there are, however, others in whom the average reaction-times are as short as in normal subjects, and in whom the other complex-characteristics are lacking, although neurotic symptoms are undoubtedly present. These rather rare cases are found especially among very intelligent and educated, chronically ill people who, after many years of practice, have learned to control their outward behaviour and therefore display very few if any traces of their

461

neurosis. Superficial observation would take them for normal, yet at some points they show disturbances that betray the repressed complex.

995   After investigating the reaction-times I turn my attention to the type of association, to find out what type I am dealing with. If it is a predicate type I draw the conclusions on which I have already enlarged; if it is a complex-type I try to determine the nature of the complex. With the necessary experience one can free one's judgment from the subject's statements to quite an extent and, under certain circumstances, almost without any previous knowledge of him, can read the most intimate complexes from the results of the experiment. I first look for the reproduction-words and tabulate them; then I pick out the stimulus-words that show the greatest disturbances. In many cases, merely tabulating these words is sufficient to unearth the complex. In some cases, one is obliged to put a question here and there. It may be best if I illustrate the point by means of a concrete example:

996   The patient was an educated woman of thirty years of age, who had been married for three years. Since her marriage she had suffered periodically from states of agitation in which she was violently jealous of her husband. The marriage was in every other respect a happy one and in fact the husband gave no grounds for jealousy. The patient was sure that she loved him and that her agitated states were absolutely groundless. She could not imagine how this situation had come about and felt quite at a loss. It should be noted that she was a Roman Catholic and had been brought up to practise her religion, whereas her husband was a Protestant. This difference of religion was stated to be of no consequence. A more thorough anamnesis revealed an astounding prudishness: for instance, no one was allowed to talk in the patient's presence about her sister's confinement, because the sexual implication caused her the greatest agitation. She never undressed in her husband's presence but always in another room, and so on. At the age of twenty-seven she was supposed to have had no idea how children were born. Her association test gave the results shown in Fig. 8.

997   The stimulus-words that stood out because of their strong disturbing effect were these: *yellow, to pray, to part, to marry, to*

quarrel, old, family, happiness, unfaithful, anxiety, to kiss, bride, to choose, contented. The following stimulus-words produced the strongest disturbances: *to pray, to marry, happiness, unfaithful, anxiety,* and *contented.* These then are the words that clearly pointed towards the complex. The conclusion that can be drawn from this is: that she was not indifferent to the fact that her husband was a Protestant, that she was again thinking about prayer and felt there was something wrong with the married state; that she was unhappy; she was false—that is, she was having fantasies about being unfaithful; she suffered from anxiety (about her husband? about the future?); she was dissatisfied with her choice (*to choose*) and was thinking about *parting.* The patient therefore had a divorce-complex, for she was very dissatisfied with her married life. When I told her this result she was very shaken and at first tried to deny it, then to gloss it over, but finally she gave in and admitted it. Moreover, she produced a great deal of material, consisting of fantasies about being unfaithful, reproaches against her husband, and so on. Her prudishness and jealousy were merely a projection of her own sexual wishes onto her husband. She was jealous of her husband because she herself was unfaithful in fantasy and could not admit it to herself.

998   It is impossible in a lecture to give a review of all the practical applications of the association experiment. I must be content with having put before you at least the main points.

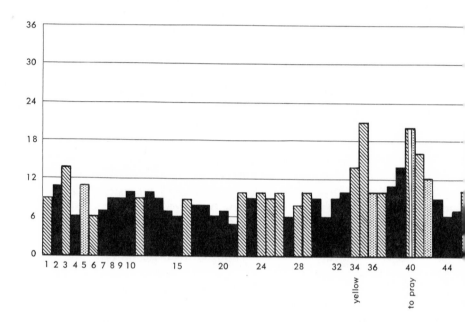

FIG. 8. Columns that are shaded ▨ = incorrect reproductions; ☐ = repetitions of the stimulus-words; ▦ = associations where the patient either laughed or made a slip of the tongue and where she used several words instead of one. The heights of the columns represent the length of the reaction-time. For the stimulus-words corresponding to the numbers, see the list in par. 941*

*[In the original editions, this graph was reproduced using three colours in addition to black: blue, green, and yellow with striped effects when two or three factors applied. As a coloured graph is mentioned in the holograph, it may have been shown as a slide or chart during the lecture. The graph has been simplified and corrected in detail for this presentation.]

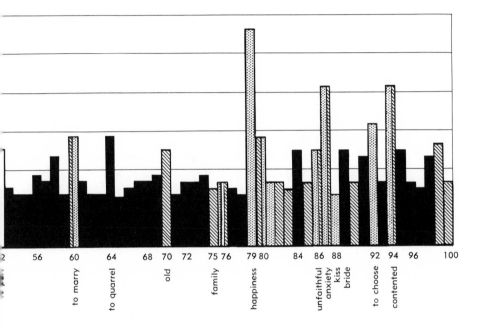

THE FAMILY CONSTELLATION[1]

999   *Ladies and Gentlemen*: As we have seen, there are many different ways in which the association experiment may be used in practical psychology. I should like to talk to you today about yet another use of this experiment, one that is, in the first place, of merely theoretical importance. My pupil, Doctor Fürst,[2] made the following investigations: she applied the association experiment to twenty-four families, consisting altogether of one hundred subjects. The resulting material amounted to 22,200 associations. This material was processed as follows.

1000   Fifteen clearly defined groups were formed according to logical-linguistic criteria and the associations were arranged as follows:[3]

	Husband	Wife	Difference
I. Co-ordination	6.5	0.5	6
II. Sub- and supraordination	7	–	7
III. Contrast	–	–	–

---

[1] [For bibliographical history, see n. 1 to the preceding lecture, "The Association Method." This lecture has also been translated from the German holograph, in consultation with the Brill version. In the holograph, Jung's title was "Die familiäre Constellation," which Brill rendered as "The Familiar Constellations" in the 1909, 1910, and 1916 publications.

[Jung had previously published "Associations d'idées familiales," *Archives de psychologie* (Geneva), VII:26 (Oct., 1907), 160–68, the content of which is similar to that of the present paper; it is omitted from the *Coll. Works*. He again presented four of the graphs, and commented on the cases, in 1935 in "The Tavistock Lectures," Lecture III (1968 edn., pp. 83ff.).]

[2] [Emma Fürst, M.D., a member of the staff of the Psychiatric Clinic of the University of Zurich. Cf. her "Statistical Investigations on Word-Associations and on Familial Agreement in Reaction Type among Uneducated Persons" (orig. 1907).]

[3] [The holograph here contains a direction to insert all of sec. 2 at p. 165 in the *Archives*, i.e., "Associations d'idées familiales" (supra, n. 1). Pars. 1000–1003 are here reproduced from the Brill translation, modified to conform with the present translation.]

466

iv. Predicate expressing a personal judgment	8.5	95.0	86.5
v. Simple predicate	21.0	3.5	17.5
vi. Relations of the verb to the subject or complement	15.5	0.5	15.0
vii. Designation of time, etc.	11.0	–	11.0
viii. Definition	11.0	–	11.0
ix. Coexistence	1.5	–	1.5
x. Identity	0.5	0.5	–
xi. Motor-speech combination	12.0	–	12.0
xii. Composition of words	–	–	–
xiii. Completion of words	–	–	–
xiv. Clang associations	–	–	–
xv. Defective reactions	–	–	–
Total	–	–	173.5

$$\text{Average difference} \quad \frac{173.5}{15} = 11.5$$

001   As can be seen from this example, I utilize the difference to demonstrate the degree of the analogy. In order to find a basis for the sum of the resemblance I have calculated the differences among all Dr. Fürst's subjects, not related among themselves, by comparing every female subject with all the other unrelated females; the same comparison has been made for the male subjects.

002   The most marked difference is found in those cases where the two subjects compared have no associative quality in common. All the groups are calculated in percentages, the greatest difference possible being $\frac{200}{15} = 13.3$ per cent.

I. The average difference of male unrelated subjects is 5.9 per cent, and that of females of the same group is 6 per cent.

II. The average difference between male related subjects is 4.1 per cent, and that between female related subjects is 3.8 per cent. From these numbers we see that relatives show a tendency to agreement in the reaction type.

III. Difference between fathers and children = 4.2.
       ”   ”   mothers   ”   ”   = 3.5.
The reaction types of children come nearer to the type of the mother than to the father.

IV. Difference between fathers and their sons   = 3.1.
       ”   ”   ”   ”   ”   daughters = 4.9.

467

" " mothers " " sons = 4.7.
" " " " " daughters = 3.0.
V. Difference between brothers = 4.7.
" " sisters = 5.1.
If the married sisters are omitted from the comparison we get the following result:
Difference of unmarried sisters = 3.8.
These observations show distinctly that marriage destroys more or less the original agreement, as the husband belongs to a different type.
Difference between unmarried brothers = 4.8.
Marriage seems to exert no influence on the association forms in men. Nevertheless, the material that we have at our disposal is not as yet enough to allow us to draw definite conclusions.
VI. Difference between husband and wife = 4.7.
This number sums up inadequately the different and very unequal values; that is to say, there are some cases which show an extreme difference and some which show a marked concordance.

1003   The different results are shown in the graphs (Figs. 1–5). In the graphs I have marked the number of associations of each quality perpendicularly in percentages. The roman numbers written horizontally represent the forms of association indicated in the table above.

Fig. 1. The father (solid line) shows an objective type, while the mother and daughter show the pure predicate type with a pronounced subjective tendency.

Fig. 2. The husband and wife agree well in the predicate objective type, the predicate subjective being somewhat more numerous in the wife.

Fig. 3. A very nice agreement between a father and his two daughters.

Fig. 4. Two sisters living together. The dotted line represents the married sister.

Fig. 5. Husband and wife. The wife is a sister of the two women of Fig. 4. She approaches very closely to the type of her husband. Her tracing is the direct opposite of that of her sisters.

468

004   The similarity of associations of related subjects is often quite extraordinary. I will give you the associations of a mother and daughter:

Stimulus-word	Mother	Daughter
to pay attention	hard-working	pupil
law	God's commandment	Moses
dear	child	father and mother
great	God	father
potato	tuber	tuber
family	many people	five people
strange	traveller	travellers
brother	dear to me	dear
to kiss	mother	mother
a burn	great pain	painful
door	wide	big
hay	dry	dry
month	many days	31 days
air	cool	moist
coal	sooty	black
fruit	sweet	sweet
merry	happy child	little children
etc.	etc.	etc.

005   One might indeed think that in this experiment, where the door is thrown wide open to so-called chance, individuality would become a factor of the utmost importance, and that therefore one might expect a rich variety and freedom of association. But, as we have seen, the opposite is the case. The daughter shares her mother's way of thinking, not only in her ideas but also in her form of expression; so much so that she even uses the same words. What is more free, fickle, and inconsequent than a passing thought? It is not inconsequent, however, nor free, but strongly determined within the boundaries of the environment. If, therefore, even the most superficial and apparently most fleeting mental images are entirely due to the constellation of the environment, what must we not expect for the more important mental activities, for emotions, wishes, hopes, and intentions? Let us consider a concrete example, illustrated by Fig. 1.

006   The mother is forty-five years old and the daughter sixteen. Both are very distinct evaluating predicate types and differ

469

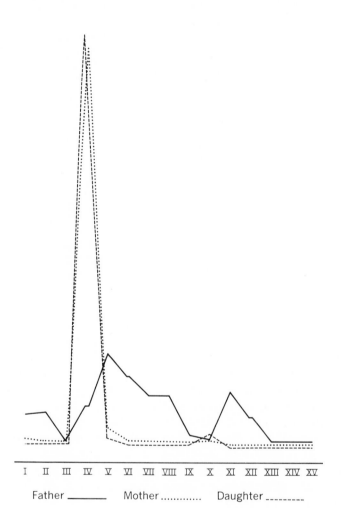

I II III IV V VI VII VIII IX X XI XII XIII XIV XV

Father _____   Mother ....   Daughter _____

1

470

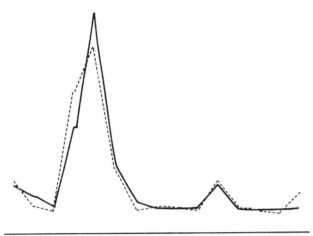

I   II   III   IV   V   VI   VII   VIII   IX   X   XI   XII   XIII   XIV   XV

Husband _____   Wife _____

2

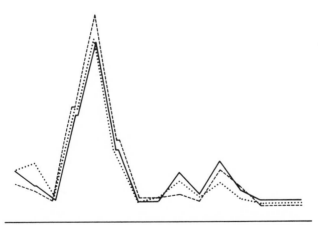

I   II   III   IV   V   VI   VII   VIII   IX   X   XI   XII   XIII   XIV   XV

Father _____   Daughter I ....   Daughter II _____

3

471

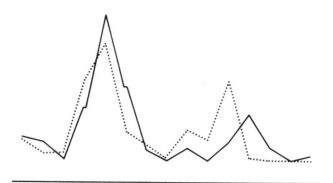

I II III IV V VI VII VIII IX X XI XII XIII XIV XV

Unmarried sister _____ Married sister ....

4

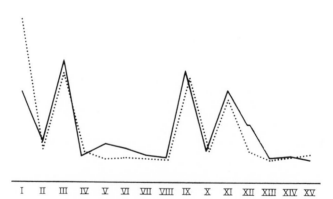

I II III IV V VI VII VIII IX X XI XII XIII XIV XV

Husband _____ Wife ....

5

472

from the father in the most striking manner. The father is a drunkard and a demoralized person. It is understandable therefore that his wife is emotionally starved and betrays this by her intense value judgments. The same reasons cannot, however, apply to the daughter for, in the first place, she is not married to a drunkard and, in the second place, life with all its hopes and promises still lies before her. It is quite unnatural for the daughter to appear as an extreme evaluating predicate type. She responds to the stimuli of the environment precisely as her mother does. But whereas, in the mother, the type is to some extent a natural consequence of her unhappy situation, this simply does not apply to the daughter. The daughter merely imitates her mother; she follows her mother's pattern. Let us consider what this can mean for a young girl. It is unnatural and forced for her to react to the world like an older woman who is disappointed in life. But it could be even more serious than this. As you know, evaluating predicate types overtly express intense emotion; for them everything is emotional. If such people are close to us it is difficult to avoid responding, at least inwardly; we may become infected and even carried away by them. Originally the affects and their physical manifestations had a biological significance; that is, they were a protective mechanism for the individual and the whole herd. If we show feeling, we can be sure that we shall evoke feeling in others. That is the experience of the evaluating predicate type. What the forty-five-year-old woman lacks emotionally, love within her marriage, she seeks compensation for in the outside world, and for this reason she is an ardent follower of the Christian Science movement. If the daughter follows this pattern she is behaving like her mother, looking for emotional satisfaction from outside. But for a girl of sixteen such an emotional state is, to say the least, very dangerous; like her mother, she is reacting to her environment, soliciting sympathy for her suffering. Such an emotional state is no longer dangerous in the mother, but for obvious reasons it is for the daughter. Once she frees herself from her father and mother she will be like her mother, an inwardly dissatisfied suffering woman. She will thus be exposed to the great danger of falling a victim to brutality and of marrying a brute and inebriate like her father.

007   This consideration seems to me important for the under-

473

standing of the influence of environment and of education. The example shows what may be transmitted from a mother to her child. It is not pious precepts nor the repetition of pedagogic truths that have a moulding influence on the character of a developing child; what most influences him are the unconscious personal affective states of his parents and teachers. Hidden conflicts between the parents, secret worries, repressed wishes, all these produce in the child an emotional state, with clearly recognizable signs, that slowly but surely, though unconsciously, seeps into his mind, leading to the same attitudes and hence the same reactions to the environment. We all know that when we are with moody and melancholy people we ourselves become depressed. A restless and nervous person infects the people around him with uneasiness, a grumbler with his discontent, and so on. Since adults are so sensitive to surrounding influences, we should certainly expect this even more among children, whose minds are as soft and malleable as wax. Fathers and mothers deeply impress their children's minds with the stamp of their personalities; the more sensitive and impressionable the child the deeper the impression. Everything is unconsciously reflected, even those things that have never been mentioned at all. A child imitates gestures and, just as the parents' gestures are the expressions of their emotional states, so in turn the gesture gradually produces an emotional state in the child, as he makes the gesture his own. His adaptation to the world is the same as his parents'. At puberty, when he begins to free himself from the spell of the family, he goes out into life with, more or less, the same kind of compromise-adaptations as those of his parents. The frequent and often very deep *depressions of puberty* arise from this; they are symptoms rooted in the difficulties of new adjustments. The adolescent at first tries to become as separate as possible from his family; he may even estrange himself from them, but inwardly this only binds him the more firmly to his image of his parents. I remember the case of a neurotic young man who ran away from home. He was estranged from and almost hostile to his family, but he admitted to me that he possessed a very special talisman; it was a casket containing his old childhood books, old dried flowers, stones, and even small bottles of water from the well at his home and from a river along which he used to walk with his parents.

oo8   The first moves towards friendship and love are constellated in the strongest possible manner by the nature of the relationships with our parents, and here as a rule one can see how powerful is the influence of the family constellation. It is not rare, for instance, for a healthy man whose mother was hysterical to marry a hysteric, or for the daughter of an alcoholic to choose an alcoholic for her husband. I was once consulted by an intelligent and educated young woman of twenty-six who suffered from a peculiar symptom. She complained that her eyes now and then took on a strange expression that exerted an undesirable influence on men. If she looked at a man he became self-conscious, turned away and suddenly said something to the man next to him, whereupon they either laughed or looked embarrassed. The patient was convinced that her glance excited indecent thoughts in men. It was impossible to talk her out of her conviction. This symptom immediately made me suspect that I was dealing with a case of paranoia rather than with a neurosis. But only three days of further treatment showed me that I was mistaken, for the symptom promptly disappeared after it had been analyzed. It arose like this: the lady had had a lover who had publicly jilted her. She felt utterly forsaken, withdrew from all society and amusements, and developed suicidal ideas. In her isolation, unconscious and repressed erotic wishes accumulated and these she unconsciously projected on to men whenever she was in their company. This gave rise to the conviction that her look excited erotic wishes in men. Further investigation showed that her unfaithful lover was mentally ill, a fact that she had apparently not realized. I expressed my astonishment at her making such an unsuitable choice, and added that she must have had a certain inclination to love mentally abnormal people. This she denied, stating that she had once before been engaged to be married, to a perfectly normal man. He, too, deserted her; and on further inquiry it was found that he, too, had shortly before been in a mental hospital for a year—another psychotic! This seemed sufficiently to confirm my view that she had an unconscious tendency to choose insane people. Where did this strange taste come from? Her father was an eccentric and in his later years was completely alienated from his family. Her love had therefore been displaced from her father on to a brother eight years her senior, whom she loved and honoured as a father. At the age of fourteen this brother became hopelessly insane. This was apparently the pattern from which the patient could never free herself, according to which she chose her lovers, and through which she was bound to become unhappy. The particular form of her neurosis, which gave the impression of insanity, probably arose from this childhood pattern. We must take into consideration that in this case we are dealing with a highly educated and intelligent woman, who was not inattentive to her inner experiences, who indeed pondered a great deal over her unhappy fate, without, however, having any idea of what caused her misfortunes.

1009   This is the kind of thing that we unconsciously take for granted in ourselves; for this very reason we cannot see what is going on but put the blame on what we think of as our innate character. I could give any number of examples of this. Patients constantly illustrate for me the determining influence of the family background on their destiny. In every neurosis we can see how the emotional environment constellated during infancy influences not only the character of the neurosis, but also the patient's destiny even down to its very details. Many an unhappy choice of profession and disastrous marriage can be traced to such a constellation. There are, however, cases where the profession has been well chosen, where the husband or wife leaves nothing to be desired, and still the patient feels uneasy and lives and works under constant difficulties. Such cases often appear to be chronic neurasthenics. Here the difficulty is that the mind is unconsciously split into two parts, of divergent and conflicting tendencies; one part lives with the husband or the profession, while the other lives unconsciously in the past with father or mother. I have treated a woman who suffered for many years from a severe neurosis which deteriorated into dementia praecox. The neurotic illness began with her marriage. Her husband was kind, educated, well-to-do, in every respect suitable for her; his character showed nothing that should in any way interfere with a happy marriage. The

476

marriage was nevertheless unhappy, all easy companionship
was impossible because the wife was neurotic.

010   The heuristically important principle of every psychoanalysis runs: *If someone develops a neurosis, this contains the negative aspect of his relationship with the person closest to him.* A
neurosis in a husband clearly shows that he has strong resistances and negative attitudes towards his wife; in a neurotic
wife there is an attitude that drives her away from her husband.
In an unmarried patient the neurosis turns against the lover or
the parents. Every neurotic naturally resists such a relentless
interpretation of the content of his neurosis and often refuses
on any account to recognize it, and yet this is always the heart
of the matter. Certainly, the conflict does not lie on the surface,
but can as a rule only be uncovered by laborious psychoanalysis.

011   Here is the history of our patient: The father was an impressive personality. She was his favourite daughter and held
him in boundless veneration. At the age of seventeen she first
fell in love with a young man. At that time she twice dreamt
the same dream, the impression of which never afterwards left
her; she even imputed a mystical meaning to it and often remembered it with religious awe. In the dream she saw a tall
masculine figure with a very beautiful white beard, at the sight
of which she was filled with a feeling of awe and delight as if
she were experiencing the presence of God himself. This dream
made the deepest possible impression on her, and she was compelled to think about it for ever after. The love-affair proved
not to be a serious one and soon came to an end. Later the patient married her present husband. Though she loved her husband she was always, in her thoughts, comparing him with her
late father, and the comparison always turned against her husband. Whatever the husband did, said or intended was judged
by this standard and always with the same result: "My father
would have done all this differently and better." Thus our patient could not enjoy life with her husband. She could neither
respect nor love him enough and was inwardly disappointed
and unsatisfied. She gradually developed strong religious feelings and at the same time marked hysteriform symptoms arose.
She began by having sentimental attachments to one clergyman
after another; she was looking everywhere for a soul-mate and

estranged herself more and more from her husband. The mental illness became manifest about ten years after their marriage, and in this condition she refused to have anything to do with her husband and child; she imagined herself to be pregnant by another man. The resistance to her husband, which had hitherto been laboriously repressed, became quite outspoken and showed itself in various ways, among other things in violent abuse.

1012   This case shows the onset of a neurosis approximately at the moment of marriage; that is, it expresses the negative attitude to the husband. What is the content of the negative attitude? It is the relationship with the patient's father, for day by day she proved to herself that her husband did not come up to her father's stature. When the patient first fell in love a symptom appeared, an extremely impressive dream or vision. She saw the man with the very beautiful white beard. Who was this man? When her attention was drawn to the beautiful white beard she immediately recognized the image. It was, of course, her father. Every time the patient began to fall in love, the image of her father arose disturbingly and so prevented her from adapting herself to a relationship with the man in question.

1013   I purposely chose this case as an example because it is a simple, obvious, and thoroughly typical one of a marriage crippled through the wife's neurosis. I could tire you out with similar examples. The misfortune is always too strong an attachment to the parents, so that the child remains imprisoned in its infantile relationships. It should be one of the most important aims of education to free the growing child from his unconscious attachment to the influences of his early environment, in such a way that he may keep what is valuable in it and reject whatever is not. It seems to me impossible at present to solve this difficult question by starting from the child's end. We know as yet too little about children's emotional processes. The first and only contribution to the literature giving actual evidence on this subject has in fact been published this year. It is the analysis of a five-year-old boy by Freud.[4]

1014   Children's difficulties are very great. Parents' difficulties, however, should not be so great. Parents could in many ways use more discretion and more forbearance towards their chil-

4 "Analysis of a Phobia in a Five-Year-Old Boy" (orig. 1909).

dren's love. The sins committed against favourite children by their parents' over-indulgence could perhaps be avoided through a wider knowledge of the child's mind. I find it for many reasons impossible to say anything universally valid about the educational aspect of this problem. We are as yet a long way from general precepts and rules; we are still doing field work shown in case-histories. Unfortunately, our knowledge of the subtler processes of a child's mind is so inadequate that we are not yet in any position to say where lies the greater fault: in the parents, the child himself, or in environmental attitudes. Only psychoanalyses like the one published by Professor Freud in our *Jahrbuch*, 1909,[5] will help us out of this difficulty. Such detailed and thorough observations should be a strong inducement to all teachers to acquaint themselves with Freud's psychology. In this psychology educationists can find far more than in the current physiological psychology.

[5][Ibid.]

II

PSYCHOPHYSICAL RESEARCHES

ON THE PSYCHOPHYSICAL RELATIONS OF THE
ASSOCIATION EXPERIMENT[1]

1015   At the second German Congress for Experimental Psychology, held at Würzburg (18–21 April 1906), Dr. Veraguth, privatdocent in neurology at Zurich, reported upon a galvanic phenomenon, which he called "galvano-psychophysical reflexes." The author conducts a current of low tension (about two volts) through the human body, the places of entrance and exit of the current being the palms. He introduces into the circuit of the current a Deprez-d'Arsonval galvanometer of high sensitivity, and also a shunt for lowering the oscillations of the mirror. With this technique, if one applies to a subject tactile, optic, or acoustic stimuli of a certain strength, the galvonometer will indicate an increase in the amount of the current, i.e., a lowering of the electrical resistance of the body. Very early in the course of these experiments it was discovered that the action of the galvanometer was not in direct relation with the strength of the stimulus but rather with the intensity of the resulting psychological feeling-tone. Of great interest is the fact that the irregularity of the galvanometer did not appear at the same moment as the perception of the stimulus, but after a latent period of one to six seconds.

1016   Somewhat later Veraguth observed that a movement (often of great intensity) occurred when the stimulus, instead of being actually applied, was merely announced to the subject. This phenomenon he terms "oscillation through expectation" (*Erwartungsschwankung*). From these observations Veraguth concludes that in this experiment *feelings* are *objectively represented*. The only difficulty in this procedure lies in the technique of the registration of galvanometric oscillations.

1 [Apparently written in English; published in *The Journal of Abnormal Psychology* (Boston), I (1907), 247–55. It was Jung's first publication in English and has never been republished. The present text contains slight stylistic revisions.]

1017 Veraguth takes photographs of the curve of the mirror's movements on a rotating film; but this method is rather difficult and expensive, and only short curves can be obtained, while for the graphic representation of feelings long curves are desirable. I have therefore constructed an apparatus by means of which curves of more than thirty to sixty feet can be taken. In such considerable periods of time many and different experiments can be made without difficulty.

1018 The principle of my apparatus is as follows: I add to the scale a movable slide with a visor. The slide, pushed forward by the hand, always follows the moving mirror-reflection. After some practice, this manoeuvre can be made very easily and exactly. To the slide is fastened a cord leading to what is called an ergograph writer, which marks the movements of the slide on a kymographic tambour fitted with endless paper, upon which the curves are drawn by a pen-point (see illustration).

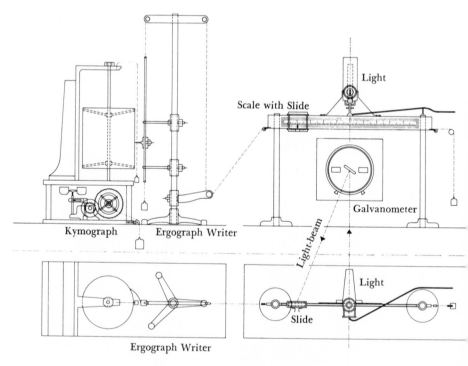

For measuring the time one may use a Jaquet chronograph, and for indicating the moment of stimulus an ordinary electric marker.

1019   With these arrangements I am able to take long curves that are especially valuable for representing feeling-tones aroused by the association experiment.

1020   As is perhaps already known, I have clearly demonstrated in the Diagnostic Association Studies[2] that strong feeling-tones often accompany the association and cause characteristic and regular disturbance in the association processes. I conduct my experiment as follows: I call a series of stimulus-words to a subject who is requested to answer as quickly as possible, saying the first word that comes into her mind. I measure the time elapsing between the stimulus-word and the reaction (the "reaction-time"). Having noted a rather large number of reactions (about one hundred), I then make the subject repeat, one by one, the answers to the stimulus-words (this I call the "reproduction method"). What will occur during such an experiment I shall illustrate by an example.[3]

Stimulus-word	Reaction	Reaction-time sec. 1/10		Reproduction
head	hair	1	4	+
green	meadow	1	6	+
water	deep	5		swim
stab	knife	1	6	+
long	table	1	2	+
ship	wreck	3	4	steamer
question	answer	1	6	+
wool	knit	1	6	+
insolent	gentle	1	4	+
lake	water	4		blue
ill	well	1	8	+
ink	black	1	2	+
swim	know	3	8	water

2 Cf. the report of Adolf Meyer, *Psychological Bulletin*, II (1905), 242–50; also August Hoch, in *Journal of Abnormal Psychology*, I:2 (1906).

3 [In the 1907 publication, the reaction-time column is headed "min./sec."; but, inasmuch as in the next par. Jung states that the reaction-times are relatively short, the column heading has been corrected.]

¹⁰²¹ In considering the reactions of this subject we find at first sight nothing remarkable. She has, with some few exceptions, relatively short reaction-times, and there are also a few incorrect reproductions. But on looking closer we discover that the reactions after *water, ship, lake, swim,* were followed by a rather long reaction-time; and at the same time we observe that with these reactions the following reproduction is incorrect.

¹⁰²² So far as we know, we may suppose that the words *water, ship,* etc., awoke lively feelings that retarded the reaction. The incorrect reproduction of the reactions is also caused, as we can prove by experience, by the interference of lively feelings. The feelings causing such phenomena are generally of a disagreeable nature and we therefore venture to suppose that these stimulus-words gave rise to a complex of ideas having some relation to water and possessing great importance for the subject. The subject, cautiously questioned, tells us that a short while ago while living through most painful and exciting experiences she had seriously thought, in a moment of desperation, of *committing suicide by drowning herself.* But as the days began to look brighter her destiny did not bring her to such an untimely end.

¹⁰²³ The complex of the intention to commit suicide, to which strong feelings are attached, betrayed itself by different psychological disturbances in the experiment. In the same or in similar fashion, all other complexes connected with the affections might naturally betray themselves. Hence the association experiment is a good means of fathoming and of analyzing the personality. According to the opinion of some German authors this method should be used to trace the guilt complexes of criminals who do not confess. At the present time many experiments are being carried out along these lines in Germany, experiments that have been of great scientific interest, but which have not, so far, produced results of undoubted practical value.[4]

¹⁰²⁴ With this experiment, however, apparently so simple, there is one great difficulty—namely, the interpretation of the disturbances; or, to express it another way, what sort of complexes

[4] See bibliography at end of this article.

486

are they that cause these disturbances ("indicators of complexes")? In reply to this question we may say that it is the *routine* of the experiments that is the main thing; and, in view of this fact, we suggest that the interpretation is at present rather an art than a science. In the future, perhaps, laws will be found for the method of interpretation. He who has not mastered this routine may easily make a wrong suggestion and thus go astray. This reproach, and especially that of arbitrary interpretation, has been made concerning my analysis; and consequently every means that helps to define the complex and its feeling-tone is useful. The "galvano-psychophysical reflex" would seem to be such a means.

1025   By representing graphically the galvanic oscillations during the association experiment, we occasionally obtain curves of very great interest, of which I wish to give some few examples. (The vertical strokes indicate the moment at which the stimulus-word was given.) It can be seen that, shortly after the pre-

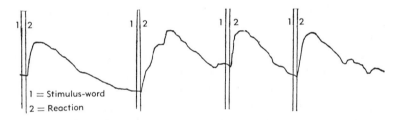

ceding reaction, the curve quickly rises and then slowly falls again. In this case every reaction is succeeded by a movement of the galvanometer. If by a special proceeding we diminish the sensibility of the apparatus, only the most intensive feeling-tones influence the current, so that occasionally we shall obtain very distinct curves that show the strong feeling-tone in a specially clear manner. The following is such an example:

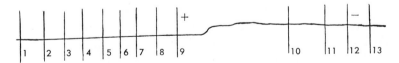

487

In the beginning we see the curve making its way horizontally without any irregularity. In this phase come the following eight reactions:

1. hot	cold	5. mouth	teeth
2. hand	foot	6. wake	wake up
3. apple	fruit	7. drink	eat
4. naughty	angry	8. bed	sleep

These reactions show nothing of interest; their feeling-curve accordingly goes in a horizontal line.

9. pretty	not pretty	11. to call on	not to call on
10. danger	no danger	12. workman	workwoman

1026   These reactions are obvious:

1. The first three are uttered in two words, which is, as a rule, unusual with this subject.

2. There are obvious and for the most part contrasting associations that are not easily intelligible.

3. A striking perseveration in the linguistic form is to be seen, beginning with *not pretty. Workman / workwoman* is rather a superficial association.

1027   It is evident that this strange phase takes its origin in *pretty.* On the curve we can see, beginning with the reaction *not pretty,* the appearance of a strong feeling-tone that lasts for a long time and disappears only with the last reaction. The linguistic perseveration (*not pretty, no danger, not to call on*) is therefore connected with a feeling, lasting probably through the same period.

1028   I had suspected from the beginning that the young man had a sweetheart. He told me that he had been married the week before. Upon my asking him whether his wife were pretty, he very characteristically replied, "Other people do not find her very pretty, but for me she is quite pretty enough." From this it is evident that the word *pretty* had hit upon a sore point.

1029   The next curve illustrates a very interesting case. The subject is a young, diligent, and gentle man, of whom I knew nothing, except the fact of his being an abstainer.

1030   In the beginning we note the curve falling slowly, then taking a rather horizontal course until the sixth stimulus-word,

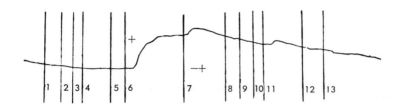

where a sudden steep rise sets in and maintains itself until the thirteenth reaction.

1031   The reactions are as follows:

1.	pay	money	4.	love	hatred
2.	snake	animal	5.	help	assist
3.	fine	beautiful	6.	*restaurant*	*non-alcoholic*

With the sixth reaction the rising of the curve begins. The reaction *non-alcoholic* indicates a very individual complex of ideas. And a very strong feeling seems to be attached to the fact that he is a teetotaler.

1032   The reaction next following is:

7. *polished*   *glass*

accompanied by a new rise of the curve. *Glass* might be another association of the *restaurant* complex. The next associations are:

8. soldier   military
9. write   letter
10. looking-glass   clear

which present nothing special and are also galvanically uninteresting.

11. *full*   *man*

(The German word *voll*, 'full', has also the occasional meaning 'completely drunk'.) This association, which distinctly indicates the idea of being drunk, is again accompanied by a rising of the curve. The next association is:

12. intelligence   prudent

489

1033   As things present themselves we may be right in supposing that there is a complex with strong feelings that has some relation to *restaurant* and *drunkenness*. When asked, the man confesses that once, when drunk, he had committed the crime of a serious assault and had consequently been sentenced to a long term of imprisonment. Because of these occurrences he had become an abstainer as a means of preventing his again getting into a similar situation. (This confession was corroborated by others as being the truth.)

1034   As may easily be understood, this event left a serious and lasting impression, deepened by the fact that his former crime had become a great social hindrance to him.

1035   These examples may serve to show that the association experiment is, under certain conditions, a suitable way of demonstrating the feeling-tones that accompany the associations. I say "under certain conditions"—for not always will one succeed in obtaining such clear and distinct curves as those shown above. The experiment possesses numerous complications, to overcome which a great deal of time and work is required. There is moreover the difficulty that the physical and physiological part of the experiment is still obscure, notwithstanding the work of Tarchanoff, Sticker, Sommer, and Veraguth. At the present time, Binswanger in Zurich is occupied with these researches. I will not here anticipate his work, which he has already finished.[5]

BIBLIOGRAPHY[6]

Works concerning the Galvanic Experiment:

1. Tarchanoff: "Über die galvanischen Erscheinungen an der Haut des Menschen, etc." (1890).

2. Sticker: "Über Versuche einer objectiven Darstellung von Sensibilitätsstörungen" (1897).

3. Sommer: In *Beiträge zur Psychiatrischen Klinik*, Vienna (1902).

5 ["On the Psychogalvanic Phenomenon in Association Experiments" (orig. 1907/8).]

6 [Jung published the bibliography with more or less full references, which will be found in the entries in the volume bibliography.]

4. Sommer and Fürstenau: "Die elektrischen Vorgänge an der menschlichen Haut" (1906).

5. Veraguth: "Le Réflexe psycho-galvanique" (1906).

Works concerning the Psychological Diagnosis of Evidence:

1. Alfred Gross: "Zur psychologischen Tatbestandsdiagnostik, etc." (1905–6).

2. Idem: "Zur psychologischen Tatbestandsdiagnostik" (1905–6).

3. Idem: "Die Assoziationsmethode im Strafprozess" (1906).

4. Hans Gross: "Zur psychologischen Tatbestandsdiagnostik" (1905).

5. Grabowsky: *Psychologische Tatbestandsdiagnostik* (1905).

6. Jung: *Diagnostische Assoziationsstudien*, Bd. I (1906).

7. Idem: *Die psychologische Diagnose des Tatbestandes* (1906).

8. Kramer and Stern: "Selbstverrat durch Assoziation" (1905–6).

9. Lederer: "Zur Frage der psychologischen Tatbestandsdiagnostik" (1906).

10. Idem: "Die Verwendung der psychologischen Tatbestandsdiagnostik in der Strafrechtspraxis" (1906).

11. Stern: "Psychologische Tatbestandsdiagnostik" (1905–6).

12. Wertheimer and Klein: "Psychologische Tatbestandsdiagnostik" (1904).

13. Wertheimer: "Experimentelle Untersuchungen zur Tatbestandsdiagnostik" (1905–6).

PSYCHOPHYSICAL INVESTIGATIONS WITH THE GALVANOMETER AND PNEUMOGRAPH IN NORMAL AND INSANE INDIVIDUALS[1]

by Frederick Peterson and C. G. Jung

1036   These investigations were carried out in the laboratory of the Clinic for Psychiatry at Zurich, to the director of which, Professor E. Bleuler, we are under obligation for the use of apparatus and material for study. The purposes of our research were to ascertain the value of the so-called "psycho-physical galvanic reflex" as a recorder of psychical changes in connection with sensory and psychical stimuli; to determine its normal and pathological variations; to study the respiratory innervation curve in the same relations; and finally to compare the galvanometric and pneumographic curves taken simultaneously upon the kymograph, under the influence of various stimuli. In word-associations the reaction-time was also registered for further comparison.

I. Apparatus Employed

1037   For the respiratory curve we used the Marey pneumograph made by Zimmerman, in Leipzig. The kymograph was made by Schüle, in Basel, and runs with a weight, making it both steady and noiseless. The stop-watch employed for reaction-time was manufactured by Billian, of Zurich.

1038   The use of the galvanometer in experimental psychology is so new and recent as to require a special description and a brief review of the scanty literature of the subject.

[1] [Originally published, in English, in *Brain: A Journal of Neurology* (London), XXX (1907):118 (July), 153–218; reprinted the same year as a small book. Frederick W. Peterson (1859–1938), M.D., was then Clinical Professor of Psychiatry, Columbia University, New York. He collaborated with A. A. Brill in the translation of Jung's *The Psychology of Dementia Praecox* (1909).

[In the present version, stylistic and terminological revisions have been made. A list of references originally at the end of the paper has been converted into footnotes.]

The first to discover the influence of mental conditions on the galvanometer was Professor Tarchanoff, who published a paper in *Pflüger's Archiv für Physiologie*, 1890, entitled "Galvanic Phenomena in the Human Skin in Connection with Irritation of the Sensory Organs and with Various Forms of Psychic Activity." He employed tubular unpolarizable clay electrodes, connected with the skin by means of hygroscopic cotton pads, 10 to 15 cm. long, saturated with saline solution. These are attached to a Meissner and Meyerstein galvanometer. Deviations of the mirror were noted through a telescope upon a scale three metres distant from the galvanometer. The scale was divided on each side of the zero point into 50 cm. and these again into mm. The galvanometer was so sensitive that a nerve-stream of a frog's sciatic nerve deflected the mirror so much that all the divisions on the scale were passed over. The electrodes were applied at various times to different portions of the body, such as the hands and fingers, feet and toes, the face, the nose, the ears and the back. Experimenting thus, he obtained the following results:

1039   Light tickling of the face, ears, or soles of the feet, with a camel-hair brush or a feather, induced, after a latent period of from one to three seconds, a deflection in the galvanometer to the extent of the whole 50 cm. of the scale. The same results were obtained by stimulating the skin with the faradic brush, with hot and cold water, and by pricking with a needle. Stimulation in analogous ways of other sensory organs, the ear, the nose, the tongue and the eye, affected the galvanometer in a corresponding manner.

1040   The experimenter then ascertained that actual stimulation was not essential to these results, but the presentation of the proposed stimulus to the imagination also brought about similar deviations in the galvanometer. He stated, furthermore, that the recollection of some fear, fright, or joy, in general any kind of strong emotion, produced the same result. The next point of interest recorded by Tarchanoff was that ordinary abstract mental exercise, such as computation, does not affect the galvanometer unless the exercise be accompanied by exertion. He also noted that the motion of expectant attention or anticipation had a marked effect upon the galvanometer. Tarchanoff regarded the phenomena he observed as due to a

493

secretory current of electricity associated with the sweat-glands. He was evidently unaware of the extraordinary value of the investigations he described in this brief paper. Like many discoveries of importance, his remarkable work lay buried in medical literature for years, and it was not until 1897 that any further contribution on this subject appeared. In that year, Sticker[2] records a repetition of the work of Tarchanoff. His conclusion was that the capillary system of blood-vessels was a factor in the perturbations of the galvanic current. He opposed Tarchanoff's idea of the centripetal excitation of a secretory current, because he found that the same deviations were noted when the electrodes were applied to anaesthetic and analgesic areas of skin (functional or organic).

1041   After a lapse of five years, Sommer[3] made some experiments with the galvanometer, but lost himself in technical and physical details, and failed completely to grasp the intrinsically valuable features of the instrument. He observed fluctuations which he attributed to alterations in resistance of the skin or to changes in contact between skin and electrodes. He thought any apparent psychic influence was due to involuntary muscular contractions induced by increased pressure on the electrodes, and concluded that, except for the reaction to tickling, no psychic influence on the galvanometer could be established with certainty. He therefore stumbled over, but missed, the one essential point.

1042   About two years ago E. K. Müller, an electrical engineer, of Zurich, read a paper before the Swiss Society of Natural Sciences (medical section) on "The Influence of Psychic and Physiological Phenomena upon the Electrical Conductivity of the Human Body." Happening to make certain experiments upon himself in relation to the resistance of the human body in the alternating magnetic field, he rediscovered the deflectibility of the mirror-galvanometer under psychic and nervous stimulation as established by Tarchanoff.

1043   O. Veraguth, a neurologist, of Zurich, was then led by Müller to experiment in the same direction. He made use of

[2] "Über Versuche einer objektiven Darstellung von Sensibilitätsstörungen" (1897).

[3] "Zur Messung der motorischen Begleiterscheinungen psychischer Zustände" (1902).

the Deprez-d'Arsonval mirror-galvanometer, nickel-plated brass cylinders for electrodes, a feeble electrical current, a horizontal celluloid scale on which the light from the mirror registered its movements, and an apparatus for photographic delineation of the fluctuations. He published some results last August (1906) in the *Archives de psychologie* (Geneva), and he gave the name "psychophysical galvanic reflex" to the phenomenon.[4] Veraguth corroborates the findings of Tarchanoff. One or two of his experiments are especially striking. If the individual under observation is read to, deviation of the mirror is noted when passages associated with emotional tone are reached. Or, if a series of unrelated words is pronounced, a test suggested to him by one of the authors of this paper (Jung), words connected with some emotional complex produce an effect on the galvanometer, while indifferent words have no effect. He concludes from his studies that only such stimuli as are associated with sufficiently intense and actual emotional tone induce a deviation in the galvanometer. He states in his paper that he is not yet in a position to explain the phenomenon, but that if change in resistance were the cause then manifold contradictions are presented to our present conceptions of resistance in the human body. He did not think it due to alterations in the quantity of blood in the parts beneath the electrodes, for the phenomenon takes place whether the hands be emptied of blood by an Esmarch bandage or supercharged with blood by artificial venous stasis. Veraguth excludes the participation of the perspiration, for the results were similar in hands made dry by formalin.

1044   As far as we know the above review covers the scanty literature of the subject, but work has been carried on for about a year in this field in the laboratory of the Psychiatric Clinic at Zurich, the most of which has not yet been published. One of

4 Veraguth presented his entire results to date for discussion at the second German Congress for Experimental Psychology, Würzburg, 1906, the transactions of which will be published early this year (1907). [See Veraguth, "Le Réflexe psychogalvanique" (1906 and 1907).]

[The following was inserted as a corrigendum slip in the *Brain* publication: "Dr. Jung wishes us to state that Dr. O. Veraguth, of Zurich, first made known to him the value of the galvanometer as a measure of psychical stimuli. It was after this demonstration by Dr. Veraguth that Dr. Jung began to experiment on his own account."]

us (Jung) has published in the *Journal of Abnormal Psychology* (Boston), for February 1907, the results of association experiments in which the galvanometer was employed, and in this
article is a drawing of the apparatus and a description of the
order of research.[5] In the same laboratory, L. Binswanger, together with Jung, has investigated the physical and physiological problems presented by the phenomenon, the results of
which will shortly be published in a separate paper,[6] though
the material conclusions of their investigations are embodied
in this paper.

1045   The apparatus employed by us is as follows: the mirror
galvanometer of Deprez-d'Arsonval; a translucent celluloid
scale divided into millimetres and centimetres with a lamp
upon it (made by Zulauf & Co., of Zurich), the scale being
placed one metre from the galvanometer; a moveable indicator
sliding on the scale and connected by a device of Jung with a
recording pen writing upon the kymograph; a rheostat to reduce the current when necessary; and one, sometimes two, Bunsen cells. The electrodes generally used are large copper plates,
upon which the palms of the hands rest comfortably, or upon
which the soles of the feet may be placed. We have also used
jars of hot water for the contact, when, as with some instances
of dementia praecox, the hands were congested and cold. Occasionally we have employed a plate of zinc for one electrode
and a plate of carbon for the other (in which case no element
was required, since the skin, sweat, and metal provided sufficient current).

II. The Physics and Physiology of the "Psychophysical Galvanic Reflex"

1046   So far as is known, it would seem that the sweat glands are
the chief factor in the production of this electric phenomenon,
on the one hand inducing under the influence of nervous
stimulation a measurable current or, on the other hand, alter-
ing the conductivity of the current. Since water contact excludes changes induced by pressure on metal electrodes, and
blanching of the fingers by the Esmarch bandage excludes
changes in connection with the blood supply, both of these
factors play but a small part in the deviations of the gal-

5 [See above, par. 1018.]
6 ["On the Psychogalvanic Phenomenon in Association Experiments."]

vanometer. Change in resistance is brought about either by saturation of the epidermis with sweat, or by simple filling of the sweat-gland canals or perhaps also by intracellular stimulation; or all of these factors may be associated. The path for the centrifugal stimulation in the sweat-gland system would seem to lie in the sympathetic nervous system. These conclusions are based upon facts at present to hand and are by no means felt to be conclusive. On the contrary, there are features presented which are as yet quite inexplicable,[7] as, for instance, the gradual diminution of the current in long experiments to almost complete extinction, when our ordinary experience teaches that resistance should be much reduced and the passing current larger and stronger. This may possibly be due to gradual cooling of the skin in contact with the cold copper plates. This can be obviated by warm water contact or by resting the copper plates upon warm sand bags. Yet there is still an inviting field for investigation here.

1. *Fluctuations of the Galvanometer from Physical Causes*

1047   If the hands, placed upon the copper-plate electrodes, be pressed down firmly, there is a slowly-increasing deviation of the galvanometer, but only to a minor degree. If the area of contact be diminished by the raising of the fingers or by lifting of the palms, there is a sudden diminution in the amount of current, marked by sudden reduction of amplitude in the excursion of the light.

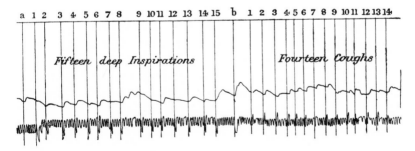

FIG. 1. Curve to show effects of deep inspirations and coughing upon the galvanometer

[7] On one occasion, with three persons in the circuit and one Bunsen cell, the sudden fall of a weight with loud noise caused a deflection of two cms.

A deep inspiration alone, or a deep expiration, without altera-tion in the contact of the hands, increases the deflection of the galvanometer, while ordinary respiratory movements do not affect it. Coughing also causes a considerable rise in the gal-vanometric wave. We are inclined to think that this rise dur-ing inspiration, expiration, and coughing may also be of psychic, that is, emotional, origin. Certainly in the curve we observe exhaustion by repetition of the command to cough or breathe deeply, as in the case of other analogous stimuli. The devi-ations brought about by altered contact, by deep inspiration and expiration, and by coughing, are all readily recognized after some experience, and are readily differentiated from those depending wholly upon psychic influences. Warm hands nat-urally permit a larger current than cold hands. The level of the curve rises when the skin in contact grows warmer or moister, and descends with increase of coldness in the skin (see fig. 1).[8]

2. *Fluctuations of the Galvanometer from Psychic Causes in Normal Individuals*

1048   *Expectation.*—As soon as the galvanometric experiment be-gins, and the circuit through the subject is closed, there is a rather rapid rise with some fluctuation of a curve induced by expectant attention. Tarchanoff was much struck by this. At-tention is, as Bleuler[9] has pointed out, nothing more than a special form of affectivity. Attention, interest, expectation, are all emotional expressions. The extent of this expectation curve rises in normal individuals, depending upon their varying de-gree of affectivity. Expectation is not only manifested at the beginning of an experiment in the galvanometer curve, but may also be observed throughout the experiment in connection with every stimulus, sensory or verbal. It is particularly strong in connection with the threat of pricking with the needle, or threat of letting fall a heavy weight. The influence of expecta-tion on the curve becomes less with each repetition of the same series of stimuli, and seems to disappear wholly with in-different stimuli; while, with the threat stimuli just referred to, which are more lively and actual, repetition may diminish the

---

[8] All tracings except figs. 9, 14, 15, and 18 have been reduced to one-eighth their size.
[9] *Affektivität, Suggestibilität, Paranoia* (1906).

curve, or at times increase it if the test case is uncertain whether the threats in the repetition are to be a real prick of the needle or an actual fall of the weight. In beginning an experiment, we therefore wait until the first influence of the emotion of expectation has subsided.

1049   *Emotion.*—Excluding the affect of attention, we find that every stimulus accompanied by an emotion causes a rise in the electric curve directly proportional to the liveliness and actuality of the emotion aroused. The galvanometer is therefore a measurer of the amount of emotional tone, and becomes a new instrument of precision in psychological research.

1050   *Imagined emotion.*—The amount of deflection seems to stand in direct relation to the *actuality* of the emotion; but, as Tarchanoff pointed out, the presentation of an outlived emotion to the imagination deviates the galvanometer, such deviation depending naturally upon the facility of the subject in living over the old emotion in his imagination. The following experiment, tried upon one of the writers, is an illustration: The list of stimuli was placed before him, while the reader of the deviations called off at intervals Nos. 1—2—3—4—5—6, allowing time for concentration upon the idea, and for the rise and subsidence of the wave. Between the periods of concentration on the emotional images, the subject allowed his eyes to wander at random about the room, and his mind to run on indifferent objects that he saw.

An Experiment in the Deflection of the Galvanometer in Imagined Conditions

	Amount of deviation of galvanometer
(1) Expectant attention.	
(2) Imagined threat of prick with needle	4.3 cm.
(3) Imagined threat of fall of heavy weight	1.6 cm.
(4) Imagined grief	2.8 cm.
(5) Thought of an amusing story	1.8 cm.
(6) Thought of a painful illness in 1888	1.6 cm.

1051   *Series of stimuli used.*—A series of stimuli, sensory and verbal, strong and indifferent, intellectual and emotional, was arranged and tested upon numerous normal individuals, besides which word associations were used in connection with the galvanometer. In some of the experiments the subject was in an adjoining room, the electric connections and signals being easily adjusted for this purpose. The following is the series of stimuli:

    (1) A loud whistle.
    (2) Actual fall of a weight with a very loud noise.
    (3) Multiply 4 by 5.
    (4) Multiply 9 by 11.
    (5) Multiply 8 by 12.
    (6) Sudden call of subject by name.
    (7) Where do you live?
    (8) What is the capital of Switzerland?
    (9) What is the capital of France?
    (10) How old are you?
    (11) Are you married?
    (12) Were you engaged once before?
    (13) Have you been long at your present employment?
    (14) Threat of prick with needle after counting 1—2—3.
    (15) Threat of allowing heavy weight to fall after counting 1—2—3.
    (16) What is your first name?
    (17) What is the first name of your wife?
    (18) Is she pretty?
    (19) We have now finished.

1052   The verbal stimuli were varied to a slight degree with various individuals, to adapt them to different conditions and circumstances, but the general character of the stimuli was the same.

1053   These stimuli were ordinarily repeated three times for each individual, normal or pathological, and subsequently the series of word stimuli were given for the word associations, and these were also repeated once or twice. From seventy curves, fig. 2 (H., nurse, Series 3) is selected as a general illustration of the galvanometric curve. This man was emotional and in the third series here presented the curves are smaller and more rounded than in the first and second series. At the same time they serve to show the character of the emotional curve. Stimuli 3, 4, and 5, although they were but simple multiplication, induced an emotional curve, because H. was a nurse and was embarrassed at doing mental arithmetic before experimenters. Stimuli 8, 9,

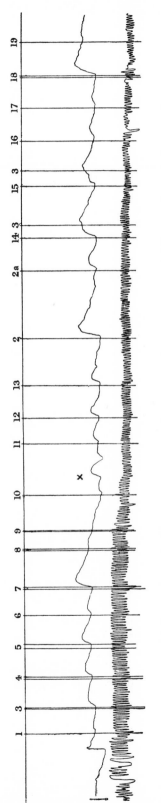

FIG. 2. Galvanometer and pneumographic curves in a normal person (H., a nurse). The numbers at the top of each stimulus line correspond to the series of nineteen mixed stimuli printed in the text. 2 and 2a representing two falls of the weight occurred between 13 and 14 instead of between 1 and 2 in this curve, which was the second repetition of the series. Between 10 and 11 someone entered the laboratory

and 10 were practically exhausted in this third trial and show very little. Between 10 and 11 someone entered the room. The weight was let fall twice between 13 and 14 instead of at 2, and being unexpected produced a large and a smaller wave of alarm. The threatened prick of the needle at 14 and threat of fall of large leaden weight at 15 still produced large waves, and show how strongly actuality in an apprehension influences the curves. Again, at 18 the inquiry if his wife was pretty, she being far from it, induced a lively emotion and correspondingly high wave, for this question was here a surprise as well, not having been asked in the preceding series.

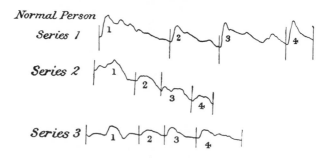

Fig. 3. Repetition of same stimulus questions in a normal person (H., a nurse) three successive times to show gradual exhaustion of emotional wave in the galvanometer curve. In 3rd series, question 1, someone entered the laboratory and caused an extra wave

1054   *Exhaustion of stimulus by repetition.*—When the first series of stimuli is recorded, the curves are usually characterized by

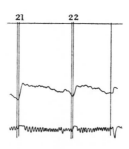

Fig. 4. Here G., a nurse, is asked about a quarrel with another nurse, H. The fluctuating galvanometer waves 21 and 22 represent the wavering emotions aroused

abrupt ascent and descent with rather sharp summits. The curves diminish in size and the summits become more rounded in each repetition, showing a slower excitation and slower reaction of the emotion. This is well illustrated in fig. 3, where several curves induced by the same stimuli in the first, second, and third series in the same individual are reproduced. Wave No. 1 in Series 1 also exhibits in the descent the fluctuating character of an emotion which is slowly and waveringly passing off. This is even better shown in fig. 4, from Case G., who was asked questions calculated to produce a complex emotional state such as the galvanometer perfectly indicates. In quite a number of instances the heights of the waves of the three successive series were measured and the following two illustrations are selected as examples of the differences in height (in milli-

Table 1: Case of H. Diminishing Excursions of Galvanometer in Successive Stimulations

Stimuli ——— Case of H	4×5	9×11	Call by name	Where do you live?	Capital of Switzerland?	How old are you?	Are you married?	Were you engaged before?	Have you been a nurse long?	Threat with needle	Threat with weight	Average
Series 1	34	18	5	38	14	24	18	27	26	36	22	24
Series 2	11	12	4	18	9	9	6	4	6	25	59+	10.4
Series 3	8	8	4	18	1	3	6	9	9	18	13	8.4

Table 2: Case of G. Diminishing Excursions of Galvanometer in Successive Stimulations

Stimuli ——— Case of G	4×5	8×12	Where do you live?	Capital of Switzerland?	Capital of France?	How old are you?	Were you once engaged?	Have you been a nurse long?	Do you like the work?	Threat with needle	Threat with weight	Average
Series 1	9	10	7	7	8	5	10	5	8	17	15	8.6
Series 2	6	6	4	7	4	6	4	5	6	14	17	6.2
Series 3	3	5	3	5	3	4	6	4	5	16	15	5.4

NOTE. In the averages of these two tables the eleventh column of figures was not included as the emotion of expectation that the weight would really be dropped modifies especially the second trial, while in the third trial there was less of such expectation.

metres) of the curves of the stimuli in the three series. Waves were selected which had not been affected in any of the series by interruptions, change of contact, coughing, or deep inspirations.

1055   In these tables the falling off of the height of the emotional curve is very well shown, and in both the livelier affects produced even in repetition by actual threats of the needle and weight are typical. In Series 2 of the first table the threat with the weight raised the curve to over fifty-nine because the subject thought that the weight would actually fall in this experiment, whereas before it was a threat only.

1056   *Latent time.*—It was noted by Tarchanoff that the galvanic wave began to rise from one to three seconds after a stimulus was given. We have verified this period of latent time in all normal conditions, but the latent time varies with different people and at different times. In the curves that we have thus far taken we could not well complicate the apparatus with a chronograph adjustment, and have estimated the space of latent time in a number of normal cases by measuring the distance of the curve from the moment of stimulation to the beginning of ascent of the emotional curve, taking the measurements in millimetres. The kymograph drum revolved slowly. The following results were obtained. Nurse B. with the series of mixed stimuli given above showed in the first series an average of 2.06 millimetres; the repetition of the second series averaged 2.55 millimetres; with Nurse G. and the same series of mixed stimuli in Series 1 the average was 1.85, in the second 1.76, and in the third or final series 2.32 millimetres. Dr. P. with the same series showed an average latent period in the first trial of 3.15, and in the repetition an average of 4.40. Dr. R. with the same series had an average period in the first trial of 4.05 millimetres, and in the second trial of 4.50 millimetres. In a series of word-associations Dr. R. showed at first an average period of 2.95 millimetres, and in the repetition immediately after the average was 4 millimetres. With word-associations Nurse H. showed in the first series an average latent period of 2.26; in the repetition or second series the latent period was increased to 3.55, and with a third trial of the same words the latent period had become 4.14. These figures with regard to the latent period show therefore that with repetition there is an increase of the latent period of time simultaneously with the rounding off and diminishing amplitude of the curve, both corresponding with exhaustion of the power of the stimulus. We were unable to determine in this investigation that there was any marked difference in latent time in relation to the various forms of stimulation whether physical or psychic, and when psychic with or without answer to questions or words, though such differences will probably be discovered by further experiment directed to this end.[10]

1057   *Normal individual variations of galvanometer curve.*—We find considerable difference in the curves made by the galvanometer in normal persons. In some the waves are of rather

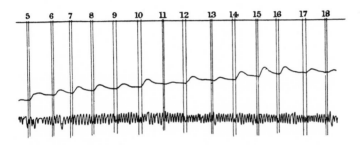

FIG. 5. Dr. R., normal curve with rather indifferent word-association stimuli. Unemotional type

small and even excursion, corresponding to the unemotional or phlegmatic nature of the subject. In other waves there is wide excursion, with fluctuating or bifurcated waves, rapid ascents and descents, expressing great emotional lability. These normal variations are illustrated in figs. 5 and 6.

[10] With a stop-watch we estimated that the time of revolution of the drum was 4.5 in five seconds. Hence the latent time in the above normal individuals was about as follows:

Latent time in seconds	B.	G.	Dr. P.	Dr. R.	Dr. R. Word Assoc.	H. Word Assoc.
First series	2.28	2.05	3.5	4.5	3.27	2.51
Second series	2.83	1.95	4.88	5	4.44	3.94
Third series		2.57				4.6

III. The Pneumograph as an Indicator of Psychic Processes

1058   The relation of the respiratory innervation curve to psychic processes in both normal and pathological conditions has not yet been thoroughly investigated. Mosso was one of the earlier investigators (1879–1893) in the physiological application of the pneumograph and could reach no satisfactory conclusions from a study of the respiratory curve under sensory stimulation. Delabarre[11] states that respiration increases in frequency and depth with attention to sensory stimulation, and with

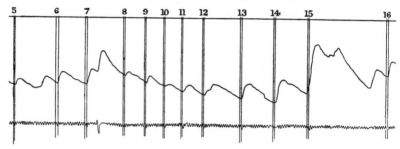

FIG. 6. H., an attendant, normal curves, very labile emotions. The numbers here correspond to the series of mixed stimuli; 15 is threat of weight

mental processes increases in frequency and diminishes in depth. Lehmann[12] states that every pleasant impression increases the depth of breathing, and that strong unpleasant impressions are accompanied by several deep respiratory movements. Mentz[13] employed pleasant and unpleasant acoustic stimuli in a study of the pulse and breathing, and as regards respiration observed with strong stimulation first slowing and then shortening of the respiratory movements. He noted also a marked influence of attention on the results. Involuntary attention generally induced prolongation of breathing, while voluntary attention often caused abbreviation of the movements. Pursuing his studies further he investigated the action of pleasant and unpleasant stimuli and of the effects upon pulse and respiration. As regards the former, pleasant feelings

11 *Über Bewegungsempfindungen* (1891).
12 *Die Hauptgesetze des menschlichen Gefühlslebens* (1892).
13 "Die Wirkung akustischer Sinnesreize auf Puls und Atmung" (1893).

lengthened the pulse curve and unpleasant ones shortened it, and he regards the respiratory curve as running a parallel course. With affects there was prolongation of the respiratory movements, and with increasing strength of the affects an increasing height or depth of the breathing curve. Zoneff and Meumann,[14] finding nothing sufficiently definite in literature in relation to the correspondence between respiration and circulation and psychic or emotional processes, have made an exhaustive research upon normal individuals, employing various stimuli, optic, acoustic, gustatory, cutaneous, and psychic (arithmetical problems and space conceptions), and studied at the same time the effects of voluntary attention and pleasant and unpleasant impressions upon the breathing and pulse. They found that as a rule attention produced acceleration of the breathing, especially at the end of the stimulation, and in addition to acceleration the breathing might become more shallow or be inhibited. This inhibition may appear as shallow and more rapid breathing, or there may be a partial or complete standstill of the respiration, which is greater in direct proportion to the degree of attention. Complete inhibition was found more often in attention to sensory than to intellectual stimulation. There were variations in the results in different individuals. There were fluctuations in the curves which they considered as being due to fluctuations in attention. In relation to pleasant and unpleasant stimuli, they concluded that all pleasant sensations cause shallowing and acceleration of the breathing, and all unpleasant sensations deepening and slowing of respiration, or, in other words, that the former diminish and the latter increase respiratory function. In experiments with diversion of the attention together with stimulation, they found that emotional effects upon breathing and pulse ceased. In experiments with concentration of attention on stimulus and sensation, attention strengthened the effects of both pleasant and unpleasant feelings upon the curves. While their work is the best that has yet appeared upon this subject, it must still be confessed that experiments of this nature carried out upon the trained assistants or students connected with the laboratory are more or less artificial, and this, together with the extremely simple character of the stimulation, would make their

14 "Über Begleiterscheinungen psychischer Vorgänge im Atem und Puls" (1900).

criteria for the more complex emotional phenomena with which we have to deal only relatively valuable.

1059   Martius and Minnemann[15] in a thoroughly iconoclastic and yet excellent work point out many fallacies in the studies of Lehmann, Menz, and Zoneff and Meumann, artifacts of a mechanical nature, and wrong conclusions as to the relations between affects and pulse and breathing curves. They themselves find the normal respiratory curve inconstant, subject to variations due to age, temperament, perseveration of affect, reactions from the affect, embarrassment from the experiment, undue interest in the procedure, etc., and their chief conclusion is that the main changes in breathing in emotional conditions consist of quickened or lengthened tempo, with diminished height in either case.

1060   Believing that a study of the inspiratory curve would throw the most light upon the relation of respiratory innervation to psychic processes, we set before ourselves several problems for consideration, viz., the character of the usual respiratory curve, the character of the curve in stimulation without verbal reaction, the influence of verbal reaction with indifferent stimuli upon the curve, whether distinct emotional complexes affected uniformly the pneumographic curve, whether there were marked disturbances of the respiratory without corresponding changes in the galvanometric curve, and, finally, what influence attention has on both galvanometer and pneumograph. We have not been able as yet to reach satisfactory conclusions on all of these points, for the material already available is more than we have yet had opportunity to investigate thoroughly; but so far as they go the results obtained are of interest. The figures in the table for one of the cases given here show a regular, though not constant, relation between the galvanometric and the pneumographic curves.

1061   To obtain these relations it is necessary to select an experiment in which the galvanometric curve has not been influenced greatly by the several sources of error, and the simultaneous pneumographic curve has not been modified too much by verbal reaction, coughing, etc. Taking the typical curves of several such series, measurements were made to determine the relative number of inspirations synchronous with the ascending

[15] *Beiträge zur Psychologie und Philosophie* (1905).

Measurements to Show the Relation in Frequency and Amplitude
of Inspirations to Ascending and Descending Portions
of the Galvanometer Wave

Nurse B. Series 1	Whistle	Weight falls	4 × 5	9 × 11	8 × 12	Where do you live?	What is the capital of Switzerland?	Are you married?	Threat of needle	Threat of fall of weight	Average
Average distance apart of inspirations in the ascending galvanometer curve	2.6	2.83	2.75	2.5	2.2	2.62	2.5	1.87	2.6	2.2	2.46
Average distance apart of inspirations in the descending galvanometer curve	2.18	2.36	2.5	2.14	2.42	2.2	2.3	2.42	2.5	2.3	2.33
Average height of inspirations with ascending galvanometer curve	15.8	15	14.5	14	12.8	11.25	12.5	13.6	16.4	14.6	14
Average height of inspirations with descending galvanometer curve	14.33	13.41	13.75	13	11	9.8	11.7	13	16.4	14.23	13

galvanometer curve, and also with the descending galvanometer curve. The amplitude of each inspiration was also measured and averaged for the same purpose, and the measurements are recorded in millimetres. It will be seen that the ascending portion of the galvanometer curve, which is the result of an emotional stimulus, is accompanied by fewer inspirations as well as by deeper ones. While this seemed to be a general rule in this instance, we find variations in different individuals with the same mixed series of stimuli, and in some cases the reverse. The stimuli in the tables were unpleasant rather than pleasant to the subject. But the determination of the quality of the emotional tone in any such experiment is very difficult. The forced and artificial situation of the subject in itself induces unpleasant feelings, and any pleasant stimulus must therefore simply bring about a certain relief or relaxation in a situation of unpleasant tension. The nervous tension during an experiment must naturally influence the breathing, and a pleasant stimulus is apt to produce only a temporary lessening of such tension. This is a criticism we would make of the Zoneff and Meumann experiments, and of experiments with the pneumograph in general. It is altogether probable that there are more inexplicable influences at work in relation to the pneumographic curve than we are at present able to comprehend. There are many respiratory fluctuations which have nothing to do with the emotions, but are the result of physical or intellectual processes, with the enforced quiet of body of the subject, with the disposition to speak, with tendencies to cough or to swallow, etc. Furthermore, there will be a difference in the curve if the stimulus occurs during an inspiration or an expiration, and there are individual variations dependent upon temperament or upon lability of the emotions.

1062   We have, therefore, not been greatly impressed with the value of a possible relation between the galvanometric and pneumographic curves since this is not constant, and the more comparative study we have given to the two synchronous curves, the more we have been impressed with a surprising divergence between the influences at work upon them. We have studied hundreds of waves in every conceivable manner. For instance, we have taken series of galvanometric curves and carefully measured the length of each inspiration, and the intervals between inspirations, as related to the point of stimulus, to the latent space before the ascent of the galvanometer wave, to the ascending curve, to the crest, to the descending curve, and to the space next to the point of stimulus, without developing any regular and constant relationship of correspondence, though we think this may ultimately be shown to exist in some degree. On the contrary, we have found thus far that the influences at work upon the two curves reveal an astonishing regularity of difference. When the emotions are very labile, and show the most marked excursions in the galvanometer curve, the respiratory curve is often regular and even (fig. 7). On the other hand, in instances both normal and pathological, where the galvanometer curve is marked by little fluctuation, or even by none, as in some cases of catatonia, there will often be most decided variations in the pneumographic curve. We often note a change

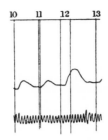

FIG. 7. Dr. P., normal good-sized galvanometer curves with fairly regular respiratory curve

in character in the pneumographic curve, not so much with each separate stimulus, but during the whole course of a series of stimuli as if expectant attention and nervous tension diminished the inspirations during the early part of the series, and as if there were a relaxation during the later half with longer inspirations (fig. 8). There does not seem to be the intimate and

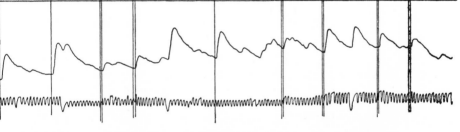

FIG. 8. Dr. S., a patient with paranoid dementia (Case No. 3). Extraordinarily labile emotions expressed in galvanometer curve. Considerable tension in pneumographic curve from stimulus 2 (fall of weight) on, with relaxation and deeper breathing beyond stimulus 7. An example of perseveration of tension for a long period in the pneumographic curve

deep relationship between the respiratory function and the unconscious emotions that exists between the sweat glandular system and these emotions. It is a matter of everyday experience that the respiration is influenced by our conscious emotions, especially when they are strong, as instanced in such expressions as "bated breath," "breathless with astonishment," etc. Such in-

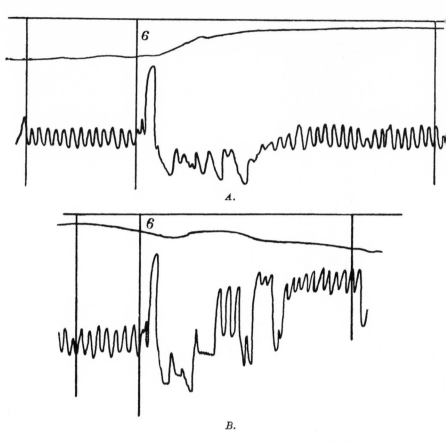

FIG. 9. J., acute catatonic stupor (Case No. 10). *A* is a wave selected from the series in which 6 is sudden call by name. The galvanometer curve is slight, but the change in the pneumographic curve is notable. *B* is the same stimulus in the repetition of the series. (Fig. 9 is reproduced actual size of the tracing)

hibitions of breathing are noticeable in many pneumographic curves, particularly in association with expectation and tension. But perhaps the emotions of the unconscious, roused up by questions or words that strike into the buried complexes of the soul, reveal themselves in the galvanometer curve, while the pneumographic curve is comparatively unaffected. Respiration is an instrument of consciousness. You can control it voluntarily while you cannot control the galvanometer curve. The respiratory innervation is closely associated with speech innervation, anatomically and functionally, and the physical connection in the brain is, perhaps, one of the closest and earliest. Let us take these remarkable curves of a case of acute catatonia (figs. 9A and 9B), which may be regarded as a psychological experiment in diverting both attention and ordinary emotion. Attention and all other emotions being practically diverted by the pathological process, the galvanometer curve is slight (indeed, in the *second* repetition it was a straight line), but the sudden call of the patient by name produced the extraordinary fluctuations in the respiratory curve, though nothing was apparent in his outward demeanour to show that he was conscious in any degree of the stimulus. He may have been conscious of the call, but we had no means of determining this. In the repetition the same fluctuations occurred, proving that they were not fortuitous. The only reasonable explanation of this phenomenon, in our opinion, is that the call of the name developed a disposition to speak, stimulated the hearing centre, and the closely-associated speech centre, the motor innervation from which acted upon the respiratory muscles. Ordinarily a sudden call by name, which is one of the strongest and deepest of stimuli, produces an answer. In this instance the call by name was a stimulus that acted as in a simple reflex process, and led to motor manifestations in the respiratory muscles connected with the motor speech centre, analogous to the contraction of the eyelids in response to a sudden flash of light. Fig. 10 is another instance of almost like character.

1063   While inconstancy of emotional variations in the respiratory curve and in correspondence with the galvanometer curve has been the rule in our findings thus far, we have learned that inhibitions, when they occur as an expression of expectant attention or of other emotions, are almost always shown in the expiratory curve and not in the inspiratory, which would accord with our idea that active, intellectual, emotional or conscious innervation is chiefly associated with inspiration, whereas expiration is rather a physical process or relaxation, prone to be inhibited, but not otherwise affected by the active respiratory nerves.

1064   In reiterating our opinion that the galvanometer curve is probably more intimately connected than the pneumographic curve with the subconscious emotional complexes, we would add that there is a greater tendency also to persistence in the pneumographic curve when emotion is expressed in it, for the

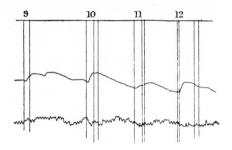

FIG. 10. Miss S., paranoid dementia (Case No. 2), stimuli 9, 10, 11, 12, correspond to numbers in the mixed series printed in the text. The noteworthy changes in the respiratory curve are due to her constant "disposition to speak." She did not speak except in answer to the questions given, but she apparently whispered most of the time between audible answers. Sometimes there was slight movement of the lips, when real whispering was not apparent

galvanometer curve subsides rather quickly with the fall of the emotion, while the pneumographic curve may show traces of conscious reminiscence of the emotional stimulus for a much longer time. The galvanometer is rather an index or measure of acute feeling-tone.

1065 Thus far, for the purposes of this study of the curves under normal conditions, we had made some forty series of curves in eight normal individuals, educated and uneducated. After this we made some thirty series of curves in eleven cases of dementia praecox of different types, viz.: Dementia paranoides three, hebephrenia two, and catatonia six cases (three chronic and three acute), and to these tests we will now turn our attention.

IV. The Galvanometric and Pneumographic Curves in Dementia Praecox

1066 Before recording the results of our experiments in dementia praecox it is necessary to say something of the psychology of the disorder. The chief characteristic in the mental condition of these patients is a peculiar disturbance of the emotions. In chronic conditions we have, as Kraepelin has clearly shown, an "emotional atrophy." In acute conditions there is a species of "inco-ordination" or "ataxia" between affectivity and concepts,

514

well demonstrated by Stransky.[16] The emotional disturbance has also been called "inadequate emotional tone." But these phrases represent rather the superficial impression that these patients make upon the physician. As soon as one examines the phenomena analytically and critically, the difficulty of attaining to a common point of view as regards all the morbid emotional symptoms is found to be extraordinary. We see at once that in most cases of dementia praecox none of the emotions is either changed or destroyed. We find, indeed, on closer analysis that many normal feelings are present. Cases with complete loss of emotion are exceptional. Elementary affects, such as fright, anxiety, pleasure, anger, embarrassment, shame, etc., are usually preserved. There is even at times an increased affectivity, or real nervous sensitiveness, present. Furthermore, in cases where one would expect more or less diminution of affectivity from their previous conduct and life, the elementary feelings are still maintained. The disorder is then shown in what Janet calls the *fonction du réel*[17] or the psychological adaptation to the environment. It is hardly to be expected that we should find characteristic disturbances in such patients by our experimental method (psychogalvanic), since they would lie in quantitative differences between the various feeling-tones. Even if there were qualitative changes, these would be too small for recognition.

1067   One of the chief factors in psychological adaptation to the environment is attention, which renders possible all the associations necessary to normal existence. In dementia praecox, especially the catatonic form, there are marked disorders of attention, which are shown by lack of power of voluntary concentration; or, otherwise expressed, objects do not excite in the diseased brain the affective reaction which alone permits an adequate selection of intellectual associations. This defective reaction to stimuli in the environment is the chief feature of dementia praecox. But this disorder is neither simple nor elementary; on the contrary, it is very complicated. What is its origin? There is in the psychology of dementia praecox still another characteristic that throws light upon the problem. By means

16 "Zur Kenntnis gewisser erworbener Blödsinnsformen" (1903); "Zur Auffassung gewisser Symptome der Dementia Praecox" (1904).
17 "Acting up to realities."

of word associations and subsequent analysis we find in these cases, among other abnormal manifestations, certain thought-complexes associated with strong emotional tone, one or several of which are fundamental complexes for the individual and embody as a rule the emotions or experiences that immediately preceded the development of the mental disorder. In suitable cases it is possible without much trouble to discover that the symptoms (delusions, hallucinations, insane ideas) stand in close relation to these psychological antecedents. They in fact, as Freud has shown, determine the symptoms. Freud applied his method particularly to hysteria, in which he found conscious or unconscious constellations, with strong affective tone, that may dominate the individual for years, or even the whole life through, by the force they exert upon associations. Such a morbid complex plays the part of an independent being, or soul within a soul, comparable to the ambitious vassal who by intrigue finally grew mightier than the king. This complex acts in a particular way upon the psyche. Janet has described it in an excellent manner in his book.[18] The complex robs the ego of light and nourishment, just as a cancer robs the body of its vitality. The sequelae of the complex are briefly as follows: Diminution of the entire psychic energy, weakening of the will, loss of objective interest and of power of concentration and of self-control, and the rise of morbid hysterical symptoms. These results can also manifest themselves in associations, so that in hysteria we find clear manifestations of emotional constellations among their associations. But this is not the only analogy between dementia praecox and hysteria. There are numerous others, which we cannot describe here in detail. One may, however, call attention to the large number of undoubted catatonic processes which were formerly called "degenerative hysterical psychoses." There are many cases, too, of dementia praecox which for years cannot be distinguished from hysteria. We call attention to the similarity of the two disorders here in order to show that our hypothesis of the relation between "psychological adaptation to environment" and an emotional complex is an established fact in the matter of hysteria. If we find in dementia praecox similar conditions, we are justified in assuming that here, too, the general disturb-

18 *Les Obsessions et la psychasthénie* (1903).

516

ances of mind may have a close causal relationship with an underlying complex. The complex is naturally not the only cause of dementia praecox, as little as it is of hysteria. Disposition is also a chief agency, and it is possible that in the disposition to dementia praecox affectivity brings about certain irreparable organic disturbances, as for instance metabolic toxins.

1068   The difference between dementia praecox and hysteria lies in certain irreparable sequelae and the more marked psychic disturbances in the former disorder. Profound general disturbances (delirium, severe emotional crises, etc.), exceptional in hysteria, are usual in dementia praecox. Hysteria is a caricature of the normal, and therefore shows distinct reactions to the stimuli of the environment. In dementia praecox, on the other hand, there is always defective reaction to external stimuli. There are characteristic differences in relation to the complex. In hysteria the complex may with very little trouble be revealed by analysis, and with a good prospect of therapeutic advantage in the procedure. But with dementia praecox there is no possibility of its being thus influenced. Even if, as is sometimes possible, the complex may be forced to reproduction, there is as a rule no therapeutic result. In dementia praecox the complex is more independent and more strongly detached, and the patient more profoundly injured by the complex than is the case in hysteria. For this reason the skilled physician is able to affect by suggestion acute hysterical states, which are nothing but irradiations from an excited complex, while he fails in dementia praecox where the inner psychic excitement is so much stronger than the stimuli from the environment. This is also the reason why patients in the early stages of dementia possess neither power of critical correction nor insight, which never fail in hysteria even in the severest forms.[19]

1069   Convalescence in hysteria is characterized by gradual weakening of the complex till it vanishes entirely. The same is true in the remissions of dementia praecox, though here there is always some vestige of irreparable injury, which, even if unimportant, may still be revealed by study of the associations.

1070   It is often astonishing how even the severest symptoms of dementia praecox may suddenly vanish. This is readily understood from our assumption that the acute conditions of both

19 Raimann, *Die hysterischen Geistesstörungen* (1904).

hysteria and dementia praecox are the results of irradiations from the complex, which for the time conceal the normal functions that are still present. For example, some strong emotion may throw a hysterical person into a condition of apathy or delirium, which may disappear the next moment through the action of some psychological stimulus. In like manner stuporous conditions may come and go quite suddenly in dementia praecox. While such patients are under the spell of the excited complex, they are for the time completely cut off from the outside world, and neither perceive external stimuli nor react to them. When the excitement of the complex has subsided, the power of reaction to the environment gradually returns, first for elementary and later for more complicated psychological stimulation.

1071 Since, according to our hypothesis, dementia praecox can be localized in some dominating psychological complex, it is to be expected that all elementary emotional reactions will be fully preserved, so long as the patient is not completely in the control of the complex. We may, therefore, expect to find in all patients with dementia praecox who show psychological adaptation in elementary matters (eating, drinking, sleeping, dressing, speaking, mechanical occupation, etc.) the presence of some adequate emotional tone. But in all cases where such psychological adaptation fails, external stimuli will produce no reaction in the disordered brain, and even elementary emotional phenomena will fail to become manifest, because the entire psychic activity is bound up with the morbid complex. That this is an actual fact is shown in the results of our experiments.

1072 The following is a brief *résumé* in each case of the features that are of interest for us here:

(1) H., male, aged 43, teacher of languages. First insane ten years ago. Well educated and intelligent. Entered an asylum for a time in 1896. Passed through a light period of catatonia with refusal of food, bizarre demeanour, and auditory hallucinations. Later constant persecutory ideas. In August 1906, he murdered one of his supposed persecutors, and since then has been in this asylum. Very precise and correct in his dress and conduct, industrious, independent, but extremely suspicious. Hallucinations not discoverable. Diagnosis—*Dementia paranoides.*

(2) Miss S., aged 61, dressmaker. Became insane about 1885. In-

numerable bizarre delusions, delusions of grandeur, hallucinations of all the senses, neologisms, motor and language stereotypy. Conduct orderly, neat, industrious, but rather querulous. Is on parole and shows considerable independent activity. Diagnosis—*Dementia paranoides.*[20]

(3) Dr. S., male, aged 35, chemist. Became insane about 1897. Very intelligent and reads numerous scientific books. Has many wants and makes many complaints. Extremely careful in dress, and is extraordinarily neat. Numerous grandiose ideas and hallucinations. No catatonic symptoms. Diagnosis—*Dementia paranoides.*

(4) Mrs. H. O., aged 44, farmer's wife. Became insane in 1904 with an attack of hebephrenic depression. Since the end of 1906, in a second attack of similar character. Speaks only in whispers. Somewhat inhibited, anxious, and hears very unpleasant voices. Works industriously and spontaneously. Neat in dress and in care of her room. Diagnosis—*Hebephrenic depression.*

(5) Mrs. E. S., aged 43, merchant's wife. Became insane in 1901. Occasionally light maniacal excitement, never confusion at first, but rapid dementia. Now greatly demented, inactive, and vexes other patients. Unemotional, indifferent, and untidy in dress. Without interest in her husband or surroundings. Chatters a great deal, but quite superficially, and it is impossible in any way to arouse in her any of the deeper emotions. Diagnosis—*Hebephrenia.*

(6) A. V. D., male, aged 39. Entered the asylum in 1897. From the beginning quiet, unemotional, somewhat timid and anxious. Speech fragmentary and indistinct, and most of the time talks to himself. Makes meaningless gestures with the hands. Has to be cared for by the attendant in all matters. Cannot work. Shows neither homesickness nor desire for freedom. Automatism on command and at times catalepsy. Diagnosis—*Chronic catatonic stupor.*

(7) Sp., male, aged 62, factory worker. Became insane in 1865. In the early stages several attacks of catatonic excitement. Later chronic stupor with occasional raptus. In one attack of raptus tore out one of his testicles with his hand. At another time suddenly kissed the attendant. During a severe physical illness at one time he suddenly became quite clear and approachable. Speaks only spontaneously and at long intervals. Works only mechanically when he is led to it. Stereotyped gestures. Diagnosis—*Chronic catatonic stupor.*

[20] [This is probably the case that Jung dealt with in detail in "The Psychology of Dementia Praecox" (1907). See especially par. 198 and pars. 364–84 in *Coll. Works*, vol. 3; also *Memories, Dreams, Reflections*, pp. 125–28 (both edns.).]

(8) F., male, aged 50. Became insane in 1881. At first, for a long period, depressed inhibition. Later, mutism, with occasional outbursts of abusive language on account of voices and numerous hallucinations. At present constant hallucination, though he is quiet, speaking only when addressed, and then in a low, fragmentary manner. Occasionally outbreaks of abuse because of the voices. Works mechanically, and is stupid and docile. Diagnosis—*Chronic catatonia.*

(9) J. S., male, aged 21. Became insane in 1902. Stupid, stubborn, negativistic, speaks spontaneously not at all or very seldom, quite apathetic and without affectivity, sits the whole day in one place, wholly disorderly in dress. Once in a while demands release with some irritation. Diagnosis—*Mild catatonic stupor.*

(10) J., male, aged 21, student of philosophy and very intelligent. Became insane about 1901, when he had a short attack. The second attack came in December last (1906). At times excited, wholly confused, and strikes about him. Incessant hallucinations. Wholly wrapped up in his inner mental processes. In occasional intervals of some lucidity, the patient states quite spontaneously that he has no feeling at all, that he cannot be either glad or unhappy, that everything to him seems wholly indifferent. Diagnosis—*Acute catatonic stupor with raptus.*

(11) M., male, aged 26, merchant. Became insane in 1902. At first maniacal excitement. Later dull apathy and occasional exhibition. Then gradually increasing stupor, with complete detachment. Now mutacismus, and tears out his beard, but at other times rigid and cataleptic. Diagnosis—*Acute catatonic stupor.*

1073   The galvanometer curves in many of the tests with dementia praecox were extraordinary. As in normal individuals we found, where there was reaction at all, a gradual exhaustion of the power of the stimulus in repetitions of the same series, so that the waves became smaller in the second, and still smaller and more rounded in the third series. In some cases, where the waves were small in the first series, they disappeared altogether in the third. In fig. 8 we have a good example of a very labile galvanometer curve from a case of dementia paranoides, in which we have abrupt and high ascents, at times with large bifurcations. This was the second series of this patient, and the curves are smaller than in the first. They may be compared with the labile normal curve of fig. 6, which was the first series; and also with fig. 10, another case of paranoid dementia, but in which the galvanometer wave is rather unemotional, while the pneumographic curve shows in this instance such marked changes owing to the disposition to whisper. The type of galvanometer curve, shown in fig. 8, is also characteristic of curves we have taken in hysteria.

1074   In the hebephrenic type there is nothing especially noteworthy in the curve, either in respect of great lability or smallness of wave. In the catatonic forms of dementia praecox, especially in the acute forms, however, we observed extraordinary variations from the normal in the character of the curve. Not only is the latent time longer, but the waves are almost always of gradual ascent, and very small if present at all. Figs. 9A and 9B, from a case of acute catatonic stupor, present illustrations of curves brought about by the sudden calling of the name. The galvanometer curve is exceedingly slight, but the pneumographic curve shows the singular changes previously mentioned. In fig. 11 (p. 522) we show three galvanometer curves. The upper one is from a normal person, with the series printed in the text. The middle one is that of a case of chronic catatonic stupor (Sp.), which is characterized by almost no reaction to any stimuli until 14 is reached, when the threat of pricking with a needle (and the actual prick where the line crosses the up wave) produced a great rise in the curve. A slighter rise occurred at 15, the threat to let the weight fall. This is an example of reaction to an elementary emotion in a chronic case where some emotional tone is still present. The lowest line in fig. 11 represents the galvanometer curve of an acute case of catatonic stupor (J.), and here it is seen that the line is perfectly straight, that not one of the mixed series of stimuli printed in the text had the slightest effect; whistle, dropping of the weight with a loud noise, sudden loud call by name, actual hard pricks with the needle—nothing brought out a response in the galvanometer. The pneumograph could not be applied in this case. Our experience with the six cases of catatonia is that such curves are characteristic for the type, and bear out our idea of the psychology of the disease as recorded above.

1075   Another feature of importance in these cases is the matter of latent time. It will be remembered that latent time, before the rise of the galvanometer wave, was estimated by us to vary in normal persons between two and five seconds. In fact, the norm is three seconds for first series, and 3.77 seconds for subsequent series. In the following tables, one relating to latent

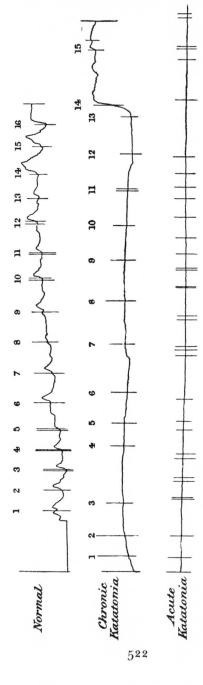

FIG. 11. Three galvanometer curves for contrast. The first curve is a normal one, with series of mixed stimuli (Miss B., a Canadian). The second curve is that of Sp. (Case No. 7), one of chronic catatonic stupor. Note presence of elementary emotion at stimulus 15. The third curve is that of J. (Case No. 10, acute catatonic stupor). No change whatever in the galvanometer curve to any of the mixed stimuli

space on the kymograph, and the other to latent time, only seven of the eleven cases of dementia praecox appear, for in the others the waves were so slightly marked or so uncertain that the facts could not be satisfactorily determined. One of these patients (Dr. S.) was tested with both the mixed series and a series of word associations.

Latent Time in Millimetres of Distance from Stimulus to Beginning of Ascent of Galvanometer Emotional Wave in Cases of Insanity

NAMES AND DIAGNOSIS	Miss S. Dementia paranoides	Dr. S. Dementia paranoides	Dr. S. Word association	Sp. Chronic catatonia	A. V. D. Chronic catatonia	F. Chronic catatonia	J. Acute catatonia	M. Acute catatonia
Series I	3.13	3.75	4.01	3.2	2	4.77	7.16	24.25
Series II	2.66	3.87	5.81		5	5.5	17.3	
Series III	3.93	4.22						
Series IV		5.46						

Latent Time in the Same Cases of Insanity as Above Estimated in Seconds

NAMES AND DIAGNOSIS	Miss S. Dementia paranoides	Dr. S. Dementia paranoides	Dr. S. Word association	Sp. Chronic catatonia	A. V. D. Chronic catatonia	F. Chronic catatonia	J. Acute catatonia	M. Acute catatonia
Series I, mixed stimuli	3.47	4.16	4.45	3.55	2.22	5.3	7.95	26.94
Series II	2.93	4.3	6.45		5.55	6.11	19.22	
Series III	4.36	4.68						
Series IV		6.06						

1076   In the first case, a woman with dementia paranoides, the latent time is within normal limits. In the second case, also dementia paranoides, Dr. S., the normal was overstepped only in the fourth round of the same mixed series, but, with the same patient using word association, the latent time was excessive (6.45) in the first repetition of the same words. In the third case (Sp.), a case of chronic catatonia, the first series showed a latent time of 3.55 seconds, but there were no waves whatever in the repetitions. The four succeeding patients, all cases of catatonia, show increase of latent time, and the two acute cases of catatonia present an astonishing interval of space and time between the stimulus and the galvanometer wave.

1077   The following table will better show the differences in latent time between the normal and cases of dementia praecox, especially in the averages given at the end of the table.

Comparative Table Showing Latent Time in Galvanometer Curve of Normal Cases and of Dementia Praecox

										Average	Average of distribution
Normal	Series I	2.28	2.05	3.5	4.5	3.27	2.51			3.01	.73
	Series II and III	2.83	1.95	4.88	5	4.44	3.94	2.57	4.6	3.77	.99
Dementia Praecox	Series I	3.47	4.16	4.45	3.55	2.22	5.3	7.95	26.94	7.25	5.09
	Series II and III	2.93	4.3	6.45	5.55	6.11	19.22	4.36	4.68	6.70	3.13

1078   The average of distribution is obtained by subtracting the ordinary average from the larger numbers in the series, or the smaller numbers from the average. The sum of these differences is divided by the number of items, which gives what is called the average of distribution or the average of differences —a useful method of showing wide fluctuations in pathological conditions.

V. Association Experiments

1079   Galton, Wundt, Kraepelin, Aschaffenburg, Sommer, and others have introduced into psychology a very simple experiment in which a word is called out to the subject, who must respond as quickly as possible with the first word that occurs to him. The reaction-time between the stimulus-word and the response can be measured with a one-fifth-second stop-watch. It was originally expected that this method would reveal certain intellectual differences in various individuals. But from the results of investigations carried out in the Psychiatric Clinic at Zurich, it has been found that it is not intellectual factors but the emotions that play the chief part in determining these associations. Two persons, of the same social class, one intelligent, the other unintelligent, even with differences in the character of their intellectual development, may still produce similar associations, because language itself has many general word connections which are familiar to all sorts of individuals belonging to the same circle of society.

1080   There are certain well-marked differences between the word associations of educated and uneducated persons. For instance, the uneducated prefer inner connections with deeper meaning, while the educated very often select simply superficial and linguistic associations. As has been ascertained at the Zurich Clinic, this difference depends upon the fact that the uneducated fix their attention more closely than the educated upon the actual meaning of the stimulus word. But attention, as has been shown by Bleuler, is nothing more than an emotional process. All affective processes are more or less clearly connected with physical manifestations, which are also to be observed in conjunction with attention. It is therefore to be expected that the attention roused by every association should have an influence upon the galvanometer curve, though this is but one of the affective factors represented in an association experiment.

1081   We observe, as a rule, considerable variation in reaction-time, even with quick and practised subjects. One is inclined to explain such irregularities, which are apparently accidental, by supposing that the stimulus-word is unusual and difficult or that the attention is momentarily relaxed for some reason or another. Such may at times be the case, but these reasons are not sufficient to explain the frequent repetition and long duration of certain reaction-times. There must be some constant and regular rule to account for them. This disturbing factor has been found at the Zurich Clinic to be in most cases some characteristic thought-complex of intrinsic importance for the personality of the subject. The following series will illustrate our meaning:

Stimulus-word	Reaction-word	Reaction-time
head	hair	1.4
green	meadow	1.6
water	*deep*	*5*
stick	knife	1.6
long	table	1.2
ship	*sink*	*3.4*
ask	answer	1.6
wool	knit	1.6
spiteful	friendly	1.4
lake	*water*	*4*
sick	well	1.8
ink	black	1.2
swim	*can swim*	*3.8*

1082   The four italicized numbers are abnormally long reaction-times. The stimulus-words are quite ordinary, are not difficult, and are such as commonly carry numerous current connections. By questioning the patient, we learn that recently, when greatly depressed, he had determined to commit suicide by drowning. *Water, lake, ship, swim* were words that excited this complex. The complex brought about lengthening of the reaction-time. This phenomenon is quite usual, and is to be observed constantly and everywhere in association studies. Lengthened reaction-time may therefore be regarded as a complex indicator, and be employed for the selection from a series of associations of such as have a personal significance to the individual. It is self-evident that associations of this kind are apt to be accompanied by lively emotional tone. The explanation would be simple if the subject were always conscious of the complex which had been excited. But it is extraordinarily common for the subject to be unconscious of the complex disturbed by the stimulus-word, and to be unable to answer questions relating to it. It is then necessary to employ the psychoanalytic method, which Freud uses for the investigation of dreams and hysteria. It would carry us too far to describe here the details of this method of analysis, and readers must be referred to Freud's *The Interpretation of Dreams.*

526

083   The cause of the interference with the reaction must be sought for in the strong emotional tone of the complex. Individuals with good powers of introspection often affirm that they could not respond quickly, because of the sudden crowding into consciousness of a number of words among which they could find none suitable for the reaction. This is easily understood, for strong affects always collect numerous associations around them, and, on the other hand, an assemblage of associations is always accompanied by an intense emotional tone. In some cases we have an opposite condition from the above, and the subjects are not able to react because of a vacuum in consciousness, in which event the complex hinders reaction by simply not appearing in consciousness. Thus the underlying thought-complex sometimes carries too much into consciousness, and at other times too little, in either case disturbing the uniform flow of psychic functions. It acts like a peace-breaker in the psychic hierarchy. Such being the behaviour of the complex under normal conditions, it is easy to understand how it may play the chief part in abnormal mental states based upon disordered affectivity.

084   Lengthened reaction-time is not the only index of a complex. If the stimulus-word causes a sudden embarrassment and brings out some striking and unusual reaction-word, it is certain that a complex has been struck, so that any reaction out of the ordinary may also be regarded as indicating the presence of an emotional thought-complex.

085   It is not infrequent to observe a lengthened or disturbed reaction also in the second reaction after some critical stimulus-word, so that we have a persistence of the affect to the next following reaction, a fact which also may be taken to indicate the existence of a complex.

086   And, finally, we have in the method of reproduction another excellent aid for the discovery of the complex. When the series of stimulus-words has been finished, the list is gone over again, and the subject is simply asked to repeat the word he had given before in response to the stimulus. We then notice that where stimulus-words touched upon a complex, the memory plays false and the subject tends to react with some other word than the one first given. This paradoxical phenomenon depends altogether upon the influence of a strong emotional

tone. The complexes are often unpleasant and create a natural resistance in the individual; but they are not always unpleasant or painful, and even with such complexes as the subject would be perfectly willing to reveal, there is yet an inhibition present which shows itself in like manner. The cause of defective reproduction must lie in the general nature of the complex as already described, in a certain independence of the complex, which comes and goes according to factors peculiar to it, and not at the behest of consciousness, and which yields the self-generated associations, and not such as are sought by consciousness. We—that is, our conscious selves—are on the whole in a sense the resultants of competitions in the unconscious.

1087   It is thus that affective factors present themselves everywhere in our associations; and it is of interest to ascertain whether the psychogalvanic reflex runs a parallel course with the complex indices just described; whether it does so regularly or has a preference for certain constellations; whether differences exist when a complex is conscious or unconscious, etc.

1088   Wherever possible, we have employed the pneumograph at the same time with the galvanometer in these association studies to determine whether parallel disturbances were present.

1089   The association question is many-sided, and there are numerous methods by which to study it. We shall try in the following pages to present our method and to confine ourselves more especially to our method of investigation, rather than to bring forward too prominently results which, owing to the small number of individuals examined, are valuable as case material but cannot be looked upon as having general application.

1. The Results Obtained with Association Tests

1090   (1) When the experiment is ended we measure the heights of the galvanometric curves and arrange them in a table, with other results of the tests. As the table shows, we made one repetition of the experiment in this instance; in other cases two repetitions were made.

1091   (2) We then determine the arithmetical average of the galvanometric deviations, which in this instance is 4.9 mm. These figures are naturally only relative and, with our apparatus, cor-

Case 1.—*Uneducated man, aged 40, normal, two series of word associations, each twenty-four words (Nine words given as example)*

	SERIES I				SERIES II		
No.	Height of galv. curve in mm.	Reaction-time one-fifth sec.	Association	Reproduction	Height of galv. curve in mm.	Reaction-time one-fifth sec.	Reaction
1	9	9	table/chair	ditto	7	7	ditto
2	4	9	sit/on a chair	ditto	3	15	ditto
3	4	11	garden/vegetable	ditto	3	6	ditto
4	3	14	red/apple	ditto	4	5	ditto
5	3	9	write/with pencil	ditto	4	7	ditto
6	6	40	full (no reaction)		2	6	cask
7	3	8	good/sugar		9	9	apple
8	6	6	forest/wood	ditto	4	5	ditto
9	5	10	tavern/drink	ditto	2	5	ditto

respond to only one-half of the actual movement of the mirror of the galvanometer. (The actual figure would be 9.8 mm.)

092   (3) We then determine the probable average (Kraepelin) of the reaction-times in the following manner: The figures are arranged in a column in the order of their size, and the middle number is taken, which in this instance is 1.8 seconds. The probable is here preferred to the arithmetical average, because occasionally very high numbers occur in such tests, where the reaction-times are much more liable to increase than to diminish. An arithmetical average would be unduly influenced by the occasional presence of one or more large numbers, and would not give us the actual average of the reaction-time.

093   (4) In the second series the average of the galvanometer deviations was 4.8 mm., and that of the reaction-times 1.2 seconds. We observe, therefore, a reduction in the average height of the galvanometer curve, which is clearly due to lessening of the power of the stimulus in the repetition. The same phenomenon is also seen in the average of the reaction-times, which is shortened. The fact that every reaction is accompanied by a galvanometer movement is due to the emotion of attention

which accompanies each reaction and is great enough to produce notable physical changes.

1094   (5) We note that in the second series certain associations (the sixth and seventh) are repeated with a change of words. These defective or changed reproductions indicate that the psychological constellation for the respective associations had changed in the short time (a little over one-half hour) that had elapsed since the first series had been given. We know that associations which belong to certain complexes are those that may, because of inner conditions, suffer change within a short period of time. We may, therefore, expect that such false reproductions carry with them particular emotional phenomena; and this is actually the case here. The arithmetical average of the altered reproductions is 5.7 mm., while in the first series the average for the same associations was 4.5 mm. Furthermore, the altered reproductions in the second series show an excess of some 0.8 mm. over the average of the stimulation of the first series. The average of the reaction-times for the altered reproductions is 1.2 seconds, and for the correct reproduction 1 second, as would be expected. We learn from this that the supposition that the altered reproductions are affective phenomena would seem to be justified. We will not here enter into details in relation to the psychoanalysis of such manifestations, as we do not wish to forestall an especially careful study of this question now being made in this clinic by Binswanger.[21]

1095   (6) From the above consideration one would also expect that those associations which are changed in the repetition should also present some sort of affective signs in the first series; but, contrary to our expectation, we see in this case that the average height of the galvanometer deviation for the words subsequently changed in repetition is 4.8 mm., while the average for the unaltered reproductions is 5 mm. This difference is, of course, small, and no particular deduction could be drawn from one case. It is to be noted that the average reaction-time for the associations subsequently wrongly reproduced is 1.9 seconds, and for the words correctly reproduced 1.8 seconds. Perhaps there is here a slight indication of the phenomenon to which we refer.

21 [See n. 6, supra.]

096   (7) In the preceding paragraphs we have frequently inti-
mated that there is a certain connection between affectivity and
the length of reaction-time, and this has been already carefully
determined in the work of one of us.[22] One may expect to have,
as a rule, large galvanometer curves with long reaction-times,
always, however, with the limitation that only such lengthened
reaction-times are considered as are connected with associations that directly excite complexes, and not the long reaction-times which may follow immediately after reactions
that excite complexes. These latter are frequent and are examples of perseveration. In order to discover the actual com-
plex-exciting association it is necessary to employ the psychoanalytic method, and for this purpose a more suitable material
is needed than is at our disposition. We, therefore, content ourselves here with simply determining the average height of all
galvanometer curves in relation to reaction-times which lie
respectively above and below the probable average.

097   In Series I, the average of galvanometer curves connected
with long reaction-times is 4.5 mm., and with short reaction-
times 6.1 mm.

098   In Series II, the galvanometer curves with long reaction-
times average 5.7 mm., and with short reaction-times 4.4 mm.

099   The two results are contradictory. The cause of this lies
in factors already alluded to and in other difficulties which
must be the subject of later study.

100   (8) The alteration of the psychological constellation of
Series II already mentioned may be manifested in the galvanometer curve alone, without any change in the reproductions.
This matter might be thus explained. In the first trial only
certain meanings are attached to the stimulus-word by the
subject; i.e., not all of the associations belonging to it are
excited at the first trial, while at the second trial another series
of new connections may be aroused. We very often meet this
phenomenon in our psychoanalytic investigations.

101   It is of the greatest importance for the study of intellectual
processes in the individual to know how his associations are
presented to consciousness, whether he has quick and complete

22 "The Psychology of Dementia Praecox"; "Experimental Observations on the
Faculty of Memory" (supra); and other works on the association test.

command of all related associations. This point is of the utmost value for testing intelligence, since many persons may appear to be stupid during investigation because their associations are not at immediate command, and on the other hand stupid persons may seem to be relatively intelligent simply because they have good command of their associations. We may perhaps also expect to discover important differences between educated and uneducated intellects; the galvanometric experiments seem to open to us endless vistas.

1102   In this case 41.6 per cent of the associations in Series II show an increased galvanometric curve with an average plus difference of 2.3 mm. It is possible that later investigations may show us that this result has considerable psychological significance for the individual, because this subject was quite unintelligent.

1103   (9) After a marked galvanometric deviation we frequently observe that there is an inclination to successive large curves, if the succeeding stimuli are not too quickly given. This is not unexpected because it is a general psychological experience that strong affects induce great sensitiveness. If therefore we take the average of the curves which follow unusually strong galvanometer curves and compare them with the arithmetical average of all the curves, we find that after unusually high curves, the average height in Series I is 5 mm. and the reaction-time two seconds in contrast with the general averages of 4.9 mm. and 1.8 seconds. In Series II these figures are reversed, for here the average has a difference of plus 0.6 mm. while the average of the reaction-times shows a difference of minus 0.5 seconds. The relations are not quite definite.

1104   (10) The whole of Series I shows a rather uniform course, for the average of distribution amounts only to 1.6. The deviations are relatively not very high. The highest curve is 12 mm., and the association connected with it is *stupid / am I*, which was for this individual a clear egocentric stimulus which evidently struck a strong emotional complex.

1105   Fig. 12 is a portion of the curve in this case. In this, one notes the even course and uniform emotional value of each association. The accompanying pneumographic curve is undisturbed.

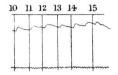

FIG. 12. Portion of curve in word association of a normal subject

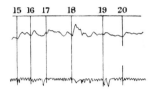

FIG. 13. Portion of curve corresponding to the association *stupid / am I*

106   Fig. 13 shows the portion of the curve in which the association *stupid / am I* (reaction No. 18) occurred. This portion is marked by a very high many-pointed wave. The pneumographic curve is altered here, as it is also in reaction No. 19, though the latter has little emotional tone. But No. 19 has, however, a very long reaction-time (4.8 secs.), which is to be looked upon as a persisting intellectual disturbance from reaction No. 18. We observe here one of the numerous instances where the pneumographic curve and the reaction-time show evident disturbances, while the galvanic curve is unaffected. According to our hypothesis, this is owing to the fact that the galvanometer indicates only acute affective conditions, and not the more lasting intellectual after-effects, these latter being often well registered by reaction-time and pneumograph. The reaction-time shows how long the mind requires to detach itself from its conscious or unconscious preoccupation, and turn to the new stimulus. The respiration, because of its close relation to consciousness (susceptibility to voluntary influences), is also affected by intellectual processes, while the galvanometer seems to be influenced directly only by the unconscious.

Case 2.—*Uneducated but rather intelligent man, aged 38*

1107   (1) We have arranged in the following table the results of three series of associations of twenty-four words each:

Series I	Arithmetical average of galvanometer curves	5.6 mm.
Series II	Arithmetical average of galvanometer curves	7.2 mm.
Series III	Arithmetical average of galvanometer curves	5.9 mm.
Series I	Probable average of reaction-times	1.8 sec.
Series II	Probable average of reaction-times	1.3 sec.
Series III	Probable average of reaction-times	1.0 sec.

1108   The reaction-times are what we expect, but the galvanic curves show an unexpected increase in the second series. Our first supposition would be that this is owing to some physical change; for instance, better contact from increased warmth of the hands, or a change of posture of the body that increased the pressure of the hands upon the electrodes. Such conditions may not only interfere with the experiment, but also render comparison of results difficult. But it is also possible that the psychological constellation changed in the second series, causing thereby greater deviation of the galvanometer. If we take the first fifteen curves of Series II, we find the average to be 4.7 mm., which is much less than the average of Series I. But if we take the last nine curves of Series II, we find the average to be 11.3 mm., and that the cause of the great difference lies where the principle of loss of power in repeated stimulation does not seem to be effective. It is possible that after the fifteenth reaction there was a physical disturbance, which increased the height of the curves.

1109   We find that the probable average of the reaction-times of the first fifteen and last nine reactions both amount to 1.8 seconds, while the average of the galvanometer curves of the first fifteen reactions shows only a difference of minus 0.2 mm., as compared with the last nine curves. Now, if a physical change occurred toward the end of Series II, we might expect no change in the purely psychological reaction-times. This is, however, not the case. For the increased galvanic curves in the last nine reactions correspond to an increase of the reaction-times (1.4 seconds, as compared to 1 second of the first fifteen reactions). There is, therefore, a parallel between the galvanometer increase and the increased reaction-times, from which we

534

may conclude that the increase depends upon an altered psychological constellation.

1110   We have already mentioned that a change in the constellation is due to the arousing of complexes. The reactions occur in this wise:

No.	Associations	SERIES I			SERIES II	
		Reaction-time	Gal. curve	Reproduction	Reaction-time	Gal. curve
1	money/round	1.8 sec.	3 mm.	ditto	1.2 sec.	12 mm.
2	high/tree	1.4 sec.	7 mm.	ditto	1.4 sec.	4 mm.
3	go out/morning	2.0 sec.	8 mm.	ditto	1.4 sec.	6 mm.
4	floor/dirty	1.8 sec.	5 mm.	ditto	1.8 sec.	9 mm.
5	wages/large	1.2 sec.	6 mm.	ditto	1.2 sec.	19 mm.
6	pay/debts	3.4 sec.	9 mm.	ditto	3.0 sec.	15 mm.
7	apple/red	2.4 sec.	5 mm.	ditto	1.4 sec.	27 mm.
8	nurses/many	1.6 sec.	4 mm.	ditto	1.8 sec.	5 mm.
9	five/small	1.8 sec.	5 mm.	ditto	1.2 sec.	5 mm.

1111   While as a rule the reaction-times are shortened in Series II, the galvanometer curves are higher. It seems as if the affects first really manifested themselves in Series II after having been inhibited in Series I. As is shown, the largest increases are connected with the associations *money / round, floor / dirty, wages / large* (the subject is an attendant or nurse and receives small wages), *pay / debts, apple / red,* and *nurses / many.* It is easy to understand that five of these associations might arouse strong sentiments. The strong reaction with *apple / red* is incomprehensible. But we have frequently noticed that quite indifferent associations following immediately upon strong emotional associations show in repetition sudden increase of galvanic reaction, as if the emotional tone were postponed. It is possible that we have such a phenomenon here, but we have no means of proving it. Affects are always inhibited if some other strong emotional complex displaces them. This was evidently the case here, because the unusual experiment excited the subject, so that he probably did not grasp the stimulus-words in all their personal relations. In Series II he was quieter and could comprehend better, in consequence of which emotional tones were more easily developed than before. This phenomenon is theoretically very important, since it indicates how affects are repressed in normal persons. Inhibition of affects plays a powerful role in psychopathology. (See the works of Freud, Bleuler, and Jung.)

1112 This experiment also illustrates well that reaction-time and galvanometer curve do not mean the same thing. We see here again how clearly the reaction-time reveals a greater intellectual freedom than in Series II, whereas the galvanometer curves are considerably higher than those of Series I.

	Galv. Curve	Reaction-time
(2) The altered reproductions of Series II average	6 mm.	1.7 sec.
The altered reproductions of Series III average	7 mm.	1.0 sec.
The unchanged reproductions of Series II average	7.3 mm.	1.3 sec.
The unchanged reproductions of Series III average	5.8 mm.	1.3 sec.

1113 Here, too, the relations are somewhat obscure, which may be owing to the occurrence of very few altered reproductions. Only half of the above numbers coincide with our expectations.

(3) Galvanometer curves with long reaction-times average in Series I	6.4 mm.
Galvanometer curves with short reaction-times average in Series I	6.4 mm.
Galvanometer curves with long reaction-times average in Series II	8.1 mm.
Galvanometer curves with short reaction-times average in Series II	4.2 mm.
Galvanometer curves with long reaction-times average in Series III	6.8 mm.
Galvanometer curves with short reaction-times average in Series III	4.1 mm.

1114 The first test is undecided, but the two following present figures which correspond with our expectation. (In Case 1 above recorded the first test also gave a contradictory result.)

1115 (4) In Series II, 41.6 per cent of the associations show an average difference of plus 3.2 mm. compared with Series I. In Series III, 45.8 per cent of the associations show a difference of plus 2.6 mm. as compared with Series II.

1116   These figures prove, as already mentioned, that Series II presents a considerably altered constellation. In Series III there are still more psychological constellations changed. It is to be regretted that there was not a much larger material at hand for the further investigation of matters so important for the psychology of the individual.

(5) Series I.   Probable average of reaction-times in associations with unusually high galvanometer curves   2.2 sec.

Series I.   Arithmetical average of the corresponding galvanometer curves   5.2 mm.

Series II.   Probable average of reaction-times in associations with unusually high galvanometer curves   1.6 sec.

Series II.   Arithmetical average of the corresponding galvanometer curves   12.0 mm.

Series III.   Probable average of reaction-times in associations with unusually high galvanometer curves   0.8 sec.

Series III.   Arithmetical average of corresponding galvanometer curves   7.0 mm.

1117   The curves in Series II and III do not, while those of Series I do, correspond to expectation. The reaction times in Series I and II are what we anticipate. Therefore, of six items, four coincide with our expectation.

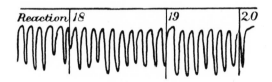

FIG. 14. Portion of pneumographic curve in Case 2 (word association, normal individual)

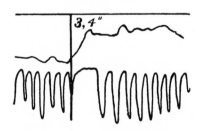

FIG. 15. Galvanic and pneumographic curve corresponding to the word association *pay/debts*. (Figs. 14 and 15 are reproduced the actual size of the tracing)

537

1118   (6) Series I. Presents in general a uniform character. The average of distribution is only 1.5 mm. The highest curve measures 9 mm., and this is connected with the association *pay / debts*, which, as we have seen, also preserves its high emotional value in Series II.

1119   Series II is much more irregular. The average of distribution is 3.8 mm., a very high figure, which well illustrates the general irregularity of the series. The highest curves of this series have already been described.

1120   Series III presents, on the other hand, another series with uniform character. The average of distribution is only 1.8 mm. The highest curve occurs with the association *wages / large*, and amounts to 11 mm., and in Series II it also had a high value. Such concord shows clearly that these figures are not accidental.

1121   The pneumographic curve presents no peculiarities. In Series I, with indifferent associations, this curve has the aspect shown in fig. 14.

1122   Fig. 15 is the galvanometric and pneumographic curve belonging to the association *pay / debts*. In this we observe a marked inhibition of respiration during and after the critical association.

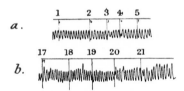

FIG. 16. (*a*) Respiratory curve, with word associations No. 1 to 5 in Case 2. (*b*) Curve, same case, associations No. 17 to 21

1123   The psychic excitation referred to previously in the last nine associations of Series II seems to manifest itself also in the pneumographic curve, as apparently evidenced in figs. 16(*a*) and 16(*b*).

1124   Fig. 16(*a*) is a portion of the respiratory curve during associations 1 to 5. Fig. 16(*b*) represents associations 17 to 21. The difference is marked. We can hardly be mistaken in supposing that the change in respiration is the expression of a certain excitation, which is in harmony with our previous assumptions.

Case 3.—Uneducated man of moderate intelligence, aged 28, lively, excitable temperament. Normal. Three series of associations, each with twenty-three words

1125   (1) Series I.   Arithmetical average of

galvanometer curves	14.2 mm.
Series II. Arithmetical average of galvanometer curves	6.5 mm.
Series III. Arithmetical average of galvanometer curves	2.0 mm.
Series I. Probable average of reaction-times	2.4 sec.
Series II. Probable average of reaction-times	2.2 sec.
Series III. Probable average of reaction-times	2.0 sec.

The curves of Series I reach a considerable height, but the stimulus diminishes rapidly and intensely in power in the succeeding series. The reaction-times shorten uniformly, but are still in general somewhat long, as we observe not infrequently among emotional people.

	Galv.	Reaction-time
1126 (2) The altered reproductions of Series II average	7.9 mm.	2.0 sec.
The unchanged reproductions of Series II average	1.8 mm.	2.2 sec.
The altered reproductions of Series III average	3.5 mm.	2.2 sec.
The unchanged reproductions of Series III average	1.3 mm.	2.1 sec.

The galvanic curves correspond in both series to our expectation, but the reaction-times in Series II are contradictory, which, however, is changed if we do not employ the probable average (as is ordinarily done by us in all cases) but the arithmetical average, when the average time for altered reproduction is 2.8 sec., and for the unchanged only 2.4 sec.

1127 (3) The galvanic curves with long reaction-times in Series I average	17.8 mm.
The galvanic curves with short reaction-times in Series I average	12.7 mm.
The galvanic curves with long reaction-times in Series II average	9.8 mm.

The galvanic curves with short reaction-times in
    Series II average   3.6 mm.
The galvanic curves with long reaction-times in
    Series III average   2.1 mm.
The galvanic curves with short reaction-times in
    Series III average   0.0 mm.

All of these figures are in perfect accord with our hypothesis.

1128   (4) In Series II, 17.3 per cent of the associations have an average difference of plus 5.8 mm. In Series III, 17.3 per cent of the associations have an average difference of plus 2.8 mm.

1129   These figures show that the constellation in the latter series is not very much changed, with the exception of a few associations. We may conclude that all the strong emotional relations of the stimulus-words were brought out in the first test. We should say here that Case No. 3 was well accustomed to this kind of experiment, while cases No. 1 and No. 2 were not.

1130   (5) Series I. Probable average of reaction-times
following associations with unusually high
galvanic curves   2.8 sec.
Series I. Arithmetical average of the corresponding
galvanic curves   22.3 mm.
Series II. Probable average of reaction-times following associations with unusually high galvanic
curves   1.8 sec.
Series II. Arithmetical average of the corresponding
galvanic curves   11.4 mm.
Series III. Probable average of reaction-times following associations with unusually high galvanic curves   1.2 sec.
Series III. Arithmetical average of the corresponding galvanic curves   1.7 mm.

The galvanic curves are what we would expect in Series I and II but not in Series III. The reaction-time is what we expect only in Series I.

	Galv.	Reaction-time
1131 (6) Series I. Average of associations altered in subsequent reproduction	14.2 mm.	2.4 sec.
Series I. Average of association unchanged subsequently	13.5 mm.	2.0 sec.

Series II. Average of associations altered in subsequent reproduction	8.7 mm.	2.2 sec.
Series II. Average of associations unchanged subsequently	3.6 mm.	2.0 sec.

All of these figures coincide with what we expect.

1132   (7) The general course of Series I is very irregular. The average of distribution is 7.6, the highest number we have yet observed. In the tests with Cases 1 and 2 the various phases of stimulation were shown in strong, but much differentiated, emotions, but in this case with a lively temperament there was a continual and marked fluctuation of emotions, and hence the high average of distribution.

1133   Series II is more uniform, and the average of distribution is 5.4, and in Series III this average is only 2.3.

1134   The highest galvanic curve in Series I measures 51.5 mm. and is connected with the association *the sun / burns.* Why there should be here so strong a reflex innervation could not be understood without further examination. The subject himself could not explain why he had any particular emotion at this moment. But the connection was shown in the following associations. The other high curves (37, 21 and 18 mm.) occurred with the associations *floor / parquet, pay / write, warm / the stove.* These three associations showed constant and similar disturbances in all three series, as illustrated in this table:

	SERIES I			SERIES II			SERIES III	
	Galv.	Reaction-time	Reproduction	Galv.	Reaction-time	Reproduction	Galv.	Reaction-time
floor	37 mm.	3.0 sec.	ditto	13 mm.	3.2 sec.	ditto	2.5 mm.	3.0 sec.
warm	18 mm.	1.2 sec.	ditto	31 mm.	2.2 sec.	ditto	7.0 mm.	2.0 sec.
pay	21 mm.	2.0 sec.	ditto	4.5 mm.	0.8 sec.	ditto	7.5 mm.	2.2 sec.

1135   All the reproductions were altered. With one exception all of the galvanometer curves were considerably above the averages for each of the series. As to the nine reaction-times, four were above, and two coincided with the probable averages. It seemed justified from these observations to assume that a strong emotional complex lay behind them. But when questioned the subject answered that he had had no particular thoughts in connection with these reactions, and was evidently unconscious of any special complex. Yet even if a subject asserts that no complex is present, this is not conclusive in the face of so many indications pointing to interference by a complex. In this instance we distracted his attention from the matters in hand and asked what personal significance the word *floor* had for him, when suddenly he said with surprise and embarrassment that

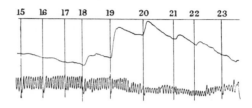

FIG. 17. Portion of a curve to show emotional effect of certain word associations

recently a *stove* in his dwelling had become defective and *burned* the *floor* to such an extent that he had not only to *pay* for a new stove, but also for an entire new floor which was a hardship for him. Besides this there had been great danger from fire. Thus all the disturbances above related were perfectly explained, including the strong emotional tone of the association *the sun / burns.*

1136 We learn from this interesting episode that the galvanic phenomenon, like reaction-time and alteration of reproductions, may give evidence of the existence of an unconscious complex. We cannot go into further detail regarding this fact here, but the investigations of Binswanger already mentioned also throw much light on the subject.

1137 The group of associations described above gives an unusually fine picture in Series II of emotional effect upon the curves (fig. 17). At the beginning we have indifferent reactions. Reaction No. 18 is *floor*, 19 *warm*, 20 *wages / small*, and 21 *pay.*

1138 The respiratory curve also shows the reactions very clearly. In general, inspiration is increased, which is especially characteristic for this particular case in connection with expectant

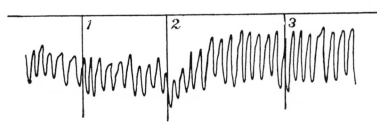

FIG. 18. Expectation curve in Case 3 (reproduced actual size of tracing)

attention. The condition during the unconscious complex excitation seems therefore to have had a certain resemblance to the tension of expectation. An example of this tension of expectation in this case at the beginning of a test is shown in fig. 18.

Case 4.—An educated woman, aged 25, used to these experiments. Three series of word associations, eighteen words in each

1139   (*A*) Series I.   Arithmetical average of galvanic

curves	6.8 mm.
Series II. Arithmetical average of galvanic curves	1.9 mm.
Series III. Arithmetical average of galvanic curves	0.9 mm.
Series I. Probable average of reaction-times	1.2 sec.
Series II. Probable average of reaction-times	1.0 sec.
Series III. Probable average of reaction-times	1.0 sec.

The galvanic curves show very rapid diminution, while the reaction-time is very short and the lowest limit is soon reached.

	Galv.	Reaction-time
1140 (*B*) The altered reproductions of Series II average	7.5 mm.	1.6 sec.
The unchanged reproductions of Series II average	1.6 mm.	1.0 sec.
The altered reproductions of Series III average	0.0 mm.	1.0 sec.
The unchanged reproductions of Series III average	1.0 mm.	1.0 sec.

The result in Series II is what we expected, but this is not true of Series III, perhaps because only very few altered reproductions occur.

1141   (C) The galvanic curves with long reaction-
        times in Series I average   11.6 mm.
        The galvanic curves with short reaction-times in
        Series I average   5.2 mm.
        The galvanic curves with long reaction-times in
        Series II average   5.4 mm.
        The galvanic curves with short reaction-times in
        Series II average   0.8 mm.
        The galvanic curves with long reaction-times in
        Series III average   1.0 mm.
        The galvanic curves with short reaction-times in
        Series III average   1.5 mm.

The figures in Series I and II are what we expected, but not in Series III, perhaps because most of the curves had already sunk to zero.

1142   (D) In Series II, 5.5 per cent of the associations
        show an average plus difference of   6.0 mm.
        In Series III, 11.1 per cent of the associations show
        an average plus difference of   2.7 mm.

In this case also we note a great readiness of the association to appear fully on the first stimulus, so that the constellation does not change much later on.

1143   (E) Series I. Probable average of reaction-times
        following associations with unusually high gal-
        vanometer curve   1.1 sec.
        Series I. Arithmetical average of corresponding gal-
        vanometer curves   6.5 mm.
        Series II. Probable average of reaction-times follow-
        ing associations with unusually high galva-
        nometer curves   1.0 sec.
        Series II. Arithmetical average of corresponding gal-
        vanometer curves   1.2 mm.

The figures in Series III are omitted, because most of the galvanic curves were reduced to zero. The figures given in the above two series do not accord with our expectation.

544

		Galv.	Reaction-time
1144	(F) Series I. Average of associations altered in subsequent reproductions	4.3 mm.	4.0 sec.
	Series I. Average of associations unchanged subsequently	4.4 mm.	1.2 sec.
	Series II. Average of associations altered in subsequent reproductions	6 mm.	1.2 sec.
	Series II. Average of associations unchanged subsequently	1.6 mm.	1.0 sec.

These figures are what we should expect.

1145   (G) Average of distribution in Series I   5.5
         Average of distribution in Series II   2.2
         Average of distribution in Series III   1.6

1146   We find as usual the greatest variation in the figures in the first series. With lessening power of the stimulus in the repetitions, a levelling tendency is manifested as regards this variation in the power of the stimulus. The highest curves are found in the following associations:

	SERIES I			SERIES II			SERIES III	
	Galvanometer	Reaction-time	Reproduction	Galvanometer	Reaction-time	Reproduction	Galvanometer	Reaction-time
ball/dance	4.3 mm.	4.0 sec.	0	7.5 mm.	1.6 sec.	ditto	12 mm.	0.8 sec.
dress/red	9.0 mm.	1.8 sec.	ditto	2. mm.	0.6 sec.	ditto	0 mm.	0.8 sec.
pretty/ugly	7.5 mm.	1.4 sec.	ditto	3. mm.	0.8 sec.	ditto	3 mm.	1.2 sec.

1147   The galvanic curves are much higher than the average in all three series for the association *ball / dance*. The intensity of the affect here is shown by the fact that while fifteen out of eighteen reactions in the last series caused no deviations of the galvanometer, this particular association induced a deflection of 12 mm. In this instance the subject expected to go in a

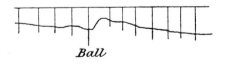

Ball

FIG. 19. Wood association *ball/dance* in Case 4

545

few days to a fancy dress ball, but despite much search had not yet found a suitable costume. She was, therefore, in a state of anxiety concerning it. The association *dress* and *pretty* are self-evident.

1148   The reaction-times were rapidly shortened in the repetitions, because of her natural aptitude in speech. It is evident that at times the galvanic phenomenon is more helpful than lengthened reaction-times in demonstrating emotional states.

1149   Fig. 19 is a curve from Series III in this case representing the well-marked association *ball / dance*. Repetition of the association test is to be recommended when one desires to bring out more clearly very strong emotional complexes.

2. *Résumé of the Tests with Word Associations in Normal Individuals*

1150   Our limited material, consisting of the word associations in one educated woman and three uneducated men, leads us to bring forward with much reserve a *résumé* of our results. We know that they must be regarded as only preliminary, and as being of questionable value, but at the same time they foreshadow features of interest for future enquiry and investigation. Our intention in this work is chiefly to point out indications, and our presentation of results must be taken in this sense.

1151   (1) The average positive difference of a galvanic curve, produced by an association whose reaction-time exceeds that of the probable average of the same series, is 2.7 mm.

1152   Taking into consideration the above-mentioned limitations this figure seems to express that in certain cases there is a clear parallelism between the length of reaction-time and the height of the galvanometer curve. This method appears, therefore, to afford a psychophysical proof of the hypothesis of one of us (Jung), that very long reaction-times are affective phenomena.

1153   (2) Altered reproductions show an average difference of 2 mm. over unchanged reproductions.

1154   (3) Such associations as are changed in the reproductions of the following series present an average difference of plus 6.8 mm. over such as are reproduced subsequently unchanged.

1155   These two figures, especially the last, seem to offer a psychophysical confirmation of the hypothesis of one of us (Jung), that altered reproductions are affective phenomena.

1156   The remaining methods embodied in the text of our work have little right to a special summing up here, because of the scantiness of our material, and also because of some contradictions in our results.

3. Word Associations in Dementia Praecox

1157   There were but two of our cases of paranoid dementia that could be used for a test of word associations with the galvanometer.

Case 1.— Male, aged 36, very intelligent, academic education. Speech well preserved. Two series of associations, with twenty-four words each

1158   (A) Series I.   Arithmetical average of heights
          of galvanometer curve   11.6 mm.
        Series II.   Arithmetical average of heights of gal-
          vanometer curve   4.6 mm.
        Series I.   Probable average of the reaction-times   6.6 sec.
        Series II.   Probable average of the reaction-times   4.8 sec.

The average height of the galvanometer curves falls in both series within normal limits, which is not the case with the reaction-times showing excess. Our four normal subjects presented the following average:

Series I. Galvanometer curves 7.8 mm.   Reaction-times 1.8 sec.
Series II. Galvanometer curves 5.1 mm.   Reaction-times 1.4 sec.

From these figures it is seen that the patient offers a strong contrast in the length of the reaction-times.

		Galv.	Reaction-time
1159	(B) The altered reproductions in Series II average	4.7 mm.	6.0 sec.
	The unchanged reproductions in Series II average	3.4 mm.	2.8 sec.

These figures coincide with the normal, and are what we should expect. But we note that the unchanged reproductions present a much lower value in the reaction-time than the altered reproductions.

547

1160   (C) The galvanometer curves with long reaction-times in Series I average   13.1 mm.

The galvanometer curves with short reaction-times
in Series I average   10.3 mm.

The galvanometer curves with long reaction-times
in Series II average   3.8 mm.

The galvanometer curves with short reaction-times
in Series II average   4.0 mm.

In this table the figures in Series I, but not those in Series II, are what we expect.

1161   (D) In Series II, 12.5 per cent of the associations show an average plus difference of 4.5 mm.

1162   (E) Series I. Probable average of reaction-times
following associations with unusually high galvanic curves   4.0 sec.

Series I. Arithmetical average of the corresponding
galvanic curves   10.0 mm.

Series II. Probable average of reaction-times following associations with unusually high galvanic
curves   7.6 sec.

Series II. Arithmetical average of the corresponding
galvanic curves   3.2 mm.

In this table, only the reaction-time of Series II is in accordance with our expectation.

	Galv.	Reaction-time
1163 (F) Series I. The associations with altered reproductions in the following series average	9.8 mm.	6.6 sec.
Series I. The associations with unchanged reproductions in the following series average	13.5 mm.	5.4 sec.

Only the reaction-time here is what we expect.

1164   (G) The average of distribution in Series I was 5.8. The average of distribution in Series II was 3.4. These figures are similar to those of Case 4 among the normal.

1165   The highest galvanic curve occurred with the reaction *love / a psychic process* (30 mm.), and here was also the longest re-action-time (27.2 sec.). The next highest curve was connected with the reaction *wife / marriage-law* (29 mm.). The patient is single, and having had with *love* a strong emotional tone, it was not surprising that *wife* should also evince a similar intensity. Another high curve was found in the association *sick / at-heart* (26 mm.). The patient still had some insight into his condition, and knew that he was confined in the asylum because of his mental malady, hence the strong emotion connected therewith. The word *handsome* produced a curve of 25 mm. The patient is very vain, and pays extraordinary attention to his dress. The contents of the association present the symptoms of affectation, which is evident from his external appearance. Most of his associations showed a definition character which, in educated people, always indicates a certain amount of affectation. The following are examples:

write	activity
shoes	footwear
hat	an article of clothing
house	building construction
to sit	condition of rest
money	medium of exchange
proud	adjective

1166   The long reaction-times may be due to this affected manner of expression, though this can hardly be the only cause.

Case 2.—Woman, single, aged 62, uneducated, medium intelligence. Speech mingled with neologisms. Three series of associations with twenty-five words each

1167   (*A*) Series I.   Arithmetical average of the galvanic curves   7.9 mm.
Series II.   Arithmetical average of the galvanic curves   3.6 mm.
Series III.   Arithmetical average of the galvanic curves   2.5 mm.
Series I.   Probable average of reaction-times   10.8 sec.
Series II.   Probable average of reaction-times   6.4 sec.
Series III.   Probable average of reaction-times   6.0 sec.

As in the former case, the galvanic deviations are of medium height, while the reaction-times are extraordinarily long.

	Galv.	Reaction-time
1168 (*B*) The altered reproductions in Series II average	3.6 mm.	6.6 sec.

549

The unchanged reproductions in Series II
average   3.6 mm.   5.2 sec.
The altered reproductions in Series III
average   2.5 mm.   7.4 sec.
The unchanged reproductions in Series III
average   2.4 mm.   4.6 sec.

The reaction-times accord with our expectation, as in the former case, much better than the galvanometer curves.

1169   (C) The galvanometer curves with long reaction-times in Series I average   9.6 mm.
The galvanometer curves with short reaction-times in Series I average   6.0 mm.
The galvanometer curves with long reaction-times in Series II average   4.7 mm.
The galvanometer curves with short reaction-times in Series II average   2.6 mm.
The galvanometer curves with long reaction-times in Series III average   2.8 mm.
The galvanometer curves with short reaction-times in Series III average   2.5 mm.

The figures in all three series are what we expect.

1170   (D) In Series II, 28.0 per cent of the associations show an average plus difference of 4.7 mm. In Series III, 24.0 per cent of the associations show an average plus difference of 4.8 mm.

1171   (E) Series I. Probable average of reaction-times following associations with unusually high galvanic curves   11.6 sec.
Series I. Arithmetical average of corresponding galvanic curves   11.8 mm.
Series II. Probable average of reaction-times following associations with unusually high galvanic curves   5.8 sec.
Series II. Arithmetical average of corresponding galvanic curves   3.7 mm.
Series III. Probable average of reaction-times following associations with unusually high galvanic curves   8.0 sec.
Series III. Arithmetical average of corresponding galvanic curves   2.5 mm.

Twice the reaction-times are what we expected, the galvanic curves only once, and in Series III the arithmetical average is the same.

		Galv.	Reaction-time
1172	(F) Series I. The associations with altered reproductions in the following series average	9.0 mm.	10.4 sec.
	Series I. The associations with unchanged reproductions in the following series average	6.3 mm.	12.4 sec.
	Series II. The associations with altered reproductions in the following series average	3.3 mm.	6.6 sec.
	Series II. The associations with unchanged reproductions in the following series average	4.0 mm.	4.8 sec.

We find in this table that only the galvanic curves in Series I and the reaction-times in Series II are what we expected.

1173   (G) The average of distribution in Series I was 4.9.
The average of distribution in Series II was 2.8.
The average of distribution in Series III was 1.6.

1174   The highest galvanic curve (21 mm.) is found in the association *sun / sun-time*, and here the reaction-time is 14.0 seconds. It is difficult to explain this excessive deviation. The preceding association is *stout / constitution* (15 mm., and 14.8 seconds reaction-time). The patient is very stout, which she thinks due to supernatural influences. She complains much of this "forced" disfigurement. In Series II these two associations caused no deviations, but in Series III *stout / constitution* suddenly induced the largest deflection of the whole series, viz., 14.5 mm., whereas the average was only 2.5 mm. There was a curve of 20 mm. with the association *ugly / disfigured by great suffering*, and with this a reaction-time of 12.0 seconds. The contents of this association are concerned with the same theme as *stout / constitution*. Another high curve occurred with *high / highest action* (19 mm. and reaction-time 11.2 seconds). This association was subsequently altered twice in the reproductions. It is

551

connected with the delusion of the patient that she had accomplished the "highest work."

1175   The associations are typically affected and show a distinctly morbid character. The following are examples:

diligent	high esteem—payment
love	to be lovable—wedding
snake	to point out as extraordinary
high	highest action—highest distinction
ugly	disfigured by great suffering

1176   *Résumé*: In our tests with word associations in the two cases of dementia praecox the only striking fact has been the great lengthening of reaction-times. In the relations between the galvanometer curves and associations we have found nothing different from the normal. From the material of Jung, who has analyzed a large collection of association experiments in dementia praecox, we learn that in by far the greater proportion of these cases there is no particular lengthening of reaction-time. Therefore a long reaction-time cannot be considered as characteristic for all cases of dementia praecox. It is of value in some cases. It is only present when the patients suffer from certain hindrances to thought, which are often present in this disease.

1177   When we examine the associations of such patients we find that the hindrance to thought (lengthened reaction-time) is especially manifested where complexes constellate the association, which is also the case in normal individuals. This phenomenon first led Jung to think that the specific pathological factor in dementia praecox depends upon some complex. A complex in fact plays a great role in the associations of our two patients here described. The reaction-times are extraordinarily long where connected with a complex. The complex constellations are also very numerous, as well as the altered reproductions related to them. In our normal cases we found an average of 30 per cent of altered reproductions in Series I, while the patients had 51 per cent. Besides this, the character of the associations presents abnormalities almost constantly, especially around the complexes.

1178   From these indications we may conclude that little of a pathological nature can be found in the general and regular mechanisms of thought, but rather in the manner and method of reaction of the individual to his complexes. We find in both of these patients an increased influence of the complex upon association, which corroborates the results of innumerable analyses of dementia praecox by Jung. This phenomenon has an important and general clinical significance, because, when carefully analyzed, nearly all the symptoms are found to be determined by an individual complex, often manifested in a very convincing way. This is particularly true for delusions and hallucinations. A series of other symptoms is more often dependent upon indirect disturbance of association by the complex. This state of affairs explains why we do not discover any elementary disturbances, even in quite intense mental disorder; the dementia is shown only in the most delicate psychological relations. Therefore we shall look in vain, for the present and for a long time to come, among these patients for simple, elementary disturbances common to all cases.

1179   NOTE.—Since this article was put into type we have found that Féré,[23] carrying a current through a subject with various sensory stimuli, made the following observation: "Il se produit alors une déviation brusque de l'aiguille du galvanomètre. . . . La même déviation se produit encore sous l'influence d'émotions éthéniques; c'est à dire qu'elle se produit dans toutes les conditions où j'ai signalé précédemment une augmentation de volume des membres mise en évidence par le pléthysmograph." This clearly shows that Féré made the discovery two years before Tarchanoff.

[23] "Note sur des modifications de la résistance électrique sous l'influence des excitations sensorielles et des émotions" (1888), p. 217.

FURTHER INVESTIGATIONS ON THE GALVANIC PHENOMENON AND RESPIRATION IN NORMAL AND INSANE INDIVIDUALS[1]

by Charles Ricksher and C. G. Jung

1180   The changes produced by various causes in the electrical resistance of the human body have been studied for many years, but as yet no definite results have been reached. Charles Féré was the first to report on the changes produced by emotion. In a communication made to the Société de Biologie in 1888[2] he noted that there was a decrease in bodily resistance when various sensory stimuli were applied, and also that emotion produced a similar decrease. R. Vigouroux had been working on the problem of electrical resistance in the human body with patients from the Salpétrière and had reached the conclusion that the old view of resistance being caused by the epidermis was wrong and that the true cause was the condition of the superficial circulation. He thought that variations in resistance were caused by an increased or decreased superficial circulation. Féré accepted these conclusions and added that "l'étude de la résistance électrique peut trouver une application dans les recherches des psycho-physiologues."

1181   Nothing new was reported for several years. In 1890, A. Vigouroux published a report on the study of electrical resistance in melancholics but added nothing to our knowledge. Tarchanoff, Stricher, Sommer, and Veraguth have all summarized the work of the French investigators. The first person to do real psychological research using the galvanometer was Veraguth, who in 1906 worked with this instrument and with Jung's association experiments. In the same year work was be-

---

[1] [Originally published, in English, in *The Journal of Abnormal Psychology* (Boston), II (1907–8):5, 189–217. Charles Ricksher (1879–1943), M.D., was then Assistant Physician, Danvers Insane Hospital, Hathorne, Massachusetts. In this version, stylistic and terminological revisions have been made.]

[2] [For this reference and others following, see bibliography at end of the paper.]

gun in the Psychiatric Clinic in Zurich to try to determine the cause of electrical resistance of the body and the changes produced in the bodies of normal and insane individuals by different stimuli. The apparatus used consisted of a circuit containing a single low-voltage element, a Deprez-d'Arsonval galvanometer of high sensitivity, a shunt for lowering the oscillations of the mirror, and two brass plates upon which the subject of the test places his hands and thus closes the circuit. The galvanometer reflects a beam of light onto a celluloid scale to which is attached a movable slide with a visor, which, pushed by hand, follows the moving mirror-reflection. To the slide is attached a cord leading to what is called an ergograph writer, which marks the movements of the slide by means of a penpoint on a kymograph-drum fitted with endless paper. For measuring time a Jaquet chronograph was used and for the moment of stimulus an ordinary electrical marker.

1182   The problem of the cause of resistance was first approached; the results given are those obtained by Jung and Binswanger and are as yet unpublished. Resistance was found to vary greatly in different individuals with different conditions of the palmar epithelium. That the epidermis was the seat of resistance was proved by the fact that when the electrodes were placed under the skin resistance was enormously decreased. This was done by piercing the skin of each arm with a surgical needle and using the needles as electrodes.[3]

1183   The French investigators were unanimous in ascribing the changes in resistance to changes in the blood supply of an area, caused by dilation and contraction of the vessels, the greater the blood supply the lower the resistance and vice versa. That the blood supply was not a chief factor was proved by exsanguinating the area in contact with the plates with an Esmarch bandage, whereupon it was found that the galvanic phenomenon still appeared.

1184   That the changes in resistance are not due to changes in contact, such as pressure on the electrodes, is shown by the fact that when the hands are immersed in water, which acts as a connection to the electrodes, the changes in resistance still occur. Pressure and involuntary movements give a deflection entirely different from the usual result of an affective stimulus.

3 Experiments by Veraguth and Jung and Binswanger.

1185   The time that elapsed between a stimulus and the change in resistance, as shown by the galvanometer, suggested some change in the sympathetic nervous system or in some area controlled by it. The sweat-glands seemed to have most influence in the reduction of resistance. If the sweat-glands were stimulated there would be thousands of liquid connections between the electrodes and tissues, and resistance would be much lowered. Experiments were made by placing electrodes on different parts of the body, and it was found that the reduction in resistance was most marked in those places where most sweat-glands are located. It is well known that both emotion and sensory stimuli influence the various organs and glands, heart, lungs, sweat-glands, etc. Heat and cold also influence the phenomenon, heat causing a reduction and cold an increase in resistance. In view of these facts the action of the sweat-glands seems to be the most plausible explanation of the changes in resistance.

1186   The following experiments were made in the winter and spring of 1907, with a view to determining the effect on the galvanic phenomenon and respiration of a series of simple physical and mental stimuli in a number of normal and insane subjects. The galvanometric changes were noted by the apparatus described above. The respiration was recorded by means of a Marey pneumograph attached to the thorax and leading by means of a rubber tube to a Marey tambour, to which is attached a pen-point that writes on the kymograph-drum.

1187   The results of pneumographic experiments of various authors are very conflicting. Delabarre[4] found that attention to sensory impressions increased the frequency and depth of respiration. Mosso, in his work on the circulation in the brain, could come to no satisfactory conclusions. Mentz found that every noticeable acoustic stimulus caused a slowing of the respiration and pulse. Zoneff and Meumann found that high grades of attention cause a very great or total inhibition of respiration, while relatively weaker attention generally produces an increase in the rate and a decrease in the amplitude of the respirations. Total arrest of respiration was found relatively more frequently in sensory than in intellectual attention.

4 Remarks by Delabarre, Mosso, and Mentz are quoted from Zoneff and Meumann.

Martius notes great individual differences and comes to the conclusion that there is an affect type differing from the normal, shown by slowness of the pulse and respiration.

1188   The experiments of these authors were all made on a limited number of subjects, usually students. Our experiments with the pneumograph were generally made on uneducated men, attendants in the clinic, and our stimuli were quite different from those used by the other investigators. It is possible that the great difference in our results may in part depend on these facts.

1189   In our experiments care was taken to have the conditions as nearly equal as possible. It was found that different positions of the body, leaning forward or backward, for example, caused a change in the level of the respiratory curves. Slight movements of the body and of the limbs did not influence the curves. The tambour itself can cause changes in the recorded curves. The tambour must contain the same amount of air in every case, otherwise the curves will be different. The curve registered is not an exact one, owing to defects in the instruments. In deep inspirations the rubber covering becomes tense and, when the pressure in the chest changes, the elasticity of the rubber causes the respirations to be registered in a different way from that in which they really occur.

1190   It cannot be assumed that the respiratory curves represent ordinary normal respiration but only the kind of normal respiration to be expected under experimental conditions. No one can breathe naturally with a recording apparatus on his chest and with his attention more or less directed to it. The release from the tension of the experiment is seen at the end of the experiment when the respirations become deeper and the level of the curve changes. The pneumograph could not be used on women because of their clothing, nor could it be used with many of the insane subjects because of their excitability.

1191   The plethysmograph was not used because with it the sources of error are too numerous. Martius has shown that, even when the arm and instrument are encased in plaster of Paris, there occur involuntary movements that make correct interpretation of the results difficult.

1192   In the galvanic experiment many sources of error have to be considered. Chief among these is the deflection caused by movements of the hands. An increase or decrease in the pressure of the hands upon the electrodes causes an instantaneous change in the position of the reflection of the galvanic mirror. This change is sudden, and it is almost impossible to produce deliberately a change in the position of the reflection like one caused by an affective mental process. The natural change of position of the hands is shown by an almost vertical rise or fall of the galvanic curve as shown on the kymograph-drum. To prevent, as far as possible, involuntary changes of position, bags of sand were placed on the hands, thus preventing any but deliberate movements. It was found that quite extensive movements of the body could be made without influencing the galvanometric curve. Deep inspirations and sighs cause a greater or lesser rise in the curve. In the same curve a sigh occurring after an affective process seems to cause a more extensive rise than one occurring before. Deliberate long inspirations cause little or no disturbance. It must therefore be assumed that sighs are caused by some affective complex, or that they cause such a complex to come into consciousness or they produce an unconscious emotional condition.

1193   The subjects were physicians and attendants, as well as patients suffering from various mental diseases.

1194   The experiment may be divided into six parts: in each part a different stimulus or series of stimuli of the same kind, physical or psychological, was used. Before each stimulus or series of stimuli the subject was told in a general way what was going to happen. In many individuals, after a short period of waiting for a stimulus, there were changes in respiration and in the galvanic curve. These expectation-curves will be discussed later.

1195   The measurements of height are in each case the real, i.e., the vertical height. The respiratory rate is given as so many per centimetre, which is a purely comparative measurement. For the quiet periods we give the average rate per centimetre for ten centimetres at the beginning and end of each period.

1196   Part I of the experiment consists of a quiet period of four minutes. The subject was asked to sit as quietly as possible and was told that no stimulus was going to be applied. In Part II, the stimulus was a leaden weight allowed to fall about three feet onto the floor. In Part III, the subject was asked to say spontaneously, after a minute or so, a word or a short sentence, and then to remain quiet. Part IV consists of three physical stimuli: a low whistle, a weight dropped onto the floor, and a picture (picture post-card) shown to the subject. Part V consists of four sentences spoken by the investigator. The first two were usually some familiar proverb, such as "The pitcher goes often to the well but is broken at last"; the third and fourth were of a more critical nature as they referred directly to the subject himself or to his habits. In several cases single words, such as *eye* and *face*, were given. Part VI is again a quiet period of four minutes. The results of each part will be given here, and the normal subjects, fifteen in number, will be considered first.

NORMAL SUBJECTS

1197   *Part I.* The galvanometric curve is usually higher at the beginning than it becomes a short time later owing to feelings of expectation and tension caused by the unusual position and the strange experiment. As a rule the curve shows many irregularities caused by the subject's hand and body movements as he settles into a comfortable position; such movements are also the result of expectation, muscular tension (this is not, however, an important factor), and of various emotionally charged complexes. In the course of the quiet period there are seen oscillations of the galvanic mirror that cannot be accounted for by any movement of the hands or body, by any respiratory change, or any conscious thought or association. We have therefore attributed them to the indefinite *feeling* caused by some still unconscious complex. Everyone has experienced these vague feelings, sad or gay, that come without apparent cause, last only a short time, and are soon forgotten. Such a curve was clearly shown in the case of a well-educated physician, with a considerable power of self-analysis, who could not remember any affective thought that had occurred to him during the period.

1198   The inspirations at the beginning of the quiet period are usually deeper and more frequent than at the end. At the beginning they average 2.91 per cm. and at the end 2.79 per

559

cm. The average height of the inspirations at the beginning is 12.41 mm., at the end 12.26 mm. In our cases the respiratory curve does not show any great or constant change of level.

1199   In *Part II* (stimulus a falling weight) the galvanometric curves show great individual differences. In one case, that of an attendant who was very nervous and frightened by the experiment, the galvanometric deflection was 54 mm. In another case, also of an attendant, but of a very phlegmatic disposition, the deflection was only 4.6 mm. The average deflection for fifteen subjects was 20.6 mm.

1200   The longest reaction-time, i.e., the time from the moment of stimulus to the beginning of the rise of the galvanic curve, varies from 1.5 to 5.5 seconds. This time, while showing individual variations, is usually shorter in cases showing the greatest galvanic reactions, and averages 2.87 seconds. The time required for the curve to reach its maximum height corresponds roughly to the height, a curve of 54 mm. requiring 11.5 seconds and one of 10 mm. requiring 2.5 seconds. The average time is 6.93 seconds.

1201   The inspirations show individual differences in rate and amplitude, and the respiratory rate does not vary as much as the height of the galvanometric curve, as the following table shows:

Height of Galv. Curve	Inspir. before Stim.	Rise of Galv. Curve	Fall of Galv. Curve
54. mm.	3.5 per cm.	3.86 per cm.	3.92 per cm.
18.8 mm.	3. per cm.	2.72 per cm.	2.5 per cm.
4.6 mm.	3. per cm.	2.5 per cm.	2.3 per cm.

1202   Thus the change in rate for a galvanic curve of 54 mm. is not as great as for a curve of 4.6 mm. Whether the respiration is slowed down or speeded up during the rise of the galvanic curve seems to depend on the individual. The majority, however, show a decrease of speed during the rise and an increase during the fall of the galvanic curve.

1203   The average number of inspirations before the stimulus is 3.05 per cm., during the rise of the galvanic curve 3.02 cm., and during the fall 3.09 per cm.

1204   The amplitude of the inspirations does not vary in proportion to the rate. Before the stimulus the average height of the

560

inspirations is 11.75 mm., during the rise of the galvanic curve 10.73 mm., and during the fall of the curve 11.45 mm.

1205   *Part III* (spontaneous speaking). In this part the average height of the galvanic curve is lower than in the preceding part, being 17.9 mm. As a rule the curves of the different subjects show little variation in height. Some of the curves show irregularities before the moment of speaking, caused partly by indecision and partly by preparation for speaking. In normal subjects the galvanic curve begins to rise at the moment of speaking or even a little before.

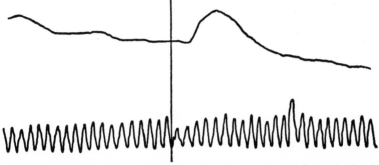

Fig. 1. *Stimulus a falling weight.* Resistance was very high at the beginning of the experiment and fell throughout the quiet period and up to the moment of stimulation, as shown by the vertical line. The latency time and the decrease in rate and amplitude of respirations are clearly shown

1206   The number of inspirations per centimetre decreases during the rise of the galvanic curve and continues to decrease as the curve falls. The average rate before speaking is 3.5 per cm., during the rise of the galvanic curve 3.15 per cm., and during the fall 3.04 per cm. The average height of the inspirations before speaking is 10.08 mm., during the rise of the curve 10.57 mm., and during the fall 11.75 mm. Thus the height increases as the rate decreases.

1207   In *Part IV* there are three stimuli: a falling weight, a whistle, and a picture. In each case the stimulus is not merely a sensory, visual, or auditory one, but has also a psychological component. Almost every stimulus, when perceived or received into consciousness, is associated with affective complexes. A low whistle is heard not only as a sound but also as a call, and is associated with many past experiences; a picture calls up many other associations. Naturally the personal equation comes into play here to a very great extent.

1208   The measurements are:

	Weight	Whistle	Picture
Height of curve	17.94 mm.	18.2 mm.	19.72 mm.
Latency time	2.55 sec.	2.82 sec.	3.03 sec.
Time to reach top of curve[5]	6.95 sec.	9.88 sec.	7.47 sec.

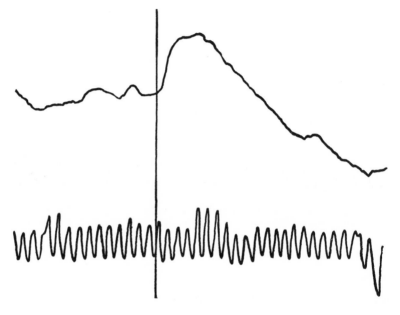

Fig. 2. *Spontaneous speaking*. The vertical line indicates the moment of speaking. The irregularities before speaking are clearly shown in the galvanometric curve. In the respiratory curve the decrease in amplitude during the rise of the galvanometric curve is clearly shown

In these cases the latency time increases with the height of the galvanometric curve. The time for the curve to reach its maximum varies in the different cases.

1209   In every case the respiratory rate increases during the rise of the galvanic curve; in one case it decreases and in two increases during the fall. The amplitude of the respirations varies in the same way, being lower during the rise and increasing

[5] [Hereafter abbreviated as Height, Latency, Time to top.]

in height as the affect passes off. Expressed in tabulated form, the measurements are:

	Inspirations per cm.			Height in mm.		
	Weight	Whistle	Picture	Weight	Whistle	Picture
Before stimulus	3.01	2.75	2.88	12.02	12.05	12.46
Rise of curve	3.33	2.77	3.02	10.56	11.35	10.90
Fall of curve[6]	2.76	3.06	3.09	12.32	12.13	11.33

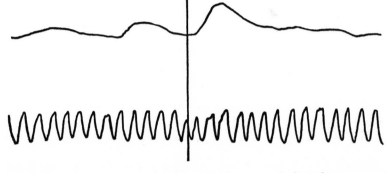

FIG. 3. *Stimulus a whistle.* A small expectation curve, before the movement of stimulus, is shown. The latency period, and the changes in the respiratory rate and amplitude, are clearly shown

1210   *Part V.* Four short sentences or words were used as stimuli. The sentences were spoken by the investigator, and time was allowed between each for the galvanic curve to return to its lowest level. The measurements are:

	Sen. 1	Sen. 2	Sen. 3	Sen. 4
Height	14.62 mm.	14.48 mm.	19.42 mm.	11.12 mm.
Latency	3.32 sec.	3.1 sec.	2.83 sec.	3.15 sec.
Time to top	8.13 sec.	5.82 sec.	7.67 sec.	5.95 sec.

As can be seen from the table, the height of the galvanic curve gradually decreases in the second and fourth sentences, while the curve of the third sentence is higher. The gradual decrease in the height of the galvanic curve is to be expected and can be explained by the gradual fading out of the affect. The first two sentences were trite, but the third usually referred to the subject or could be referred by him to himself, hence the

6 [Hereafter abbreviated as Before, Rise, Fall.]

stronger innervation and the increase in the height of the galvanic curve.

1211   The latency time and the time required for the curve to reach its maximum height bear no constant relation to the height of the galvanic curve.

1212   The respiratory curves vary greatly for the different sentences. In response to two sentences the respiratory rate decreases and in two it increases during the rise of the galvanic curve. The amplitude of the inspirations is always lower while the galvanic curve is rising and while the affect is acting, and slowly increases as the affect wears off, as the following table shows:

	Inspirations per cm.				Height in mm.			
	Sen. 1	Sen. 2	Sen. 3	Sen. 4	Sen. 1	Sen. 2	Sen. 3	Sen. 4
Before	2.84	2.97	2.71	3.05	12.85	12.59	13.74	12.23
Rise	3.04	2.78	2.57	3.41	11.63	11.27	12.81	11.76
Fall	3.09	2.74	3.13	3.46	12.13	11.98	13.38	13.07

1213   *Part VI* is a second quiet period of four minutes. As a general rule this part shows fewer irregularities than the first, because the subject has become accustomed to the experiment and is comfortably settled in his place. One marked feature of this part is the change of level of the respiratory curve as soon as the subject is told that the experiment is over and he is released from the involuntary tension in which he has been held.

1214   The respiratory rate is slower than in the first quiet period. At the beginning the inspirations are 2.41 per cm. as compared to 2.91 per cm. in the first curve. At the end they are 2.71 per cm. as compared to 2.79 per cm. in the first curve. The height of the inspirations is 12.57 mm. at the beginning as compared to 12.41 in the first curve, and 12.17 mm. at the end as compared to 12.26 mm. in the first curve.

1215   What we have designated expectation curves are changes in the galvanic curve that occur while the subject is waiting for the stimulus. Naturally they vary according to the individual. Some of our subjects showed no trace of an expectation curve, whereas in others we found quite marked expectation curves. These curves are more frequent in the early part of the experiment and are especially marked in Part II while the subject is waiting for the fall of the weight. In height they vary with the reactions to the stimuli but are nearly always lower than these.

1216   The average height of expectation curves is 15.70 mm. This high average is due to the fact that a subject who has an intense galvanic reaction to a stimulus will have many and strong expectation curves. The time required for the curve to reach its maximum averages 10 seconds; to fall to the former level, 12 seconds.

1217   The inspirations from the beginning to the top of the curve average 3.06 per cm.; during the fall they average 3.3 per cm. The average respiratory amplitude during the rise is 10.18 mm.; during the fall, 10.56 mm.

Fig. 4. *Expectation curve.* Showing changes in electrical resistance and respiration due to anticipatory attention

1218   That there are great individual differences in the galvanic reactions will be seen from the average of distribution of the various averages, expressed as a coefficient obtained by taking the average of the sum of the differences between each figure and the average of all the figures.

Part	II:	weight	8.09
Part	IV:	weight	8.71
		whistle	2.75
		picture	6.64
Part	V:	sentence 1	4.7
		sentence 2	4.42
		sentence 3	7.63
		sentence 4	3.98

1219   This coefficient shows, when large, that there is a great diversity in the numbers of which an average is taken; when low, that the numbers are nearly equal. Two of our subjects had extremely high galvanic curves, and therefore the average and coefficient are greater than they would have been had these two cases been omitted. On this account, our averages are probably higher than those of other observers.

1220   The pneumographic results are interesting because they differ from those obtained by other investigators and because they show a different relation between the rate and amplitude from what one would expect.

1221   The following table shows the averages of all the averages of respiratory rate and amplitude and the average of distribution of each.

	Inspir. per cm.	Coefficient	Height in mm.	Coefficient
Before	2.94	0.16	12.19	0.62
Rise	2.97	0.19	11.28	0.50
Fall	3.11	0.13	12.19	0.47

1222   It can be seen that the respiratory rate increases from the moment of stimulus while the amplitude decreases during the action of the affect and increases when it passes away. The coefficients in all cases are low and show that the numbers of which an average was taken are about equal.

1223   The relation between the respiratory rate and amplitude during the rise and fall of the galvanic curve and the high and low galvanic reactions is interesting. These relations were obtained by taking the averages of the sums of the respiratory rates and amplitudes of the high and low reactions of each individual before and after the stimulus. They are:

During rise
 high rate   decrease 0.05 per cm.
       amplitude decrease 1.17 per mm.
 low   rate   decrease 0.06 per cm.
       amplitude decrease 1.06 per mm.

1224   Thus during the rise the decrease in rate is practically the

566

same in both high and low reactions but the decrease in amplitude is greater in the higher reactions.

During fall
- high
  - rate — decrease 0.066 per cm.
  - amplitude — increase 1.601 mm.
- low
  - rate — decrease 0.001 per cm.
  - amplitude — increase 0.819 mm.

1225 During the fall of the galvanic curve the rate decreases more in the greater than in the lesser reactions, while the amplitude also increases more in the greater than in the lesser reactions.

1226 During the rise of the curve it is probable that part of the bodily innervation is expended on the various affective muscular tensions, etc., and consequently the more the individual reacts with other innervations the less will be expended on the respiration. This would explain the decrease in rate and amplitude in the greater reactions. During the fall of the galvanic curve more innervation is probably concentrated again on the respiration but chiefly on the depth; the rate decreases in some of the greater reactions.

1227 The relations of the rate and amplitude before and after the reaction show that there is an increase in the rate and amplitude after high reactions and a decrease in the rate and increase in the amplitude after low reactions.

1228 The following table was obtained by comparing the rate and amplitude before stimulus with the rate and amplitude during the rise of the galvanic curve, and the rate and amplitude during the fall of the galvanic curve with those occurring during the rise of the galvanic curve.

Before stimulus
- high
  - rate — increase 0.156 per cm.
  - amplitude — increase 0.213 mm.

After reaction
- low
  - rate — decrease 0.091 per cm.
  - amplitude — increase 0.093 mm.

This table shows that the differences in respiratory changes are much greater in cases of higher galvanic reactions.

1229 So far as could be determined there was no regular relation between the height of the galvanic reactions and the individual bodily resistance at the beginning of the experiment.

567

ABNORMAL SUBJECTS

1230   These subjects were patients suffering from epilepsy, dementia praecox, general paralysis, chronic alcoholism, and alcoholic dementia and senile dementia.

1231   The conditions of the experiment were exactly the same as in the case of normal subjects except that in many cases the pneumograph could not be used.

Epilepsy

1232   There were nine subjects in this group, the majority being seriously demented. Among these were included one case of traumatic epilepsy with congenital imbecility and one case of epilepsy with hysteria. One subject was examined immediately after an attack of *petit mal*. In this case the reactions to ordinary stimuli were slight or nil, but when the patient was threatened with a needle there was a galvanometric deflection of 20 mm. This change was very slow and the curve remained high for several minutes. The threat of a prick of a needle is a very strong stimulus and causes reactions in nearly every case where dementia is not marked. In this case the whistle produced a fluctuation of 4 mm. and the weight one of 2.8 mm. The other stimuli were without effect. The latency time for the whistle was 5 seconds and for the needle 15 seconds. It required 21 seconds for the curve produced by the needle to reach its maximum.

1233   In this group the differences between the reactions to physical and to psychological stimuli are more marked than in normal subjects. In all cases the quiet period shows little change. Only one subject shows what could be considered an expectation curve.

1234   Five subjects reacted to the falling weight, Part II. The reactions vary from 3.2 mm. to 35.6 mm. The greatest reaction was in the case of epilepsy and hysteria. The three cases not reacting were severely demented. The averages for the cases reacting are:

Height	7.5 mm.
Latency	2.25 sec.
Time to top	6.00 sec.

1235   The pneumographic measurements are:

	Inspirations per cm.	Average height in mm.
Before	2.6	12.28
Rise	2.6	9.73
Fall	2.71	10.81

1236   The galvanometric reaction is only about one-third as high as the normal. The pneumographic measurements are almost the same as those of the normal cases.

1237   Spontaneous speaking (Part III) could only be tried in three cases. In these cases there was a latency time averaging 2 seconds, in contrast to the normal cases where the curve begins to rise at the moment of speaking. The measurements for the three cases are:

Height	14.66 mm.
Latency	2.0 sec.
Time to top	5.5 sec.

1238   These measurements are lower than in normal subjects. The pneumographic results are:

	Inspirations per cm.	Average height in mm.
Before	3.5	10.92
Rise	3.3	11.52
Fall	2.9	13.62

In normal cases the amplitude decreases from the moment of stimulus; here it increases.

1239   Part IV, three physical stimuli, weight, whistle, and picture, failed to cause any reaction in three demented cases.

1240   The measurements for five cases are:

	Weight	Whistle	Picture
Height	26.6 mm.	23.6 mm.	15.4 mm.
Latency	2.3 sec.	3.5 sec.	2.83 sec.
Time to top	6.6 sec.	6.75 sec.	5.3 sec.

1241   In the normal cases the greatest reaction was to the picture. The weight, the stimulus calling up the fewest associations,

569

caused the smallest reaction. The pneumographic measurements in three cases are as follows:

	Inspirations per cm.			*Average height in mm.*		
	Weight	*Whistle*	*Picture*	*Weight*	*Whistle*	*Picture*
Before	2.8	3.0	2.7	8.05	8.23	8.34
Rise	2.5	2.96	3.6	7.1	9.37	6.51
Fall	3.11	3.1	2.9	6.74	8.38	8.03

1242   In the normal cases the height is always less during the rise of the galvanic curve, here it varies very much.

1243   Part V, sentences, caused comparatively slight reactions in all cases. In four demented cases there were no reactions. The measurements for four cases are:

	Sen. 1	*Sen. 2*	*Sen. 3*	*Sen. 4*
Height	13.4 mm.	7.8 mm.	4.5 mm.	4.5 mm.
Latency	3.0 sec.	3.3 sec.	5.0 sec.	3.0 sec.
Time to top	3.6 sec.	5.0 sec.	5.0 sec.	2.0 sec.

1244   The reactions decrease in intensity from the first to the third sentence. The pneumographic curves give the following measurements:

Inspirations per cm.

	Sen. 1	*Sen. 2*	*Sen. 3*	*Sen. 4*
Before	3.5	3.0	3.0	4.0
Rise	4.0	3.0	3.0	3.0
Fall	3.1	3.3	3.3	2.5

Average height in mm.

	Sen. 1	*Sen. 2*	*Sen. 3*	*Sen. 4*
Before	7.2	6.7	5.6	7.0
Rise	6.1	7.5	6.0	5.5
Fall	6.8	6.0	6.6	5.5

1245   Part VI, the second quiet period, shows nothing.

1246   In all these cases of varying degrees of dementia the galvanic fluctuations were in direct relation to the degree of mental dullness, seriously demented cases having little or no reaction. In such seriously demented cases the reactions are similar to those of the subject cited above, tested after an attack of *petit mal*: only those stimuli tending to cause pain are reacted to. The problem of this phenomenon is entirely a question of lack of associations.

Dementia Praecox

1247   The cases in this group were in various stages of the disease. The reactions therefore vary considerably. Each form of the disease will be discussed separately.

Catatonia

1248   There were eleven cases of catatonia varying from those in complete stupor to those in a convalescent condition. Our results are high because one convalescent gave reactions that were those of a normal person. Cases in a condition of stupor give practically no reaction to ordinary stimuli; for cases in a depressive state the reaction is also less marked.

1249   The curve for the quiet period varies according to the condition of the subject. In patients who are actively hallucinated it is very often quite irregular; in patients in a stuporous condition it is very nearly a straight line.

1250   The pneumograph was not used.

1251   Part II (falling weight) caused a reaction in almost every case, the reaction varying from 1.8 mm. in a very depressed patient to 6 mm. in a patient with active hallucinations and 43.2 mm. in a convalescent. The average deflection for eleven cases was 6.8 mm.

1252   Part III (spontaneous speaking) was not possible with these subjects.

1253   Part IV (three physical stimuli) caused various reactions, as in normal cases. In five cases of patients in a stuporous, depressed condition, the whistle caused no reaction.

1254   The weight caused a deflection of 6.3 mm., the whistle 2.4 mm., and the picture 3.9 mm. As in the groups of epileptics the weight caused the greatest reactions.

1255   Part IV (four sentences) in every case gave smaller reactions than the physical stimuli. The subject who reacted to the weight with 43.2 mm. reacted to the sentences with a deflection of from 6 to 14 mm. The averages for the four sentences are:

Sentence 1	2.01 mm.
Sentence 2	2.3 mm.
Sentence 3	2.6 mm.
Sentence 4	1.9 mm.

1256   The second quiet period curve shows nothing.

Hebephrenia

1257   There were eleven subjects suffering from this form of the disease. The measurements, while not markedly different from those of the former group, are quite different from the normal.

1258   As in the former group, the quiet curve is irregular whenever the patient has marked hallucinations.

1259   The weight (Part II) caused a weaker reaction than in the former group, the average deflection being 5 mm.

1260   Spontaneous speaking (Part III) in four cases gave an average deflection of 2.6 mm.

1261   The three physical stimuli (Part IV) caused the following reactions: weight, 6.8 mm.; whistle, 3.5 mm.; picture, 4.4 mm. As in the former groups, the weight caused the greatest reaction.

1262   Part V (sentences) caused a greater reaction here than in the former group but a much smaller average reaction than the physical stimuli. The measurements are:

Sentence 1	2.6 mm.
Sentence 2	1.3 mm.
Sentence 3	3.8 mm.
Sentence 4	4.2 mm.

Paranoid Group

1263   There are four subjects in this group, one in an early stage, two somewhat demented, and one seriously demented. The latter reacted to none of the stimuli. The pneumograph was used in two cases.

1264   The quiet period is almost that of a normal subject.

1265   Part II (falling weight) called forth weaker reactions than those in the two preceding groups, the average being 4.8 mm. The latency time averages 3 sec. and the time required for the curve to reach its maximum 7 sec. The rise and fall of these curves is much slower than in the normal cases. The pneumographic measurements of two cases are:

	Inspirations per cm.	*Average height in mm.*
Before	2.5	13.1
Rise	2.94	8.1
Fall	2.63	11.8

These are very close to the measurements obtained in the normal cases.

1266   Part III (spontaneous speaking) was tried in two cases, giving an average deflection of 4.6 mm. The pneumographic measurements are those of the normal cases:

	Inspirations per cm.	Average height in mm.
Before	3.2	11.78
Rise	2.92	9.2
Fall	2.52	10.76

1267   Part IV (three physical stimuli) gives measurements similar to those of the normal subjects in that the reaction to the picture is the greatest. The measurements are:

	Weight	Whistle	Picture
Height	5.8 mm.	5.4 mm.	7.0 mm.
Latency	2.5 sec.	2.0 sec.	2.0 sec.
Time to top	6.0 sec.	6.0 sec.	5.5 sec.

1268   The pneumographic measurements for the depth of inspirations are about those of a normal subject. The rate varies in every case, apparently quite freely.

	Inspirations per cm.			Average height in mm.		
	Weight	Whistle	Picture	Weight	Whistle	Picture
Before	3.0	2.7	3.0	11.90	11.61	16.91
Rise	2.78	3.2	4.0	9.32	9.50	11.25
Fall	2.95	3.16	2.91	12.54	11.53	11.31

1269   Part V. The reactions to the sentences are but little higher than those in the other forms of dementia praecox. The measurements are:

	Sen. 1	Sen. 2	Sen. 3	Sen. 4
Height	5.2 mm.	3.2 mm.	2.6 mm.	3.0 mm.
Latency	3.0 sec.	5.0 sec.	3.0 sec.	3.0 sec.
Time to top	4.5 sec.	5.0 sec.	2.0 sec.	1.0 sec.

The pneumographic curves for the first two sentences only are given, those of the other two being unusable.

	Inspirations per cm.		Average height in mm.	
	Sen. 1	Sen. 2	Sen. 1	Sen. 2
Before	3.2	3.0	12.52	13.58
Rise	3.16	2.99	12.16	12.1
Fall	2.5	2.48	13.0	12.22

1270   The second quiet curve is regular in all cases.

Chronic Alcoholism

1271   There are three cases in this group, confirmed alcoholics, but showing no dementia. The galvanometric measurements only are given. The subjects reacted fairly rapidly, and most of them responded more intensely than normal subjects to all stimuli.

1272   The first quiet period shows nothing.

1273   Part II (falling weight) caused a deflection of 23.3 mm., greater than in any of the other groups.

1274   Part III (spontaneous speaking) caused a deflection of 18.6 mm.

1275   Part IV (three physical stimuli, weight, whistle, and picture) caused the following deflections: weight, 24 mm.; whistle, 24 mm., picture, 28 mm. These reactions are greater than those of the normal subjects. The relation of the reactions to the various stimuli in these and in normal subjects is almost the same in all cases, that to the picture being the greatest and those to the weight and whistle being very nearly the same.

1276   Part V (the four sentences) caused reactions generally greater than in the normal cases, being: Sen. 1, 8.6 mm.; Sen. 2, 16 mm.; Sen. 3, 20 mm.; Sen. 4, 14 mm.

Alcoholic Dementia

1277   There were three cases of alcoholic dementia, which may be contrasted with the last group. In this group the reactions are all weaker than in the cases without dementia, and the smaller reactions to psychological stimuli are especially striking.

1278   The weight caused a deflection of 9.06 mm., as compared to 23.3 mm. for the last group.

1279   Spontaneous speaking caused a reaction of 6.8 mm.

1280   The reactions to the three physical stimuli, weight, whistle, and picture, are very interesting. The picture caused a deflection of only 7.6 mm., as compared to the weight, 16 mm., and the whistle, 13 mm. The reactions are directly proportional to the physical nature of the stimuli. The picture, which in normal cases caused the greatest number of associations and the greatest affects, here caused the fewest associations and the slightest reactions.

1281   The reduction of the reactions to mental stimuli is again seen in the sentences, where they are slight.

Sen. 1	Sen. 2	Sen. 3	Sen. 4
3.3 mm.	1.3 mm.	5.6 mm.	2.5 mm.

The reduction here is proportionally much greater than in any of the other groups.

General Paralysis

1282   Nine cases of general paralysis were examined. Two were in a condition of euphoria and one in a period of remission. The other six cases were in a condition of dementia and apathy and gave hardly any reactions to the various stimuli.

1283   The quiet period shows nothing at all for the cases of dementia; in the other cases a few irregularities can be seen.

1284   Part II (the falling weight) caused strong reactions in the two euphoric cases and the case in remission, but no reaction at all in the demented cases.

Height	21.1 mm.
Latency	2.2 sec.
Time to top	6.6 sec.

1285   The pneumographic measurements in these cases are nearly normal.

	Inspirations per cm.	Average height in mm.
Before	3.25	8.7
Rise	3.1	7.2
Fall	3.4	9.6

1286   The pneumographic measurements for two cases giving no galvanic reactions are:

	Inspirations per cm.	Average height in mm.
Before stimulus	2.5	21.37
After stimulus	3.0	22.3

1287   Spontaneous speaking could not be attempted.

1288   Part IV (three physical stimuli) in the three cases caused the following reactions:

	Weight	Whistle	Picture
Height	9.4 mm.	25.8 mm.	15.05 mm.
Latency	2.5 sec.	2.3 sec.	2.6 sec.
Time to top	4.0 sec.	7.0 sec.	4.1 sec.

¹²⁸⁹ The high average reaction to the whistle is due to the reaction of the patient in a period of remission whose reaction was 70 mm. It will be observed that the weight in these cases caused the smallest reaction. The pneumographic measurements for the three cases are:

	Inspirations per cm.			Average height in mm.		
	Weight	Whistle	Picture	Weight	Whistle	Picture
Before	3.0	3.0	3.65	5.5	5.5	7.9
Rise	3.0	3.0	3.2	4.5	9.1	7.9
Fall	3.0	2.9	3.5	4.8	8.8	7.8

¹²⁹⁰ In the case of two patients giving no galvanic reaction the pneumographic measurements are:

	Inspirations per cm.			Average height in mm.		
	Weight	Whistle	Picture	Weight	Whistle	Picture
Before	2.0	3.0	2.0	20.5	20.45	18.5
After	2.0	2.5	2.0	21.12	20.50	19.0

¹²⁹¹ Part V. The results for three sentences are given. Four subjects reacted to these stimuli.

	Sen. 1	Sen. 2	Sen. 3
Height	16 mm.	9.58 mm.	18 mm.
Latency	4 sec.	2.5 sec.	1.5 sec.
Time to top	5 sec.	4.7 sec.	5.5 sec.

¹²⁹² These reactions are nearly the same as those of the normal subjects. The pneumographic measurements for these cases are:

	Inspirations per cm.			Average height in mm.		
Before	3.5	3.0	3.0	7.4	7.1	10.3
Rise	4.0	3.3	3.3	10.0	8.6	9.0
Fall	4.0	4.6	4.5	11.0	8.1	9.2

¹²⁹³ The pneumographic measurements of two cases giving no galvanic reaction are:

	Inspirations per cm.		Average height in mm.	
	Sen. 1	Sen. 2	Sen. 1	Sen. 2
Before	2.75	3.0	20.75	20.40
After	2.75	2.75	21.30	21.50

¹²⁹⁴ Paretics in a condition of euphoria and in a stage of remission, when dementia is not pronounced, react well to the vari-

576

ous stimuli. They take a very active interest in the experiment and this may account for the fairly large galvanic reaction. Paretics in a demented condition give no reactions to simple stimuli and correspond to other cases of dementia.

Senile Dementia

1295 There were eleven cases of senile dementia. Most of these cases did not react to the stimuli. In some cases even the prick of a needle caused no galvanic fluctuation.

1296 The weight caused a reaction in three cases. The average deviation for the three cases was 5 mm.

1297 Spontaneous speaking (Part III of the experiment) could not be attempted on account of the dementia.

1298 The three stimuli (Part IV) gave smaller measurements than those obtained in any other disease, the weight causing an average deflection of 1 mm., the whistle 1.8 mm., and the picture 4 mm. The relatively high reaction caused by the picture is interesting.

1299 The mental stimuli, sentences (Part V), caused very little reaction.

Sen. 1	Sen. 2	Sen. 3	Sen. 4
0.6 mm.	0.6 mm.	0.2 mm.	0.8 mm.

1300 The following table gives a survey of the galvanic measurements in mm. of all the subjects:

	Weight	*Spont.*	*Weight*	*Whistle*	*Picture*		Sentences		
						1	*2*	*3*	*4*
Normal	20.6	17.9	17.94	18.2	19.72	14.62	14.48	19.42	11.12
Epilepsy	7.5	14.66	26.6	23.6	15.4	13.4	7.8	4.5	4.5
Catatonia	6.8	—	6.3	2.4	3.9	2.01	2.3	2.6	1.9
Hebephrenia	5.0	2.6	6.8	3.5	4.4	2.6	1.3	3.8	4.2
Paranoid D. P.	4.8	4.6	5.8	5.4	7.0	5.2	3.2	2.6	3.0
Chronic alcoholism	23.3	18.6	24.0	24.0	28.0	8.6	16.0	20.0	14.0
Alcoholic dementia	9.06	6.8	16.0	13.0	7.6	3.3	1.3	5.6	2.5
General paralysis: euphoria and remission	21.1	—	9.4	25.8	15.05	16.0	9.58	18.0	—
General paralysis: dementia	—	—	—	—	—	—	—	—	—
Senile dementia	5.0	—	1.0	1.8	4.0	0.6	0.6	0.2	0.8

577

1301   This table shows that in every case the physical stimuli cause a smaller galvanic fluctuation than the psychological ones, but in the cases where intellectual deterioration is marked the reduction is proportionally greater than in the other cases.

1302   The intensity of the reaction seems to depend partly on the attention paid by the subject to the experiment. In cases of dementia praecox, where internal complexes dominate the affectivity and attention, the reactions are slight; in alcoholism and in general paralysis, euphoric state, where excitability is very great, the reactions are correspondingly greater. In organic dementia, where all associative power is lost, the reactions are almost nil. In dementia senilis, where dementia was very marked, even the prick of a needle failed to cause any response.

1303   The pneumographic measurements in these cases are nearly the same as those found in normal cases. There is evidently no rule for the rate but the amplitude usually decreases while the galvanic phenomenon persists.

1304   That the galvanic fluctuation is caused by the psychological[7] and not the physical factor of a stimulus is shown by the following facts:

1305   The reaction is greatest when the stimulus is such as to call up a large number of associations, e.g., the picture.

1306   A stimulus causing doubt and perplexity is accompanied by a marked galvanic fluctuation, e.g., where the stimulus is a simple word.

1307   In cases of dementia, where associations are few, the reactions are correspondingly weaker.

1308   The physical intensity of a stimulus does not bear any regular relation to the force of the galvanic reaction.

1309   The strength of the reaction changes exclusively according to psychological constellations. This is beautifully shown in one normal case where an ordinary whistle caused only a slight reaction, but the whistle-call of a society to which the subject had belonged as a schoolboy caused a very great fluctuation.

1310   If the attention is not directed to the stimulus the reaction is small or nil. We therefore have no reactions in cases where

7 Binswanger, "On the Psychogalvanic Phenomenon in Association Experiments" (orig. 1907/8).

attention is seriously disturbed. This can be proved by letting the subject count or draw lines on a paper at the beat of a metronome. In this case the reactions are almost nil.

Summary

1311   From the above experiments we conclude that:

(1) The galvanic reaction depends on attention to the stimulus and the ability to associate it with other previous occurrences. This association may be conscious but is usually unconscious.[8]

(2) In our experiments greater galvanic fluctuations are caused, as a rule, by physical than by psychological stimuli. This may be due to the fact that they occurred before the psychological stimuli, early stimuli nearly always causing greater reactions than later ones.

(3) While normal reactions vary greatly in different individuals, they are nearly always greater than pathological reactions.

(4) In depression and stupor, galvanic reactions are low because attention is poor and associations are inhibited.

(5) In alcoholism and in the euphoric stage of general paralysis, reactions are high because of greater excitability.

(6) In dementia, reactions are practically nil because of the lack of associations.

(7) Reactions show great individual variation and within certain rather wide limits are entirely independent of the original bodily resistance.

The pneumographic measurements may be summarized as follows:

(1) The inspiratory rate varies according to the individual and no general rule can be given.

(2) The amplitude of the inspirations generally decreases during the rise of the galvanic curve.

(3) This decrease in amplitude, however, has no relation to the height of the galvanic curve but varies according to individuals.

(4) In cases of dementia where there is no galvanic reaction, changes of respiration exist but are very slight.

8 [*Orig.*: subconscious.]

BIBLIOGRAPHY[9]

Delabarre: *Über Bewegungsempfindungen* (1891).

Féré: "Note sur des modifications de la résistance électrique sous l'influence des excitations sensorielles et des émotions" (1888).

Idem: "Note sur des modifications de la tension électrique dans le corps humain" (1888).

Mentz: "Die Wirkung akustischer Sinnesreize auf Puls und Atmung" (1893).

Mosso: *Über den Kreislauf des Blutes im menschlichen Gehirn* (1881).

Sommer: In *Beiträge zur Psychiatrischen Klinik*, Vienna (1902).

Sommer and Fürstenau: "Die elektrischen Vorgänge an der menschlichen Haut" (1906).

Sticker: "Über Versuche einer objektiven Darstellung von Sensibilitätsstörungen" (1897).

Tarchanoff: "Über die galvanischen Erscheinungen an der Haut des Menschen . . ." (1890).

Veraguth: "Le Réflexe psycho-galvanique" (1906).

Idem: "Das psycho-galvanische Reflex-Phänomen" (1906).

A. Vigouroux: *Étude sur la résistance électrique chez les mélancoliques* (1890).

R. Vigouroux: "Sur la résistance électrique considerée comme signe clinique" (1888).

Idem: "L'Électricité du corps humain" (1888).

Zoneff and Meumann: "Über Begleiterscheinungen psychischer Vorgänge in Atem und Puls" (1900).

[9] [Jung published this bibliography with more or less full references, which will be found in the entries in the volume bibliography.]

APPENDIX

1

STATISTICAL DETAILS OF ENLISTMENT[1]

1312   As a member of a medical board I had the opportunity last autumn to make a few observations that may be of interest to some of my colleagues and stimulate them to make similar investigations.

1313   The enlistment at which I was present took place in Lucerne and its environs. The first day of the enlistment produced much strikingly inferior human material. At least, that is how it struck me—it was the first time I had taken part in an enlistment. If I remember rightly, not even half of the recruits were fit. Later on it became even worse. There are places where not even 30 per cent of the male population are fit; it must be emphasized that these places are not industrial towns, but villages in rich and fertile country. The impression that the first day of enlistment made on me, namely the fact that so many mentally inferior men came for examination, induced me to note how many manifestly imbecile men had presented themselves. Since a somewhat too biassed judgment regarding the diagnosis of mental deficiency is attributed to the psychiatrist, I noted only those cases that had also immediately struck the psychiatric layman as idiots. I omitted a number of cases where, after a short examination,[2] I was convinced that I was faced with mental deficiency, in which, however, imbecility was not immediately apparent to the layman. The material under examination consisted of 506 men, of whom 47 (that is, as much as 9.2 per cent) were patently imbecile! 211 men

---

1 [Translated from "Statistisches von der Rekrutenaushebung," *Correspondenz-Blatt für Schweizer Aerzte* (Basel), XXXVI:4 (Feb. 15, 1906), 129–30. Jung served as an officer in the Swiss Army medical corps from 1901 to 1930.]

2 One must take into consideration that the formalities of enlistment create for many people an unusual situation, owing to which they get into a state of persistent stupefaction (so-called emotional stupidity), which makes them appear more stupid than they really are.

from the town presented themselves; of these 5.6 per cent were imbecile. 232[3] men came from the country; of these 13 per cent were imbecile. The big difference between town and country might be explained by the fact that it is mainly the intelligent and enterprising people who converge on the towns, while the unintelligent and torpid remain in the country. The difference between town and country probably does not mean more than a symptom of the present tendency to migrate into the towns. The imbecility of my cases was so obvious that, where there had been any question of criminal offences, the psychiatrist present had stated that the accused were not responsible for their actions. Should my figures be confirmed throughout, then approximately 9 per cent of Swiss adolescents would not be responsible for their actions! This is a terrifyingly high figure which casts a curious light on the level of intelligence of our people, particularly of the rural population. The even higher figures for physical unfitness raise the question of whether there has always been an inferiority of this kind or whether we are faced with degeneration. In any case, an investigation of this problem in connection with enlistment would, for various theoretical and economic reasons, be worthwhile.

1314   In this connection one should consider the fact that, in the enlistment district about which I am reporting, the farmers are alleged to have the curious custom of delivering all their milk to the cheese-factories and of feeding their children on coffee and brandy (a similar custom is reported from the canton of Bern).

1315   When examining those conscripts who reported some ailment to the Commission, I was struck by the large number of alcoholics. To avoid misunderstandings, I noted only those cases that also impressed my colleagues as alcoholics. I therefore included only the cases that revealed themselves as chronic alcoholics through tremor, heart or liver symptoms, and perhaps through signs of polyneuritis. My material comprises 78 men, nearly all of them between the ages of 20 and 30. Of these, 10 (that is 12.9 per cent) had to be discharged as unfit for military service owing to chronic alcoholism. No statistical survey, however, reports this figure because these people are

[3] The rest came from the semi-urban population of Kriens; they were therefore omitted.

not classified under the heading of alcoholism; they are entered under the more decent title of the alcoholic sequela—for instance, dilatation of the heart or hypertrophy of the heart, chronic gastric catarrh, chronic nephritis, etc. One refers to these alcoholics with a kind of euphemism that certainly often originates in commendable personal consideration but which ultimately leads to a highly detrimental obscuring of the fact that our army annually loses a disproportionately large number of strong men because of alcoholism. What makes matters even worse is the fact that it is the most vigorous age-group that is in question and not the older age-groups. One wonders what conditions are like in the militia if we get such figures for the regular recruits!

NEW ASPECTS OF CRIMINAL PSYCHOLOGY[1]

Contribution to the Method Used for the Psychological
Diagnosis of Evidence (Tatbestandsdiagnose)[2]

1316   The very simple experiment designed to induce an individual to respond to a given stimulus-word with the first word that crosses his mind has become the point of departure of a long series of psychological problems that are of interest not only to the psychologist but also to the jurist and the psychiatrist.

1317   It is not my intention to give here a review of all association experiments; I only wish to indicate one of the possible applications of these experiments, which may interest practical psy-

---

1 [Translated from "Le nuove vedute della psicologia criminale; Contributo al metodo della 'Diagnosi della conoscenza del fatto' (Tatbestandsdiagnose)," *Rivista di psicologia applicata* (Bologna), IV:4 (July–August, 1908), 285–304. The article in Italian was translated by L. Baroncini from a German manuscript that has not been discovered. Part of the article was incorporated in Jung's lecture "The Association Method" at Clark University, 1909; see supra, par. 929, n. 1, and infra, n. 10.]

2 [Editorial note in the Italian, apparently by the editor of the *Rivista*, G. Cesare Ferrari, director of the provincial mental hospital at Imola:

"*Tatbestandsdiagnose* is one of those words without meaning, at least for us, that only the Germans can coin. The subject to which this inappropriate word refers is, however, so important that we must try to find a significant term.

"It is not the first time that this difficulty has arisen; terms such as 'associations with a diagnostic purpose,' 'involuntary self-accusation by means of associations,' 'diagnosis of complexes of ideas,' and others have been proposed. Each of these is, however, open to criticism.

"Baroncini, who has translated Jung's original work into Italian, tries to be faithful to the German phraseology of the text. He proposes, however, to correct the term to 'psychological diagnosis of evidence' (*diagnosi della conoscenza del fatto*), a logical substitution that has the disadvantage of needing two pages of interpretation. For lack of a better term, we accept this phrase and we suggest that the organizers of the Congress for Psychology in Geneva may improve on it."]

chologists and criminologists. This is the so-called "diagnosis of evidence" (*Tatbestandsdiagnose*), i.e., the psychological diagnosis of a crime.[3] This term is somewhat pretentious; in practice, those in favour of the method content themselves with more modest results than the infallible diagnosis of a crime. Notwithstanding this limitation, there are some, and they are not a few, who deny any value to the use of the experiment and who maintain that it is without any interest: but as so often, this exaggeration only shows how one falls from one extreme into the other. On the one hand, workers in this field dare not hope that they can arrive at a psychological procedure that will permit them to make a sure diagnosis after only a few preliminary investigations. Medicine, however, possesses quite a number of such methods that have won acceptance only after a laborious struggle. In the field of psychology progress cannot be made any more easily. On the other hand, one must recognize the facile opposition that is based on initial failure of the method; some, like Heilbronner, deny that any application of the experiment can be of value. So the opposition degenerates into a scepticism that arises not from knowledge and serious criticism, but from a deplorably superficial judgment.[4]

1318　　The problem of the diagnosis of evidence is at present of the greatest importance to psychologists; to criminologists it is only of academic interest, since we are still far from its practical application in court: this must be the honest and fair appreciation of the experiments we are going to report.

1319　　The technique is very simple. Let us take an example: a bag containing jewellery, such as a gold bracelet with blue stones, a diamond brooch in the shape of a butterfly, a ring shaped like a snake, and a brooch in the form of a lizard with

---

[3] For the history, literature, and technique of the experiments, see my "The Psychological Diagnosis of Evidence," supra.

A good illustration of the laboratory experiments and of many questions about the method can be found in Alfred Gross, "Kriminalpsychologische Tatbestandsforschung" (1907).

The use of the association experiments for criminological purposes was first suggested by Wertheimer and Klein [1904].

For the general importance of the association experiments, see the Diagnostic Association Studies edited by me (1906).

[4] J. G. Schnitzler, medical dissertation, Utrecht, 1907 [= "Experimentelle Beiträge zur Tatbestandsdiagnostik" (1909)].

emerald eyes, was stolen from a hotel. There were also a green leather wallet containing a cheque drawn on the Banca Commerciale Italiana and three banknotes of fifty lire each, and a bottle of Odol.

1320   The hotel porter and two other employees were suspected of the theft and arrested. Apart from the hotel proprietor, only the culprit could have known the contents of the bag. Such a state of affairs lends itself admirably to the association experiment. Here are examples of the words chosen for it: *gold, fifty, three, bracelet, blue, bank, snake, stone, diamond, lizard, green, leather, butterfly, wallet, cheque, banknote, Odol*, etc. These were distributed among approximately twice the number of other words, chosen for having the smallest possible reference to the evidence. This was done because we wanted to demonstrate how words derived from the evidence, which is known in its minutest particulars only to the culprit, affect people subjected to the experiment.

1321   How then, generally speaking, do the stimulus-words "act"?

1322   Needless to say, the subject must consent to the experiment and must obey the instructions. Without his co-operation one cannot, of course, achieve anything. The instruction usually given is this: "You must say, as quickly as possible, the first word that the stimulus-word suggests to you." It is possible for the subject to cheat by not saying the first word that comes to his mind, but in order to reveal the deception, we measure the reaction-time with a stop-watch. If the subject does not say the first word that occurs to him, it is tantamount to rejecting it and he has to look for another; this needs a certain time, which is measurable. A long reaction-time should therefore not mislead the experimenter. The subject of the experiment may well go to the trouble of prolonging his other reaction-times nearly to the same extent, whether they belong to critical words or to others without special meaning. But this deception is as a rule easily seen through since it is known that the reaction-time in educated people is about 1.5 seconds and in uneducated people 2.0 seconds; on the other hand, as the subject deliberately influences the reaction-times, these are as a rule unduly prolonged because it is difficult consciously to judge the lapse of time. Apart from these possible deceptions, every other effect of the critical stimulus-words will result from a disturbance of attention. This disturbance arises from the fact that the critical stimulus-word brings back to the mind a content with a strong feeling-tone; this attracts the attention and captivates it for a moment, producing a slowing down of the reaction if a familiar word does not at once present itself. The reproduction method[5] also brings into relief another fact, namely, that reactions to critical words (i.e., those words that revive contents of consciousness with a strong feeling-tone) are more easily forgotten than reactions to words without special meaning. Reactions that immediately follow critical reactions are also often forgotten (perseveration of the disturbance of attention). Why they are so easily forgotten has not yet been sufficiently explored; nor do I wish to enter into any theoretical speculations.

1323   It often happens that the subject is startled by the critical stimulus-word. This is another disturbing factor, which first affects the reaction-time and then the verbal form of the reaction itself: the subject believes that he has not properly understood or has really misunderstood, or he mechanically repeats the stimulus-word. As, in his embarrassment, he cannot find a word of no special significance, he replaces it with a phrase (and this is against the rules) and then, in uttering this phrase, makes a mistake. In these short moments, which are of immense intrinsic value, he produces many blunders that betray him, such as we all, in our daily lives, also commit for the same reasons, even though as a rule unconsciously. In one case, a student who took part in the experiment, and who was usually very much in command of himself, betrayed himself by making at each critical word a certain small gesture of the hand which he omitted when the word had no special meaning for him.

1324   All these small disturbing elements in the experiment I have termed "complex-characteristics" (*Complexmerkmale*);

---

[5] In the reproduction method, one first collects a large number of associations, then one requests the subject to say again the words with which he had reacted to the various stimulus-words. One then finds that it is mainly such associations as indicate complexes that are easily forgotten. Cf. my "Disturbances of Reproduction in the Association Experiment," supra.

this means that they are pointers revealing the influence of a complex of ideas with a particular feeling-tone.[6] These are the complex-characteristics in question:

1. Prolonged reaction-time[7] in the critical reaction or in the one immediately following.
2. Reaction with two or more words, although the subject usually reacts with one word only, according to the instructions.
3. Repetition of the stimulus-word.
4. The stimulus-word (especially the one following the critical word) is misunderstood.
5. Failure to react (i.e., where the subject does not know how to react).
6. *Lapsus linguae* when pronouncing the reaction-word.
7. Translation of the stimulus-word, or of the reaction, into a foreign language.
8. Reaction in the form of an unusual expression.
9. The reaction has a singular content or may be meaningless.
10. Perseveration of the reaction-word in respect of content and of form.
11. Interpolation of "yes" or of other interjections before or after the reaction-word.

1325   Characteristics 8, 9, and 10 are somewhat arbitrary and can therefore be omitted in an exact computation.

1326   It may be objected that these deviations cannot with certainty be reduced to psychological disturbances determined by ideas with a special feeling-tone (complexes). This does not in fact appear when the association experiment is used specifically for what we have called the diagnosis of evidence, whereas it becomes quite clear in the case of the accurate analytical examination of the experiments made without a diagnostic purpose. These findings receive considerable support from measuring oscillations of body-resistance to the galvanic current during the association experiment.[8]

1327   Now, given that these deviations are caused by critical stimulus-words, we may justifiably admit that we are faced with

---

[6] A classification of the complex-characteristics can be found in par. 935, supra.

[7] See my "The Reaction-time Ratio in the Association Experiment," supra. I call "prolonged" those reaction-times that exceed the probable mean of all the reaction-times observed during the investigations.

[8] Cf. especially the investigations of Binswanger, "On the Psychogalvanic Phenomenon in Association Experiments."

a disturbing inner factor, i.e., an idea with a strong feeling-tone. If, then, with a particular subject these deviations occur mainly in connection with critical reactions—i.e., in response to stimulus-words derived from actuality—then we can confidently assume that with the word that influences the subject a complex is operative that refers to actual facts. This complex may embrace simply the subject's general knowledge about a particular crime; should stimulus-words refer to this crime then a certain emotion is bound to arise in response to every one of these stimulus-words. But it may also turn out that the disturbing complex is one that points to a feeling of guilt in the subject.

1328 An innocent suspect, as well as a guilty one, will of course show a certain emotion in response to critical stimulus-words. We do not yet know whether this emotion exerts the same perturbing influence over each of them, or whether the reaction of the innocent can be qualitatively distinguished from that of the guilty; only further experience can decide this question.

1329 In the case of our hypothetical crime only the guilty party knows the details of the facts, whereas innocent suspects hardly know the general outline. From the experiment it appears that all the critical stimulus-words have a disturbing effect on the porter, whereas in the other two employees most of the critical reactions are quite normal. From this we may conclude that suspicion must very probably fall on the porter and that his guilt appears to be established; moreover, the complex-characteristics are, significantly enough, recognized through those stimulus-words the importance of which cannot by any means be known to the innocent.

1330 We have no absolute proof of guilt, but it is clear that in such cases the experiment may provide valuable pointers for further investigation. This will happen especially when there is a large number of suspects and when the elements of suspicion about some of them lack a solid basis; in such a case we can, with the help of the experiment, eventually succeed in tracing those on whom graver suspicion must fall. Let us, however, repeat that the results of the experiment will not provide absolute proof of guilt but, at best, merely a valuable addition to the circumstantial evidence. If one has to do with only one suspect and if there are no facts with which to confront this person, then the results are unquestionably most unreliable.

1331   Some two years ago I published a case from my practice, in which a thief confessed his crime as a result of strong evidence arising from the association experiment.[9] A short time ago I was concerned with another case of theft that from the technical point of view lent itself very well to the experiment; like the first case, it was entirely successful.[10]

. . . .

Critique and Qualitative Analysis

1332   Faced with these results, the reader who is without a thorough knowledge of the method is bound to ask himself this question: Is it not possible that one of the three suspects who was not the subject of this research would, on examination, present an even greater number of signs of guilt? This is of course *a priori* possible, but in practice one always begins with the subject to whom the evidence points most clearly; in our case this was definitely the nurse A. From this reasoning my concept of the experiment clearly emerges: it should only, in the first place, show us which of the subjects presents the maximum number of complex-disturbances. Then we have the suspect who shows himself most disturbed, either because he is really the culprit or because the fear of appearing guilty causes great agitation. Nurse B appeared very agitated during the experiment and this prejudiced me against her, even though she did not show distinct signs of a guilt-complex. Nurse C was relatively calm but nevertheless the complex-characteristics were more numerous. This discrepancy needs to be examined further. Why do the innocent usually show signs of a guilt-complex? The answer to this question presents no difficulties. Nurse B knew all the particulars of the case and during the experiment Nurse C had an inkling of its importance. It is therefore easy to understand why words like *theft, to steal,* and *police* created in them an unpleasant feeling that in its turn produced the characteristic disturbance of the experiment.

9 "The Psychological Diagnosis of Evidence," supra.
10 [The case report is omitted here, as it is reproduced in "The Association Method," supra, pars. 957–82. The present paper, however, contains further analysis of the case, which follows.]

Here we have the explanation of why even the innocent can show a not inconsiderable number of signs of guilt-complex. What distinguishes them from the guilty are not (at least as far as we know at present) qualitative differences but mainly quantitative ones.

1333   It is nevertheless surprising that Nurse B, who had been given exact information about the circumstances of the theft and who was evidently affected by strong emotion, showed fewer signs of guilt-complex than Nurse C, who was the calmer of the two. Only psychoanalysis, applied to each association, can throw light on this question.

1334   In Nurse C the words *watch, chain, silver*, produced evident complex-disturbances; now, by an unfortunate coincidence, both the watch and the chain had been broken a few days before. The word *to hide* also has a disturbing influence; Nurse C had a short time before taken away her evening meal and hidden it, something that was absolutely forbidden in the hospital. *Fear, to discover, innocent, suspect, to lie* are all disturbing words: it was known that through negligence she had mislaid or lost a garment belonging to one of the patients. It suddenly occurred to her during the experiment that this incident was being enquired into, since nothing had so far been discovered about it; and that was why signs of guilt-complex appeared in response to these words.

1335   The interference of other individual complexes seriously compromised the results of the investigation but this was unavoidable. One of the few measures that could be taken to this end would be to use a long series of stimulus-words (100–200) of which as many as possible would refer to definite details of the case and would be of similar categories since, if they were, they would produce disturbances owing to the intellectual work involved. *A priori* one would regard as most suitable words that are apparently of no special significance and that yet have a special significance in relation to the case (the so-called "exchange" [German, *Wechsel*], according to Freud's apt expression[11]).

---

[11] Freud, "Psycho-analysis and the Establishment of the Facts in Legal Proceedings" (1906). [See the Standard Edn., IX, 106, where, however, the term "exchange" (*Wechsel*) does not occur. In a letter to Jung of 1 Jan. 1907, Freud uses *Wechsel* in precisely this sense. It is possible that Jung was recalling Freud's

1336   Let us therefore try to assess the importance of words that have a direct reference to the case as compared with those that have only a general connection with the theft.

1337   First we shall again calculate the probable mean of the reaction-times; we shall, however, reduce the numbers of B and C as if the reaction-times of these subjects had the same general probable mean as those shown by A (11.0).

Probable Mean of Reaction-times
(reduced to the level of that of the culprit)

	A	B	C
Special stimulus-words	15	15.1	12.2
General stimulus-words	18	11.0	14.6

1338   We can see that the general stimulus-words have a very strong influence on the guilty nurse A. The special stimulus-words have the same effect on the guilty A and on the innocent B, whereas on B the general stimulus-words show very little effect. In this case the expected confirmation was not forthcoming.

1339   Let us now investigate the same question from the point of view of complex-characteristics.

Average Number of Complex-characteristics per Reaction

	A	B	C
Special stimulus-words	1.2	0.9	1.0
General stimulus-words	1.5	0.7	1.1

1340   We find here in essence a state of affairs similar to that in the reaction-times, i.e., [in the case of A and C][12] the general stimulus-words exercise a stronger influence.

1341   Let us now examine the disturbances of reproduction from the same point of view.

Incorrect Reproductions

	A	B	C
Special stimulus-words	0.4	0.2	0.2
General stimulus-words	0.6	0.2	0.3

usage in that letter but by mistake cited the 1906 article. See *The Freud/Jung Correspondence* (in press).]

[12] [Bracketed words added by translator.]

¹³⁴²   This shows that the figures for disturbances of reproduction are larger for the general stimulus-words [for A and C].

¹³⁴³   Little can be expected, for the time being, from the study of such associations as follow immediately upon critical associations; this is because we do not know when, in what individuals, or in what complexes a particularly strong perseveration may exert a disturbing influence on the experiment. One could presume that perseveration would appear mainly after very intense emotion, but it is not at all certain that this would be shown by the experiment. Should it prove to be true, it could turn out to be one of the origins of disturbance associated with perseveration. Another cause may be found in the fact that quite often the total range of the preceding stimulus-word is not readily understood, so that soon enough other ideas suddenly appear, not infrequently carrying strong feeling-tone. But all these contingencies demand very accurate investigations. Until these are completed, we shall not be able to benefit from whatever emerges from the research—according to which, words referring in a special way to the evidence leave in their train more disturbances in the post-critical associations than general stimulus-words do.

¹³⁴⁴   The most intense after-effect was produced in the culprit by the following stimulus-words; I give the reactions with the ordinary reactions that follow them.

Stimulus-word		Reaction	Reaction-time	Reproduction[13]
(1) banknote		money	15	—
mountain	r	to climb	26	—
to play		to sing	15	—
(2) suspect (noun)		nobody	43	+
bottle		water	17	—
fire		wood	9	—
(3) to hide		to lose, to look for	18	—
sofa		seat	17	—
night		day	6	+
(4) chain		round the neck	19	—
(5) silver		gold	10	+

---

13 The sign — means incorrect reproduction; +, correct reproduction; the letter "r," repetition of the stimulus-word.

(6)	money	r	centime	34	–
	wine		beer	8	+
(7)	open	r	free	6	+
(8)	key		keyhole	19	+
	house		courtyard	13	–
	lamp		light	8	+

1345   Just as we have found that it is *on the whole* the general stimulus-words that work with the utmost intensity, so we now see that the strongest single impact is made by those stimulus-words that refer particularly to the evidence. This shows that the general stimulus-words usually have a strong effect, whereas the special stimulus-words sometimes have an intense effect and sometimes a weak one.

1346   The only way in which we can do full justice to these results is to apply them as much as possible to practical cases since, for reasons not far to seek, laboratory investigations are always rather incomplete.

1347   I am confident that with this work I have awakened a certain interest in experiments of this kind and have encouraged others to follow in this direction. It is only by the work of many, directed always towards the examination of practical cases, that we can hope to make the diagnosis of a particular case a matter of greater certainty.

3

THE PSYCHOLOGICAL METHODS OF
INVESTIGATION USED IN THE PSYCHIATRIC
CLINIC OF THE UNIVERSITY OF ZURICH[1]

1348   1. Rapidity of apperception: short exposure of simple pictures.

2. Working through psychological material and fidelity of reproduction: retelling of three fables. The first fable contains two similar simple situations which, however, differ from each other by one important nuance. The second fable is similar but more complicated. The third fable is in principle similar, but contains a whole series of similar situations.

3. Fatiguability of the will: Kraepelin's method of reckoning.

4. Emotionally charged contents ("complexes"): Jung's association method.

5. Psychogenic mechanism and symptom-determination: Freud's psychoanalytic method.

[1] [Translated from "Die an der psychiatrischen Klinik in Zürich gebräuchlichen psychologischen Untersuchungsmethoden," *Zeitschrift für angewandte Psychologie* (Leipzig), III (1910), 390. The item is a contribution to a "survey of clinical methods for the psychological testing of the insane," along with six other reports, from German institutions.]

4

ON THE DOCTRINE OF COMPLEXES[1]

¹³⁴⁹   It is difficult to express in a short summary the doctrines laid down in my two books, "Diagnostic Association Studies" and "The Psychology of Dementia Praecox." What I state here must necessarily be incomplete and superficial.

¹³⁵⁰   My theoretical views on the neuroses and certain psychoses—especially dementia praecox—are founded upon the psychological outcome of the *association experiment.* These experiments are used for the demonstration of certain intellectual types, but I must here mention that an important point was formerly disregarded, namely, the disturbing influence of the experiment on the subject. Thus, in my practice of using a series of *stimulus-words,* and allowing the subject to react to them, that is to give answers to each word, the reactions often do not come with equal smoothness, but very irregularly, or with lengthened intervals; or there appear other disturbances such as repetitions of the stimulus-word, slips of the tongue, several reaction-words instead of one, etc. These irregularities were formerly regarded as mere faults of the experiment, and not taken into further consideration. In collaboration with Riklin, however, I have now given special attention to these disturbances. Noting at which stimulus-words they occur, we find that it is principally where a stimulus-word refers to a personal matter, which, as a rule, is of a distressing nature.

¹ [In March 1911, Dr. Andrew Davidson, the secretary of the Section of Psychological Medicine and Neurology, Australasian Medical Congress, invited Jung, Freud, and Havelock Ellis to send papers to be read before the Congress in Sydney, September, 1911. All three responded, and subsequently the papers were read and in 1913 published in the *Australasian Medical Congress, Transactions of the Ninth Session,* II, part 8. It is not known whether Jung's paper (pp. 835–39) was written in English or whether this is a translation. It is published here with only stylistic alterations. For Freud's paper, "On Psychoanalysis," see vol. XII of the Standard Edn., pp. 205ff.]

Often the relation between the two is not clear at first glance, but is rather of a "symbolic" character, it is in fact an "allusion." Usually there are only a few personal matters to which the disturbances of the experiment refer. Riklin and myself have introduced for this "personal matter" the term *complex*, because such a "personal matter" is always a collection of various ideas, held together by an emotional tone common to all. With practice and experience one may easily attain the faculty of collecting those stimulus-words which will most likely be accompanied by disturbances, then of combining their meanings and deducing therefrom the intimate affairs of the subject. It is obvious that this procedure is of special importance in a psychological examination of patients. (It is important also to note the use of the procedure in criminology; I, myself, have detected by its means two cases of theft.) Here I must mention that nearly all the German authorities have pronounced against the method, but its use is generally recognized in Switzerland and in the United States of America. French and English psychiatrists are as yet unfamiliar with the method.

¹³⁵¹   The experiment, which I perform usually with a hundred specially selected and collocated stimulus-words, serves as an indication of the psychic contents of a patient and his mode of reaction. This is of special importance with regard to the neuroses, the psychic origin of which present-day observers no longer doubt. Somatic states are never the real, but only the predisposing causes of the neuroses. The neurosis itself is of psychic origin, and emanates from "special psychic contents," which we call a *complex*. It has been discovered that the complexes revealed by association experiment are either pathogenic conflicts or at least nearly such, so that by association experiment the pathogenic complex is easily located. If one wishes to penetrate still further into the psychological connections of a neurosis, one must have knowledge of Freud's psychoanalytic method. But for a superficial grasp of the psychic contents of a neurosis the association experiment is quite sufficient. It is interesting to find that the experiment discloses thought-complexes, which were not mentioned at all in the history of the case. The obvious reason for this is the distressing character of the complexes. At the outset, patients do not talk to the doctor quite frankly about more private matters, and it is pre-

cisely these matters which have the most important bearing on the genesis of the neurosis. That these painful private matters are mostly conflicts of a distinctly psychosexual nature is to the unprejudiced judge of human nature a matter of course. Occasionally the psychosexual conflict is very deeply hidden, and can be discovered only by psychoanalysis. In many cases the aroused complex is by no means approved by the patient, who even tries in every way to deny, or at least to weaken, the existence of the complex. Since it is therapeutically important to induce the patient to self-recognition, i.e., to a recognition of his "repressed" complexes, one must take this fact into careful consideration, and proceed with corresponding care and tact.

1352   The association experiment provides the means of studying experimentally the behaviour of the complex. Experience teaches us the close relation between complex and neurosis. We must assume that the complex is a thought material, which stands under special psychological conditions, because it can exert a pathogenic influence. In the association experiment we first observe that it is the intention of the subject to react quickly and correctly. This intention is disturbed by the interference of the complex, so that the association, contrary to expectation, is either turned from the sense of the complex or replaced by fragmentary allusions, or is in general so disturbed as to render the subject altogether unable to produce a reaction, although he may be unaware that the complex is independent of his intentions. The same observation is confirmed by applying the so-called *reproduction method.* If after the finished association experiment we let the subject repeat all the reactions to the different stimulus-words, we find the uncertainty of recollection (the so-called faulty reproduction) usually at those places where the complexes have interfered (though we must not lose sight of the perseveration factor of the complex). Therefore, the "faulty reproduction" is also to be regarded as a sign of the complex, and this is theoretically interesting because it shows that even the moods associated with a complex are subject to certain exceptional conditions, that is, they are inclined to be quickly forgotten or replaced. The uncertainty of the subject towards the complex-associations is characteristic; they are to the individual either of an obsession-

600

like stability, or they disappear totally from the memory, and may even cause false memories—as may be well observed *in nuce* during the experiment. This points also to the complex and its association material having a remarkable independence in the hierarchy of the psyche, so that one may compare the complex to revolting vassals in an empire. Researches have shown that this independence is based upon an intense emotional tone, that is upon the value of the affective elements of the complex, because the "affect" occupies in the constitution of the psyche a very independent place, and may easily break through the self-control and self-intention of the individual. The "affect-intensity" of the complex can be easily proven psychophysically. For this property of the complex I have introduced the term *autonomy*. I conceive the complex to be a collection of imaginings, which, in consequence of this autonomy, is relatively independent of the central control of the consciousness, and at any moment liable to bend or cross the intentions of the individual. In so far as the meaning of the ego is psychologically nothing but a complex of imaginings held together and fixed by the coenesthetic impressions, also since its intentions or innervations are *eo ipso* stronger than those of the secondary complex (for they are disturbed by them), the complex of the ego may well be set parallel with and compared to the secondary autonomous complex. This comparison shows the existence of a certain psychological similarity, because the emotional tone of the secondary complexes is also based upon coenesthetic impressions, and, further, both the ego and secondary complex may be temporarily split up or repressed, a phenomenon which may be observed with particular clearness in hysterical delirium and other "cleavages" of personality. Especially in those states where the complex temporarily replaces the ego, we see that a strong complex possesses all the characteristics of a separate personality. We are, therefore, justified in regarding a complex as somewhat like a small secondary mind, which deliberately (though unknown to consciousness) drives at certain intentions which are contrary to the conscious intentions of the individual. Hysterical symptoms are the products of those counter-endeavours; they originate from the complex, and are all the more intense and obstinate the greater the autonomy of the complex is. I may say here that the superstition held by all races that hysterical and insane persons are "possessed" by demons is right in conception. These patients have, in fact, autonomous complexes, which at times completely destroy the self-control. The superstition is therefore justified, inasmuch as it denotes "possession," because the complexes behave quite independently of the ego, and force upon it a quasi-foreign will.

1353 By means of the association experiment, aided by Freud's psychoanalytic method, I have succeeded in proving that all neuroses contain autonomous complexes, whose disturbing influences have a disease-producing effect. Amongst the psychoses, Kraepelin's dementia praecox has undoubtedly proved itself a "complex disease," at least in its initial stages. (I regard the noted but still unconfirmed anatomical alterations as secondary.) In this disease the autonomy of the complexes may sometimes be observed with surprising distinctness; for instance, the overpowering force of "voices," the obsessions arising from catatonic impulses, etc.

1354 The objection that neuroses and dementia praecox are totally different affections, and cannot possibly be founded upon the same disturbances, I can only meet here with the suggestion that more or less autonomous complexes occur everywhere, even in so-called normals. The question is, to what extent are the complexes really autonomous, and in what form does the reaction take place? The researches of Freud and his school have shown how hysteria reactively deals with the complexes, while the work of the Zurich school has shown a characteristic and different behaviour of dementia praecox; with this, however, I cannot deal here at length. I may say only that certainly in both the neuroses and dementia praecox the symptoms —whether of a somatic or of a psychic nature—originate from the complex as has been described in detail by the school of Freud. While in hysteria there occurs usually a continuous accommodation to the surroundings, in consequence of which the complexes are subjected to continual alterations, in dementia praecox on the contrary the complexes are fixed, so that they usually arrest the progress of the general personality; this we call dementia. In estimating the extent of this dementia some authors have gone much too far in assuming that the repulsive and degenerate exterior of the patient is the result of an equally great interior decay. This is quite incorrect, because the patients still possess a very vivid life of fantasy, of which, however, they are able only in exceptional cases to give utterance. In these fantasies, of which in some instances the patients are quite unconscious, they deal with the fixed complex in a way which is intensely interesting to the observer. In fact, this is the workshop where delusions, hallucinations, etc., are produced from really sensible connections. The direction of thought is, however, entirely turned away from reality, and prefers thought-forms and material no longer of interest to modern man; hence many of these fantasies appear in a purely mythological garb. Owing to the loss of the recent biological train of suitable thought, there is apparently substituted an antiquated form. (I may refer here to a similar conception of the hysterical symptom by Claparède and Janet.)

¹355   In this short summary I have been forced to restrict myself entirely to indications and assertions. Proofs have not been offered, because the subject has already reached the extent of a special science, a science which may be called "Analytical Psychology,"² or after Bleuler, "Deep Psychology" ("Tiefenpsychologie").

¹356   In conclusion, I would draw attention to the following publications. An account of all works on association methods will be found in:

Jung. *Diagnostische Associationsstudien.* Band I and II. J. A. Barth, Leipzig.³

A summary of these methods in the English language appeared in *Lectures and Addresses delivered before the Departments of Psychology and Pedagogy,* in celebration of the 20th anniversary of the opening of Clark University, Sept., 1909, Worcester, Mass., 1910.⁴

These lectures contain an account of the practical application of the experiments in a case of theft.

² [This may be Jung's first use of the term "analytical psychology." However, see "General Aspects of Psychoanalysis," a paper which he delivered in London on Aug. 5, 1913; the term is introduced in par. 523. The term "deep psychology" did not gain acceptance; the usual form is "depth psychology."]

³ [Jung's papers are in the present volume; those of his collaborators are available in the M. D. Eder translation, *Studies in Word-Association.*]

⁴ ["The Association Method," comprising three lectures. See supra, par. 929, n. 1.]

Further details may be found in:[5]

Jung. *Die psychologische Diagnose des Tatbestandes.* Marhold, Halle.

Peterson and Jung. "Psychophysical Investigations with the Galvanometer and Pneumograph in Normal and Insane Individuals." *Brain.* Vol. 30. 1907.

Jung. "On Psychophysical Relations of the Association-experiment." *Journal of Abnormal Psychology.* Vol. I.

Details concerning my conception of the neuroses and psychoses may be read, partly in Vol. I of my *Diagnostische Associationsstudien,* partly in Jung, "The Psychology of Dementia Praecox"—*Journal of Nerv. and Ment. Dis.,* New York, 1909; also in Jung, *Ueber die Psychologie der Dementia Praecox;* Marhold, Halle; and in Jung, *Der Inhalt der Psychose.* Deuticke, Vienna.[6]

Proofs of the resumption of antiquated forms of thinking are as yet published only in part. A general presentation of the problem may be found in:

Jung. "Wandlungen und Symbole der Libido." *Jahrb. f. Psychoanalyt. u. Psychopath. Forschungen.* Deuticke, Vienna. Band III. 1911.[7]

[5] [These three papers are in the present volume, the first translated as "The Psychological Diagnosis of Evidence."]

[6] [These two works are in vol. 3 of the *Coll. Works,* the latter translated as "The Content of the Psychoses."]

[7] [Translated as *Psychology of the Unconscious* (1916); revised version translated as *Symbols of Transformation,* vol. 5 in the *Coll. Works.*]

ON THE PSYCHOLOGICAL DIAGNOSIS OF EVIDENCE[1]

The Evidence-Experiment in the Näf Trial

The method of investigating crime called "psychological diagnosis of evidence" was thought out and first published thirty years ago in the *Archiv für Kriminologie*, vol. XV, pp. 72–113.

In that paper, entitled "Psychological Diagnosis of Evidence: ideas on psychological experimental methods of ascertaining whether or not a person had taken part in a particular crime," all that is essential in the method and its technique was described and can be referred to there.[2]

1357   In a letter of October 31, 1934, the Criminal Court of Canton Zurich, in the case of Hans Näf, dental technician of Mogelsberg, asked for an opinion on the following question: "Would the interrogation of the accused by me reveal anything that would be of considerable significance for the judge who has to decide on the guilt or innocence of the accused?"

1 [Translated from "Zur psychologischen Tatbestandsdiagnostik: Das Tatbestandsexperiment im Schwurgerichtsprozess Näf," *Archiv für Kriminologie* (Leipzig), C (1937), 123–30. It followed a detailed account of the case from the criminological standpoint by H. W. Spiegel, "Der Fall Näf: Mord und Versicherungsbetrug, Selbstmord oder Unfall?", pp. 98–122.]

2 [The paper referred to in this headnote was by Wertheimer and Klein, "Psychologische Tatbestandsdiagnostik" (1904). In Jung's brief 1905 paper, "On the Psychological Diagnosis of Facts" (*Coll. Works*, vol. 1, par. 479), he attacked Wertheimer and Klein for not crediting the work of the Zurich Clinic, "from which they appropriated their seemingly original ideas." Wertheimer responded with a statement in the *Archiv für die gesamte Psychologie*, VII (1906), 1/2, 139–40, indicating that his first work was published prior to Jung's. Jung then published a retraction in the *Zeitschrift für angewandte Psychologie*, I (1907/8), 163, acknowledging that Wertheimer and he had arrived at the same conclusions independently of one another. Thirty years later, in the present publication, Jung took occasion again to give primary credit to the work of Wertheimer and Klein.]

¹³⁵⁸   For my information, copies of the following documents were handed to me:

1. A graphological opinion given by Dr. Pulver[3] on March 21, 1934.

2. Psychiatric opinion of the director of the Canton Asylum, Burghölzli, of August 10, 1934.

3. The act of indictment from the Police Court, Zurich.

¹³⁵⁹   A further basis for my opinion was the result of a so-called "evidence-experiment."

I. THE EXPERIMENT

¹³⁶⁰   Since the expert opinion of the psychiatrist had already established the mental state and the character of the subject, I was concerned only with a psychological examination of the accused with regard to a possible guilt- or innocence-complex. Such an examination is called the evidence-experiment. In principle it consists in an association experiment distinguished from the usual form, in which stimulus-words are used without any ulterior motive, in that so-called critical stimulus-words taken from the evidence are interspersed with the others. In the case under consideration a list of 407 stimulus-words was used. (The experiment took more than three hours.) Of these 407 words, 271 were neutral, 96 referred to the evidence, and 40 were of an emotional nature and referred to the history and conditions of life of the subject.

¹³⁶¹   Examples of evidence-words: *murder, death, to die, gas, suicide, rubber tubing, morphia, advantage, fraud, to rub out, letter, table, floor, accident, to marry, bottle, syringe, beer, ampoule,* etc.

¹³⁶²   Examples of emotional stimulus-words: *theft, stumbling, girl, to despise, to despair, peace, anxiety, unjust,* etc.

¹³⁶³   Experience has shown that stimulus-words referring to very emotionally charged contents of consciousness cause considerable disturbances in reaction; i.e., the subject cannot comply with the instruction to respond as quickly as possible to the stimulus-word with the word that immediately comes to his mind. The usual disturbances, which in technical language are called complex-characteristics, are these:

---

[3] [Max Pulver (1889–1952), Swiss graphologist, poet, and scholar of religion.]

1. A reaction-time longer than the average (measured with a stop-watch).

2. Repetition of the stimulus-word by the subject (as if he had not heard it properly).

3. Mishearing of the stimulus-word.

4. Expressive movements (laughing, twitching of the face, etc.).

5. Reaction with more than one word.

6. Strikingly superficial reaction (purely mechanical, according to sound, etc.).

7. Meaningless reaction.

8. "Failure" (failing to give a reaction).

9. Perseveration, i.e., a disturbing influence on subsequent reactions.

10. Defective reproduction (i.e., after the experiment we try to find out whether the subject remembers the reactions he gave the first time).

11. Slips of the tongue (stammering, etc.).

1364   To this list should be added the use of foreign words; this happens in 27 out of 34 cases (i.e., approximately 80 per cent of the cases) with critical words. In the case under observation we very often observed a slight movement of the left index-finger; this happened with 81 per cent of the critical stimulus-words and is therefore regarded as a complex-characteristic.

1365   The exact observation, measurement, and recording of the complex-characteristics thus served the purpose of ascertaining emotionally charged contents as well as of establishing their character.

II. The Results of the Experiment

1. *The Reaction-time*

1366   Stimulus-words that had no personal meaning, excluding those that immediately followed a critical stimulus-word and therefore were disturbed through perseveration of the affect, resulted in a mean reaction-time of 2.4 seconds.

1367   Stimulus-words referring to the evidence had to be divided into two groups according to their reaction-time; namely, those with a long and those with a short reaction-time. In the latter group we usually found a perseveration-phenomenon which made itself noticeable by a prolonged reaction-time of the association immediately following. When the reaction-time of a critical association was long, then the reaction-time of the following association without personal meaning was short; i.e., it equalled the mean of the reactions without personal meaning. When the reaction-time of the critical association was short, then the following one was long. This resulted in the following picture:

Reaction-time after critical stimulus-word:
First group: long 3.2 secs.
             short 2.5 ''
Second group: short 2.4 secs.
               long 3.3 ''

1368   Expressed in words: the evidence-words produce, either directly or indirectly, a reaction-time the mean prolongation of which is 0.8 and 0.9 seconds.

2. The Complex-characteristics

1369   The experiment reveals the following distribution of the complex-characteristics described above:

Associations without personal meaning contain 0.6 complex-characteristics
Evidence stimulus-words contain 2.2 complex-characteristics
Emotional stimulus-words contain 2.0 complex-characteristics

1370   Stimulus-words that are taken from the evidence produce, it appears, almost four times as many disturbing elements as stimulus-words without personal meaning; the disturbing influence of the former surpasses that of the emotional stimulus-words by 0.2.

3. Incorrect Reproductions

1371   The incorrect reproductions were numbered together with the complex-characteristics. In 31.7 per cent of all reactions the memory failed. No less than 77 per cent of these mistakes occurred in the critical reactions and in those immediately following them (disturbed by perseveration). The memory fails:

In 32.5% of the emotional associations
In 36.0% of the evidence-associations

608

In 20.5% of the associations without personal meaning (outside the range of perseveration).

Expressed in words: the critical stimulus-words that are taken from the evidence had the greatest disturbing influence on the memory.

4. *Maximally Disturbed Associations*

1372   Among the 407 associations of the total experiment there are 36 that are maximally disturbed, i.e., that are characterized by four complex-characteristics, or by a particularly long reaction-time, or by strong perseveration. Of these, 29 belong to the evidence stimulus-words and 7 to the emotional stimulus-words. Computed in percentages of the total number (96) of the evidence stimulus-words, there were 30.2 per cent; of the emotional stimulus-words (40), 17.5 per cent. This means that the evidence stimulus-words produced 30.2 per cent maximal disturbances and the emotional stimulus-words only 17.5 per cent. Such stimulus-words as were recognizable beforehand as without personal meaning did not produce any maximal disturbances at all.

1373   Since the disturbances of the normal experiment always indicated the presence of affective contents (apart from accidental external influences which, however, were absent in this experiment), this rule applies, of course, in great measure to maximal disturbances.

1374   The following were the maximally disturbed associations:

Stimulus-word	Repetition, Interjection, or Misunderstanding	R.T.[3a]	Reaction	Finger-movements	Reproduction	Number of C.C.[3a] in the critical & post-critical reactions
1. suicide	(yes)	5.0	to make-death	–	–	5/1
2. to die	(sigh)	8.8	death	+	–	5/3
3. stupid	–	6.0	not intelligent	–	–	4/2
4. to scorn	+	9.4	not to love	–	–	4/2
5. smell	–	3.0	notice nothing[4]	+	–	5/3

[3a] [R.T. = reaction-time; C.C. = complex-characteristics.]
[4] [Original in Swiss dialect.]

Stimulus-word	Repetition, Interjection, or Misunderstanding	R.T.	Reaction	Finger-movements	Reproduction	Number of C.C. in the critical & post-critical reactions
6. gas	–	3.2	poison methane	+	–	5/5
7. cow	++	6.8	mammal	+	–	5/5
8. drunk	+	5.2	intoxication	–	–	4/2
9. hose	–	2.0	rubber	–	+	1/4
10. month	+	5.8	Little bell of the month⁴ (flower?) part of the year	–	–	5/1
11. to marry	–	2.6	dear—yes	–	–	4/2
12. truth	–	3.6	is best—yes	–	–	4/2
13. beer	–	6.0	I like it, I dare say⁴	+	–	6/2
14. bottle	–	1.8	wine, beer	–	+	2/6
15. ampoule	–	4.0	adrenalin	+	–	5/2
16. to inherit	–	4.0	disinherited	+	+	5/1
17. intoxication	–	3.0	silly feeling	–	–	4/1
18. inheritance	–	4.0	without—	+	–	5/3
19. marriage	–	10.0	married	–	–	3
20. picture postcard	–	5.2	for sending	+	+	4/2
21. ground	–	3.2	air etc.	–	–	4/2
22. twenty-two	–	3.0	February	–	+	4/2
23. peace	–	3.0	unpeaceful	+	–	4/1
24. brush	+	4.0	to clean	–	+	3/5
25. soap	–	4.0	fatty	–	+	2/4
26. tap	–	2.8	brass	+	+	3/3
27. to despair	+	8.8	don't know	+	–	5
28. *heimlich* (cozy, secret)	–	2.8	*nicht-unheimlich* (not-uncanny)	+	–	4
29. illustrated	–	10.0	don't know what it's called	–	–	5/2
30. anxiety	+	3.6	to press	+	–	4/1
31. calf	+	4.8	cow	+	–	4/1
32. success	–	4.0	unsuccessful	–	–	4/1
33. to kill	–	3.6	how can I express myself?— unpleasant— to suffer	++	+	3/4
34. periodical	+	2.8	subscription	–	+	3/4
35. syringe	–	2.4	for injecting	+	–	4/3
36. injecting	–	3.6	injection	+	–	5/1

⁴ [Original in Swiss dialect.]

1375   As we have already mentioned, of the 36 stimulus-words 29 are taken from the evidence. Of these, 18 are designations of definite concrete phenomena, namely: *smell, gas, drink, hose, beer, bottle, ampoule, intoxication, picture postcard, ground, brush, soap, tap, illustrated, to kill, periodical, syringe,* and *injecting.* These constitute 62.0 per cent of the maximally disturbed evidence-reactions. In the total experiment 96 evidence stimulus-words occur and of these 53.1 per cent designate concrete phenomena. Thus the maximally disturbed reactions occur mainly in response to concrete evidence stimulus-words, and this exceeds the normal expectation by 9 per cent. In other words: it is precisely the concrete details of the evidence that prevail over the more general aspects of the evidence.

1376   To summarize:

1. The evidence stimulus-words prevail over the emotional stimulus-words by 12.7%.

2. Among the evidence stimulus-words, those prevail that refer to concrete or otherwise distinctive details of the evidence by 9%.

5. *The Minimally Disturbed Critical Associations*

1377   25 per cent of the evidence stimulus-words and the same percentage of emotional stimulus-words are minimally affected, i.e., less than 2 complex-characteristics. Among them there are stimulus-words of which one would under normal conditions have expected a certain effect; for instance, the wife's Christian name and the following words: *woman, to abort, cocaine, to do in, death, murder, morphia, to rub out, accident, money, poisonous, last will and testament, gaol, punishment, loss, judgment,* etc. To the stimulus-word *total,* the subject reacted with *to kill* after only 2.8 seconds.

1378   Among the evidence stimulus-words with minimal effect there are 37.5 per cent stimulus-words that refer to concrete content of the evidence, while there are 62.0 per cent among the maximally disturbed ones. This shows that the evidence stimulus-words are distinguished from the other categories by their appreciably stronger effect.

611

The Expert Opinion

1379   It must be stated, in the first place, that an association experiment will, under these conditions, result as a rule in appreciably higher degrees of disturbance with critical reactions. The reason is that the critical stimulus-words invariably stir up already-existing affects which in their turn disturb the associations. The general picture of disturbance will therefore not necessarily mean a great deal. It would, however, be a most aggravating piece of circumstantial evidence in the case of a defendant who at the preliminary inquiry had not been made acquainted with the evidence and therefore could not possibly know the details. In our case every detail of the evidence is known, even the incriminating details. Therefore the disturbance of the critical reaction is not relevant in evaluating the psychological situation. So only a consideration of small variations can promise some success. Consequently I devised the experiment in a certain way: I selected general stimulus-words that are assumed to be affectively potent, in order to obtain a yardstick for the general emotional make-up of the subject; then I selected general and special stimulus-words obtained from the evidence, in order to determine whether the general emotional situation or the special concrete evidence is in the foreground of the affective interest.

1380   Experience has shown that a defendant who is sure of his innocence will concentrate more on the general fact of the injustice of being suspected than on any particular detail of the evidence, which is for him irrelevant. For him it is not the particular concrete details that carry a guilty and therefore confusing affective charge but the stimulus-words referring to the indignation roused by his sense of justice and to his fear of possible conviction. As our findings demonstrate beyond doubt, one subject is much less affected by the general emotional stimulus-words than by those referring to the evidence; among these, the particular concrete details prevail that carry weight for the judicial proof of guilt.

1381   The reaction to the stimulus-word *brush* was: "I pronounce the word *brush*"; the subject is startled and repeats *brush* as if he had not properly understood the word. Then he hesitates for 4 seconds until he can say *cleaning*. The next stimulus-

612

word, *to force,* which follows immediately, finds him unprepared because his attention is still disturbed by *brush.* So he also repeats this stimulus-word; the reaction takes as much as 6.2 seconds. Contrary to the instructions, which he usually follows, he lapses into dialect.[5] The stimulus-word *soap,* which would in itself be harmless, produces such an after-effect that the subject cannot find any reaction at all to the stimulus-word *important* that follows, although he has a considerable vocabulary and is quite able to react quickly according to his educational standard.

1382　　Such processes are responsible for the disturbances in 62 per cent of the concrete evidence-reactions. From this fact it must be concluded that it is mainly the subject's ideas referring to the concrete details of the evidence that carry the strongest affects, and that other affects recede into the background.

1383　　That this diagnosis is not incorrect is proved by the fact that the subject himself spontaneously states, with every sign of affect, that the maximally disturbed associations to *suicide* and *to die* have touched on his suicidal ideas. Just as his ideas revolve round the theme of suicide, so they move round the concrete details of the evidence. This is statistically corroborated by our findings.

1384　　It must be emphasized that, apart from the suicide-complex, out of four stimulus-words referring to stupidity (*stupid, sheep, cow, calf*) no less than three are maximally disturbed. This fact can only be understood as meaning that the subject experiences a very strong inner conflict because of a piece of stupid behaviour.

1385　　The maximal disturbance at *to marry* and *marriage* indicates complications that can only be interpreted as meaning that his married life was no simple matter but of a problematical character.

1386　　Likewise, the stimulus-words *to inherit* and *inheritance* elicit a maximal disturbance, which proves that these words too point to a background full of conflict and complication.

1387　　The stimulus-words *clandestine* and *truth,* with maximal disturbance, indicate that the subject was not prepared to respond to these ideas.

---

5 [The two German words actually used are *zwingen* (standard) and *forziere wolte* (dialect), both meaning 'to force.']

1388   To summarize, and in reply to the original question, it must therefore be stated that the subject's psychological situation, as revealed by the experiment, in no way corresponds to what one would empirically expect in an innocent person. To assess the signs of a guilty conscience, however, must be left to the discretion of the judge.

BIBLIOGRAPHY

BIBLIOGRAPHY

A. LIST OF PERIODICALS CITED, WITH ABBREVIATIONS

Allg. Z. Psychiat. = *Allgemeine Zeitschrift für Psychiatrie und psychisch-gerichtliche Medizin.* Berlin.

Amer. J. Insan. = *American Journal of Insanity.* Baltimore.

Année psychol. = *Année psychologique.* Paris.

Arch. ges. Psychol. = *Archiv für die gesamte Psychologie.* Leipzig.

Arch. Kriminalanthrop. = *Archiv für Kriminalanthropologie und Kriminalistik.* Leipzig.

Arch. psychol. = *Archives de psychologie de la Suisse romande.* Geneva.

Beitr. Psychol. Aussage = *Beiträge zur Psychologie der Aussage.* Leipzig.

Brain = *Brain. A Journal of Neurology.* London.

C.R. Soc. Biol. Paris = *Comptes rendus hébdomadaires des séances et mémoires de la Société de Biologie.* Paris.

J. Abnorm. Psychol. = *Journal of Abnormal Psychology.* Boston.

J. Psychol. Neurol. = *Journal für Psychologie und Neurologie.* Leipzig.

Jb. Psychiat. Neurol. = *Jahrbuch für Psychiatrie und Neurologie.* Leipzig and Vienna.

Jb. psychoanal. psychopath. Forsch. = *Jahrbuch für psychoanalytische und psychopathologische Forschungen.* Leipzig and Vienna.

Jurist.-psychiat. Grenzfr. = *Juristisch-psychiatrische Grenzfragen.* Halle.

Med. Wschr. St. P. = *St. Petersburger Medizinische Wochenschrift.* St. Petersburg (Leningrad).

Mschr. Kriminalpsychol. = *Monatsschrift für Kriminalpsychologie und Strafrechtsreform.* Heidelberg.

Mschr. Psychiat. Neurol. = *Monatsschrift für Psychiatrie und Neurologie.* Berlin.

617

Neurol. Zbl. = *Neurologisches Zentralblatt.* Leipzig.

Pflüg. Arch. ges. Psychol. = *(Pflügers) Archiv für die gesamte Psychologie.* Bonn and Leipzig.

Psychiat.-neurol. Wschr. = *Psychiatrisch-neurologische Wochenschrift.* Halle.

Psychol. Bull. = *Psychological Bulletin.* Lancaster, Pa. and New York.

Rev. phil. = *Revue philosophique de France et de l'Étranger.* Paris.

Rif. med. = *Riforma medica.* Rome.

Riv. psicol. = *Rivista di psicologia applicata.* Bologna.

Samml. Abh. pädag. Psychol. = *Sammlung von Abhandlungen aus dem Gebiete der pädagogischen Psychologie und Physiologie.* Berlin.

Wien. klin. Rdsch. = *Wiener klinische Rundschau.* Vienna.

Z. angew. Psychol. = *Zeitschrift für angewandte Psychologie.* Leipzig.

Z. ges. Strafrechtswiss. = *Zeitschrift für die gesamte Strafrechtswissenschaft.* Berlin.

Z. Psychol. Physiol. Sinnesorg. = *Zeitschrift für Psychologie und Physiologie der Sinnesorgane.* Leipzig.

Zbl. Nervenheilk. = *Zentralblatt für Nervenheilkunde und Psychiatrie.* Berlin.

B. GENERAL BIBLIOGRAPHY

ASCHAFFENBURG, GUSTAV. "Experimentelle Studien über Assoziationen." In: KRAEPELIN, *Psychol. Arb.*, I (1896), 209–99; II (1899), 1–83; IV (1904), 235–374.

BECHTEREW, W. M. VON. "Über die Geschwindigkeitsveränderungen der psychischen Prozesse zu verschiedenen Tageszeiten," *Neurol. Zbl.*, XII (1893), 290–92.

———. "Über zeitliche Verhältnisse der psychischen Prozesse bei in Hypnose befindlichen Personen," *Neurol. Zbl.*, XI (1892), 305–7.

BINSWANGER, LUDWIG. "On the Psychogalvanic Phenomenon in Association Experiments." In: JUNG, *Studies in Word-Association*, (1918), pp. 446–530. (Orig. 1907/8.)

BLEULER, PAUL EUGEN. *Affektivität, Suggestibilität, Paranoia.* Halle, 1906; 2nd edn., 1926. (See "Affectivity, Suggestibility, Paranoia," translated by Charles Ricksher, *New York State Hospital Bulletin* (Utica), Feb. 1912.)

————. "Consciousness and Association." In: JUNG, *Studies in Word-Association* (1918), pp. 266–96. (Orig. 1905.)

————. "Upon the Significance of Association Experiments." In: Ibid., pp. 1–7. (Orig. 1904.)

————. "Versuch einer naturwissenschaftlichen Betrachtung der psychologischen Grundbegriffe," *Allg. Z. Psychiat.*, L (1894), 133–68.

BONHÖFFER, KARL. *Der Geisteszustand des Alkoholdeliranten.* Breslau, 1897.

BOURDON, B. "Recherches sur la succession des phénomènes psychologiques," *Rev. phil.*, XXXV (1893), 225–60.

BREUER, JOSEF, and FREUD, SIGMUND. *Studies on Hysteria.* Translated by James and Alix Strachey. In: FREUD, Standard Edition, 2. (Orig.: *Studien über Hysterie*, 1895.)

BREUKINK, H. "Über Ermüdungskurven bei Gesunden und bei einigen Neurosen und Psychosen," *J. Psychol. Neurol.*, IV:3 (1904), 85–108.

BRILL, A. A. "A Case of Schizophrenia (Dementia Praecox)," *Amer. J. Insan.*, LXVI (1909–10), 53–70.

————. "Psychological Factors in Dementia Praecox, an Analysis," *J. Abnorm. Psychol.*, III (1908–9), 219–38.

CATTELL, JAMES McKEEN. "Psychometrische Untersuchungen," I and II. In: WUNDT, *Philosophische Studien*, III (1885), 305–36, 452–92.

CLAPARÈDE, ÉDOUARD. *L'Association des idées.* Paris, 1903.

————. "Association médiate dans l'évocation volontaire," *Arch. psychol.*, III (1904), 201–3.

———— and ISRAÏLOVITCH, D. "Influence du tabac sur l'association des idées," *C.R. Soc. Biol. Paris*, LIV (1902), 758–60.

COLUCCI, CESARE. "L'Allenamento ergografico nei normali e negli epilettici," *Rif. med.*, Anno XVIII, vol. I (1902), 424–28.

CORDES, G. "Experimentelle Untersuchungen über Assoziationen." In: WUNDT, *Philosophische Studien*, XVII (1899), 30–77.

DELABARRE, E. BURKE. *Über Bewegungsempfindungen.* Freiburg i. Baden, 1891. See *Rev. phil.*, XXXIII (1892), 342–43, a review of it.

FÉRÉ, CHARLES SAMSON. "Note sur des modifications de la résistance électrique sous l'influence des excitations sensorielles et des émotions," *C.R. Soc. Biol. Paris*, 3 Mar. 1888.

FÉRÉ, CHARLES SAMSON. "Note sur des modifications de la tension électrique dans le corps humain," *C.R. Soc. Biol. Paris,* 14 Jan. 1888.

――――. *The Pathology of the Emotions.* Translated by R. Park. London, 1899. (Orig.: *La Pathologie des émotions,* 1892.)

FREUD, SIGMUND. The Standard Edition of the Complete Psychological Works. Translated under the general editorship of James Strachey. 24 vols. London, 1953–

――――. "Analysis of a Phobia in a Five-Year-Old Boy." Translated by Alix and James Strachey. Standard Edition, 10, pp. 5–147. (Orig.: "Analyse der Phobie eines 5-jährigen Knaben," 1909.)

――――. "Five Lectures on Psycho-Analysis." Translated by James Strachey. Standard Edition, 11, pp. 3–55. (Orig.: "Über Psychoanalyse," 1910.)

――――. "Fragment of an Analysis of a Case of Hysteria." Translated by Alix and James Strachey. Standard Edition, 7, pp. 7–122. (Orig.: "Bruchstück einer Hysterie-Analyse," 1905.)

――――. *The Interpretation of Dreams.* Translated by James Strachey. Standard Edition, 4, 5. (Orig.: *Die Traumdeutung,* 1900.)

――――. *Jokes and Their Relation to the Unconscious.* Translated by James Strachey. Standard Edition, 8. (Orig.: *Der Witz und seine Beziehung zum Unbewussten,* 1905.)

――――. "The Neuro-Psychoses of Defence." Translated by John Rickman. Standard Edition, 3, pp. 45–61. (Orig.: "Die Abwehr-Neuropsychosen," 1894.)

――――. "On the History of the Psycho-Analytic Movement." Translated by Joan Riviere. Standard Edition, 14, pp. 3–66. (Orig.: "Zur Geschichte der psychoanalytischen Bewegung," 1914.)

――――. "The Psychical Mechanism of Forgetfulness." Translated by James Strachey. Standard Edition, 3, pp. 287–97. (Orig.: "Zum psychischen Mechanismus der Vergesslichkeit," 1898.)

――――. "Psycho-analysis and the Establishment of the Facts in Legal Proceedings." Translated by James Strachey. Standard Edition, 9. (Orig.: "Tatbestandsdiagnostik und Psychoanalyse," *Arch. Kriminalanthrop.,* XXVI:1 (1906), 1–10.)

――――. *The Psychopathology of Everyday Life.* Translated by Alan Tyson. Standard Edition, 6. (Orig.: *Zur Psychopathologie des Alltagslebens,* 1904.)

――――. "Screen Memories." Translated by James Strachey. Standard Edition, 3, pp. 303–22. (Orig.: "Über Deckerinnerungen," 1899.)

———. See also BREUER.

FUHRMANN, M. *Analyse des Vorstellungsmaterials bei epileptischem Schwachsinn.* Dissertation, Giessen, 1902.

FÜRST, EMMA. "Statistical Investigations on Word-Associations and on Familial Agreement in Reaction Type among Uneducated Persons." In: JUNG, *Studies in Word-Association* (1918), pp. 407–45. (Orig. 1907.)

GALTON, FRANCIS. "Psychometric Experiments," *Brain*, II (1897), 149–62.

GRABOWSKY, ADOLF. "Psychologische Tatbestandsdiagnostik," *Beilage zur Allgemeine Zeitung* (Tübingen), 15 Dec. 1905.

GROSS, ALFRED. "Die Assoziationsmethode im Strafprozess," *Z. ges. Strafrechtswiss.*, XXVI (1906), 19–40.

———. "Kriminalpsychologische Tatbestandsforschung," *Jurist.-psychiat. Grenzfr.*, V:7 (1907).

———. "Zur psychologischen Tatbestandsdiagnostik," *Mschr. Kriminalpsychol.*, II (1905–6), 182–84.

———. "Zur psychologischen Tatbestandsdiagnostik als kriminalistisches Hilfsmittel," *Beitr. Psychol. Aussage*, II:3 (1905–6), 150–53 (436–39). (Reprinted from *Allgemeine Österreichische Gerichtszeitung*, LVI, no. 17.)

GROSS, HANS. "Zur Frage des Wahrnehmungsproblems," *Beitr. Psychol. Aussage*, II:2 (1905–6), 128–34 (258–64).

———. "Zur psychologischen Tatbestandsdiagnostik," *Arch. Kriminalanthrop.*, XIX (1905), 49–59.

HEILBRONNER, KARL. "Die Grundlagen der psychologischen Tatbestandsdiagnostik," *Z. gess. Strafrechtswiss.*, XXVII (1907), 601–56.

———. "Über epileptische Manie nebst Bemerkungen über die Ideenflucht," *Mschr. Psychiat. Neurol.*, XIII (1903), 193–209, 269–90.

HOCH, AUGUST. Review of Jung, "Über das Verhalten der Reaktionszeit beim Assoziationsexperimente" and "Experimentelle Beobachtungen über das Erinnerungsvermögen" (= papers 3 and 4 in present vol.) and "Zur psychologischen Tatbestandsdiagnostik" (= final paper in Coll. Works, 1), *J. Abnorm. Psychol.*, I:2 (June 1906), 95–100.

ISSERLIN, MAX. "Über Jung's 'Psychologie der Dementia praecox' und die Anwendung Freud'scher Forschungsmaximen in der Psychopathologie," *Zbl. Nervenheilk.*, XXX, n.s. XVIII (1 May 1907), 329–43.

JANET, PIERRE. *Les Obsessions et la psychasthénie.* 2 vols., Paris, 1903.

JERUSALEM, M. "Ein Beispiel von Assoziation durch unbewusste Mittelglieder." In: WUNDT, *Philosophische Studien*, X (1892), 323–25.

JUNG, CARL GUSTAV. "The Analysis of Dreams." In: *Freud and Psychoanalysis.* Coll. Works, 4.

————. *Analytical Psychology: Its Theory and Practice. The Tavistock Lectures* [1935]. New York and London, 1968. To be included in Coll. Works, 18.

————. "Associations d'idées familiales," *Arch. psychol.*, VII:26 (1907), 160–68.

————. "A Case of Hysterical Stupor in a Prisoner in Detention." In: *Psychiatric Studies.* Coll. Works, 1.

————. *Freud and Psychoanalysis.* Coll. Works, 4.

————. *Memories, Dreams, Reflections.* Recorded and edited by Aniela Jaffé. New York and London, 1962. (Diff. paginated edns.)

————. "Psychological Conflicts in a Child." In: *The Development of Personality.* Coll. Works, 17.

————. "On the Psychological Diagnosis of Facts." In: *Psychiatric Studies*, Coll. Works, 1.

————. "On the Psychology and Pathology of So-Called Occult Phenomena." In: *Psychiatric Studies.* Coll. Works, 1.

————. "On Simulated Insanity." In: *Psychiatric Studies*, Coll. Works, 1.

————. *Psychiatric Studies.* Coll. Works, 1.

————. *The Psychogenesis of Mental Disease.* Coll. Works, 3.

————. "The Psychology of Dementia Praecox." In: *The Psychogenesis of Mental Disease.* Coll. Works, 3.

————. "The Significance of the Father in the Destiny of the Individual." In: *Freud and Psychoanalysis.* Coll. Works, 4.

————, ed. *Studies in Word-Association.* Translated by M. D. Eder. London and New York, 1918.

KANT, IMMANUEL. *Critique of Pure Reason.* Translated by J.M.D. Meiklejohn. London and New York (Everyman's Library), 1934.

KRAEPELIN, EMIL. *Experimentelle Studien über Assoziationen.* Freiburg, 1883.

————. *Psychiatrie: Ein Lehrbuch für Studierende und Ärzte.* 7th edn., 2 vols., Leipzig, 1904. (Cf. *Clinical Psychiatry; a Text-book for Students and Physicians*. Abstracted and adapted from the 7th German edn. by A. Ross Diefendorf. New edn., rev. & augmented, New York, 1907.)

———. "Über den Einfluss der Übung auf die Dauer von Assoziationen," *Med. Wschr. St. P.*, n.s., VI (1889), 9–10.

———. *Über die Beeinflussung einfacher psychischer Vorgänge durch einige Arzneimittel*. Jena, 1892.

———, ed. *Psychologische Arbeiten*. 9 vols., Leipzig, 1896–1928.

KRAFFT-EBING, RICHARD VON. *Psychopathia Sexualis*. Translated by F. J. Rebman. London, 1901. (Orig. 1886.)

KRAMER, F., and STERN, W. "Selbstverrat durch Assoziation," *Beitr. Psychol. Aussage*, II:4 (1905–6), 1–32.

KRAUS, O. "Psychologische Tatbestandsdiagnostik," *Mschr. Kriminalpsychol.*, II (1905), 58–61.

LEDERER, MAX. "Die Verwendung der psychologischen Tatbestandsdiagnostik in der Strafrechtspraxis," *Mschr. Kriminalpsychol.*, III (1906), 163–72.

———. "Zur Frage der psychologischen Tatbestandsdiagnostik," *Z. ges. Strafrechtswiss.*, XXVI (1906), 488–506.

LEHMANN, ALFRED. *Die Hauptgesetze des menschlichen Gefühlslebens*. Leipzig, 1892.

LIEPMANN, HUGO. *Über Ideenflucht, Begriffsbestimmung und psychologische Analyse*. Halle, 1904.

MARTIUS, GÖTZ, and MINNEMANN, C. *Beiträge zur Psychologie und Philosophie*, vol. I, part 4. Leipzig, 1905. (Martius, "Über die Lehre von der Beeinflussung des Pulses und der Atmung durch psychische Reize," pp. 411–513; Minnemann, "Atmung und Puls bei aktuellen Affekten," pp. 514–51.)

MAYER, A., and ORTH, J. "Zur qualitativen Untersuchung der Assoziationen," *Z. Psychol. Physiol. Sinnesorg.*, XXVI (1901), 1–13.

MEIER, C. A. *Die Empirie des Unbewussten*. (Lehrbuch der Komplexen Psychologie C. G. Jungs, 1.) Zurich, 1968.

MEIGE, HENRY, and FEINDEL, E. *Tics and Their Treatment*. Translated by S.A.K. Wilson. London, 1907. (Orig. 1902.)

MENTZ, PAUL. "Die Wirkung akustischer Sinnesreize auf Puls und Atmung." In: WUNDT, *Philosophische Studien*, XI (1893), 61–124, 371–93, 563–603.

MEYER, ADOLF. "Normal and Abnormal Associations" (review of Jung and Riklin, "Experimentelle Untersuchungen über Assoziationen Gesunder" = paper 1 in present vol.), *Psychol. Bull.*, II:7 (1905), 242–50. (251–59 continues with review of other association studies by Jung, Wehrlin, and Riklin.)

MINNEMAN, C. See MARTIUS.

MOSSO, ANGELO. *Über den Kreislauf des Blutes im menschlichen Gehirn.* Leipzig, 1881.

MÜLLER, E. K. "Über den Einfluss psychischer und physiologischer Vorgänge auf das elektrische Leitvermögen des menschlichen Körpers," *Schweizerische Naturforschende Gesellschaft: Verhandlungen*, LXXXVII (1904), 79–80 (summary of paper read 1 Aug. 1904 to Section for Medicine).

MÜLLER, GEORG E., and PILZECKER, A. "Experimentelle Beiträge zur Lehre vom Gedächtnis," *Z. Psychol. Physiol. Sinnesorg.*, Ergänzungsband I (1900).

MÜNSTERBERG, HUGO. "Die Assoziation sukzessiver Vorstellungen," *Z. Psychol. Physiol. Sinnesorg.*, I (1890), 99–107.

———. *Beiträge zur experimentellen Psychologie.* 4 vols., Freiburg, 1889–92.

NUNBERG, HERMANN. "On the Physical Accompaniment of Association Processes." In: JUNG, *Studies in Word-Association* (1918), pp. 531–60. (Orig. 1910.)

PICK, ARNOLD. "Zur Psychologie des Vergessens bei Geistes- und Nervenkranken," *Arch. Kriminalanthrop.*, XVIII (1905), 251–61.

PIÉRON, H. "L'Association médiate," *Rev. phil.*, XXVIII (1903), 147.

RAIMANN, EMIL. *Die hysterischen Geistesstörungen.* Leipzig and Vienna, 1904.

RANSCHBURG, PAUL, and BALINT, EMERICH. "Über quantitative und qualitative Veränderungen geistiger Vorgänge im hohen Greisenalter," *Allg. Z. Psychiat.*, LVII (1900), 689–718.

———, and HAJÓS, LAJOS. *Beiträge zur Psychologie des hysterischen Geisteszustandes.* Leipzig and Vienna, 1897.

RIKLIN, FRANZ. "Analytische Untersuchungen der Symptome und Assoziationen eines Falles von Hysterie (Lina H.)," *Psychiat.-neurol. Wschr.*, 46–52 (1905), 449, 464, 469, 481, 493, 505, 521.

———. "Cases Illustrating the Phenomena of Association in Hysteria." In: JUNG, *Studies in Word-Association* (1918), pp. 322–53. (Orig. 1906.)

———. "Hebung epileptischer Amnesien durch Hypnose," *J. Psychol. Neurol.*, I:5/6 (1902), 200–25.

———. "Die diagnostische Bedeutung des Assoziationsversuches bei Hysterischen," *Psychiat.-neurol. Wschr.*, 29 (1904).

———. *Wish Fulfilment and Symbolism in Fairy Tales.* Translated by William A. White. New York, 1915. (Orig.: *Wunscherfüllung und Symbolik im Märchen*, 1908.)

———. "Zur Psychologie hysterischer Dämmerzustände und des Ganser'schen Symptoms," *Psychiat.-neurol. Wschr.*, 22 (1904), 185–93.

RÜDIN, ERNST. "Über die Dauer der psychischen Alkoholwirkung." In: KRAEPELIN, *Psychol. Arb.*, IV:1 (1901), 1–44.

———. "Auffassung und Merkfähigkeit unter Alkoholwirkung." In: KRAEPELIN, *Psychol. Arb.*, IV:3 (1902), 495–522.

SCHNITZLER, J. G. "Experimentelle Beiträge zur Tatbestandsdiagnostik," *Z. angew. Psychol.*, II (1909), 51–91. (Extracted from medical diss., Utrecht, 1907.)

SCHÜLE, HEINRICH. *Klinische Psychiatrie.* Leipzig, 1886.

SCRIPTURE, E. W. "Über den assoziativen Verlauf der Vorstellungen." In: WUNDT, *Philosophische Studien*, VII (1889), 50–146.

SMITH, WILLIAM. *Zur Frage der mittelbaren Assoziation.* Dissertation, Leipzig, 1894.

SOMMER, ROBERT. *Lehrbuch der psychopathologischen Untersuchungsmethoden.* Berlin and Vienna, 1899.

———. "Zur Messung der motorischen Begleiterscheinungen psychischer Zustände," *Beiträge zur Psychiatrischen Klinik* (Berlin and Vienna), I (1902), 143–64.

———, and FÜRSTENAU, ROBERT. "Die elektrischen Vorgänge an der menschlichen Haut," *Klinik für psychische und nervöse Krankheiten* (Halle), I (1906):3, 197–207.

STERN, WILLIAM. "Psychologische Tatbestandsdiagnostik," *Beitr. Psychol. Aussage*, II (1905–6), 145–47 (275–77).

STICKER, GEORG. "Über Versuche einer objektiven Darstellung von Sensibilitätsstörungen," *Wien. klin. Rdsch.*, II (1897), 497–501, 514–18.

STRANSKY, ERWIN. *Über Sprachverwirrtheit.* (Sammlung Zwangloser Abhandlungen aus dem Gebiete der Nerven- und Geisteskrankheiten, VI, 4/5.) Halle, 1905. (See review by Lewandowsky, *Zbl. Nervenheilk.*, XXVIII, n.s. XVI (15 Nov. 1905), 879, answered by Stransky, ibid. (15 Dec. 1905), 963–64.)

———. "Zur Kenntnis gewisser erworbener Blödsinnsformen," *Jb. Psychiat. Neurol.*, XXIV (1903), 1–149.

STRANSKY, ERWIN. "Zur Auffassung gewisser Symptome der Dementia Praecox," *Neurol. Zbl.*, XXIII (1904), 1074–85, 1137–43.

TARCHANOFF, J. "Über die galvanischen Erscheinungen an der Haut des Menschen bei Reizungen der Sinnesorgane und bei verschiedenen Formen der psychischen Tätigkeit," *Pflüg. Arch. ges. Physiol.*, XLVI (1890), 46–55.

THUMB, ALBERT, and MARBE, KARL. *Experimentelle Untersuchungen über die psychologischen Grundlagen der sprachlichen Analogiebildung.* Leipzig, 1901.

TRAUTSCHOLDT, MARTIN. "Experimentelle Untersuchungen über die Assoziation der Vorstellungen." In: WUNDT, *Philosophische Studien*, I (1883), 213–50.

VERAGUTH, OTTO. "Le Réflexe psycho-galvanique," *Compte rendu du IIme Congrès allemand de psychologie experimentale.* Würzburg, 1906. (See report by E. Claparède: *Arch. psychol.*, VI (1907), 162–63.)

———. "Das psycho-galvanische Reflex-Phänomen," *Mschr. Psychiat. Neurol.*, XXI (1906), 387.

VIGOUROUX, A. *Étude sur la résistance électrique chez les mélancoliques.* Thesis, Paris, 1890.

VIGOUROUX, R. "L'Électricité du corps humain," *C.R. Soc. Biol. Paris*, 11 Feb. 1888.

———. "Sur la résistance électrique considerée comme signe clinique," *Le Progès médicale*, 21 Jan., 4 Feb. 1888.

WALITSKY, MARIE. "Contribution a l'étude des mensurations psychometriques des aliénés," *Rev. phil.*, XXVIII (1889), 583–95.

WEHRLIN, K. "The Associations of Imbeciles and Idiots." In: JUNG, *Studies in Word-Association* (1918), pp. 173–205. (Orig. 1904.)

WERTHEIMER, MAX. "Experimentelle Untersuchungen zur Tatbestandsdiagnostik," *Arch. ges. Psychol.*, VI (1905–6), 59–131.

———. "Zur Tatbestandsdiagnostik," *Arch. ges. Psychol.*, VII:1 (Mar. 1906), Literaturbericht, 139–40.

———, and KLEIN, JULIUS. "Psychologische Tatbestandsdiagnostik," *Arch. Kriminalanthrop.*, XV (1904), 72–113.

WEYGANDT, WILHELM. "Zur psychologischen Tatbestandsdiagnostik," *Mschr. Kriminalpsychol.*, II (1905), 435–38.

WRESCHNER, ARTHUR. "Eine experimentelle Studie über die Assoziation in einem Falle von Idiotie," *Allg. Z. Psychiat.*, LVII (1900), 241–339.

Wundt, Wilhelm. "Sind die Mittelglieder einer mittelbaren Assoziation bewusst oder unbewusst?" In: Wundt, *Philosophische Studien,* X (1892), 326–28.

———, ed. *Philosophische Studien.* 20 vols., Leipzig, 1883–1902.

Ziehen, Georg Theodor. "Die Ideenassoziation des Kindes," *Samml. Abh. pädog. Psychol.,* I:6 (1898), III:4 (1900).

———. *Introduction to Physiological Psychology.* Translated by C. G. van Liew and O. W. Beyer. London and New York, 2nd edn., 1895. (Orig.: *Leitfaden der physiologischen Psychologie,* 1891; 2nd edn., 1893.)

———, ed. *Sammlung von Abhandlungen aus dem Gebiete der pädagogischen Psychologie.* 8 vols., Berlin, 1898–1906.

Zoneff, P., and Meumann, E. "Über Begleiterscheinungen psychischer Vorgänge im Atem und Puls." In: Wundt, *Philosophische Studien,* XVIII (1900), 1–112.

INDEX

INDEX

associations, classification of (*cont.*): 32; internal, 14–24, 412; linguistic connection, 35*f*; objective type, 458; perseveration, 33*ff*; predicate, 19–24; repetition, 35; sound, 27*f*, 412; subordination, 17; superordination, 17*f*; synthetic, 19*ff*; *see also specific entries, e.g.,* egocentric reactions; perseveration; sound associations

attention, 4, 137*f*, 415, 525; blunting of, 52*f*, 55, 60, 70, 73–77; degree of, 146*f*; in dementia praecox, 515; distraction of, *see* distraction; disturbances of, 44, 50, 52*f*, 55, 70, 73, 139*f*, 320, 589; in galvanometer and pneumograph experiments, 498, 556

attention phenomenon, 150*f*

attentive reaction, 43*f*

attitude phenomenon, 73*f*, 76

audition colorée (synesthesia), 56*f*

Australasian Medical Congress (1911), 598*n*

autohypnosis, 53

automatism, 402*ff*, 406; linguistic, 55

autonomy (autonomous complexes), 601*f*

B

Balint, Emerich, 10*n*, 23, 141, 226*n*, 415*n*

Baroncini, L., 586*n*

Binswanger, Ludwig, 490, 496, 530, 542, 555, 590

black man, dream of, 389–93, 405*f*

Bleuler, Paul Eugen, 3, 73, 204*n*, 262*n*, 290, 320, 332*n*, 386*n*, 492, 498, 525, 536, 603

blood: dreams of, 384, 390; hysterical attitude towards, 354, 404

Bonhöffer, Karl, 172*n*

Bourdon, B., 12, 36

breathing, *see* respiration

Breuer, Josef, 191*n*, 272, 288, 331*n*

Breukink, H., 198

Brill, A. A., vi, 439*n*, 466, 492*n*

brother: in dreams, 396–99; neurotic attachment to, 476

Burghölzli Cantonal Hospital, 200, 379*n*, 606

C

catatonia, 43, 172*n*, 287; galvanometer and pneumograph experiments in, 510, 512*ff*, 524, 571; in hysteria, 516

catatonic stupor, 519*ff*

cats, dream of, 384*ff*

censor, 251

centrifugal sound-shift, 29*f*, 32

centripetal sound-shift, 30*ff*

children, parents in character development of, 474*f*, 478*f*

chorea, hysterical, 353*ff*, 374*f*, 400–406

chronograph, Jaquet, 485, 555

chronoscope, 232

clang, *see* sound associations; sound-shift

Claparède, Édouard, 12, 172, 174, 221, 223, 409*n*, 603

Clark University, Worcester, Mass., 439*n*, 603

cleanliness compulsion, 355, 396

Colucci, Cesare, 198

complex(es), 128, 136, 290, 321*f*, 324*f*, 526*ff*, 598*ff*; concealed, 458; definition of, 321, 599; doctrine of, 598–604; masked reactions, 109; sexuality in, 82, 256*f*; suppression and, 150*f*; the unconscious and, 86–92; *see also specific entries, e.g.,* erotic complex; feeling-toned complexes

complex-characteristics, 261*ff*, 273, 284, 287, 295, 382*f*, 426*ff*, 589*f*, 606*ff*

complex-constellation, *see* constellations

complex-constellation type, 149, 159*ff*, 204, 458, 460

complex-image, 418*f*

compound words as reactions, 26

concepts: abstract, 20*f*; common intermediate, 29; concrete, 20*f*

consciousness, association and, 245, 253

constellations (complex-constellations), 78, 80–83, 90*f*, 94*f*, 97, 100*f*, 103*ff*, 108*f*, 115, 122*f*, 125, 130, 135*f*, 290*f*, 322, 426*f*; definition of, 322; emotionally charged, *see* emotionally charged complexes *and* feeling-toned complexes; in epilepsy, 211, 218*f*; family, 466–79; in hysteria, 382*f*; in imbeciles, 81, 200; reaction-time and, 109, 122*f*, 216*n*, 217, 237, 244*f*, 262, 278*f*, 284, 324–28

constellation type: complex, 149, 159*ff*; simple, 149, 156*ff*

co-ordination in association, 14–17, 20, 23, 73, 92

Cordes, G., 8*f*, 30, 175*n*, 319

crime, *see* evidence, psychological diagnosis of

D

Davidson, Andrew, 598*n*

death, obsession with, 292*f*, 300, 309*ff*, 316

definition type, 458*ff*; *see also* explanation of stimulus-word

Delabarre, E. Burke, 506, 556

dementia, 602*f*

dementia paranoides, *see* paranoia

dementia praecox, 252, 328, 424*f*, 476; association in, 547–53; complexes in, 602; dreams in, 395*f*; galvanometer and pneumograph experiments in, 496, 514–24, 547–53, 571*ff*; hysteria and, 576*ff*; nature of, 514–18

Diagnostic Association Studies (*Di-*

agnostische Assoziationsstudien), 3*n*, 291, 429, 485, 587*n*, 598, 603*f*

dinner table, dream of, 394–98, 405

directional idea, 138

distractibility, 52

distraction: acoustic disturbance, 108*f*; effects of, 137*ff*; experiments, averages, 163–71; in hysteria, 359*f*, 362; motor excitation and, 52; by surroundings, 111*f*; of uneducated subjects, 103

dogs, dreams of, 386–89

dreams: in dementia praecox, 395*f*; erotic, 312; father in, 393*f*, 477*f*; in hysteria, 383–400; INSTANCES, *see* black man; blood; brother; cats; dinner table; dogs; father; fire; fire alarm; money; mother

drowning, water associated with, 325–28, 486, 526

drowsiness, 52*f*, 70, 100*f*

E

eating, symbolism of, 394*f*

Eder, M. D., vi

egocentric reactions, 33, 141*f*, 144, 146, 149*f*, 156–62, 176*f*, 178, 184; in epilepsy, 210, 212, 214*f*; of imbeciles and idiots, 200, 206*ff*

ego-complex, 245, 250*f*, 290, 601

ego-consciousness, 245, 289

electrical resistance, 483, 554*f*

Ellis, Havelock, 598*n*

emotion: in association, 210; in dementia praecox, 514*f*, 518; in galvanometer experiments, 499, 503*f*

emotional attitudes, classified, 458*ff*

emotionally charged complexes, 72, 77, 82, 94*f*, 104, 109, 115–19, 122, 127*f*, 290, 321*n*, 418*n*, 606*f*; definition of, 72*n*; in hysteria, 360; of imbeciles, 206; reaction-time and, 234*ff*; slips of the tongue and, 214*ff*; in value judgments, 57, 62; *see also* feeling-toned complexes

in reproduction disturbances, 427f
reproduction, disturbances of, 426–38
reproduction method, 273f, 290f, 325f, 461, 527f, 600; in criminal investigation, 456f, 589; in galvanometer experiments, 485
respiration: galvanometer experiments, 497f, 508–14, 559–65; pneumograph experiments, 506–14, 556ff, 566f; see also pneumograph
rhyme as response, 28, 78, 113, 151n, 247
Ricksher, Charles, 554n
Riklin, Franz, 3, 199f, 203f, 223, 229, 252n, 263n, 286, 287n, 290, 328n, 332n, 353n, 421n, 598f
Rüdin, Ernst, 42n

S

St. Vitus's dance, see chorea
Salpétrière, 554
schizophrenia, see dementia praecox
Schnitzler, J. G., 587n
school-complex, 401f
Schüle, Heinrich, 320n
screen memories, 286f
Scripture, Edward Wheeler, 174, 319
senile dementia, 577
sentence: as reaction, 125, 203f, 207. 210f, 416; as stimulus, 559, 563f
sexual complexes, 82, 256f; in dreams, 384–400; in hysteria, 373–81, 400–406; see also erotic complex
sexuality in psychoanalysis, 306–16
simple-constellation type, 149, 156ff
slips of the tongue, 214, 247, 257f, 260
Smith, William, 42n, 174
Sommer, Robert, 5, 223, 319f, 409, 490, 494, 524, 554

songs, 104ff, 118, 252f, 257f
sound associations (sound reactions), 27f, 138ff, 144, 146, 169–73, 320, 412, 414f
sound-shift, centrifugal and centripetal, 29–32
speech motility, 76f
speech-phenomena, 13; see also entries under linguistic
Spiegel, H. W., 605n
split personality, 309
Stern, William, 318, 330
Sticker, Georg, 490, 494, 554
stimulus-words, 319; attitudes towards, 147ff; defining of, 201; experimental procedure, 5ff; explanation of, 205f, 208–12, 448–51, 458f; forgetting, 272; grammatical form, influence of, 184–89, 229–32; language problems, 6f; not understanding, 108f; reaction and, as association, 9f; reaction-time and, 229–32, 263–67; repetition of, 33, 175f, 208f, 213ff, 218f, 451
stop-watch, use of, 222f
Störring, Gustav, 290
Stransky, Erwin, 515
stupidity: definition type and, 459; emotional, 86, 176, 199f, 583n; hysterical, 81
subjective type, 148f
suicide, by drowning, water associated with, 325–28, 486, 526
suppression of feelings, 149ff
Switzerland, German language in, 6f
synesthesia (audition colorée), 56f
synonyms: in foreign language, 113, 115; as responses, 25

T

Tarchanoff, J., 490, 493ff, 498f, 504, 553f
teachers, influence of, 475

THE COLLECTED WORKS OF

C. G. JUNG

THE PUBLICATION of the first complete edition, in English, of the works of C. G. Jung was undertaken by Routledge and Kegan Paul, Ltd., in England and by Bollingen Foundation in the United States. The American edition is number XX in Bollingen Series, which since 1967 has been published by Princeton University Press. The edition contains revised versions of works previously published, such as *Psychology of the Unconscious*, which is now entitled *Symbols of Transformation*; works originally written in English, such as *Psychology and Religion*; works not previously translated, such as *Aion*; and, in general, new translations of virtually all of Professor Jung's writings. Prior to his death, in 1961, the author supervised the textual revision, which in some cases is extensive. Sir Herbert Read (d. 1968), Dr. Michael Fordham, and Dr. Gerhard Adler compose the Editorial Committee; the translator is R. F. C. Hull (except for Volume 2) and William McGuire is executive editor.

The price of the volumes varies according to size; they are sold separately, and may also be obtained on standing order. Several of the volumes are extensively illustrated. Each volume contains an index and in most a bibliography; the final volume will contain a complete bibliography of Professor Jung's writings and a general index to the entire edition.

In the following list, dates of original publication are given in parentheses (of original composition, in brackets). Multiple dates indicate revisions.

* Published 1957; 2nd edn., 1970.   † Published 1973.

* Published 1960.   † Published 1961.
‡ Published 1956; 2nd edn., 1967. (65 plates, 43 text figures.)

* Published 1971.　　† Published 1953; 2nd edn., 1966.
‡ Published 1960; 2nd edn., 1969.

* Published 1959; 2nd edn., 1968. (Part I: 79 plates, with 29 in colour.)

9. (*continued*)
The Prophecies of Nostradamus
The Historical Significance of the Fish
The Ambivalence of the Fish Symbol
The Fish in Alchemy
The Alchemical Interpretation of the Fish
Background to the Psychology of Christian Alchemical Symbolism
Gnostic Symbols of the Self
The Structure and Dynamics of the Self
Conclusion

*10. CIVILIZATION IN TRANSITION
The Role of the Unconscious (1918)
Mind and Earth (1927/1931)
Archaic Man (1931)
The Spiritual Problem of Modern Man (1928/1931)
The Love Problem of a Student (1928)
Woman in Europe (1927)
The Meaning of Psychology for Modern Man (1933/1934)
The State of Psychotherapy Today (1934)
Preface and Epilogue to "Essays on Contemporary Events" (1946)
Wotan (1936)
After the Catastrophe (1945)
The Fight with the Shadow (1946)
The Undiscovered Self (Present and Future) (1957)
Flying Saucers: A Modern Myth (1958)
A Psychological View of Conscience (1958)
Good and Evil in Analytical Psychology (1959)
Introduction to Wolff's "Studies in Jungian Psychology" (1959)
The Swiss Line in the European Spectrum (1928)
Reviews of Keyserling's "America Set Free" (1930) and "La Révolution Mondiale" (1934)
The Complications of American Psychology (1930)
The Dreamlike World of India (1939)
What India Can Teach Us (1939)
Appendix: Documents (1933–1938)

†11. PSYCHOLOGY AND RELIGION: WEST AND EAST
WESTERN RELIGION
Psychology and Religion (The Terry Lectures) (1938/1940)

* Published 1964; 2nd edn., 1970. (8 plates.)
† Published 1958; 2nd edn., 1969.

A Psychological Approach to the Dogma of the Trinity (1942/1948)
Transformation Symbolism in the Mass (1942/1954)
Forewords to White's "God and the Unconscious" and Werblowsky's "Lucifer and Prometheus" (1952)
Brother Klaus (1933)
Psychotherapists or the Clergy (1932)
Psychoanalysis and the Cure of Souls (1928)
Answer to Job (1952)

EASTERN RELIGION

Psychological Commentaries on "The Tibetan Book of the Great Liberation" (1939/1954) and "The Tibetan Book of the Dead" (1935/1953)
Yoga and the West (1936)
Foreword to Suzuki's "Introduction to Zen Buddhism" (1939)
The Psychology of Eastern Meditation (1943)
The Holy Men of India: Introduction to Zimmer's "Der Weg zum Selbst" (1944)
Foreword to the "I Ching" (1950)

*12. PSYCHOLOGY AND ALCHEMY (1944)
Prefatory note to the English Edition ([1951?] added 1967)
Introduction to the Religious and Psychological Problems of Alchemy
Individual Dream Symbolism in Relation to Alchemy (1936)
Religious Ideas in Alchemy (1937)
Epilogue

†13. ALCHEMICAL STUDIES
Commentary on "The Secret of the Golden Flower" (1929)
The Visions of Zosimos (1938/1954)
Paracelsus as a Spiritual Phenomenon (1942)
The Spirit Mercurius (1943/1948)
The Philosophical Tree (1945/1954)

‡14. MYSTERIUM CONIUNCTIONIS (1955-56)
AN INQUIRY INTO THE SEPARATION AND
SYNTHESIS OF PSYCHIC OPPOSITES IN ALCHEMY
The Components of the Coniunctio
The Paradoxa
The Personification of the Opposites
Rex and Regina   (continued)

* Published 1953; 2nd edn., completely revised, 1968. (270 illustrations.)
† Published 1968. (50 plates, 4 text figures.)
‡ Published 1963; 2nd edn., 1970. (10 plates.)

* Published 1966.
† Published 1954; 2nd edn., revised and augmented, 1966. (13 illustrations.)
‡ Published 1954.

The Development of Personality (1934)
Marriage as a Psychological Relationship (1925)

18. MISCELLANY
Posthumous and Other Miscellaneous Works

19. BIBLIOGRAPHY AND INDEX
Complete Bibliography of C. G. Jung's Writings
General Index to the Collected Works

See also:

C. G. JUNG: LETTERS
Selected and edited by Gerhard Adler, in collaboration with Aniela Jaffé.
Translations from the German by R.F.C. Hull.
VOL. 1: 1906–1950*
VOL. 2: 1951–1961

* Published 1973. In the Princeton edition, the *Letters* constitute Bollingen
Series XCV.